Mac OS® X Secrets®

Panther Edition

Mac OS® X Secrets®
Panther Edition

Benjamin Levisay

Wiley Publishing, Inc.

Mac OS®X Secrets® Panther Edition

Published by
Wiley Publishing, Inc.
111 River Street
Hoboken, NJ 07030-5774
www.wiley.com

Copyright © 2004 by Wiley Publishing, Inc., Indianapolis, Indiana

ISBN: 0-7645-4228-1

Manufactured in the United States of America

10 9 8 7 6 5 4 3 2 1

1BR/SS/QW/QU/IN

Published by Wiley Publishing, Inc., Indianapolis, Indiana
Published simultaneously in Canada

WILEY

About the Author

In his capacity as MIS and Web master for the XRX corporation (publishers of Knitter's Magazine and Knitter's Books), **Benjamin Levisay** gained wide-ranging experience in the maintenance of high-end graphics workstations. This included learning the software, implementing solutions, and then training graphic artists and technicians on how to use new technology. His experience as troubleshooter and consultant eventually lead to the formation, with two partners, of MacDoctors, an Apple and Adobe reseller and service provider, in Southeastern South Dakota. MacDoctors has positioned itself as a vital resource in its service area, able to provide highly specialized hardware and networking solutions along with consulting and training services for the graphic arts community.

Benjamin serves as the principal trainer and prepress consultant for his company. His specialties include font management, image manipulation, and digital asset management including inline managed color workflow. With respect to the latter, he is becoming increasingly more in demand to provide color calibration and proofing solutions to MacDoctors' clientele.

In 2001 Benjamin coauthored *Photoshop 6 In Depth*. Other books, with subject matter that coincides with his areas of special expertise on the Macintosh platform, figure in his future plans.

Benjamin Levisay lives in Sioux Falls, South Dakota. He is married and the father of three children.

Credits

Acquisitions Editor
Michael Roney

Project Editor
Kenyon Brown

Technical Editor
Pieter Paulson

Copy Editor
Maarten Reilingh

Editorial Manager
Robyn Siesky

Vice President and Executive Group Publisher
Richard Swadley

Vice President and Executive Publisher
Bob Ipsen

Vice President and Publisher
Barry Pruett

Project Coordinator
Erin M. Smith

Graphics and Production Specialists
Beth Brooks
Sean Decker
Carrie Foster
Lauren Goddard
Jennifer Heleine
Joyce Haughey
Lynsey Osborn

Quality Control Technicians
Laura Albert
John Greenough
Andy Hollandbeck
Brian Walls

Proofreading
Nancy L. Reinhardt

Indexing
TECHBOOKS Production Services

This book is dedicated to my mother who continues to remind me how uncommon it is to find (or use) common sense.

Foreword

You don't need this book.

The talisman of twenty-first century technology that is today's Macintosh running Mac OS X continues the tradition begun twenty years ago with the first Mac: it just works. Back then, pundits and PR folk enjoyed comparing the Mac to a toaster, a device so simple to operate that it didn't need a manual. And that hasn't changed. Plug the Mac in, turn it on, and it just works. If all you want to do with your Mac is read and write some email, balance your checkbook, and browse the Web, the Mac is a perfect choice. It's simple. It's friendly. You don't need a manual. You don't need this book.

But beneath the elegant aluminum, titanium, or white plastic housing of today's Mac is an intricately engineered computational marvel, an assemblage of advanced circuitry and software that can sequence genomes, generate movie magic, combine to form one of the world's fastest supercomputers, and help teach hundreds of subjects to millions of school kids from Bangor to Burbank. The strength and stability of Mac OS X's Unix foundation, graced with a user interface that is not only clear and inviting but simply beautiful, and running on some of the most powerful and advanced hardware available on the market gives you a tool of unrivalled flexibility and capability.

The Mac may be simple on the surface, but the more you know about your Mac, the more exciting, the more satisfying, the more intellectually and emotionally rewarding working with it becomes. Your Mac is an enabler. And so is this book.

Mac OS X Secrets presents the tips, tricks, shortcuts that can make you more productive and creative with your Mac. But it does more: it goes beneath the surface and behind the scenes to tell you the untold stories of how—and why—the Mac does all that the wonderful things that it does. On its own, each tip and secret in this book can be interesting and instructive, but taken all together, they can be nothing less than inspiring. With this book you can not only do what you never thought possible, you will think of doing things you never thought of doing before.

You don't need this book. But you're going to be very happy that you have it.

—Michael E. Cohen
Interactive Media Developer
Santa Monica, CA

Preface

I've been told (by other writers) that writing a preface for a book is one of the hardest parts of a book project. What you may not know is that many authors (including myself) write the preface last. So as you read this, this is your first chance to hear from me. But I've been talking to you for 32 chapters before this, so to me, we're already old friends.

The preface does give me a unique opportunity. How many times do you get a chance at a planned reintroduction to an old friend? I promise I won't squander it trying to make you think that I'm cooler than I am. (As you read these pages, you'll see that's not true anyway.) Instead, I'll try to stay on task and explain what I've been talking to you in this book for the past couple of months.

This book's goal is to help you get the most out of your Mac while running Mac OS X Panther (10.3). And the concept for this book is not mine. It goes back to the early days of IDG Books Worldwide, when David Pogue wrote the first several editions. The idea for this all-new edition is to write a comprehensive, real-world, tips-based book about using your Macintosh with the latest and greatest version of Mac OS X, as well as with some of the main applications for the Mac. If you're not already a Mac expert, I expect that some of the tips and techniques in these pages may be a little more advanced and technical than you're used to. However, I've strived to make everything in these pages accessible and useful for any user level, and I predict that your efficiency and productivity in using your Mac will be "kicked up several notches" after you've spent some time with me here. I won't disappoint you.

There is more. Besides the Tips, Cautions, Web site references, and hip Notes, the real cool stuff in this book are the Secrets. The Secrets are kind of hard to explain. They vary depending on the subject matter. I like to think of them as tips or sidebars plus. Some of the Secrets are anecdotal. Some of the Secrets are kind of technical. Some of the Secrets are how-to in nature. And some of them are just plain fun! You may find that you know some of them, but I doubt you'll know them all. One of the contributors on this project compared the Secrets to Cliffs Notes for Macintosh uber-geekdom. I don't know if I agree with that, but I suppose this text could help you along your way toward being a super-user.

Along the way I've tried to keep a sense of humor and conversational style that you will find entertaining. So welcome to the start of our conversation. I hope you have as much fun hearing from me as I did talking to you.

How the Book Is Organized

Mac OS X Secrets is organized to provide a wide range of insanely useful information to any Mac user, and to be dipped into randomly as necessary. (I'll be flattered if you read this cover-to-cover, but you don't have to do that, as this is meant to be a reference.)

Part I kicks off with six chapters on getting to know Panther better than most people, peppered throughout with cool Secrets and techniques that will tame the beast in order to customize it for your needs and get it running like a powerful wildcat. From the Dock to System Preferences to utilities, you'll find plenty you can use here.

Part II provides a major helping of Secrets and techniques for getting more out of the productivity apps you will use with your Mac, including valuable tips for word processing, desktop publishing, graphics, and sound. This part also covers automating your Mac operations with AppleScript, a very productive strategy.

Part III is loaded with advice and Secrets for getting the most out of Apple's digital lifestyle applications, including iTunes, iPhoto, iMovie, iDVD, and more.

Part IV features several chapters covering the killer app of computing today: getting online while staying safe and sane. Here you'll make sense of e-mail options (including combating spam), learn how to get more out of instant messaging, learn the ins and outs of Safari and other popular Web browsers, get more out of Apple's .Mac and iDisk services, and even how to build your own Web page using he best Mac tools available.

Part V delves deeply into connection Secrets — printing, using digital cameras and scanners, getting the most out of CD and DVD drives, hooking up your own network (yes!), and dipping your feet (just slightly... don't worry) into the powerful world of Unix for even more productivity. This part also contains a professional troubleshooting chapter, which could save you a great deal of time and money when things go wrong.

The appendix offers an array of online resources that'll point you to the applications that are referenced throughout the book. You'll find a comprehensive list of Web sites that provide useful information and advice.

Conventions Used in this Book

As I said in the preface, this book is a thorough look at Panther, Apple's newest OS. Along the way, I use some different icons to pull out different kinds of information. I thought it might be useful if I explained the icons and their uses here before you start into the main text.

You'll notice in this book that I use different icons to present different kinds of information. These icons flag small sidebars that call attention to the following things...

insider insight   This icon gives you an insider's glimpse in the computer or technical world.

caution   This self-explanatory icon is usually presented after a section where I've told you to do something and then thought of something that could go wrong.

on the web   Occasionally there are quick Web site references that I feel don't fit well into the body of the text. In those cases, I use the On the Web icon.

note   I use this icon in a few different ways throughout the book. Sometimes I use this to show something new in Panther from a previous version of OS X. And sometimes I use this to show something new in OS X from pre–OS X operating systems.

tip

I use this icon when a Secret that I had is too short to be used at a Secret.

cross ref

I use this icon to direct you to important information that appears in other chapters or the appendix.

We Interrupt This Chapter . . .

The idea for this icon was to let our very talented TE (Technical Editor) Pieter Paulson talk to you throughout the book. We did this in a fashion that usually shows Pieter either commenting on or disagreeing with something that I have said.

My contact with Pieter is usually reserved for the Author Review process where he, Maarten, and Kenyon give my work back with notes and corrections so that I can go through and try to make it more correct and work better for you. (This process is sometimes referred to by authors as "death by a thousand paper cuts.") Needless to say, the process, although necessary, is not that much fun. So, it was a great change of pace to be able to have an open dialog with Pieter throughout the book. I hope you find these exchanges entertaining; I think they prove that there is usually more than one way to look at or do something.

Besides all of these icons, there is one main icon that makes this a Secrets book. That is, of course...

Secret

...the Secrets style

When you see this icon, you are looking at what makes this book unique to other OS X books. These Secrets contain a lot of different kinds of information. In some of the Secrets, I give you a way around problems while in other secrets I try to give you extra (or very specialized) information. The Secrets (in each chapter) are listed at the front of each chapter.

These Secrets were collected by many people. I'd like to encourage you to e-mail me <macdrben@mac.com> with your own secrets so that the next edition of this book can have even more great secrets in it. If I find that your Secrets are really great, I'll make sure that you're acknowledged in the next book and I might even hire you for some research!

Let's see. What else?

```
In the Unix chapter or when I talked about AppleScript or the Terminal I
used the Code Style to show command-line text. It isn't pretty, but it gets
the job done.
```

Also, you know that you're looking at a URL, if you see the Code style peeking at you in an otherwise normal paragraph!

I used a few other conventions in this book, like numbered lists to show an order of things to do and bulleted lists to show features. And like other books, I referenced figures in the text and then used figure captions to further explain diagrams and screen shots.

Acknowledgments

Many thanks are owed and need to be given:

First and foremost is my dear wife Krista who took on a lot during the writing of this book. As far as I'm concerned, she remains the unnamed coauthor of anything that I write.

And thanks to my kids — not only for lending their likenesses in many of the figures in this book, but also for forcing me to stop every so often to goof off. (It's important to play on a regular basis to keep from getting too old.)

We all need to recognize the original author of this version of the book, Gene Steinberg. The outline and much of the concept of this book are his. Due to time constraints, Gene was unable to finish this book and I didn't get the privilege of working with such a great author. Throughout the book, I tried very much to keep things in his style and to use as much of his work (already done) as I could. Thanks, Gene!

My editors, Mike Roney, Kenyon Brown, Pieter Paulson, and Maarten Reilingh, deserve a lot of thanks for coping with a relatively new author who didn't always react to the editorial process with the grace that I should have.

When I took over the book, it was already behind schedule. To get it back on track I needed to bring in some help with some of these chapters. Among those heroes were Scott Stoel, Erik Tollefsrud, Michael Cohen, Dennis Cohen, Ilene Hoffman, and my partner Larry Lamb.

And speaking of Larry Lamb, I need to thank him, again, as well as my other partner Dan Meinke for allowing me the extra time away from the office to work on the book. Eric, Colleen, George, and Garret (the staff at MacDoctors) also deserve my thanks for helping take up the slack at work.

I also need to thank my agent, Margot Maley Hutchinson, for dealing with some of the more unpleasant aspects of the book writing process and for knowing when to tell me to get over it and when to take up the fight for me.

We used a lot of different software in this book, but some of the systems software companies were really helpful. So, I would also like to thank the folks at Adobe, Insider Software, Unsanity, and Ambrosia. These companies are now my favorite software developers. (I wish dealing with Apple was as easy.)

And finally, I would like to thank my dad who continues to provide a sounding board when I need to talk about my writing projects and my business world.

Thank you all!

Contents at a Glance

Contents

Part III: Secrets of Apple's Digital Lifestyle Applications 373

Chapter 12: Mac OS X Application Overview 375

Chapter 13: "The Beat Goes On" with iTunes, GarageBand, and the iPod 401

Part I

Dissecting Mac OS X

Part I kicks off this book with six chapters that will help you get to know Panther better than most people. The chapters are peppered with cool secrets and techniques that will tame your Mac "beast" in order to customize it for your needs and get it running like a powerful wildcat. From the Dock, to system preferences, to utilities, you'll find plenty of useful information here.

In This Part

The Elements of Mac OS 10.3

Chapter

1

◆ ◆

Secrets in This Chapter

◆ ◆

Have you seen some of the mock switcher commercials that are floating around the Internet? There's one in particular that I like a lot, called pissed, about a young guy, a self-proclaimed "Mac person," who installs OS X for the first time. As he restarts his computer into this new OS, his first words are "What the #%*@?!"

Apple's release of OS X on January 5, 2000 brought strong reactions (positive and negative) from people. Everyone liked the stuff going on under the Unix hood. But few people fell in love with the interface right away.

Traditionalists hated the new interface. And loyalists were cautiously optimistic that they would eventually "learn to love it." I didn't like it at all. I didn't know where anything was and I had lost my ability to color label items (brought back to us in this version of OS X).

As a Macintosh service provider, I found more people who didn't like the new OS than those who did. And that didn't change much until Jaguar was released (on August 23, 2002 at 10:20 pm around the country). That's when I found the OS friendly enough to switch over from OS 9.2.2 to OS 10.2.1. (Yes. Unlike this time, I was smart enough then to wait for a .1 revision of the OS before I joined the rest of bleeding edge upgraders.)

And I still missed labels. And I hated switching to Suitcase because my ATM Deluxe didn't work any more. And . . . . Well let's suffice it to say that I had a myriad of rants that kept me feeling self-righteous for hours at a time. But over time, I started to like some of the cool new features. I liked the navigation by panes. I liked that I could hide the Dock. I liked that I had a screen saver with a password. And I liked how stable it was. (Yes. I find that having the desktop up and running can be considered a nice interface feature as well.)

Six months later I found myself among the converted. I was one of those people who did learn to love it. And as a Macintosh service provider, I found myself actually dreading having to work on my customer's Macs who were still working in pre–OS X computers. A little over a year later I found myself nervous about giving up my tame Jaguar for a not-yet-housebroken Panther. But I did it under the same assumption that I would eventually learn to love it.

This time it didn't take a few months. I was hooked right away. All of the really cool stuff that I liked about Jaguar was there, plus some improvements in the Finder and the other iApps. I went from Jaguar to Panther without batting an eye (or a whisker).

They even brought back my color labels. And when I launched my Panther version for the first time and saw that my OS 9 (and earlier) files with color labels on them were showing up in Panther with the labels intact, I could have sworn my computer purred (or maybe that was me).

Dissecting the Finder

"Dissecting" is such a loaded word. It brings forth images of high school biology class and frogs. It start things off with the assumption that we are going to explore this way past the level where normal people would consider comfortable or interesting. I promise that we'll try not to live up to that expectation — too much. This won't be an awful experience.

What is the Finder? Some people say that the Finder is the desktop. That's not accurate. The desktop is actually just a part of the Finder. The Finder is your common user interface to deal with the Mac OS in a graphic context. It's a program, just like any other that's running. But, you can't deal well with the others in the GUI unless the Finder is running.

In this chapter, I break the Finder down into bite-sized components. We'll look at the Finder windows, the Finder preferences, the other menus, the contextual menus, the files themselves, a cool little interface enhancement called Fast User Switching, and a few other features of the Finder.

The Dock and the Apple Menu are large enough "new" features that I've set aside Chapters 2 and 3 (respectively) to explore those parts of the Finder.

This all sounds like a lot to go through. But I keep things clear and concise. And I use a lot of figures to help illustrate what I'm talking about. (Okay class . . . first take your frogs out of the jars. . . .)

The New User-Centric Experience

If you haven't yet moved to any version of OS X yet, you will find that there are some significant changes in where things are kept. For instance, the Desktop folder is actually four levels down on your hard drive (HD). And it changes depending on how you log in.

The Main Screen

You also don't have the same old pre–OS X system folder (called System Folder in pre–OS X). It has been replaced with a folder called System at the top level of your HD. There is also a folder called Library at the top level of your HD that isn't to be confused with the Library folder in the System or in four directories down (in your User folder) at the same level as your desktop (shown in Figure 1-1). Confused? You're not the first.

So why, you may ask, have things changed so much? The reason for this is Apple's (and Unix's) user-centric approach to the OS. PC people have had this kind of thing for years. And we need to give them their due. It's a good idea — not only for security but also for preserving a customized user experience. (Hmm. You'd think PCs would have better security if they've been able to have this kind of thing for years.)

Everything you do is centered on you as a user. Your specific settings and preferences are all kept in your User folder, which you can lock down and not share with anyone. And Apple's upgrade system is designed to help in moving your User folder(s) forward into new versions of the OS.

Before you get distracted by it, the row of icons along the bottom of the screen is called the Dock. We're not going to talk about that here. If you're in a hurry to know more about the Dock, skip ahead to Chapter 3.

Let's get back to the Finder. As you can see from Figure 1-1, the desktop consists of a number of elements that might be familiar to you.

The hard drive icon is shown in the upper-right corner of the desktop. The open window that you see (in Figure 1-1) is the open hard drive shown in a Finder window. We'll get to the items shown on the top and side of this window shortly. Items on the desktop are shown here (in Figure 1-1) on the desktop and in the Desktop folder in the logged-in User folder.

Figure 1-1: Down, down, down, and down again to the Desktop folder. Welcome to your new desktop and OS environment.

First Look at a Finder Window

The Finder windows treat your information more like a browser than traditional Classic Finder windows. Clicking on a folder or volume opens a window. Clicking on folders within an open window replaces the open window with the new window. According to Apple, this saves users from having to continually close windows after themselves.

Two new browser-like features of the Finder window are the Forward and Back buttons (represented by two arrows) in the upper-left corner (shown in Figure 1-2).

Figure 1-2: Use the Forward and Back buttons (two arrows in the upper-left of the Finder window) to navigate like you would in a browser.

Secret

Command-Click for a New Window

If you're not a fan of windows that open to replace the previous one, or you just want to open a folder into a new Finder window, hold the Command key down when you double click on a folder or volume.

At the top of every window or document, you will also see three little colored icons (shown in Figure 1-2). The green button maximizes the window. The red button closes the window. And the yellow button minimizes the window or document into the Dock (as shown in Figure 1-3). If you haven't tried that one yet, do. It's quite a kick.

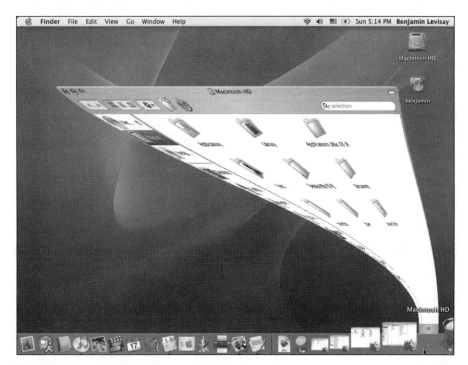

Figure 1-3: This is the ultra cool genie effect.

Selected icons also react differently in OS 10.3.x. Figure 1-4 shows an icon on the desktop that is not selected. Clicking one time on that same icon (shown in Figure 1-5) shows a new raised label and gives a button-like appearance to the icon itself.

Figure 1-4: A folder icon. It looks innocent enough, doesn't it?

Figure 1-5: The same folder icon is selected and feeling special.

Double-clicking on that selected icon opens a familiar window (shown in Figure 1-1 earlier in this chapter).

Using the Document Name to Find Out Where You Are

All of the new directories can be confusing. Here's a secret to help you know and go where you want from where ever you are.

The path or directory information for any document can be gotten by holding the Command key down while clicking and holding on the name at the top of the window (shown in Figure 1-6). A menu will pull down showing the complete directory to the top level. Click on any of the folders or directories in that pull-down menu (shown in Figure 1-7) and you will cause a Finder window to open into that directory.

Figure 1-6: One simple ⌘-click on a window can show four levels down.

Figure 1-7: A close-up of the pull-down from the window shows the Directory Path. Choose any folder and you're there.

This also works on documents open in other applications. The OS will switch the Finder into a new window to show the directory chosen from the document.

Looking at the Information in Different Views

We have examples of data in different views as we progress in this chapter. So, for now, I just point out that there are three different views in a window. Use the three buttons (Figure 1-8) next to the arrow buttons to control the views in the Finder window.

Figure 1-8: It's not a traffic light on its side. It's the new Window controls for Mac OS X.

- ◆ **Icon view** is depicted in Figure 1-9. Icons float freely with only the icon and name showing. You can turn a window to icon view by clicking on the first button above the View text (shown in Figure 1-8).
- ◆ **List view** is depicted in Figure 1-23. This view allows for the viewing of date, size, kind, and any other information available when the Show View Options menu item is selected from under the View menu. (We get into more depth for those options in the next section.) You can turn a window to list view by clicking on the second button above the View text with four horizontal lines on it on the top of a Finder window (shown in Figure 1-8).
- ◆ Column **view** is the new OS X way of viewing information (shown in the first figure in this chapter, Figure 1-1). This is the new way of listing and navigating directories in OS X. This is the way that you will see most Finder windows shown throughout this book. Gone are the different kinds of ancillary information that is available in list view. But the icon and name information are still available just like in icon view. You can turn a window to Column view by clicking on the on the third button above the View text with three vertical panels on it on the top of a Finder window (shown in Figure 1-8).

We Interrupt This Chapter . . .

I think Column view is one of the coolest things about OS X. It offers file and preview information right in the window (shown in Figure 1-56). But critics such as Pieter seem to see it as decidedly un-Mac Like.

Pieter: List view or icon view? Personally, I prefer list view because I like to customize the various columns that are displayed and use that capability to sort the various files in the directory. Likewise, I like being able to change the width of these columns because I tend to use long, very descriptive filenames that can be a problem in Column view. Icon view is okay, but seems inefficient when you have a limited amount of screen space in which to work.

Benjamin: The best reason to at least try Column view is that Change Is Good. Column view gives you the best way to navigate through directories and drill down to a single file. And thanks to Quartz and QuickTime, PDFs, QuickTime movie clips, MP3s, and a number of other file formats can be played and/or previewed in the Column view. It's great!

If you like one of the other window views, great. Use them/it. But you should give Column view a try. If you refuse to try something this useful just because it's new, then you are probably on the wrong platform. The mantra, lest we forget, is "Think Different." (Just my not-so-humble opinion.)

Figure 1-9: The default insertion point is at the bottom of the sidebar list.

More New Features of the Finder Window

Opening a new (Finder) window quickly presents you with a number of new things — both from the Classic window and from previous versions of OS X windows. There are new icons across the top of the window and familiar icons (if you've upgraded from Jaguar) along the left side of the window.

The Sidebar

The left side of the window is a major step toward a *user-centric* OS from the previous version of the OS. Many of these icons were default icons on the toolbar of the Finder window in Jaguar. The main difference here is that you can choose to add items to the left side of the Finder windows.

---

note | Adding an item to the top or side of a Finder window makes those items show up in *all* Finder windows.

By moving a folder to the left, from within the window, you get an insertion point that can be moved up or down (as shown in Figure 1-9). The folder will then be set at the insertion point (shown in Figure 1-10).

Figure 1-10: This folder, added to the sidebar, can be moved up the list, or removed by selecting the folder and hitting the delete key.

The Finder window and the Finder menus are closely linked. And we'll get into those in more depth later in this chapter, but to show you how to further customize the sidebar, we need to break out of the window and deal with the Finder's preferences.

The Finder Preferences

This is new stuff! The Finder has gotten complex enough to now need a separate set of dialog boxes to control the way that you deal with a Finder window. I'm not a fan of more dialog boxes, but these are relatively simple (Mac-like) and easy to use.

To get at the Finder preferences, select Preferences from the Finder menu (shown in Figure 1-11).

Figure 1-11: ⌘-, (Command-comma) will open the new Preference options for the Finder.

General Finder Preferences

The General panel (shown in Figure 1-12) presents itself first when the Finder Preferences are opened.

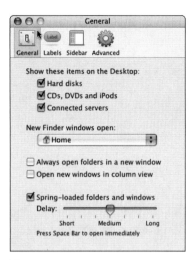

Figure 1-12: What you see on the desktop, the behavior of new windows, and control of spring-loaded folders are set in the General preference panel.

The default settings are to show the Hard disks, CDs, DVDs, and iPods, and Connected servers on the desktop.

New Finder windows (⌘-N) are set to open to the home folder by default. You also have the option here to always open folders in a new window (in case you hate the browser-like way that windows open by default). And you can choose to always have windows open in column view.

Spring-loaded folders (if you use that feature) are also controlled here.

Labels Finder Preferences

If you haven't noticed by now in either my opening text or in some of the screen shots, *labels are back!* (Hooray!!!) Okay. I just needed a minute there.

I show you labels later in this chapter, but we're in the Finder Preferences, so I have to show you how to change the label names here.

The second panel in the Finder Preferences is the Labels panel (shown in Figure 1-13). You don't have a lot of control here, but you can change the text associated with the colors available to you.

Sidebar Finder Preferences

Here's where we needed to get when I took us off course. The third panel in the Finder Preferences is the Sidebar panel (shown in Figure 1-14). This panel allows you to check or uncheck items that you want or don't want (respectively) in the sidebar.

If you feel like having any of these items not appear in the sidebar, feel free to uncheck them. (I won't hassle you or lecture you about it.)

Figure 1-13: You can't change the colors to custom colors, but there's still reason to celebrate. Labels are back!

Figure 1-14: All the items, except the Computer, are checked by default.

Advanced Finder Preferences

The most useful Preference panel is the Advanced preference panel (shown in Figure 1-15).

It's the most useful because it allows you to turn off the warning you get before you empty the Trash. (I find that particular warning annoying enough that I think whether you want to turn it off should be a question asked in initial set-up of the User when the OS is installed so that intelligent people don't have to be irritated with it ever again.)

Figure 1-15: Be smart. Turn the Trash warning off and just pay attention when you empty the trash.

You can also choose to show all the file extensions, usually hidden because we are smart enough to be on a Mac.

The Select button offers multiple languages for searching for file contents. If you have need of additional languages, check them here.

The Toolbar

Jaguar and OS 10.1.x had navigation aids on the top bar of Finder windows. And as I said before, the idea here is to create a more browser-like window to view and navigate through your files.

In Jaguar, I got used to it, but often found it just a little too much. It's been simplified now, by moving some of the items like the Applications and home folder to the sidebar. We've already covered the three colored buttons, the Back and Forward buttons, and the three View buttons in previous sections of this chapter. And I'll get to the new Action pull-down menu that looks like a gear (shown below in Figure 1-16) to the right of the View buttons later.

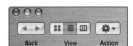

Figure 1-16: The standard new buttons on the top bar.

These buttons as well as the Search field on the far right at the top of a Finder window (shown in Figure 1-17) are the default options for Finder windows. In these next few sections, I show you how to customize your top bar.

Adding Your Items

Almost anything can be added to the top bar of a Finder window. Let me show you how to add your items to complete the user-centric experience.

Drag an application or a folder from the desktop or Finder window (as shown in Figure 1-17).

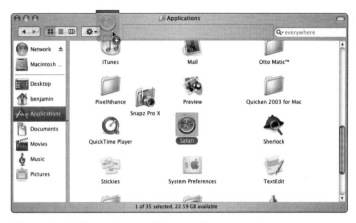

Figure 1-17: Dragging the Safari application to the top bar.

tip If you have problems moving items to the top bar, it's because the space there is flexible. To avoid problems in putting applications, folders, and/or documents in the top bar, drag them just to the right (as close as possible) of the new Action menu.

If you do it right, your application will appear on the toolbar (as shown in Figure 1-18).

Figure 1-18: Safari is now conveniently accessible from the toolbar.

tip There isn't a lot of room on the top bar, so don't junk it up with stuff you don't need. Sometimes less is more.

The Action Menu

As nonlinear as the OS (and this book) is, I have to try to put things in some kind of order. So before I go into more detail about how to customize the top bar, I need to make another slight detour into the Action menu.

The Action menu is a new, contextually sensitive menu that Apple has added to the Finder window in Panther (shown in Figure 1-19).

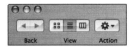

Figure 1-19: The little arrow and gear icon that looks like a button is actually a menu.

The cool thing about the Action menu is that it changes, depending on the view and/or what is selected in the window, to give you possible Finder actions for those views and/or item(s).

Selecting an alias in a Finder window and then clicking and holding on the Action menu gives all of the options available for that alias (as shown in Figure 1-20).

Figure 1-20: Among the contextual possibilities for a selected alias is the option to Show Original. All of the other options would be available for any other kinds of non-alias files.

Many of these contextual options are also available from the from the menu bar at the top of the screen. And for those of you who dabble in the PC world, this may look decidedly PC-like. My advice is to get over it and take advantage of the new features.

Some of the most useful that are fairly new to the Mac are the Copy "name of document" and the Create Archive of "name of document" (as shown in Figure 1-20). By far the one that I'm the most excited about is the Color Label option (shown in Figure 1-21). This, of course turns a file or folder to the color chosen (as shown in Figure 1-22).

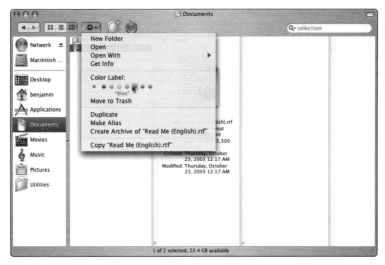

Figure 1-21: Copy, Open, Label, Trash, etc. . . . Actions-a-plenty.

Figure 1-22: In living color. Labels are back!

Later on in this chapter, I show you how to get at these same contextually aware options right from the file itself without the Action menu.

View Options

The Action menu is a great place to take us back to more customization of your Finder windows. From any Finder window view choice, but without selecting any file(s) within the window, you can click on the Action menu and get the Show View Options choice (as shown in Figure 1-23). You can also get at the View Options by selecting the Show View Options (⌘-J) under the View menu (as shown in Figure 1-24).

Depending on which view your topmost (or selected) Finder window is in, you will get some variation of the View Options (shown Figure 1-25). If you are in List view you will get options that apply to List view Finder windows. Likewise, you will get corresponding choices in Column or Icon view.

Figure 1-23: Show View Options is also an Action menu choice.

Figure 1-24: And when all else fails you can try the Finder's View menu.

Figure 1-25: These options tell you that your Finder window is in List view. If you don't see the options you want, then you're in the wrong view in your uppermost Finder window.

tip

In all of the views, you have the choice to affect all windows (in the selected view mode) or just the forward Finder window. You should decide that before you start changing the icon or text sizes, or any of the other View Options.

If you don't know how you want your windows to look and you want to experiment for a while, make sure you choose the This window only option at the top of the View Options palette (shown in Figure 1-25).

More View Option Choices in Icon View

With View Options, you can use a picture background in icon view Finder windows. This choice is available in Finder windows in icon view only.

To place an image in the background of your Finder window, follow these steps:

1. Open a Finder window and put it in icon view.
2. Select Show View Options from either the Action menu on the Finder window or from the bottom of the View menu at the top of the screen.
3. When the View Option palette opens, choose Picture at the bottom of the dialog box under the Background section.
4. Click on the Select button to the left of the Picture option in the View Option palette. This will open up a Select a Picture dialog box (as shown in Figure 1-26).

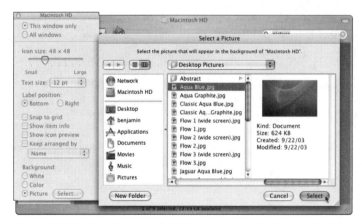

Figure 1-26: Any picture can be the background to your Finder windows.

5. Navigate through the Select a Picture window to the image you want as your background and then click on the Select button in the Select a Picture window.

Now the picture you chose in the Select a Picture window (in Step 5) will show up in the Finder window (shown in Figure 1-27).

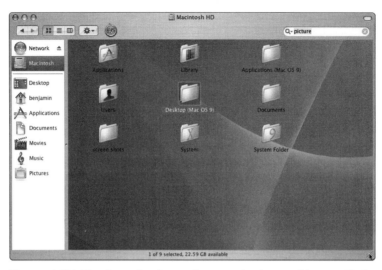

Figure 1-27: Your icons floating against your background in your Finder window.

A Few Tips for Choosing Images for Your Desktop

Large pictures and busy pictures don't always work very well for background. Here are a few simple rules for background pictures for your Finder windows.

Photos usually work best if they are simple and screened back. If you open your photo in a photo editor and screen the opacity back to 20 or 30%, you may find the image easier to take as the background behind the data you want to get at.

Large images and very small images don't always look very good. You may need to reduce or enlarge your images to make them work better as Finder window backgrounds.

And most importantly, be original. Apple gives you this option to express yourself. Don't use a background image that comes with the OS like I did with the example shown in Figure 1-27. If you're going to spend the time customizing your Finder windows, make them either interesting or personal.

A Few Remaining Things You Can Do to Your Finder Windows

At this point, you're probably wondering what the heck else there could possibly be to do to customize a Finder window. Mercifully, there's not too much more. I'll be brief.

Earlier in this chapter, I showed you how to put your own items in the top bar of a Finder window. Apple also has some ideas about other things you may (or may not) want to add to the top bar of your Finder window.

Just like the other things you add to the sidebar or top bar, these things will appear on all windows regardless of the view chosen. To get at the these choices, open a Finder window and choose, Customize Toolbar from the View menu (in the Finder) at the top of the screen (shown in Figure 1-28).

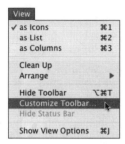

Figure 1-28: The Customize Toolbar option is only available under the View menu if there is a Finder window open and to the front.

When you select that menu option, a pane drops down from under the toolbar. This pane gives you Apple's extra choices for items you may want to add to the toolbar like an icon to add a new folder (shown in Figure 1-29).

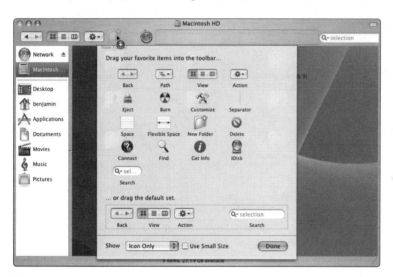

Figure 1-29: This is a place where less can be better. Choose what you want here. Don't add everything.

You also have the option to show the items on the toolbar as Icons Only, Text Only, or as Icons and Text. You can click the Use Small Size check box to let you get more items on the toolbar.

Add, Delete, or Move Items on Your Finder Window Toolbar

If you find that you have too many things on the toolbar or need to rearrange items on the top bar, all you have to do is hold down the Command key and either drag them off or around the toolbar.

Stop the Insanity

If you're a died-in-the-wool pre–Mac OS X person and you just can't cope with all of the new options along the top or the bottom, Apple has thought of you too.

By clicking on the small oval icon in the upper-right corner of a window you will collapse the toolbar and the sidebar, leaving you with a window in whatever view it was before you collapsed them (shown in Figure 1-30).

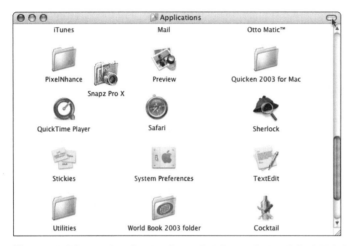

Figure 1-30: Longing for the Good Old Days of Mac OS 9? This is as close as we get.

And that's it for the Finder window.

Working from the Menus

You've seen some of the menus already, and more are covered in detail later. But just to be thorough, let's take a survey of the menus across the top of the screen when you are in the Finder.

Let's start at the left side of the screen and move to the right.

The Apple menu

On the far left is the Apple menu (Shown in Figure 1-31). Chapter 2 covers the Apple menu so we won't get into the options under the Apple right now.

The Application Menu

The immediate right of the Apple menu you will find the application menu. This menu can be called the Finder menu when the Finder is the forward application.

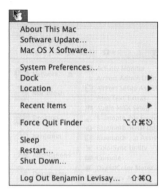

Figure 1-31: It's not the same Apple menu you knew from your Classic days.

Secret

Use Application Switching to Move between Applications and the Finder

If the application name is not the Finder (to the right of the Apple), then you will need to switch from the application you are in to the Finder.

A quick way to do this is to hold the Command and Tab keys down at the same time. An Application Switcher will appear hovering over the top application (shown in Figure 1-32).

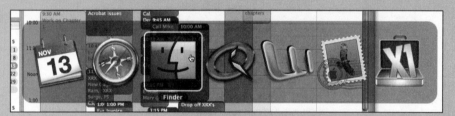

Figure 1-32: Command-tabbing the Application Switcher is a great way to see what applications you have running.

Then you click on the Finder (or other application you want to switch to) and that application will become the forward application.

After you get to the Finder as the forward application, you can click and hold the Finder menu (shown in Figure 1-33). We've already been to this menu (earlier in the chapter) when we accessed the Finder preferences.

Figure 1-33: The Application menu is the place where you can choose (among other things) to hide the application you are currently in.

A new feature to the Finder menu is the Secure Empty Trash option — which does exactly what you think it does. It securely empties the trash. It works like a virtual shredder.

It's also important to note that this is where you can access the Mac OS services. We'll get into the services later on in this book.

The File Menu

The File menu (found to the immediate right of the Application menu) is probably familiar to Mac users of any genre. Many of the standard File menu options are available in this menu (as shown in Figure 1-34). You might notice that some of the old key command combinations have changed.

Figure 1-34: The File Menu. Have I mentioned that labels are back?

Some of the new options (other than labels) from the old Classic File menu, that you can find under this menu are the Open With, Create Archive, Move to Trash, Eject, and Burn Disc. Some of these used to be under the old Classic Special menu. Some, like Create Archive, are brand new to Panther.

The Edit Menu

Just to the right of the File menu, you will find the Edit menu. This is also a familiar menu to Mac users. Clicking on the Edit menu will allow you to get at those common actions like Cut (⌘-X), Copy (⌘-C), Paste (⌘-V), and Select All (⌘-A) that you are used to using all the time (shown in Figure 1-35).

Figure 1-35: If you make mistakes as much as I do, you'll want to remember the Undo command (⌘-Z) under the Edit menu.

Special Characters is also one of the new OS X options under the Edit menu.

The View Menu

Just to the right of the Edit menu (while you're in the Finder) you'll find the View menu. We've been in this menu earlier in this chapter when we customized the toolbar and when we accessed the Show View Options. Clicking on this menu gives us other choices for organization as well (shown in Figure 1-36).

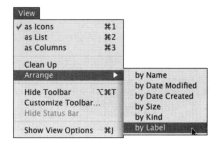

Figure 1-36: Now that Labels are back you have one more choice in how to arrange your data.

At the top of this menu, you can choose to view your data as Icons (⌘-1), as a List (⌘-2), and as Columns (⌘-3).

The Go Menu

The Go menu, located just to the right of the View menu (while you're in the Finder) is new to OS X. This menu replaces some of the features of the Classic Chooser and some of the features of the Classic Apple menu. By clicking on the Go menu you will see that you have access to all the places that your Mac can take you (shown in Figure 1-37).

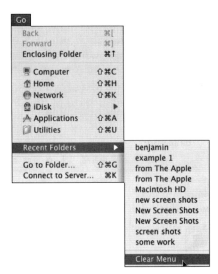

Figure 1-37: Recent applications and documents are in the Apple menu. But if you need to get at the folders that you've been to recently, you will find that option here in the Go menu.

Many of these options you can access through the sidebar in the Finder window. But if you've turned those features off, here's another place you can reach them.

New to this version of the OS is an expanded iDisk submenu that allows you to access more than just your own iDisk. You can also choose to access an Enclosing Folder, which is a new Go menu feature.

You can access network volumes via the Connect to Server (⌘-K) menu option. We'll explore the Connect to Server options and dialog boxes in Chapter 29.

The Window Menu

The Window menu, to the right of the Go menu (while you're in the Finder), will allow you to access any open Finder window. Clicking on a window name (shown in Figure 1-38) will bring that window to the front.

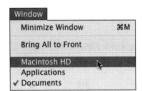

Figure 1-38: This specialized menu provides another way to minimize a selected Finder window.

The Help Menu

The Help menu, to the right of the Window menu (while you're in the Finder) has one option only. You can choose Help (⌘-?). When you are in the Finder this will show up as Mac Help (shown in Figure 1-39).

Figure 1-39: The Help menu changes depending on which application is forward.

We look at the Help feature(s) in more depth later in Chapter 7.

The AirPort Menu

If you don't have any third-party software installed on your computer (like Norton AntiVirus, QuickKeys, StuffIt Deluxe, Remote Desktop, Timbuktu, etc.) that add menus to the top of your top menu bar, then the first menu you will encounter (to the right of the Help menu) will be the AirPort menu (shown in Figure 1-40).

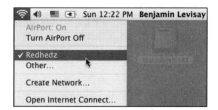

Figure 1-40: The signal strength of your AirPort connection is indicated by the curved signal bar in the AirPort menu icon itself. Four solid bars indicate a strong signal.

If your AirPort is turned off or if you don't have an AirPort card installed on your computer, the icon for the AirPort menu will look like an empty outline of the signal bars. You can also open the Internet Connect.

Multiple available AirPort networks will be listed by name (if they are published) under this menu if the AirPort is on. The network that you are on will be shown with a check next to it (shown in Figure 1-40).

The iChat Menu

If you have set up your .Mac account or an AIM account through iChatAV, then you will have an iChat menu available to the right of the AirPort menu. In this menu, you have access to most of your iChat AV settings and options (shown in Figure 1-41).

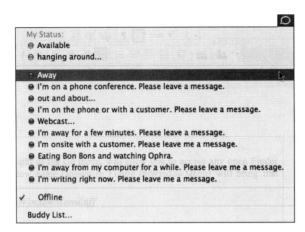

Figure 1-41: Accessing the Buddy List at the bottom of the iChat menu will cause iChat AV to connect and log in.

The Available and Unavailable status messages are available in the menu. And if iChat AV is connected, the available people in your Buddy List will appear in the menu with their AV options.

We Interrupt This Chapter . . .

A short dispute about the "handiness" of this menu popped up during editing.

Benjamin: Through out this book, you will find that I have a "problem" when Apple offers overly redundant options. The iChat menu is one of those not-too-useful options. To use iChat well, you need to have it open. When you have it open, all of the options are available to you. This menu just provides you with more ways to accidentally connect iChat to the Internet.

Sometimes less is more. This menu is one of those cases.

Pieter: While this menu is a tad cluttered, okay, very cluttered, iChat gives you many options to customize the way that you communicate with your friends and co-workers over the Internet. Personally, I kinda like the ability to select different away messages to let people know what I am doing and why I am not answering their messages as if they were the most important people in the world. However, Ben is right in that it is simple to make an accident and turn on iChat without meaning to. On the other hand, in this very connected world, why would you ever want to turn off iChat? Just kidding.

The Volume Menu

The volume can be controlled using the Volume slider menu to the right of the iChat menu (shown in Figure 1-42). Drag the slider up and down to control the volume.

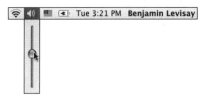

Figure 1-42: The rounded volume bars on the icon of the Volume menu also indicate the volume. Two bars indicate half (approximately) volume.

Turn the Volume Up, Down, or Mute the Volume from the Keyboard

The Volume menu is not nearly as useful as F3 (Mute), F4 (Volume Down), and F5 (Volume Up) keys. You will know if you are affecting the sound by a slightly transparent speaker symbol with a level indicator below it. You will also hear a sound rising and falling as you turn the sound up or down (respectively).

The Keyboard Input Menu

The Keyboard Input menu, located to the right of the Volume menu, allows for direct access to some of the features in the International settings in the System Preferences (shown in Figure 1-43).

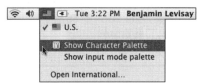

Figure 1-43: The flag icon itself actually represents the language that is set for the keyboard.

Selecting the Show Character Palette option under the Keyboard Input menu will open the Character palette where you can view and select characters in a variety of sets and categories (shown in Figure 1-44).

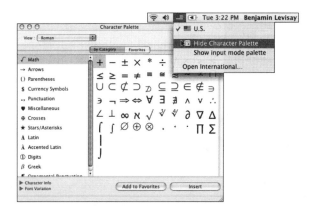

Figure 1-44: Extensive work with text and unusual characters make this palette very useful.

Choosing the Keyboard Input menu again gives you the choice of hiding the Character palette without closing it, as shown in Figure 1-44.

> **note**   Closing the Character palette is not available if you have more than one language palette installed.

The Battery Menu

If you have a laptop, you will find another menu to the right of the Keyboard Input menu. This menu's icon will show up as a plug inside a battery (shown in Figure 1-45). When the PowerBook is plugged into an AC source, the icon looks like status bar within a battery indicating the level of charge.

Figure 1-45: The menu allows different views for the battery as well as direct access to the Energy Saver controls in System Preferences.

The Date & Time Menu

This menu is located to the right of the Battery menu. The Date & Time menu shows the Date just below it by clicking on the time itself (shown in Figure 1-46).

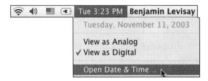

Figure 1-46: The menu offers Analog and Digital views of the time. The bottom choice offers direct access to the Date & Time controls in System Preferences.

Push (or Drag) Your Icon Menus Around

Secret

If you don't like the arangement of your icon pull-down menus (to the right of the Help menu) you can hold down the Command Key while you click on those Icons and move them around to change the order.

While your at it, you can also drag the menus off the top bar by holding down the Command key and dragging them down. You'll have to go into the appropriate System Preference or launch the appropriate application to get those menus back.

The User Menu

The last menu (that comes with the OS) is the User Menu, located in the upper-right corner of the screen (if you have Fast User Switching enabled in the System Preferences). Clicking on this menu lists all the users available on the computer (shown in Figure 1-47).

Figure 1-47: The check marks in front of the user pictures and names indicate that the accounts are active and have been logged into.

This menu is new to OS X in Panther. It allows for quick access to the Login window, but, more importantly, it allows for a new Panther feature, Fast User Switching. In Panther, it is possible to be logged into more than one account at a time. If you are, you can switch between the users by select the users in this menu.

We get into more depth about users and Fast User Switching in Chapter 6.

Contextually Speaking . . .

Contextual menus seem to make a lot of Mac people uncomfortable. Perhaps they seem too PC-like to use. Maybe people find them too new.

But contextual menus are *not* new. In fact, Apple has had contextual menus in the Finder since OS 8.x. And most applications now are contextually aware. In fact, if you've used FinalCut Pro or FinalCut Express, you will find that using the contextual menus are almost essential to do what you want to do.

The idea of contextual menus did start in the world of the PC. (You've got to give the Devil his due!) The idea was that for any object there were certain actions or commands that either applied or didn't apply. And because those actions could be known by the OS, it could present a list of options that apply.

Assume that you are working with a Mac, right out of the box, bundled with the Apple Pro Mouse that came with the computer. In order to access a contextual menu you will need to Control-click (Control key and mouse click) on an object. When you Control-click on an object the cursor will appear with a small ladder next to it, indicating that you are about to access a contextual menu.

Clicking one time on an object before you Control-click on it will select the file, folder, volume, or application (shown in Figure 1-48) prior to accessing the contextual options of that object.

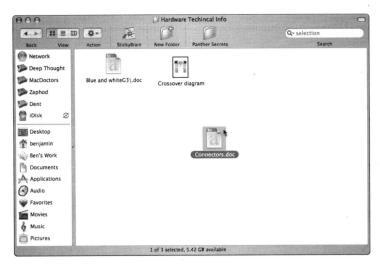

Figure 1-48: The highlighted icon shows a selected document ready for contextual access.

Holding down the Control key and clicking again on that same file will open up a menu with the available OS actions and commands (shown in Figure 1-49), as well as contextual options from third-party programs that add contextual modules (shown in Figure 1-50).

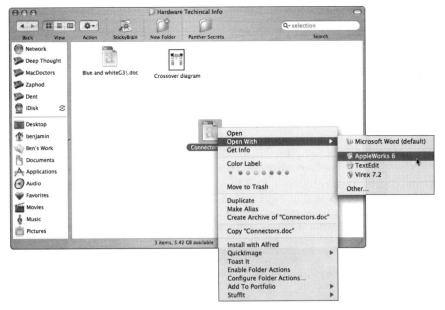

Figure 1-49: Among all the things that contextual commands can do, you can choose to open a document in various applications and of course to add a color label.

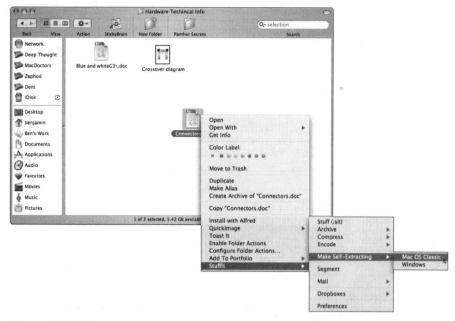

Figure 1-50: StuffIt Deluxe adds contextual modules so you can access all of StuffIt's features by Control-clicking on an item(s).

Items on the desktop also have contextual menus available to them (as shown in Figure 1-51).

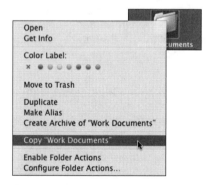

Figure 1-51: You can now copy files and folders by Control-clicking on a file or folder and choosing Copy "item name."

We Interrupt This Chapter . . .

This started as a note about giving the Devil his due with regards to two-button mice . . .

Benjamin: What I'm about to say may sound very Un-Mac-like. Apple is famous for its sleek design and easy functionality. But the Apple Pro Mouse has not evolved with the OS.

The reason that Mac users don't use (and most often don't know about) contextual menus is that the mouse is a one-button mouse. Although I understand the standpoint of making the experience easy, this mouse design is stunted and parochial. PC users have had two-button mice for years to take advantage of the contextual menus. Another handy thing, the scroll bar, is a great way to read through e-mail pages and look at Web sites.

And there are lots of third-party mice that have at least two buttons with a scroll wheel — so if you want it, you can get it. I just don't understand why Apple hasn't come out with a two-button mouse like every other computer manufacturer. Perhaps Apple doesn't think we're smart enough to handle all the options that they've given to us through the OS.

This is a case where Apple should think of function over form.

Pieter: Personally, I use a two-button mouse and love it, but then again I also use Windows- and Unix-based computers daily, so I am used to it. The original idea that Steve Jobs and the original Lisa and Macintosh engineers had was for a computer that required as little training as possible. Thus, the engineers felt that producing a mouse with two buttons would create an interface element that required a user to learn what each button does. Not exactly a point-and-click experience. Microsoft looked at what Apple did with one button and what workstation makers did with three buttons and settled on what they felt was a compromise, the two-button mouse. However, this did entail a higher cost of training, because users were forced to learn what each button did; and then there was the whole issue of how to deal with left-handed people, like Bill Gates. In the end, all sides have stuck with their style of mouse. Even three-button mice are still popular in the workstation market, simply because users that grew up with each operating system are used to them.

Searching Like a Pro

Much to-do has been made about searching in the Mac OS. And I have seen articles that are just too darn long about how to search for items on you computer. We're not going to do that. This section of the chapter is short.

Unlike Classic, finding files no longer happens in Sherlock. That application is now exclusively used for various Internet searches. We talk about Sherlock in Chapter 12.

To search for files in Panther, you have two options. You can search for files through the Finder window or you can choose Find from under the File menu (⌘-F) in the Finder.

If you want to look for a file within a specific folder or directory, you would be best served searching for the file(s) using the Search field in a Finder window's toolbar. To search in a directory or folder, open a Finder window to the directory (or folder) that you want to search and type the name of the file, folder, or application you want in the Search field in the upper-right corner of a Finder window's toolbar (shown in Figure 1-52).

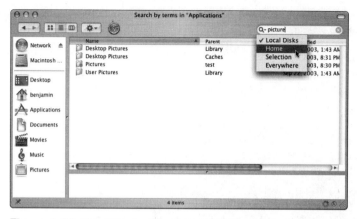

Figure 1-52: The fast searching feature of the window search will cause the results to update as you continue to type, changing those results.

The default setting for the window search is for the selected directory. If you do not find the file you are looking for in the selected directory, you can pull down a menu from the small magnifying glass icon that expands your search to the Home folder, the Local Disks, or Everywhere (as shown in Figure 1-52).

note When you expand Finder window searches to any of the other directory choices, the search criteria at the top of the Finder window do not change to help you remember where you started the search from.

Clicking on any of the search results shows a directory path in the bottom panel. The search window is also just like any Finder window. You can drag, copy, delete, and launch any document from the search results.

The other method for searching for files is by typing ⌘-F and launching the Find application. Find (shown in Figure 1-53) allows you to search in the same places as the Finder window search.

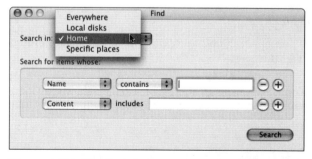

Figure 1-53: The Find dialog box can be as simple to use as the window search option.

The Find dialog box has a lot of expanded features that the Finder window search does not. You can choose to search by ten different categories and multiples of those to help in your search (as shown in Figure 1-54). This is the method you'll want to use if you need to "Search like a Pro."

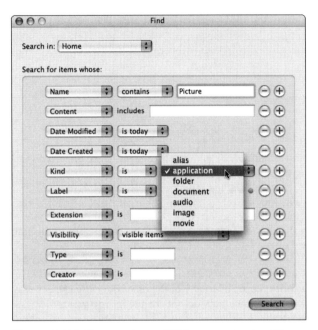

Figure 1-54: The search possibilities are extensive. The search permutations are large enough that I don't care to work them out.

Digging into the Files

Looking at the files in more depth will help you understand and use the Finder more like an expert. Having said that, I can tell you that what we cover here is a real snooze fest to all but the biggest Mac geeks. But the material needs to be covered, and this is as good a place as any to cover it, so let's press on.

Info in Column View

If you look at a file or application in the Column view, you will be able to see a lot of information about that file or application (shown in Figure 1-55). Data shown includes the item's icon or preview, its name, kind, size, date created, date modified, and version.

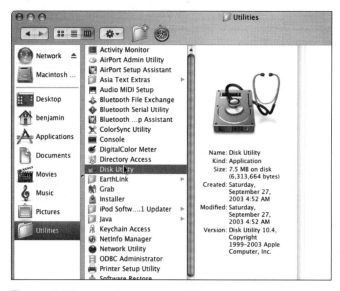

Figure 1-55: Icons show up in the Column view for applications and some files.

Beside the usual information, you will see previews of some files such as PDFs, some text files, QuickTime clips, and lots of image file types (shown in Figure 1-56).

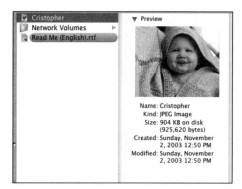

Figure 1-56: Previews show up in the Column view for many kinds of data files.

Get Info

After you have a file selected, you can choose to get a lot more information about them by either Control-clicking the document to access the Get Info option in the contextual menu (shown in Figure 1-57) or by selecting Get Info (⌘-I) in the File menu.

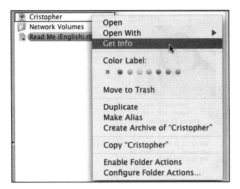

Figure 1-57: Accessing the Get Info option.

File Info

Now that you have the File info open, you will be confronted with a lot of options. The Info dialog box is broken down into six parts: General, Name & Extensions, Open with, Preview, Ownership & Permissions, and Comments.

General Info

The first thing you see when you open up the Get Info panel is the document name on the top (shown in Figure 1-58). The General info shows the icon preview (not the image preview), the size of the document, the location of the document, the date the document was created, the date that the document was last modified, the Stationery Pad option, and the ability to lock the document so that it can't be modified further.

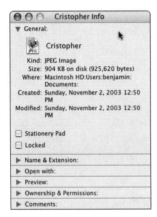

Figure 1-58: The General info is almost identical to the information available through the column view file info.

Secret

Using the Stationery Pad Option to Protect Your Files

There is a little-used option in the General info section of the document info called Stationery Pad. When you click on the Stationery Pad check box you give that document Stationery properties. This becomes apparent the first time you try to double-click on a file that has this Stationery Pad option checked and a copy of the document is immediately created in the same directory (as shown in Figure 1-59).

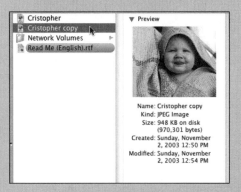

Figure 1-59: The Stationery Pad option treats the file like a master file and makes usable copies of it.

You should be careful with this feature. Every time you double-click on a document with the Stationery Pad option selected, a new copy will be created.

Name & Extension

By turning the little disclosure triangle to the left of the Name & Extension section of the document Info box, you get the name of the document with the extension and the option to hide (or not) the file extension (shown in Figure 1-60).

Figure 1-60: You can also use this name field to change the name of the document.

Open with

Just below the Name & Extension section of the document Info box, you will find the Open with section of the document Info box. In this part of the Info box you can choose which application you want to set to open the document by pulling down the application choice menu (shown in Figure 1-61).

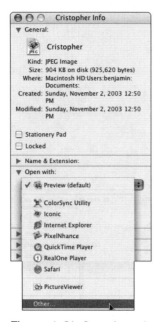

Figure 1-61: Sometimes the applications that the Mac OS thinks may work well to open your document may not work so well.

Many of the choices that the OS understands will appear in the menu. If the application you want to use doesn't appear in the list, you can select the Other option at the bottom of the menu and choose the application you want to use to open the document (shown in Figure 1-61).

The only other thing that the Open with feature of the document Info box will do is allow you to specify the newly selected application to open all documents like the one that you are getting the Info about. To do that, click on the Change All button (shown in Figure 1-62).

---

caution   The ability to make all documents open with the application you select (by clicking on the Change All button in the Open with selection in the document Info box) is a very powerful option. In fact, it's almost too powerful. You can cause a lot of problems for yourself if you don't know what you are doing.

If you don't have a reason to do this (and even sometime when you do), you should avoid using this feature.

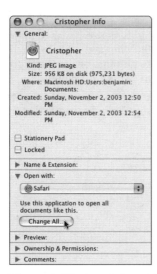

Figure 1-62: The choice of Change All button is grayed out until the application is first changed.

Preview

Below the Open with section of the document Info box, you will find the Preview info section (shown in Figure 1-63). Other file types show movie information or play audio.

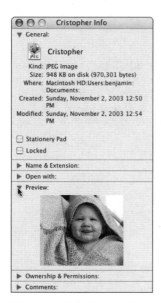

Figure 1-63: There isn't any way to affect the Preview information. You can only look at the preview of this picture of my son Cristopher when he was a baby.

Ownership & Permissions

This is the part of the document info that gets complicated because we have to get further into users and permissions. Understanding this part of the document Info box can be useful in the cases where you are having problems with documents or applications on your computer. If you aren't having problems, you should leave this stuff alone!

The first option you have in this section is to choose or change your access to the document. This is done by pulling down from the You can drop-down list in the document Info window (shown in Figure 1-64).

Figure 1-64: Sometimes these three options are enough.

When you need more access to a file's permissions or privileges, you can get there by clicking on the disclosure triangle next to the Details label in the Ownership & Permissions section of the document Info box. What you get is an expanded area where the ownership, group, and other access can be set or changed (shown in Figure 1-65). Before you can change some of the items in this area you have to click on the lock icon next to the Owner drop-down list.

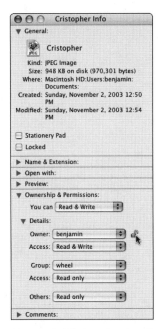

Figure 1-65: The Details allow a lot of control of a document's permissions after you unlock them.

After the Ownerships are unlocked, you can change the user to another owner (shown in Figure 1-66), change the Group (shown in Figure 1-67), and/or set the access for Others.

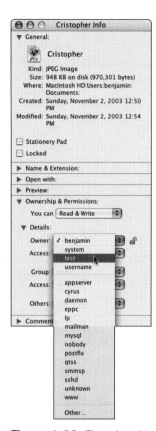

Figure 1-66: Changing the document's owner.

After you've set or changed the ownership and/or privileges, you will need to Authenticate to prove to Panther that you have sufficient privileges to make these changes. This happens when you try to close the document Info box and the Authenticate dialog box comes up and asks you for your Administrative Password (shown in Figure 1-68).

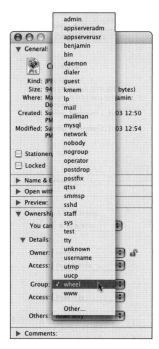

Figure 1-67: Changing the Group privileges for a document.

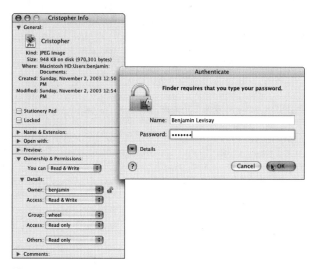

Figure 1-68: If you're not an administrative User or don't know the password, don't muck around with the Ownership & Permissions.

Comments

The Comments field in the document Info box, located at the bottom of the Info box, is good for one thing — storing comments (shown in Figure 1-69).

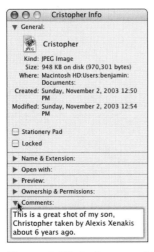

Figure 1-69: In the case of this document, I thought it was important to note the name of the photographer and the relative date about this picture of my son.

Secret

Comments Can Be Used to "Tag" Your Files

Unless you go looking, most people don't see the text in the Comments. As an added security feature, you can put your information and/or relevant creation and ownership information here. I've even seen people put their phone and address information in the Comments.

My Favorite Third-Party OS Menu Enhancer

I like almost everything about OS X. I like the Dock. I like the new Apple menu. And I like the logic behind it all. But I just couldn't get over not having an application menu in the upper-right corner of the screen like I had in my pre–OS X days. Maybe it's just a character defect, but I went out and found myself a third-party *haxie* when I moved to Jaguar, and I'll probably never move forward without it.

There is more than one option for an application menu utility or haxie. The one that I found that I liked the best with regards to its look and to the preference options it had is ASM from Frank Vercruesse Products which can be found online at www.vercruesse.de/software.

Before you add an application menu to the upper-right corner of the screen, you might want to turn off the Fast User Switching menu. You can do this by clicking on the Accounts icon in the System Preferences. If you click on the Login Options under the Users, you can disable Fast User Switching, which will turn off the Fast User Switching menu.

After you've installed and registered this shareware (registering shareware is the right thing to do), you can access the ASM preferences in the Other section of the System Preferences. ASM preferences allow you to set preferences for the entire menu bar (shown in Figure 1-70), the menu settings for the menu itself (shown in Figure 1-71), and some other useful special features (shown in Figure 1-72).

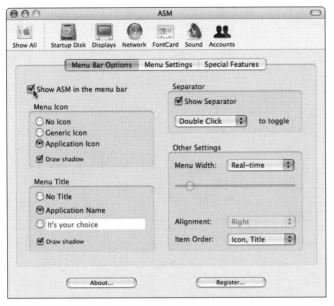

Figure 1-70: I chose to make the menu bar look like my menu bar used to look in OS 9.x.

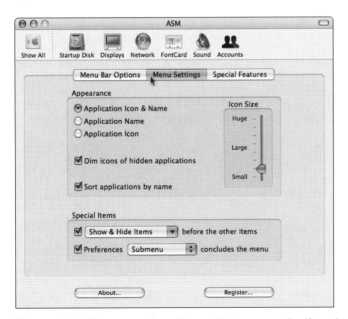

Figure 1-71: The appearance of the pull-down menu itself can be changed in the Menu Settings preferences.

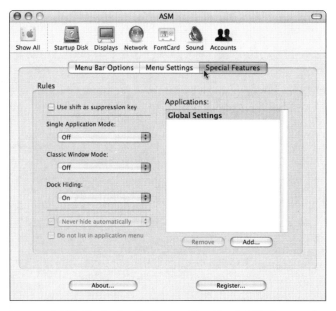

Figure 1-72: Single Application and/or Classic Window mode may trip your trigger, but they're not for me.

Many of the ASM preferences are overly complex, in my opinion. I wanted to add a simple application menu to the upper-right corner of the menu bar. To that end, I found that the default settings (with a minor change or two) gave me the application menu that I was looking for (shown in Figure 1-73).

Figure 1-73: This is the menu that I wanted and that's what I got from the ASM preferences shown in Figures 1-70 through 1-72. If you like this ASM look as well, feel free to copy my prefs.

Summary

So, we looked at the desktop and learned that it wasn't as close to the surface as we thought. We also found that a desktop, like a lot of things in this user-centric OS, can be distinctly you.

We explored some of the new Finder window views and options. And when we were done with that, we explored the Finder window options some more. We looked at the new options on the toolbar and explored the entirely new sidebar. We even showed you how to add a picture to the background of a Finder window in icon view. And if you didn't catch my enthusiasm about the labels being back, then you just weren't reading. If you read through these sections, you can now consider yourself an expert in Finder window use.

We explored the menus at the top of the screen, contextual menus, and searching for files.

After that, we dug into the files themselves and learned how to learn more about any file on your computer. This includes some time spent on messing around with file permissions. If you read all the way through that section, you're not an expert, but you're a better person that I am. (I wrote it and I don't want to read it all the way through.)

But we ended the chapter well by looking at my favorite OS haxie that gives us back the Classic-like application menu.

In the next chapter, we go through what the Apple menu is and what the Apple menu can be.

Putting Power in
the Apple Menu

Chapter

2

The Apple menu is the unique identifier that separates the men from the boys, or at least the Mac OS from all other operating systems. It's not just the symbol of the company; it's also an important navigation feature for your Mac, a place where you can access system settings and a number of other mission-critical functions.

The Origin of the Apple Logo

Secret

Did you know that the same person who created the IBM logo, Rob Janoff, who was the head of the art department at Regis McKenna Advertising, originally designed the progenitor to the famous Apple menu? It was 1977 when he designed the famous logo that bears the shape of an Apple someone had the temerity to bite into. It was said to signify knowledge, and represented the Bible's depiction of the apple that was the fruit of the tree of knowledge. The bitten into part is also considered a take-off of the word *byte*, part of the computer lexicon even in those early days of the PC era.

The finished logo debuted at the first West Coast Computer Faire. The present version of the Apple menu, consisting of a single shaded color, first appeared in the PowerBook G3 in 1998.

But this oh-so-useful feature has a long and checkered history, and has appeared in three basic forms over the years. As I explain in the next section, each has its advantages and disadvantages, and it all depends on what you're used to and the sort of features you like.

To be fair, the Mac OS X version (as you see in Figure 2-1), which has existed without much change since the operating system's initial release, does have a good deal of intelligence behind it, even if the ability to customize it to your taste is severely limited. For one thing, it incorporates some of the features of the Special menu, so it's no longer necessary to go to the Finder simply to restart or shut down your Mac.

note   When he first unveiled the revised Apple menu circa Mac OS X, Steve Jobs even hinted that there may be other changes afoot that would reduce reliance on the Finder for certain functions. But that hasn't happened, at least not yet.

Avoid Getting Second-Guessed by Your Mac

Secret

Apple knows that some Mac users can't make up their minds, which is why you have to OK an acknowledgement prompt when you try to restart, shut down, or log out. But if you resent second-guessing, just hold down the Option key when you access those commands. Mac OS X will obey you without question, although you've still got to prepare for a short delay, from 15 to 30 seconds, before it happens in either case.

Figure 2-1: This edition of the Apple menu is, as some people put it, a mixed bag.

Some of the commands are pretty self-explanatory, and many are really useful if you know what to do with them. Let's break it down. . . .

Dissecting the Apple Menu

You should consider the Apple Menu as being more than just one menu. It's more like several menus that have been combined into one place to make your access of the OS a little easier. Let's take a look at the Apple Menu by sections.

The Normal Commands

The bottom five choices in the Apple Menu are Force Quit, Sleep, Restart, Shut Down, and Log Out.

You could, if you wanted, free yourself of a crashing application by way of the Force Quit command in the Apple menu, although, frankly, if an application locks up real tight, it may not be all that easy to access. But there's always the alternative, ⌘-Shift-Escape.

While Windows forces you to endure various and sundry promotions for different digital hub-type products as you traipse through its wide array of wizards and information screens, Mac OS X keeps this irritating practice to a minimum. I'm sure you're all grateful about that. The Get Mac OS X Software command, for example, does nothing more than take you to a page at Apple's Web site where you can download a decently rich collection of applications, some of which are actually free. Who coulda thunk it?

Sleep, Restart, and Shut Down are all well-known commands from the days of pre-OS X, under the Special menu.

---

note We revisit some of these commands later in this chapter when we compare the OS 9 and OS 10.3 Apple menus.

Using the Apple to Know Who You Are

The Log Out option at the bottom of the Apple menu is new (as you can see in Figure 2-2). In Panther, the name of the user has been added — presumably as a construct of the Fast User Switching that we talk about in Chapter 1.

Figure 2-2: The Apple gets personal. To know who you are, look at your choice for logging out.

Using the Apple to Know What You Are

Just under the Apple Menu (shown in Figure 2-3) you will see a choice that has been around for a while. About This Mac brings up a dialog box (shown in Figure 2-4) that gives you a brief overview of what kind of computer you're using, which OS you are running, and how much RAM you have.

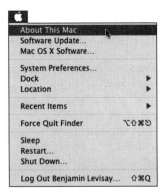

Figure 2-3: If you need to know fast, it's at the top of the list.

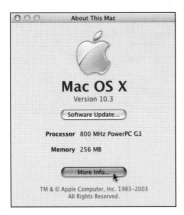

Figure 2-4: The About This Mac dialog box shows the essentials right away with buttons to take you to more information.

A Quick Way to Find Your Mac Serial Number

Want more information than just the Mac OS version in the About This Mac window? Just click the version number once to see the operating system build number. This is the number that Apple's developers use when developing Mac OS X. On recent Macs, a second click will yield your Mac's serial number, which saves you the drudgery of poking behind your Mac or looking for the box that you put beneath a dozen other boxes in the garage when the Apple demands to know that information before allowing you to have some technical support.

The More Info button will bring up Apple System Profiler (shown in Figure 2-5), so you can discover all you ever wanted to know about your system and then some. You learn more about that handy application in Chapter 12.

You can also get to the Software Update part of the System Preferences from either the second menu option under the Apple (shown in Figure 2-3) or by clicking on the Software Update button on the About This Mac dialog box (shown in Figure 2-4). We cover software updates when we get to System Preferences in Chapter 4.

Apple has also included a direct link to their Web site in Panther. The third item under the Apple (shown in Figure 2-3) will launch a browser and take you directly to a redirect page on the Apple Web site. You will end up (for now) at www.apple.com/downloads/macosx/. This convenient (if not a touch self serving) Web link will allow you to search for the latest and greatest OS X applications, utilities, screensavers, updates, and so on.

Figure 2-5: The system profiler has changed looks but not functionality.

More Shortcuts to the System Preferences

Just under the Mac OS X Software option (under the Apple) you will see a direct link to System Preferences and to the Dock controls (shown in Figure 2-6).

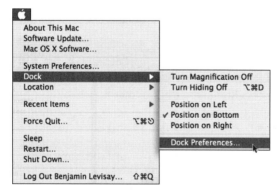

Figure 2-6: The Dock submenu gives direct control of the Dock. And the System Preferences menu option gives one more way to get to the System Preferences.

We Interrupt This Chapter . . .

A few offhand remarks by me about Apple's propensity toward leading us (over and over) to the System Preferences lead to the following discussion . . .

Benjamin: It's at this point that I started to realize that Apple seems somewhat obsessed in making the System Preferences available to us. You can get to the System Preferences through the Dock (next chapter), the Software Update (both under the Apple and on the About This Mac dialog box), the Dock Preferences options in the Dock submenu, the Network Preferences options in the Location submenu, and under the Applications part of the Recent Items submenu if you have recently opened System Preferences.

This is just my opinion, but perhaps "less would be more" here.

Pieter: Apple seems intent on making the Apple menu a lot like the Start menu in Windows, in other words, a common and unchanging menu that stores many commonly used user tools. While this is a worthy goal from a user interface viewpoint, I miss the ability to customize my Apple menu that I had back in earlier versions of Mac OS. The downside to this and to making the System Preferences so accessible is that you remove some of the ability to personalize your Mac OS experience and, unless you lock things down, you make access to some of the most powerful utilities available in Mac OS X a bit too easy.

Using the Apple to Know What You've Done

We skip past the location for now, and look at the Recent Items submenu shown in Figure 2-7.

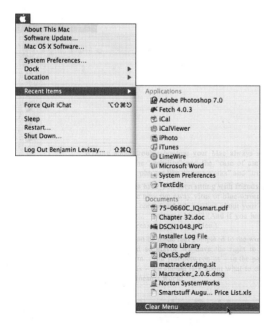

Figure 2-7: The most useful part of the Recent Items menu is the Clear Menu at the bottom.

Recent Items is something that Mac OS pre–OS X has had for quite awhile. At this point, it's appropriate to show the evolution of the Apple menu by comparing the Panther and Classic Apple menus.

Comparing the Apple Menu for Classic and Mac OS X

When the Mac OS X Public Beta first appeared in September 2000, observant Mac users wondered, "What did they do to the Apple menu?" All you saw was an Apple logo in the center of the menu bar, and clicking on it did, well, nothing.

Fortunately, Apple realized that you can't take away cherished features of this sort without forming battle lines, so changes were made, and they showed up in the first official release of Mac OS X, version 10.0.

> **note** All right, I realize that other Mac features have yet to be restored under Mac OS X. So, hold the cards and letters please. If all goes well, you might even see some of these in a future version, no doubt in a spiffy new form in keeping with Apple's penchant for wowing its customers, or at least giving them something new to learn. (Take your choice.)

But it wasn't the Apple menu you knew and loved. The original was simply a listing of the items inserted into a single folder, Apple Menu Items (see Figure 2-8). For this new version, Apple felt it had to tamper with success and take it in a new direction.

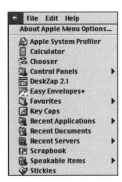

Figure 2-8: A quick visit to the Classic environment shows that this Apple menu just won't go away. It just appears when you switch to a Classic application.

Secret

You Can Have Your OS X and Classic Apple at the Same Time . . .

. . . just not in the same place. Yes. It's true.

A little know feature of the Classic System Preferences (shown in Figure 2-9) is that you can show your Classic status in the menu bar. Many people go right past this feature because they can't see the value of knowing if Classic is on or not. Especially because launching a Classic application will either bring Classic to the front or launch it anyway.

Secret

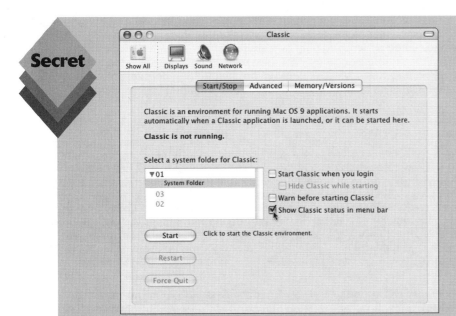

Figure 2-9: The Show Classic status in menu bar check box option doesn't hint at Classic Apple menu goodness, but it's there for those who are curious enough to go looking for it.

But because not very many people use this extra menu, you never get to see that the Classic Apple Menu Items are available for the Classic environment under this special menu (shown in Figure 2-10), located toward the right side of the top menu bar.

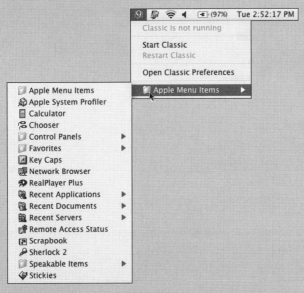

Figure 2-10: The Apple Menu Items submenu only affects items in the Classic environment.

In a sense, the original Mac OS X version 10.0 was a mixture of the old and the new and then some. If you recall back in the heady early days of the Mac OS, prior to System 7.0, the Apple menu could be customized only by installing startup programs, most commonly known as INITs. These little programs were designed to enhance the functions of your Mac, such as providing a fancy font menu or, in some cases, letting you completely redesign the interface. (The famous ClickChange comes to mind.)

The World of INITs

Secret

You do remember the word INIT, right? All right, maybe you're not as old as I am, but the word was short for initialization, and referred to a program that loaded code when you started your Mac. Some of these little programs also had a front end, called a control panel, that you could use to change settings. INIT took a long time to disappear from the lexicon of Mac users. (And frankly, some of my friends still use it.) For System 7 and beyond, Apple decided to separate INITs into extensions, the ones without the user interface, and control panels, the ones with. But old-time Mac users still use the term INIT to refer to such things.

To install one of these INITs, you just popped it in the System Folder and restarted. If the INIT had a user interface, it would be listed among your roster of control panels that you called up from the Apple menu. But what goes around comes around; Mac OS X's System Preferences application, as you see in Chapter 4, comes across as, in some part, a variation on this theme.

Back to our little history lesson: The version of the Apple menu that premiered beginning with Mac System 7.0 was a whole lot smarter than earlier versions because it was so supremely extensible. With the addition of the Apple Menu Options control panel (see I got the term right!) a few years later (see Figure 2-11), you could regulate the number of recent items, including network servers, and many regret the way it was changed because the ability to modify some of these Apple menu options under Mac OS X ar relatively limited.

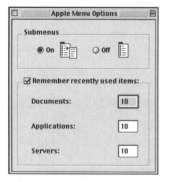

Figure 2-11: Enter the number of recent items to be displayed in each category and Apple Menu Options will make it so.

HAM and Rye

Did you know that Apple Menu Options was once a third-party commercial program? In the early 1990s, a now-defunct software publisher known as Microseeds introduced a product called HAM, which was short for Hierarchical Apple Menu. No wonder they gave it an abbreviation. In 1995, Apple acquired the program for its 7.5 upgrade, renamed it, but kept most of the features, which included adding submenus to the Apple menu, and allowing you to configure the number of recent items. It stuck, and the utility was last updated in 2001, at version number 1.1.9. I'm sure many of you hope that perhaps one of the Mac OS X Apple menu enhancers might also be acquired by Apple for a future version of Mac OS X, or at least serve as inspiration.

However, the Mac OS X seemed a step backwards with sharply reduced opportunities for user setup. Of course, you can adjust the number of Recent Items listed, courtesy of the Appearance preference panel (as shown in Figure 2-12), and you can setup additional locations for networking, courtesy of the Location submenu (shown in Figure 2-13).

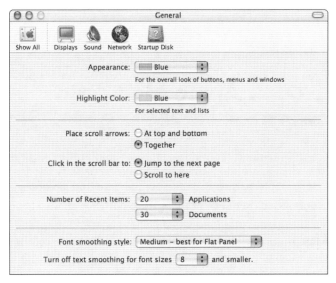

Figure 2-12: As with old Apple Menu Options, you can set the number of recent items, but they are limited to increments of 10 and top out at 50.

Using the Apple Menu to Know Where You Are

The last built-in option of the Apple menu that we're going to talk about is the Location submenu.

Even though the Apple menu (Panther edition) has fewer features than the one it replaces, there's still some handy stuff there. For example, if you're a Road Warrior, you no doubt have to connect to lots of different networks, or, at the very least, use different ISP access numbers.

First, create a separate Location in the Network Preference panel of System Preferences for each place you're going to visit. That's explained in more detail in Chapter 29. Then just select the new spot from the Location submenu in the Apple menu. Just give it a name that makes sense, such as Las Vegas Casino or Secret Hideaway. Those sets of network settings will appear under the Location submenu under the Apple menu (shown in Figure 2-13).

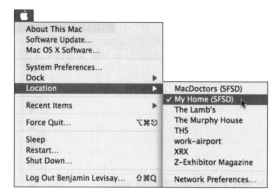

Figure 2-13: Make sure that the names of your sets mean something to you.

And that is where it stands . . . unless, of course, you decide to give the Apple menu a little help, and that forms our next topic.

Tricking the Mac OS X Apple Menu with Third-Party Software

Ah, frustration rears its ugly head. Yes, the new Apple menu is pretty nice, and I really appreciate the ability to restart without visiting the Finder, but it doesn't meet the needs of folks who became accustomed to that extensible Apple menu of yore. Fortunately, where Apple fails to innovate, third parties will take over and get the job done.

Rather than prolong the agony, let's give two of those third parties a chance to shine.

FruitMenu Haxie

"Apple menu" is trademarked, so the folks who run Unsanity, developers of lots of cool Mac OS X add-ons, had to pick a different name for this *haxie*.

---

note

A "haxie" is a new term that has been used (if not coined) by such software developers like Unsanity. In fact the term haxie has become almost synonymous with Unsanity and its products.

While Mac OS 9 (and earlier) had an the Extensions and Control Panel model that developers could add to to make "improvements" to the OS, that construct is not available for OS X.

The answer to this has been the development of APE (Application Enhancers) and other kinds of System Enhancers. APE haxies allow third-party modules to modify the way applications work and operate.

Other (non APE) haxies can include modifications of the System that can cause severe problems. These haxies should be researched and used with some care.

Yes, the Mac OS X version of the Apple menu can be configured. But configuration is limited to the number of recent applications and documents, within a limited range. That's rather disappointing if you were used to customizing the Mac OS 9 version to a fare-thee-well.

Using FruitMenu

With FruitMenu (see Figure 2-14), you not only have the ability to make the Apple menu your own, but also you can spruce up contextual menus. You can also assign hot keys for specific menu items (shades of NowMenus, a cool menu modifier from the Classic Mac OS days).

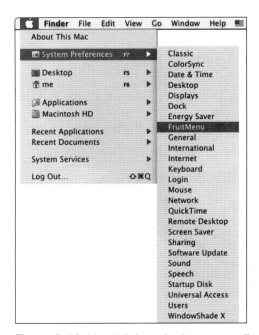

Figure 2-14: Now this is an Apple menu to die for.

If I listed all the features in FruitMenu, I'd end up devoting this chapter to nothing else, so I'll be brief. Here are some of the useful things you can do:

♦ Add files and folders and even complete disks to both the Apple menu and contextual menu.

♦ List individual items in System Preferences for direct access via the Apple menu.

♦ Create custom Apple and contextual menus for various applications.

♦ Easily move items to a selected folder using the Gather Items in New Folder feature for contextual menus. Ultra cool.

Installing FruitMenu

FruitMenu installs within System Preferences as a preference pane, which is used to configure the utility (see Figure 2-15). You have the option to install only for your user account, or system wide. There is also an Uninstaller, because Unsanity installs some system components that aren't so easy to remove manually. Fortunately, the removal process just takes a few seconds.

> **note** FruitMenu is demoware, which means it'll run for 15 days and then stop dead in its tracks if you don't buy a user license. That should, though, give you plenty of time to see if it gives you the Apple menu of your dreams.

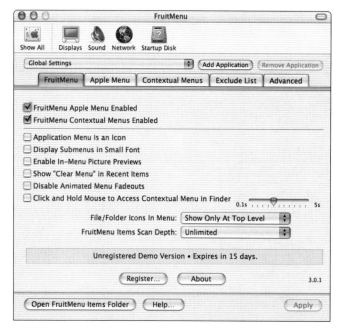

Figure 2-15: Use this preference panel to configure FruitMenu to your needs and desires.

> **note** You might wonder what all these system extras do to performance. Can they affect system responsiveness in the same fashion as Classic Mac extensions? The answer is that it depends. How's that for dodging the question? But it's also true. The people at Unsanity say that you will experience a minor speed hit with one of their haxies when launching applications, but it's usually not enough to be noticeable under normal circumstances.
>
> Curious to know more? Just hook up to www.unsanity.com and check it out.

Keeping It Simple with Classic Menu

Compared to the huge feature set of FruitMenu, Sig Software's Classic Menu (shown in Figure 2-16) might seem underpowered. But if all you need is the simple ability to add the items you want to the Apple menu without the fuss or the slight slowdown from installing a system add-on, you might prefer it.

When you launch Classic Menu for the first time, it will change the Apple icon to something resembling the Classic version (which you can change in the application's preferences), and it makes a Classic Menu Items folder within the Preferences folder of your personal Library folder. The developers anticipate your needs by popping in a few aliases to commonly used items, including your Applications and Users folders, plus your startup drive. You can go the rest of the route simply by dragging an item in the Finder to the Apple icon. That's all you have to do to make things happen.

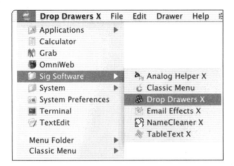

Figure 2-16: Classic Menu is a simple Apple menu fixer-upper; and it's easy to configure.

It All Starts with a Control-Click

Secret

Must you access the original Apple menu after installing Classic Menu? Well, if you must, just Control-click the Apple icon and you will accomplish this worthy task. Or if you prefer to just exit Classic Menu for good, go to the submenu with that name, and choose Quit. Now you're back to normal — or as normal as you can get under the circumstances.

note

So how many levels does Classic Menu's hierarchical menu support? Here it has an advantage over the Mac OS 9 edition, which was limited to five submenus without a little third-party trickery. With Classic Menu, I managed to get 10 submenus before I gave it up and went back to work. (My publisher was screaming something about missing deadlines.)

You can get your copy of Classic Menu direct from Versiontracker.com or from www. sigsoftware.com/.

We Interrupt This Chapter . . .

Our fearless technical editor, Pieter Paulson can't stop being opinionated, so I'll let him have his due.

Pieter: I find that FruitMenu is a much nicer and more robust package than Classic Menu. While Classic Menu is an application and not a hack like the Unsanity offering, it just doesn't have the breadth of features that FruitMenu does. Should Sig Software revise Classic Menu, they could easily change my mind, but for now, the menu altering software of choice in my mind is FruitMenu.

Gene: Opinions, opinions. Can't we all just get along? All right, you wanted to know what I think. Well, this is something really rare, but I also vote features over stability, with this cautionary note. Although those haxies can do wonders to enhance system performance, it's not a good idea to pile them high. I'd rather have a few working right than a lot creating a system slowdown or a possible instability.

Summary

All this just for an Apple menu? Well, now you know how it came to be and how it arrived at where it is now.

In the next chapter, we focus on the Dock, probably the most controversial feature of Mac OS X, and one that is also eminently configurable, though it sometimes takes a little help from outside parties.

The Dock and Its Secrets

Chapter 3

Secrets in This Chapter

" W hat's that weird thing on the bottom of the screen?"

That was probably one of the more complimentary comments at the initial unveiling of Mac OS X's Aqua interface, when Apple first unleashed its new taskbar and application-switching palette, the Dock (see Figure 3-1), upon an unsuspecting public.

Figure 3-1: Love it, hate it, the Dock will not be ignored.

I remember when I wrote an article about the operating system's new features, and my editor added the descriptive phrase "cartoonish and goofy" into my text. I didn't object. Compared to the drab Windows taskbar, Apple wanted something pretty, but it had to be functional too in order to make sense.

Now if you want to find a historical precedent for the Dock, you can look at that original launching bar from NeXT's OS, on which Mac OS X is based.

Dissecting the Dock

Like it or hate it, when you get accustomed to the Dock, you'll find it packs a lot of power if you use it just right. So let's look at the sum of the parts and see if it doesn't begin to grow on you after a while, or at least you don't object to it so much.

Even though some people have never really taken to the Dock, there is a method to Apple's madness. First and foremost, what applications do you have open? Under the Classic Mac OS, you just looked at the application menu to see what you were using (later versions let you choose between simple icon and full label display); the rest appeared with a pop-up menu, a fact lost on some novice Mac users.

The best way of showing you what the Dock does is to compare it to (when possible) what other OS features used to do.

Dock Replaces Several Classic Mac OS Features

As you'll learn in the next chapter (see I'm setting you up for that already), Apple has done a few things to simplify features and functions that used to require several utilities to control. Here's what the Dock replaces, at least in part:

◆ **Application Menu:** First and foremost, what applications do you have open? Under the Classic Mac OS, you just looked at the application menu (which was located in the upper-right corner of the screen) to see what you were using (later versions let you choose between simple icon or full label display); the rest appeared with a pop-up menu, a fact lost on some novice Mac users. Now active applications are shown in the Dock with a small black triangle under them (shown in Figure 3-2).

Figure 3-2: Applications not kept in the Dock will be shown in the Dock when they are open.

Click and Hold on an Active Application to Add It to the Dock

Save a step. Once you've launched an application, you can keep it in the Dock after quitting by holding the icon and choosing Keep in Dock from the pop-up menu (shown in Figure 3-3). Hint: This option won't be listed if the item has already become a kept icon in the Dock. Stay, stay!

Figure 3-3: Using the Keep In Dock menu option is a one-time choice.

♦ **Apple menu:** One of the functions of the Apple menu was the ability to place items in a folder, Apple Menu Items, and have them immediately show up in the menu. This was a great way to access frequently used applications, files, and folders. The Dock is now your main repository for this feature.

♦ **Control Strip:** As you may recall if you've been using Macs for awhile, the Control Strip (see Figure 3-4) was a floating palette, where you could access a number of control panels, and provide special control functions for some applications. Some of those functions now appear in the menus at the top of the screen (shown in Figure 3-5), but access to all of System Preferences are available from the Dock via the System Preferences when the System Preferences application is open (shown in Figure 3-6).

Figure 3-4: A well-populated Control Strip handling many important Classic Mac OS features via a click.

🖥 ◯ ☎ ◀ꞏ) Fri 2:58:25 PM 🔊

Figure 3-5: The top menu bar also shows different System controls. Some of these menu options replace Control Strip functionality.

Figure 3-6: This Menu is only available by clicking and holding on the System Preferences in the Dock when the System Preferences are already open.

> **note**
>
> Mac OS X applications can be configured to add extra functions in the Dock, so that you can click and bring up a menu allowing direct access to extra control functions. Apple's iTunes is one notable example of how well the feature works.

A Guide to Dock Management

So, what's to manage? You drag an icon to the Dock to keep it there, and you drag it away to remove it? That's the beginning and end of it.

Well, no, there's a little more to the Dock than just that. This little section of basic uses and a few cool tips empowers you to use the Dock in ways you never considered before.

note Don't despair if the Dock isn't doing all that you want it to. Courtesy of some of the cool utilities I cover at the end of this chapter, you'll be able to take the Dock into regions that you've never previously explored. Or, at the very least, you'll be able to restore some Classic Mac OS features that you cherished and missed.

The Dock from End to End

Simply stated, there are actually two Docks, combined into one palette and separated by a divider. The left side displays your applications, both the ones that are open and any others that you've placed there previously. The right side displays the rest of the bunch, consisting of documents and folders and even entire drives that have been placed there or minimized. (The Dock doesn't show open documents unless they have been minimized).

That covers the basics, and now here's the rest of the story on using the Dock on a day-to-day basis:

◆ Whenever an application is launched, its icon will magically appear in the Dock (if it's not already there) and in either case, will bounce up and down as it's opening. Once launched, the icon will have a tiny black arrow below it. As with other Dock features, the bouncing effect can be disabled if it annoys you.

note All right, here's an exception to the rule: Some applications run in the background and do not display Dock icons. An example of this is SnapzPro X, a nifty shareware screen capture program from Ambrosia Software, which I consider the best of the breed and totally essential if you, like me, must capture screen images on a regular basis.

Secret

Option-Click Your Way to a Cleaner Desktop

Too much desktop clutter? Hold down the Option key when you click on any application in the Dock. This will hide the other applications, and give you a pristine desktop, except for the 20 documents you may keep open in that application. This Option-clicking trick also works when you click on a Finder window. When you Option-Click on a Finder window from an active application, the Active application will be hidden. There are, by the way, some cool shareware utilities that do this stuff automatically and save you some wear and tear. I cover some of that stuff in Chapter 1 and in the shareware section at the end of the book.

◆ If an application needs to put up an alert prompt, the icon will bounce continuously until you click on the icon to see what's up. With a Web browser, for example, it may just want to tell you that the site can't be found. Some applications even put information in a Dock icon. For example, AOL for Mac OS X shows the number of unread e-mails on the left of its icon, and the number of new instant messages at the right. Apple's Mail shows the number of unread e-mails, and Print Center shows you the page number of the document that's being processed.

Use Key Command to Put Items in the Trash

One of the biggest criticisms of the Dock is that it's a moving target, and makes moving things to the Trash much too difficult, because you are apt to miss your target. This is particularly true when it comes to using the option to magnify the icons (not my favorite feature, but that's just me).

A better way to move something to the trash is by using selecting the file(s) and using the ⌘-Delete key combination. That's the only way to always get a hole in one.

◆ When you click the yellow icon in a Finder or document window, it'll minimize the item to the appropriate spot on the Dock in a flourish. Click the icon again in the Dock and it will be restored to full size.

> **note**   If you prefer the original Window Shade effect of the Classic Mac OS, where a single click reduced a window to its title bar, don't despair. I let you in on a way to achieve that capability later in this chapter. So, hang in there.

Minimizing in "Slow-Mo" for a Cool Effect

Remember that famous demonstration that Steve Jobs made when OS X was unveiled, where you minimize something to the Dock and it moves in ultra-slow motion? This is no parlor trick, or gussied up version of Mac OS X. It's something you can do yourself, to amaze your friends, freak out your boss, or make your family think you've finally gone over the edge.

All you have to do is hold the Shift key when you click the yellow button to minimize a window. Shades of that old TV show, *The Six Million Dollar Man,* which made me become sick and tired of slow motion in a single season. This Shift key gambit also works when you click on a minimized icon in the Dock to restore it.

And if you tire of the special effect, release the Shift key and let your Mac OS go about its business at regular speed.

◆ To add an icon to the Dock, just drag it to the appropriate side. The Dock doesn't have the sense to alphabetize its icons, so you must drag it to the appropriate place. If an application icon is not kept in the Dock, it'll vanish when you quit the program.
◆ You cannot remove the icon of an open application, but if it's closed you can click and drag any icon away. It'll vanish in a puff of smoke.

> **note**   Third-party utilities can alter some of the special effects the Dock displays, as you'll see at the end of this chapter.

◆ When you click and hold on an application icon, you'll see a pop-up menu with such basic choices as the ability to show the actual location of the application and to quit a program (refer to Figure 3-3). You also have direct one-click access to your open documents. And as I explained earlier, some applications even include commands to control special functions, such as the ability to play your songs in iTunes and to rearrange the replay order. Just like the System Preferences example (shown in Figure System_DockMenu), the iTunes must be launched for these kinds of menus to work.

What to Do When Good Dock Icons Go Missing

Secret

Why is there a question mark on the Dock where there used to be a Dock icon? That's the Dock telling you something, that the application it originally pointed to is history. Sometimes, it happens when you install a new version, although the Dock should be smart enough to sort that out. The solution is to drag the icon off the Dock and replace it with the current version of the application — or reinstall the application if that's necessary.

◆ Press on a folder or disk icon, and you'll see a multileveled, hierarchical menu allowing you to drill down through folder by folder to get to the file you want (see Figure 3-7). This is one of the Dock's best features, and a really quick way for you to find your stuff.

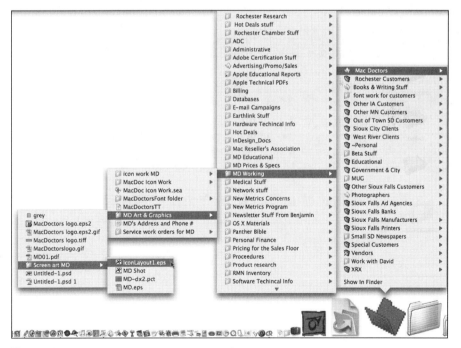

Figure 3-7: This menu may indeed go on forever.

◆ Pressing on a single document or file (on the right side of the dock) gets you the option of showing that file in the Finder (as shown in Figure 3-8).

Figure 3-8: For files you use all the time, keeping them in the dock is a great way to open them and to find them on the hard drive.

◆ The Trash is a permanent resident of the Dock. It functions as it did in pre-Dock operating systems. Drag a file to it, and it enlarges to show that the Trash is filled. Emptying the Trash is accomplished by choosing Empty Trash from the Finder's application menu. Hold down the Option key to bypass the confirmation prompt; you know, the one you see in Figure 3-9.

Figure 3-9: Make up your mind, pilgrim. Delete it or not.

Secret

Option-Click the Trash Icon to Empty the Trash without a Warning

When you click and hold the Trash icon, you'll see an Empty Trash command, which bypasses the Option prompt. Use it wisely, because there's no turning back.

Remaking the Dock in Your Own Image

The Mac OS X offers a few ways to modify the dock to your taste, within a limited range.

You can see your Dock preferences in several ways: By choosing Dock from the Apple menu and selecting what you want from the submenu, by Control-clicking the divider bar that separates the two halves of the Dock, or by accessing the Dock preference panel from System Preferences.

Fast Prefs

The submenus from the Apple menu and the Dock divider provide the most immediate result (see Figure 3-10). These preference commands are also available by clicking and holding on the divider bar in the dock which shows the same preferences in a slightly different way (shown in Figure 3-11).

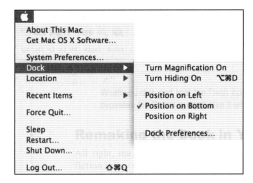

Figure 3-10: If you like your prefs fast and dirty.

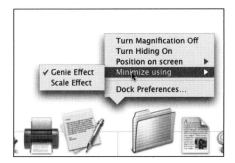

Figure 3-11: You have direct access to the Genie and Scale effects from the Dock preferences from the Dock.

Here's a brief look at what they accomplish:

◆ **Turn Magnification On:** Depending on your point of view, this may be the neatest or the most irritating Dock feature (see Figure 3-12). When you move your mouse towards a specific icon, that and the icons around it jump in size. (The amount can be customized, as you'll see shortly.) This is a boon if you like your Dock real small and just need to make it larger to make the most important stuff readily visible.

Figure 3-12: If you want your Dock to show a life of its own, use the Turn Magnification On option.

◆ **Turn Hiding On:** You detest the Dock, or have a small screen, perhaps on that original Bondi Blue iMac, and don't want it to intrude. This option makes it invisible until you bring your mouse down to the bottom of the screen, at which time it magically appears so you can do your thing with it.

◆ **Position on screen:** Choose Left, Bottom, or Right from the submenu under the Apple. If you choose Right, you will get a vertical Dock on the right side of your screen (see Figure 3-13). This may not be enough to satisfy your needs, but it'll do, I suppose, unless you are really picky about position. (And don't fret, I get to that later in this chapter too.)

Figure 3-13: Right-wing, left-wing, or center (bottom), depending on your political or design temperament.

Dragging Your Dock Around

Here's a fast way to move the Dock to a different position in your screen. Hold down the Shift key and start to adjust the divider bar in the Dock. Now drag it in the direction you want to move it to. The Dock automatically jumps to the new position on the left, right, or back to the bottom of the screen. If it doesn't work the first time, don't get frustrated. It sometimes takes a little practice to get the adjustment and dragging sequence just right.

◆ **Minimize using:** The famous genie effect is the default, but the scale effect is optional. Go ahead and pick your poison. A minimized window or document is *not* an application, so they will be stored on the right side of the dock divider (shown in Figure 3-14).

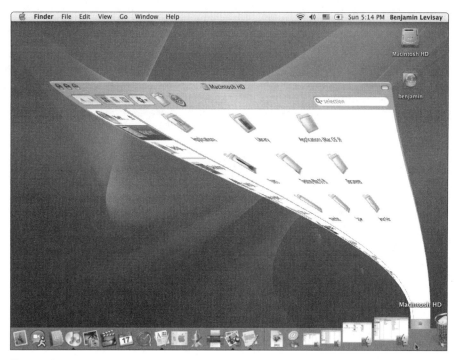

Figure 3-14: The scale effect is actually more efficient and faster, but the genie effect is just too darn cool.

Secret

How to Keep Your Dock from Moving When You Add Items to It

In addition to placing folders or drives in the Dock, you can drag items into docked folders or drive icons. This can be a slightly confusing process, but we have a solution.

Here's what happens: When dragging something to the right end of the Dock, the system has to account for the possibility that you actually want to place the item you're dragging *on* the Dock, not inside a previously docked item. So, when you are hovering over your drive and folder icons on the right side, the Dock shuffles around, evacuating some space for you to place the items it thinks you *might* want to place. Meanwhile, you're only trying to put the things in a docked folder. Depending on your Dock's size and magnification factor, it can get pretty slippery trying to place the item above the folder you want to put it in.

Thankfully, holding down the Command key while hovering over the Dock will cause the Dock to stop in its tracks, allowing you to safely and easily drop the transported items into the correct folder or drive icon. Now some of us might suggest that Apple goofed here, and should have done things the other way around, and that is to leave the folder and drive icons static, so you can drop things inside them, and present the moving target with the Command-key option. But I'm just a book writer, not an operating system architect, so what do I know? (No comments please!)

Slow Prefs

Opening up the actual preference dialog box takes you a little longer, but you'll be rewarded for your trouble with a greater ability to customize your Dock experiences.

When you choose Dock Preferences from the Dock submenu in the Apple menu, from the Dock's contextual menu, or from System Preferences, you get the dialog box shown in Figure 3-15.

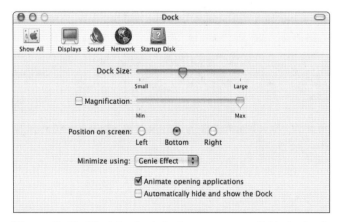

Figure 3-15: All of the Dock Preferences are available in the System Preferences.

Here you can adjust the following six Dock preferences:

◆ **Dock Size:** Move the slider to take it up a size, or down a size. (Or save yourself the bother and drag the Dock's divider bar to do it directly (as shown in Figure 3-16)).

Figure 3-16: Show some muscle and push your dock around with the divider bar.

◆ **Magnification:** If the magnifying effect is too imposing, this particular preference lets you regulate it to a more suitable size. Or, you can make it even more imposing. Slider bars are like that.

◆ **Automatically hide and show the Dock:** What can I say? This is just a repetition of the preference discussed previously.

◆ **Position on screen:** Ditto. No further explanation needed.

◆ **Minimize using:** Another preference you've seen before and don't need to see again, or maybe you do.

◆ **Animate opening applications:** If you don't like the image of bouncing balls on your Dock, you can turn it off with this option. Programs will just open, and will only signify their operation by a startup or splash screen as well as the appearance of that telltale arrow below the applications.

Secret

Control-Click Your Folder and Volumes in the Dock for Faster Access

In designing the Dock, Apple has prioritized its behavior for tweaking it, rather than using it. Now this may not be the smartest approach. I mean, how often do you tweak the Dock, versus *use* the Dock? Anyway, if you want to click on a Docked drive or folder icon with the intention of digging down into nestled folders, you will notice a pause before the root of the contents of the drive or folder pops up. The reason for this pause is for the system to give you a chance, by way of your mouse activity, to tell the system that you are dragging it of the Dock.

Of course, if you really wanted to do this, you would simply drag the item off the Dock. If you wanted to burrow down, however, Apple assumed you'd be expecting to wait for the Docked item's contents to appear anyway, so they decided to let you wait a second more, so that a grace period exists for those occasions when you want to drag an item *off* the Dock, rather than burrow in.

What's the end result? This interface scheme makes Mac OS X seem slower, intentionally. Now why would they do that, especially when users of older Macs are yelling at Apple already about performance lapses? In any case, there's solace for this dilemma. Let your Control key come to the rescue.

If you Control-click on a Docked drive or folder, its contents pop up as soon as your hardware system can muster. On an entry-level G4, for example, clicking on the main drive icon in the dock will take about a second to bring up its contents. Control-clicking makes the action almost instantaneous. See how fast Mac OS X really is. Now why must you gum up your ergonomic workflow to grab the Control key when you want to work quickly? As I said before, we only explain the rules, we don't make them.

We Interrupt This Chapter . . .

This is getting to be habit forming, but oh well.

Pieter sayeth: "The Dock is all right, such as it is, but why do you have to drag the mouse over it to see what an icon stands for?"

Gene responds: "Pieter, your batting average is awesome. My sentiments exactly. Any basic level application launcher can be set to show both. Maybe having labels displayed full time may upset Apple's design sensibility, and maybe you'll get used to what those icons stand for, but I still find myself looking twice when I need to choose between iMovie and iDVD. Yes, I know the latter has an optical disk icon, but the shape is the same, and it's easy to miss your target if you move a little too fast."

Secret

Shortcuts for the Dock

Like other Mac OS features, the Dock has its rich resource of keyboard shortcuts.

Here, in no special order, is a list of some of the best of the breed, all in one place. Just remember that all of these shortcuts require you to directly address the Dock (hello, Dock) when you try them:

- **Command-click application icon:** This one opens the folder that contains that application in the Finder. No more hunting for its location.
- **Option-click application icon:** All right, I mentioned this before. This one switches to that application, and hides one you previously used.
- **Command-Option-click application icon:** Even better. This one hides *all the other* applications when you switch to a new one.
- **Command-Option-D:** Switches between hiding and showing the Dock.
- **Command-Tab:** Cycles between the present application and the previous (or next) one. If you press the Tab key repeatedly, you'll move among all open applications, which will be highlighted as you access them. Neat.
- **Command-Shift-Tab:** Reverses the above operation. As they said in that old comic book: 'nuff said.
- **Option-drag vertical divider bar:** Option-drag it up and down and the Dock resize operation will lock into full sizes, such as 32 pixels, 64 pixels, etc. If you are into exact sizes, as I am, this is the way to satisfy your obsessive-compulsive impulses.

Using Third-Party Utilities to Put the Dock on Steroids

Wouldn't it be nice if you could put the Dock on the top of the screen, or let it sit at the far left or right? Why must it be centered, when the capabilities to move it anywhere you want are already present in the operating system?

Wouldn't it be nice if you can make the Dock walk all over the screen? All right, that's stretching things a little bit, but a smart programmer may just make it happen some day. You read it here first.

The key issue is that some people regard the Dock as an unnecessary annoyance, or lacking important features, and could just as well do without. But it's really not so easy to tell the Dock to just go away, although hiding it, as you read earlier, isn't so hard.

Rather than tell Apple to redesign the Dock to your taste, there are handy utilities out there that, more or less, replace the Dock or make it do things more to your liking.

> **note** Before going further, let me point out that I'm just providing a basic cross-section of Dock enhancers, replacements, and so on. So please don't write me asking why your favorite (or the one you wrote) wasn't included. When I checked for suitable candidates for this chapter, I soon realized I'd never run out of suitable prospects, so I had to be highly selective.

A-Dock X

What can this be? Well, it's not a Dock replacement so much as an extra Dock with such neat features as the ability to create a custom skin, including a Classic Mac OS look (see Figure 3-17), spring-loaded folders, hot keys, nested folder browsing to ten levels, and the ability to exclude items, if that's what you want.

Figure 3-17: If you love the look of Mac OS 9, you'll just adore this Dock replacement.

Even more interesting, if you must visit Mac OS 9 from time to time, you'll be pleased to know there is a version for your Classic Mac OS as well. You can learn more via this direct link to the publisher's Web site: http://jerome.foucher.free.fr/ADock.html.

Dock Detox

As I said earlier in this chapter, the Dock has an annoying habit of letting icons bounce when they have to tell you something. Now I happen to think that's a good idea, because you shouldn't sit in ignorance if a message has to get through.

But if you find the symptom annoying, as some do, and prefer that an application keep its messages to itself until *you* want to communicate with it, Unsanity's Dock Detox is the freeware program that'll keep your stomach from heaving in sync with the bouncing icon. Not that I think that happens terribly often, but I can see how more than one icon in bouncing mode can get a mite upsetting. Get a copy from www.unsanity.com/haxies/dockdetox/.

> **note** According to the folks at Unsanity, Dock Detox includes a development kit that lets application developers grab a hold of those icon bounce requests and display visual feedback in a less jarring fashion to alert you of problems. Perhaps a skull and crossbones if a document fails to print or someone holding up their hands in despair if the Web site you want isn't available?

Dock Switcher

For some, one Dock is more than enough, but for others you need more, much more. And that's where Dock Switcher comes in. It's another system preference (see Figure 3-18) that adds several extra Dock options, and then lets you configure a separate Dock for different purposes, such as Internet applications, multimedia applications, and lots more.

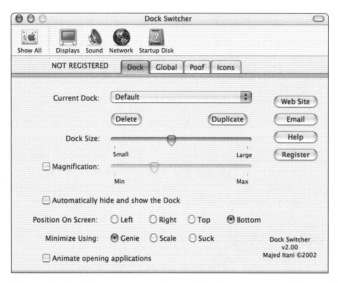

Figure 3-18: This program lets you pick from among different Docks.

Now let me clarify one thing, before we get too far astray. You don't actually see more than one Dock at a time. This shareware program lets you set up hot keys that allow you to change Docks, depending on your needs, your moods, or whether you just want to amaze and influence your friends over your magical powers.

The publisher says the number of Docks you can create is "unlimited," but I suppose it'll get confusing after two or three. Anyway, if you want to give this one a try, go to http://ilearnat.com/ and you'll never be forced to live with a single Dock again.

Launcher

Did I say Launcher? Well, yes indeed. All right, you can run the Classic Mac OS Launcher, but it won't recognize those special Mac OS X applications known as packages, which hide a folder containing application files behind a single icon. But Brian Hill looked at the Launcher and did one up for Mac OS X (see Figure 3-19). There's not much to say about this version, except that it inherits the luscious Aqua look and feel, but also operates in a way that's pretty much like the Mac OS original.

What this means is that this Launcher works very much in the same fashion as the one you knew and loved. Just drag an item into a palette to add it. You can manually place an item in your Users/Library/LauncherItems folder/subfolders. You can learn more than you ever wanted about Launcher, which is shareware, from http://personalpages.tds.net/~brian_hill/launcher.html.

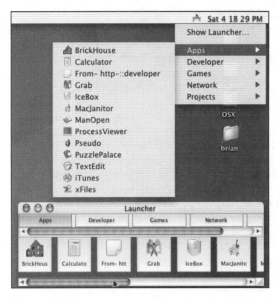

Figure 3-19: The venerable Launcher gets a Mac OS X facelift from this third-party adaptation.

TinkerTool

Installed as a preference panel (see Figure 3-20), this is one of the original Mac OS X system enhancers. But we're just concerned with the Dock features here, so let me tell you just about those. You'll have to go back to Chapter 1 for the other stuff. Fair enough?

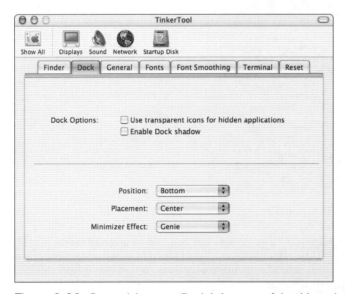

Figure 3-20: Customizing your Dock is just one of the things that TinkerTool can do.

Now, even though Apple limits your Dock maneuvering to only three positions, TinkerTool's authors realize that isn't enough, so they also let you position the Dock at the top or sides of the screen. And if the genie or scaling effect doesn't do it when it comes to minimizing a window, TinkerTool adds a "suck in" feature. The other neat Dock display option is to use transparent icons to display the infamous hidden or background applications, so you know what's happening behind the scenes. A copy of this free program is available for download direct from www.bresink.de/osx/TinkerTool2.html.

> **note**
>
> Perhaps you're wondering why a program such as TinkerTool can handle Mac OS X features that Apple hasn't implemented. The secret is that those features are there, but normally you'd have to use the command line to get to them. With TinkerTool and similar programs, all they are doing is putting on a pretty, easy-to-access front end and calling those commands behind the scenes, so you don't have to. If you like it easy, this is the way to go.

Ugly Dockling

Here's a shareware utility that helps you organize your Dock in an Apple menu-like structure. Here's how it works: Ugly Dockling puts, well, an ugly — or at least different looking — duck icon in the Dock. To add items to it, be they applications, documents, or folders, you just drag them to a simple Finder contextual menu and, presto, they show up in the Ugly Dockling pop-up hierarchical menu (see Figure 3-21).

Figure 3-21: Make my Dockling ugly.

Simple enough? Now to be fair, I should also tell you that you could make your own folder on your desktop, drag it to the Dock, and put whatever you want inside and it would have a similar result. But if you like the contextual menu convenience and the look of that Dockling icon go and visit the publisher's site at www.bkeeney.com/Utilities.html and download a copy.

WindowShade X

All right, if you don't like the way the Dock minimizes a window, maybe you prefer the way it was done under Mac OS 9. If that's the case, give WindowShade X, another haxie from Unsanity, a whirl. As you see in Figure 3-22, this utility works on a document window in the same way as its Classic counterpart, and that is to minimize it to a title bar with a single click.

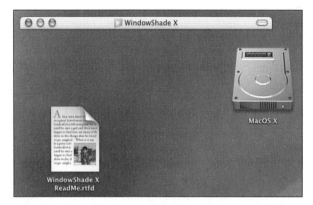

Figure 3-22: Now you can close your windows again.

WindowShade X installs as a preference panel. Besides minimizing, it also lets you adjust the shading and stacking of windows, as well as how an inactive document window will look. There are also adjustable hot keys that let you selectively minimize windows in the normal fashion. More information can be had at www.unsanity.com/haxies/wsx/.

A Few Words about Killing the Dock

All right, some of you don't simply want to hide the Dock. You want to zap it, kaput, history, never to return. All right, I investigated a few hacks that do just that, but I don't recommend them, for the simple reason that they eliminate an important method of switching applications. Now I suppose if you prefer to try an alternate application launching program, such as Brian Hill's Mac OS X Launcher or Unsanity's WindowShade X, you won't have to fret over this.

If that's your choice, let me suggest you give Killdock a try. You can find out more about this freeware utility from http://madej.ca/killdock/. All I'd suggest here is that you use it with caution, and feel secure in the knowledge that a simple restart or login and log out process should restore your Dock to full functionality.

And, in fact, after you look at it a while, you might actually come to like the Dock, or at least not resent it as much. You know that old song about becoming accustomed to its face. . . .

Summary

If you still can't get connected with the Dock, you can always hide it, keep your mouse away from the corner of the screen on which it's lodged, and use one of those Dock substitutes instead. But that requires a trip to the Appendix for the real skinny.

In the next chapter, I introduce you to every bitty, little panel in System Preferences and show you what they do, what they don't do, and what you'll want to change to make your Mac sing for its supper (or lunch, depending on your feeding hours).

The Power of System Preferences

Chapter

4

◆ ◆

Secrets in This Chapter

◆ ◆

Think of your Mac as the Starship Enterprise (unless that totally geeks you out). Almost everything is controlled from the bridge. Communications, weapons, sensors, access control, you name it; and the bridge is where you interface with the different systems aboard your starship. Your Mac's bridge is System Preferences.

If you're new to Mac OS X and come from either Windows or a pre–Mac OS X background, you can also think of System Preferences as being a control panel analogue. System Preferences are where you establish both system-wide and user-specific preferences relating to hardware, connectivity, and general Mac operation and appearance.

Some System Preference panes are essential if you want your Mac to be anything more than a hermit. The Accounts pane is where you create/maintain/delete user accounts, including your own. Use the Network pane if you want to connect to the Internet or any other computers or printers on your local network. If you have any "old" (OS 9 or earlier) software that you need to employ, Classic is where you establish the OS 9 System Folder that operates your software time portal. There are more, but you get the drift, and we'll see how more of them are used as this chapter develops.

System Preferences Displayed

The System Preferences window (shown in Figure 4-1) displays icons for your System Preferences panes (also called panels), divided into five categories: Personal, Hardware, Internet & Network, System, and, for non-Apple-supplied preference panes, Other.

Figure 4-1: The System Preferences window displays your choices organized into categories by default.

At least, this is the default display. If you find it more difficult to remember in which category a pane resides, you have the following ways to simplify your search (and get at your System Preferences):

+ You can choose View⇨Organize Alphabetically (shown in Figure 4-2) to remove the categorization and sort the icons by name in the.

Figure 4-2: You can view the System Preferences alphabetically or you can open an individual preference panel by selecting it from the menu.

+ You can choose the pane you want from the View menu, which lists all your Preferences panes in alphabetic order. Choosing to view the Preferences in alphabetical order from the View menu will remove the categories from the main System Preferences window (shown in Figure 4-3).

+ You can Control-click (or click-and-hold) the System Preferences Dock icon (shown in Figure 4-4) and choose the pane you want from the contextual menu that appears (shown in Figure 4-5).

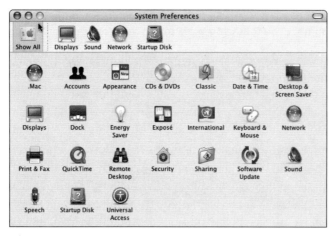

Figure 4-3: If Categories aren't important to you, this is a more simple view of your preferences.

Figure 4-4: The little light switch with the Apple on it in the Dock gets you to the System Preferences by clicking on it.

♦ You can access System Preferences from the Apple menu (shown in Figure 4-6).

♦ And you can access System Preferences directly in the Applications folder (shown in Figure 4-7).

♦ Another way you can organize System Preferences is to put the your most commonly used Prefs into the System Preferences toolbar. You do this by dragging a preference button from the main window to the toolbar, as shown in Figure 4-8 (top and bottom).

Figure 4-5: Holding the mouse down on the System Preference icon in the Dock, after the System Preference application is launched gives you a menu to select any System Preference panel.

Figure 4-6: The Apple menu gives you one more way to get to the System Preferences.

Figure 4-7: The System Preferences are located in the Applications folder on your hard drive.

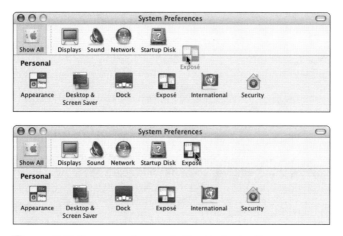

Figure 4-8: Drag a preference button to the toolbar.

There are a few more ways to get at System Preferences, but I think this is probably enough options for you.

It's important for you to realize that the System Preferences application is a GUI to help you get at various part of your OS. All of these preferences are found in one of the Library folders on your hard drive in the form of a PreferencePane. Some of these PreferencePanes are necessary for the system to work. So, if you don't know what you're doing, you should keep your customization restricted to what you can and cannot do in System Preferences itself.

How to Look at the System Preference Package Contents

The Apple-supplied preference panes are found in /System/Library/PreferencePanes. Each of the icons in this folder is either an alias pointing to another preference pane (e.g., Internet.prefPane points to Mac.prefPane) or a folder masquerading as a single icon. If you Control-click one of these icons and choose Show Package Contents from the contextual menu that appears, you can burrow down and see all the interface elements comprising the preference pane.

Thanks to OS X's Unix underpinnings and the permissions system, you can't do any real harm by looking inside unless you do so as the root user, a definite no-no.

The preference panes that appear in the Other category are located in /Library/PreferencePanes for those accessible to all users or your home directory's Library/PreferencePanes folder for those you keep for yourself.

You'll note that neither the Bluetooth pane nor the Ink pane appear in Figure 4-1. These are hardware-specific preference panes that System Preferences won't even display unless the requisite hardware (a Bluetooth wireless networking interface or a compatible graphics tablet respectively) is attached to your Mac. So we're going to skip these two preference panels in this chapter.

Additionally, some of the prefPane icons (see the first Secret) have different names than those you see in System Preferences — the name System Preferences displays is contained in the package's info.plist file (under the key `CFBundleName`). For example, Localization.prefPane appears in System Preferences as International.

The only way for me to show you System Preferences and do a good job with it is to take you through all of your options (at least a quick looking at each one). Because System Preferences is arranged by category (shown in Figure 4-1), we might as well use that as our structure.

cross ref As I take you though the various preferences in each of the category, you will run across preferences that are covered in a lot of detail in other parts of this book. For the sake of space, I'm going to refer you to those sections of the book for more information rather than duplicating the same in-depth coverage of the relevant preferences.

Changing the Category Names in Your System Preferences

Category names are found in the `NSPrefPaneGroups.strings` file, concealed within the System Preferences application package and within the lproj folder for the language of your Mac (in my case, that is the English.lproj folder).

Moreover, the NSPrefPaneGroups.plist file, located in the System Preferences package's Contents/Resources folder, contains the listing of which preference panes belong to each group.

Thus, exercising suitable caution and administrator privilege, you could edit these files to reorganize the System Preferences display to something more suited to your work style.

Personal Preferences

Normally, there are six preferences in the Personal section of the System Preferences window. As the heading suggests, these preferences affect personal settings.

Appearance

The Appearance preference panel gives you control over the look of your windows, buttons, and menus (shown in Figure 4-9).

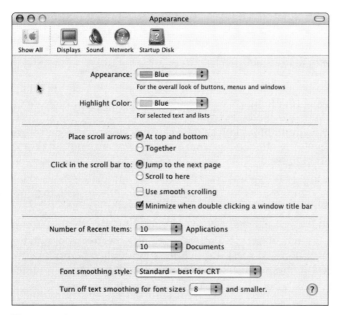

Figure 4-9: The Appearance panel is reminiscent of the OS 9 Appearance and General control panels.

In the Appearance preference panel, you can select the Highlight Color, the position and characteristics of the scroll bar, the number of recent Applications and Documents (displayed in the Apple menu), and the size of the Finder font with smoothing choices.

The best way to learn about these options is to play with them for a while to see how they affect your Finder.

Desktop & Screen Saver

Panther combined the Desktop preference panel and the Screen Saver preference panel of Jaguar (and other previous versions of OS X) into one preference panel called Desktop & Screen Saver that accesses both.

The Desktop section of this preference panel allows the selection of pictures in either Apple's preset folders (shown in Figure 4-10) or in other user-created folders. The selected image shows itself in the preview window above the list of image folders. The same image also shows on the desktop as soon as it is chosen.

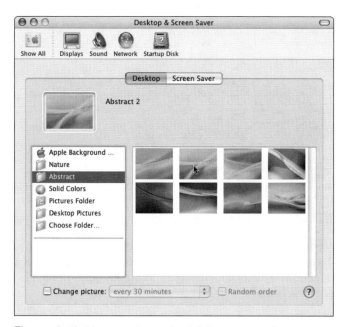

Figure 4-10: You can choose Apple's images or colors, or you can use your own images for the desktop.

A fairly cool thing that you can do with Apple's or your own folder of pictures is to choose to have those images change at specified intervals. To do this, select the Change picture option and select the time interval (shown in Figure 4-11). This changes your preview icon to three images with three arrows connecting them. This indicates that the selected group of images (from the list under the preview) will be changed at the specified intervals from the menu at the bottom of the screen.

The Screen Saver section of the this preference panel shows the Screen Savers list on the left side of the panel. Apple screen saver modules are at the top of the list and user-added screen savers are on the bottom (shown in Figure 4-12). The selected screen saver in this list is shown in the preview window to the right of the Screen Savers list.

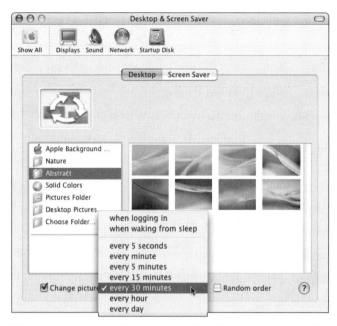

Figure 4-11: Scheduling and changing pictures at very fast intervals ties up processor speed.

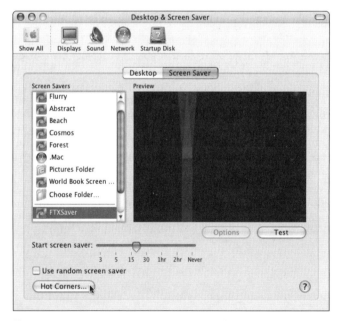

Figure 4-12: There is a divider line between the system's screen savers and the user's screen savers.

You can set the time that the screen saver starts by using the time slider. Use the Hot Corners button at the lower-left corner of the preference panel to bring up the Active Screen Corners dialog box (shown in Figure 4-13). With this dialog box you can set how the screen saver behaves when you drag and leave your mouse in that (hot) corner.

In order for the Screen Saver time settings to be used, the settings for the Energy Saver (shown later in this chapter) need to be set later than those of the Screen Saver's.

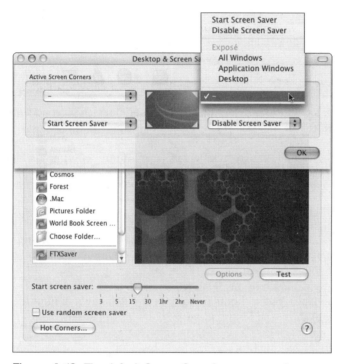

Figure 4-13: The default Screen Saver hot corner options are to start the screen Saver in the lower-left corner of the screen and the disable the screen Saver in the lower-right corner of the screen.

note The corners can be used for Screen Savers and Panther's new Exposé (shown later in this chapter). You need to be aware of Exposé Hot Corner settings and Screen Saver Hot Corner settings while setting either and/or both. Exposé and the Screen Saver cannot share the same Hot Corner settings.

The user-added screen savers are (most often) third-party screen savers that you add to your OS. Those screen savers are installed by moving them into the Screen Savers folder in your home Library folder (shown in Figure 4-14).

Figure 4-14: The Screen Savers folder shows the only user-added screen saver added to this user's folder. This is the FTXSaver shown in Figure 4-12.

You may not find the folder named ScreenSavers in your Library folder if you have never added a third-party screen saver before. You have to create this folder in your Library folder (⌘-Shift-N and then names it "ScreenSavers") first before you add any screen savers.

Dock

The Dock is one of the most notable features of OS X. It's perhaps the first thing that people either love or hate about OS X. And the preference panel in System Preferences is where you control it.

The Dock has its very own chapter in this book (Chapter 3). If you want to see everything there is to see about the Dock, including its preference panel (shown in Figure 4-15), you can see it all in that chapter.

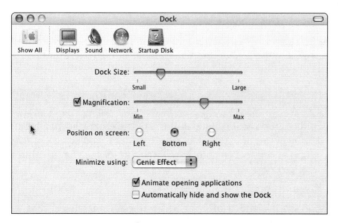

Figure 4-15: The Dock preference panel can also be accessed from the Apple menu and from the Dock itself.

The Dock preference panel allows you to control of the dock size, the magnification, the position of the Dock on your screen, the animation type, the animation of opening applications, and the ability to automatically hide the Dock.

Exposé

Some might quibble with my characterization of Exposé (see Figure 4-16) as a critical preference pane, but that's just because they have yet to use Exposé. If you suffer from a proliferation of open windows, and those of us who use a number of applications simultaneously or run programs like Photoshop with lots of palettes definitely experience this difficulty, Exposé is a heaven-sent gift.

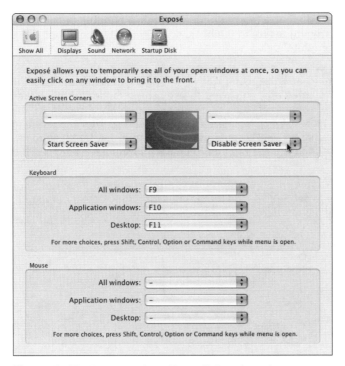

Figure 4-16: You can activate Exposé's functions three ways.

Exposé organizes the open file and folder windows on your desktop as follows:

- ◆ Tile miniatures of all windows so that, as you glide the mouse over them, their names appear and you can click the one you want brought to the front.
- ◆ Tile miniatures of just the windows in the front-most application (very handy when you have overlapping palettes in Photoshop).
- ◆ Move all windows out of the way like scurrying mice so that you can click on something on your desktop.

By default, these three functions are activated by the F9, F10, and F11 keys, respectively. Using the Keyboard section, you can change the keystroke used to invoke one or more of them. The Active Screen Corners (which Exposé shares with the Screen Saver) area lets you specify activation just by moving the mouse to the appropriate corner. Further, you can use one or more of the corners to activate or disable the screen saver. Finally, you can use the Mouse area to dedicate the functionality to buttons on a multibutton mouse or trackball.

There is more written about Exposé as well as examples of each of the three features in Chapter 7.

International

The International settings (via the International preference panel in System Preferences) won't be talked about anywhere else in the book, so I take a little more room here to make sure you cover them completely.

Simply put (in deference to myself) the International settings allow you to set up your computer so you can read or write using different languages. The first step toward that end is to select the languages that you want to use. The selection of these languages is done in the Language section of the International preference panel in the System Preferences (shown in Figure 4-17). You are able to see and reorder the languages in the Languages list. You can select the languages shown in that list by clicking on the Edit button where another dialog box allows you to check and uncheck languages (shown in Figure 4-18).

The Formats section (shown in Figure 4-19) of the International preferences in System Preferences allows you to set and control the formats for dates, times, numbers, and units of measurement.

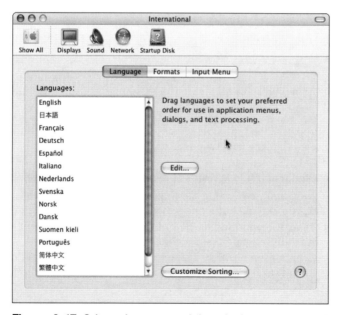

Figure 4-17: Select a language and drag the language up or down to reorder them.

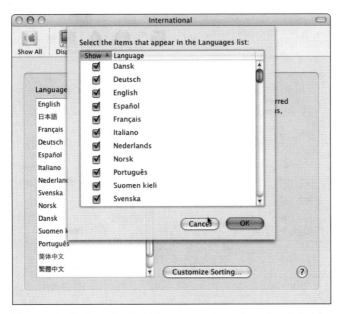

Figure 4-18: The displayed languages are selected and deselected in the drop-down language dialog box after clicking on the Edit button.

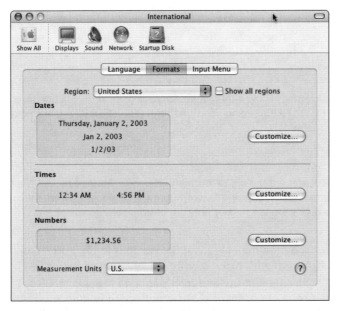

Figure 4-19: The format choices affect how the dates, times, and numbers appear in Finder windows and other applications.

By clicking on the Region menu (shown in Figure 4-20) you can select another regional Formats set (other than the United States).

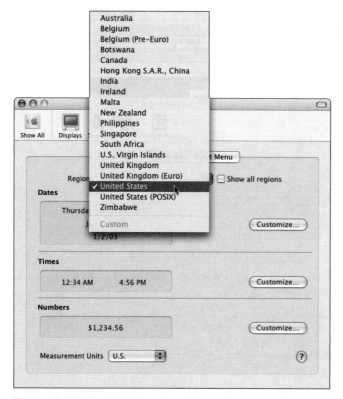

Figure 4-20: The default settings show only regions for your preferred language (in the Languages pane). If you don't see the region you want, select the Show all regions option next to the Region pull-down menu.

> **tip**
>
> Only the most recent custom settings are saved. If you choose a different region, you can return to your custom settings by choosing Custom from the Region pull-down menu. But if you customize a region's settings, your previous custom settings will be lost.

Clicking on the Customize button next to any of the sections in the Format area opens a drop-down dialog box (shown in Figure 4-21) allowing you options for that section.

One of the really useful things about the multiple language support in OS X is that you write in multiple languages in applications that support those languages. Those choices can even be different than the keyboard setting that you are using for that application and/or document.

The Input Menu section (shown in Figure 4-22) of the International preferences in System Preferences is where you control that kind of functionality.

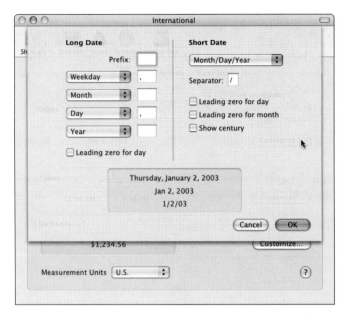

Figure 4-21: Clicking on the Customize button next to the Date section brings up this drop-down dialog box.

Figure 4-22: This Input Menu section shows that Character Palette, Keyboard Palette, and the input menu in menu bar option are all selected.

Another Way to Get at Your Key Caps

As you can see from the Input Menu section of the International settings, this is where the Key Caps utility that you had become so fond of in Jaguar, went when you upgraded to a Panther OS. And if you turn on your Input menu you still have access to the same thing.

But if you want to have your old Key Caps utility back, all you have to do is find it in the Utilities folder of a Jaguar system and copy it over. You'll find that it still runs just fine in Panther.

Clicking on the Option button at the bottom of this preference panel opens a drop-down dialog box (shown in Figure 4-23) that allows you to change your input menu shortcuts.

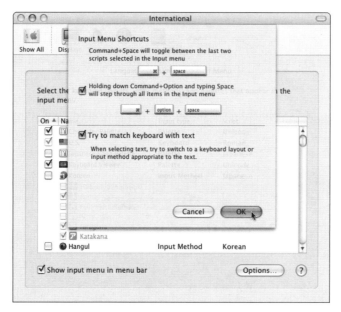

Figure 4-23: The Try to match keyboard with text option is one of the more useful features of the Input Menu Shortcuts. This allows the OS to try to find the best match for a keyboard depending on what you're doing.

It's important to note that not all applications are supported with International options. Only applications that support Unicode (a worldwide standard for encoding multilingual text) can view languages that Mac OS X supports. (These languages are listed in the Languages pane of International preferences.)

This is not a hard-and-fast rule. There are non-Unicode applications that do understand and are able to use text in more than one language that may or may not be in the Languages list. There are also some applications that will support one language only.

If you find a language selection grayed out so that you cannot select it in a given application, that's a good indication that either that application does not support that language, or there is a problem with the settings for that language. You should check the documentation that is bundled with that application for language and Unicode compatibility.

> **tip**   There are additional languages available for installation from the second CD on your Panther install discs.

Security

The main function of the Security preference panel (in the System Preferences) is to control the FileVault. The idea of the FileVault is to secure your home folder by encrypting its contents. It does this on the fly (and in the background), so you won't be bothered by the process.

You have access to the FileVault from both the Security preference panel (shown in Figure 4-24) and through the security section of the Accounts preference panel (shown in Figure 4-25). Only the admin account can access this feature.

Figure 4-24: The password control for the screen saver is also now controlled from the Security preference panel.

Figure 4-25: Turning FileVault on and off as well as changing the password is available from the Accounts panel as well as the Security panel.

Choosing to change the master password causes a drop-down dialog box to appear where you can change your master password (shown in Figure 4-26).

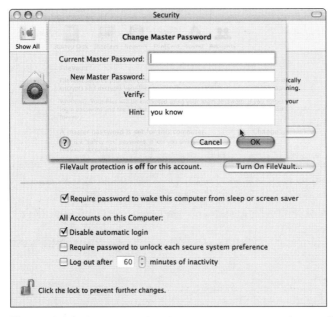

Figure 4-26: If you have already set a master password, you will need it to change the password. Don't lose or forget your master password. It cannot be retrieved.

At the time this was written, there was a lot of online discussion about FileVault causing problems with some configurations and applications. You should check the Apple discussion boards and online FAQs to see if FileVault will cause any problem for your particular setup before you start using it.

Also, *make sure you have your master password written down in a place where you can find it!*

That brings us to the end of the Personal preferences. Next, we'll cover the Hardware preferences.

Hardware Preferences

As I said before, if your computer had a Bluetooth module (internal or external) and/or a graphics tablet plugged into it, then there would be two additional hardware preference panels than those that you see in Figure 4-1.

If you have either of these (or other) additional hardware items on your computer, you can find more information about these from the Help menu in System Preferences.

For now, let's move on to the normal Hardware preferences.

CDs & DVDs

Every OS X–supported Mac includes an optical drive of some sort. The CDs & DVDs preference panel is where you tell your Mac what you want it to do when you insert a CD or DVD. Figure 4-27 shows the pop-up menu from which you can choose those preferences on a SuperDrive-equipped Mac. Because Apple provides DVD Player, iTunes, and iPhoto, you probably want DVDs to start playing in DVD Player, audio CDs to open in iTunes, and Kodak Picture CDs to open in iPhoto, but you can make other choices or even have your Mac ask you every time it detects an optical disc.

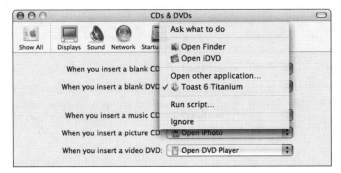

Figure 4-27: Tell your Mac what to do with optical disc types in the CDs & DVDs preference pane.

The CDs & DVDs Preferences and the media that it controls are covered in a lot more depth in Chapter 26. Please refer to that chapter to learn more about your optical options.

Displays

The Displays preference panel (in System Preferences) controls the resolution of your Display(s) (shown in Figure 4-28) and gives you access to Color Sync profile options (shown in Figure 4-29).

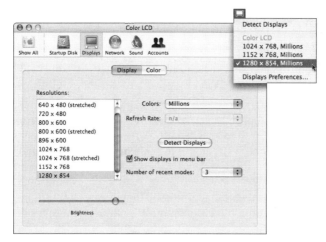

Figure 4-28: The display menu can be turned on and off from the Display preference panel.

The Display section of the Display preference panel is where you control the brightness of your monitor as well as the number of colors that your screen displays.

The brightness controls can also be adjusted using the F1 (Brightness Down) and F2 (Brightness Up) keys on your keyboard.

Secret

Quick Access to the Display Preferences

You can jump directly to the System Preferences Display panel by holding down the Option key while pressing one of the keyboard's brightness level keys.

The Color section of the Display preference panel allows you to choose preset display profiles from the Display Profile list as well as click the Calibrate button and create a new/customized display profile yourself. Depending on your level of expertise, you might want to leave this alone (shown in Figure 4-29).

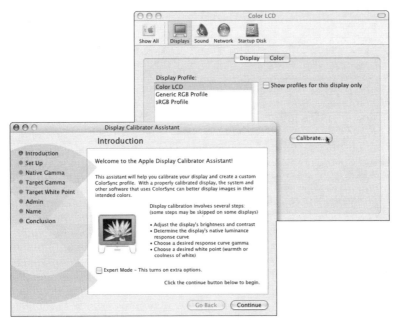

Figure 4-29: Checking the Show profiles for this display only option limits the choices in the Display Profile list.

Energy Saver

You might think that Energy Saver is primarily for laptops, to conserve battery life. It's true that the PowerBook line was the genesis for Energy Saver, but blacking your screen when it's not in use can prolong the monitor's life and putting the Mac to sleep when you're away cuts down on electricity costs (you Green thing, you). The Energy Saver panel (in System Preferences) is shown in Figure 4-30.

The Sleep and Options tabs are pretty self-explanatory, and not particularly interesting. The Schedule tab, though, is the first time this popular feature from OS 9 (turning your Mac on and off automatically) has been present on OS X. The first row lets you specify an automatic power-on time for every day, weekdays, weekends, or a specific day of the week. The second line lets you choose either an automatic sleep time or a shutdown time for every day, weekdays, weekends, or a specific day of the week.

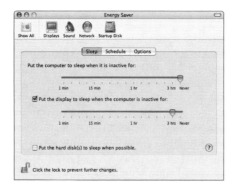
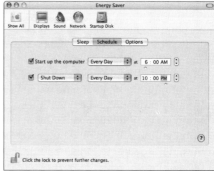

Figure 4-30: Energy Saver's three tabs let you control how and when your Mac sleeps, lets you turn it on and off at a set time, and control various sleep/wake aspects as well as whether the Mac should automatically restart after a power failure.

Keyboard & Mouse

The Keyboard & Mouse preference panel (in System Preferences) is somewhere you might not go. If you like the feel of your mouse, trackpad, and keyboard, there would be no need.

The first section of the Keyboard & Mouse preference panel is the Keyboard section (shown in Figure 4-31). Here you control the Key Repeat Rate and the Delay Until Repeat sliders.

---

note   The following screen shots are from my laptop. Desktop Macs will probably not have the trackpad option.

The second section of the Keyboard & Mouse preference panel is the Mouse section (shown in Figure 4-32). Here you have as much control over your mouse as you can get. You can change the tracking speed, the scrolling speed, and the double-click speed.

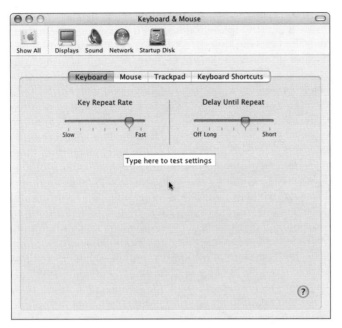

Figure 4-31: Use the Type here to test settings field to check on the changes you make to the two sliders.

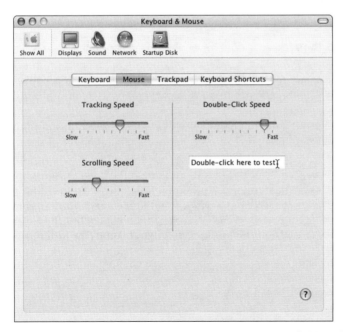

Figure 4-32: You can use the Double-click here to test field to check on the changes you make to the Double-Click Speed slider.

The third section of the Keyboard & Mouse preference panel is the Trackpad section (shown in Figure 4-33), if you have a laptop that is. And if you do have a laptop, this section gives you control over the tracking speed, the double-click speed, and how you want to use the trackpad.

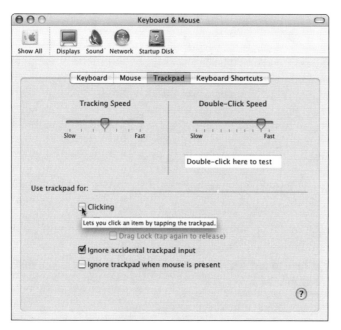

Figure 4-33: You can set the trackpad itself to be sensitive to tapping so that you can tap to click.

The fourth section of the Keyboard & Mouse preference panel is the Keyboard Shortcuts section (shown in Figure 4-34). This section allows you to add and remove shortcuts for your keyboard.

And if you get in over your head while creating and removing shortcuts, clicking on the Restore Defaults button does just that.

Print & Fax

The Print & Fax preference panel (in System Preferences) controls printing and faxing. In the Printing section of the Print & Fax panel (shown in Figure 4-35), you can set up printers, choose how printers are selected in the print dialog boxes, choose the default paper size, and choose to share (or not) printers connected to your computer with other computers on your network.

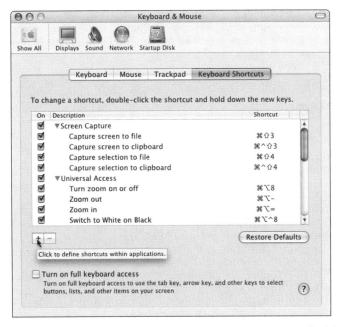

Figure 4-34: You can choose to add or remove any and all of the shortcuts using the plus and minus buttons below the shortcuts list.

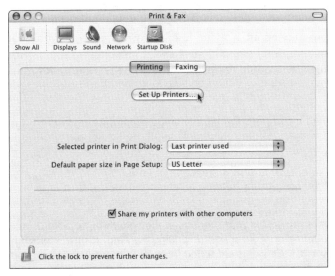

Figure 4-35: Clicking the Set Up Printers button launches the Printer Setup Utility in the Utilities folder — allowing you to access the features of this utility.

New to Panther is the idea that you can choose to fax directly from the OS. The setup for this is handled in the second section of the Print & Fax panel. In the Faxing section, you can choose to receive faxes on your computer, as well as how and where faxes go when they are received (as shown in Figure 4-36).

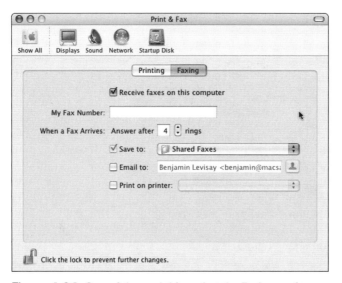

Figure 4-36: One of the cool things that the Faxing preference can do is prompt the receiving computer to e-mail a notice of the incoming fax to yourself or someone else.

Faxes coming in and out depend on a phone line being plugged into your modem port and for the your phone settings in this preference panel to be correct.

More of the printing setup is covered in Chapter 22 where printing has its very own chapter.

Sound

Panther's Sound panel (in System Preferences), shown in Figure 4-37, is your audio control center. This is where you set both the Alert volume (that annoying beep telling you that you've done something the Mac doesn't understand) as well as the separate main volume level. The main volume level you set is used, for example, as the maximum volume at which QuickTime or iTunes plays.

note   Remember that the level you set for your speakers at the bottom of the Sound pane is the maximum volume for other audio actions, including the Alert volume, QuickTime, and iTunes. In other words, their sliders are scaled from mute to the maximum main volume setting.

The sound controls can also be adjusted using the F3 (Mute), F4 (Sound Down), and F5 (Sound Up) keys on your keyboard (if your Mac supports this feature).

Figure 4-37: The Sound pane is where you specify settings for (top left) sound effects, including alert/sound effect volume, (top right) audio output device, and (bottom left) sound input device.

Secret

Quick Access to the Sound Preferences

You can jump directly to the System Preferences Sound panel by holding down the Option key while pressing one of the keyboard's sound level keys.

note Most of the time, the Output choice is moot. The only time it will really make a difference is when you have a Mac with multiple audio-out ports.

Internet & Network Preferences

This set of preferences is self explanatory, but probably the greatest source of problems for end users. In my work, we spend a lot of time with customers with Preference problems. Eight out of ten times in phone support situations, we direct our customers to one of the Internet or Networking preferences. So before you call me (just kidding), let's look at these preferences.

.Mac

.Mac is a yearly online subscriptions service provided by Apple to its customers at the nominal price of $100 per year. And while a lot has been written about the merits of the .Mac features, I think it's one of the best things you can buy to help you take full advantage of your Mac.

We Interrupt This Chapter . . .

The benefits of the .Mac account are great, but the message can sometimes be contradictory.

Benjamin: Of the many cool things that .Mac has as one of its features, the Virus protection software is probably not my favorite. On the one hand, Apple touts itself as the platform of choice to use if you want to avoid viruses. On the other hand, Apple touts the virus protection software offered with its .Mac account as a great value-added feature. I think that virus software is a good idea. I don't think Apple's propaganda machine(s) can promote it both ways.

Pieter: Well here is one area that I have to agree with Apple's marketing department. Viruses come in many forms — there are macro worms and viruses that exploit holes in applications like Microsoft Word or Entourage and there are also viruses that exploit the seemingly bottomless well of operating system holes, usually those in the many Microsoft operating systems. Apple is correct that Mac OS X Panther is very secure and resistant to most viruses simply because it is based upon its Unix lineage. However Panther is not all you run on your Mac; you use applications like Microsoft Entourage to send and receive e-mail or use Word to write and read documents. That's where the antivirus really comes into play. The antivirus software helps limit your vulnerability to downloading an infected file that could cause your copy of Entourage to go berserk and spew out hundreds of infected e-mails or one that causes Word to start deleting critical files.

The features of .Mac aside, you use the .Mac preference panel (in System Preferences) to let your computer know about your .Mac account so that it's the .Mac's OS-integrated features (like Mail or the iDisk) can take full advantage of the account's capabilities with the OS.

The first section of the .Mac preference panel is where you put your .Mac username and your password for the account (shown in Figure 4-38).

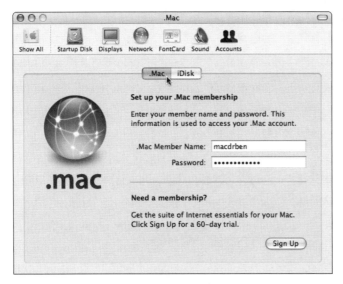

Figure 4-38: If you don't have a .Mac account you can click on the Sign Up button to get one.

Another part of the .Mac account is the iDisk. The iDisk is the 100MB of space that comes with your .Mac account. You can store files, personal Web sites, and other data on your iDisk. Clicking on the second section of the .Mac preference panel takes your computer online to check the status of your iDisk (shown in Figure 4-39) and then displays the space usage of your iDisk in the preference panel window (shown in Figure 4-40).

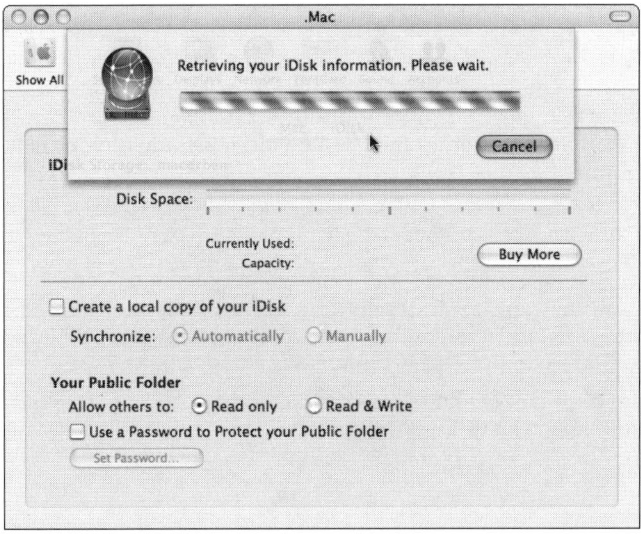

Figure 4-39: The iDisk query only works if you are online and have a .Mac account.

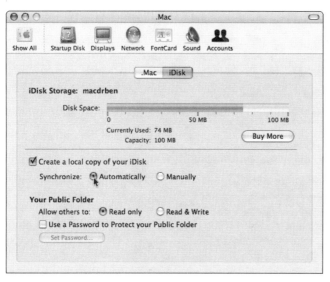

Figure 4-40: You can purchase additional space for your iDisk using the Buy More button under the iDisk storage status bar.

> **note** Panther gives you the option of creating a copy of your iDisk on your computer. When you choose this option, a mirror of your iDisk is created that you can work in. The really cool part about this is that any work you do on your local iDisk will be synchronized in the background when your computer is online and can make a connection to your .Mac account.

The Public folder of your iDisk, can be password protected. This password can be set and changed using the Set Password button in the Public Folder section of your iDisk preference panel (shown in Figure 4-41).

Network

The Network panel (in System Preferences) is your communications console (shown in Figure 4-42). All your Internet and local networking connections are defined here. We could spend a whole chapter, and then some, just talking about all the Network pane options, but we're not going to do that. Well. Okay, we are. It's Chapter 29.

But here, let's just hit the high points and point you to Chapters 29 and 30 to get the complete lowdown on Network (and its sibling, Sharing).

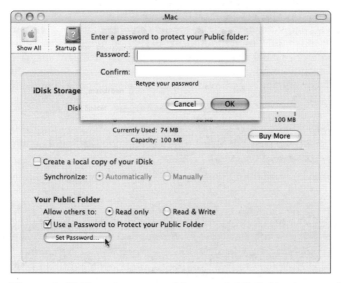

Figure 4-41: Type the password for your Public Folder (on your iDisk) in the drop-down dialog box.

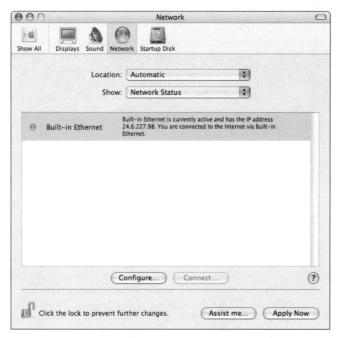

Figure 4-42: The Network pane is communications central, where you establish how your Mac connects to the Internet and how it is known both on the Internet and on your local network.

It isn't completely obvious, but the key item on this pane is the Show pop-up menu. From it you select whether you see your network status, as shown in Figure 4-42, one of your connection types (e.g., built-in Ethernet, modem, or AirPort), or a list of available network ports that you can enable or disable and reorder into a priority list. This last is an important aspect of OS X's multihoming network technology; when you make a connection request, it attempts one connection type after another until it finds one that works or runs out of options.

tip

Select a connection type on the Network Status view and click the Configure button as a shortcut to the Show connection-type view.

Secret

IP over FireWire

Probably one of the best but least-advertised features available in OS X is IP over FireWire. With your Mac's multihoming ability to maintain multiple, simultaneous network connections, connecting two Macs via a FireWire cable adds FireWire to the list of available connections in the Connection Type tab. At that point, you can connect one Mac directly to your cable or DSL modem and share the connection via FireWire (use the Sharing panel to turn on the sharing), and get FireWire transfer speeds between your Macs, as well.

QuickTime

QuickTime is a core technology of the Mac OS. QuickTime is available for both the Mac and the PC. Many applications use QuickTime conventions and protocols. The QuickTime Player (in the Applications folder) as well as Safari use QuickTime for streaming and/or other video encodings. Because of the variety of QuickTime uses, the ability to control QuickTime is needed on the Mac. These controls are found in the QuickTime preference panel in the System Preferences.

The first section in the QuickTime Preferences is the Plug-in section (shown in Figure 4-43) where the QT plug-in modules for applications like Safari are controlled. You can choose to play movies automatically, save movies in disk cache, and enable kiosk mode.

You can also change your MIME (Multipurpose Internet Mail Extensions) settings from this preference panel. Clicking on the MIME settings button causes a drop-down dialog box to appear (shown in Figure 4-44) in the preference panel that allows you control of all of the MIME options.

note

MIME (Multi-Purpose Internet Mail Extensions) is a protocol that allows people to exchange different kinds of data and files on the Internet: audio, video, images, application programs, and other kinds, as well as the ASCII text handled in the original protocol, the Simple Mail Transport Protocol (SMTP).

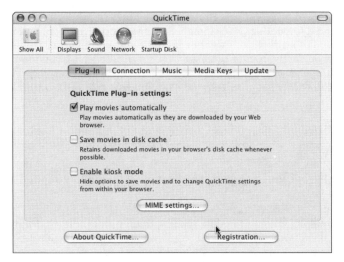

Figure 4-43: Play movies automatically is a default plug-in setting.

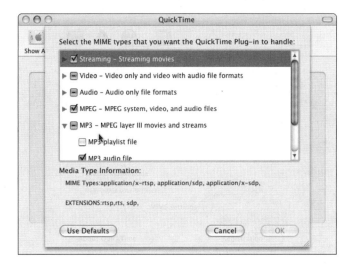

Figure 4-44: Some of the MIME settings that can be played via QuickTime work better when other applications take care of them. You shouldn't mess with these settings unless you have a reason to do so.

The Connection section of your QuickTime Preferences (shown in Figure 4-45) allows you to control the speed and protocol of QuickTime and streaming. The Connection Speed pull-down menu (shown in Figure 4-46) needs to be set to a speed in order for things like movie trailers to display correctly in your browser window. Additionally you may find that some kinds of other QuickTime streaming applications (like Caststream Player) need to have the protocol and Port IDs set manually (shown in Figure 4-47) via the Transport Setup button.

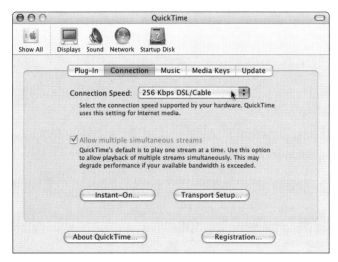

Figure 4-45: Besides setting the Connection Speed you can choose to allow multiple simultaneous streams for speeds below 56K.

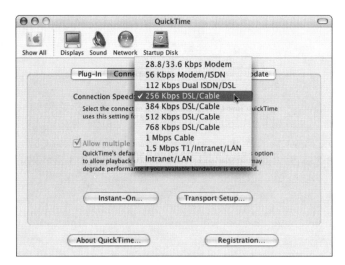

Figure 4-46: Some applications require that you have alt least 256 Kbps or 384 Kbps to make the streaming work. You can try lying to your settings about your speed to make things work as long as your bandwidth is not too far from what you say it is.

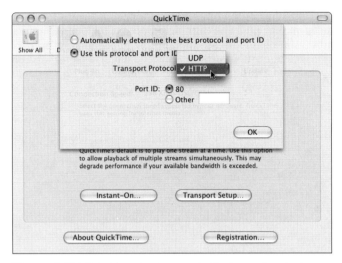

Figure 4-47: Selecting the Automatically determine the best protocol and port ID option is the default. Sometimes certain applications and/or network environments require that you try other Transport Setup settings to make streaming work.

Unless you have additional hardware and software installed, you will probably see only one choice in the Music section of the QuickTime preferences (shown in Figure 4-48). And if you don't have any additional hardware or software, you can leave this one alone.

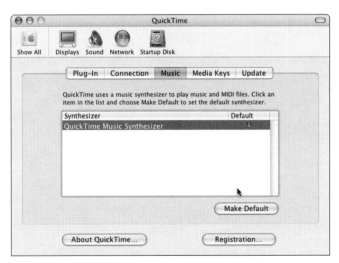

Figure 4-48: The QuickTime Music Synthesizer is QuickTime's built-in option for the music synthesizer. For most of us, this is all we need.

The Media Keys section of the QuickTime preferences (shown in Figure 4-49) is the place where you create media keys that give you authorized access to secured media files. To do this, click on the Add button below the Media Keys list to prompt a drop-down dialog box to appear from the top of the preference panel (shown in Figure 4-50). Here, name your category and key. Click the OK button to add your newly created media key to the Media Keys list (shown in Figure 4-51).

Figure 4-49: Add, Delete, or Edit your media keys in the Media Keys preference panel.

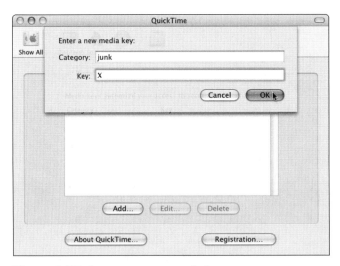

Figure 4-50: Create your new media key.

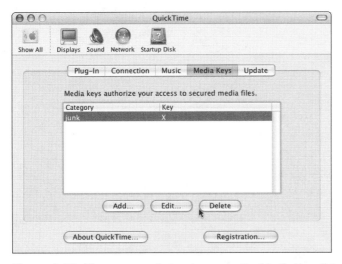

Figure 4-51: Your new media key is now in the Media Keys list.

The last section of the QuickTime preference panel is the Update section. Clicking on the Update button (shown in Figure 4-52) allows you to update your Apple and third-party QuickTime software.

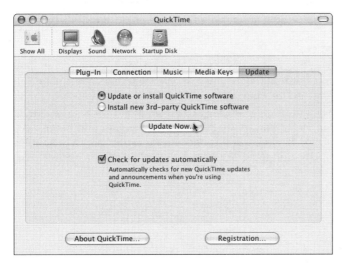

Figure 4-52: Besides updating your QuickTime software manually, you can choose to have your system check for updates automatically.

If there are updates available, you are prompted with QuickTime Component Install screen (shown in Figure 4-53) where you can choose to customize your installation.

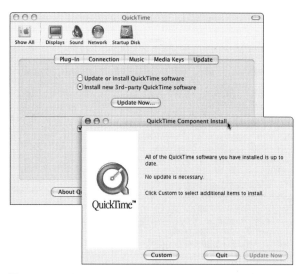

Figure 4-53: This is the update screen for the third-party QuickTime software. If your Apple QuickTime software is up-to-date, it with not give you this window.

I should note here that if you do regular Software Updates (in the Software Updates preference panel shown later in this chapter), your QuickTime software will most likely always be up-to-date.

Sharing

The Sharing preferences pane is divided into three parts (not unlike Gaul, according to Julius Caesar, for all you Latin buffs). There are Services, their corresponding Firewall settings, and a section for Internet sharing.

The Services section of the Sharing preferences (shown in Figure 4-54) controls the activation of all available services. For another user to access your computer, using one of these services, that user has to have the right account information (user name and password), a network connection of some kind, and the relevant service enabled on your computer.

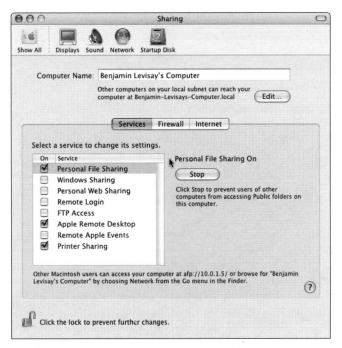

Figure 4-54: Personal File Sharing, Apple Remote Desktop, and Printer Sharing are shown as active services for my computer. Even if another user had my username and password, they would not be able to access my computer if these services were turned off.

Central to the idea of sharing my computer across the network is my computer name. The name of your computer on the network is displayed at the top of the Sharing preference panel with the name.local. To change this, click on the Edit button and change the Local Hostname (shown in Figure 4-55).

After you turn on services in your Sharing section, you have the option to turn on corresponding Firewall settings. Clicking the Start button causes a blocking of access to all but the checked services and ports (shown in Figure 4-56). Once started, clicking the Stop button allows network communication to all active services and ports.

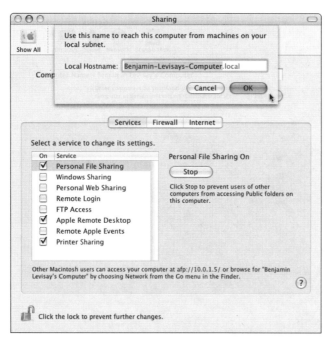

Figure 4-55: If you are on a big network, you may want to check the names of the other computers on the network before you name your own computer.

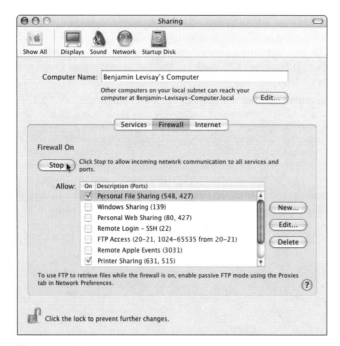

Figure 4-56: You cannot check a Firewall option manually. Firewall options match the corresponding services activated in the Services section of the Sharing preferences.

> **tip** Turning on Firewall options may cause programs like iChat that need other open ports and protocols not to work. If you find you have trouble with your Internet or network applications, try turning off the Firewall services as part of your troubleshooting efforts.

The third section of the Sharing preferences, Internet (shown in Figure 4-57), is a little different than the other two. This is the place where you can choose to allow your computer to share files across the Internet using selected/enabled ports.

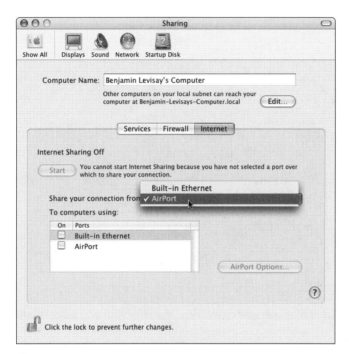

Figure 4-57: You have to select and enable a port before you can start Internet sharing.

I should note here that if you are behind a firewall you may experience problems with Internet sharing. Opening up ports may be required to get around this. This is kind of an advanced thing to do, so make sure you know a good Mac guy that you can call for help. An Apple authorized service provider (shameless self promotion) would be a good choice for help with this kind of problem.

System Preferences

As this heading suggests, in this section, we're going to talk about preferences for the System category. Let's get started.

Accounts

How to set up multiple users has its very own chapter in this book, Chapter 6. And in that chapter, we cover the Accounts preferences in detail. So, if Accounts is what you want to know about, turn in your book to Chapter 6 and get comfortable.

Here, let me say that the Accounts preference panel (shown in Figure 4-58) is the place where you manage your and other accounts on your computer.

Figure 4-58: The top user is always the administrative user. This account cannot be deleted (without a lot of fuss).

You can choose to add and delete users, change passwords, set your Address Book Card, set pictures, set security features, and set access privileges for other users and startup items for yourself.

A Neat Unix Login Trick

Even though we aren't getting into all of the login options in the Accounts settings in this section, I couldn't resist giving you a little Unix login trick as a way of saying "thanks for playing our game. You've been a great contestant."

One of the oft-touted tricks for OS X is logging into a pure Unix environment. To accomplish this, a couple of things have to be done in Login Options first. Because you need to type >console in the Login window, you must make sure that Display Login Window has the Name and Password radio button checked. If you have Fast User Switching selected, you have to make sure that all users are logged out before logging in as >console. If any user (including you) is logged in, the pure Unix login will fail.

Classic

Now that we're now into computers that no longer boot into OS 9.x, we have to rely on Classic mode to run older non–OS X native applications. The idea of Classic is that we can run an emulated OS 9 environment inside of OS X. And although there is a difference in services and options between applications running at the same time between OS X and Classic, it's not a bad workaround.

You can launch Classic mode by launching a Classic application. You can also launch and manage Classic behaviors inside the Classic preference panel in System Preferences.

The first section of the Classic preference panel is the Start/Stop section. In this section, your hard drive(s) is listed in the window (shown in Figure 4-59) that allows you to select which Classic System Folder you want to have start up when Classic mode is launched. You can also set Classic to automatically launch when the computer is started up and give you a warning when it does.

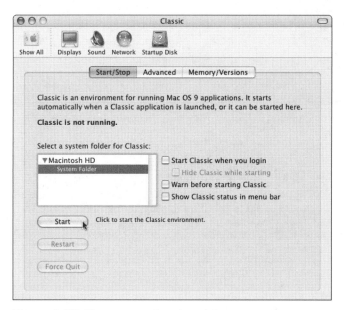

Figure 4-59: If your menu bar doesn't have enough menus yet, you can add another one for Classic mode by checking the Show Classic status in menu bar option in this preference pane.

If Classic is not yet running, clicking on the Start button under the System Folder list window causes a screen to launch showing Classic mode booting up (shown in Figure 4-60).

Figure 4-60: The extensions that you see loading in the Classic window are services that are available only to applications running in Classic. They won't apply to applications running in Panther.

What to Do If Classic Acts Up

Secret

Classic is just like any other OS X application. If it gives you any trouble (and it might), you can choose to Force Quit that application by selecting the Force Quit button from the Classic preference panel or by selecting Force Quit from the Apple Menu (or pressing ⌘-Option-Escape) and choosing Classic as the application to Force Quit.

And if you do have trouble with your Classic mode you can further troubleshoot the problem in the Advanced section of the Classic preference panel. Here you can choose other startup options like turning off the extensions (shown in Figure 4-61) to help you launch and keep Classic mode stable. You can also control Classic sleep options and rebuild the desktop database from the Advanced preferences.

Once you have Classic stable and working well, you're free to use your Classic applications. Because your system's resources are now being used by both OS 9 and OS X, you may want to see how Classic is using/draining your RAM. To do this, click on the Memory/Versions section of the Classic preferences to see which applications are running, what version those applications are, and how much RAM they are using (shown in Figure 4-62).

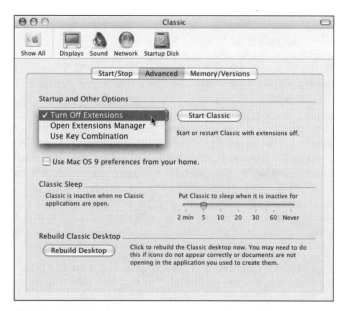

Figure 4-61: You have to start or restart Classic from this preference panel in order to get the options chosen here to take effect.

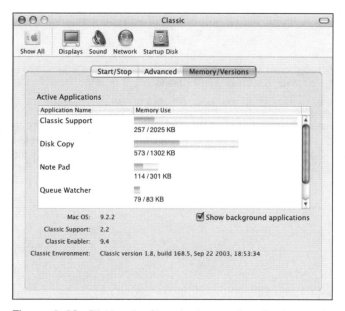

Figure 4-62: Clicking the Show background applications option shows you things like Queue Watcher and Classic Support. Although they are not applications as such, they use RAM and so you should include them in this view.

Date & Time

You'll find it very important for your Mac to know the correct time and date. Without this knowledge, you'll have no way to track when files are created or modified, when e-mails are sent or received, and the Mac won't know when to notify you of To Do items in iCal or any other organizer program. Figure 4-63 shows the three tabs of the Date & Time preference panel in System Preferences.

The Set Date & Time automatically check box and drop-down menu lets your Mac check a highly accurate clock via the Internet. If you don't have an always-on connection such as cable or DSL, you might want to uncheck this to prevent your Mac from dialing in to set the time at various odd hours. Of course, you can set the date and time manually by typing in the text boxes or just clicking in the calendar or dragging the clock's hands (but only if Set Date & Time automatically is unchecked).

Use the Time Zone tab to tell the Mac where you're located. Knowing where you are lets the Mac convert times on e-mail and other items into local time for you, so that you don't have to know what the time difference is between where you are and where the file or e-mail originated.

The Clock tab is where you specify whether a clock appears, and if so, if it is in the menu bar or a window and whether it is analog or digital. Further, you can specify the format displayed. If it is a window, you can even specify the level of transparency. Finally, you can tell your Mac to announce the time at set intervals and choose the voice used.

note Changing the format of the clock doesn't affect how dates and times are displayed in the Finder. For that, click the Open International button in the Date & Time tab.

Setting the Time in the Terminal

Assuming that you don't have an always-on Internet connection, you can set the time and date from the Unix command line in Terminal. Just type `sudo date ` *`yyyymmd-`* *`dhhmm.ss`* and press the Return key. That's a 4-digit year, 2-digit month, 2-digit day of month, 2-digit hour, 2-digit minute and (optional) 2-digit second. When asked for your Administrator password, enter it and press Return again. For example 9:50 A.M. on December 15, 2003 would be `200312150950.00`.

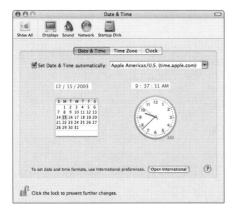 

Figure 4-63: The Date & Time pane has three tabs: (top left) Date & Time is where you set the date and time, (top right) Time Zone is where you tell the Mac in what time zone you reside, and (bottom left) Clock is where you specify what type of clock, if any, you want displayed and whether it should chime.

Software Update

One of the handiest, simplest, and cleverest ideas in OS X, the Software Update preference panel in System Preferences (Figure 4-64), lets you tell your Mac to call home for any updates to OS X or many of the applications Apple chooses to include with it (such as Safari, iMovie, iTunes, iSync, and so forth) on a schedule, or manually upon your request. Best of all, you can have it download the updates automatically as a background process and notify you when they're ready. Then, you can install them at your leisure. (You might not want to interrupt what you're doing to install an update requiring a restart immediately.)

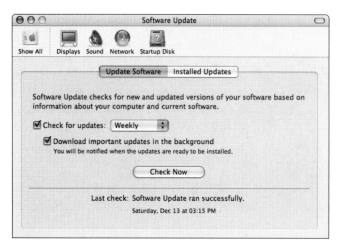

Figure 4-64: Software Update frees you from having to search to see whether an Apple software update is available — it checks and lets you know on a regular schedule what updates are available.

Software Update checks with Apple to see what's new — what updates Apple has made available that are not currently installed on your Mac. The truly paranoid among us choose Update⇨Install and Keep Package, just in case we ever need to reinstall Panther or a specific application (like iPhoto or iDVD). We still have to run the updater, but we don't have to download it again. Additionally, if you have more than one Mac (maybe you bought the five-license Panther package), you can use the update packages on each one without having to download them on every Mac.

The Installed Updates tab lists all the updates you've installed, as well as when you installed them (as shown in Figure 4-65). Click the Open as Log File button to see the log displayed in the Console utility.

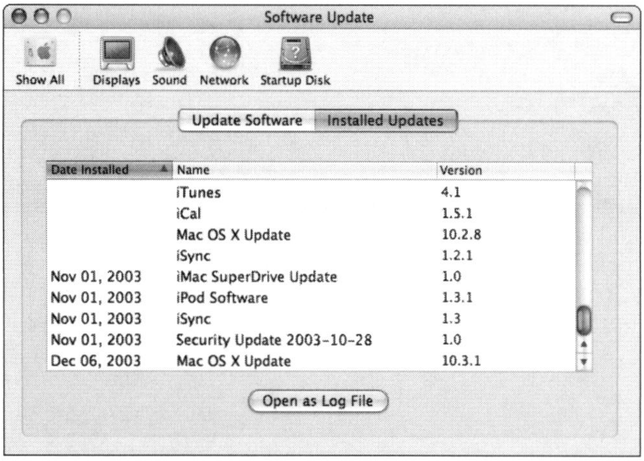

Figure 4-65: Software Update's Installed Updates tab tells you what you have installed and, if installed under Panther, the date it was installed.

A Way to See the Dates for Pre-Panther Updated Software

The log file is, no surprise here, named Software Update.log and is located in /Library/Logs. Even though the extension, .log, tells OS X to launch Console by default, it is really just a text file and you can open it in TextEdit, BBEdit, or any other text editor. Panther's Installed Updates tab doesn't recognize date formats other than *yyyy-mm-dd* followed by *hh:mm:ss –nnnn* where the nnnn is your adjustment from Greenwich Mean Time. Earlier versions of Software Update stored the date and time in a more human-friendly form known as the *long date format*. An example of long date format would be: Wednesday, November 27, 2002 12:45:00 US/Pacific. That's why old entries don't display the date when you view them in Software Update's Installed Updates tab. If you really want the old dates displayed as well, you can use a text editor to convert to the condensed format Panther employs.

Using Receipts to Look at the Installer Types

If you look in /Library/Receipts, you'll find a collection of .pkg files. These packages include the installation code and language resources for all the files you've installed using Apple's Installer utility, the installer used by Software Update. Other vendors use Apple's Installer, so the contents of this directory shows you everything you've installed using Installer. If only StuffIt InstallerMaker and Vise used the same receipt scheme, you would be able to track everything you've used an installer application to install or update. Of course, you would still have to deal with drag installs separately.

Speech

The Speech preference panel (in System Preferences) is also covered in quite a bit of depth in Chapter 10 where we look at Speech recognition by Panther, as well as third-party applications like ViaVoice and iListen. So, if you want to get gabby with you're Mac, head on over to Chapter 10 and talk away.

For the sake of this section, I'd like to show you that the Speech preference panel is broken down into three sections. The Speech Recognition section gives you OS control over Apple's built-in speech recognition capabilities (shown in Figure 4-66 top left). The Default Voice section allows you to choose a voice personality for how your computer talks to you as well as to change the speech rate (shown in Figure 4-66 top right). And the Spoken User Interface section gives you control over talking alerts and some other spoken items (shown in Figure 4-66 bottom left).

Startup Disk

The Startup Disk preference panel (in the System Preferences) is one of the simplest preference panels on you computer. It has one feature. You can choose which valid OS/System folder you want the computer to boot up into the next time it restarts (shown in Figure 4-67).

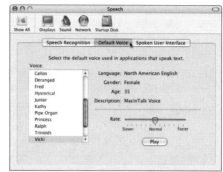

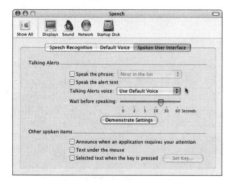

Figure 4-66: The Speech options in System Preferences control how Speech is used by the OS only. Third-party applications use separate preferences.

Figure 4-67: Once you've selected the System folder/OS you want your computer to start up in, you can click on the Restart button to restart your computer into that system.

If you choose to restart your computer into an OS 9.x OS, you can choose the OS X System folder from within the Startup control panel (available from under the OS 9 Apple menu items in the Control Panels folder) to get your computer to reboot back into Panther.

A Quick Way to Get Back to OS X on a Dual-Bootable Computer

If you are having trouble getting your computer to boot back into OS X, you can restart your computer and hold down the X key. This forces your computer to find a valid OS X (hopefully Panther) System folder that your computer can boot back into.

A Quick Way to Get All Your Bootable Choices

If you have several valid (or even invalid) System folders, and you can't get your computer to boot into any of them, you can give yourself more choices by holding down the Option key when you reboot. This causes the Boot Manager screen to appear (with some delays). Here you can choose which System you want to boot into.

When the clock stops spinning, the choices that your computer understands are shown on the screen. Select the one you want and click on the arrow button on the right side of the screen to choose it.

Universal Access

The Universal Access preference panel (in System Preferences) has come along way over time. This is the place where you go for help if you have trouble seeing, hearing, or using the computer keyboard and mouse. You use the various settings inside of Universal Access to compensate and to make your computer user-friendlier. At the top of all of the sections, the invitation, "When using the computer, I have difficulties with," prompts you to choose how the Universal Access sections can help you.

As you navigate through the Universal Access settings, you notice that the computer starts talking to you about the options as you move through it.

In the Seeing section of the Universal Access preferences, you can adjust screen contrast and zoom options to make your computer screen easier to see (shown in Figure 4-68). You can also invert the screen for even greater text clarity.

In the Hearing section of the Universal Access preferences, you can make the screen flash instead of hearing an alert sound (shown in Figure 4-69). You can also access the Sound preferences using the Adjust Volume button to turn the Alert sounds up.

Figure 4-68: The zoom options are the most commonly used, but you can also switch to a white-on-black screen as a contrast device.

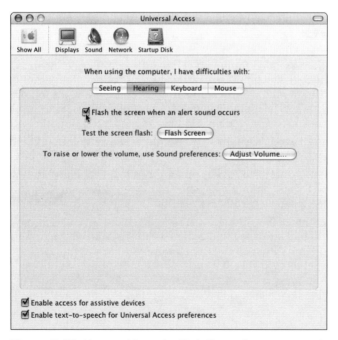

Figure 4-69: You would use the Flash Screen button to test the screen flash for notices. If you are not able to see the flash well, you can adjust the brightness settings from the keyboard or adjust the contrast settings in the Seeing section of the Universal Access preferences.

The Keyboard section of the Universal Access preferences allows you to adjust the way your keyboard receives keystrokes (shown in Figure 4-70). The Keyboard options allow for help in difficulties pressing more than one key at a time and in difficulties with initial or repeated keystrokes.

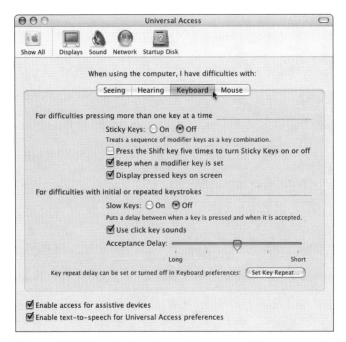

Figure 4-70: The Set Key Repeat button provides access to the key repeat delay feature.

And the Mouse section of the Universal Access preferences allows you to adjust the way you make mouse commands available through the keyboard (shown in Figure 4-71). You can set speed and delays for mouse keys in this section of preferences.

In all of the Universal Access sections, you can select or deselect two options: Enable access for assistive devices and Enable text-to-speech for Universal Access Preferences. Even if you don't use either of these, you might as well leave them selected.

Some AppleScripts can utilize these options to provide additional functionality to your OS. (See Chapter 11 for more details on this.)

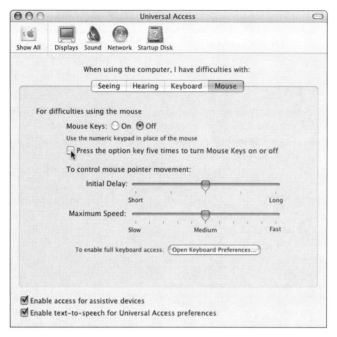

Figure 4-71: You can jump to the full keyboard settings by clicking on the Open Keyboard Preferences button.

Other Preferences

As I mentioned at the beginning of the chapter, you can have preference panes in addition to the ones Apple provides. My System Preferences (shown in Figure 4-72), for example, contains 12 additional preference panels. Some are haxies. Some are for additional hardware. And one (Remote Desktop) is even for a piece of software made by Apple.

Figure 4-72: Because these are not common, they are not separated into the other categories. And, what the heck, Other works as well as anything else.

If you click on one of these Other preference panels, you get additional controls for hardware and/or software that you have on your system. Because I use a Kensington two-button mouse, I have the Kensington MouseWorks software installed on my computer. When I installed the software, the installer placed a MouseWorks preference panel in System Preferences. Clicking on this preference panel opens up additional control options for my Kensington mouse (shown in Figure 4-73).

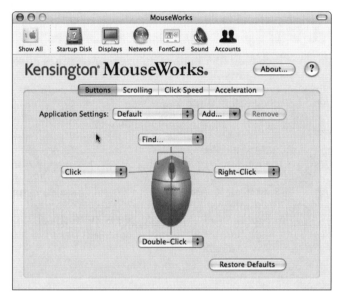

Figure 4-73: My Kensington Iridio still works without the MouseWorks preferences (using the OS Mouse settings), but Kensington gives me additional options with its preference panel.

The third-party preference panels shown in this chapter are just a few of the freeware, donationware, shareware, and commercial preference panes available. Just do a search on Version Tracker for the string "preference pane," and you'll find many third-party panes that might provide you with functionality you crave. To remove a third-party preference pane, make sure you've quit from System Preferences and then just remove the prefPane file from the Library/PreferencePanes folder in which you've installed it.

What to Do When You're Having Trouble Removing Preferences

Secret

Sometimes, when you remove a user-installed preference pane, System Preferences shows it as still present. You can remedy this by quitting from System Preferences and deleting the com.apple.preferencepanes.cache file located in your home directory's Library/Caches folder.

note

Not all preference panes are of equal importance or utility to all users. Some, though, like Orwell's pigs, are more equal than others. Contrary to the glitz and hype, setting a desktop pattern or a screen saver is not a critical activity. They're fun, they make your Mac experience more personal, but they aren't really necessary to successful operation.

A Guide to Third-Party Preference Enhancers

I mentioned much earlier in this chapter that third-party preference panes appear in the Other category and are installed in either /Library/PreferencePanes or ~/Library/ PreferencePanes, depending upon whether they are available to all standard accounts or just your account. If you search Version Tracker (www.versiontracker.com/macosx/) for preference pane, you'll see a list of at least a dozen. We'll just hit on a couple of the ones I think are most useful.

Déjà Vu, a backup utility bundled with Roxio's Toast 6 Titanium (www.roxio.com) is another very common third-party preference module. This one is also available separately from Propaganda Productions (http://propagandaprod.com). Other popular preference panes include Unsanity's WindowShadeX (www.unsanity.com), providing alternative window minimization effects; More Internet (www.monkeyfood.com/software/morein-ternet), where you can set protocol helpers as you did in OS 9's Internet Config; and SharePoints (www.hornware.com/sharepoints), a utility making it easier to share individual folders with specific users and groups.

More Internet

In days of yore (Mac OS 8 and 9), there was Internet Config with which the user could specify what application handled what Internet protocol or file type. Mac OS X just about eliminated that user oversight. You can still specify your e-mail client (by running Mail and setting it or a different mail client in its preferences). Similarly, you can specify the browser used to deal with http and https protocols in Safari's (or Internet Explorer's) preferences. In addition to distributing the control to the four winds (two winds?), you no longer get to specify your FTP client (you might want RBrowser, Fetch, or Interarchy to handle ftp) or your news client. The OS X news (or nntp) default is, believe it or not, to use Outlook Express, a Classic application, rather than Thoth, MT-Newswatcher, Hogwasher, MacSoup, or even Entourage, all of which are native OS X news clients. The freeware More Internet preference pane (shown in Figure 4-74) returns the power to you.

caution

If you use Internet Explorer as your Web browser, make sure it isn't running when you change settings in More Internet, or they might not stick. Internet Explorer includes a similar capability in its preferences and frequently overwrites these settings with whatever it has cached. Thus, if you quit Internet Explorer, it flushes its cache, you have those as your starting point, and you can make any changes you wish, having them show up in Internet Explorer the next time you launch it.

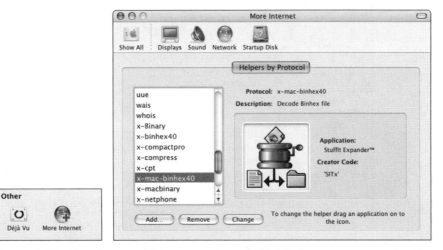

Figure 4-74: More Internet (left) presents the pane (right) where you can associate the application of your choice with the Internet protocol or file type.

Just select the protocol in the list and, if it isn't what you want, click the Change button and choose a new application relationship from the sheet that appears. If the protocol you're interested in isn't in the list, click the Add button, name it, and give a description in the sheet that appears, then select the new entry from the list, click Change, and select your application.

SharePoints

Another very popular pre–OS X functionality became much harder to use in OS X: general file sharing. In olden times, you could easily create users and groups of users and specify which shared directories they could access. With OS X's much more rigid Unix permissions structure, sharing has just about been relegated to users who have physical accounts on your Mac; so, creating groups necessitates navigating the scary waters of NetInfo. SharePoints (Figure 4-75) makes the older, less rigid capability available. "Normal" Shares lists those items shared via the standard OS X mechanisms. You can create users who don't have accounts on your Mac in the Users & "Public" Shares tab, create groups in the Groups tab, and oversee Apple File Sharing in the AFS Properties tab and Samba properties (Windows file sharing) in the SMB Props tab.

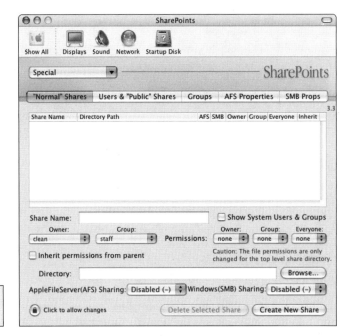

Figure 4-75: The SharePoints icon in Other (left) presents file-sharing on steroids (right), a complete, slightly less complex, and localized approach to the best of OS X and OS 9 file-sharing capabilities.

Summary

System Preferences is your Mac's command- and control-center. The various preference panes are your interface consoles to their respective functionality.

If you have trouble locating the preference icon you want in the default category, you can sort, change the view to alphabetic, use the Dock icon's contextual menu, or simply choose from the View menu.

You can add preference panes to the ones Apple provides, either for all account holders or just for your own account, but if you remove one that you've added, you might need to find and delete the cache file, as well.

In the next chapter, we look the Utilities, which go hand-in-hand with System Preferences as Apple's tools to help you harness the power of your OS.

Secrets of the Utilities Folder

Chapter

5

◆ ◆

Secrets in This Chapter

◆ ◆

Think of the Utilities folder (hidden near the bottom of your Applications Folder) on your Macintosh as your trusty toolbox. Back in the days of OS 9, your toolbox was almost empty. Just Disk Copy, Drive Setup, and Disk First Aid lived there. With the advent of OS X, the Utilities box is filled with a cavalcade of handy gadgets that show you what your Mac is thinking, how fast it is thinking, and where its thoughts are wandering. Instead of a couple of wrenches and a screwdriver, you now have a full complement of tools (even the one used just to open cans of paint. This is OS X. We don't use a flat screwdriver. We use the correct tool to break the seal on our paint cans.)

If the whole toolbox comparison doesn't make you just want to pop open your Utilities folder and start exploring, think of it more along the line of Batman's utility belt. Many of you familiar with the Dark Knight will know that whenever he is in a situation that seems impossible, he will pull the exact tool he needs to escape, be it a bat-boomerang, bat-blowtorch, bat-parachute, bat-truth serum, bat-can opener, bat-squeegee — anything needed at that particular moment to save the day.

And that is what the applications in your utility folders can do for you. So, when you are fooling around with your utilities, you are not just a Mac user, you are the resourceful super-hero Panther Man (or Panther Woman), and you can call your trusty buddy still using OS 10.2 Jaguar Boy (or Jaguar Girl.)

I can see you on the big screen already, examining the Activity Monitor to see what processes are taxing your CPU, then busting out your Digital Colorimeter to get the hex number for that color that looks oh-so-sweet on your monitor for your own Web page, then, when all hope seems lost, using the command line in Terminal to FTP a jpeg to your server. You might not get invited to join the Justice League of America, but you will probably impress some of your buddies with your intimate knowledge of Panther.

Looking at Your Utilities Folder

A quick glance at the contents of your Utilities folder (shown in Figure 5-1) reveals a lot of tools that, frankly, most users will never need to use. In fact, most will never even need to open the Utilities folder at all. Not that you will never use the tools, it is just that Apple offers different ways to get to them other than going directly to the source. For instance, if you ever access About This Mac in your Apple menu, and click the More Info button (shown in Figure 5-2), the System Profiler window opens. So, while your utilities are tucked away on your system, Apple makes it easy to access the ones you will use most often.

So, now that you know a little bit about what your utilities are, let's have a quick look at each of them.

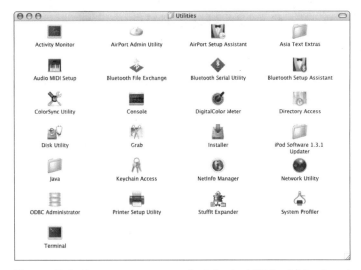

Figure 5-1: You may never use what's in the Utilities folder, but the tools are there in case you need them.

Figure 5-2: If you've hit the More Info button on the About the Mac dialog box, you've made a trip to the utilities folder without even knowing it.

Utilities for Processes, Setup, and Troubleshooting

This section covers utilities that can best be described as system or process utilities. When you are troubleshooting, you may find yourself looking at these applications.

Activity Monitor

You can use this tool to monitor your Mac's processor, network, disk activity, and disk usage. This is like the information you get on the dash of you car. It shows how fast your Mac is running, what programs are hogging your processor's resources, and other information (Figure 5-3).

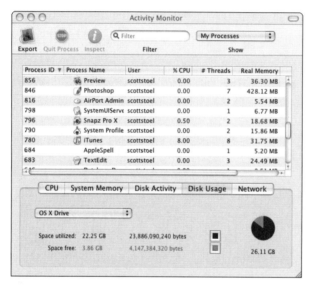

Figure 5-3: The Activity Monitor also allows you to see how much of the processor's (possibly more than one processor's) power each program is using. In this screenshot, iTunes is using 8 percent of the CPU's capacity. Photoshop, a resource hog if there ever was one, can use most of the CPU just by applying one of its many filters.

By double-clicking on an process name in the Activity Monitor, you bring up a window that provides more information than you would ever need about any of the programs you are running.

You can also find out a lot about other processes happening on your machine in the Activity Monitor, such as where your Mac is allocating its RAM, how much disk space you have available, how hard your hard drive, or drives, are working, and how active your network is.

And if the information provided in the main window of the Activity Monitor isn't enough, the utility offers three different ways to monitor your machine's performance graphically (shown in Figure 5-4). You can even change the Activity Monitor's Dock icon so that you can keep and eye on your machine without giving up much screen real estate. Just select Dock Icon underneath the Monitor Menu and pick which monitor you want the icon to be.

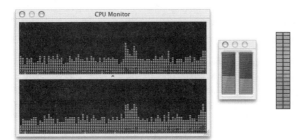

Figure 5-4: The Activity monitor offers three different ways of watching how hard your CPU is working (from left to right): the CPU Monitor, CPU usage, and the floating CPU window. The dual windows and bars indicate the presence of a Mac with dual processors.

Secret

Use the Activity Monitor to Force Quit an Application When Nothing Else Works

Next time one of your programs becomes unresponsive (i.e., freezes), launch your Activity Monitor. There you can see if it really is not working. You can then double-click on the icon to bring up additional information on the program. This window offers a Quit button, which when clicked gives you the option to force quit the program. This often gets results even when the Option-Command-Escape key combination doesn't work.

Console

The Console is the viewfinder into the inner workings of your system. Each line in the Console is a text log of the little conversations Panther is having with each of your programs, and the messages your programs are sending each other (shown in Figure 5-5). To the layperson, a system log can be pretty dry reading. But to a programmer or a System's Administrator, it offers invaluable troubleshooting and debugging information.

Figure 5-5: The system logs displayed in the Console can back up your claim, "The ColorSync Utility has crashed twice in the last five minutes. . . ."

Secret

Use the Console to Find Out When Your System or Application Last Crashed

If you are every really interested in the stability of your programs (or just incredibly bored), you can always find out the last time one of your favorite programs crashed just by checking the Console utility. First, click on the Logs button at the top of the Console window to reveal your log collection. Click the triangle in front of ~/Library/Logs, and then click CrashReporter. The CrashReporter holds a record of all the programs that have crashed on your Mac. When you select one of the program names, it reveals the last crash report. Scroll to the top of the report (by default it shows you the last part of the screen). In the second line of the report, it tells you the last time the program crashed.

Directory Access

This utility will probably only interest you if you are a network administrator, and, in fact, this is one of those utilities that you might think you will never use.

However, Panther has added many features to Directory Access that allow easier integration with Windows computers and file servers that you may wish to browse (shown in Figure 5-6).

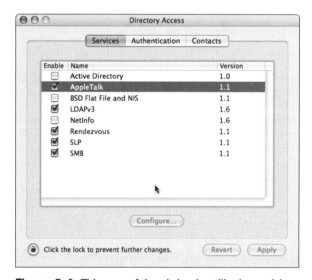

Figure 5-6: This powerful and simple utility is a quick way to see what services you have on.

Troubleshooting AppleTalk with the Directory Access Utility

As this book is written, Panther is very new. And like all new OS's, there are some reported "bugs" in the OS. One of those bugs concerns AppleTalk.

It seems that there are some computers that will not create an AppleTalk connection to a network even if they are correctly plugged in and configured within the Network controls in the System Preferences. Sometimes restarting helps and sometimes it doesn't.

One solution that we found is to launch the Directory Access utility and enable by checking (or unchecking and rechecking) the AppleTalk service in the list (shown in Figure 5-6). More times than not, this fixes the AppleTalk connectivity problem.

Keychain Access

The keychain keeps track of your passwords for Web sites, servers, applications, and anything else for which you need a password (shown in Figure 5-7). You can use Keychain Access to create different keychains and add information to them, but that sort of distracts from the simplicity of one centralized location for your passwords. If you have a lot of passwords to look after, if you frequently forget passwords, or if the security of your system is a major concern (i.e., you have a lot of different users, or your Mac is in a public area) this utility will make your life much easier. As a security measure, Keychain also lets you lock and unlock your keychain so that only you can control access to your passwords.

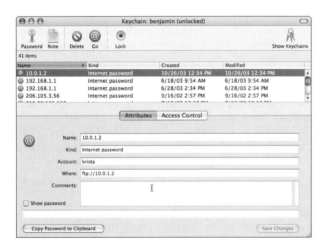

Figure 5-7: The Keychain window shows the keychains for you (your username) as indicated at the top of the window.

Bring Keychain to the Menu Bar

Secret

If you are a keychain-a-holic, you can put an icon on your menu bar to open keychain access, lock and unlock your various keychains, and lock your screen when you are away from your Mac. Under the View menu, select Show Status in Menu Bar and a little padlock icon appears toward the right end of your menu bar. Now you can exercise your paranoia, er, I mean, due caution in no time flat, without wading through menus to find Keychain Access.

System Profiler

Formerly the Apple System Profiler, this utility lets you know what hardware and software is installed on your Mac, how much memory is installed, and what peripheral devices are installed. It can help you troubleshoot any problems you are having on your Mac (shown in Figure 5-8).

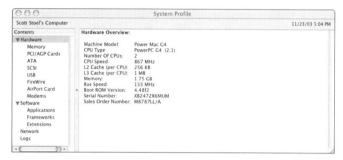

Figure 5-8: Just by opening the System Profiler, you can learn a lot about your Mac right down to the serial and sales order numbers.

A quick look at the System Profile window lets you know exactly what you can learn about your machine, but it is more than that. It can tell you about your mouse; just click USB under Hardware and scroll down until you see your mouse. And if you are e-mailing a mouse recommendation to a friend, you can copy this information right out of the System Profile window and paste it into your e-mail or any other document for that matter.

If you want to know how much RAM you have in your machine, click on Memory under Hardware and it shows you how many slots you have and what sort of memory is installed in each slot.

Now, how does that help you troubleshoot? Well, say your Zip drive stops working. You know you have a Zip drive and it is installed. You can check the System Profile, and if it doesn't indicate you have a Zip drive, it could be that a power cord or some other connector has become loose, so you can crack open your case and try to better fasten the connections. If System Profiler can see the hardware and your apparatus continues to not work, you could need a driver update. Any way you look at it, if it's supposed to be there and your System Profiler can't see it, there is something wrong.

Setup Assistant

The Setup Assistant isn't really a process utility, but it doesn't go anywhere else, so I'm tacking it on the end of this section.

The Setup Assistant is a lot like the old Apple Setup Assistant from Jaguar. If you skipped some of the screens when you created your user, it repeats the interview screens you had to answer when you first logged on to your Mac. If you are already connected to the Internet, you don't need to use this ever again.

If you did complete these screens, the Setup Assistant will assume that you want to add or modify your Internet connection when you launch it (shown in Figure 5-9).

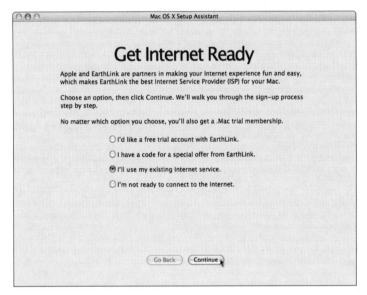

Figure 5-9: If you are not connected to the Internet, you'd better get with it, because you have issues that the Setup Assistant will never be able to solve.

More Control with the AirPort Utilities

Apple bundles a variety of tools to help you configure and manage an AirPort network as well as to just help you join an existing AirPort network. Some of the networking is covered in Chapter 29, but for now, let's look at what the Utilities folder offers for control over AirPort.

AirPort Admin Utility

If you don't have a Mac with an AirPort card, you will never need this utility. If you do have the necessary hardware, you can use this utility to monitor your connections in your AirPort network, update the base station firmware, or set up a connection manually instead of using the AirPort Setup Assistant (shown in the next section).

Double-clicking on the AirPort Admin Utility brings up a Select Base Station window that shows visible, local AirPort Base Stations (shown in Figure 5-10). To make changes to a specific base station, click on the base station in the list and then click on the Configure icon at the top of the Select Base Station window.

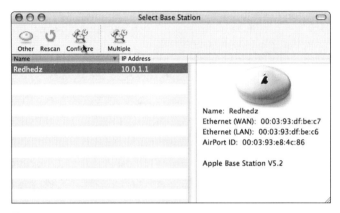

Figure 5-10: Visible base stations also display their name, WAN, LAN, AirPort ID, and base station software version information.

If you have a password on your AirPort base station (and you should), you will be prompted to enter it prior to entering the configuration screens for the base station (shown in Figure 5-11).

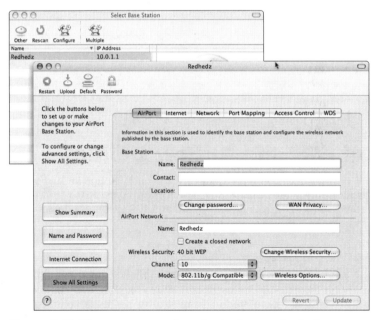

Figure 5-11: The name you see here for the base station is the same name shown in the Select Base Station window.

All of the AirPort settings (Internet and network connections) are covered in Chapter 29, but for now suffice it to say that here is where you edit or change the way your AirPort Base Station interacts with the Internet and your computer.

Secret

Use the AirPort Admin to Help You Avoid Other Wireless Interference

Microwaves and some other electronic devices/appliances devices can cause signal interference with an AirPort network if they are located near an AirPort Base Station or a computer on an AirPort network.

Apple has given us some help with this. Choose the Wireless Options button on the bottom of the AirPort section of the base station's settings window to get an option to select Enable interference robustness (shown in Figure 5-12).

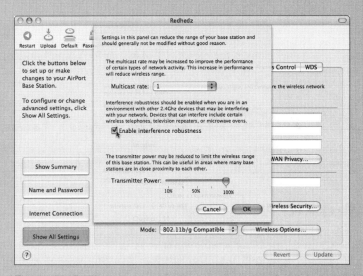

Figure 5-12: Changing the Multicast rate may also help you help AirPort signal performance. Trial-and-error is the rule for these settings.

Click the OK button and then click the Update button and you will have given your base station that extra edge that might make the difference between a stable or unstable AirPort network connection.

If all of these settings seem a little bit too technical, I suggest you move to the next utility.

AirPort Setup Assistant

If you have the proper hardware for a wireless network, the AirPort Setup Assistant will ask you a few questions to help you configure your network (shown in Figure 5-13).

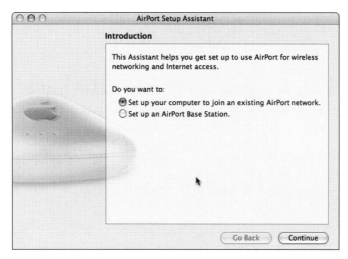

Figure 5-13: For a novice, this is the easiest way to join an AirPort network or set up a base station from scratch.

A Few Utilities You Probably Won't Use

This is probably an unfair statement about the following utilities. What I should have said is that these are a few utilities that most people won't use, but that others will find extremely useful.

Asia Text Extras

This is an example of Apple's forward thinking regarding Mac marketing, especially toward the Chinese-speaking developer. The Asia Text Extras folder (shown in Figure 5-14) features the Chinese Text Converter utility that makes encoding conversions between simplified Chinese and traditional Chinese, and the IM Plugin Converter, which converts a user-defined text file to a Chinese Input Method Plugin data file. This is probably very handy, if you speak Chinese. And with over a billion people that do, it is nice to see Apple planning for that vast market.

Audio MIDI (Musical Instrument Digital Interface) Setup

This utility lets you configure audio input and output devices connected to your Mac. The panel offers two tabs (shown in Figure 5-15).

The first tab is Audio Devices, which is a control panel for all your input devices — microphones, keyboards, and so on — and your external speakers. This isn't much use on a Mac out of the box, which features one input jack (for a microphone) and one output (the speaker).

The second tab, MIDI Devices, allows you to add and remove MIDI devices.

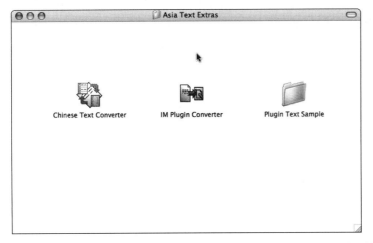

Figure 5-14: Utilities that you will probably leave alone, but you should be glad Apple has thought of them.

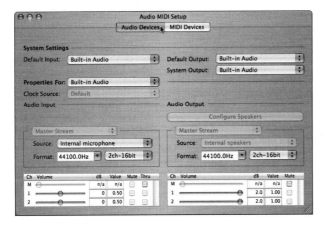

Figure 5-15: If you're making music with your Mac and other equipment hooked up to it, you need to learn the options of this utility.

The Java Folder

Java is the Sun Microsystems contribution to the programming world, and is chiefly used to write small programs, called *applets*, which are placed on Web pages. Java applets provide animated features, sound effects, and games, although that is not the limit of Java as a programming language.

Inside the Java folder (shown in Figure 5-16) are a few tools used to access applets written with Java. First is the Applet Launcher. This lets you run Java applets on your computer or on the Internet without having to use a browser. From the launcher you can type in a URL where an applet is posted on the Web, or browse your machine to find an applet stored on your Mac.

If this doesn't sound very useful, that's easy to understand. Most browsers are Java-enabled and any applet you download from the Web can run in your browser window. (The Web is filled with free Java applets to download, and lots of them are games.)

Also, in your Java folder is the Java Plugin Settings (shown in Figure 5-16). This program allows you to configure options for Java applets in your Web browser. This is mainly used by Java developers and system administrators. (But isn't that true with all the fun stuff?) Changing these setting may prevent applets from running on your Mac.

The last resident of your Java folder (see Figure 5-16) is Java Web Start. This is a Sun program that allows you to download Java applications on the Web without having to go through an installation process. It's a feature that has a lot of promise, but I'm not exactly sure what that promise is.

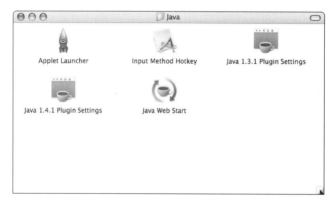

Figure 5-16: Java . . . it isn't just for breakfast any more.

Let's Talk About (and With) Bluetooth

Bluetooth is an technology where we talk about networking, protocols, hardware, and specific functions available to other protocols as well as just to Bluetooth. If this sound like much ado about nothing, then you you'd be mistaken. Maybe I need to explain Bluetooth a little more. Bluetooth is a universal standard and specification that enables devices like Bluetooth-enabled mobile phones, computers, handheld PIMs, and any other Bluetooth-enabled appliances to communicate wirelessly with each other. A Bluetooth device contains a Bluetooth chip that is either integrated (as with the new Apple laptops) or is an external module (sold by third parties like D-Link) that is usually plugged in via USB.

Bluetooth (as it's being used by the Mac these days) can connect devices within a range of approximately 30 feet. And unlike other wireless connection methods, a Bluetooth connection is relatively secure.

One of the coolest examples of Bluetooth technology (in the market place) is Bluetooth-enabled mobile phones that can make contact with wireless Bluetooth-enabled head-phone/microphones. Those same Bluetooth-enabled phones can also be synced (using Apple's iSync) with a Bluetooth-enabled computer's address book, so that the sharing of addresses can be quick, secure, and wireless.

For the sake of looking at these next few utilities, we will assume that you have a Bluetooth-enabled computer. (If you don't, there's not much point in looking at this section.)

You can read more on the wild world of syncing with Bluetooth in Chapter 16, networking in depth with Bluetooth in Chapter 29, and general Bluetooth preferences in Chapter 4.

Bluetooth File Exchange

Bluetooth File Exchange is the utility that enables the discovery and connection of other Bluetooth devices and/or computers. (No matter how you get there, this is the utility that it uses.)

The easiest way for me to show you the Bluetooth File Exchange utility is to take you through the steps of sending and receiving a file:

1. Launch the Bluetooth File Exchange utility (located in the Utilities folder in the Applications folder) or select the Send File command from the Bluetooth menu located in the right-hand group of menu bar icons (shown in Figure 5-17).

Figure 5-17: The Bluetooth menu can be turned on and off from the Bluetooth pane in System Preferences and will be an option only if your computer has a Bluetooth module built-in or added externally.

2. In the Select File to Send dialog (shown in Figure 5-18), select your file(s) and click on the Send button.

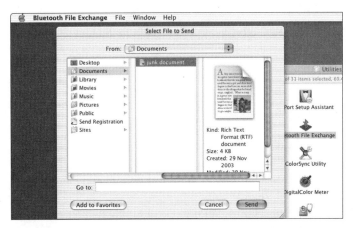

Figure 5-18: The file(s) sent via the Bluetooth File Exchange utility must be selected before selecting the destination.

3. The file selection screen will be replaced with the Send File: <name of file> box. The first thing you will need to choose is the Device type. Since you are sending a file to another computer you need to select "Computers" from the Device Type pull-down menu (shown in Figure 5-19).

Figure 5-19: Choosing Computers is a little more useful than deciding if your computer is a laptop or a desktop model.

4. The second selection in the Send File dialog is the Device Category. Because there are no devices in the Device list window, you need to select Discovered Devices from the Device Category pull-down menu (shown in Figure 5-20).

Figure 5-20: The first time you select a category you need to use Discovered Devices.

5. After you make these two choices in the Send File dialog, click on the Search button to see if there are any Bluetooth-enabled computers within range (shown in Figure 5-21).

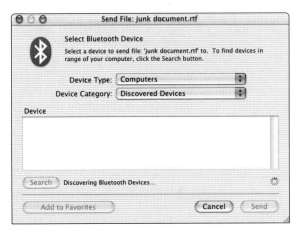

Figure 5-21: The spinning symbol (above the grayed out Send button) and the text displaying "Discovering Bluetooth Devices..." indicate that the computer is searching for local Bluetooth-enabled computers.

6. If you do have a Bluetooth-enabled computer within range, it will show up in the Device window (shown in Figure 5-22). Highlight the computer/device and then click on the Send button to send the file(s) you selected in Step 2.

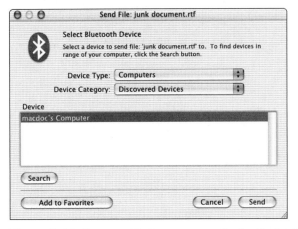

Figure 5-22: Because this is a computer (in the Device list), the name of the device is set in the File Sharing pane in System Preferences on that computer.

7. The next part of this process happens on the computer that you are sending the file to. If you go to that computer, you will see a dialog box prompting you to Accept or Reject the incoming file (shown in Figure 5-23) sent via the Bluetooth Exchange utility. Click on the Accept button to receive the file.

Figure 5-23: Notice that the dialog box shows you the name of the computer/user sending the file(s), which is set the in File Sharing controls in the System Preferences of the sending computer.

8. Once you have received the file, you get another dialog box prompting you to either open the file, show the file(s) in the Finder, or to cancel (shown in Figure 5-24).

Figure 5-24: This dialog box, as well as the behavior of other similar Bluetooth dialog boxes, can be controlled from the Bluetooth pane in System Preferences.

9. Choosing the Show In Finder button in Figure 5-24 opens a window showing you the file in the directory it was placed (shown in Figure 5-25).

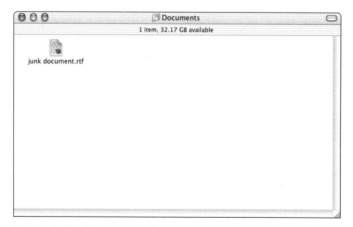

Figure 5-25: The default place to store Bluetooth Exchanged documents is in the user's Documents folder.

If any of these steps do not behave in the way that you think that they should or you want to change their behaviors, you can set some of these options in the Bluetooth preferences pane accessible in the Hardware section of System Preferences (shown in Figure 5-26).

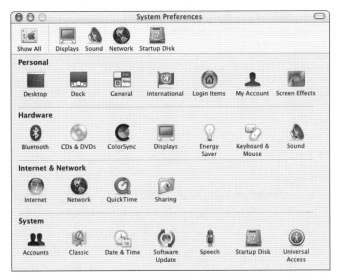

Figure 5-26: All of the settings for Bluetooth devices can be accessed through System Preferences, which is covered in more depth in Chapter 4.

Bluetooth Serial Utility

The Bluetooth Serial Utility allows you to select and define a Bluetooth device as a port to be used by other features of your OS. This utility uses the discovery capability of the Bluetooth File Exchange utility behind the scenes and has the same kind of control when you are setting up Bluetooth ports.

As with the Bluetooth Exchange utility, the best way for you to understand how this works is to take you through the addition of a Bluetooth serial port. Please follow along with me with the following steps:

1. Click on the Bluetooth Serial Utility (in the Utilities folder in the Applications folder) to open a window showing a list of the Bluetooth serial ports (shown in Figure 5-27).

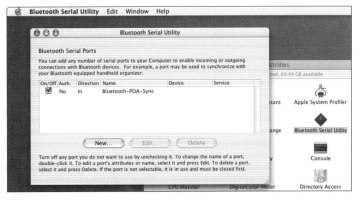

Figure 5-27: The Bluetooth-PDA-Sync is preset to help you use a PDA or phone with iSync.

2. Clicking on the New button (in Figure 5-27) presents you with a new screen which asks you to name your port, select your port direction, and select the port type (shown in Figure 5-28).

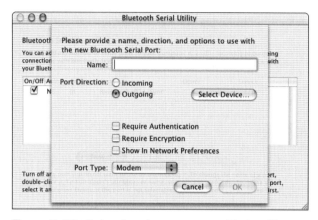

Figure 5-28: Only select the port type as Modem if you are going to be using the Bluetooth device as an Internet connection or fax connection alternative to your computer. There are special options in the Network preferences and the Printing and Faxing preferences of the host computer for modem options.

3. Change your port type accordingly and then click on the Select Device button. This presents you with the Select Bluetooth Service window (shown in Figure 5-29). For the sake of this example, you are going to choose another computer's OBEX Object Push service as the service to name/use.

4. Select the Device Type, Device Category, the Device itself, and the service, and then click the Select button (shown in Figure 5-29).

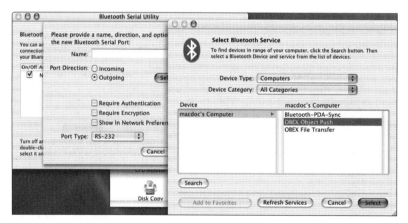

Figure 5-29: If the Select Bluetooth Service window looks a lot like the Bluetooth Exchange window, that's because the Exchange discovery technology is being used in this window.

5. After selecting the Bluetooth service, you will be back to the previous screen that now shows the device and service above the Require Authentication option. Now you can name your Bluetooth serial port, select your port direction (in this case Outgoing), select your port type (shown in Figure 5-30), and click OK.

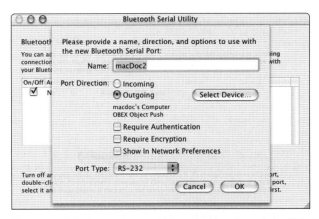

Figure 5-30: Knowing the device name and service will help you name the serial port. If you have a lot of Bluetooth serial ports, make sure you name each port something that makes sense.

6. You are now back to your main Bluetooth Serial Utility window, which shows your newly created Bluetooth serial port (shown in Figure 5-31). If you need to make a change to this port, highlight the port in the list and click the Edit button.

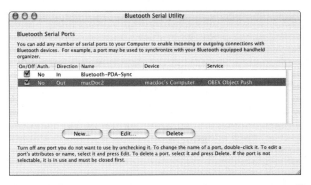

Figure 5-31: You can choose to turn these ports on or off after you have added them by selecting or deselecting them using the check boxes in front of each port.

7. Not only can you now rename, but you can also add additional security to your newly added port; you can then change your mind and select or deselect the Require Authentication and Require Encryption options, and/or show that port in the Network preferences for other uses (shown in Figure 5-32).

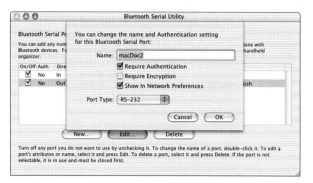

Figure 5-32: These options give more security to your Bluetooth connection/serial port.

8. The newly edited port now shows that Authentication has been turned on. (See Yes indicated in the second column of the Bluetooth Serial Ports list shown in Figure 5-33.)

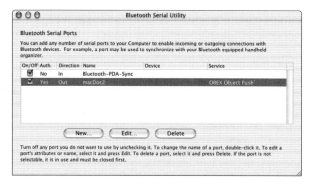

Figure 5-33: If you don't want or need the Bluetooth Serial Port anymore, you can also select it and click the Delete button to remove it altogether.

As I say in Step 7 (shown in Figure 5-32), you can choose to make these serial ports available in the Network preferences. I go into *why* you would do this in Chapter 29, but for now, by launching System Preferences (either from the Apple Menu or the Applications folder) and then clicking on the Network preferences, you can see how these choices have affected the Network setting's choices.

By selecting the Network Port Configurations from the Show menu, you see the newly created Bluetooth Serial Port (shown in Figure 5-34). If the port is turned on in the Network Port Configurations, it is one of the menu items available in the Show pull-down menu (shown in Figure 5-35).

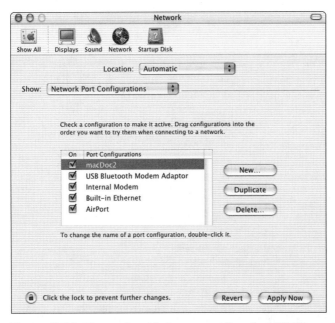

Figure 5-34: The newly added port, as well as the USB Bluetooth Modem Adaptor choices, is available on this Bluetooth-enabled computer.

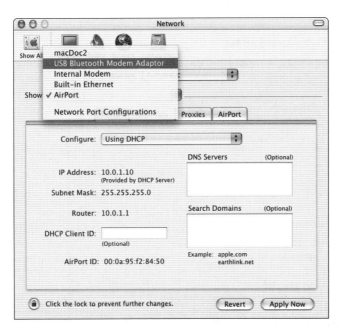

Figure 5-35: All ports turned on in the Network Port Configurations show up in the Show pull-down menu.

Use the Bluetooth Menu to See What Devices You've Already Set Up

If you look under the Bluetooth menu (from the top of the screen), you can see devices that have already been added to your computer, like the Apple Wireless Mouse (shown in Figure 5-36).

Figure 5-36: Almost all Bluetooth utilities and services can be reached from under the Bluetooth menu.

If you don't see the device you're looking for you can quickly find it by selecting Browse Device from under the Bluetooth menu.

And for added security you can shut off all Bluetooth services from this same menu.

Bluetooth Setup Assistant

Double-clicking on this utility launches a dialog box that asks you a few questions that will help it configure your Bluetooth settings (shown in Figure 5-37).

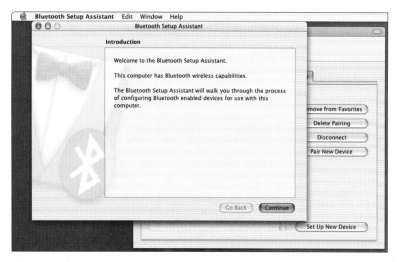

Figure 5-37: You can access this utility by double-clicking the Bluetooth Setup Assistant in the Utilities folder in the Applications folder, or by clicking on the Set Up New Device button from within the Bluetooth settings in System Preferences.

New Uses for the Graphic Utilities

The Mac platform has long reigned supreme as the most graphic and graphic-friendly OS in use. And while creating a new suite of utilites, Apple didn't forget to give us a few good utilites that help us handle color.

ColorSync Utility

Formerly, this utility was invaluable to those in the graphics design business and virtually no one else. If you live and die by color, this was the place for you. But otherwise, you didn't bother.

But now, with Panther, ColorSync adds an extremely cool and useful feature that you can use no matter who you are.

Open the ColorSync Utility and skip over the menu bar selections until you get to the last one called Filters. Click on that one.

Looking at the available filters (shown in Figure 5-38), you might be prompted to ask the profound question, "So what?" Well, I'll tell you what. Each one of these is what Panther calls a Quartz filter. It allows you to take an image and convert it using a different profile without opening it in an image-editing program like Photoshop. So, theoretically, you can have one image and use ColorSync to convert so it will look good on any output device you are going to use.

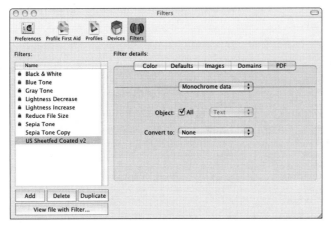

Figure 5-38: The filters window lets you use prefab profiles or construct your own custom profiles.

Still sounds like the realm of graphic designers, right? Well, they benefit too. They benefit a lot. But if you have that one printer that always prints too dark you can use the Lightness Increase selection (shown in Figure 5-39) and that will lighten the whole image, and you will get a better printout without editing the original image.

Print

Printer:	Adobe PDF
Presets:	Standard
	ColorSync
Color Conversion:	Standard
Quartz Filter:	Lightness Increase

(?) (Preview) (Save As PDF...) (Fax...) (Cancel) (Print)

Figure 5-39: ColorSync offers its filters in the print dialog box. Just select the ColorSync tab and then select whatever Quartz filter best suits your output device. If it is destined for a fax machine you may want to select "Black and White." If the document is bound for a black and white laser printer, you may want to select "Gray Tone."

But what if you have to send the image out to a service provider and you want it altered according to your profile. Well, that is easy enough. You simply click the View File with Filter button and browse for the file you want to assign a new profile. Make sure the file is a copy of the original, because ColorSync will apply the profile to the file and won't give you a Save As option. A new window opens that displays your file and the list of filters (shown in Figure 5-40). Assign a filter to your image and hit Apply. Now close the window. ColorSync asks you if you want to save the changes. Remember ColorSync applies the changes to the file you selected. Once you do, there is no getting your original image back.

Secret

Use ColorSync to Resize Images

ColorSync will do more than convert color spaces for you. You can make a filter that does nothing to the color of the file, but will resize the image by percentage or by maximum and minimum pixel dimensions. Once again, and I can't get enough of this, all without opening the file in another image editor. . . .

DigitalColor Meter

This utility is the color freak's best friend. Whether you are a print designer or html coder, this tool is incredibly handy. With it, you can determine the color of anything on your screen, and then copy the information in a variety of methods to your other programs (shown in Figure 5-41). DigitalColor Meter also can take the RGB (Red, Green, & Blue) information and convert it into CIE, Lab, and Tristimulus values.

---

insider
insight

Lab describes color in terms of *luminance* or its lightness component (L) and two chromatic components: the *a* component (green and red) and the *b* component (blue and yellow).

Figure 5-40: ColorSync lets you apply multiple filters to an image, and you can view all the changes you made by clicking on the history button. Although you can view your changes, you cannot undo any of them.

(Tristimulus values were set by the CIE [Commission Internationale de Eclairag] as an alternate way to measure color based on the response of the three photoreceptors in the human eye, and the values are expressed with the coordinate values X, Y, and Z. Now aren't you glad you asked?)

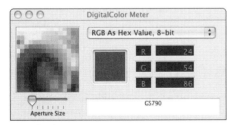

Figure 5-41: To keep DigitalColor Meter in front of your other applications, and thus always available, just open the preferences and select "Float window above other apps."

Here are a few of the main commands you will use if you decide to use the DigitalColor Meter utility:

- ◆ **Option-⌘-C:** This key combination will copy a 56 x 53 pixel sample of the color you captured onto your clipboard.

- ◆ **Shift-⌘-C:** This key command will copy the numeric value of the color you captured. If you are running DigitalColor Meter in RGB as Hex Value, 8-bit mode, you can take that information and paste it right into your HTML code. How's that for slick?

- ◆ **Shift-⌘-H:** This key combination toggles the Hold feature and keeps the value of whatever color was captured at the moment you hit the key combination. Hitting the key combination again switches the feature off and you can once again troll for that perfect color.

We Interrupt This Chapter . . .

You wouldn't think that an argument could start over the DigitalColor Meter, but I tend to be graphically inclined and have strong options about these kinds of things. So, I'll claim responsibility for starting this one.

Benjamin: If Apple were serious about making the DigitalColor Meter a useful tool for designers, it would take the monitor values and allow for conversion to CMYK values as well. Print designers work mainly in the CMYK color space and having a utility to make that conversion would eliminate an extra step needed in design programs such as Photoshop. And while we are at it, why not have the DigitalColor Meter record the numbers in a manner that could be pasted directly into Photoshop's color picker. Now that is a tool that print designers would embrace.

Pieter: While CMYK would be a great addition, Apple still needs to leave some room for Adobe and Quark to make the killer applications that help sell Macs. Personally, I don't miss CMYK because I don't do much print work and tend to just work on Web pages and such. Knowing what a color looks like on the printed page is just not that important to me. Apple, as far as I can determine, developed DigitalColor Meter to make it easy for a person, such as myself, to get the exact color values of a color that I like and then use those values to create the Web pages of my dreams.

The Disk Utility Gets New Powers

With Panther, the fine folks at Apple have combined two utilities from Jaguar, Disk Copy and Disk Utility, to make one full-service disk tool. Disk Utility now handles all your disk needs from creating disk images and burning CDs and DVDs to partitioning drives. So, in order to understand this cool utility, first you will create a disk image from a folder and burn a disc from that image, and then you are going to tend to your neglected hard drives.

Creating and Burning a Disk Image

Open Disk Utility. Select Images⇨New⇨Blank Image. The New Blank Image dialog box appears and gives you several options including naming your new disk image, and specifying where you want to put it on your drive and what size it will be. In Figure 5-42, Size is specified as 660 MB (CD-ROM 12 cm), Encryption as none, and Format as read/write disk image. I like to choose read/write because then I can drag something off the disk if I later decide not to save the file. Make your settings and hit Create.

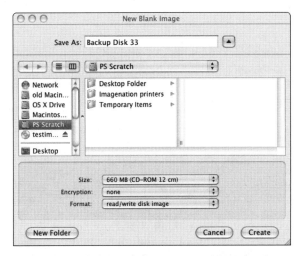

Figure 5-42: The New Blank Image dialog box allows you to select the location of the image, as well as choose the Size options, Encryption options, and Format options.

When you create a new blank disk, it is like setting up a temporary partition on your drive. Your actual disk image file (with the .dmg suffix) resides wherever you place it, and may be buried as deeply on your hard drive as you want it, but the disk image has another icon that acts just like another hard disk or any other removable media on your hard drive. You can use Get Info to find out the capacity of the drive, and you can even eject the disk and the info will still be safe in your disk image file. To open the "disk" again, just double-click on the disk image file.

Now because you chose a size for your disk, Disk Copy lets you know when you attempt to put too much data on it. This way, you create a disk image that can hold only as much as a standard CD can hold (shown in Figure 5-43). Another benefit of setting this limit is that Disk Copy alerts you when you are ready to burn a CD, and start a new backup, thus keeping your hard drive clear for your other projects.

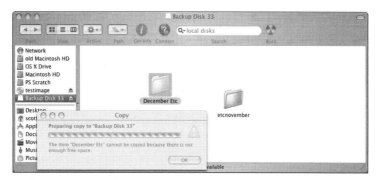

Figure 5-43: Disk Utility helps you show a little restraint by not allowing you to make an image larger than your backup media. It's like having a maid clean your house only when it's filthy, not every Thursday whether you need it or not.

Once you fill your backup disk image, it is time to burn a copy for your records. Insert a blank CD into your Mac. If you have your CD player set to ask you what program to open, select Open Finder. If you're an mp3-burnin' fool, you might want to go into System Preferences and change your CD preferences to open the Finder, or at least ask you what program you want to open when you insert a blank disc. Once the blank disc shows up, simply drag your disk image to the CD icon and Select Burn Disk from the File Menu or if you have the Blank CD in the sidebar of a Finder window, click the 50s-era bomb shelter sign (the Burn icon) next to the CD's icon. If everything works as it should, your Mac provides you with a disc that contains an exact copy of your disk image. You can use the newly burned disc to restore disks, view backed up files, or gleefully re-create a child's CD game that was mutilated during a rousing game of let's-see-how-much-pressure-a-CD-can-take-as-I-bend-it-out-of-a-slot-loading-iMac.

Testing and Repairing a Disk

Disk Utility makes verifying and repairing your hard drives a breeze. You might even forgo third-party disk repair software, although right on the Disk Utility window, Apple suggests using third-party products if Disk Utility fails. That's not exactly a rousing vote of confidence in the product, but when it comes free with the OS, who can complain?

Disk Utility offers two great features that you can use on your Mac regularly to keep your hard drives happy, and a happy hard drive is a fast hard drive. And even more importantly, it is a drive that is less likely to send files into oblivion or just plain quit.

The first of these items is the Verify Disk feature (shown in Figure 5-44). In your Disk Utility window, select a drive or partition and select Verify Disk. (You will not be able to do this if your only drive is your startup drive. To verify the startup disk you have to reboot from your Panther Disk.) If the Verify Disk returns with a problem, click Repair Disk and hope for the best. As Apple advises, if this doesn't work you might have to get one of the many commercially available disk utility programs such as Norton Utilities, Disk Warrior, or Tech Tool Pro. But Disk Utility should handle some of the problems you encounter.

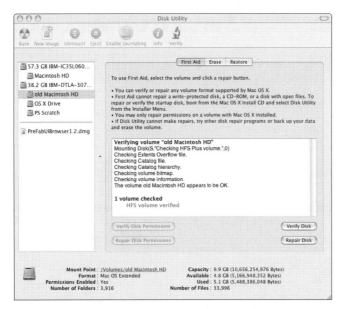

Figure 5-44: Panther's Verify Disk and Repair Disk features resemble the old Disk First Aid from OS 9.

The Verify Tool keeps your disk in order, but how can you increase your Mac's speed? In your Disk Utility First Aid window there are two buttons labeled Verify Permissions and Repair Disk Permissions. Every once in a while, one of many permissions associated with OS Xin general, become damaged. When this happens, programs may not open or your Mac may run slower than, well, Disk Utility verifying disk permissions. Verifying or repairing permissions is a good thing to do, especially when you install new software or update your system.

To verify your permissions just click the Verify Permission button and go.

How to Protect Yourself by Making Your Hard Drive S.M.A.R.T.

Wouldn't it be nice if before your disk just up and explodes, or silently commits suicide, that you would get a little warning? Well, most drives include S.M.A.R.T. (Self-Monitoring, Analysis and Reporting Technology) hardware developed by IBM that allows hard drives to examine themselves for problems.

To find out if your disk is ready to give up the ghost, click on a disk in the left column of your Disk Utility window. At the bottom of the window, there is a line called S.M.A.R.T status. If your disk is verified, your disk is fine, but if you see a message in red letters that reads, About to fail, you'd better back up your files and start shopping for a new drive, because your hard drive will not be with you very much longer.

Using the Not-So-Used Service Utilities

Some utilities are actually used by other applications or menu options. I like to think of these utilities as Service utilities. Here's a look at those utilities that you're not likely to use by actually double-clicking on the applications themselves . . . although you can.

Grab

This utility is for capturing screen shots. It's also the application that the Grab service accesses when it's used. It duplicates the function of your keyboard shortcuts for screen shots (Shift-⌘-3 for a screen dump, Shift-⌘-4 for shooting a selection). The only real difference is that Grab saves your file as a TIFF instead of a PDF, and you can set Grab to take a timed shot (ten seconds).

When you double-click on the Grab utility/application, your menu changes to allow you to choose a Selection, Window, Screen, or a Timed Screen for ten seconds (shown in Figure 5-45).

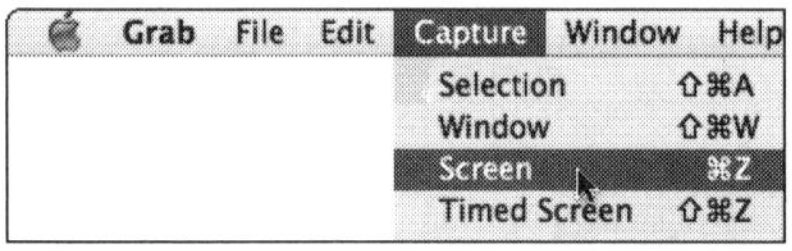

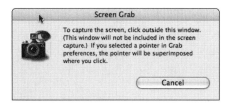

Figure 5-45: Selecting the Screen (⌘-Z) is one way to capture the screen as a picture.

After you select the Screen option from under the Capture menu, you will be prompted with a Screen Grab dialog box (shown in Figure 5-46).

Figure 5-46: The Screen Grab dialog box allows you to select the screen (behind the box) by clicking on the screen or to cancel by clicking on the Cancel button.

These other Grab Capture options can be accessed through the Grab submenu in the Services menu under one of the application's menus (shown in Figure 5-47) if there are objects that can be grabbed.

Choosing Mail⇨Services⇨Grab⇨Selection brings up a prompting dialog box titled Selection Grab (shown in Figure 5-48). You can then click and drag over the area that you want to select with the Grab utility. Clicking again on the selection will complete the selection.

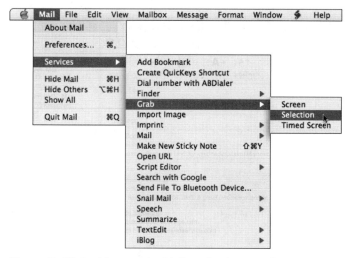

Figure 5-47: In this case, the Mail application can Grab through the Services the Screen, a Selection, or a Timed Screen. Only options that apply to what is up in the application will be listed in the Services window.

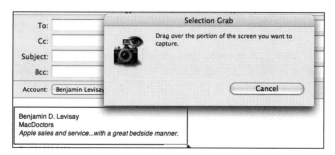

Figure 5-48: A red line will appear around your selection.

The selected area is then available for you to use. In the mail application (shown in Figure 5-48) the selected text is turned into an image and automatically placed inline at the point where my cursor was located.

Hard Drive Update 1

This utility is not in all Utility folders. It has been added to one of my computer's Utility folders through the software update process.

This utility updates the firmware for some hard drives installed in certain Mac models containing the G4 chip and helps extend the life of the drive. Most drives do not need this update. If you run this utility and it indicates that an update is needed, it also allows you to quit the program and back up your files before continuing with the update.

You really should take the hint in this case and back up your files. There are horror stories galore from those who have run this utility, from kernel panics to the OS not being able to see the drives after the utility is run.

This utility really applies to a few G4 models only and the problem does not exist in the current line of Mac computers. But still, it gives you the warm fuzzies seeing a dialog box that tells you everything is all right (shown in Figure 5-49), doesn't it.

Your drive's ATA Firmware is up-to-date with Hard Drive Update 1

OK

Figure 5-49: G4 models that use IBM/Hitachi Deathstar hard drives require a firmware update. For the rest of us, Hard Drive Update lets us know everything is okee-dokee.

Installer

You will never need to use this utility. When you install a program, Installer is the software that drives your Mac's installer and other software installers.

StuffIt Expander

This is another utility that is used automatically when you download or double-click on a *stuffed* item. If you don't have StuffIt Deluxe installed on your computer, StuffIt Expander will be used by your OS as the default application for opening compressed files.

NetInfo, Network Utility, and the ODBC Administrator

These three utilities are kind of "all by themselves." Since there isn't a real section to talk about them in, we'll talk about them here.

NetInfo Manager

This utility comes with one of Apple's most stern warnings, "Do not make changes to the NetInfo data unless you are the administrator of the computer, or have a specific task to accomplish."

But that is not going to stop us from looking around a bit, eh? But also be aware, you are on your own here. NetInfo Manager is an extremely powerful utility that if misused, or even looked at wrong it seems, will mess your Mac up for life, or at least until you reinstall your OS, so be careful.

Now let's start messing things up. Double-click on the NetInfo Manager icon, and let's have a look.

What is NetInfo?

NetInfo is a central database of user accounts, groups, passwords, printers, and other information. You can use NetInfo Manager to change any of this information, such as passwords, or delete information such as users, groups — anything. You, however, are not going to do anything big, but you are going to do a little exercise that will show you what is accessible from NetInfo Manager.

Using NetInfo Manager

When you open NetInfo Manager, you get a dialog box that shows the hierarchy of the information stored on your computer (shown in Figure 5-50). Most of this will make no sense to you unless you are a network administrator or a software developer, and even then there is a lot of things here you will never use.

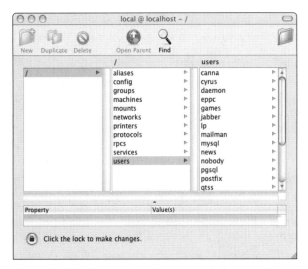

Figure 5-50: Get ready to do some real damage. NetInfo Manager is one of the most powerful tools on your Mac. Don't let it fall into the wrong hands, even if they are yours.

In the first column, you will see a slash, which represents the root of the NetInfo database. In the second column, you find a list of subdirectories contained in the root directory. The one we want to look at is at the bottom. It's called users. Now you might see yourself getting into familiar territory. The NetInfo database contains a bevy of system information including the users that are configured on your Mac as well as services, rpcs, etc. Now, notice the pane at the bottom of the dialog box. There's lots of information about your account displayed there, but it is grayed out. Click on the lock and enter your password to make that information accessible and editable. Here you can change your password, the shell your terminal window runs the next time it opens, your password hint, and a host of other things. You can also do things that will confound you and make your Mac impossible to use until you restore these values. And if you cannot remember these values, well, you're in trouble.

So, now that you have been warned by Apple, NetInfo Manager, and me, go ahead and try something relatively harmless, such as changing your picture in your home account.

If you go into System Preferences and click Accounts, you get a list of the users on your machine. Click on your home account and then click the Picture tab. There you have a place where you can select new photos, but we are going to change this information in the NetInfo Manager.

Now, go back to your NetInfo Manager window and look at the properties in the lower pane, you will find a property called picture. Double-click on the filename directly to the right and it allows you to edit the pictures path. Type in **/Library/User Pictures/Sports/8ball.tif.** If you already use the eight ball for your picture, type in **Baseball** where 8ball is (remember that filenames are case sensitive). Don't worry, you can always switch it back. Click the lock to prevent further changes. NetInfo Manager then asks you if you are sure you want to confirm your modification. Hit Update this Copy.

Now, let's go back to the Accounts window of your System Preferences. Instead of your previous image, your account is now represented by the eight ball. If you don't like the eight ball, you can easily change it to something else in the Accounts window. You don't have to go to all that work in the NetInfo Manager.

Now what you did was very minor in the scheme of things, but it shows just how far-reaching and powerful the NetInfo Manager is. When you are using this utility, your hand is strong, probably too strong. Caution is the watchword when you are using this super-charged utility.

Network Utility

This utility gathers information about your network, its users, and the World Wide Web. It has several tools that allow you to poke around the Internet. Among them are Ping, Traceroute, Whois, Finger, and Port Scan. These are tools your network administrator uses quite a bit, but the average user will be called to open this utility only rarely. And many of the tools you have here are readily available on the Web.

For example Whois is available on many sites on the Internet. Whois (*Who is*, get it?) offers information, such as ownership, addresses, fax numbers, and phone numbers for about any URL on the Internet. What is nice about the Network Utility is that it lists several places to look for Whois information in one spot.

You can use your Network Utility to troubleshoot your connections to other computers and devices on your network. Select Ping on your Network Utility window (shown in Figure 5-51). Type in the URL or IP address and hit the Ping button.

ODBC Administrator

The ODBC Administrator (shown in Figure 5-52), which arrived on the scene with Jaguar, lets you connect databases with applications that conform to the Open Database Connectivity standard (developed by Microsoft). ODBC is an emerging standard for SQL-based database engines.

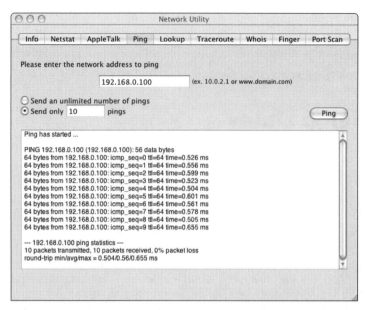

Figure 5-51: Pinging is sending tiny packets of information at another computer or apparatus on the Web just to see if it will respond. Pinging another device on the Web will tell you if your basic connection is good.

Figure 5-52: Data sources set up in this list are available only to the user who sets them up.

ODBC enables you to access files from a variety of database types, including Access, dBase, Oracle, DB2, and Excel. In order to use this utility, a separate database needs to be set up for each database that is accessed.

This is really a tool for database administrators that have need for it. You probably will not need it, but now you know as much as anybody does. Run with it.

The Printer Setup Utility

The reason that we've broken the Printer Setup Utility into its own section is that this will probably be used by most users, regardless of their expertise or special uses.

If OS X has an equivalent to the Chooser (from Mac OS 9.x and earlier) then the Printer Setup Utility is it.

This is the utility you use to set up and access printers.

Double-click on this utility to access the Printer List window and to add or remove printers using the appropriate buttons in the window's menu bar.

The Printer Setup Utility used to be called the Print Center in Jaguar. In Panther, the name not only changed, but you now get a visual way to see shared printers (shared from other computers) in the list. If you look at the bottom of the printer list you sill see a Shared Printers heading where you will see the printers themselves as well as the computers sharing them (shown in Figure 5-53).

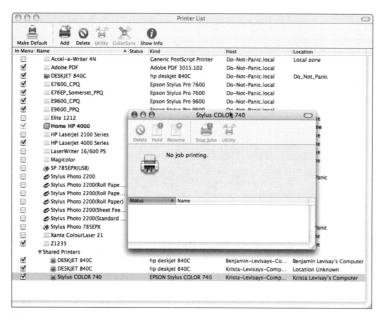

Figure 5-53: Double-clicking on one of the shared printers will open up a printer queue window just like any of your regular printer queues in the Printer List.

Clicking or unclicking the boxes in front of these printers will force them to show or hide (respectively) in the printer selection menus when you print documents from other applications.

---

tip

Because the Printer Setup Utility is a commonly used item, you may want to provide a quick way to get at it.

For most of my novice customers, I usually drag the Printer Setup Utility to the Dock, onto the Sidebar of a Finder window, or into the toolbar of a Finder window. You tend to print from within applications, so I think it works best in the Dock.

You can also access this utility from the System Preferences application by clicking the Setup Printers button. For more on printing in Panther check out Chapter 22.

And Now, Behold . . . the Terminal

To call the Terminal a utility, with no offense meant to the rest of the utilities, is an insult to the Terminal. The Terminal is where you, when you get the right eyes, can behold the power of Panther's Unix foundation.

We take all of Chapter 31 to look at Unix and the Terminal. But I think this is important enough in the world of OS X that you get a look at Terminal and Unix and what you can do here, as well. (A little repetition can be a good thing.)

The GUI interface is Apple's gift to the world. (Well, actually Xerox's, but we can get into that some other time.) But the Terminal is where Unix is honed into a rock-solid OS. And it is also where, by learning just a few tricks, you can make your GUI-dependent friends and coworkers gasp in awe, cringe in terror, become insane with jealousy, or just say "neato."

The Most Powerful Utility — the Terminal

Remember earlier in the chapter I likened the Utilities folder to the utility belt worn by the Caped Crusader? Well, the Terminal is that tool you can use when no other tool can help you. If you need a list of every .m4a (the extension for the ACC format your iTunes converts your CD tracks to) in your Music folder and you want it saved as a text file in your home folder just type

```
find ~/Music/ -iname "*.m4a" > mymusic.txt
```

This is only one example of the many things you can do in the Terminal that you can't do in the Aqua interface. If you look around you will find many other quick commands that will do similar things, quick and easy. And shortly, we learn how to use FTP, a free (you guessed it) file transfer protocol client that comes with OS X and is accessible from the Terminal.

But beware, when you work in the Terminal. You are in the domain of the geek. By that, I mean for the uninitiated it is an unsafe place to play, where you are a two-keystroke command and filename away from permanently deleting valuable information from your hard drive, no chance to fetch it out of the trash. In a lot of ways, it was wise for Apple to tuck this powerhouse app away in the Utilities folder, away from prying eyes. But for those that seek it out, the rewards can be great.

How to Use FTP, or Sticking It to the Man 101

It used to be there were plenty of people out on the World Wide Web who wanted to create and freely distribute FTP programs. And while that's still true, there are also a lot more programs on the market for FTP service that cost money. So, that is why I call this section "How to Use FTP, or Sticking It to the Man 101." And by, "the man," I mean everyone who charges money for an FTP program.

Now to be fair, there are advantages to commercially available FTP programs. They are easy to use and they often have security features (like SFTP) that are unavailable with Panther's free program. But when you tell your boss you can save about thirty bucks a workstation just by learning a handful of Unix commands, you will earn his or her admiration and the enmity of your coworkers.

But it's principle that counts. And anytime you do something for free that everyone else pays for, that makes you all warm on the inside. As I said before, this books covers Unix more thoroughly in Chapter 31. But some things, such as free FTP, are too cool to put off until then. The following exercise will give you a chance to get your feet wet in a simple Unix app that will make you want to learn even more about what's under Panther's hood.

Getting started with FTP in the Terminal

First, open a Terminal window. Open the FTP program by simply typing `ftp` and hitting the Return key. The terminal provides you with an `ftp>` prompt.

Now type `ftp` and the name of the host of the FTP site, for example `ftp ftp.apple.com` to access Apple's FTP site (shown in Figure 5-54).

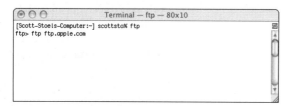

Figure 5-54: Although the command line can be daunting, once you get the hang of it, you will never want for another FTP client.

When the program connects to the site, Terminal asks for a name. (For Apple's site, you can log in using the name anonymous.) Type in the username here and hit Return.

Terminal displays that the username is okay and tells you it needs a password. (Apple's site requires you to enter an email address as a password.) Enter the password and hit Return.

If the information you provided is correct, Terminal will tell you are logged in.

At this point, you can do whatever it is you need to do. To find out what is posted on the site, type dir or ls. Terminal provides a list the files and directories on the site.

To download a file, type get, then the filename. Hit Return and your download will begin. To place a file on the server type put and the filename from your local directory, and hit Return. Your file will begin uploading.

---

tip
When using the Terminal, it's important to remember that names are case-sensitive and spaces are not handled.

To change directories on the FTP site, simply type cd then the directory name. (Remember, *directory* is just another name for a folder.) If you are successful, Terminal tells you that the directory you changed to is the new working directory. To view the contents of the new working directory, just type ls or dir.

Figure 5-55 shows how this process works. First, I asked for a list of the files on the site (ls), and then Terminal retuned a list of files and directories. (directories have a d at the beginning of the list line.) Then I changed the directory to public_html by typing cd public_html. Then I asked for a display of files in the public_html directory. Terminal replied with a list of the files and directories. Then I decided to download the file index.htm so I typed get index.htm. The download began, and when it was finished Terminal informed me my transfer was complete and provided me with a new prompt. As far as conversations go, it was successful, but it wasn't the sort of witty exchange you'd find in a Woody Allen movie.

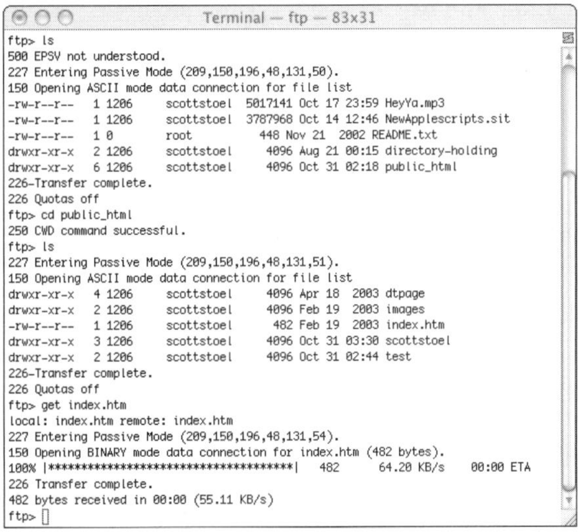

```
⊙ ⊙ ⊙                 Terminal — ftp — 83x31
ftp> ls
500 EPSV not understood.
227 Entering Passive Mode (209,150,196,48,131,50).
150 Opening ASCII mode data connection for file list
-rw-r--r--   1 1206    scottstoel 5017141 Oct 17 23:59 HeyYa.mp3
-rw-r--r--   1 1206    scottstoel 3787968 Oct 14 12:46 NewApplescripts.sit
-rw-r--r--   1 0       root           448 Nov 21  2002 README.txt
drwxr-xr-x   2 1206    scottstoel     4096 Aug 21 00:15 directory-holding
drwxr-xr-x   6 1206    scottstoel     4096 Oct 31 02:18 public_html
226-Transfer complete.
226 Quotas off
ftp> cd public_html
250 CWD command successful.
ftp> ls
227 Entering Passive Mode (209,150,196,48,131,51).
150 Opening ASCII mode data connection for file list
drwxr-xr-x   4 1206    scottstoel     4096 Apr 18  2003 dtpage
drwxr-xr-x   2 1206    scottstoel     4096 Feb 19  2003 images
-rw-r--r--   1 1206    scottstoel      482 Feb 19  2003 index.htm
drwxr-xr-x   3 1206    scottstoel     4096 Oct 31 03:30 scottstoel
drwxr-xr-x   2 1206    scottstoel     4096 Oct 31 02:44 test
226-Transfer complete.
226 Quotas off
ftp> get index.htm
local: index.htm remote: index.htm
227 Entering Passive Mode (209,150,196,48,131,54).
150 Opening BINARY mode data connection for index.htm (482 bytes).
100% |***************************************|   482    64.20 KB/s    00:00 ETA
226 Transfer complete.
482 bytes received in 00:00 (55.11 KB/s)
ftp> ▯
```

Figure 5-55: Here is an example of an FTP session.

---

tip
FTP can transfer files in either a text mode or a binary mode and while it is usually right about which format to use, sometimes it is best to set the type manually.

Moving from the GUI to the Terminal

The Terminal is a command-line interface, but it also works with your GUI interface. If you need a pathname to a particular folder on your Mac, just click on the folder and drag it to your prompt in the Terminal window. This action pastes the pathname to the folder in the Terminal window. This works great if you need to change your local directory for downloading files from the FTP site (ftp defaults to your home folder), and saves a lot of typing. It also keeps you from having to memorize all those paths.

Here are a few of the other commands you already used, and some additional commands to play with.

- ♦ **ftp:** In Terminal, this command opens the FTP program.
- ♦ **binary:** This command changes the mode to transfer to binary. You will need to do this if you are uploading images to the FTP site.
- ♦ **put:** put *filename* places a file on the FTP site.
- ♦ **get:** get *filename* retrieves a file from the FTP site.
- ♦ **mput:** Use this command to place or retrieve several files from an FTP site.
- ♦ **delete:** delete *filename* deletes a file on the FTP site.
- ♦ **dir** or **ls:** Lists the files in a directory.
- ♦ **cd:** Changes the directory.
- ♦ **lcd:** Changes the directory on your machine.
- ♦ **close:** Ends a session with a particular FTP host.
- ♦ **quit:** Quits the FTP program and returns you to a shell prompt.
- ♦ **man ftp:** Bring up a file with all the commands for the programs. Use this if you want to learn more about FTP in Terminal.

Fast FTP

If you have an FTP site that you visit regularly, you can save a few keystrokes by saving a Terminal window just for working with that site. When you save a Terminal window, you are given the option to execute a command when the window opens automatically (shown in Figure 5-56). Just type in `ftp`, then the host name, then save the window. Now when you open the window from the Terminal menu, or double-click on its icon, it will execute the command and then ask you for your name and password.

Customize Your Terminal Settings for a Cooler Command-Line Experience

Now just because you are you are using Terminal, it doesn't mean you have to submit to the Spartan appearance of the usual command-line interface. From the Terminal menu, select Window Settings to open the Terminal Inspector dialog box. Select Color in the drop-down menu. There you can customize the color of your cursor, your text, and the background color of the window. You can even select an image for the background. The image stretches to fit the background, so you can get that funhouse effect in your normally staid Terminal window.

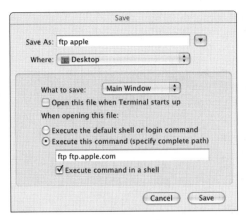

Figure 5-56: Preserve your keyboard; automate your opening command in Terminal's Save dialog box.

Tuning in to the iPod Software Updater

And last but not least, we have the iPod Software Updater which is downloaded via the Software Update Preference panel. This is a utility that doesn't fall under any of the categories above, so I thought I'd drop it in on the end of this chapter.

From time to time Apple provides updates for its iPod to make the iPod more compatible to other applications and current OS versions. Updating an iPod is done by plugging an iPod into your computer via FireWire and then running the iPod Software Updater.

You can also use this updater to wipe out your iPod so that you can start over with it (with iTunes, your Address Book, etc.) from scratch.

The iPod Software Updater is located in the iPod Software (version number) Updater folder in the Utilities folder in the Applications folder. At this writing, the most current version of the iPod Software Updater is 2.0.1.

Double-clicking on the iPod Software Updater, opens a screen that allows you to update or restore (erase) your iPod to factory settings (shown in Figure 5-57).

Because the iPod has its own OS (of sorts), and because you mainly use it as a jukebox for your iTunes, erasing your iPod every so often isn't a bad thing to do — as long as you back up any other files you may be keeping on your iPod (if you are using it as a FireWire HD).

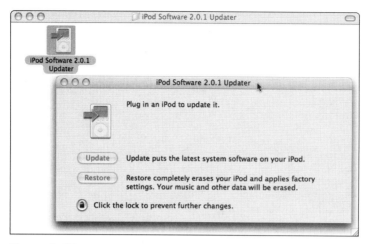

Figure 5-57: Before you can erase or update your iPod, you will need to have it plugged in and you will need to click the lock in the lower-left corner and enter your administrative password.

Summary

If you want to get up close and personal with Panther, the Utilities folder is the place to go. But if you are content just using Panther as the environment you run your other programs in, you'll never need to open the folder. The Utilities folder is full of powerful applications, and if you want to kill an afternoon and learn a lot about your Mac, start exploring your Utilities folder ASAP.

Secrets of Setting Up Your Mac for Multiple Users

Chapter
6

♦ ♦

Secrets in This Chapter

♦ ♦

A dmittedly, the whole user thing is kind of hard to wrap your head around if you're coming from the pre–OS X world. This is new in the Unix world of OS X and can take a little getting used to. (We talk a little about where things are in Chapter 1.)

One of Apple's premises is that there will be more than one user on a computer and that everyone's user experience should be separate from everyone else's user experience. This is not only a good organizational model, but also a good model for security, as you learn later on in this chapter.

There are those that would tell you that if you are the only user on a computer that you could skip this kind of a chapter. Those people would be *wrong!* Multiple users are at the heart of not only the OS's architecture, but also of the feature and problem sets that you will have to deal with.

So sit back in your favorite reading chair, pour yourself a cup of whatever, and read on.

Advantages of Having Multiple Users

As I said before, one of Apple's premises is that there will be more than one user on a computer (shown in Figure 6-1). And that if you set up different user accounts on your Mac (running OS X), everyone using your Mac will have their own account.

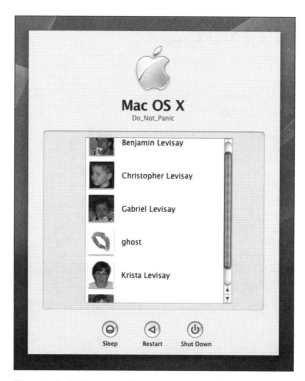

Figure 6-1: These are the user accounts I set up for my family. You shouldn't use these. Get your own wife and kids.

The really cool thing about this is that if you set up multiple users, you can protect your-self from other people mucking around on your computer. You will be able to isolate your documents and settings from the other user's documents and settings.

And if you have kids, you can limit their access to the computer's features.

So, you can give yourself online access but deny it to your kids. Or let's say that you're writing a book about Panther, but your kids like to use your computer for going to lego.com. By creating a new user, I (I mean you) can protect your valuable (and insightful) Panther Secrets manuscript from death by what I like to call Kiddie Click.

The First User Is You

But I'm getting ahead of myself. Before thinking about additional users, you should note that you have already set up one user — yourself. Your user settings were automatically created when you went through the installation process. If you haven't noticed, it's prob-ably because Apple's default setting is to log you in to your account automatically when you start up your computer.

If you want to quickly get to the main login screen, you can access it by logging out. By selecting Log Out *Username* (Username is you, okay?) in the Apple menu (shown in Figure 6-2), you temporarily bypass the automatic login.

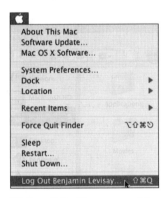

Figure 6-2: The name of the current user is always shown under the Apple menu.

You can change Apple's default so that every time the computer is started or restarted a user must be selected as shown in Figure 6-1, (or the user's name has to be typed in) and a password must be entered (shown in Figure 6-3). (You make these changes in the Accounts preference panel in System Preferences as described later in this chapter.)

Assuming that the Mac is yours, by default your user was probably set as an administra-tor (or Admin) of the computer. Regardless of any other accounts you may create, you will always be the Admin. All others accounts created after yours are limited in some ways, even if those users are given administrative privileges, as well.

Figure 6-3: Once a user is selected in the Login list, the password must be entered before that user can log in.

The Architecture of User Privileges

Before looking at the controls for users and accounts, you must understand what you can and can't do with those privileges and limitations. This is the theory prior to the practice.

As I said, the first user (which we'll assume is you) is the main administrator (or Admin) of the computer. All other users can and/or will be limited as described in the following passages.

Applications

Applications can be set to be used by all users or just users you select. This can be done in more than one way.

You can install a specific application into a user's home folder (described later in the chapter) and then that application will be visible to that user only (shown in Figure 6-4).

You could also restrict the user's access to specific applications through the limitations section of the Accounts control panel for non-administrative users.

Work Data

Data can also be *protected* from other users by being stored inside a user's home folder. This includes data that you have saved on your desktop (because your desktop is in your home folder).

A good example of this would be a financial program used by several users. Such a program may be stored in the Applications folder, but the individual financial database files would be stored in each user's home folder. This would give all users access to the program without giving them access to each other's sensitive data.

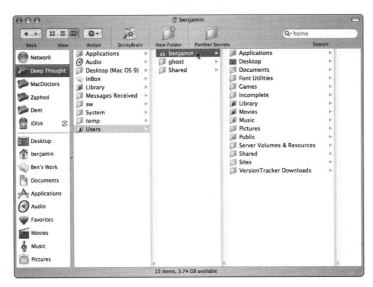

Figure 6-4: A user's folder can also be home to an Applications folder containing applications available to that user only.

Internet Data

Strictly speaking, Internet data is the same as work data, but you may not realize it because you don't save it in the same way. When I talk about Internet data, I'm talking about your e-mail settings, your Safari favorites, your iChat buddy lists, and so on. All of this data is saved without knowing it to various places in your home folder — usually in home folder's Library folder.

This means that every user can set up the e-mail program for their own account and keep their e-mail separate from all other users. The same goes for the addresses stored in Address Book, Favorites stored in Safari, and any other Internet preferences.

All of the Other Preferences

If you can change it in System Preferences, then this data is saved specifically for the logged-in user. That means that screen savers, desktops, Finder window preferences, keyboard preferences, and so on can all be customized for each user.

This is especially handy when you have limited one of the users on your computer and you want to simplify the Dock by pulling out everything that they don't have access to. You can do this in that person's user account without affecting your own Dock.

And if you have users that have special needs, you can enable helpful functions in Universal Access just for that user.

What Other Users Can't Do

Although it is possible for you to set another user as an administrator, he or she will still not have all of the capabilities that you (the first main user) have.

Users can't change the date or time, energy-saving preferences, file-sharing preferences, networking preferences, or the startup disk. Nor can a secondary administrative user change some of the login options.

And although other administrative users have access to most places on the computer, they still do not have access to the main (your) home folder/account. (It's good to be the king.)

Auto Login Options and Fast User Switching

Before we get into the individual account preferences, we need to explore the two ways that we deal with logging in to the computer.

Automatic Login

By clicking on the Accounts icon in System Preferences (located in the Applications folder on the top level of your hard drive), you are presented with the users and their respective settings. Clicking on the Login Options below the list of users gives you your various login options (shown in Figure 6-5).

Figure 6-5: These login settings have to be accessed by the main (first) administrative user.

Among the things you can set in this preference panel, you can choose to log in automatically as any user or not to login as anyone when your computer is first started up. If you do set a new user as the user that the computer will automatically log in as, you must provide the password of that user to change the login options (shown in Figure 6-6).

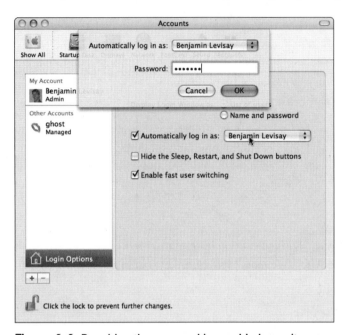

Figure 6-6: Requiring the password is an added security measure to make sure that enabling the automatic login option isn't a way to bypass security.

Fast User Switching

A new feature of Panther is Fast User Switching, which not only allows multiple users to be logged in on the same computer at the same time, but also allows for fast switching of users.

The option to enable Fast User Switching is located on the same screen as the automatic login option. To enable Fast User Switching you simply need to check the box (shown in Figure 6-7). When you enable Fast User Switching, you are prompted with a warning that cautions you to make sure that you trust the other users before enabling this option.

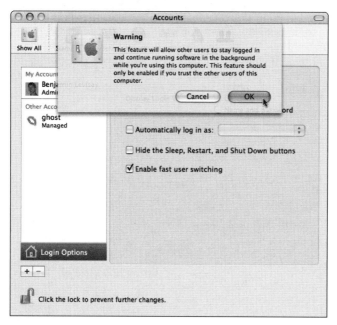

Figure 6-7: Enabling Fast User Switching is interrupted by a warning only.

We Interrupt This Chapter . . .

Fast User Switching is something that everybody thinks is a good idea. The warning that we are prompted with when this feature is enabled does draw some interesting conversations.

Benjamin: The first time I saw the warning (after enabling Fast User Switching), I thought I must have misread. So, I looked again. This warning seems a little on the useless side to me. Even when Fast User Switching is enabled, you still need to give your password each time you change users. And it seems a little subjective to make for a very good warning.

But after thinking about the way that Apple guards its own security and attacks rumor sites that try to give people previews of its breaking news or products, this warning doesn't seem out of character for Apple at all.

Pieter: The main reason for this warning is that it does not terminate applications that you might be running in the background under your username and with your level of access. One common hacker trick on Unix is using a tool to cause an application that is running in the background to crash in such a way that the hacker can then access the application that they crashed and impersonate you. Then they can issue commands to the operating system that would normally be usable by you only.

While this is not much of a problem at home, it could easily be a problem for Macs located in an open computer lab. In general, for home users, fast switching is a great idea as you most likely know all your users and hopefully trust all of them. For a computer lab or someplace where you do not know all your users and trust is in short supply, fast switching probably is not a good idea.

Once you have the Fast User Switching enabled, you get a Fast Users Switching menu in the upper-right corner of your screen. All users are shown in this list (shown in Figure 6-8).

Figure 6-8: The main administrative user is always shown at the top of the Fast User Switching menu.

Making Fast User Switching Fast

Secret

Just having the users listed in the Fast User Switching menu doesn't mean that user switches happen quickly. To do that, users have to have been logged in.

Log in to each user you want to switch between quickly at the beginning of your computer-using session by selecting each user, in turn, from the Fast User Switching menu and entering their respective passwords.

Users that you can quickly move between (that have already been logged in) show a check mark in front of those users in the Fast User Switching menu.

Understanding Your Account Preferences

Working with accounts and the preferences can be a lot like deciding which came first, the chicken or the egg. So I think the best way to get through this is to start with the various preference panel settings and then moving from there to what that means to the user. This may seem a bit fragmented, but, bear with me, I bring it all together at the end.

note Access to account preferences changed in Panther from Jaguar and other versions of OS X. The Accounts, Login Items, and My Account system preferences that were accessed by three separate system preference icons (respectively) are now located in the (one) Accounts system preference. None of the options have been lost; they've just been consolidated.

When I say "understanding your account preferences," I'm assuming that you are the primary, first, administrative user of the computer. If you are not, some of these things will not apply to you.

You, the User

After clicking on the Accounts icon in System Preferences, you see a list of accounts and account options (Password, Picture, Security, Startup Items). The main administrative account is the one at the top of the accounts list under My Accounts (shown in Figure 6-9). By clicking the main administrative account (you) in this list, you are given your account options.

The Password tab of your Accounts preferences shows you your Name, Short Name, Password (with Verify field below it), and a Password Hint field.

Secret

You Can't Change Your Short Username

Don't pull your hair out in a futile effort to change the short username in your account preferences. The user account short names are not just names; they are also the directory name in the Users folder (the user's home folder) that contains all of your settings.

You cannot change any of the short names of any of the users no matter what you try to do.

The other thing that you can set in this panel is your Address Book Card. To do this, click the Edit button next to the Address Book Card label (shown in Figure 6-9).

Figure 6-9: Users can specify their own Address Book Card.

This launches the Address Book application and allows you to specify which Address is you (shown in Figure 6-10).

Figure 6-10: Your user address is marked with a small "me" in the lower-left corner of the icon or picture selected for your address.

Setting Your Security

We'll skip the Picture tab in the Accounts preference panel for now and move to the Security tab. (I cover the Picture tab later in this chapter when I dissect all of the user settings of another user).

Security is handled in two places on your computer. The first is in the Accounts panel in System Preferences and the second is in the FileVault preference panel, in the new-to-Panther Security panel in System Preferences.

Security Options in the Accounts Panel of System Preferences Security

The Security section in the Accounts preference panel for each user in System Preferences offers the option of changing the master password (from FileVault), to turn FileVault on or off for each account, and to specify whether a user is an administrator. Although you, the main administrative user, can't choose to not be an administrative user (shown in Figure 6-11).

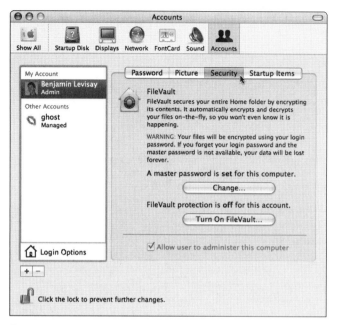

Figure 6-11: You are an administrative user by default, which is why that option is grayed out.

The Security Panel in System Preferences

The Security panel in System Preferences is the other, new place where security is handled on your computer.

Among the other things that you can do in this preference panel, you can change the master password for the your account, set your password to be used when waking from sleep or a screen saver (previously controlled in the Screen Saver preferences in Jaguar), and disable automatic login for all accounts on the computer (shown in Figure 6-12).

> **note**
>
> Not only is the Security panel in System Preferences new to the OS, but so is FileVault.
>
> The idea of FileVault is to allow your entire home folder to be encrypted, using a high-performance 128-bit algorithm for added security. The home directory is then decrypted and then re-encrypted on the fly as you use your home folder so that you don't even know that it's happening.
>
> If you do utilize this, however, you want to make sure you have a record of your password. If you forget the password, it cannot be retrieved and the data will be lost to you.

Figure 6-12: When you log in as the administrator, you can choose to disable automatic login from this preference panel. However, resetting the automatic login option back in the Accounts panel of System Preferences overrides this choice.

caution

Besides the password issue, there are some other issues that have arisen with regards to the FileVault.

At the time that this chapter was written, there were a good deal of reports about FileVault losing some kinds of information and/or not working well with some kinds of applications. While Apple will surely work these issues out (or disprove them), in short order, I'd be remiss in not suggesting that you check Apple's discussion boards and/or help sites like Macfixit.com to find out if you will have any problems in using FileVault with your applications and hardware.

Setting Your Startup Items

As noted earlier in this chapter, Jaguar's Login Items panel has been consolidated into the Accounts preferences in System Preferences. To be more specific, they have been replaced with the Startup Items in the Account preferences panel in System Preferences.

To access the new Startup Items, click on your user in the Accounts preference panel and then click on the Startup Items button to the far right. This gives you a list of the items that are selected to start up when you log in or start up (shown in Figure 6-13).

To add applications to this list, click on the Add button (plus sign) below the list of Startup Items (shown in Figure 6-13). This opens a dialog box that allows you to browse and select an application through the Finder (shown in Figure 6-14).

Figure 6-13: Clicking the check boxes in front of the Startup Items hides (or not) any application that is launched when you log in.

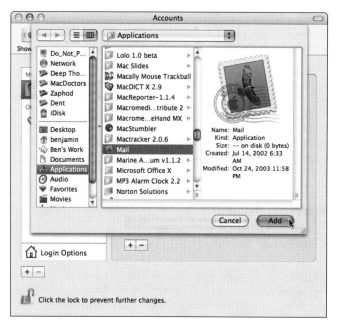

Figure 6-14: Once you've selected the application you want to add to your startup items, click the Add button.

Your newly added application then shows up in the list of Startup Items (shown in Figure 6-15).

Figure 6-15: Some Startup Items are added manually and some are added when applications are installed. You can choose to add, using the Add button (plus sign), or delete, using the Delete button (minus sign), any Startup Item you want at any time.

The Startup Items load in the order that they are listed in the panel. You can change that order by dragging items to any position in the list (shown in Figure 6-16). You can drag more than one item at a time, if you wish.

When you're done setting all of your Account preferences, close the System Preferences window or move on to setting the Account preferences for other user(s).

Figure 6-16: Changing the loading order of some Startup Items can be a useful way to avoid system problems that can occur when certain background or "helper applications" start up after other applications start up that need those background applications.

Setting Other User's Account Preferences

So now that we have a good understanding of the permissions and preference panel of your (administrative) Account settings, let's move on to setting the preferences for other users. Some of this may seem repetitive, compared to the last section, but you need a complete picture; so, please bear with me.

Setting the Password for Another User

The first preference panel that you see when you select another user (in the user's list in the Accounts preference panel in System Preferences) is the Password preference panel. This panel offers most of the same options available to the administrative user, as described in the previous section.

Like the administrative user, you cannot change the Short Name, but you can change almost everything else (shown in Figure 6-17).

The only thing missing from this preference panel is the ability to edit or set the Address Book Card. The Address Book Card can only be set to "me" when you (or someone) are logged into the computer as that user and accessing the Accounts preference panel (in System Preferences) as said user.

Figure 6-17: The first thing that you notice when selecting another user in the Accounts list is that the Startup Items button is replaced by a Limitations button. We get to that later in this section.

Setting the Picture for Another User

We skipped setting the picture in the administrative user section, mostly because I knew we'd be covering it here, and partly because it was my picture and I didn't want to mess with such a good looking picture. (Humor . . . or my attempt at it.)

If you don't have a custom image for use as the user's icon, you can select one from a set of images called Apple Pictures. These options show up in the Picture section of the Accounts preference panel in System Preferences (shown in Figure 6-18).

You can choose one of these images or you can click on the Edit button to modify or choose another picture to be used to represent the user. This brings up an Images dialog box (shown in Figure 6-19) that allows you to select Recent Pictures from the top pull-down menu, or to drag an image onto the Images dialog box to use for the user.

Figure 6-18: The selected user icon shows in the square to the left of the Edit button in the Picture tab of the Accounts panel.

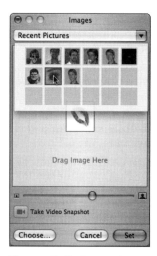

Figure 6-19: By moving the slider under the Drag Image Here area, you can zoom in or out and effectively crop the part of the picture you want to use.

Clicking on the Choose button in the Images dialog box allows you to browse the Finder to locate the desired picture. You can also use the Camera button to take a video snap shot if you have a FireWire Web cam hooked up to your computer. (I cover this in more depth in Chapter 19.)

Once you have your image captured, sized, and/or chosen, click on the Set button located in the bottom-right corner of the Images dialog box (shown in Figure 6-19).

Setting the Security for Another User

Setting the Security options for another user (in the Account preferences panel in System Preferences) is a little different than for the main administrative user. Here you can choose whether to give the user administrative privileges (shown in Figures 6-20 and 6-21).

Figure 6-20: If you choose to allow the user to have administrative privileges, the Limitations button is grayed out.

If you choose, you can also change the master password in another user's settings (shown in Figure 6-22). This will be applied system-wide and will therefore require an administrative password to accept the changes.

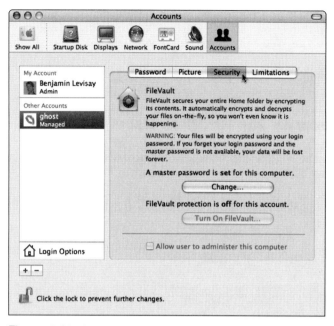

Figure 6-21: If you don't choose to allow the user to have administrative privileges, the Limitations button is available to allow you more choices for user restrictions.

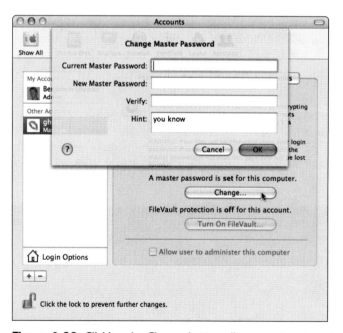

Figure 6-22: Clicking the Change button allows you to set or change the master password for the computer.

Setting Limitations for Another User

If you chose to turn off the administrative privileges for the selected user (if you've set them that way) in the Accounts preference panel (in System Preferences), you will have Limitation options available to you.

In the Limitations section of the User Preferences, you have three options. You can choose No Limits, Some Limits, and Simple Finder.

Limitations: No Limits

Choosing No Limits in the Limitations section (shown in Figure 6-23) for a non-administrative user (in the Accounts preferences in the System Preferences) is as close as you can get to giving a user administrative privileges, just short of actually giving the user administrative privileges.

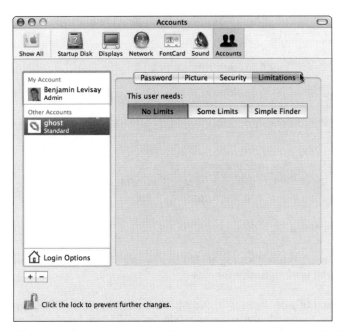

Figure 6-23: There are no additional options needed when No Limits is selected for a user in the Limitations tab of the Accounts preference panel.

Selecting the No Limits option allows the selected user complete access to all applications (including those in OS 9), utilities, and anywhere else on the HD not secured by an administrative or other user's settings.

The biggest differences between selecting No Limits as opposed to allowing the user to be an administrator, is that the user, while having access to everything, won't have the privileges necessary to install new applications or to modify any other user's settings.

Limitations: Some Limits

When you select Some Limits in the Limitations section for a user (in the Accounts preference panel in System Preferences), you start to have a lot of options to selectively restrict different kinds of user access.

With a simple check mark, you can allow a user the following options: Open all System Preferences, Modify the Dock, Change the password, limit which applications they can run, and Burn CDs and DVDs (shown in Figure 6-24).

Figure 6-24: Some Limits imply just that. You should choose this Limitations option only if you have specific things that you want to disable for a user.

Selecting the triangle next to Applications in the Application list reveals all of the applications in the Applications folder on the computer (shown in Figure 6-25), but not in the Utilities folder which is in the Applications folder. Utilities are handled in the Utilities list. You can then check or uncheck specific applications that you want the user to have access to.

> **tip**
>
> A dash (–) in the Allow check box in front of Applications in the Application list indicates that some of the applications are on and some are off. A check mark in the same place would indicate that they were all on.

Utilities (located within the Applications folder) and Applications (Mac OS 9) (located at the top level of the hard drive) can also be opened and set in the same way that the applications can be.

The last set in the list, Others, allows for the addition of items that do not reside in any of the above-mentioned folders. To add items to the Others set, select Others and then click the Locate button on the right under the Application list (shown in Figure 6-26).

Figure 6-25: Applications as well as the other items in this list can be turned on or off.

Figure 6-26: The Others set is Apple's attempt to allow you to control applications not resident in any of the listed places in this section.

After you click on the Locate button a Finder-like window opens allowing you to browse and select an application you want to add to the Others set (shown in Figure 6-27).

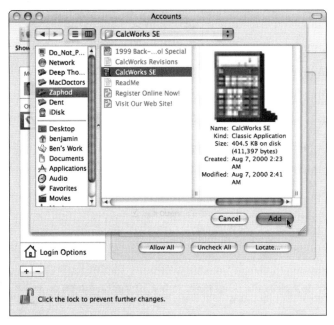

Figure 6-27: Browsing through alternate folders or volumes, you add an application to Others by selecting the application and clicking on the Add button.

After you add the application to the Others section in your Application list, you can still choose to allow or not allow the user to have access to the application by checking or unchecking the box to the left of that item (shown in Figure 6-28).

Limitations: Simple Finder

For a little less control but for a little more ease of use, the Simple Finder option is available in the Limitations tab of the Accounts preferences panel in System Preferences.

The Application list is the same as in the Some Limits section, but the options Open all System Preferences, Change password, Modify the Dock, and Burn CDs and DVDs are gone (shown in Figure 6-29).

Figure 6-28: Items located and added to Others in the Applications list do not show up in the Others in the Application list for other users.

Figure 6-29: The Simple Finder is probably the option that you would choose for a child's access on your computer.

One great thing that stands out about the Simple Finder is that the Dock is also simplified to allow the user to only use those applications showing in the My Applications folder in the Dock (as shown in Figure 6-30).

Figure 6-30: A user with the Simple Finder set for them doesn't have access to the HD itself, and therefore the real Applications folder, so you have to plan ahead when setting applications for a user limited to Simple Finder.

User Privileges Are Indicated in the User List

Under each user listed under Other Accounts in the Accounts preference panel in System Preferences, you can see the icon, the name of the user, and then Admin, Managed, Standard, or Simplified.

Each of these words indicates a level of user access with Admin having the most access and Simplified having the least.

The User in the Finder

Once you've set all of the user privileges for the account, you can close the Accounts preference panel. You can then see that user in the Finder in the Users folder (shown in Figure 6-31).

Figure 6-31: All users set up in the Accounts preference panel of System Preferences are shown as folders or directories in the Users folder of that computer.

File Sharing Changes with Users and OS X

Unlike file sharing in pre–OS X, not all folders on your computer can be shared to different users. This can be hard for users to get used to. (I show you a few clever strategies for greater versatility of file sharing and file access in Chapters 29 and 30.)

Apple's default architecture here is to allow other users to access the Public folder in each user's folder. Any file you place in the public folder can be shared by turning on Personal File Sharing in the Sharing preference panel in System Preferences.

The Drop Box is also a new OS X construct. The idea with the Drop Box is that users can place documents into this folder but cannot access or see any items placed in the Drop Box. So you get a one-way place for files from external users. You, of course, can see freely access anything placed in your Drop Box.

The only way external users can circumvent the rules regarding accessing the Public folder or folders within the home folder is if they log in to your computer using your username and password. If they do that, then the external user has complete access to mounted volume(s) as well as your home directory (covered in more depth in Chapter 29).

The Sites folder is also new to OS X. This is a place where you can store a Web site or other files that you want people to access through the Internet, via Rendezvous, or some other protocol (covered in more depth in Chapter 29).

Adding and Deleting a User

To add a user, simply click on the Add button (plus sign) under the Accounts list in the Accounts preference panel in System Preferences. After you click on this button (shown in Figure 6-32), you go through the process of setting all of your user preferences like you did in the previous section.

Figure 6-32: When you set up a new user from scratch, you can set/change the short name until you save the settings.

After you have your user settings done, you can exit the Account settings and see the newly added account in the Users folder as a new directory (shown in Figure 6-33).

Nothing that you've seen so far in this section is all that new from the previous section. But we're working up to deleting a user.

To delete a user, simply select the user and click on the Delete button (minus sign) under the Accounts list in the Accounts preference panel in System Preferences. This prompts a warning dialog box to drop down from the top of the Accounts preference panel (shown in Figure 6-34). This warning asks you if you are sure you want to delete the selected user. It also gives you the option to delete the user immediately or to save the user data in a specially created Deleted Users folder in the Users folder.

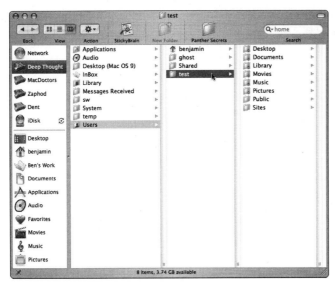

Figure 6-33: Your newly added account is just like any other user account.

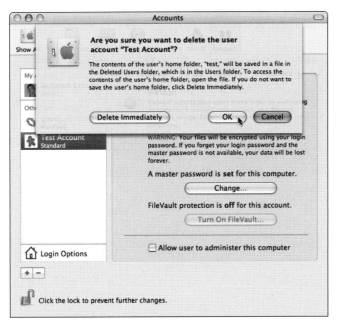

Figure 6-34: If you want to disable a user but not throw all of the user data away *do not* choose the Delete Immediately button.

When you click OK (as opposed to Delete Immediately) in the warning dialog box (shown in Figure 6-34), you create a disk image file (.dmg suffix) of the archived user folder in the newly created Deleted Users folder (shown in Figure 6-35).

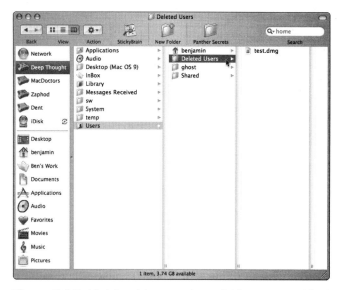

Figure 6-35: All deleted, but saved user folders are saved in the Deleted Users folder. You can choose to throw these users away later when you know you no longer need them.

If you find you need that user information again, you only have to double-click on the user.dmg file and it opens into a mounted volume (shown in Figure 6-36) on the desktop that you can access or copy back into the top level of the Users folder.

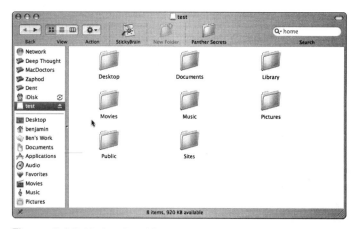

Figure 6-36: Notice that this user's archived folders are not protected in the same way as other folders are protected within the Users folder.

Understanding the Shared Folder

There isn't a lot of mystery to the Shared folder except that new users usually don't understand what it does. This is not a place where you put documents or data that you want to share with other networked users.

Instead, it is a place where applications as well as other users put shared resources and data that other users may need or want when they access those applications (shown in Figure 6-37).

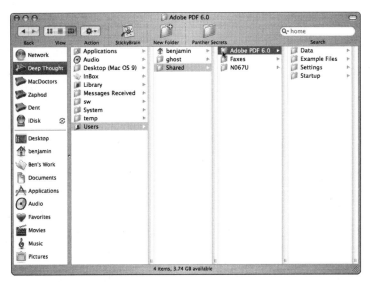

Figure 6-37: Documents or data put in the Shared folder are available to all users, even if they only have Simple Finder access set for them.

Summary

In this chapter, you've looked at users and privileges. It's really just that simple. What we find when we strip away all of the preference panels is that different users can be set to have different kinds of user experiences. Some of these differences are cosmetic. Some of these differences are about access to options on the computer.

In the next chapter, you look at a few third-party OS X programs and what common elements make them OS X programs.

Part II

Application Secrets Revealed

Part II provides you with a major helping of secrets and techniques for getting more out of the productivity applications you will use with your Mac, including valuable tips for word processing, desktop publishing, graphics, and sound. This part also covers automating your Mac operations with AppleScript.

In This Part

The Raw Essentials of a Mac Program

Chapter

7

◆ ◆

Secrets in This Chapter

◆ ◆

My own dirty little secret is that I came to the Mac platform from the Wintel platform about eight years ago. I had an Apple IIc with two floppy drives (living large at the time) when I was a kid and learned how to use Apple BASIC and run some machine language. But I left Apple and went to a DataTrain running DOS and Windows 3.1.

insider
insight   **As it turns out, Apple's version of BASIC (Beginners All-purpose Symbolic Instruction Code) that came on the early pre-Mac Apple computers, was licensed by a small software company that you might have heard of . . . Microsoft.**

And I was happy in my little DOS and Windows 3.1 world (living even larger). I think I had 16MB of RAM, 256 colors on my 14" screen, a dot matrix printer, and 100MB of hard drive space. I was the king of the world. So what that I had to watch my system die and rebuild it from scratch every time I installed a new program? So what if I had to relearn how everything worked with each new application that I installed? And so what if I had to keep a journal of what and where things lived and how to deal with my documents? (At the end, my journal was several hundred pages of cryptic steps and instructions that only I could make any sense of.)

I remember once how I got my computer to make a sign for me that I used at my job. I had to install my system twice and the program three times. It took me all week to install, learn, and then output a sign that I could have drawn by hand (even with my own limited artistic ability) in a few hours. If nothing else, this was a testament to just how much of a geek I am that I made my computer do what I wanted it to do.

And for many years, I thought this was normal. And then about eight years ago I went to work for my Dad's publishing company and learned that there was an easier way to deal with things. I discovered the Mac. My first ride was an LC. After the initial shock of the desktop and how easy it worked, I was hooked.

The thing that most impressed me was the fact that all of my applications behaved a lot like each other. They seemed to have the same kinds of functions in the same relative places. And as I used more different kinds of applications, I found my own mental model of a Macintosh application evolving to the point where I could use what I know about any application I'd already run on any new application that I came across. I found that on the Mac, I could learn software very quickly because I'd already learned a great deal of the program in other programs. Now if that isn't ideal, I don't know what is.

So, in this chapter, I'm going to show you those things that are common to Macintosh applications. Along the way, you learn how to install applications and switch between them.

As you read through this chapter, you will see a lot of similarity to the things that we cover in Chapter 1 about the Finder, which is the first Macintosh application. By the end of this chapter (with some review of Chapter 1), you should have a head start on learning your next new Macintosh application. You too may see the patterns necessary to look like an ubergeek.

You won't be living large in the way I was with Windows 3.1 on my DataTrain with my 100MB of HD space . . . but we all have to come to terms with the fact that we can't have it all.

The Elements of the Mac OS Interface

The Mac OS interface is as much the Finder as it is the application (running inside the Finder) itself (with a few exceptions). Present and prominent when most applications are loaded (with or without a document) are the Apple menu (in the top-left menu), the Dock (on the bottom of the screen), the hard drive (on the right side of the desktop) if you've chosen to have it on the desktop (shown in Figure 7-1). When one or more documents are open with an application, you will see these same items (more or less), along with any palettes associated with the application (shown in Figure 7-2).

Figure 7-1: Your Finder and desktop; the Apple menu is shown here with a few items on the desktop.

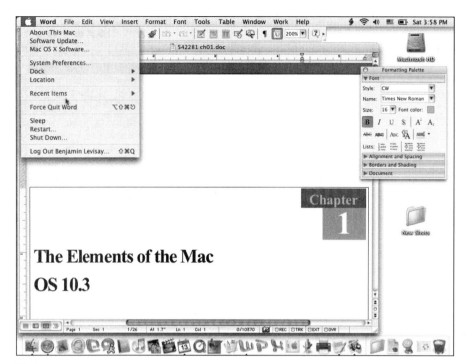

Figure 7-2: All of the same items are shown with Word X and a Word X document up on the screen. An additional toolbar and palette are shown here.

If you're interested in the elements of the Finder itself, turn to Chapters 1, 2, and 3. The Finder, the Apple menu, and the Dock (respectively) are covered in those three chapters.

For now, I want to talk about the elements common to most all (other than the Finder) applications.

The application shown in Figure 7-2 is Word X for the Mac. The document that is loaded happens to be the Word document for Chapter 1 of this book. Word, like other applications, adds its own toolbar(s) and optional palette(s) to help you use the program more easily. These toolbars and palettes vary from program to program and between users with different preferences. We're going to skip looking at these toolbar(s) and optional palette(s) that differ from application to application and look at the elements that are similar — for now.

Looking at Two Applications

For the sake of this section as well as many others in this chapter, I compare features of two different kinds of applications from two different software manufacturers. These applications are Word X from Microsoft (used to write this book), which has been around for OS X for almost two years now, and Adobe Photoshop CS from Adobe (used for editing many of the figures in the last part of writing this book), which has only been out for about one month at the time this chapter was written.

Common Things When Launching Applications

The first thing to know about applications is that you can launch them. You can double-click on them in a Finder window or you can put them in the Dock and click on them (shown in Figure 7-3 and Figure 7-4) to launch the applications.

Figure 7-3: Active or launched applications are shown in the Dock with a small triangle under them.

Figure 7-4: Moving your mouse over an item in the Dock causes the name of the application or document to appear over the selected item.

Another common thing about Mac applications is that when you launch an application you usually get a startup screen showing startup graphics from the manufacturer, version information, and licensing information (shown in Figures 7-5 and 7-6).

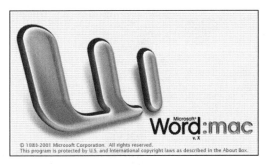

Figure 7-5: Your own personal information is usually shown on these startup screens. I removed my info for reasons of privacy.

Figure 7-6: Some startup screens display the status of the startup process. This startup screen shows that the program is initializing.

The other way to launch an application is to double-click on a document (created or set to be opened by that application) or that document's alias. Documents are any file(s) that contain your work. The application can be used without these specific documents, but these applications are ideally suited to open these documents and manipulate the information contained in them. Double-clicking a document or its alias launches the application(s), gives you the startup screens (shown in the previous figures), and then opens the documents in your screen surrounded by the menus and palettes that are a part of those applications (shown in Figures 7-7 and 7-8).

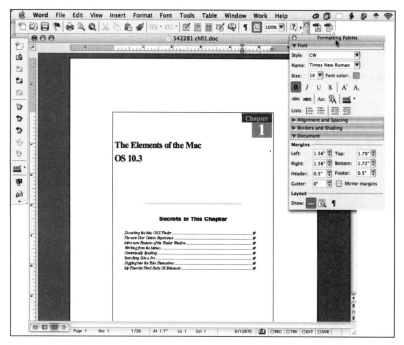

Figure 7-7: This is a work document opened in Word X. It's the same document shown in Figure 7-2, but here the document is shown at 100 percent.

Photoshop File Edit Image Layer Select Filter View Window Help
Camp_Snoopy_Family.psd @ 100% (RGB/8#)
Navigator Info Histogram
Color Swatches Styles
History Actions
Open
Crop
Crop
Layers Channels Paths
Background

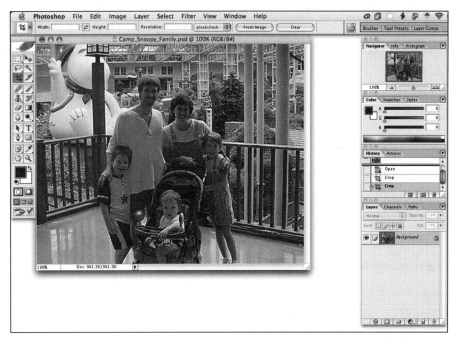

Figure 7-8: This picture is also a document, shown here open in Photoshop CS. It doesn't contain text but it does contain data that can be edited. This document is also shown at 100 percent.

The Common Menus of a Mac OS Application

Some menus are common to almost all applications. They allow access to key built-in OS technology as well as normal application functionality. All of the menus for these programs are covered here, but let's start with the common menus first.

If you look at just the menu bars themselves for Photoshop CS, Word X, and the Finder you see that the common menu choices between Word X (shown in Figure 7-9) and Photoshop CS (shown in Figure 7-10) are the ones that they share with the Finder (shown in Figure 7-11).

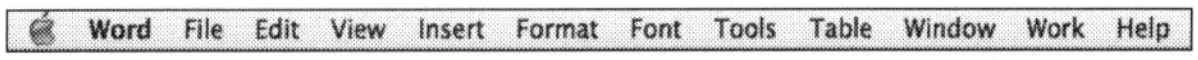

Word File Edit View Insert Format Font Tools Table Window Work Help

Figure 7-9: The Word menu choices contain most of the Finder's menu choices.

Photoshop File Edit Image Layer Select Filter View Window Help

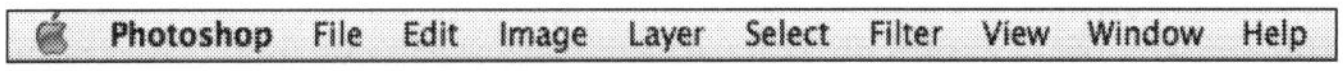

Figure 7-10: The Photoshop CS menu choices contain most of the Finder's menu choices.

Finder File Edit View Go Window Help

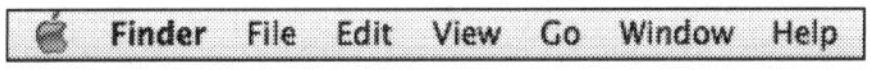

Figure 7-11: The application menu is to the right of the Apple menu. Each program, including the Finder, shows its name in this place.

The Go menu is the only menu that the Finder has that these two applications don't have.

The Application Menu

To the right of the Apple menu (covered in depth in Chapter 2) is the name of the active application. This is the application menu.

Application menus (shown in Figures 7-12, 7-13, and 7-14) give access to application preferences, system services, as well as information about the application itself.

Figure 7-12: The Finder application menu does not contain the Quit command (⌘-Q) like other application menus.

Figure 7-13: You can select to Hide (⌘-H) your application from the application menu.

Figure 7-14: Application menus sometimes include options of registration information or access for plug-ins or add-ons for that application.

The File Menu

The file menu is located to the right of the application menu. The File menu, as indicated by the name, is where you get at your work or file(s). This is where your work starts and finishes.

Like the application menu, the File menus are different between applications like the Finder (shown in Figure 7-15), Word X (shown in Figure 7-16), and Photoshop CS (shown in Figure 7-17).

There are common things you can do in these menus such as opening and making new documents. With applications that work with documents, like Photoshop CS and Word, you also have the options to save, save as, and print. (The Finder doesn't do these things because it doesn't work directly with documents.)

Figure 7-15: The File menu for the Finder is very different from other application File menus. Among some of the more powerful options under the Finder's File menu, you can move items to the trash, get information for data, make aliases, and choose colors for the label of the selected document or folder.

File	
Project Gallery...	⇧⌘P
New Blank Document	⌘N
Open...	⌘O
Open Web Page...	
Close	⌘W
Save	⌘S
Save As...	
Save as Web Page...	
Versions...	
Web Page Preview	
Page Setup...	
Print Preview	
Print...	⌘P
Send To	▶
Properties...	
1 542281 ch07.doc	
2 542281 ch05.doc	
3 Connectors.doc	
4 opener.doc	
5 apple menu.doc	
6 MAC_PS Temp 120203.dot	
7 TOC April 8th Update.doc	
8 542281ch02resub.doc	
9 PS Word Sample 122302.doc	

Figure 7-16: Among the options in Word's File menu is access to the Project Gallery. This is an example of an application-specific option for Word that you won't find in the File menus of other applications.

File and Document Usually Mean the Same Thing

Secret

Applications like Word allow you to access the properties of a document from under the File menu (shown in Figure 7-16). This kind of information can be accessed from under the same menu in Photoshop CS by a different option named File Info (shown in Figure 7-17).

Some software developers refer to "documents" and some refer to "files." If you don't see one, look for the other.

The names changes but the song (and the function) remains the same.

The Edit Menu

The Edit menu is located to the right of the File menu. The Edit menu, as indicated by the name, is where you select options to modify or edit your work or file(s). This is where you start working on your work.

Like the File menu, the Edit menus are different between applications like the Finder (shown in Figure 7-18), Word X (shown in Figure 7-19), and Photoshop CS (shown in Figure 7-20).

Figure 7-17: Recent documents are shown in the Photoshop CS File menu in the Open Recent submenu. In contrast, Word X displays recent files at the bottom of its File menu.

There are common things you can do in these menus such as undoing (⌘-Z), selecting all (⌘-A), cutting (⌘-X), copying (⌘-C), and pasting (⌘-V) data and selections from documents. These are common editing commands that are universal on the Mac. These commands are very identifiable as Mac-like application features. Such features are one of the cornerstones of what makes a Mac application a Mac application.

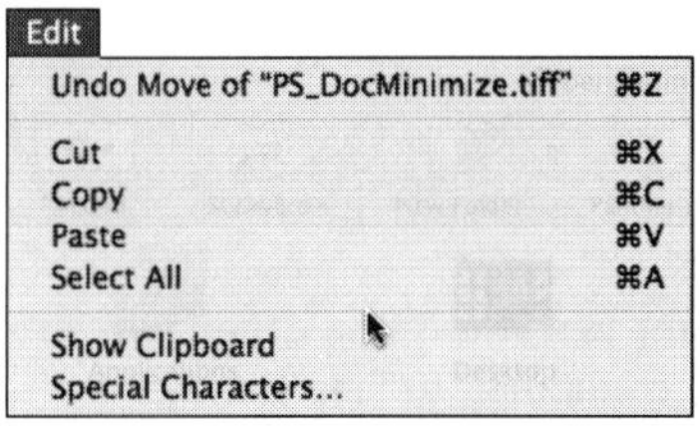

Figure 7-18: The top five commands under the Edit menu are almost universal on the Mac platform.

> **note**
> For the first time the Copy command under the Edit menu in the Finder can be used to copy entire files rather than just the filenames.

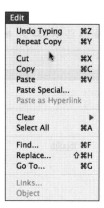

Figure 7-19: Some applications like Word X allow not only for an undo but a repeat of the last action or edit.

Figure 7-20: Some even more sophisticated programs like Photoshop CS and Word X allow you to undo an almost unlimited number of steps by continuing to Step Backward.

Copy and Paste Works Between Applications

One of the really cool things about the Finder is that there is a place called the Clipboard that can be accessed from under the Edit menu while the Finder is foremost (shown in Figure 7-18).

The Clipboard is a place where text, pixels, or other data that is copied (Command +C) or cut (⌘-X) is stored until it is pasted (⌘-V). Because the data that is selected and copied (or cut) from an application is stored in the Finder, it is available to any other application/document that has access to those same features (all document applications).

This means that you can copy text from an application like AppleWorks and paste it into a document open in Word X.

Also in the Edit menus of applications that work with documents, like Photoshop CS and Word, you have special options that apply to documents. The options to Find and/or Find and Replace are examples.

The View Menu

The View menu is located to the right of the Edit menu. The View menu, as indicated by the name, is where you choose how you want to view your work or file(s). The View menu offers many different options depending upon what kind of data the application deals with.

Like the Edit menus, the View menus are different between applications like the Finder (shown in Figure 7-21), Word X (shown in Figure 7-22), and Photoshop CS (shown in Figure 7-23).

In the Finder, you can choose to view files and folders in different ways on the desktop or in Finder windows. In applications that deal with documents, you can usually choose how large you want that document(s) to be on your screen by zooming in or out. Other than that, commands are all very specific to each application.

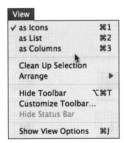

Figure 7-21: View options seem limited here, but there are a lot more options for viewing your files and folders than you would think by looking at this menu. Check out Chapter 1 to see most of the options.

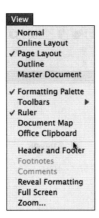

Figure 7-22: Besides the document size (Zoom), there are very few similarities between the View menus in Word X and Photoshop CS.

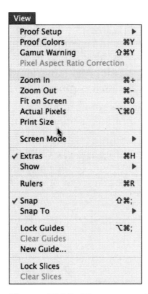

Figure 7-23: There are only a few similarities in the View menu options between Photoshop CS and Word X. Notice that there are a lot of key commands in this Photoshop CS menu. This is because these view options are very similar (common) between Photoshop CS and other OS X applications from Adobe.

The Window Menu

The Window menu is located to the left of the Help menu. The Window menu, as indicated by the name, is where you choose which windows or documents (files) you want to select; presumably to work on. The main function of the Window menu is to allow access to all open windows or documents open in the application that the Window menu is being selected from.

Like the Edit menus, the Window menus are different between applications like the Finder (shown in Figure 7-24) and applications like Word X (shown in Figure 7-25) or Photoshop CS (shown in Figure 7-26), which handle documents.

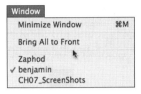

Figure 7-24: Both of the command options in the Finder's Window menu are available in all applications.

Figure 7-25: Word X's Window menu acts a lot like the Finder's Window menu. The open documents are at the bottom of the menu.

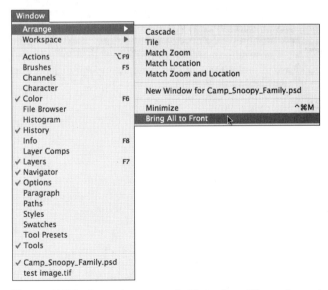

Figure 7-26: Open documents in Photoshop CS are shown in the Arrange submenu. Tile, the command to show all documents on the screen without overlapping them, is a common option for all programs that can open multiple documents.

The Help Menu

The Help menu is usually located to the far right of all the application menus. (It's usually the last menu.) The Help menu, as indicated by the name, is where you go for Help.

Some applications, like the Finder contain only the help command (Mac Help, ⌘-?, shown in Figure 7-27). Other applications, like Word X, show a variety of help options to "help you" more easily get to the specific help section you want (shown in Figure 7-28). And still other applications, like Photoshop CS, try to include help and tutorials in the help menu (shown in Figure 7-29), that may or may not be helpful.

We Interrupt This Chapter . . .

Okay. Yes. If you sensed a little parting shot at Adobe's help system the section on help menus, you would be correct. Pieter caught it and he called me on it.

Benjamin: I personally think that Adobe had gotten a little too "user friendly." I wish they could separate the tutorials from the help a little more. Now it seems like I have to wade through too much information to find a short concise sentence to answer my questions. It seems as if Adobe has taken the stance that you should never use three words when twelve will do.

Pieter: Ben, it is always a fine balance between too much information and too little, alas in this day and age, many publishers tend to err towards the side of too much as you have noticed. However, for a new user, or even a user of moderate experience, it is critically important that Adobe and other publishers provide them with clearly written instructions on how a command can be used. All the power in the world is useless if a user cannot figure out how to access it. While things may be self-evident once you see how they work or are very comfortable with an application and as such the help files seem too simplified, for a new user they may provide just the right amount of information. That's the balancing act — providing clear and concise information for the experts, like us, and making things easy to understand and educational enough to allow even a beginner to learn the application and all its features.

Figure 7-27: Simple and Direct. Just like I like a Help menu.

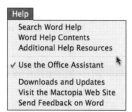

Figure 7-28: Word X's Help menu allows you to turn of the Office Assistant. If you've ever used Word before, this little animated icon shows up to help you out by giving tips.

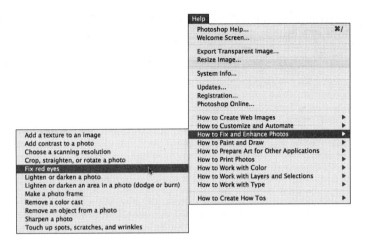

Figure 7-29: The Photoshop CS Help menu (or Help ad nauseam as I call it) also allows you to make contact with the Adobe Web site to check for updates — which is a very helpful feature.

Another feature of the help system in Photoshop CS is that it will open your browser and make contact with the Adobe Web site for additional support. This is a very sophisticated feature that can help a new user get up to speed more quickly on a program like Photoshop CS.

The way that Help works in the Finder and other applications in OS X (and in particular, Panther) is important enough to go into a little more detail.

Working With Help in Panther

Photoshop CS's Web-based help system notwithstanding, you will probably have need of Apple's built-in help system and Help Viewer, which provides access to help that has been packaged onboard your computer.

Apple allows the placement of Help library files in a variety of places. The Help Viewer application finds and uses those help files when you call for them.

The great thing about Apple's help system is that enables both narrow and broad searching comparable to the Find command that searches for files on your computer (see the "Searching like a Pro" section in Chapter 1).

To get help, follow these steps:

1. From the application you are in (or need help from), select the help option for that application from under the Help menu (shown in Figure 7-30).

Figure 7-30: This is the Preview Help menu. The application is usually shown in the menu options itself.

2. If the Help doesn't use a browser like Safari (the way the Photoshop CS does), the Help Viewer application launches (shown in Figure 7-31).

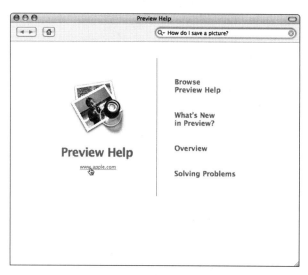

Figure 7-31: The Help Viewer shows the name of the application in the title bar and some main navigation screen or table of contents for the application as provided for in that application's library.

3. For specific questions, type your question in the search field at the top of the Help Viewer and hit the Return key on your keyboard.

4. Your Help Viewer screen shows the results of your search by topic and relevance (shown in Figure 7-32).

5. If the results are not what you need, you should consider that the application that you are using is not the one ideally suited for the question. If that's the case, you can open up your search by clicking on the pull-down menu next to the magnifying glass icon next to the help search field (shown in Figure 7-32).

6. After this is done, the help search expands to include all help files. The results can be viewed by relevance (shown in Figure 7-33).

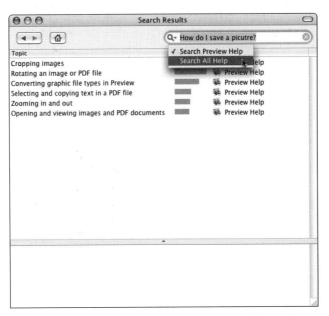

Figure 7-32: Help Viewer can access the help files of all applications on your computer.

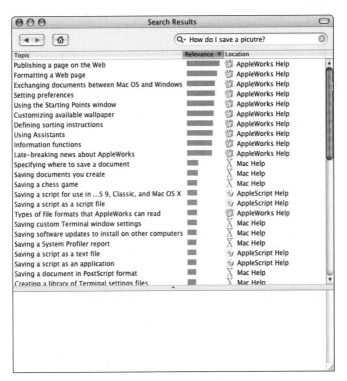

Figure 7-33: The application library is shown in the location column. To preview the information, click on the topic. To change the view to the topic, double-click the topic.

If you're interested in the applications that provide help libraries or if you want to choose a different help library, you can view or select said libraries from under the Library menu when the Help Viewer is up (shown in Figure 7-34).

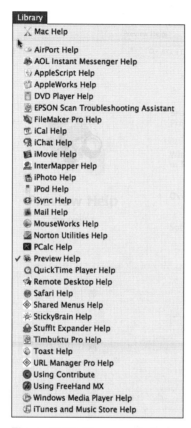

Figure 7-34: These applications are not the only ones that have help in them. These are just the ones that use Apple's help system and Help Viewer.

You Can Get Help for Help

In Apple's very logical way, they have allowed for help in getting help.

Once you have the Help Viewer open, because the Help Viewer is also an application with a help library, you can choose Help Viewer Help from under the Help menu (shown in Figure 7-35).

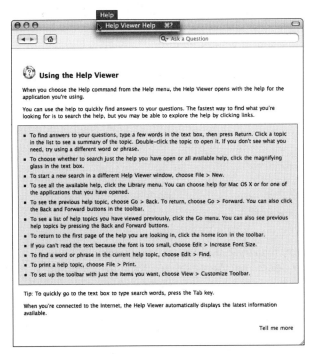

Figure 7-35: You can get quick Help help instructions from the Help Viewer Help or click on the "Tell me more" link on the bottom-right corner of the Help Viewer Help screen.

Some Menus That Aren't All That Common

Some menus are not universal and although we could ignore them to try and make the point about the common aspects of Mac applications, you'd miss out on learning how some Mac applications deal with data. You may even see some commonalities.

Application-Specific Word X Menus

Word X's menu options can seem like overkill, but Word users on both Macs and PCs are very used to the editing capabilities that these menus and palettes (shown later in this chapter) provide.

The Word X Insert Menu

The Insert menu (shown in Figure 7-36) in Word does exactly what you'd think it does. It allows you to insert all kinds of things into a document. This menu (or something similar) is common to text editing programs and page layout programs (covered in more depth in Chapter 8).

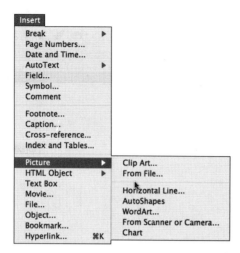

Figure 7-36: The most common thing that you might insert in a document is a picture. You can choose your own image or select from Word's clip art files, usually installed on your computer when you install Word X.

The Word X Format Menu

The Format menu (shown in Figure 7-37) in Word allows for very precise control of certain aspects of a document. Again, most word processing, text editing, and page layout programs have something similar or have similar features in other menus.

The nearest equivalent to the control over a document/file that Photoshop CS has would be the Image menu (shown later in Figure 7-42).

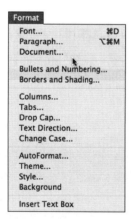

Figure 7-37: The Format menu is actually kind of a poor substitute to the Formatting Palette that is part of Word X.

The Word X Font Menu

Not all word processor programs have a dedicated Font menu as Word X does (shown in Figure 7-38). Most have submenus for Fonts (shown later in the chapter in Figure 7-43) under a Font or Type submenu. And some programs don't have a font menu at all. Instead, they have a Font menu choice that opens the Apple Font Browser dialog box to select fonts, sizes, and styles.

Figure 7-38: Fonts can be selected under the Fonts menu in Word X or from under the Name pull-down menu in Word X's Formatting Palette.

If You Don't Have a Font Menu You Can Add One

Secret

If your program doesn't have a Font menu or if the Font menu shows all of the fonts in one long list and you would like them grouped into families, you can purchase third-party software to do just that for you.

My favorite two helper applications for adding Font menu functionality are FontSight from Stone Design (`www.stone.com/FontSight/`) which adds a Font menu if your application doesn't have one, and the haxie FontCard from Unsanity (`www.unsanity.com/haxies/fontcard/`) that gives you a lot of control over how fonts display and are grouped in OS X.

The Word X Tools Menu

The Tools menu in Word X is very useful. This is where you go for Spell Checking, among other things (shown in Figure 7-39). Almost all word processing programs and page layout programs have some of these functions.

If you don't find options like Spell Checking in menu like Tools in your word processor or page layout program, you might find them in the Edit menu.

Figure 7-39: Word X is part of the Office X suite that contains Entourage (an e-mail and address book program), so there are options like Envelopes, Labels, and Address Book that directly access data from those programs.

The Word X Table Menu

The Table menu (shown in Figure 7-40) is something that can be very handy. Tables can be very helpful if you've got data that you want to display that doesn't format well in paragraph form.

Most page layout programs have this feature, but not all text editors do.

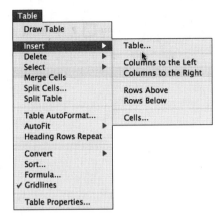

Figure 7-40: Notice that the Table menu includes the ability to insert tables, table columns, and table rows. It's interesting that these options aren't in the Insert menu (shown in Figure 7-36).

The Word X Work Menu

The Work menu (shown in Figure 7-41) is a uniquely Word thing. You add documents to the Work menu for quick access. I have never had need to use this, but I imagine that Microsoft had some use for it when they added it.

Figure 7-41: The Word document for this chapter is shown here added to the Work menu.

So much for Word X's "other menus." Now let's look at the application-specific menus for Photoshop CS.

Application-Specific Photoshop CS Menus

Photoshop CS doesn't have fewer menu options; it only looks like it at first glance. If you pull down the menu in Photoshop CS, you see a lot of submenus that give you the same kind of control (if not more) to image documents that Word X has over text documents.

The Photoshop CS Image Menu

The Image menu in Photoshop CS (shown in Figure 7-42) won't be found in Word X. This menu is used in image editors to control things like resolution, image size, and color modes. (These are things that make more sense if you work in programs like Photoshop CS.)

The Image menu is there to control those features that are inherent to an image. I know that sounds overly simplistic, but let's leave it at that.

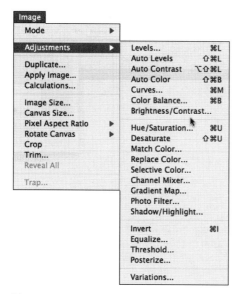

Figure 7-42: Most of the color correction controls are located in the Image menu under the Adjustments submenu.

The Photoshop CS Layer Menu

The options in the Layer menu (shown in Figure 7-43) are not necessarily a Photoshop model so much as they are a graphic program model. The idea of layers is that you have different levels or *layers* on a document that contain information that affect other layers or the whole document.

Most of Adobe's programs work on the layer premise. And other page layout programs, like QuarkXpress 6, also understand and utilize layers.

The Photoshop CS Select Menu

The Select menu in Photoshop CS (shown in Figure 7-44) is reminiscent of the Edit menu in that you can select items. Photoshop needs the Select menu and controls because of the many ways that Photoshop CS allows you to get at data.

Figure 7-43: Photoshop allows for the control and styling of layers, including the required Drop Shadow layer style that *must* be applied to text at least once to make you feel like a real artist (smile).

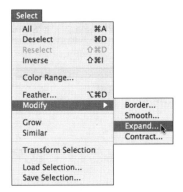

Figure 7-44: The Select menu in Photoshop CS allows you to select and/or make modifications of a selection.

The Photoshop CS Filter Menu

Modifiers, called filters, are part of how Photoshop works. These are plug-ins that allow for effects or other modifications to be done.

The Filter menu in Photoshop CS (shown in Figure 7-45) contains built-in filters. And an entire industry has been created to create and sell third-party filters for programs just like Photoshop CS.

Figure 7-45: Filters are grouped into submenus. The submenu heading gives you clues to what the filters do.

Adding Additional Plug-ins and Filters

If you have other filters or plug-ins from a previous version of Photoshop (that are all compatible with your current version), you can select to add that Plug-ins folder in the Plug-ins & Scratch Disks Preference panel in Photoshop CS.

If you aren't sure or you don't want to move everything, you'd be better off reinstalling or moving the individual plug-in or folder you're trying to get at.

What Makes a Mac Document a Mac Document?

I know that this seems like we're getting off topic, but applications make documents. And how documents behave is as much a part of what makes a Mac a Mac as anything else. In this section, we look at the parts of the documents shown earlier in this chapter in Figures 7-7 and 7-8.

The Workings of the Title Bar

An open file or document contains information about the document itself. This information can be modified by the application. There is also information as well as the ability to manipulate the document around the open document frame itself.

The Document Name

All documents show the names or titles of the document in the top bar of the open document itself (shown in Figure 7-46 and Figure 7-47).

Figure 7-46: The Word document's name and window controls are shown at the top of a document. Some documents, like Word documents, show an icon of the document type next to the document name.

Figure 7-47: The Photoshop document's name and window controls are shown at the top of a document. Some documents, like Photoshop documents, show a small preview of the image next to the document name.

Closing and Minimizing a Document

There are also three colored buttons on the left side of a document's title bar. These three buttons work just as they do for windows in the Finder. The red button closes the document. The yellow button minimized the document to the Dock (shown in Figures 7-48 and 7-49). And the green button changes the set sizes of the document.

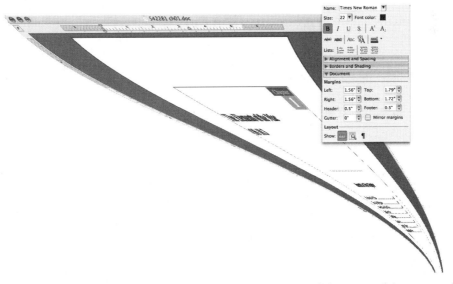

Figure 7-48: Documents always minimize toward the lower-right corner of the screen where minimized documents are stored in the Dock.

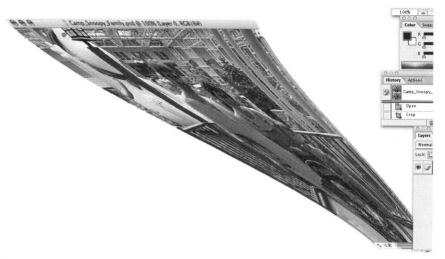

Figure 7-49: The Genie Effect document animation can be turned off in System Preferences to allow for faster minimizing of documents. But where's the fun in that?

Double-Clicking on the Title Bar Minimizes a Document

Secret

Besides clicking on the yellow button, double-clicking on the top title bar on a document causes it to minimize into the Dock.

The ⌘-M key combination minimizes documents in some, but not all, applications.

Directory Access from the Title Bar

You can also access the directories of documents by Command-clicking on the names of the documents on their title bars (shown in Figures 7-50 and 7-51). This action gives a directory path pull-down menu of that document. You can open any of the directories in a new Finder window by selecting it in the pull-down menu.

The Workings of the Bottom and Side of a Document

Besides the top bar there are more controls along the bottom and side of a document that make it Mac-like.

More document information along the bottom of the document

In very simple documents, there isn't any additional information along the bottom of a document. But for more sophisticated programs that make more sophisticated documents, software companies like Adobe and Microsoft often enable the window to display additional information about a document (shown in Figures 7-52 and 7-53).

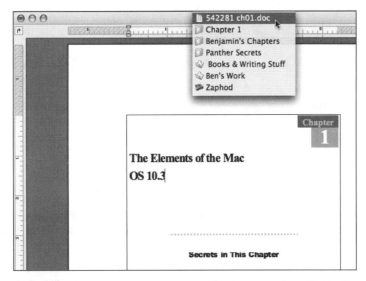

Figure 7-50: The entire directory list of a document is available through the document name.

Figure 7-51: Even the custom icons of the folders show up in the pull-down directory list from the document name.

Figure 7-52: Word documents show, among other things, layout views, word counts, and page number information.

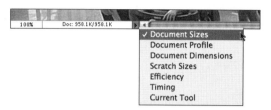

Figure 7-53: Photoshop documents show the document size in percentage as well as providing a pull-down menu for access to a lot of other information relevant to that document and to Photoshop.

Sizing a Document from the Lower-Right Corner of a Document

All documents and windows can be sized by dragging their bottom-right corner. The sizing corner can be identified by the three diagonal lines (shown in Figure 7-54 and in Figure 7-55).

Figure 7-54: Pulling on the sizing corner resizes a document or window.

Figure 7-55: Documents or windows can be sized out (by dragging down and to the right) or sized in (by dragging up and to the left).

Scrolling within a Document on the Side and Bottom of a Document

All documents (or Finder windows)that can't or aren't seen completely within the window containing them shows a scroll bar on the side and/or on the bottom of document or window (shown in Figure 7-56 and in Figure 7-57).

The scroll bars usually consist of arrows at the top and bottom on the right side and/or on right and left on the bottom of a document. Between these arrows is a colored bar that moves either by clicking on arrows, dragging the colored bar, or clicking on the white part of the bar between the two arrows.

Figure 7-56: The scroll bars in Word documents allow for "splitting" a document screen. .

Figure 7-57: The larger colored section in this scroll bar (in proportion to the size of the entire scroll bar) compared to the smaller colored section in the Word scroll bar indicates that the Photoshop document isn't as large (respectively and in terms of overall pages) than the Word document.

Hidden Contextual Commands within the Document

The last thing that we look at in the document itself is the contextual options. Just like in the Finder, control-clicking on a document produces a contextually sensitive menu with options that are relevant to that document or to selections in the document.

Since pixel data is different than type data, different contextual options are available for a selection (highlighted text) made in a Word document (shown in 7-58) than in a selection (pixel selection made by the Marquee tool) made in a Photoshop CS document (shown in Figure 7-59).

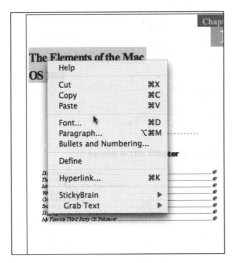

Figure 7-58: Some of the Edit menu, Format menu, and the Help menu functions from Word X are available to this selected text via this contextual menu.

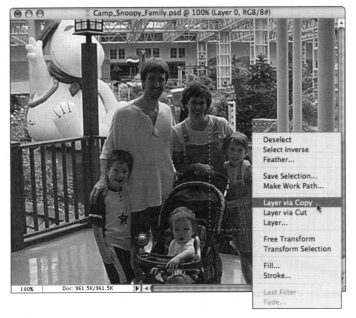

Figure 7-59: Some of the Selection menu and Layer menu functions from Photoshop CS are available to the selected pixels via this contextual menu.

Opening and Saving Documents with a Mac Application

Common actions like printing, opening, or saving a document (and the dialog boxess that go with those actions) are also a part of what makes a Mac application a Mac application.

We have an entire chapter (Chapter 22) devoted to printing, so we'll skip it in this chapter and work through opening and saving documents. Although there are a lot of additional dialog boxes that are part of opening and saving document with a Mac application, it isn't necessary to show two applications doing the same kind of function. So we'll switch off between Photoshop CS and Word X as we go through this section.

Opening a Document

Opening a document inside an application starts from under the File menu in a Macintosh application. You select the Open or Open Document command (usually ⌘-O) to get at the Open dialog box (shown in Figure 7-60).

Figure 7-60: The Open dialog box allows you to browse for files in Column or List view. Column view is not only the default but also a much more efficient way of navigating through the hierarchy of your hard drive or network volumes to find the file you want to open.

The main purpose of the Open dialog box is to navigate through your mounted volumes to find the file you want to open. That is true of *all* Open dialog boxes.

Once the Open dialog box is open, different applications give you different options. To that end, most Open dialog boxes allow quick directory menu (shown in Figure 7-61) to facilitate getting to common or recently visited directories.

Figure 7-61: The directory of the current document is shown at the top of this directory menu. The other items below it are Recent Places that have been used by this and/or other programs.

Some Open dialog boxes allow you to select the kind of documents recognized by the application (shown in Figure 7-62). You will occasionally need to change this setting in order to allow your application to select and open a particular kind of document.

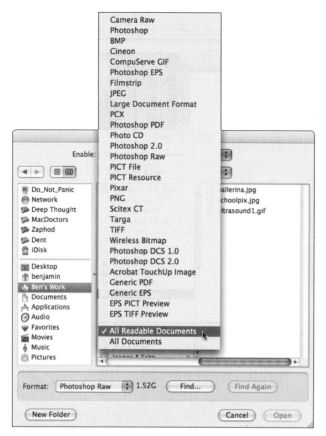

Camera Raw
Photoshop
BMP
Cineon
CompuServe GIF
Photoshop EPS
Filmstrip
JPEG
Large Document Format
PCX
Photoshop PDF
Photo CD
Photoshop 2.0
Photoshop Raw
PICT File
PICT Resource
Pixar
PNG
Scitex CT
Targa
TIFF
Wireless Bitmap
Photoshop DCS 1.0
Photoshop DCS 2.0
Acrobat TouchUp Image
Generic PDF
Generic EPS
EPS PICT Preview
EPS TIFF Preview
✓ All Readable Documents
All Documents

Figure 7-62: Selecting the All Readable Documents option from the Enable format menu is probably the safest and most useful choice. Selecting All Documents is probably not as useful.

Secret

You Can Force and Change Which Applications Are Set to Open Your Files

Over time, you may find that you have accumulated several programs that do some of the same kinds of things and open the same kinds of files. You may also find that the default program that you want to use to open your files (so that you can work with them) isn't the program that is launched by the Finder when you double-click your document(s) or file(s).

There are two other good ways to open your file in the application you choose (other than by selecting the file through the Open (⌘-O) command and dialog boxes.

The first way is old-school Mac magic. You can take your file and drag it on top of the application or an alias to the application in the Finder (which could be located in your Dock or elsewhere in your Finder). If the file can be opened by the application, the application should open the document. If it can't, then it can't.

The second way is new to OS X. You can select the file or document in question (clicking on the file one time or highlight it) and then choose Get Info (⌘-I) from under the File menu in the Finder or from the Contextual menu. The third option is the Open With section in the file's Info box. Here you can not only specify which application will open this document (until this preference is changed again), but also specify that application to open all files or documents like it.

Some Open dialog boxes allow you to open the selected document for a read-only session or to open a copy of said document instead of the original (shown in Figure 7-63).

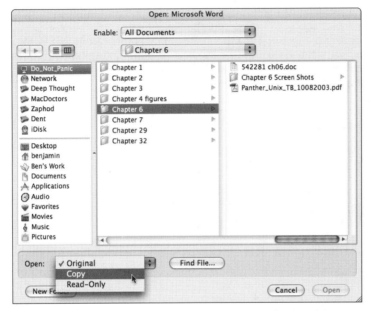

Figure 7-63: Word also allows you to search for a file by clicking the Find File button, rather than trying to navigate through your directories for the file you want to open.

Saving a Document

Actually, I'm taking you through the Save As option rather than just saving. They work the same way and if you can do one you can do the other.

Although not all applications work this way, most documents in most OS X applications have the Save and Save As options under the File menu. Selecting Save As from under the File menu with a Word X document returns a Save As dialog box to drop down off of the title bar of the document you are saving (shown in Figure 7-64).

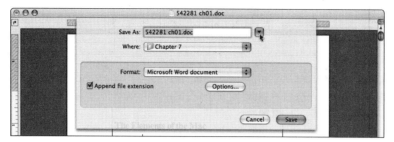

Figure 7-64: The default dialog box for saving documents is usually simple, with a single Where menu to help you save your file to the appropriate directory.

By clicking on the small arrow to the right of the Save As text field (shown in Figure 7-64) you get a window that is just like the Open dialog box (shown in Figure 7-65). As in the Open dialog, the Save dialog box can be viewed in both Column and List view. These views are there to help in navigating through your hard drive or other mounted volumes to the desired folder or directory that you want to save your file in.

Figure 7-65: Custom icons and labels are visible in both the Open and Save dialog boxes.

Programs like Word that allow sophisticated documents to be created, also usually allow different file format options when those same documents are saved. Word X does this with a Format menu at the bottom of the Save and Save As dialog boxes (shown in Figure 7-66).

Occasionally after you've selected the directory and format of your file, the application prompts you with a warning, preferences for that format or application (shown in Figure 7-67), and/or additional file options (shown in Figure 7-68).

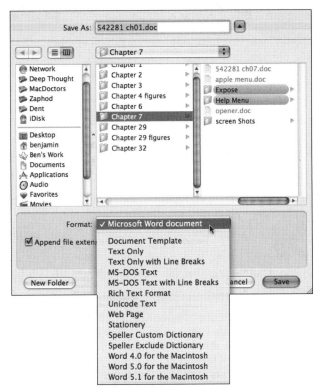

Figure 7-66: The default format for Word X documents is the Microsoft Word document format. Unless you have a specific reason to save a file in other than the default format, the default format works just fine.

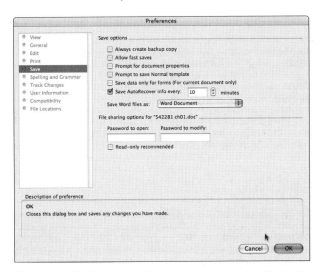

Figure 7-67: Additional Save options may be available through your application preferences.

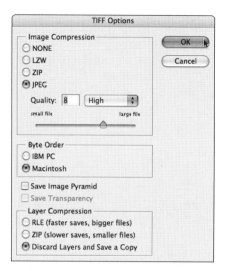

Figure 7-68: Saving TIFFs in Photoshop require that you make additional choices for compression and image compatibility.

Sometimes these kinds of dialog boxes can be bypassed by setting preferences so that they won't come up when saving a document in a program like Word, as in Figure 7-67. And sometimes these additional dialog boxes are just a part of the Save process that you must go through when you save files like TIFFs in Photoshop CS, as in Figure 7-68.

Common Places to Save Documents To

Apple always tries to steer you toward the Documents folder within your home folder as the place to save documents. That's fine. Feel free to do so.

But if you have other directories that you save files to a lot, you should drag that folder into the sidebar of one of your Finder windows. Thereafter, you can click on that folder in the sidebar of the Save, the Save As, and the Open dialog boxes to quickly get at those documents.

You can also place file and folder aliases in the Favorites folder (usually located in the sidebar) to help you organize your most-visited items.

It's your computer. It's your time. You might as well make one help you make the most of the other.

About Installing Applications and How to Avoid Bad Installations

You might think that this is a section should go in Chapter 32 (the Troubleshooting chapter), but I think it's appropriate to talk about installing applications here. This isn't so much a troubleshooting section as it is a preventative maintenance and strategy section.

Typical Mac OS X Installations

First, you should understand a little more about the architecture of an application. Most complex applications are not simply contained in the Applications folder on your hard drive (or in their respective folders inside the Applications folder). Applications also tend to put pieces in other places on your computer. Although most application support files are placed (somewhere) in the Library folder in the Home folder, they can put support files in the System folder as well. Applications also occasionally put library files in one or more places in the Library folder on the top level of the hard drive on your computer.

These support files tie in, update, and sometimes replace definitions and plug-in information in a variety of different places. And these are just some of the things that can happen when you install an application.

In the "old days" of the OS 9.x and earlier, we had similar problems with extensions, control panels, and preferences. Conflicts between versions of these files were very common. We call these kinds of problems extension conflicts. Apple even included a built-in control panel called the Extensions Manager to help us help ourselves by being able to turn extensions and control panels on and off and to build sets for greater stability.

Now we have far too many library and preference files to be able to manage with such a control panel, even if there was one for OS X. Fortunately, OS X is very stable and applications that are unstable don't usually take down the whole system or other applications. Part of that is because it's Unix. Part of that is because applications run in protected memory. And part of that is because it's a Mac, built by Apple, which knows what it's doing.

Avoiding Installation Problems

Having said that, we need to recognize that bad things *can* happen when applications are installed. Here are a few tips to help you have clean installs and avoid really bad problems from bad installs. These are not rules so much as suggestions. The list below is not in any order. You need to be mindful of all of them all at the same time.

- **Turn off sharing and other services.** In your System Preferences you will find the Sharing preferences panel. If you have any services turned on, you should turn them off. This has less to do with simplifying what's going on in your computer than it does with making sure someone isn't accessing your computer via file sharing while you're doing an installation.
- **Turn off applications and background applications.** You shouldn't have to do this with normal applications. Native Mac X applications run in protected memory so this shouldn't be necessary. However, it can't hurt.

  Mac Classic applications run in a shared memory model under Classic emulation.

  Background applications, haxies, and programs that check for viruses can cause problems when installing a new application. Quitting those programs before you install a program is also not a bad idea.

Secret

You Can Use the Activity Monitor to See What Applications Are Running

By double-clicking on an application in the Activity Monitor (located in your Utilities folder) you bring up a window that provides you with more information than you would ever need about any of the programs you are running. (See Chapter 5 for a better look at the Activity Monitor.)

◆ **Verify and repair your permissions.** Many of the problems that you run into in OS X center on permission issues. You can verify and repair permissions on your startup drive by using the Disk Utility in your Utility folder. (See Chapter 5 for a better look at the Disk Utility.)

◆ **Dismount network volumes.** It's a good idea to dismount volumes so that you don't accidentally install your application on a network drive.

◆ **Don't do other things on your Mac when you're installing an application.** As I said before, Mac OS X native applications run in protected memory. And because an installer is an application, you should be able to do other things while an installer is running. Having said that, I'd urge you to *not* do other things. Better safe than sorry.

◆ **Do your homework.** Read the documentation and the Read Me files. Check the version numbers and compatibility. Look at the FAQs online. Look at the known issues online. Check reviews of the software. And read what has not worked for others. (Make sure you're taking advantage of other peoples' pain and suffering.)

Doing your homework also means that you should talk to your reseller. If your reseller won't give you presales support about the product then *don't buy from them any more.*

◆ **Use your common sense.** This is a lot harder than it sounds. What I mean by this is that you need to look for problems. If you're installing something and it gives you a choice that sounds like it might do something to your system that might not be good, then *stop.* Don't just click buttons and pray to the installation gods to take care of you.

This also goes back to presales support from your reseller. You should find yourself a reseller that you can trust and then support them so that they can support you.

◆ **Don't do big upgrades and major installations during a deadline.** I think this falls under the "well . . . duhh" category. If you have an important big project or an important deadline and your system is working great, then leave well enough alone until your gig is done.

◆ **Have a recent backup.** This is the magic bullet. If you do nothing else in this list, do this. If you have a good, recent backup and your system falls apart after an install, you're golden. See Chapter 32 for a large section on how to set yourself up with a backup system.

◆ **Know where and who to go to for help.** If you don't have a local Apple reseller or Apple specialist, then find the closest one to you and get to know them. You need to find someone who is Apple certified and can do in- and out-of-warranty work on your Mac. Support that Apple reseller or Apple specialist with sales and service work and you'll be able to lean on them when you need them It's a win-win relationship.

As I said, these are not rules so much as suggestions. Try to know a bit about what you're installing and who makes it.

The bottom line for this (and any other Mac problem you may have) is to build yourself a support system and to use your head.

Switching Between Applications Courtesy of Apple

Much ado has been made about switching between applications. I think that this is mostly because applications are more stable and work with each other more in OS X than they ever have in Apple's history.

And Apple has devoted quite a bit of its Eye-Candy expertise in giving you some cool ways to switch between applications.

The Dock

The first thing that confronts you in OS X is the Dock. The Dock always shows you active applications whether they hidden or not. Some background applications are not shown in the Dock, but for the most part you won't be switching between those anyway. Open applications in the Dock are indicated by small triangles under the icons for those applications (shown in Figure 7-69). Clicking on an open application in the Dock brings that application to the front.

Figure 7-69: This Dock animation is controlled by the Dock preferences accessed from under the Apple.

Command-Tabbing

Holding the Command key down and then pressing the Tab key brings up a bar in the center of the screen showing all of the active applications (shown in Figure 7-70). Pressing the Tab key again switches to the next application in the Application Switcher bar.

Figure 7-70: The Application Switcher bar grows until it reaches the sides of the screen and then the icons shrink to accommodate more applications, just like the Dock.

The animation and visual effect is new in Panther, but Command-tabbing through open applications has been around for a while.

Exposé

If much ado has been made about application switching in Panther, then Exposé is the reason and the star of Apple's switching options. Unlike the previous application-switching feature of the OS, both the graphics and the way that Exposé's features work are entirely new in Panther.

The idea behind Exposé is that the desktop is a virtual place. Apple's thinking behind this is that because it's virtual, there's no reason why we have to allow ourselves to be bound by stodgy architectures and conventions that over-emulate a real desktop which, if you're like me, gets overly cluttered with documents and projects with very little effort at all. Exposé's answer to this is to allow you to press a key and see it all. You essentially zoom out, select what you want, and then zoom in on what you've selected in miniature, and then select what you want.

In the next few sections, we look at the three main features of Exposé as well as its preferences. I'm going to spend a little time going through Exposé in this section so get comfortable.

Application Windows

Exposé allows you to get control of the open documents or windows associated with a single application. The idea here is that with a simple keystroke (F10 is the default key) all documents from a single application (shown in Figure 7-71) will come forward and shrink to show visuals of those windows or documents shown in Figure 7-72).

Figure 7-71: Three documents are shown here in the background and by the Window menu, opened in the Preview application.

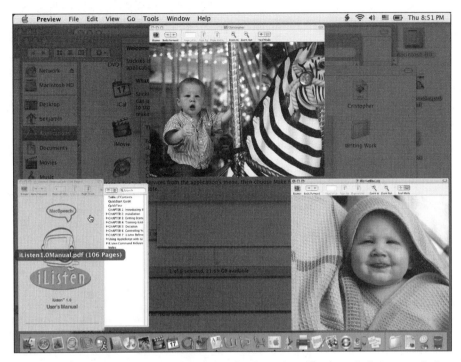

Figure 7-72: Pressing F10 (the default key for Exposé application window control) shows the open documents. Running the mouse over a document darkens it and shows the name of the document, indicating that it is selected.

Once you have the documents all up in Exposé's Application view, you can select one of those documents by running the mouse over that document and releasing the application windows Exposé key. You don't even need to click to mouse to select the document.

All Windows

As cool as that is to do with windows or documents within one application, it is even cooler to see with all open windows and documents in all open applications. Holding down the key set for All windows in Exposé (F9 is the default key) gives you visual access to everything open on your computer (shown in Figure 7-73).

After you have all of the documents and windows up in Exposé's All windows view, you can select one of those documents by running the mouse over that document and releasing the Application window's Exposé key. And because multiple documents from multiple applications are open, this has the added feature of being another way to switch between applications.

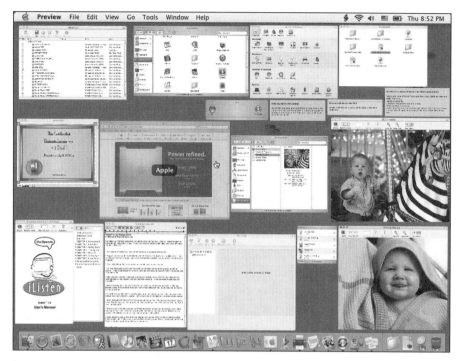

Figure 7-73: The more windows and documents that are open, the smaller Exposé makes documents to fit on the screen.

Secret

A Cool Exposé Animation Trick

Exposé is a Cocoa application. All Cocoa animations (like minimizing a document into the Dock) can be slowed down by holding the Shift key down.

Try holding the shift key down and then pressing the F9 key (Exposé's default key for All applications control). You will see all the windows slowly shrink into position.

Desktop

The best use of the desktop itself is something that I think Apple and its customers have struggled with for years. The reality of the desktop, regardless of well-placed work folders, such as Documents in each user's home folder, is that it's where people tend to put their work and other things that they are working on. Right or wrong, sloppy or not, the desktop is where some people put things while they're figuring out where they should put things. Apple has finally realized that this is the case and has given us a way to get directly to the desktop.

So, unlike the previous two features of Exposé, clicking on the Desktop Exposé key (the default key for the Desktop option in Exposé is F11) takes all of the open documents and windows and moves them up and out to the sides (shown in Figure 7-74 and in Figure 7-75) so that a user can see and select files, folders, or even other applications on the desktop.

Figure 7-74: Pressing F11 (the Exposé Desktop default control key) shows an animation of the windows and documents moving to the sides of the screen to show the desktop.

The desktop is a part of the Finder, so clicking on the desktop or an item on the desktop has the added benefit of switching from whatever application you were in to the Finder.

Exposé Preferences

As I've indicated while covering the features of Exposé, there are default keys set for the various Exposé options. If these references indicated to you that you had some control over those settings and perhaps other Exposé preferences, you'd be right (and intuitive in my opinion — pat yourself on the back).

You will find Exposé in the Personal row of the System Preferences (shown in Figure 7-76). The System Preferences can be accessed from in the Applications folder, on your Dock, or from the Apple menu.

Figure 7-75: The edges of the documents and windows are shown here. After the windows are out of the way, you can select and open objects on the desktop.

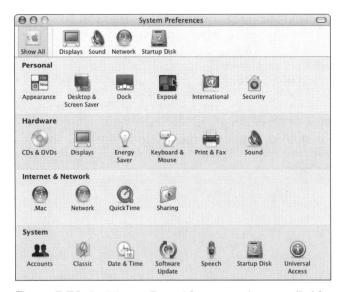

Figure 7-76: Apple's new Exposé feature can be controlled from the System Preferences.

Clicking on the Exposé icon in the System Preferences gives you access to controls for the hot corners (shown in Figure 7-77), the keyboard shortcuts (shown in Figure 7-78), and optional mouse controls for Exposé (shown in Figure 7-79).

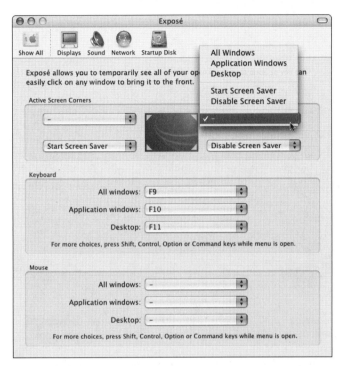

Figure 7-77: Hot corners can be set for both Exposé and the screen saver in this preference panel. Make sure you consider both preferences when you change your settings.

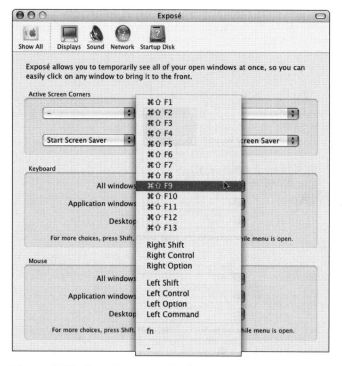

Figure 7-78: If you have your F9, F10, and/or F11 keys set for other uses or applications, you can change the default keys in the pull-down menus in the Exposé preference panel.

In my opinion, Exposé is the juggernaut of Apple's new Finder options. It took me a while to start using it. Now that I do, I have trouble working on pre–OS 10.3 systems that don't have this feature.

But if you find that Apple hasn't given you enough application switching features, there are always third-party options.

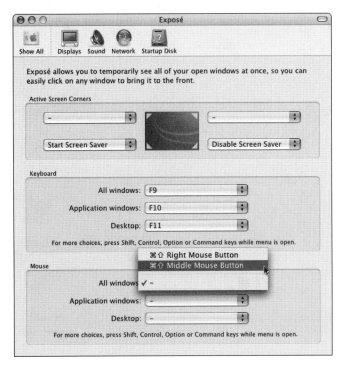

Figure 7-79: Optional mouse controls are also available for Exposé. This is useful for people with third-party mice with more than one button.

Third-Party Solutions for Applications Switching

If, after going through all of Apple's (new and old) application-switching features, you still find your OS wanting, there are more third-party solutions than you can shake a stick (or is that "stick a shake") at.

ASM

If you read Chapter 1, you have already seen this one. ASM is my *favorite* third-party utility. ASM is a Finder menu from Frank Vercruesse Products, which can be found online at www.vercruesse.de/software.

Before you add an application menu to the upper-right corner of the screen, you might want to turn off the Fast User Switching menu. You can do this by clicking on the Accounts icon in System Preferences. If you click on the Login Options under the users, you can disable Fast User Switching, which turns off the Fast User Switching menu. For more information about this, please refer to Chapter 6.

What I was looking for, and what I got from this little utility was a simple application menu in the upper-right corner of the menu bar. To that end, I found that the default settings (with a minor change or two) gave me the application menu that I was looking for (shown in Figure 7-80).

Figure 7-80: ASM . . . the Finder menu is back.

I'm not going to go through all of the preferences for ASM here. You can see the preferences for ASM at the end of Chapter 1 in this book.

PopApp

PopApp, a Freeware application by Peter Ammon, can be found online at www.people. cornell.edu/pages/pa44/popapp.html. It is a simple little utility that gives a floating application circle around the mouse when keys that you have specified are pressed (shown in Figure 7-81).

Figure 7-81: This hovering palette of active applications appears around your mouse, wherever it may be on the screen, when you hit the PopApp Keys.

This simple application needs to be launched manually or at login (see Chapter 6 for more information on startup items). When it's opened, you are confronted with a preference panel (shown in Figure 7-82) that allows you to change the layout and change the key commands. You can also change the size of the icons in PopApp (shown in Figure 7-83).

Figure 7-82: The first time you launch PopApp you must set your preferences. Hit the Apply button to change or set the preferences. Don't quit the application or PopApp won't work.

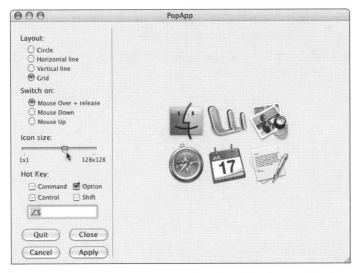

Figure 7-83: Change the layout or the size of the icons in PopApp to suit your sensibilities.

PopApps is cute and simple, but the application needs to be to use. It also can be a bit of a juggling act to get the key commands and mouse to switch applications. It's not my favorite helper application, but it is a good example of a simple floating application switcher that doesn't get in the way.

ParaDocks

ParaDocks, by PCV, can be found online at www.pcv-soft.com/. This is also a freeware application, like PopApps. I really like this utility a lot. It allows you to create a hovering button bar of the active applications (shown in Figure 7-84), that can be either horizontal or vertical (shown in Figure 7-85) with transparency control of the button bar itself.

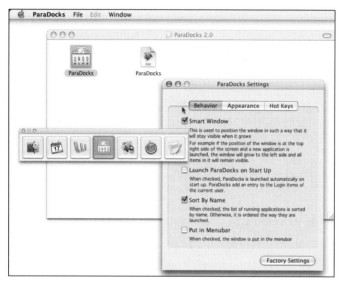

Figure 7-84: This little utility is reminiscent of another utility called HoverBar in the old classic OS's.

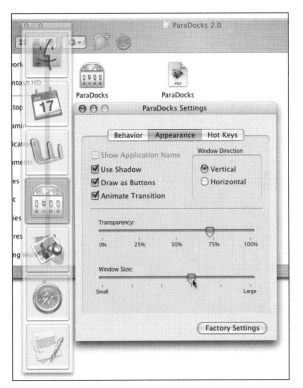

Figure 7-85: This semi-transparent ParaDocks tool bar becomes solid when you click on an application.

ParaDocks preferences also allow you to put the tool bar on the top menu bar (shown in Figure 7-86). And it allows for all the key commands for all of ParaDocks to be changed by you, the user (shown in Figure 7-87).

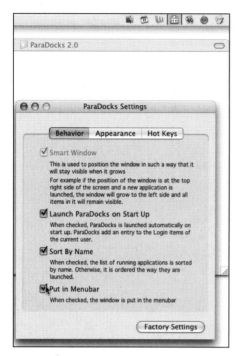

Figure 7-86: The menu bar option is for those who don't like clutter on their desktop.

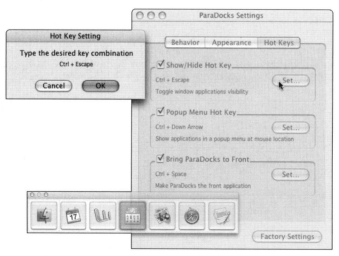

Figure 7-87: If you have as many key commands set as I do, you'll more than likely have to change ParaDock's default key commands.

Wrapping Up Third-Party Switchers

These are just a few of third-party switching applications. I chose these because — well no reason in particular other than I liked them. There are a lot more third-party enhancers online. If you're interested, you might try sites like Versiontracker.com or Macupdate.com and do a search for similar applications.

---

caution

I have a few cautionary words about these kinds of applications, switching enhancers, and haxies . . .

Some of these little application enhancers are a lot of fun. Some of them are very useful. And some are even both. But some of these (not necessarily the ones listed or not listed in this book) can be fairly toxic to your system.

Please remember that freeware is the same thing as you-install-the-program-and-you-take-your-chances. And some shareware isn't much better.

If your system is stable and you have a good system of backups, then feel free to experiment with some of these enhancers. You should still read the reviews online and be careful.

If your system isn't stable, then you need to take care of that before you start messing around with third-party solutions like this.

Summary

As so, with a look at a few third-party application switchers, we end this chapter.

In this chapter, you learned that you can count on seeing certain features in Mac applications and documents. You saw that those menus shared by the Finder (the first application open on your Mac) are the ones that you are going to see in most other applications. And you saw that some applications have additional menus that pertain to the kinds of data or documents for which they were created.

You also looked at the Open and Save dialog boxes to see how the programs and the Finder help you to navigate through the files on your hard drive.

And last, we looked at how the Finder and third-party solutions can help you switch between applications. Exposé, I believe is the real winner here.

In the next chapter, you'll put some of these fundamentals to work while looking at word processors and page layout programs.

Word Processing and Desktop Publishing

Chapter

8

◆ ◆

Secrets in This Chapter

◆ ◆

Whenever a new technology is announced, its survival depends on finding a so-called killer app, and for computers one of the first killer apps was word processing. Those of you old enough can remember back to those dark days of the typewriter when each time you pushed a key you made an irrevocable change to your document. You actually needed to know how to spell. (Gasp!)You could be 245 words deep into a page of brilliant prose, and then on the last line, misspell a word, and the entire sheet was ruined. All the white-out in the world couldn't restore your sheet to its original pristine beauty.

Now fast forward a few years to a fanciful world, where there are many programs that check your spelling as you go; they even check your grammar. Your document no longer needs the printed sheet to exist. It can live tucked away on your hard drive as a series of cleverly encoded zeros and ones, endlessly editable, ultimately customizable.

But this still isn't enough for some (including me). You want all the benefits of word processing and you want it to look good. So, page layout, or desktop publishing, programs pick up where the word processing programs left off, allowing you to combine your words with photos and art, or even manipulate your words into creative shapes.

It used to be that there was a clear defining line between the capabilities of a word processing program and a layout program but that line has blurred as developers add more and more capabilities to each type of software suite. Today, desktop publishing programs now have robust spell-checking engines and word processing programs have some layout abilities.

In this chapter, I take a very quick look at some of the main word processor programs. I make some comparisons, talk about some features, and even look at two page layout programs and how they are different from word processors.

Word Processors — Killer Apps or Killer Yawns?

Despite the obvious uses and benefits of word processing programs, they just are not as romantic as some of the other less useful (but super-cool) programs that run on your machine. Out of all software applications, word processors are by far the most used. Most consider word processing a replacement for the typewriter, and, in many ways, it is. For many users, it is all about the words; in that respect, your Mac is just a typewriter, albeit a very smart one.

What Are Word Processors Good At?

Word processing is much more than being able to input and edit text. A good word processor puts an abundance of tools right at your fingertips. The main tool people think of is a spell checker, but many programs come with thesaurus capabilities as well, so you can find that just-right word. Word processors also give you a variety of typographical tools that enhance the look of your documents. Word processors offer convenient ways to present your information, such as tables. They can help you index your text, and, if you make your living with words, they can count your words so your brilliant story or chapter is just the right length.

In short, word processors make all the difficult things about composing and formatting text easier.

The Nuts and Bolts of Word Processing

Here are a few of many features that are common on word processing programs:

◆ **Justification and Alignment:** These allow you to align text to both left and right margins, and specify margin and tab settings. You can also center your text on a line.

◆ **Copy, Paste, and Delete:** Word processors let you copy selections of text and place them in other areas of the document, or in a new document. You can also delete text from a document.

◆ **Search and Replace:** You can specify a word or phrase and replace every instance in a document to a different word or phrase.

◆ **Discretionary Hyphenation:** You can set your document to hyphenate or break text that ends a line. Later, when a document is changed, that word, if it moves to the middle of a line, will not be hyphenated.

◆ **Pagination:** This automatically divides the document in sections to fit on the selected output media. If you are printing on letter-sized paper, your document will flow one way, if you change it to a different-sized document, your word processing program will reflow the text.

◆ **Page Numbering, Headers, and Footers:** You can number the pages of your document sequentially and place standard information at the top and bottom of each page.

◆ **Footnoting and Index Generation:** This feature is invaluable for those cursed with writing heavily referenced text, common in academia. Word processors take your footnotes and place them at the bottom of the appropriate pages when a document is paginated. Index generation creates an index based on the text of your document.

◆ **Spell Checking and Correcting:** As mentioned earlier, word processors take the words in your document and compare them against a dictionary. They alert you to items not found in a dictionary and offer alternate spellings and a way to correct the error. Most word processing documents offer you a way to add to a dictionary words such as proper names, or words most dictionaries are too prim to include such as your favorite profanities.

These features have been included in word processors for over a decade now, and you probably take them for granted. But if you think back to a time before word processors you can imagine the intestine-shuddering excitement at seeing a word automatically hyphenate at the end of a line or having a footnote jump from page to page depending on the location of the reference. All of these things required meticulous planning to make them work correctly on the typewritten page. Frankly, it took the fun out of typing. Now, even the most rudimentary word processors include these features.

Secret

The Origin of the Term "Word Processing"

IBM engineer Ulrich Steinhilper coined the expression "word processing" in the late 1950s. The phrase is a translation of the German word "textverarbeitung." Steinhilper felt it was a more accurate term for typing. IBM later used the term to market their Magnetic Tape Selectric Typewriter. This cutting edge product (for 1964) could record typed information and retype a document as many times as needed.

I found a list of word processing software offerings from 1986 and there were over 25 packages available (including AppleWrite III, a precursor to AppleWorks). Surprisingly, a search on the Internet for the same software names today yielded many matches, and several of those listed almost two decades ago are still available, and, even more surprisingly, available for Mac OSX.

Let's have a quick look at some of the more popular word processing programs available for the Mac today.

Microsoft Word

You can't get around it. Microsoft Word is a behemoth both in the world of word processing and on your hard drive. Often criticized as *bloatware,* it is the word processing program that all word processing programs are measured by. It is probably the most used program in the world, the Mac world included. I know people who have very little nice to say about the folks in Redmond, but when asked what they use for a word processor, nine times out of ten they say "Word," and then they begin to offer lame excuses why they do. For good or ill, Word is the industry standard for word processing and will probably continue to be for some time to come. And despite its detractors, it offers some interesting features.

Multiple Selections

Have you ever needed to grab several sentences out of a paragraph and place them someplace else? It was a lot of clicking and dragging, to say the least. With Microsoft Word, you can select multiple lines of text from different parts of your Word document. Just select a line of text, then hold down the Command key and select the next portion of text you need to copy (shown in Figure 8-1). Then place the cursor where you want to paste your text and select Paste under the edit menu or hit the key combination ⌘-V.

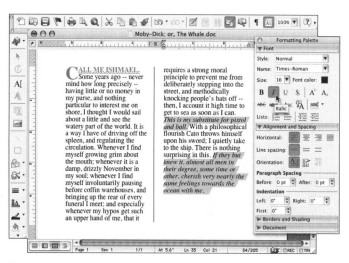

Figure 8-1: You can select multiple areas of text and reformat them easily in Microsoft Word. This feature is also available in Nisus Writer Express, covered later.

You can also use this tool to edit as you go. If you put your sentences down in the wrong order and your want to select a new sequence for the sentences, simply select them in the order you wish them to appear, copy them, and when you paste them back, behold they are arranged in the desired order.

Turn Off That Annoying Select Whole Word Feature

Microsoft Word ships with one of the most annoying presets ever. Annoying to the tune of I'd-rather-stick-my-head-in-a-meat-grinder-than-endure-this-any-more annoying. When you go to select text in Word, it automatically selects the whole word.

To turn this agonizing feature off, go to your Preferences, which you can find under Word in your menu bar, and select Edit. Uncheck the box next to When selecting, automatically select entire word. Now when you go back to your document, you can select chunks of words.

Project Gallery

For those who are either time-short or creatively challenged, Microsoft ships with a boat-load of templates for letterheads, catalogs, menus, almost everything you can think of (shown in Figure 8-2). Word even offers a ready-made Web template that you can use as a start for your own site. Word supplies the look. You supply the content.

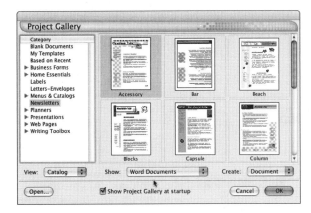

Figure 8-2: The Project Gallery lets you access all of your templates in one convenient place.

Also, when you save your documents as templates in your "My Templates Folder," you can access them through the Project Gallery as well. With this, you can turn Project Gallery into a project manager by creating new folders in your My Templates folder. If you have many categories of documents you work with, this is a great way to keep them organized.

Integrated Contacts

Have you ever typed a letter and needed an address and been forced to open your contacts in Entourage (the e-mail and address program that ships as part of the Office X suite with Word X) and copy and paste from there? Well, Microsoft has added a feature that allows you to access this information right from Word. Under the View menu, select the Contact submenu from Toolbars to add the Contact Bar to your interface. You can get your contact's name either by typing the first few letters of the name in the Type Contact Name field, or just select the inverted triangle to the right to access a drop-down menu of all the names in your contact list. To place the address, just click on the Include Address button for a drop-down menu of your contact's address (shown in Figure 8-3).

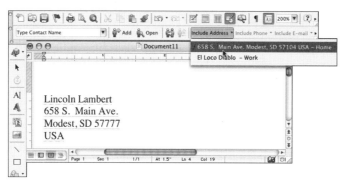

Figure 8-3: Not only can you access your contacts form Word, you can also edit them. To access that information just click the Open button and change your contact's information without even opening Entourage.

Of course, if you're using Mail and Address Book, Apple's own e-mail and address programs (respectively), this is not going to be a real useful feature for you. But Microsoft had the right idea. This idea is the same as Apple's vision of the Address Book; a program containing data that can be accessed from many other programs. But that's a different discussion altogether.

Secret

Preview Word Documents in Safari

If you want a quick way to preview Word documents without having to open Word, you can download a plug-in for Safari at www.schubert-it.com that allows you to display a text only preview of Word documents in Safari.

This is a heckuva timesaver if you've ever had to wait for Microsoft to read all the fonts on your machine at startup before you could proceed any further.

A Few Last Comments about Word

Microsoft Word can even save for the Web, but if your document gets too complicated, say you use two columns in a layout; the option is grayed out in your File menu as unavailable. So while Microsoft advertises this feature, remember you have to keep things simple for it to work.

But all in all, Word is the most capable and accepted word processor there is. And it should be, it costs about $230 and the upgrade weighs in at nearly $100. Part of that cost is the complete feature set, but the rest is that it is the industry standard. And as long as Microsoft can keep putting out a usable product, it seems they can charge whatever they want.

This book (and many other books and manuscripts I've written) was written in Word to take advantage of cross-platform compatibility as well as the powerful comment and revision features. If you're going to be a writer, working with other publishers, you'll probably need Word.

AppleWorks

AppleWorks is Apple's answer to Microsoft Office and contains six different applications, including one that handles word processing. AppleWorks comes free on consumer Macintosh models, and for those who want to buy it, it costs about $80.

AppleWorks has a full set of features for text editing. It also offers drag-and-drop table creation, and tools to create mail-merge documents. It has a huge library of clip art if you like to add some color to your documents. Apple's offering in the world of word processing also features a customizable autosave.

AppleWorks now also claims you can read and write Microsoft Word files. While that may be technically true, the documents lose something in the translation process (shown in Figure 8-4). Certain formatting does not transfer, and some font information does not make the translation either.

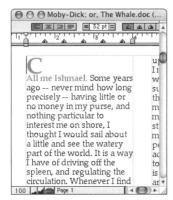 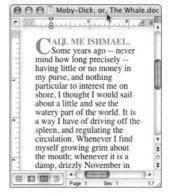

Figure 8-4: Even a drop cap was too much of a challenge for the Word-to-AppleWorks conversion (left). The conversion from AppleWorks to Word, even when you save your document as a Word file, doesn't fare any better (right).

Movies in AppleWorks

If you want to send a multimedia presentation to your friend with a Mac, you can embed movies into your AppleWorks document (shown in Figure 8-5). Just select Insert from the File menu and browse for a movie on your system. (Under the File Format pull-down menu in the Open dialog box, make sure you change the selection from AppleWorks to All Available so you can see all the document in your folders.) Once you have your image placed, just double-click on it and watch away.

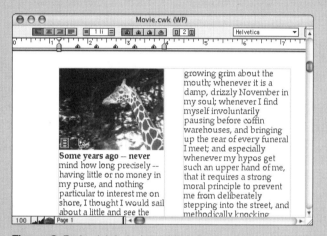

Figure 8-5: AppleWorks is multimedia savvy; you can place movies and even sounds into your document.

But if you think you are going to send this to someone who has Word only, it won't work. (You can, however, place movies in Word.) This is just for your AppleWorks friends. Also, make sure you send the movie in the same folder as the AppleWorks document because AppleWorks doesn't embed the movie data.

For the average consumer who just needs something for basic word processing, AppleWorks should be more than enough program for them. It holds many of the capabilities of its more expensive relative Word, but at a much lower price, and if you buy an iMac, eMac, or iBook, you get it on the house from the folks at Apple.

Mariner Write

The next in the field of popular word processing programs is Mariner Write. Mariner Write costs about the same as AppleWorks but doesn't offer the additional spreadsheet, drawing, and database capabilities. It can read Microsoft Word files, and when you save files from Mariner Write into Word format, the results are impressive (shown in Figure 8-6).

Word processing programs often have interfaces that are, to be polite, inelegant, but Mariner Write has an easy-to-use, intuitive interface (shown in Figure 8-7). All of the tools you regularly use are easy to get to.

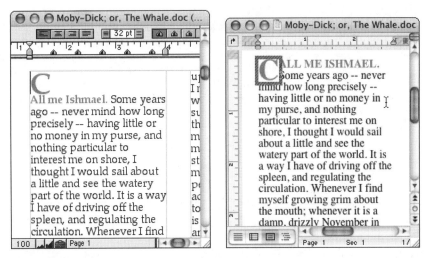

Figure 8-6: Mariner Write (left) and Microsoft Word (right) played together better than any of the other word processing products we looked at.

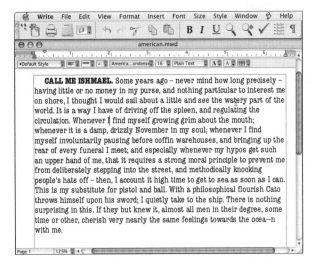

Figure 8-7: Mariner Write manages to keep all of its tools handy without cluttering up the interface.

Mariner Write has some other features that make it an attractive option to Word. It has mail-merge capabilities. It has an extensive spelling dictionary, and drag-and-drop copying and pasting of text. The program also features a fast WYSYWYG font menu, and it is true WYSYWYG, taking advantage of OS X font-smoothing capabilities.

Mariner Write can save files in only a few formats, but the ones it does are the most important formats. It does a good job saving to Word formats and PDF formats, and that's really all a word processor needs to do the job.

Mariner's Mighty Contextual Menu

One secret about Mariner Write that people need to know is it has the most powerful contextual menu (shown in Figure 8-8) of the word processing programs I looked at. It allows you to access almost every tool you need with a Control-click (or right-mouse click for you two-button mousers out there). This tool is hands-down the best way to avoid clutter in an interface and Mariner Write has it mastered.

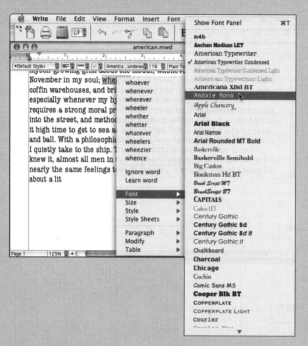

Figure 8-8: Mariner Software finds the cure for busy interfaces with Mariner Write's super powerful contextual menu.

Nisus Writer Express

Nisus Writer is a no-nonsense word processor that is lean and quick and takes up less than 10 megabytes of space on your hard drive. It also takes less out of your wallet as well, costing about $50.

The interface is clean, and it follows the OS X theme of having drawers for interface elements rather than menu bars (shown in Figure 8-9). All the important items are accessible in the drawer, but when the window is set to a smaller size, the interface becomes cramped and difficult to navigate.

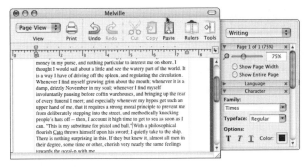

Figure 8-9: Nisus Writer Express looked the most at home in Panther out of the programs we looked at, all decked out with a drawer, even.

The program has advanced features, including the ability to make multiple selections, an extremely accessible thesaurus feature and it is able to open Word Documents (Figure 8-10).

Nisus Writer Express lacks a save to PDF feature, but that is easily worked around by using the print dialog box and saving as a PDF which we cover in more depth in Chapter 22 of this book.

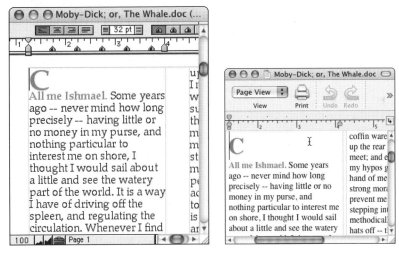

Figure 8-10: Nisus Writer Express (right) was able to get the text from Word (left), but failed to get the drop cap format to copy over.

Macros in Nisus Writer Express

Nisus Writer Express comes with a ready-made collection of mouse click–saving macros ready to run (shown in Figure 8-11). And because Nisus is so customizable, you can assign a key combination to any of the macros.

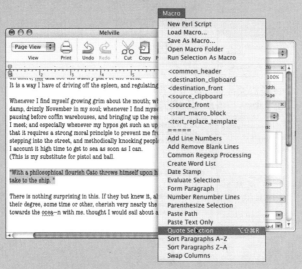

Figure 8-11: Nisus Writer Express's macros are available in the Menu bar.

Simply access the Menu Keys in the Preferences window, Select the macro you want to assign a key to and set the key combination in the right part of the Menu Keys pane. Don't worry about selecting a key combination that is already in use. Nisus Writer Express displays a message at the bottom of the screen telling you a certain key combination has been reserved for something else.

Think Free Write

Think Free Office has been marketed as an alternative to Microsoft Office. And at $49.95 for the whole suite, it is going to have a lot of takers. Think Free Write is the word processing section of the suite and has many of the features of its Microsoft competitor. And some that belong to it alone.

The first thing that you notice when you open Think Free Write is that despite the familiar feature set, this program is an entirely different animal than any other word processor program we've looked at. Think Free Office was written entirely in Java, so it is platform-independent. All the features and formats for Think Free Write travel back and forth between Windows, Linux, and Mac platforms without additional file conversion processes.

But still, there is something weird about this program. Look, for example, at the Open dialog box (shown in Figure 8-12). It just looks odd, and not as elegant as the Aqua interface. Also, the print dialog box left a lot to be desired. The only options available are which pages you want printed, how many copies, if you want to print the page number, and if you want to print the background image. That's it. There's no option to save the file as a PDF. That can be remedied by setting up your default printer to Adobe PDF, but this still is the only program I've seen that does not offer that option in the print dialog box.

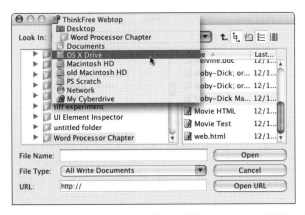

Figure 8-12: Things look a little off in the world of Think Free Office.

And despite its claims to be able to open Word documents, it failed to open the document (the opening chapter to *Moby Dick*) I used to test the other word processor contenders ability to open Word files. Think Free Office is a great idea, and a great price, but it has a lot off growing to do.

Although Think Free Write may not (in my opinion) be worth the price, the entire suite is a great deal for those people that need to have limited access to Microsoft Word and Excel documents but don't feel like shelling out hundreds of dollars.

Viewing Web Pages in Think Free Write

Secret

Think Free Write has a really neat feature that other word processing programs lack. You may have noticed the open dialog box (shown in Figure 8-12) has a field at the bottom where you can type in a URL. You can open and view Web pages in Think Free Write. From there, you can click the dandy little HTML icon in the menu bar and edit the source code for the file. Then, you can save the changes and upload the pages back up to your site using the Publish command.

Comparing Apples and, Well, Apples

We've looked at a few different word processing programs and they offer a wide range of abilities at an even wider range of prices. If you think you need tools other than word processing, it might be in your interest to get a copy of AppleWorks or Think Free Office, which come with spreadsheet and presentation capabilities. If you absolutely have to have compatibility with the rest of the word processing world, it might be better for you to plunk down the coin needed to get Microsoft Word.

If you want something that doesn't hog all the resources on your computer, you might want to avoid Microsoft Word and head toward Nisus Writer Express or AppleWorks. (AppleWorks was the surprise winner in our completely unscientific test of how much real memory a word processing program uses, with Nisus following close behind. Word gobbled up four times as much memory as AppleWorks.)

In the end, you have to weigh the capabilities of each program against the cost. All of them have free demos that last about thirty days so you can easily give them a test drive. Just remember to save all your documents as Word files or Rich Text Format so you can open them up again in whatever program you decide to buy.

The Nuts and Bolts of Layout Programs

People use layout programs to assemble type and graphics on the page and prepare them for output, whether on a printer, to film, or straight to a printing plate. Layout programs were the basis for the desktop publishing revolution and continue to be where most of the heavy lifting is done in that field.

Layout programs are where the many elements of a printed piece are assembled for output. There are essentially three things that a layout program helps you put together:

- ♦ **Type:** This is the printed text that is placed on the page. Type imported into a layout program has usually passed one way or another through a word processing program before it arrived at the layout stage.

- ♦ **Bitmap Art:** These files are usually photos where the information is defined on the pixel level. Adobe Photoshop is the best-known image editor, but there are several others available.

- ♦ **Vector Art:** This is art that is calculated and drawn using mathematical equations. If you remember quadratic equations from junior high math class, this is what they are, except way more complicated. Vector art is great for type and line drawing because its lines are crisp at any scale.

A successful layout program takes all these elements and is able to convert them to something a printer can understand, mainly PostScript. PostScript is the language invented by the folks at Adobe to describe how the various elements you use in your layout are arranged on a page — in other words, more math. But with a good layout program, you never see the math, and you are allowed to remain blissfully ignorant of all the ugly little equations that make up the nuts and bolts of your creative design.

Secret

How to Look at Your Raw PostScript Code

If you choose not to be blissfully ignorant, here is a way you can look at the raw code for a postscript document. Open any vector program and draw a simple shape. (The simpler the better, even a circle in the middle of a page generates an avalanche of code.) In your Print dialog box, Select a printer and set your output options to print to a PostScript file. Then hit Print. Now find that file, change the extension to .txt, and open the file with a word processor. Then you are able to view the raw PostScript code.

For more fun, save your text file, this time with a .ps extension. Double-click on the file and Preview converts the file to a PDF and displays it on your screen. Now take a break, because things are just getting a little too wild.

Desktop Publishing Information You Need to Know

Knowing two things will endear you to your service provider.

This first is CMYK. (We talk more about CMYK in Chapter 9) These are the four colors a traditional offset press uses to create the final printed product. Sometimes you can add spot colors, but to get started, your base is CMYK, not RGB, not LAB. For full color work, anything else will have to be converted to the CMYK color space by you or your service provider. And if your service provider does it, you'll be charged for the trouble.

The second thing you need to know is that the files you use in your layout program must be in the right format. Just because it shows up on your screen or prints on your printer in your home or office, is no guarantee that it will print for your service provider. Imaging devices, such as image setters and computer-to-plate devices, are finicky beasts. And even if your file goes through an imagesetter, sometimes it won't print correctly, and if the problem is not caught until your printed piece rolls off the press, you will have a very expensive correction to make.

Here are a few hard-and-fast rules, which if followed, should put you on good footing with your service provider.

◆ **Use PostScript fonts.** TrueType fonts are simply not appropriate for a digital workflow. You can also use OpenType fonts because these contain PostScript information that imagesetters can read. You can tell the difference by selecting the font file and using the Get Info command under the File menu in your finder. You can also tell be looking at the font file's icon (shown in Figure 8-13).

KozMinStd-Regular.otf   04b-03.bmap   04b-03.suit

Figure 8-13: You can determine your font's type by examining the icon. From left to right, the fonts are OpenType, PostScript, and TrueType.

◆ **All of your placed art should be in either TIFF or EPS format.** Even older imagesetters can understand these formats. And make sure they are CMYK files. JPEGs may be the standard for the Web, but they are still a gamble in the world of print. And if you have any type placed in vector images, it is best to convert the type to outlines or paths.

◆ **Know what colors you're using.** If your piece is a two-color job (typically black and a second color), make sure the second color has the same name throughout your piece. If you have some art brought in from a vector program like Adobe Illustrator, and the second color is called Red make sure that the second color, when added in your layout program is also called Red, not red or Pantone Red. Just because the color looks the same on the screen doesn't mean an output device will see it as the same color. Red and red are two different colors to the always-picky imagesetter.

If you can do these things, you should get on well with your service provider. Here is another thing you can do to put yourself in their good graces. Give them a call and ask them how they prefer your files to be set up. Then there is no confusion on how you need to create your piece. And if you want to go one step further, bring them donuts or pizza. These people are generally easily bribed, and a little food goes a long way to putting them into a good mood.

Get It All Together with Collect for Output

Getting all the pieces of your file to your printer can be an even bigger challenge than getting your files in the right format. Most layout programs do that ugly task for you. Check your layout program for the Collect for Output or Save for Service Provider command. This command takes all of the digital assets (an expression meaning your graphic files) and assembles them in one location, ready to send to your printer.

Type Control

The way you present your type affects the way you communicate. If your text cannot be read, or if it is laid out in a confusing manner, no matter how good it looks it has failed because no one can understand it. Legibility is paramount. Just because you have a collection of hundreds of fonts doesn't mean you need to use them all. Restraint is the key to making your typography work in your design.

Think of it this way, you have seen many photographs in your life and when you think of the ones that are most striking, I'd bet many of them are done in black-and-white. They could have easily been shot in color, but by limiting the spectrum of the image, the results are more dramatic. Limit the use of your fonts and you will achieve a clean look that effectively conveys your message and doesn't drive your audience to distraction.

Word processors are excellent tools for getting your text into shape so it reads well, but layout programs can make your text aesthetically pleasing and make it more readable. The concern you want to deal with when you are working with type is how the characters look together. Do they need more space between them? Or do they need to be placed further apart?

So for starters, let's explore two basic terms in typography: leading and kerning. Leading is the space between lines of text. It gets its name from the thin strips of metal printers used put in between lines of type.

A good rule of thumb is to set your leading to be at about 120 percent of point size. That is, if you have 10-point type, the best setting for leading is 12 points (shown in Figure 8-14). However, if you have a particularly long line of type, you might want to open up the leading a little to make it easier for your eye to move to the next line.

Kerning is the adjustment of space between characters. Sometimes the default spacing in your layout programs can leave gaps. You can adjust the kerning between letters to give your text a more balanced look (Figure 8-15). When you decrease the space between two letters that is known as negative kerning. Some character pairs that need more attention as far as kerning matters to are Wa, Ta, and Ye.

Often confused with, but related to kerning, is tracking. Kerning is how two characters are spaced. Tracking is the adjustment of space between characters over blocks of text. Tracking adjusts how open or how dense your text looks. Apply too much negative tracking and your text will look cramped. Apply too much positive tracking and your text will look scattered and unconnected.

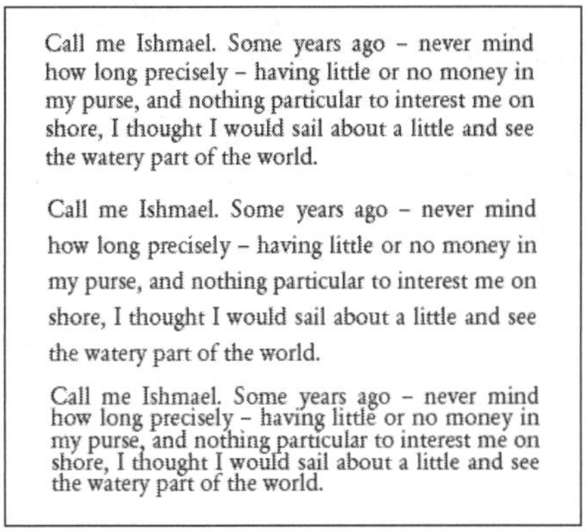

> Call me Ishmael. Some years ago – never mind how long precisely – having little or no money in my purse, and nothing particular to interest me on shore, I thought I would sail about a little and see the watery part of the world.
>
> Call me Ishmael. Some years ago – never mind how long precisely – having little or no money in my purse, and nothing particular to interest me on shore, I thought I would sail about a little and see the watery part of the world.
>
> Call me Ishmael. Some years ago – never mind how long precisely – having little or no money in my purse, and nothing particular to interest me on shore, I thought I would sail about a little and see the watery part of the world.

Figure 8-14: The top paragraph is set using the 120 percent setting formula for leading. The paragraph immediately below is easy to read, but it doesn't look very balanced. The bottom paragraph is too close together, with the text's ascenders and descenders violating each other's space.

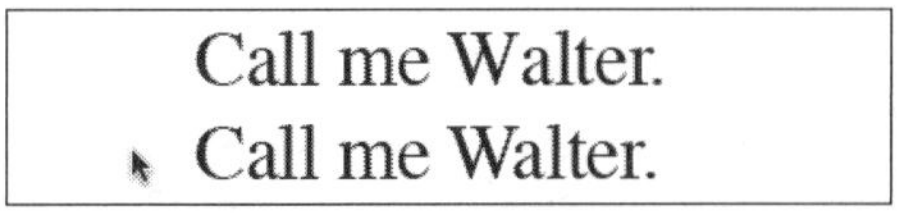

> Call me Walter.
> Call me Walter.

Figure 8-15: By bringing the *W* and *a* closer together, the text in our butchered opening sentence of *Moby Dick* is much smoother.

Bending the Rules of Typography

Secret

There are no rules in the world of typography that cannot be broken (or at least bent). One rule that is near and dear to the hearts of many is that using all uppercase letters is to be avoided because words in all caps are hard to read. There may be some truth to this but sometimes all-caps simply look better.

Go to a bookshelf or magazine rack and start looking at covers. All-caps are used quite often to great effect. Now imagine these same magazine and book covers if they used lowercase letters. For example, I own a small book on typography that warns of the evils of using all uppercase letters. I took a moment to look at the cover, and the title and author information was set in, you guessed it, all capital letters. In short, you have to weigh design against readability, but sometimes you can have both.

The Origins of Uppercase and Lowercase

Here's an interesting little factoid that you might not know. The terms *uppercase* and *lowercase* have their roots in the old publishing days where lead type was kept in buckets or bins and manually placed on a press by a pressman.

To make it easier for the pressman, the most commonly used letters were stored on the lower case, so that the pressman could get at those letters faster. The letters used less often, only at the beginning of sentences and for proper nouns, were kept on the upper case.

And even though we haven't done that in print shops for many years now, the terms stuck.

QuarkXpress versus InDesign

The two heavy hitters in the desktop publishing world are QuarkXpress and Adobe InDesign. Quark has been around for while and is currently the industry standard. InDesign is a relative newcomer and was marketed originally as a "Quark Killer." While that hasn't proved to be the case, Adobe's desktop publishing program is making inroads in areas that traditionally belong to Quark.

Both have a wide range of tools available for type freaks to sink their teeth into. Both can be set up to automatically create ligatures. Each can easily adjust leading and kerning. Both programs are rich and full featured, but when it comes to working with type, InDesign (shown in Figure 8-16) is the hands-down winner.

InDesign offers automatic typographic adjustment by paragraph. Quark is limited to line-by-line adjustment. InDesign offers stroke and fill for text. Quark does not. InDesign offers Optical Margin Alignment, which allows hanging punctuation and letters such as T and W to hang outside the column (shown in Figure 8-17).

In the end there are just too many things that InDesign can do that Quark can't. You can still go in and tweak your text in QuarkXpress until you get the look you want, but InDesign does it so easily and on its own. For type, InDesign is king.

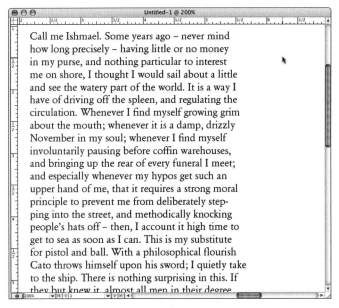

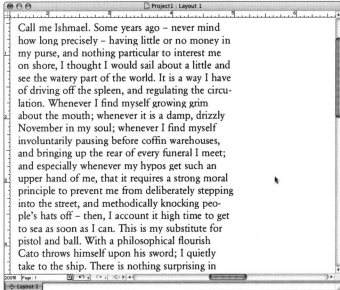

Figure 8-16: InDesign (top) puts together sweet-looking text and you don't have to lift a finger. Quark documents (bottom) take a little more work.

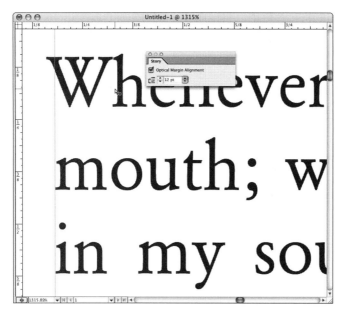

Figure 8-17: You can turn on Optical Margin Alignment in the Story palette. Did I also mention that InDesign offers magnification up to 4000 percent but Quark only goes to 800 percent?

Summary

If your gig is words, there are plenty of tools you can use on your Mac to get any job you want done. If it is word processing you want, Microsoft Word holds a virtual stranglehold on the market. (How un-Mac-like of me, eh?) But Mariner Write offers a robust competing product that costs a fraction of what the folks from Redmond have to offer.

And you learned that layout programs pick up where word processors leave off offering powerful tools to make type look good and easier to read. After some stutter-steps, those in the graphics game can confidently move out of OS 9.x (now that Quark has a native Mac OS X application) and to Panther knowing that the tools they need are there, and more powerful than ever.

In the next chapter, you'll learn some more about nontext elements, graphically speaking.

Getting Graphic with Your Mac

Chapter
9

◆ ◆

Secrets in This Chapter

◆ ◆

Graphics and Macs go together so well you'd think Frank Sinatra would have sung a song about the pair instead of "Love and Marriage." The Chairman of the Board had long since recorded that song about marital bliss when Macintosh was introduced to the world in 1984, but it is still only natural that creative professionals would gravitate toward the fledgling platform. The GUI interface offered a representation (albeit simple by today's standards) of what was familiar to them in the real world of commercial art. And in those early days, there was a cornucopia of programs to choose from, each vying for their place in the wide-open Mac graphics market.

In the summer of 1985, Aldus PageMaker was released. PageMaker was a page layout program with which you could set type and import graphics; and what you saw on the screen was indicative of what would you would see on the printed page. Soon after, software companies offered other programs to enhance the graphics power of the Mac. Adobe released Illustrator, which found immediate success. QuarkXpress was released in 1987 and quickly became the industry standard layout program. Aldus Freehand was released in 1988 as a competitor to Illustrator. The rivalry continues today with Freehand now traveling under the Macromedia banner.

In 1990, a little program called BarneyScan XP was retooled and released by Adobe as Photoshop 1 (shown in Figure 9-1 on the left). So a few short years after the introduction of the Mac, all the major players in graphic software were already on the scene. This scene continues to be robust, with new programs with ever-growing capabilities being offered in the newest version of Photoshop CS (shown in Figure 9-1 on the right). In fact, things happen so fast in the graphics arena that it is difficult for creative professionals to keep up with the expanding technology. This phenomenon has spawned the ever-lucrative third-party software tips book boom. God bless endless innovation.

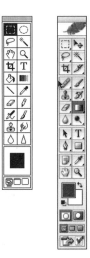

Figure 9-1: The toolboxes for Photoshop 1.07 (left) and Photoshop CS (right). As you can see most of the original tools remain, but there are several changes including, toward the bottom, the addition of a foreground and background color, that was adopted in version number 2 of Photoshop.

With Panther, Apple's devotion to supporting the graphic community continues. Although the switch to OS X was a rocky one at first for creative departments, almost every graphics program has made the leap to OS X and now graphics professionals are reaping the benefits of increased speed, stability, and capabilities of their new OS X–compatible software suites.

Books the size of this one have been written on graphics, so what we'll try to do here is expose you to the basics. I'll also spend a little extra time on Photoshop, the master of all graphics programs.

The Nuts and Bolts of Drawing on a Mac

To get started with creating graphics on a Mac, all you need is a program that you can draw with. There are dozens to choose from, but what they have in common (or not in common in the case of proprietary formats) are their output file formats.

Looking at Graphic File Formats

Selecting the right file format is the best way to make sure your audience can see your graphic as you intend it to be seen. Here are a list of common file formats and their features:

- **JPEG files:** The JPEG (Joint Photographic Expert Group) format is the king of file formats on the Internet. If you are looking at an image on the Web, an overwhelming majority of these images will be in JPEG format. JPEGS are what is called a lossy format, which means there is information that is discarded in the compression process (when the file is saved in the chosen file format), which makes for outrageous reductions in file size.

Don't Re-Save JPEGs

JPEG files can look lossless (having the same visual quality as the original) on the first compression from the original file, but if you apply additional JPEG compression to a file, your image will be chock full of artifacts, giving your picture that chunky look. JPEGs are great for display on the Web or for compression for delivery over the Web, but to tack on an additional round of JPEG compression, which strips additional information from the image, is asking for a screen full of ugly.

For best results with your images, work on them in some lossless format, and then save them out to JPEG as the last step before your online or multimedia use.

- **GIF files:** GIF (Graphics Interchange Format, pronounced with a hard G and not a J sound) files are huge (as in popular) on the Web, and perhaps no place else. GIF files can contain a maximum of 256 colors, which makes it not so good for photographic files but perfect for logos or continuous-color backgrounds. These files, especially when the colors are limited to less than 256 colors, are very small and download very quickly. GIF files are not necessarily lossless but they do have the added capability of being animated if properly prepared.
- **PNG files:** PNG (Portable Network Graphics, pronounced "ping") files were supposed to be the next big thing for Web graphics but have yet to live up to the hype. PNG files do not lose quality when compressed and are not limited to 256 colors. You can't, however, animate a PNG and they don't compress much as a JPEG can. This could explain why PNG are not more widely used.

♦ **EPS files:** EPS files are a mainstay of print graphics. EPS (Encapsulated PostScript) files can accommodate both pixel and vector information. In fact, an EPS can contain anything a Postscript file can hold. You can save a preview of an EPS file that displays in other layout and graphics programs, such as QuarkXpress or Adobe Illustrator, so you can place and preview them easier in those kinds of applications. EPS files can be raster, vector, or both (which we'll talk about later in this chapter).

♦ **TIFF files:** The TIFF (Tagged Image File Format) file format is one of the oldest and most wildly accepted formats. It travels easily from Mac to PC platforms and can contain a large amount of information. TIFFs are bitmaps, meaning each piece of information (called a pixel, a contraction of picture sample) has a value and that value is stored in the file.

Understanding LZW Compression

TIFF and GIF Files can be compressed using LZW (Lempel-Ziv-Welch are the names of the folks who developed this method of compression) compression. This is a lossless compression logarithm, so none of your image is destroyed in the process. LZW compression works best with bitmap or black-and-white images, but offers almost 50 percent compression on 24-bit RGB images, as well. While this mode of compression does save disk space, some programs require plug-ins to properly print these files.

♦ **PDF files:** The Portable Document Format was initially created by Adobe as a step toward the paperless office. Now it has become a universal medium of exchange for text and graphic files. These files travel from Mac to Windows to Unix/Linux worlds with few problems. PDFs are extremely versatile as well. You can set compression levels anywhere from high resolution for printing to low resolution screen viewing. Fonts can be embedded in PDFs and vector and raster (pixel) information can be stored. PDFs can be single images or multi-page documents. For print designers, there is a subset of PDF called PDF-x1 that is geared toward print production.

♦ **PICT files:** (abbreviated for Picture): This is the file format, developed by Apple for use in the MacDraw program that pre–OS X users are familiar with. Screenshots in pre–OS X were in this format, however in OS X they are now PDFs, so the PICT format will most likely go the way of the dinosaur.

Optimizing Your Graphics from Left to Right

Now that we have had a chance to talk about file formats and their advantages, there are also ways to make your images so that they take better advantage of the way they are compressed. Most compression techniques work from left to right along a row of pixels, that is, compression encoding is performed left to right, the same way you are reading this page. So, if you have several pixels that have the same value along the horizontal axis of your image, your compression algorithm will be more efficient. For example, open an image-editing program and create two square images of equal size, one with a gradient that is vertical, and another that is horizontal. Save each of the images using the same degree of compression. Now check the image file sizes. You will find the image with the gradient that changes values from top to bottom is smaller than the picture where the values are constantly changing along the horizontal axis.

Drawing is using Vectors

Computer graphics programs offer a variety of ways to create art. Photoshop offers you the godlike command of the pixel (or raster) universe, but its vector (lines and angles) programs like Adobe Illustrator and Macromedia Freehand that make you master of the vector universe. And vector art is where the analogy between drawing in the computer world and drawing in the real world comes the closest. There are a few differences in that analogy. For instance, everyone has grabbed a pen, but few people have applied a overlay filter to a pencil sketch. But before we get into the basics of drawing, let's look at the difference between vector and raster art.

Pixels or Lines and Angles: Vector vs. Raster

Essentially, raster images store information that describes a square of color in a file. The square is called a pixel and can be any physical size. If you have an image that is 72 dpi, the size of that square is $\frac{1}{72}$ of an inch by $\frac{1}{72}$ of an inch. If your image is 300 dpi, that square is $\frac{1}{300}$ of an inch by $\frac{1}{300}$ of an inch. Although the pixel in the 300-dpi image is much smaller (physically) than the one in the 72-dpi file, it takes the same amount of information to describe it. With this information, you can determine that a 300-dpi image, which would be suitable for high output printing, would take much more disk space, and require much more RAM to edit in an image manipulation program, than 72-dpi image, which would be suitable for display on a Web page.

Vector images are resolution-independent. The same file that you might use for a 2-inch logo on a letterhead would be the same size as the file you'd use for display on a billboard. The information is essentially a complicated math formula. The vector information for a circle would be much smaller than the same information for a raster circle. As the circle increases in size, the vector file size would remain the same, but the raster file would increase for every pixel added.

Secret

Vector Files Are Not Always Smaller

Vector art gets kudos for small files, but vector files are not always smaller. In fact, the example in Figure 9-2, the saved vector EPS file of the ½-inch gray circle is nearly six times as large as the ½-inch gray circle saved as an RGB tiff at 72 dpi. But when you enlarge the circle to 10 inches across, the TIFF file has grown three times as large as the vector file, which has remained the same size.

continues

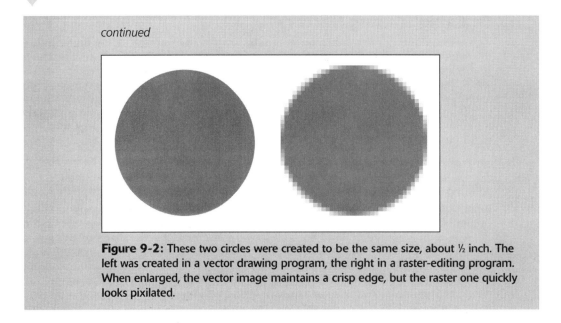

Figure 9-2: These two circles were created to be the same size, about ½ inch. The left was created in a vector drawing program, the right in a raster-editing program. When enlarged, the vector image maintains a crisp edge, but the raster one quickly looks pixilated.

Meanwhile, Back at the Vector Ranch. . . .

Now we know the ins and outs of vector and raster images, we can cover the basics. One tool in particular is nearly universal to drawing programs and is the key to becoming a vector-drawing ace.

The Pen Tool

Vector programs all offer various tools for image manipulation, but the tool that is the workhorse among them all is the pen tool. I am not oversimplifying when I say that mastery of the pen tool is key to mastering vector-drawing programs (shown in Figure 9-3).

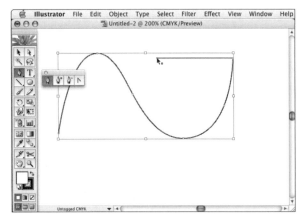

Figure 9-3: You can use the pen tool to draw straight lines or elegant curves. You can control how the curves behave by manipulating the handles or control points along the curve.

Vector control is based on the Bezier curve. A Bezier curve is defined by four points: the two end points of a line, and two control points.

note   You can thank the French for this technology behind the pen tool, in particular a man named Pierre Bezier, who developed the curve concept and the formula (called, surprisingly enough, the Bezier curve) for use in computer-assisted design programs.

But enough about math, let's see how they work in vector drawing programs.

In Adobe Illustrator CS, you can find the pen tool toward the top of the tool box. This tool has two additional features. The Add Anchor Point tool enables you to add additional anchor points to a path or remove an anchor point. (An anchor point, as opposed to a regular point, has control points so you can adjust the curve.) The Convert Anchor Point tool takes an anchor point and makes it a regular point. If you hold down the Option key while you use the Convert Anchor Point tool, you can change a regular point back to an anchor point. Now let's do some drawing. Please follow along:

1. First click on the Pen Tool. You don't need to have Illustrator to practice your pen skills. The pen tool is available in nearly every vector-based program, with a few variations, and is also available in Photoshop and other image-editing programs as well. But the example you have here is done in Adobe Illustrator CS.

2. Select a point where you want to start.

3. Release the mouse button, and move your pen tool to the next point. About one-third of the way into the curve you are trying to create, click and hold, and then drag the tool along the curve you are trying to create. Your pen tool turns into an arrow and the point sprouts two handles, which are your control points (shown in Figure 9-4).

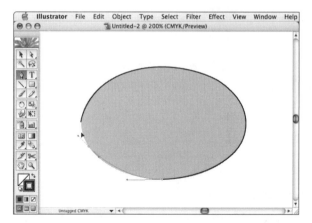

Figure 9-4: The best way to get experienced at the pen tool is practice on shapes drawn with another tool. I created an oval and traced it with the pen tool. If you are feeling wild, you can combine several shapes to hone your pen tools.

4. After you feel the curve is right, release the mouse and move on to the next point, and repeat. To close the path, move the pen tool over the starting point.

5. When you are directly over the point, a small circle appears at the lower-right of your pen tool. Click to close the path.

Once you have a grasp of the pen tool, the world of vector art will come easily. The learning curve for this tool is among the steepest of any individual tool; so don't get frustrated too quickly. Pretty soon you will be drawing intricate arabesques that will make grandma's doilies look like chicken scratches.

The Current State of Vector Editing Programs

The pen tool is the basis for all drawing programs. If not for the pen tool, we'd be combining ovals and squares, and clipping arcs out of circles to make our drawings. (Although that method can come in handy too.) But where does that leave the state of vector editing today?

Well, previously it was thought that vector and 3D go together like oil and water. Adobe Illustrator CS, however, combines these capabilities. For example, some wonderful 3D effects allow you to simulate lighting effects, a task that would take hours without the right tool. The tool, crazily enough, is called the 3D tool (shown in Figure 9-5) and it lives in the Effect menu in Illustrator CS.

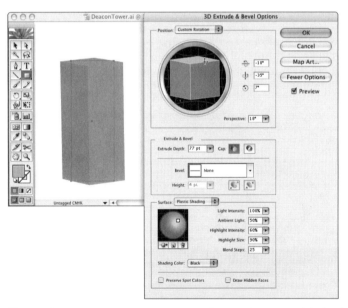

Figure 9-5: The 3D Extrude and Bevel Options feature all kinds of tools to change the look of your 3D object. This shape started as a simple rectangle. When you check on the preview you can see exactly what each tool does to your shape. For example the Extrude and Bevel section controls how deep your object becomes and how the edges are treated. This window will lead to hours of experimenting as you play with Illustrator's new 3D capabilities.

Being able to make 3D objects is great, but you are also able to place art on each side of your creation. Just create some art and drag it to your Symbols palette. (You can open it by selecting Symbols in the Window menu in Illustrator CS.) Voila, you just created a new symbol.

Now you just can't click on the 3D tool and edit what you have already done if you have left the 3D Extrude and Bevel window. To get back to editing your original object, go to your Appearance palette, accessibly under the Window menu, and double-click to open the 3D Extrude and Bevel dialog box. If you hit Preview, you see that Illustrator now lets you edit right where you left off.

To place some map art on your 3D creation, click the Map Art button to open the Map Art dialog box (shown in Figure 9-6). Now, if you click on the inverted triangle on the right side of the symbol box, you can browse through your symbols and select whatever art you want to place on your creation. Illustrator gives you and opportunity to select something new for each side, and you're able to change the size or even rotate the art to your heart's content.

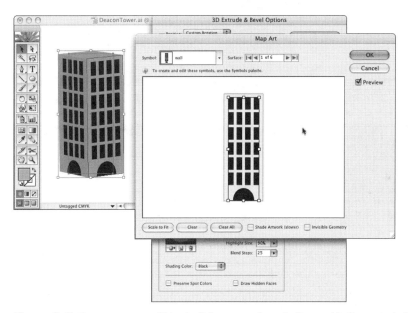

Figure 9-6: Pretty soon you'll be building complete skylines with Illustrator's 3D tool.

Now Illustrator's 3D tools are not limited to just squares or circles. With a little bit of experimenting you will find that almost any shape is possible out of this feature (shown in Figure 9-7). In fact, I predict you will see tons of illustrations in magazines, newspapers and Web pages that take advantage of this new tool, and in a couple years, 3D vector illustrations will be this year's gradient. Or is it last year's gradient? (Or this year's transparency. Or is transparency this year's gradient. I can't keep track of all these trendy effects.)

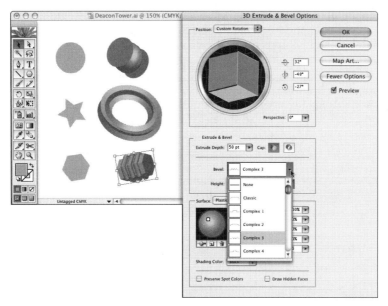

Figure 9-7: Here is an example of what you can do very quickly with a few simple shapes in just a couple minutes. You can now populate your drawings with all sorts of strange and odd widgets, just by clicking a few buttons. To give your objects some extra texture, you can select one of the many bevel styles available, and you can adjust how deeply the bevel cuts by changing the height.

A Look at Photoshop, Part One, Quick and Dirty

If there is one software program that can claim the title The Industry Standard and make it stick, it is Adobe Photoshop. No other program in the graphics field has been so dominant and consistently ahead of the competition as this image-editing program.

Throughout its development, it's added features that make it friendlier to use and a more powerful graphics editor. If you are considering a career in graphics, Photoshop is a program that can make or break you.

And as a tool to embarrass or humiliate your friends — as seen on the Internet by the plethora of people with their faces imposed on bodies of people in inappropriate situations attests — there are few that compare to Photoshop.

Getting Started

There is no way anyone can wrap arms around Photoshop in just a few pages of instruction. This program has probably spawned more forest-leveling, telephone-book thick, skull-crushing tomes than any other. Photoshop possesses a seemingly unending feature list that you could study for years and never achieve a comprehensive grasp. But once you get started learning this powerful program, you will want more.

If you don't have a copy of Photoshop, you can download a tryout version of Photoshop's less-featured, but very cool sibling program Photoshop Elements 2.0 at Adobe's Web site, www.adobe.com. Most of the material we go over in the following pages is available in that program as well, and it costs about $500 less that the full version of Photoshop. And yes, you can embarrass your friends and enemies alike with Photoshop Elements as well.

Time to Look Around

For those familiar with Adobe products, the layout of Photoshop is familiar and welcoming (shown in Figure 9-8).

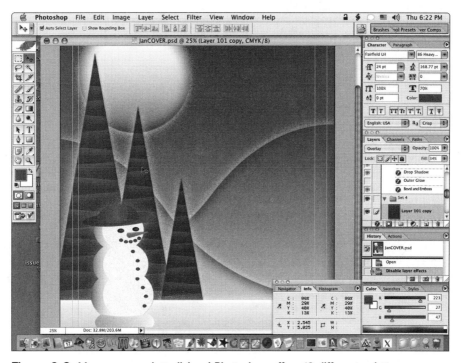

Figure 9-8: Mmmm . . . palette-licious! Photoshop offers 19 different palettes so you can easily access your tools. If you plan on keeping all these tools open, you might want to get a second monitor just for your palettes.

Looking at the Tools More Closely

So now enough of the tour, let's get to a quick-and-dirty look at some of the main tools you will be using, and how they can be efficiently used.

Marquee Tool

This tool is your basic selection tool (shown in Figure 9-9). It offers four different modes of selection (click on the marquee tool and hold to get the Options palette), Rectangular, Elliptical, Single Row, and Single column.

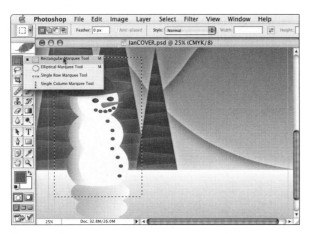

Figure 9-9: Use the Marquee tool to get that marching-ants effect around the area you want to select. If you hold down Shift, it constrains your selection to a circle or square, whichever tool you have selected.

Select the marquee tool and drag it over a selection on your open file. That area is now an active area, limiting whatever effect you decide to implement, be it a filter, adjust saturation, or just fill. This is true with all the selection tools. Wherever you place the tool will be the start of your selection. If you hold down the Option key, you can drag the marquee from the center of the area you want to select.

Secret

Adding and Removing Multiple Selections with the Marquee Tool

Sometimes you want to select an area that goes outside an area of your image. Just select the area that you don't want selected and then, select Inverse from the Select menu (or hit ⌘-Shift-I). Now the area outside the area you first selected is your selection. To add areas to your selection, just hold the Shift key while using the marquee tool. To remove areas, hold down Option while using the tool.

The Move Tool

The Move tool moves things (how appropriate) and more (shown in Figure 9-10). If you drag a selection, it moves the selection leaving the previously selected area blank. If you hold the Shift key, you constrain the movement of your selection along a 45-degree axis. If you hold down the Option key, you drag a copy of the selection to anywhere you want on that layer.

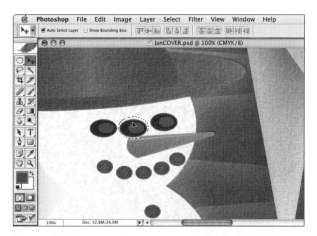

Figure 9-10: It doesn't take long to discover Photoshop's potential to create embarrassing images. Here we give ol' Frosty an extra eye.

A Better Way to Move Through and/or To Select Layers

Secret

To turn your move tool into a mean lean layer-navigating machine, just click in the Auto Select Layer check box in the Move Tool Options bar. Then whatever you click on becomes the active layer. No more negotiating through the Layer palette the old-fashioned way.

The Lasso Tool

This tool is the freehand selection tool, although I like the name lasso tool much better. This tool is perfect for selecting areas that don't have perfectly square or circular areas, which is pretty much most every situation. The handiest of the lasso tools is the polygonal lasso tool (shown in Figure 9-11). With this tool, you draw a series of straight lines to make your selection. It offers more control than the regular lasso tool, and you can use it while you are using the lasso tool just by holding down the option key.

Another cool feature of the lasso tool is the magnetic lasso tool. You can use this tool to select along areas where there are different colors; the magnetic lasso tool follows the line where there is a distinction between colors (shown in Figure 9-12). This is very handy for making paths that have to follow areas of crisp color changes.

Figure 9-11: The polygonal lasso tool lets you to make selections with a series of straight lines.

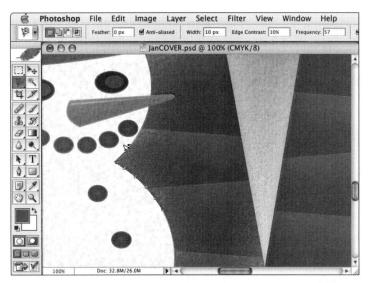

Figure 9-12: You can adjust the tolerance of the magnetic lasso tool by adjusting the width, edge contrast, and frequency settings in the Lasso Tool Options.

Secret

Get Contextual with Photoshop

You can increase the power of your selection tools (all your selection tools, not just the lasso tool) by using contextual menus. Once you make your selection, hold down the Control key and click; the contextual menu pops up (shown in Figure 9-13). Here you get a shortcut to many of the common tasks you would do following making a selection such as filling it with a solid color, putting a stroke around the selection, or heading straight to the transform contextual options.

Figure 9-13: Changing a selection into a work path (used for a variety of editing and image manipulations) is a breeze with the contextual menu.

This menu opportunity takes on even more convenience when you have a two-button mouse. Simply right-click and the contextual menu pops up.

The Magic Wand Tool

The magic wand tool is an advanced selection tool, but once mastered, it will save you oodles of time by having your image define the selection area (shown in Figure 9-14). Soon, you will be making more precise selections in less time than with any of the other selection tools in the toolbar.

The magic wand tool makes its selection based on the color of the pixel below the tool, and then depending on how the tolerance is set, it selects other pixels near it based on how close they are to the original selection color. If you want to select a color range throughout the whole image, make sure the Contiguous box is unchecked in the options bar.

Secret

Use a Channel to Make a Selection or Mask

Sometimes a color area you want to select is not clearly defined in your image, or the magic wand tool simply has trouble clearly distinguishing the area you want selected. You might find it is easier to get your target area by using one channel in your image. Just select Channels in the Window menu. In the Channels palette, switch through the channels, and pick the one with the most contrast in the area you want to select, and make your selection there. Then return to your main image and make your edits there.

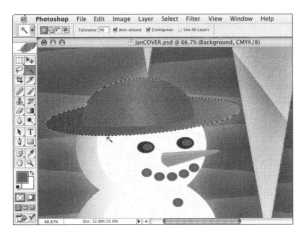

Figure 9-14: To select an area of color, place the magic wand tool over the area you wish to select. If the range of color the magic wand is selecting is too narrow, you can increase the number in the Tolerance field in the options bar above the image.

The Crop Tool

The crop tool is usually one of the last tools you apply to an image before you save the final version. Use this tool to remove the excess areas of the image to properly frame the focus of the picture. To crop an image, drag the crop tool across the area of the image you want to save (shown in Figure 9-15). Hit Return and the unwanted portion of the image is removed.

Figure 9-15: You can use the crop tool to change the aspect of an image from vertical to horizontal. If you want to have the cropped area darkened to make it easier to visualize the results of your crop, just check the Shield box in your options bar and select the color and opacity you wish the shield to have.

Change Your Perspective While You Crop

The crop tool can be so, well, square. But if you want to vary the area you crop, check the perspective box in the options bar (located just under the menus at the top of the screen in Photoshop CS) of the crop tool and drag the corners wherever you want. When you hit return to apply the crop, the area you selected reshapes to fill a rectangular area.

This is great for doing funhouse distortions on photos of people, or if you want to alter the perspective of a photo of a building. By changing the perspective this way, you can make it look as if you took a photo of a building from an impossible angle, when you were really just standing across the street.

The Brush Tool

Photoshop CS has beefed up an already beefy brush tool, with that addition of new brushes and an improved Brushes palette (shown in Figure 9-16). The brush tool acts like its name, but is useful for so many other things. In fact as you get further along in Photoshop, you will find you use this tool very little to brush on color in the traditional sense.

Figure 9-16: The brush tool is what I like to call a "bottomless feature" of Photoshop. It is so completely customizable and editable that you could never see every combination of brush available. If the collection that ships with Photoshop isn't enough you can search the Web for brush collections that other enthusiasts have posted, or you can create your own.

The brush tool is useful for making selections (especially in layer masks, but more about this later). You can use the brushes to apply custom textures and to select feathered areas for adjustment layers and masks. In fact, almost anything you can do with the standard selections tools you can do with brushes and masks. And better yet, the changes you make are usually editable.

Also, you can use it to paint. The color of the brush is whatever your foreground color is. You can determine your foreground color by looking at the bottom of toolbox. The full square displays the foreground color, the square that is overlapped by the foreground color is, you guessed it, the background color. To change colors, you can double-click on the foreground color box and the Color Picker box appears (shown in Figure 9-17). Here you can visually select the color you want, or, if you have a numeric value for your color, you can enter those numbers. If you don't have a numeric value, you can get those numbers from the Digital Color Meter utility, covered in more depth in Chapter 5.

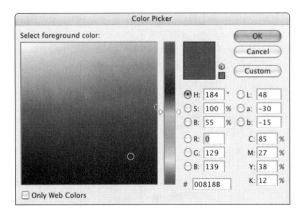

Figure 9-17: The Color Picker lets you select any color available in a variety of color spaces. If you need a specific color, such as a Pantone color, click the Custom button and Photoshop takes you to a list of custom color libraries where you can find the exact color you need.

Also, you can select colors from your Swatches palette (in the Window menu). Just click on the color you want, and your foreground color takes on the new hue.

tip

If, for some goofy reason, you actually want to paint with the brush tool, there is a collection of natural media brushes that come with Photoshop. One of the things you can do to make your digital painting look more natural is play with the Mode, Opacity, and Flow settings in the brushes option bar. That way when you are using even just one color setting, your strokes interact with each other, and the colors beneath. Each stroke adds additional "pigment" rather than just expanding the area of your set color.

And (Super Bonus Tip) when you are done, to make your digital work look more lifelike, create a new layer over your work and fill it with a 50 percent gray fill (Edit⇨Fill⇨contents use 50% Gray). Then, apply a canvas Texture (Filter⇨Texture⇨Select Texturizer⇨Canvas). Once you have done that, change the blending mode of the layer to Overlay. (Select the layer in the Layer palette and change the blending mode toward the top of the Layers palette from Normal to Overlay.) Then, adjust the opacity to tweak the amount of canvas texture you want on your masterpiece.

The Text Tool

The text tool in Photoshop is a feature that continues to improve with each update. Phototshop CS is no exception with the long awaited text-on-a-path feature and expanded warp features.

You can access the type tool in Photoshop's toolbar (shown in Figure 9-18). The text tool contains four different options, the horizontal type tool, the vertical type tool, the horizontal type mask tool, and the vertical type mask tool. The mask tools seem like a nice idea, but they are just selection tools, and you can easily use the regular type tool and make selections of the live type later, which, if you change your mind, you can change easily, because the type is still editable.

Figure 9-18: They type tool in Photoshop is similar to other Adobe products. Here some type with a light drop shadow is placed over the winter image.

To place type on an image, just select the type tool, place it on the image where you want to begin and click. Photoshop creates a new layer for your type. Then type away. You can use the Character palette to tweak your text to your heart's content. And when you are done you can check your spelling by selecting Check Spelling in the Edit menu.

Secret

Saving Vector Info within Raster Files

Now here's a Photoshop Secret that should not be a Secret; this feature was available in Photoshop 6, but many professional graphic designers are still, two versions later, failing to take advantage of this amazing trick.

If you have type or any other vector information in your image, you can keep that vector information in your file if you save it as a Photoshop EPS. When you save as a Photoshop EPS, the EPS Options window (shown in Figure 9-19) presents several options, including Include Vector Data. Check this box and hit OK. Now your type will be super crisp when it is printed, even if it is very small — effects and all. No more jagged type, no more importing your image into another program to get vector type.

continues

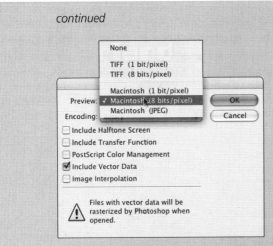

continued

Figure 9-19: The Save EPS dialog offers many options to customize your EPS, but you should check with your service provider or printer before you click any of these features. Also, beware which method of preview you use. The Macintosh JPEG option throws some RIPs (Raster Image Processors) into a tailspin.

But beware, the file will be rasterized when you open it again, and your vector information will be lost.

The Eyedropper Tool

This tool is invaluable. Think of it more as a color sampler tool. You can use it on any point on your image and get the exact color of the pixel beneath. If you wanted a sample of the average value below your dropper, you can expand the selection area to 3 x 3 or 5 x 5 pixels in the eyedropper options bar (shown in Figure 9-20). These options, including Copy Color as HTML are available in the contextual menu, which you can access by hitting the Control key while you click. The color you click on becomes the foreground color, and you can use any of your other drawing tools to apply the color on another part of your image.

note

How is the eyedropper tool an important tool for drawing on the Mac? Well, if you want to paint from a photo and you don't want to waste all that time guessing colors, it is perfect. A quick way to paint using colors faithful to your digital photo is to place your image on a layer and lock it, and then place a new layer on top of it. Use your eyedropper tool to sample the color and then switch to the brush tool and apply the color right above the sample using one of the natural media brushes.

One technique that can be very successful is to use one layer to apply broad brush strokes, hide that layer and create a new layer, and apply narrower strokes on that layer. Work your way up; layer after layer until you have one filled with the details. Turn them on and admire the first in a long line of masterpieces. You can experiment on the layers; blend modes, add filters and lighting effects, and adjust hues until you are thrilled with your creation. We'll get into layers a little later in this chapter.

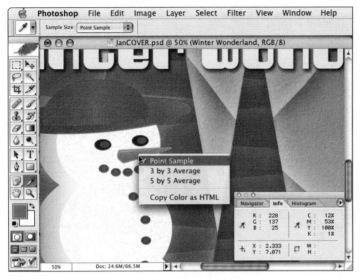

Figure 9-20: The contextual menu or the eyedropper tool allows you to copy a color as HTML hexcode, ready to paste into your HTML editor, a real timesaver for Web designers.

Photoshop Tutorial, Part Two, Fast and Filthy

Drawing with Photoshop can be fun, but the program offers many other ways you can alter images that are equally artistic, and often have amazing results. Here are a few Photoshop features that will make your images more compelling and interesting.

Filters

The first place anyone who wants to mess with their images should head to is the Filters menu. In here is a pile of Adobe-provided filters that you can use to enhance your images.

Photoshop CS has a new interface for filters called the Filter Gallery. No longer do you have to bounce up and down the menu selections to try different filter settings. Instead, Photoshop's Filter Gallery shows a preview of the effect and small images that show what each of the effects will do to the image (shown in Figure 9-21).

However not all the filters are available through the gallery; some, including one of my all time favorites the Twirl Filter (shown in Figure 9-22), have to be accessed individually.

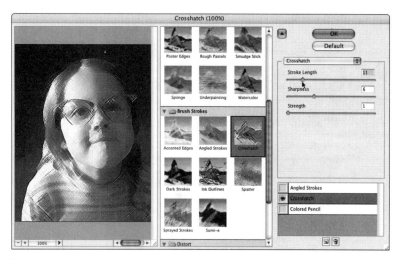

Figure 9-21: The Filter Gallery allows you to access all the art filters from one window, rather than meandering from the menu. A new feature also allows you to apply more than one filter at once and preview the effect before you apply the filter. Above we give a crosshatch effect to a photo to give it a penciled look.

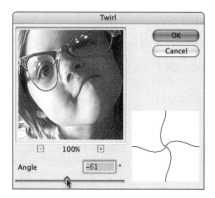

Figure 9-22: The Distortion section of the Filter menu holds several old favorites including the Twirl filter, which can turn a lovely young girl playing dress-up into a twisted ol' hag in just a few clicks of the mouse.

We Interrupt This Chapter . . .

Some of us are never satisfied. The way that the Filter Gallery works is one of those things that that brings that part of my personality out.

Benjamin: This is the kind of thing that is irritating about new features in programs — they only half work, or they only access a few of the items available. With Photoshop CS, it is the Filter Gallery, which accesses only some of the filters available. And there seems to be no rhyme or reason to what is included and what isn't. For example, none of the blur filters are available, but all of the artistic filters are. Then to muck things up further, three of the distort filters are accessible through the filter gallery and the remainder must be applied individually. The Filter Gallery is a great feature, but it would be amazing if it included all the filters.

Pieter: Like the first round of applications for Mac OS X that supported some but not all of OS X's great features, Adobe and other Photoshop filter makers can hardly be expected to rewrite all their filters to support the filter gallery. Now that it is out there and gaining the acclaim that is deserves, I think that many of the folks who produce filters for Photoshop will go through the process or making their filters compliant with the Filter Gallery. However, a lot of older filters that are no longer supported will never make the jump as the company that wrote them might have gone under, the programmer that wrote them might have passed on, or maybe the person or company who wrote them just does not like the Filter Gallery.

In addition to the Filters that come with Photoshop, there are plenty of third-party developers making filters that create that just right effect you've been looking for. Some companies to check out for their filters are Alien Skin found online at `http://www.alienskin.com/` (their Eye Candy collection is amazing) and AutoFX filters found online at `http://www.autofx.com/`.

Layers

Another way to come up with very striking compositions in Photoshop is by using the Layers palette. This is where all the cool montage work is done that you see when advertising folks juxtapose images of happy, healthy people walking in the park, flowers and a bottle of weight loss medication just above a warning that "taking this medication might cause you to lose control of your bowels." Now that is a mixed message, but marketing people work with associations, and Photoshop has given them the tools to do that right on their desktop. They have also given them to you, and we can walk though a short tutorial that can show you the power of the Layers palette.

First, Get Two Images

You need a couple of images that go together. I selected a scan of a flower from my back yard, and the lovely girl whom we vandalized earlier with the twirl filter (shown in Figure 9-23). What we are going to do is superimpose the flower over the girl. It is not fancy, but it will show you how the tools work and how you can use them to make your own, compelling images.

Figure 9-23: Select the images you want to combine for a whole new message.

Next, copy the image you want to go on top (Select⇨All or just ⌘-A on your keyboard then hit ⌘-C to copy), and paste it on the other image (Edit⇨Paste or ⌘-V). Photoshop automatically pastes the image on a new layer.

Then, adjust the image to where you want it to go using the Move tool. If the top image needs to be resized, use the Free Transform tool under the Edit menu to resize your image

Masking

Once you have your image in place, you need to create a layer mask so you can expose the image underneath.

> **note** A layer mask is essentially a grayscale image that sits on another layer. When you work on a layer mask, what you select or paint in black will be hidden and what you paint in white will show, and what you paint in gray shades will show in various levels of transparency.

Select the top layer in the layers palette, then click the Add Layer Mask button at the bottom of the Layers palette (shown in Figure 9-24), or select Add Layer Mask from the Layers menu. (Select Reveal All for the purposes of this tutorial.)

Figure 9-24: When you add a layer mask, a white rectangle appears next to the thumbnail in the layer you are masking. This is your mask thumbnail.

Remember earlier when I talked about how the brush can be a selection tool? Well in this case you are going to use a brush to select the area you want to unmask, so you can see through to the layer below (shown in Figure 9-24). I like to select a large brush with a soft edge so the images appear to fade into each other (shown in Figure 9-25).

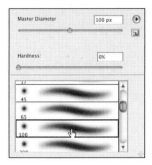

Figure 9-25: Just scroll through your brush selection to find the one that best suits your masking situation.

Now, with your brush (make sure you have the mask in the correct layer selected), start painting (make sure black is your foreground color or you won't get the results you are looking for). The image below begins to reveal itself. Keep painting until you see the amount of image you want exposed (shown in Figure 9-26). Don't worry about going too far, because you can always change the brush color to white to paint back the parts of the mask you want to keep.

Figure 9-26: Notice on the mask icon that the area where you painted is represented in black. If you want to see a full view of your mask, just Option-click on the mask thumbnail. To get back to your previous view, just Option-click the Mask thumbnail again.

Now that is all you really need to know about layer masking. From here, you can make more intricate masks with the other selection tools you have already learned. You can use the magic wand tool to create a mask from a red shirt you wore for a family photo and then use that mask to change the color to one that better goes with your eyes, as shown in Figure 9-27. You can even juxtapose a photo of your mother-in-law with kittens and daisies if you need to start making more pleasant associations in that area. You always knew your mother-in-law could use a better marketing scheme.

Figure 9-27: Here's the final product. I used the magic wand tool to add an additional white mask around the flowers à la Adobe marketing to get that clean floral look for my daughter's stationary.

What Else Is Out There? (Or, Bring Out GIMP)

Now that the Mac OS is Unix, there is a huge world of Unix apps available and included among them is the GIMP, or the GNU Image Manipulation Program.

GIMP is a full-featured image manipulation program, with capabilities very similar to Photoshop, (but think Photoshop 5). The interface (shown in Figure 9-28) is not intuitive, even for those used to other image manipulation programs. And because the Unix environment expects a two-button mouse, you end up doing a lot of double-clicking in areas you normally wouldn't. But once you get used to it, there are few things you can't do in GIMP that you can do with other raster programs. And you can't beat the price. It is a free download.

Now for the bad news. You have to get over some major techno fear to attempt the install, and even then, you are either lucky or skilled to get it to work.

The fine folks at SourceForge have made the prospect of getting GIMP easier with the Fink Project (http://sourceforge.net/projects/fink/), their initiative to make Unix programs available to Mac users to run in the X11 environment (for more about X11 see Chapter 31). But even then, you have to overcome your fear of the Terminal window, and type in pathnames to get it to work. And then, if you are used to the smooth Cadillac ride of Photoshop, the GIMP will seem like hopping behind the wheel of a less-than-mint Ford Falcon. But remember, it's free. And every time you use a free program that does something for which someone else makes you pay, you are doing your part in supporting the open source community, and keeping the big players honest, or as I like to call it, Sticking it to the Man.

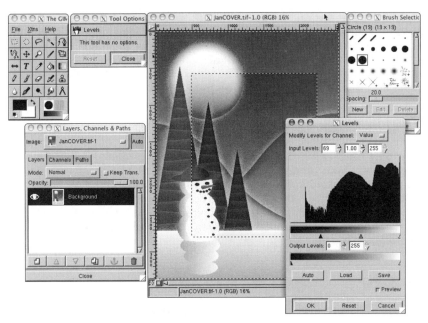

Figure 9-28: GIMP's interface might look like the cockpit of the space shuttle, but it offers many powerful features and will especially appeal to Web developers that need to do some image manipulation, but not enough to justify Photoshop's hefty ($649) price tag.

The easiest way to get the GIMP is to pay for a Mac OS X Native version is at MacGIMP. com. The going rate is about $18 for the download. You can even get it on a CD if you want to for a few dollars more. But that's not free, is it? But it is definitely worth it if you want a robust image-editing program without spending a lot of money and you don't have the time to beat your head against the wall getting the free download to work.

note   Now before you put your copy of Photoshop up for auction on eBay, there are some serious disadvantages to the GIMP. The GIMP is, well, kind of gimpy? Its biggest weakness is the program's inability to save a file in CMYK format. For print designers, that makes GIMP essentially unusable. But for the big world of Web designers, who normally dwell in an RGB world, the GIMP is a viable alternative.

Why AppleWorks Really Isn't Enough for Graphics

AppleWorks, formerly Claris Works, is a program that comes free with the purchase of a consumer Mac (iMacs, eMacs, and iBooks), or you can get it for $79 from Apple. It features two different art areas, Drawing and Painting.

The tools are unfamiliar and odd, and are not very powerful. It doesn't have much luck opening files from other formats. The word processor and spreadsheet sides of AppleWorks may act as good substitutes to other commercially available programs, but the art side of the program is only good for minor editing. It has very limited saving capabilities, so it makes it inappropriate for print production. The only reason I include it here is because if you buy an eMac, iMac, or iBook, you get it for free. And you can't really complain about that.

Summary

We have only touched on the potential for using your Mac as a mean, lean graphics machine in this chapter, and the potential is endless. The platform owes a lot to its ability to keep graphics people happy, and OS X continues allowing creative people to keep the faith in the folks from Cupertino. And with the power of Unix underneath the hood, the possibilities for the Mac to become an even more powerful graphic engine are eminently present. Graphic software companies, as well as other creative software developers are flocking to Mac. And that is always good news.

Mac OS X
Speech Secrets

Chapter

10

◆ ◆

Secrets in This Chapter

◆ ◆

Talking to your computer. Making it do what you want it to simply by speaking to it. That has been the dream of computer users since the very first episodes of the original *Star Trek* (if you'll excuse the geeky reference) when the captain and crew accessed their computer and was answered by a slightly feminine monotone voice.

And how cool is that? Forget the mouse and keyboard. Forget the contextual menus. A real power user works talks to his computer. There are just two problems. This is not the Federation and you don't have a science officer with pointed ears. In other words, the promise of the *Enterprise* computer is not available to you today.

The technology just isn't there yet. There are problems. Using the technology that is there isn't as intuitive as it should be. And there is considerable margin for misunderstanding between you and your Mac.

That being said, the technology has improved a great deal. Panther is as voice friendly as the Mac OS has ever been. And because we're both here, we might as well take a good look at how you can chat with your Mac.

In this chapter, I take you through some of the ways to talk to your Mac as well as some third-party programs that allow you to turn your Mac into your own private secretary.

Talking to Your Mac and Making It Listen

Using speech to control your Mac permits you to do such fun stuff as issue commands to control your windows, look up phone numbers, place calls, or even start instant messaging in iChat. Panther contains some robust technologies to accomplish speech, but if you want to dictate your text, you still need a third-party application.

The first part of this chapter covers Mac OS X 10.3 speech features and the second covers two applications designed for dictation; iListen by MacSpeech and ViaVoice by IBM.

Your Speech Preferences

There are two types of speech technologies bundled with Panther, and both are accessible through the Speech preference pane in System Preferences, under the System category (shown in Figure 10-1). The two types are Text-to-Speech, which you use to enable your Macintosh to speak to you, and Speech Recognition, which you use to issue verbal commands to your Mac with either your built-in or external microphone.

Figure 10-1: The System row of System Preferences contains your built-in speech controls.

As you can see, the Universal Access pane is also under the System section of System Preferences. Universal Access contains hooks to the speech panes and other kinds of access for people with special needs.

The Input Controls

If you want to issue commands to your Mac, all you need is a microphone, because all of the capabilities are built in to the system software. You can access the input volume and microphone selection in the Input tab of the Sound preference pane in System Preferences (shown in Figure 10-2).

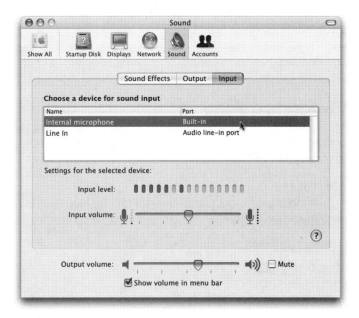

Figure 10-2: You can select a microphone, and adjust and check the input level of your microphone in Sound preferences.

If your built-in microphone isn't enough, you can use the old Apple PlainTalk microphone, included with some older Macs, or look in Apple's store (www.apple.com/store) for other compatible microphones. Prices vary from $29.95 to almost as much as you want to spend. Some, like Apple's iSight are a combined microphone and camera, and are perfect for use with iChat as discussed in Chapter 19.

---

note   Apple's iSight camera is not yet supported for speech recognition.

The ViaVoice Headphones Work Great for the OS Speech Controls

Secret

Later on in this chapter, I show you a cool program called ViaVoice from IBM. It comes with a USB headphone with a microphone. After using the headset with not only ViaVoice but also with the system software, I can tell you from experience that I get the best results speaking to my Mac with this equipment than with anything else I tried.

If you find that you're interested in buying a speech-to-text software package and a third-party microphone, you can kill two birds with one stone with this software and its packaged headphones.

The Speech Preference Pane

Let's look closely at the Speech pane to understand how to customize speech recognition just the way you want to hear it. The Speech pane has three main tabs: Speech Recognition, Default Voice, and Spoken User Interface.

Spoken User Interface

The Spoken User Interface tab is used to set preferences for talking alerts and other system communications (shown in Figure 10-3).

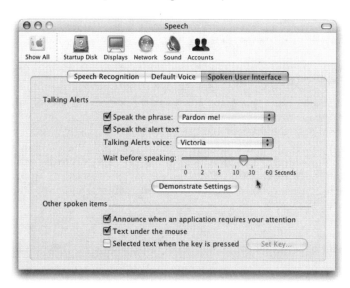

Figure 10-3: Talking Alerts and Other spoken items cover the way that your computer communicates to you with its own (user set) voice.

These are the settings you use to specify how much you want your computer to talk to you.

Unlike Jaguar (Mac OS X 10.2), Panther can speak the text in any application. This is a handy feature if you want to fold laundry or file away papers while your computer reads to you. To enable this feature you choose a keyboard key to initiate and turn off speech.

Default Voice

The second tab contains Default Voice settings. These settings allow you to choose from a variety of speaking voices that the computer uses. Panther has added some high quality voices to the mix, so that it is a more pleasant experience (shown in Figure 10-4). I highly recommend you test all the voices, as some are pretty funny — and useless to boot!

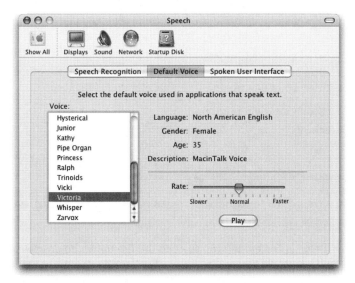

Figure 10-4: The Default Voice pane is good for a few minutes of sheer nonsensical entertainment; it's also the place to choose your computer's voice.

Secret

Vicki Has the Best Voice

The most soothing voice to listen to is Vicki. She has a more pleasant and natural sounding voice than most of the others, plus she is the computer's default voice. Victoria is also nice, but has a definite edge to her voice.

If a male voice is your choice, only Bruce and Fred are in the running; but they definitely sound mechanical.

Speech Recognition

The features of the Speech Recognition tab in the Speech preferences are almost the same in Panther as they are in Jaguar. The Speech Recognition tab also has three more options within it: On/Off, Listening, and Commands. It is important to go through each of these tabs to set up your speech recognition to function the way you want to work.

The On/Off Tab

First, let's look at all the options under the On/Off tab (shown in Figure 10-5). The main purpose of this interface is to turn the OS's Speech Recognition on and off.

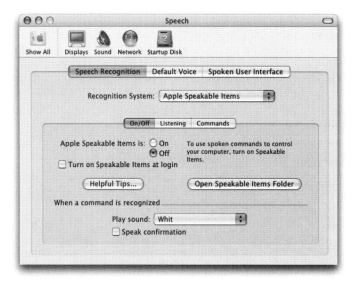

Figure 10-5: The only option under Recognition System is Apple Speakable Items, even though a scroll bar appears.

The Apple Speakable Items is Off by default, so click the On button to enable speakable items. You can also select Turn on Speakable Items at login if you want to keep the feature on when you restart. In addition, you can choose whether to play a sound or to speak a confirmation that the sound is heard, under the When a command is recognized option.

When you turn on Speakable Items, a microphone appears on your screen (shown in Figure 10-6). (When you turn it on for the first time you also get a dialog box describing helpful tips for speakable items.) You can move the microphone to any convenient location, including storing it in your Dock (just double-click it). When you click the down arrow on the bottom of the microphone, the menu items Open Speech Commands window and Speech Preferences become available.

Figure 10-6: Your microphone with the down arrow opened to show the options.

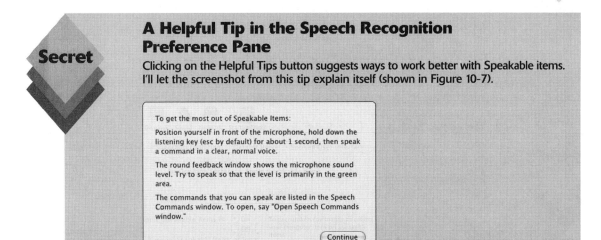

Secret

A Helpful Tip in the Speech Recognition Preference Pane

Clicking on the Helpful Tips button suggests ways to work better with Speakable items. I'll let the screenshot from this tip explain itself (shown in Figure 10-7).

To get the most out of Speakable Items:

Position yourself in front of the microphone, hold down the listening key (esc by default) for about 1 second, then speak a command in a clear, normal voice.

The round feedback window shows the microphone sound level. Try to speak so that the level is primarily in the green area.

The commands that you can speak are listed in the Speech Commands window. To open, say "Open Speech Commands window."

Continue

Figure 10-7: That there is a Helpful Tips button at all suggests that more help in future OS's may be forthcoming.

The Open Speakable Items Folder button brings up the folder. This folder contains items that can be invoked with spoken commands. There are numerous Finder scripts and a folder with application-specific scripts (shown in Figure 10-8).

Figure 10-8: Your Speakable Items folder.

You can add new items to this folder or you can create your own scripts and save them to this folder. For more information on creating AppleScripts, see Chapter 11.

tip You can download scripts to expand the capabilities of your Speakable Items folder and avoid having to reinvent the wheel. One site, Doug's AppleScripts for iTunes, includes a number of useful scripts for playing your favorite music. It can be found at www. malcolmadams.com/itunes/scripts/scripts02.php.

Secret

Turning Speech Off Completely

When you want to turn Speech off completely, open the Speech pane in System Preferences and click the Off button under the On/Off tab in Speech Recognition.

In addition, you need to go to the Universal Access pane in System Preferences and uncheck the box, Enable text-to-speech for Universal Access preferences (shown in Figure 10-9).

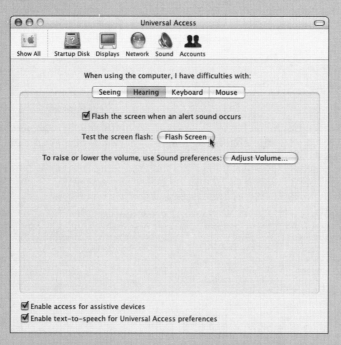

Figure 10-9: The Enable text-to-speech for Universal Access preferences check box can become checked automatically when using some speech applications.

The Listening Tab

The second speech recognition preference lies under the Listening tab (shown in Figure 10-10). In this tab, you can tell your computer to listen to you all the time or to listen only when you press a key.

Figure 10-10: The Speech pane Listening tab lets you choose when your computer is all ears.

By default, Listening Key is set to the Escape key. You can set another key when you press the Change Key button.

---

tip

The listening key should be one that is not used regularly by the system or another application. Another key that is not often used is the forward slash (/) or the tilde key (~). Forward slashes (/) may be used quite a bit if you are working with Windows users on a network.

When you choose the Key toggles listening on and off Listening Method option, you can catch your computer's attention by prefacing the command with a word, such as the default word "computer." You can choose another word, if you prefer, and then set how much time passes before the next command in the pop-up menu. Using a preliminary voice command is recommended for settings where there may be background noise that may confuse the computer. The microphone can adjust itself to consistent background noise, such as a fan, air conditioner, or computer fans, but may still have trouble with inconsistent sound, such as televisions or radio noise.

The Microphone pop-up box allows you to choose between an external microphone and your computer's built-in microphone. In Figure 10-10 an external Telex USB microphone is among the choices, because it plugged in to the USB port.

You set the microphone loudness with the Volume button (shown in Figure 10-10). Speak the phrases suggested, and adjust the volume accordingly (as shown in Figure 10-11).

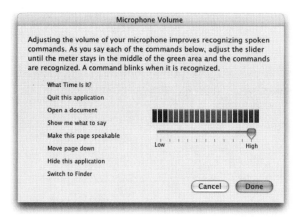

Figure 10-11: Speak in a normal voice, and make sure the microphone is not too close to your mouth; 18 to 24 inches is the recommended distance.

Commands Tab

The Commands tab defines the level of control you want to have over your computer. You can choose the command set to use in the check boxes provided (shown in Figure 10-12).

Figure 10-12: Commands sets available for use with Speech Recognition.

This area has changed a bit since Jaguar, but the functionality is the same. When you click on a command set, text appears to explain how speech recognition works for that item.

The Configure button is active for Address Book and Global Speakable Items only. Configure allows you to check Speak command names exactly as written. In Jaguar this feature was named Require exact wording of Speakable items command names. Some commands can be spoken in different ways when this feature is turned off. For example, when you want to know the time, you could ask "What time is it" or "Tell me the time."

Third-Party Speech Solutions

This is where I talk to you about turning your Mac into your personal secretary. This is where you put your feet up on the desk and dictate your letters and correspondence like the executive you always wanted to be . . . well, sort of. Two main speech recognition programs enable you to dictate to almost any text-capable application. Let's look at them.

MacSpeech iListen

MacSpeech's iListen (www.macspeech.com) is completely Panther-compatible with version 1.6.4. It supports the Services menu and you also now have control over hierarchical menus. Once installed, the iListen application is in a MacSpeech folder placed in your Applications folder. It comes with a ScriptPak for use with AppleWorks (shown Figure 10-13) and more packs. Hardware Error! Bookmark not defined. (like microphones) can be bought from their site.

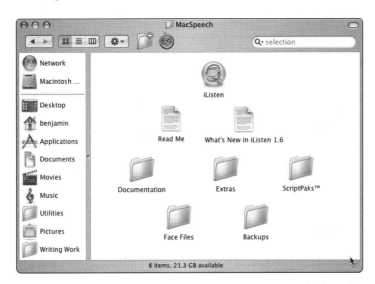

Figure 10-13: This folder contains the basic installation of iListen from MacSpeech.

At a resale price of approximately $99, it's cheaper than its main competitor (which we talk about in the next section).

Training iListen

What you find with all speech-to-text programs is that training your computer to understand your voice is a time-consuming but necessary process if you want to things to work well. When you start the program, you have to train it to recognize your voice, including accent and inflections. You should try to speak as clearly and plainly as possible. Before you can do that, you must set up a profile for your voice (shown in Figure 10-14).

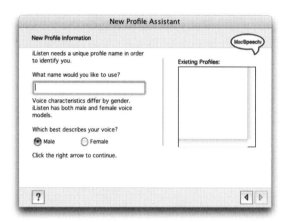

Figure 10-14: Setting up your individual profile is the first step toward training iListen to know who you are.

After you choose a name and set yourself up, you must then train the program. After that, your profile can be selected from the Profiles dialog box in iListen (see Figure 10-15).

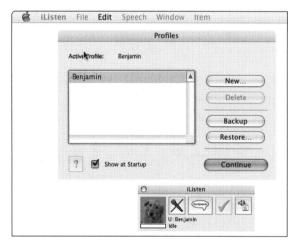

Figure 10-15: Multiple users can be set and selected in the Profiles dialog box.

Secret

Users Cannot Share Voice Profiles

Each user has such unique voice characteristics it is just not possible to share profiles. Each user can train the program for his or her own use, though.

First, the program helps you choose and set up your microphone correctly, tests the sound levels, and determines your background noise.

The Feedback palette allows you to see a character talk when you talk, turn the microphone on and off, bring the application to the front, correct improperly recognized text, and choose an audio file to be transcribed. The Message tells you the mode iListen is in and the I Heard area shows what the program heard you say. When iListen is active, the feedback palette is always available.

iListen provides stories for you to read to train your computer. The more stories you read the better the program can train itself to recognize your words reliably. The first required story is about 27 very short pages (shown in Figure 10-16).

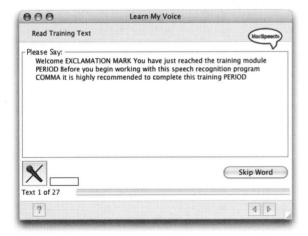

Figure 10-16: This is the first page of the first training story you read.

You must remember to read the punctuation you want, too. Although it can be tedious to read all the stories provided, it really does help the computer recognize your words correctly. After the first story is read, you can choose more stories under the Windows menu. Choose the Learn My Voice option.

tip After some experimentation, I found that reading about three or four of the stories really helped both iListen and ViaVoice to dial into my voice. Reading one story only produced (for me) just too many mistakes to make the program useful.

If you think you don't have time for that, ask yourself if you have time to correct the mistakes that your program will make if you don't teach it your voice.

The Other Modes of iListen

iListen has three modes: Dictation, Spelling, and Command. Dictation is just that — it saves your hands because it allows you to speak your great American novel right into the computer. Spelling mode lets you correct misrecognized text. MacSpeech does not recommend you use spelling mode to edit your document because it may reduce your voice recognition accuracy. The Command mode allows you to issue commands to the computer. You can invoke it to say one command and return to dictating or use it to control the computer when you're not dictating.

Secret

Drinking and Voice Training Do Mix

NO. I'm not advocating drinking alcohol while training your voice recognition software. But when training or using dictation software, make sure you drink plenty of water and juice; or watered down juice if you're calorie conscious. You don't want to get a dry throat and overtax your vocal cords. Coffee is not recommended for wetting your whistle.

iListen is easy to set up, and with patience and training it can provide you with a stress-free way to write on your feet, so to speak!

IBM ViaVoice

IBM's ViaVoice is the competitor to iListen that I referenced earlier. This program is in the update process for Panther, but many folks report that the current version works fine in Panther. ViaVoice is now supported and sold by ScanSoft, (www.scansoft.com/viavoice). IBM offers two editions: the full Mac OS X Edition and Simply Dictation Mac OS X Edition. The full version, which retails for approximately $175, has the ability to create voice commands and includes a noise-canceling USB headset. As IBM has yet to release a version that fully supports Panther, I won't go into too much detail here.

Installing ViaVoice

When you install ViaVoice you get a set of applications that are meant to interface with your other programs and settings (shown in Figure 10-17).

The similarities between MacSpeech and ViaVoice are many; but how the programs implement their technologies differ. You must also train ViaVoice, which is done with the VoiceCenter drawer menu and SetupAssistant. Each user must set up their own Voice Model with which to dictate.

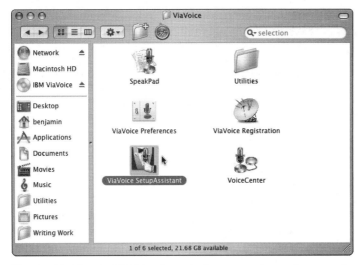

Figure 10-17: The ViaVoice SetupAssistant sets the preferences, SpeakPad, and VoiceCenter applications.

Unlike MacSpeech, ViaVoice provides its own preferences pane, accessible through Mac OS X System Preferences (shown in Figure 10-18).

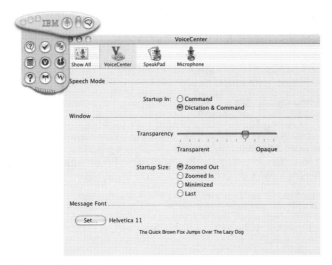

Figure 10-18: You can choose a voice to use, including sliders to control pitch and quality, a hot key to read text, and detect how sensitive the program is in recognizing your words.

Another cool thing about ViaVoice is that there is a handy little desktop control (shown in the upper-left corner of Figure 10-18) that gives you complete access all of the ViaVoice applications and preferences.

ViaVoice Preferences

A number of settings in ViaVoice Preferences will probably change in the Panther version to accommodate the new Finder and upgraded System Preferences. Already, some settings control much more detail than in MacSpeech. For example, you can specify how dates, the time, and numbers appear in dictated text. You can also choose a different voice than those offered through the Mac OS X built-in Speech, Default Voice pane. ViaVoice allows for quite a bit of customization through its Preferences pane. You can choose which commands to store in the toolbar for easy access (shown in Figure 10-19).

Figure 10-19: ViaVoice installs a Preferences pane where you control a number of settings.

Another major difference is that ViaVoice 3 dictation can be entered into the SpeakPad, instead of other applications. When your text appears as you want it to read, you can copy and paste it to another application. You can use a Train Word window to add a word to the built-in dictionary or use the Correction window to perform specific correction functions. ViaVoice also has a Commands option so that you can control your computer.

ViaVoice is a very sophisticated implementation of dictation software and includes many more customization options than MacSpeech. The current version works well in Jaguar, and seems to work fine in Panther, but it is not officially supported yet in Panther.

When Your Mac Talks Back

Before I stop talking about your Mac talking, I should tell you that OS X also has the ability to read to you through the services. To do this in any application, you only have to select (highlight) the text in a document, go to the application menu and choose the Start Speaking Text option from under the Speech Services submenu (shown in Figure 10-20).

Your results may vary with proper names and misspelled words, but it's kind of a kick to try out.

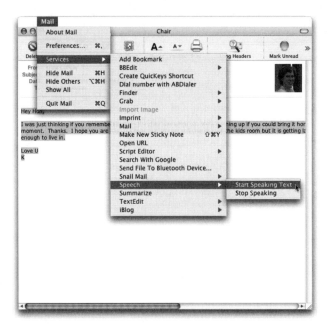

Figure 10-20: Any text that can be highlighted (selected) in any application can be read to you by your Mac.

Summary

As you can see there is a lot more to speech recognition and text-to-speech technology than is obvious at first glance. Although it may look daunting, it is a lot of fun to try out. I've introduced you to a smattering of what's available, but as this technology is advancing rapidly, there's no telling what features may be available next month!

With the advent of Bluetooth-enabled devices, as discussed in Chapter 16, and the growing sophistication of Web cams and microphones, we can expect interesting developments in speech technology with each revision of Mac OS X.

In the next chapter, we'll look at AppleScripts and other ways to automate your Mac.

Putting Your Mac on Autopilot

Chapter 11

♦ ♦

Secrets in This Chapter

♦ ♦

Macs are wonderful machines, but every once in a while some situation comes along and you say, "Why can't I do this? Why can't I just push a button and make this happen?" Despite technology's efforts, dull, repetitive tasks remain.

The problem is, as friendly as we want our computers to be, sometimes we just want our computers, well . . . to act like computers. We need something to do our grunt work, or just coast on autopilot while we sit back and wait for our servants to peel us another grape; and many times the our Macs just don't seem up to the task. That is where AppleScript comes in.

> **note**
>
> Apple's best kept secret is that AppleScript has been around for a while. Although AppleScript is making a big splash now, with its implementation in Panther, it has been around since Mac OS 7. Just over a dozen years old, it is finally being appreciated for the robust production machine it is.

In this chapter, we're going to show you that AppleScript is no longer just the domain of geeks and tinkers. It's ready for prime time. And it's ready for you. . . .

If you are thinking, "That's great, but what can AppleScript do for me?" The stock answer is "pretty much anything," which really doesn't leave you any closer to knowing AppleScript's capabilities than before you asked the question. So let's get into it.

AppleScript Explained in Plain English (More or Less)

According to folks who created it, AppleScript is an English-like language used to write script files that automate the actions of your computer and its resident applications. In short, when all your applications get together in the cyberspace of your Mac and ask, "Can't we all just get along?" all heads turn toward AppleScript. AppleScript is your Mac's lingua franca that helps all your programs, and you, become more productive.

Sounds simple, doesn't it? Well it is, and it isn't. It is true that anyone can look at AppleScript code and see the words and could read them, and maybe see a logic in its arrangement, but beyond that . . . most people see nothing.

Take for example the following AppleScript sample code included with Panther:

```
set the date_stamp to ((the current date) as string)
display dialog the date_stamp buttons {"Clipboard", "OK"} default button 2
if the button returned of the result is "Clipboard" then
    set the clipboard to the date_stamp
    display dialog "The date stamp is on the clipboard." buttons {"•"}
giving up after 2 default button 1
end if
```

Now after looking at this code could you tell what result would be? If you guessed a dialog box with a date (shown in Figure 11-1), you're today's grand prizewinner.

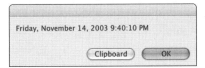

Friday, November 14, 2003 9:40:10 PM

Clipboard　　OK

Figure 11-1: Unless you are familiar with programming, this dialog box was probably a surprise to you.

It seems like a lot of code to retrieve information that you can find in the upper-right of your screen with only a glance and a mouse click, doesn't it?

The above example isn't meant to scare you away from AppleScript, but it is meant as a warning to those who heard how easy AppleScript can be and were already planning how they were going to tell their boss to take a flying leap because they were moving on to a promising and prosperous career in the lucrative field of AppleScripting. AppleScript can be easy, and later on in this chapter, you write a script that reads data from one program, records it in a manner that makes it input information for another program, which, in turn, provides additional information about the input material, all in seven short lines (six of the lines are very short) of code. Now doesn't that sound easy?

Secret

AppleScript's Humble Beginnings

Did you know AppleScript found its beginnings as an outgrowth of HyperCard? HyperCard, originally known as Wildcard, (the name was replaced at the last minute due to copyright concerns) was a Macintosh application toolkit, which gave users an easy way to create hypertext presentations. These presentations included hyperlinks that could take the user to different parts of a document or project just by clicking on them. (Sound familiar?) One of the many user-friendly features of HyperCard was an English-based scripting language called HyperTalk. The fine engineers at Apple saw great potential in a scripting language that would work with any application and AppleScript was born.

Entry-Level AppleScripting

Even if the previous scripting example dashed your AppleScript-fueled dreams of riches and leisure, there are easy ways for the everyday person to enjoy the benefits of the programming language.

Included with Panther are 170-plus AppleScripts ready to use with absolutely no scripting knowledge needed. This doesn't include the many other scripts available for download from Apple's Web site and the Web sites of AppleScript enthusiasts around the world. But before you go on, you need to know where to find these scripts on your Mac and how to make them easily accessible.

Installing the Script Menu

As mentioned, Apple includes a number of scripts with Panther that are ready to go, but where are they? You need look no further than your Applications folder. Among the fancy icons Apple uses to adorn the folders of its other apps, you can find a nondescript folder called AppleScript. Double-click on the folder to reveal the contents (shown in Figure 11-2).

Figure 11-2: Finding the AppleScript folder doesn't make you an AppleScripter, but it is the gateway to your scripting experience.

If you are ready to step into the world of AppleScript, double-click on the Install Script Menu icon. When you look toward the right side of your Finder menu bar, you notice a small scroll icon has appeared. This is your Script menu. Click on the icon (shown in Figure 11-3) to reveal all the scripting goodies Apple has provided out of the goodness of its heart.

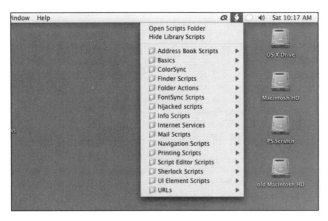

Figure 11-3: Click to Script. You're still not an AppleScripter, but you've got full access to Apple's bundled scripts.

> **note**
>
> In your AppleScript folder is a folder called example scripts (shown in Figure 11-2). If you look closely, you can see that the file is an alias for your Mac's script folder. Control-click on the folder and select Show Original from the contextual menu. This leads you to where your scripts, and many other of your Mac's mysterious behind-the-scenes information is stored, in the Library Folder.

Getting to Know Your Script Menu

Script menu is a friendly utility that lives in your Finder's menu bar, which you can use to easily access your scripts. A quick exploration of your Script menu reveals that Panther comes with almost twice the number of complimentary scripts as its predecessor Jaguar, while still including all of Jaguar's scripts.

Here are some of the categories that you can find (shown in Figure 11-3):

◆ **Address Book Scripts:** This folder contains scripts for importing information from various e-mail programs.

◆ **Basics:** This Folder holds the invaluable AppleScript help script, a script that takes you to Apple's scripting Web site, and of course, a script that opens your Script Editor, which I cover later in this chapter.

◆ **ColorSync:** Includes a collection of scripts to help you manage color on your Mac.

◆ **Finder Scripts:** This folder includes a variety of scripts that control the Finder, including scripts that can rename all the folders in a folder.

◆ **Folder Actions:** This folder contains super-cool scripts that allow you to attach script actions to folders. Much more about this later.

◆ **Info Scripts:** This is where you go if you want to find out what time it is or a script that tells you what your installed fonts look like. (The latter is a very handy script. Check it out immediately.)

◆ **Mail Scripts:** Like it says, the Mail Scripts folder holds a selection of helpful and just-plain-cool scripts to liven up your mail experience.

◆ **Navigation Scripts:** Here you can find scripts that duplicate what you can do more easily with key commands in the finder, such as ⌘-Shift-A to open the Applications folder. However, if you save them as applications and move them to the Library/Startup Items folder, your computer automatically opens these folders for you when your machine boots up.

◆ **Printing Scripts:** Contains scripts for printing, but also goes beyond printing to doing file conversion. Some of these scripts contain an interesting but invisible surprise for their users. (Hint: You will be able to tell your friends and coworkers you regularly employ Unix shell scripts to optimize your workflow . . . let the ubergeek worship, or envy, begin.)

◆ **Script Editor Scripts:** This invaluable resource for the AppleScripter contains templates to handle several different situations you will encounter as you move toward more involved scripting.

◆ **UI Element Scripts:** This folder houses useful tools for interface scripting, now a full-fledged feature of Panther (previously available as a beta only in Jaguar).

◆ **URLs:** Like the label says, this folder contains scripts that tell your browser what sites you want to view.

Upon examination, you might find many of these scripts do not apply or are not useful to you. For example, if you are not in the graphics field, and are not really concerned about fine-tuning the color of you monitor or your computer's color output, the ColorSync folder may remain unvisited for the life of you computer. But you will find that many scripts will be immensely useful, and once you install them, you will wonder how you ever got along without them.

Some of the Coolest Scripts (i.e., Shock Your Friends and Enemies)

Read on to discover how you can take advantage of several excellent AppleScript applications.

Folder Actions

With the advent of OS X and OS X networking, the Drop Box has become the hot spot for interaction of computers in an office or group setting. After you turn your Personal Sharing on, people who connect to your machine as guests can leave items in your Drop Box. But the only way you will know when something arrives is if you have your Drop Box folder on your desktop all the time, or if someone tells you they left you a file.

Apple realizes that there is such thing as too much human contact, and, for that reason (and possibly just to make you more efficient, among many others), they provide you with an AppleScript application, or applet, that helps you set up folder actions.

Folder actions let you put ordinary organizational tasks on autopilot. To use folder actions, you attach a script to a folder. Whenever a folder is modified, opened, closed, or items are added to it the AppleScript attached is automatically activated. And you are not limited to your Drop Box, actions can be attached to any folder on your system. Folder actions were part of OS 9, but were left out of OS X until version 10.2 arrived. Now they continue to be one of the most timesaving features AppleScript has to offer.

Now consider the situation mentioned earlier, files languishing unnoticed in your Drop Box, all the while one of your scheming coworkers in another cubicle is not informing you of the important file just left there, hoping, praying, you are to busy to notice. Then two hours later at the department meeting, your boss brings up the file in question and you sit there bewildered. Then the boss announces, "Levisay, frankly, I expected more of you. You disappoint me," and your rival gets the corner office and you are sent to the mailroom.

Now I hope you are not working in this sort of situation, but it only illustrates how much easier folder actions can make you life. Now, let's move on to assembling that folder action and propelling you into that corner office. Follow these steps:

1. Click on the Script menu and then select the Folder Action Setup submenu choice from under the Folder Actions Option (shown in Figure 11-4).

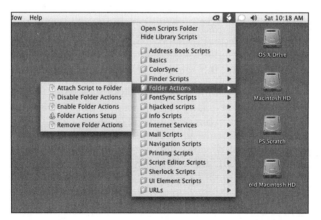

Figure 11-4: Access the folder actions option in your AppleScript Menu.

2. In your Folder Actions Setup dialog box, select the Enable Folder Actions check box (shown in Figure 11-5).

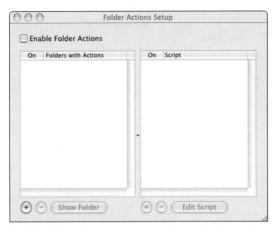

Figure 11-5: Checking Enable Folder Actions allows your folder actions to work once you get them set up. The folder dialog box offers a straightforward two-column setup for folder actions.

3. In the lower-right corner of the dialog box, click the plus sign (shown in Figure 11-5). A folder selection dialog window drops down for you to select a folder, in this case, the Drop Box in your Public folder. Click the plus sign in the lower-center of the dialog box to access a drop-down box of the scripts available to attach to your Drop Box (shown in Figure 11-6).

Figure 11-6: These are the built-in actions that can be added to the Drop Box. Once you know more about AppleScripting, you won't be content with just these.

4. For your purposes here, select add – new item alert.scpt and click the Attach button (shown in Figure 11-6). Now close the dialog box. You now have an alarm (shown in Figure 11-7) on your Drop Box that alerts you to any changes.

Figure 11-7: When you receive the alert from your folder actions script, you have the option to view the contents of your drop box just by clicking Yes.

As you may have noticed in the folder action drop-down box (shown in Figure 11-6), there are many other selections from which to choose. If you want more choices, you can add more scripts to the list by adding them to the Folder Action Scripts folder in your Scripts folder in the Library folder of your startup drive. You could even come up with a script that played the Hallelujah Chorus every time you send a project to print. Now that will raise your standing among your coworkers.

Use Your AppleScripting Powers for Good and Not for Evil

To those of you who are familiar with the Windows world, AppleScripts can sound a lot like macros — and they are. And you may have also heard about insidious virus-like macros that have been delivered across the Internet. Well, AppleScripts offer that same kind of opportunity for Mac communities' ne'er-do-wells, delinquents, crackers, and just plain bad people. AppleScripts can be written that dump files, send e-mails to your whole address list, to the president, anything. So please, even those among you who are pure evil, please use AppleScript responsibly. It is a tool, not a toy. (Well, sometimes it's a toy, but only when it is done right!)

Printing Scripts (And More!)

Some of the coolest new scripts included with Panther are to be found in the Printing Scripts section of your Script menu. Included are scripts that can print the contents of a folder and its subfolder, which is handy for creating hard copies of project elements or the contents of CDs or DVDs.

When you see the printout from one of these scripts, those of you familiar with the Terminal window will recognize the format of the printouts. It looks exactly like the output you get when you examine the contents of folders in Terminal. On further examination of the script (Option-click the Print Window script to open it in Script Editor), you can scroll down and see the telltale sign of Unix in your AppleScript:

```
do shell script
```

Apple has taken scripting one step further for you by involving shell scripts. A shell is one of the command-line interfaces Unix uses so you can operate your computer. Scripting has a long tradition in Unix, and after you master AppleScripting, there is a wide world of Unix scripting with its myriad shells and scripting languages waiting for you. And you thought AppleScript was complicated.

There are two other printing scripts that also use shell scripts to accomplish their tasks. They are Convert to PDF and Convert to Postscript. These scripts take files in JPEG, GIF, TIFF, PFD, PostScript, text, and rich text formats and covert them to files in either PostScript or PDF, whichever you decide. The script can even do certain EPS files, but not Adobe Illustrator files, which may have too much proprietary information for the script to work properly.

Nonetheless, this script is a tremendous timesaver. Converting a graphic to a PDF without having to open an application is a great production enhancer, and will also leave jaws agape when you do in seconds what takes others several minutes to accomplish outside the worlds of AppleScript and our new friend, shell scripting. As I said, let the ubergeek worship begin.

And Now, the Script Editor

Now that you have had a taste of what AppleScript can do for you without even lifting a finger (well, maybe just a few mouse clicks), you can move on to the world of editing and writing your own scripts. To do just that, look at the venerable Script Editor (shown in Figure 11-8), an app that has been around since the inception of AppleScript. In the past however, Script Editor was a Plain-Jane script editor that could do the job, and that is about it. In fact, most scripting jocks often relied on other text editors to do the heavy lifting.

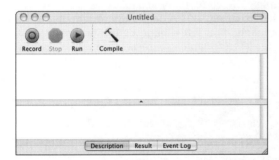

Figure 11-8: On top of all its new features, Script Editor got a little facelift courtesy of Panther.

With Panther, Apple finally has given the AppleScript community a robust editor. It now features find and replace, multiple undoes, and a Library palette for quick access to favorite scripting dictionaries (shown in Figure 11-9). It also features a Font palette that allows you to use any font active in your system for display.

But for all its improvements, Script Editor in this latest version of Mac OS is unstable. It tends to quit unexpectedly when you get many windows open, and can even quit unexpectedly when it is in the background. With OS X, this isn't the horror it was in OS 9 and its earlier incarnations when a program quitting in this manner most likely would have meant a complete system reboot. All in all, the improvements greatly outweigh the lack of stability. So, let the mantra be, when you are writing scripts in Script Editor, save and save often.

Figure 11-9: Keep your applications close, but keep your applications' libraries even closer with Script Editor's new Library palette.

The Finder Gets "Recordable" Again (Sort Of)

The move to OS X burned the AppleScript community in a lot of ways. Many scripts didn't make the migration to OS X and had to be edited or completely rewritten. The Finder was assigned a whole new set of commands that left a huge chunk of legacy work behind. And, if that wasn't bad enough, the Finder, which featured recordable actions in OS 9, was no longer recordable in OS X.

Secret

The Best Web Site to Get More AppleScript

When someone shows you a new program, shareware, or widget that impresses you and you inquire where the treasure was found, nine out of ten times they will reply, "I found it on the Web," which is a not-so-subtle way of saying, "I wouldn't tell you if you shoved bamboo skewers under my fingernails." This isn't the case with AppleScripters (most, that is). There are dozens of Web sites dedicated to AppleScripting. The quickest way to find a helpful script is to go to your favorite Internet searching site or Sherlock and type in the name of the application you are using followed by AppleScript, for example "InDesign AppleScript," With very little digging, you will be on your way to AppleScript gold. For finding scripts for Apple's own apps, the first place to look is www.apple.com/applescript/apps/. There you will find a bevy of tasty scripts to make your Mac mighty.

But Panther makes everything new again, as far as Finder recording goes, in a limited way. You can record the opening of a window (shown in Figure 11-10), you can record the relocation of a window, but the Finder will not record the copying of a file, or basically anything else. This is useful if you want to create scripts that open certain windows when you restart your machine, but it doesn't offer an easy way to make backup scripts, or a way to configure new systems for custom workflows. Apple leaves that in the hands of those who want to get into heavier scripting.

Figure 11-10: Limited Finder recording, but better than nothing.

We Interrupt This Chapter . . .

As good as Apple's newest version of the OS and AppleScript are, it seems like there are those that aren't completely happy with Apple's progress.

Benjamin: I think for all the advances Apple made with latest version of OS X, not making the Finder more completely recordable is a mistake. Although the Finder is as scriptable as any program out there, being recordable made it a fantastic education tool for those learning AppleScript. If you wanted to know the command to copy a folder, you simply hit Record in the Script Editor, and copied a folder. It was that simple. Now neophytes have to find a script that contains the command, or find an outside resource, to learn it. We can only hope Apple takes the next step and makes the Finder fully recordable.

Pieter: Hey Ben, making the Finder completely scriptable was a great idea back in the days of OS 9 when the damage you could do was fairly limited. These days however, Mac OS X gives you immense power over the operating system and the files that it controls. Allowing users to create scripts that are recorded by having the Script Editor watch users as they work in the Finder could lead to the creation of scripts of enormous power. The other major problem is that a script recorded by the administrator of your Mac would not necessarily work when executed by a user that does not have administrator rights. Lastly, because Mac OS X is based upon Unix, you do have access to the power of shell scripts; by removing the ability to easily record AppleScripts, perhaps Apple is trying not so subtly to get users to start learning shell script.

Doing Some AppleScripts Together

Now, time to get your hands dirty, or at least do a little hand coding.

You are going to start with a script that covers the basics and does some of the things a good script should. A good script should save the user time, should be clear and concise, and above all be quick to code, because you want to get on to enjoying the fruits of your labor, not belaboring code. As this may be your first stab at AppleScripting, I am going to make it as easy and pleasant as possible.

The First Secret to Creating a Good AppleScript

The secret to writing a good script is first knowing what you want it to accomplish. This may sound silly, but knowing what you want for your result is vital so you can build a proper script. AppleScripting, when done well, is very modular. Each section of a program should do one thing; these units are called blocks. When each of these blocks is a nearly self-contained unit, troubleshooting becomes a breeze. Each block should be set up so the results of the `tell` block becomes the input for the following block. AppleScript allows for comments, so use them. AppleScript ignores anything following a double hyphen (–), or surrounded with comment tags ((* or *)). Hit the return key to get AppleScript back on track. Sometimes, no matter how hard you are concentrating on writing that perfect script, you may leave it for months before you come back to it. These comments will save time spent trying to decode your earlier work. Complete comments will also make it easier for those who you share your scripts with to customize them for their own situation.

What Do You Want to Do?

Out of all my OS X programs, the one I spend the most time with is iTunes. I always, and I mean always, have it on. And if you are like me, you have so much music on your hard drive that it would take you weeks (at least a week plus a couple days) to listen to it all. Every once in a while an old gem comes along and you want to know a little more about the artist while the song is playing (shown in Figure 11-11). So, you have to bring iTunes to the front, get the artist's name, open Sherlock, type in the artist's name, and hit return to get a list of sites that have information about the artist. Now wouldn't it be nice is you had a script to do that for you? You bet it would, especially if the band in question is Commander Cody and the Lost Planet Airmen. In fact, the script you are going to write is only a few keystrokes more than the name of that late sixties band with the eclectic repertoire.

Figure 11-11: You want the skinny on our iTunes artist, without having to actually do anything?

Getting started

First, you are going to let your Mac know what program you are going to work with, which is iTunes. Type the following:

```
tell application "iTunes"
```

Normally, you would tell a program here to `activate` which would bring it to the front, but suppose you prefer to have iTunes remain in the background, so you can proceed with your next step, which is to get the artist's name:

```
set ArtistName to artist of current track
```

What you have done is ask iTunes what the artist of the current track is and set the variable `Artist_Name` to the information iTunes has provided. Now you are done with iTunes, so you are going to let your Mac know you are through with the music program and ready to move on:

```
end tell
```

There, you have finished your first `tell` block. Feels good, doesn't it.

Now, it is time to take the information you have gleaned, namely the artist's name, and pass it on to Sherlock. First, you have to wake up Sherlock:

```
tell application "Sherlock"
    activate
```

This tells your system you need Sherlock, and you want it to come to the front so you can see the results of your search. But now, you have to tell Sherlock what to look for and where:

```
    search Internet for the ArtistName in channel "Internet" with display
```

Now you have told Sherlock to look for the artist's name on the Internet, but because Sherlock has several channels it uses to search for information on the Internet, you have to tell it to choose Internet, or else it will default to the last channel used. And if the last channel used was Translation, you may end up with the Spanish equivalent for the artist in question, rather than information about the band.

Now you are done with Sherlock, so you enter your final line:

```
End tell
```

All of this code is shown in Figure 11-12.

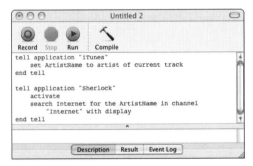

Figure 11-12: An untested script shows up in the Script Editor window as Courier (or whatever typeface you've set for untested scripting in your preferences).

Now, you have to test your miniature masterpiece. Click Compile (⌘-K) to check your grammar (shown in Figure 11-13). This alerts you to any syntax errors you might have.

Figure 11-13: After a script passes muster, the text becomes color-coded with a different color for different code elements.

After your script clears this hurdle, hit Run to see your results (shown in Figure 11-14).

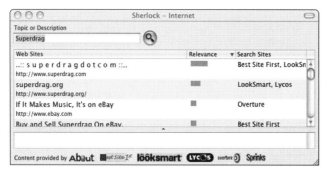

Figure 11-14: If all is right in the universe, Sherlock leaps to attention and provides a cavalcade of sites that inform you all about the artist in question.

Congratulations, you've got a useful, informative script under your belt. Although it was simple, extremely simple, it shows the power of AppleScript. Now, you just need to save the script. But with five ways to save your script, which is the right way?

Saving Your Script

In Panther, your scripts can be saved in five different formats: as text files, as script files, as applications, and two new formats —application bundles and script bundles.

As Text Files

Text files are just that, text, and Script Editor saves them with an extension of .applescript, although you can easily change the extension to be whatever you want. If you place these files in the Script menu, they will not run when you select them. They will open in Script Editor for further editing.

As Script Files

The second method is to save your script, as well . . . a script. This allows you to run the script from within the Script Menu or Script Editor. This method also allows you to edit the script later if you want to make additional changes. If you save the script as Run Only (shown in Figure 11-15), make sure to save it as a copy if you plan to change it in the future, because like the name says, the only thing you can do with that script is run it.

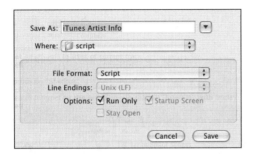

Figure 11-15: Saving you script as a Run Only keeps others from tinkering with your well-crafted code.

As Applications

To save your script as an application, simply select Application for the file format. By saving your file in this method, you can run your script simply by double-clicking it in the Finder, or by dragging a file or files on to it. The icons also appear differently in the Finder (shown in Figure 11-16).

Figure 11-16: To the left a script, to the right, a script dressed for a night on the town.

Once again, if you don't want anyone monkeying with your script after you are done with it, save it as Run Only (shown in Figure 11-17).

Figure 11-17: If you want to make yourself indispensable, turn your scripts into Run Only. From there on in, every time they make a change to their OS, they'll need you to fix their scripts.

If you save your script as an application, you have the option of having a startup screen. This works well if you have a script that has consequences you should think about, such as files being deleted. But in most cases, such as with our iTunes info script that we created earlier, it's just another annoying mouse click (shown in Figure 11-18).

Figure 11-18: And I thought AppleScript was supposed to remove clicks. . . .

Applications Scripts Versus Other Scripts: Speed Could Be the Key

Secret

What's the difference between a script and a script that has been saved as an application, other than the icon? Speed. Applications are slower, and many times noticeably slower. In a test script for Quark Xpress 6.0 that placed crop marks on an image box, the script saved as an application took over twice as long to complete its task as the exact same script saved as an editable script.

As Bundles

You can save your scripts in a new format with Panther called *bundles*. Bundles can be as script bundles or application bundles. The difference lies in what the script can contain. A bundle can contain its own support files, images, movies, sounds, whatever. The icons for bundles look the same as regular scripts and applets, but when you Command-click on the icon, you get a new option in the contextual menu, Show Package Contents (shown in Figure 11-19).

Figure 11-19: New formats get new menu options; explore AppleScript's new bundles.

Once inside you can see that this script is a different animal (shown in Figure 11-20).

Figure 11-20: Inside the bundle icon are all the pieces needed to run a script in its entirety.

The really cool thing about the bundle format, is if your script needs any multimedia pieces to make it work, it can collect these items in a form that can be transmitted to someone else's computer and it can run there without any additional installation materials. They are self-contained scripts. The bad thing is that they will be as large as the media contained within. After a few big JPEGs, a couple of QuickTime movies, and a sound file, you are going to have one humongous script that isn't very bandwidth friendly.

Another negative for the bundle format is it doesn't work on anything before OS 10.3, so you can forget about sharing these scripts with your pre-Panther pals.

But all in all, it is proof that Apple is taking another step toward making AppleScript a more powerful and flexible program building engine.

Remember to Back Up Your Scripts

Secret

AppleScripts, like any other programs, are susceptible to corruption. One day, and that day will come, when you are merrily working along, you will summon an AppleScript and it won't hop to attention, in fact it won't even whimper. So, you try to open the script in Script Editor to see what is wrong and your Mac will give you an error message. The script is gone, and without explanation. Some scripts are more stable, and others seem to have a counter on them for how many times you can use them before they go kaput. So, it is smart to keep a backup file of all your scripts so you can easily replace the bad ones when they die on you.

Other Features: GUI Scripting

While all might seem like paradise in the world of AppleScripting, there has been one dogging complaint scripters have consistently had in the past. "What about programs that do not support AppleScript, or have limited ability to be scripted?"

Late in 2001, Apple introduced its solution to just that problem with a beta version of UI Scripting, which you could download from the Apple Web site. With the release of Panther, it is included with the OS.

Getting Started with User Interface Scripting

The first thing you need to do to prepare your Mac for user interface scripting is to select the Enable access for assistive devices option in the lower portion of the Universal Access panel in System Preferences (shown in Figure 11-21).

Figure 11-21: To make UI Scripting work on your Mac, you need to enable access for assistive devices in the lower-left corner of the Universal Access pane of your System Preferences.

User interface elements are set up in a hierarchy of elements within the interface of an application. Basically what that means is that any selection in a program's interface can be found in reference to its location in the menu; that is, in a program like Microsoft Word, the Save menu item resides in the File menu bar item, which in turn resides in the menu bar of the application Word.

If this sounds complicated, it gets a little easier because Apple has a downloadable tool, called UI Element Inspector (available at www.apple.com/applescript/uiscripting/ 02.html) that can help.

When the UI Element Inspector is on, it is always in the forefront of your Finder providing information about every single element you mouse over. For instance, you can see what the UI Element Inspector displays when you mouse over the New Folder selection in the File menu of the Finder (shown in Figure 11-22).

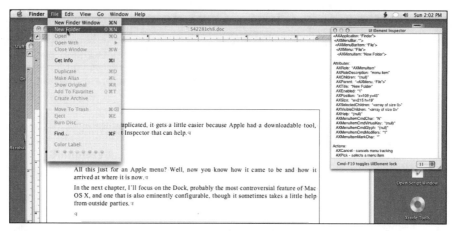

Figure 11-22: The UI inspector is not a crutch. It's a necessary part of learning to create AppleScripts.

With this information, you can draft a script that uses GUI scripting to create a new folder on your desktop.

```
tell application "Finder"
    activate
end tell

tell application "System Events"
    tell process "Finder"
        tell menu bar 1
            tell menu bar item "File"
                tell menu "File"
                    click menu item "New Folder"
                end tell
            end tell
        end tell
    end tell
end tell
```

As you noticed in the fourth line of the script, you are telling the application System Events to do something. System Events is the mysterious application (just try to find it in your applications folder, or on your system for that matter) that lets you select menu items, click buttons, enter text into text fields . . . basically run your Mac as if you were sitting in front of it directing the machine to do your bidding, except you are off somewhere having a latte, or watching cartoons or creating a confectionary masterpiece in the kitchen. The point is you are not in front of your computer's screen, and your Mac is busily working away, while you are not.

This feature of AppleScript, when it works properly, solves most of the problems not covered by AppleScript. Many programs don't offer readily available commands to print, or to make printer selections, or save as a certain type of file. UI Elements scripting covers that last bridge. On top of that, Apple includes some UI code snippets in your Script menu to help you get started.

UI Scripting Help (Really Cool Help)

Prefab offers an amazing tool called Prefab UI Browser (www.prefab.com/uibrowser/) to help with UI scripting. It is like the UI Elements Inspector except it is turbocharged for quick scripting ease. The interface (shown in Figure 11-23) allows you to target the application and make the interface selection you desire; then it generates the AppleScript code for you to cut and paste into your Script Editor window.

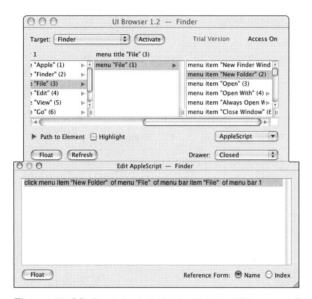

Figure 11-23: Don't be intimidated by the UI browser. One thing at a time gets you where you want to be.

And to prove there is more than one way to skin a cat (and that there are many more ways to write an AppleScript than there are to skin a cat), here is a script that does the same thing as the script you wrote using the help of the UI Element Inspector, seen through the eyes of Prefab's UI Browser.

```
tell application "Finder"
     activate
end tell

tell application "System Events"
     tell process "Finder"
             click menu item "New Folder" of menu "File" of menu bar item
"File" of menu bar 1
     end tell
end tell
```

Both accomplish the same task, creating a new folder, but they are worded in different ways. Not only is AppleScript powerful, it is forgiving. Now, while your Mac is on autopilot from all the new scripts you are going to write, you can argue with your scripting buddies what is the best way to word your scripts. Now that is a bottomless argument. Good thing you'll have plenty of free time.

Other Third-Party Editors: QuicKeys

Another third-party player in the Mac automation market is CESoft's QuicKeys. While at the time of this writing, QuicKeys did not have a full version of its software ready for OS 10.3, it did have its 2.0.2 beta 6 version that ran very well on Panther.

The idea of QuicKeys is very much like the end goal of AppleScripting, but instead it assigns certain tasks to keys on your keyboard. QuicKeys comes with several actions that are ready to go out of the box (shown in Figure 11-24), including Open Calculator (Shift-F7).

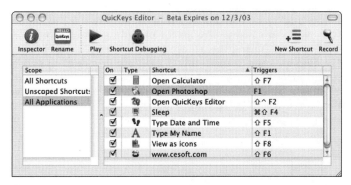

Figure 11-24: QuicKeys works with the idea of sets of actions and triggers to help you create scripts.

Recording actions is easy, simply hit the Record button and go. Don't worry about making mistakes, because you can go in later and edit your actions in the QuicKeys editor (Figure 11-25).

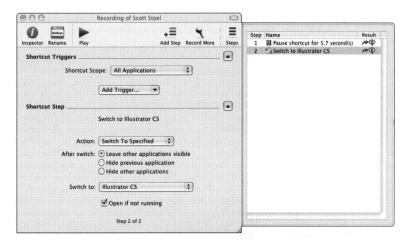

Figure 11-25: QuicKeys records everything in your action, including the pauses. You can easily delete those well-recorded moments of indecision by Command-clicking and deleting them.

Afterwards, you can select a trigger for your action, either assigning a Hot Key or adding it to your QuicKeys menu. (You can even set the trigger to start an AppleScript if you so desire.) You also can select the advanced trigger mode where you can have your action triggered at a certain time, or it can be set to repeat at any given interval. For those who want to increase their production, but don't have the time or inclination to work with AppleScript, QuicKeys offers a very low learning curve for Mac automation.

Summary

With Panther, AppleScript has finally come into its own. Automation has never been easier, and the number and quality of the tools continues to grow. Yet AppleScript, and automation on the Mac platform still have room for growth, such as more applications (including Apple's own Finder) offering the ability to record scripts, and more tools that bring automation to the average user, without having to learn to code their own scripts. In addition to the tools mentioned in this chapter are a whole slew of additional tools in the Xcode developer's kit, known collectively as Apple Script Studio. Not only can you script, but you can put an Aqua interface on these scripts so they look and run just like any other program on your Mac. For AppleScript enthusiasts and developers there is no end to the opportunity.

Part III

Secrets of Apple's Digital Lifestyle Applications

Part III is loaded with advice and secrets for getting the most out of Apple's digital lifestyle applications, including iTunes, iPhoto, iMovie, iDVD, and more.

In This Part

Mac OS X Application Overview

Chapter
12

◆ ◆

Secrets in This Chapter

◆ ◆

Did you ever notice that when you set up a new Mac or installed Mac OS X for the first time that the OS is loaded to the gills with software?

Where did it come from? How did the Applications folder fill up so fast? The answer is simply that all those great products are installed by default. Apple delivers more and more value in the shipping box, and includes many useful applications to make your life easier.

The assortment ranges from a simple word processor to Internet access software and a bunch of utilities that are designed to manage your Mac OS X user experience. Some of those utilities are so powerful that you shouldn't use them until you gain some system administration experience. The Utilities folder is covered in Chapter 5, so we look at the Applications folder in this chapter.

What You Get with Your New Mac

This chapter covers the basics of a wide range of programs that Apple includes with Panther. Some of these programs are described in complete detail elsewhere in this book; the rest are dealt with here. Here is a list of the software that Apple bundles with Panther:

> Acrobat Reader
> Address Book
> AppleScript
> AppleWorks (included with iBooks, iMacs, and eMacs only)
> Calculator
> Chess
> DVD Player
> Font Book
> iChat AV
> Image Capture
> Internet Connect
> Internet Explorer
> iMovie
> iPhoto
> iTunes
> Mail
> Preview
> QuickTime Player
> Safari
> Sherlock
> Stickies
> System Preferences
> TextEdit

These applications are found in the Applications folder (shown in Figure 12-1).

Figure 12-1: As you can see the Applications Folder is filled to the brim.

> **note**   Before I get too deep into this, I should point out that Apple sometimes changes its software bundles; and consumer Macs, such as the iMac, include different software than the pro models, for example, AppleWorks. So, if you find that you don't have something that I've written about, or vice versa, don't complain to me.

Text and Graphic Applications

Categorizing the applications is a little difficult, but it's the best way to go through them. In this first section, I'll take you though the text and graphic applications.

Adobe Reader

Don't be fooled by the simplicity of this application. Adobe Reader (formerly known as Acrobat Reader in earlier version), an Adobe, Inc. product, lets you read electronic documents made in PDF format, like the ones that companies include, in lieu of printed manuals, on product CD. Portable Document Format (PDF) files, retain all their formatting and can be read by other operating systems, such as Windows. That means that if you want to send another person a file with particular fonts, graphics, color, and formatting, you can. You only need to save the document as a PDF. If Adobe Reader didn't come installed with your Macintosh, you can download it from Adobe's site at www.adobe.com.

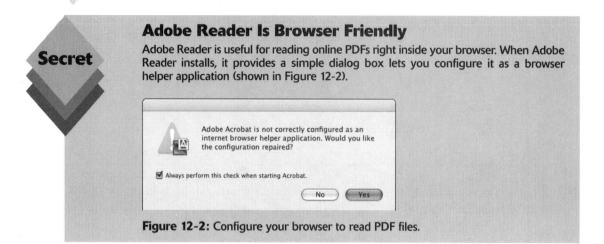

Secret

Adobe Reader Is Browser Friendly

Adobe Reader is useful for reading online PDFs right inside your browser. When Adobe Reader installs, it provides a simple dialog box lets you configure it as a browser helper application (shown in Figure 12-2).

Figure 12-2: Configure your browser to read PDF files.

Adobe Reader allows you to view your PDFs in a browser-like window with the option of looking at thumbnails of the other pages and even bookmarks, so long as they were placed within the document (shown in Figure 12-3).

Figure 12-3: This homemade PDF was laid out in Quark and then distilled (made into a PDF using Acrobat Distiller) so that it could be read by Adobe Reader in either platform.

A PDF in Adobe Reader is more than an image of a document. Depending on how a PDF is made, you can select, copy, and paste text from within it. You can also take advantage of interactive features in a PDF. You can embed links within an Acrobat PDF. Those links can reference another page in the PDF (shown in Figure 12-4, on the left) or even an address on the Internet (shown in Figure 12-4, on the right).

Figure 12-4: Graphic elements or text can be used as internal links (left) to other pages or sections in the same PDF document or as external links (right) that will launch your browser to a specific Web address.

It's important to remember that links like these can be used in Adobe Reader, but not created in Adobe Reader. You need one of Adobe's professional Acrobat programs to manage those kinds of interactive tasks.

> **note**
>
> Any Mac OS 10.2 (or higher) program that adheres to Apple's printing guidelines should give you the choice of saving a document to PDF in the standard Print dialog box. Instead of choosing Print, you choose Save as PDF. For more information on this option, see the discussion of Preview later in this chapter, and Chapter 22, which covers printing. You cannot save to PDF inside a Classic application, though. If you want to create PDF documents from scratch you can upgrade from Adobe Reader to the full Adobe Acrobat program for a fee, but Apple makes it so easy, you don't need to upgrade unless you want to produce extremely complicated PDFs.

Image Capture

Image Capture allows you to easily take your digital images off your camera and store them on your hard drive, and do amazing things. You can share your images over the Web, with others on your local network, or simply delete images. You can even scan pictures and put them back into your camera if you want.

Preview

Preview is an all-in-one PDF and graphic file reader (shown in Figure 12-5). It's not an image editor, but you can crop, resize, and rotate images. You can use the built-in tools to copy text and images to other applications. You can also read files created in graphics formats as JPG, GIF, TIF, PSD, PICT, PNG, BMP, and SGI.

Figure 12-5: Open a file, any (well almost any) file. Here you see a PDF document opened in Preview.

So, if you are getting strange files with strange-sounding extensions from your friends, you should be able to open most of them. I cover more of this stuff in Chapter 9.

Preview can be set to be the default application to read PDF files, especially helpful if your computer did not come with Adobe Reader. Also, when you preview a document prior to printing, Preview generates a PDF document based upon the printer settings and then uses Preview to display the PDF that resembles what the final printed document will look like. This document is stored in a temporary location on your hard drive.

Secret

A Quick Way to Make Preview Your Default PDF Application

If you have inadvertently made Adobe Reader the default application to view PDFs and you want to switch them to Preview, it is a simple change. Select any PDF document in the Finder (click on it once), then choose Get Info in the File menu, and click the Open with triangle. Choose Preview instead of Adobe Reader and you're done.

QuickTime Player

I'm often asked what is QuickTime and where do you find it? Well, because it's a system-level tool, the best manifestation of its existence is the player application (shown in Figure 12-6).

I cover QuickTime in Chapter 15, in the section dealing with Apple's movie-making software.

AppleWorks

If you buy a consumer model, such as the eMac, iMac, or iBook, you get a copy of AppleWorks, Apple's own integrated office suite. The AppleWorks modules are Word Processing, Painting, Drawing, Spreadsheet, Database, and Presentation (slideshow). These modules can be accessed from the Starting Points palette that appears when you launch the program (shown in Figure 12-7).

Figure 12-6: You can play and listen to MOV, MP3, and many other types of files with the QuickTime player.

Figure 12-7: AppleWorks includes a helpful Starting Points display when you start it. You can hide this display in the File menu.

It may not provide all the features that you find in Microsoft's Word or Excel, or even FileMaker Pro, but don't sell AppleWorks short. If you take stock of what you really need, this compact office suite can usually do the job. AppleWorks can open Word and Excel documents, and all kinds of graphic files. Similarly, AppleWorks can create documents that Word and Excel can handle as well.

So, if you have a professional Mac, it still may be worth buying a copy AppleWorks.

Using the Web to Help You Get Graphic with AppleWorks

Secret

A nifty feature included in AppleWorks is its ability to quickly search the Web when you need that special graphic for an invitation, report, or school paper. Just choose Show Clippings under the File menu to get at the Clippings palette (shown in Figure 12-8).

continues

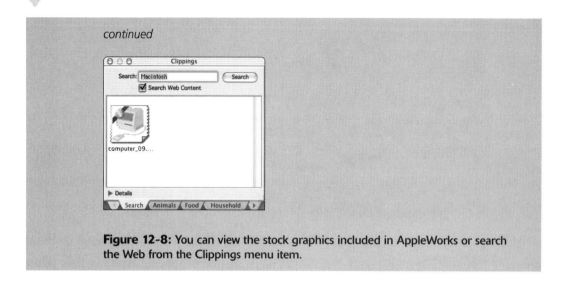

continued

Figure 12-8: You can view the stock graphics included in AppleWorks or search the Web from the Clippings menu item.

TextEdit

Once upon a time, there was TeachText, and it wasn't very good. Then there was SimpleText, and it was only slightly better. TextEdit (see Figure 12-9) is a substantial improvement over its predecessors. It's actually a tiny word processor that can even read Microsoft Word documents with pretty good accuracy. Not bad for something you get free. Chapter 8 covers other word processing options, but don't sell this robust text editor short, especially if you don't need a whole lot of fancy formatting features and crowded palettes.

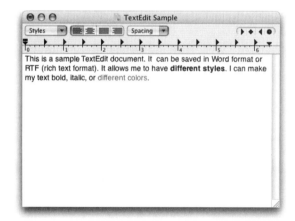

Figure 12-9: Trust me. It really does read a Word file.

Font Book

Font Book isn't, per se, a text or image application. But it is Apple's font utility so you need to see it here, close to the text applications.

Font Book (shown in Figure 12-10) is a new application in Panther. It is a consumer font management program that is provided free of charge by Apple to help you manage your fonts. It has some similarities to the more popular professional (which are not free) font management programs such as Extensis Suitcase and FontAgent.

Figure 12-10: Font Book presents your fonts in an easy-to-read display.

Font Book lets you find, view, and organize fonts. And it also allows you to install, remove, deactivate, and preview fonts. Font Book is covered in more detail in Chapter 23.

There are those that say that Font Book is good as long as you aren't using more than 100 fonts (or so). The truth is that if you use your computer for graphics at all or if you need to move between native OS X and Classic applications, you will probably need something more substantial like Suitcase or FontAgent.

We Interrupt This Chapter . . .

As usual, my opinion on this brought some comments from Pieter.

Benjamin: Font Book is a good idea, but it doesn't begin to sort out the mess that Apple has made of fonts in OS X. I applaud them for trying to deal with it, but they need either to make it a stronger application or to extend its abilities for Classic applications, as well.

Pieter: Hey Ben, for those of us who are not graphics and desktop publishing gurus, Font Book does a great job. I have only about 50 or so font families in my library and for those, Font Book does just fine with all my OS X–native applications. 'Course I don't hardly use Classic apps anymore for doing serious work where I need more than one or two fonts. Font Book lets me control the font families that I use and works great with native OS X applications, and best of all, it is free.

Secret

Getting at Those Special Characters with the Input Menu

If you used the Key Caps control panel a lot to find special characters in Mac OS 9, you'll love the new version in Panther, called Keyboard Viewer. Just choose International in the System Preferences. Click the Input Menu tab(shown in Figure 12-11), select Keyboard Viewer and select the Show input menu in menu bar option.

continues

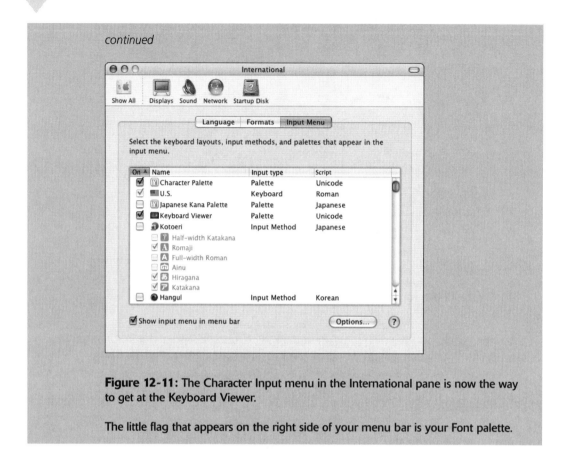

continued

Figure 12-11: The Character Input menu in the International pane is now the way to get at the Keyboard Viewer.

The little flag that appears on the right side of your menu bar is your Font palette.

A Quick Look at the iApps

The cornerstone of Apple's vision of the hub of your digital lifestyle is the suite of iApps software that manages these functions. From handling digital photos and music libraries to editing movies, the clever combination of intuitive interface and robust feature set places these applications among the best in their class.

Because these are all covered in other chapters, I'll just go cover the basics here.

iCal

It started life as a simple calendar with the ability to share and post online (see Figure 12-12), but has become more and more integrated into the Mac user experience. Even Quicken 2004 uses iCal for scheduling bill payments.

The most notable thing about iCal is the ability to use it to share information and synchronize between devices and other computers. This makes is a very powerful productivity application. Check out Chapter 16 for more on iCal.

Figure 12-12: You can use iCal to keep your schedule organized and view it by day, week, or month.

iChat

iChat could go in either in this category or the Internet category. As I was writing this, it seemed to go better here. If my organizational sense differs from yours, please excuse me.

Sometimes known as iChat AV, this is a live messaging client so you can type with coworkers and friends who are also online. The latest version (shown in Figure 12-13) extends your chatting capability to audio and video.

Figure 12-13: I avoided using the AV element here, because I didn't want to frighten off any readers.

It works with .Mac and AIM (AOL Instant Messenger) addresses, but don't tell the phone company how much you save on long distance charges because of this useful utility. Or maybe you should, so they'll think about lowering the rates. I cover more of this excitement in Chapter 19.

Secret

Using iChat AV to Spy on Yourself

Ever feel you are talking to yourself? Well there are times where you might just want to do that with iChat AV, more or less. If you ⌘-click on the name of a buddy with audio or video turned on, you can start a one-way session. I suppose this might come in handy if you want to use your iSight camera for security purposes or to keep tabs on the baby.

iDVD

If your Mac shipped with a DVD burner, better known as the SuperDrive you are able to use the latest version of iDVD (see Figure 12-14) with your Panther installation, (not to be confused with the SuperDisk, a floppy-type disk format).

Figure 12-14: I've used an image of my kids in one of iDVD's templates as a start to my first DVD.

Chapter 15 covers this program in more detail, but I will say that it allows you to make professional-caliber CDs, with motion menus and animated backgrounds, in just minutes (plus the time it takes to burn the DVD of course).

iMovie

Home moviemakers never had it so good. And iMovie (shown in Figure 12-15) has become good enough to handle simple industrial videos too. And if you're a budding Steven Spielberg, this is definitely a way to stretch your skills and give family and friends a chance to show off their acting chops.

Figure 12-15: Even your pet can be a movie star in iMovie.

As with iDVD, Chapter 15 delivers the goods on secrets and such.

iPhoto

A true blessing, iPhoto (shown in Figure 12-16) provides a way to put order in your digital photo library clutter. My personal opinion is that iPhoto was Apple's first free killer application. For the very first time you had a built-in program that allowed you to import, organize, and share your images with others.

Figure 12-16: Images are organized by date and then shared using the choices at the bottom of the iPhoto window.

If you're like me — that is, you take photos and then figure out what to do with them later — iPhoto, described in more detail in Chapter 14, is worth investigating.

iTunes

iTunes has evolved from earlier editions. It is now not only a way to organize your existing music files, but also a place to preview and purchase songs legally for a dollar a piece (shown in Figure 12-17).

We'll look at iTunes in more depth in Chapter 13.

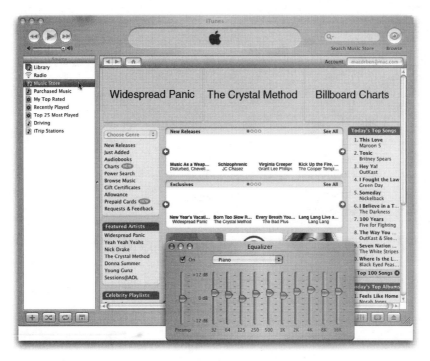

Figure 12-17: Whether you are purchasing new music through the iTunes Music Store or working with your own music, you can still use iTunes to mix and burn your own playlists.

GarageBand

GarageBand is Apple's newest iApp. It give you the ability to create your own music using real instruments or by messing around with software (virtual) instruments. Together with bundled melodies and rhythms, you can add and work on a timeline within GarageBand (shown in Figure 12-18) to create your very own music.

While not a very musically inclined person myself, I take a more in-depth look at GarageBand in the same chapter (13) as iTunes. If you want to learn more, please turn your attention there and we can be off-key together.

Figure 12-18: Like most of Apple's idea's, it's as simple as dragging and dropping elements within the window to be creative.

Internet Applications

Most of the applications in OS X can make some kind of connection to the Internet either for shopping (like iTunes) or for helping you create Web pages (like iPhoto). But there are those programs that have the Internet on the brain. These are the programs that will assist you and act as your clients or agents.to get you onto the Internet and/or do those things people do online. In this section, we'll look at those applications.

Internet Connect

The Internet Connect application (shown in Figure 12-19) allows you to start and stop connections to the Internet that require passwords. These are called authenticated accounts, because your password verifies that it is you; unless of course you've given someone else your password. Do I even have to mention that it is never a good idea to share your password with anyone? Trust me, you really never want to share a password!

Figure 12-19: Internet Connect lets you set up your modem quickly and easily.

The new Internet Connect window shows you every connection you have available only after you set them up in either the Network preference pane or in the File menu in Internet Connect.

> **note** You can edit your configured connections from the Network pane in System Preferences only, even though you view them in Internet Connect.

Secret

Troubleshooting Internet Connect with the Connection Logs

If you have problems with your Internet connection and need to seek help from your Internet provider, you may find some useful information in your Connection Log. Under the Window menu, choose Connection Log to view your connection details.

Mail

Apple's e-mail application, simply called Mail (shown in Figure 12-20), has one of the best spam filtering systems you can find. Mail is covered in depth in Chapter 18.

Address Book

While not exactly an Internet application, Address Book is so closely linked with iChat and Mail that it belongs in this category.

This is one of the heroes of Panther. Address Book (see Figure 12-21) is your system-wide Rolodex directory of all your contacts. While nothing stops you from using Microsoft Entourage or a dedicated contact manager, such as Now Contact, this is certainly an easy alternative. It's free and already started for you.

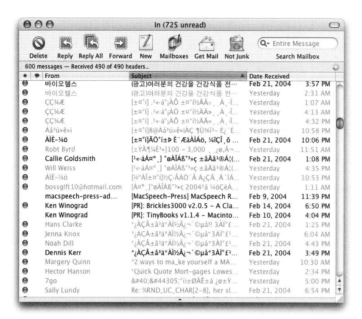

Figure 12-20: Mail color-codes your junk mail, so that you can quickly see all those wonderful spams and delete them easily. When you click something and choose Junk, Mail remembers it the next time you receive mail, too.

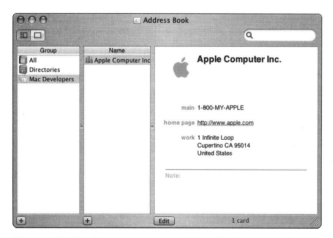

Figure 12-21: Create your own address lists by group in Address Book.

What do I mean? When you first set up your Mac or Mac OS X, your name and other contact information is entered into Address Book for you automatically.

Secret

Reading a Phone or Fax Number across the Room

I cover more of Address Book in Chapter 18. Meantime, if you can't wait for a secret, here's one that'll help those of you who, like me, find it a little difficult to read small type. (In my case, I'm sure it's just age.) Or maybe you need to see the phone number when you dial it from across the room.

Just click on the label that identifies the category of the phone number (such as Main or Work), and hold. Select Large Type from the pop-up menu (shown in Figure 12-22) and, wow, it sure gets large, doesn't it?

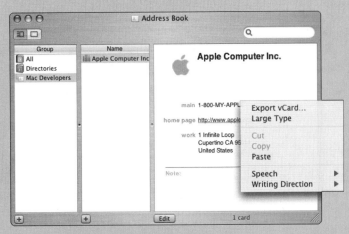

Figure 12-22: As you see, the contextual menu allows you to show the phone number in large type.

Microsoft Internet Explorer

Yes, I know Safari is the bee's knees of Web browsers, but Panther makes even Internet Explorer run faster, and, for now, Apple is still supplying it (see Figure 12-23). There's an important reason not to ignore this application, because some Web sites are, for better or worse, designed with Internet Explorer in mind and don't always look nice in other browsers.

You benefit by having lots of browser choices to ponder. I cover this whole subject and the various online options in Chapter 17.

Secret

Using the Web Archive Feature in Internet Explorer

Internet Explorer has this great save feature where you can preserve a Web page in all its original glory. From the File menu choose Save As and under Format, choose Web Archive. Your archive can be customized with the Options button to save just the text, or to include any pictures, sounds, movies, and links. No other browser includes this robust save feature.

Figure 12-23: Yes, folks, Microsoft won't be making a new Mac Internet Explorer, but the existing one still works great.

Safari

There's so much to say about Safari that it's hard to know where to start. Safari (shown in Figure 12-24) is Apple's answer to Internet Explorer. It is by far the fastest browser for OS X and supports a lot of great features that take full advantage of Panther as well as Apple's protocols and other programs.

Since Safar and Mail are closely linked, I've included a lot more screen shots and an in-depth look at Safari in Chapter 18.

Sherlock

Sherlock (shown in Figure 12-25) is like a super Find command for the Internet. While you may have used it to locate items on your hard drive in previous versions of the Mac OS, it now is an Internet-only application. The difference between Sherlock and a Web-based search engine is that you choose which sites to search in Sherlock.

You can add more channels to Sherlock simply, just click on the Other Channels folder under Collections. Sherlock can use your Address Book for location information too, which makes it easy to get directions to a business, a movie, or even a ski slope.

We'll also look at Sherlock in a little more depth in Chapter 18.

Figure 12-24: Apple's Web browser is shown here with tabbed browsing enabled.

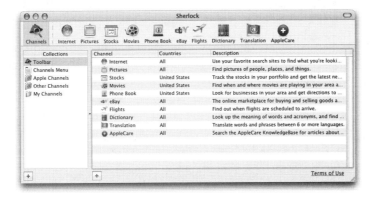

Figure 12-25: Sherlock is organized by channels, which can be seen in the toolbar.

Other Applications

Some of these applications just don't fall into well-defined categories, which I've decided is a category itself.

AppleScript

AppleScript is a system tool that lets your Mac do the work for you, rather than the other way around. You can create English-like bits of code (scripts) that perform useful short-cuts and automate repetitive tasks. Graphic artists use it to process a lot of files (such as changing the size of many photographs at once) in applications such as Adobe Photoshop and QuarkXPress. Most Mac OS X applications support some level of automation.

The AppleScript folder contains a Script Editor application to make your own scripts, plus a load of sample scripts you can build on. You can find more on AppleScript and Script Editor in Chapter 11.

Getting Started with AppleScripts

Inside the AppleScript folder is a little utility called Install Script Menu (shown in Figure 12-26). Double-click and, voilá, you now have a handy dandy list of available scripts from your Finder menu available in all applications.

Figure 12-26: As you see in the column view, AppleScript includes menu installation and removal scripts to make your life easier.

Calculator

In the past, Apple's Calculator was a bare-bones device that let you do simple arithmetic. If you wanted to go beyond the simple, you had to use a dedicated scientific calculator, or even a real handheld device.

The Panther version (see Figure 12-27) adds advanced math, including trigonometric and logarithmic features. On top of all that, you can use the paper tape feature to remind yourself of lengthy calculations. You don't have to guess if those figures in the third line of your checkbook register were forgotten or not.

Figure 12-27: The venerable Calculator has a new face and powerful new features, including a paper tape feature.

After you have done your work, you can print or save the results for your files. The most fascinating feature of all may be the Convert menu, which lets you convert most anything from volume to foreign currency rates. You can even use your Internet connection to track the latest goings on in the highly volatile currency markets. Knowing how often things change just makes me glad I don't trade in that arena.

Chess

All right, just how smart is your Macintosh's processor? Can you beat it at chess? Here's your chance (see Figure 12-28). To play, just click a piece and move it and your Mac responds with a move of its own. You can set the preferences so that you play against the computer or watch the computer match wits with itself. May the better mind win. You can also customize Chess to fit your needs too. You have four choices for board pieces, can choose to hear your moves, or make the computer a stronger opponent; all within the Preferences panel.

Secret

You Can Get Your Mac to Help You Learn (or Do Better in) Chess

If you're not an assured chess player yet, don't despair. Choose Show Hint from the Moves menu and a big red arrow will point the way to your next maneuver. No cheating, please!

Figure 12-28: The wooden board and pieces are just elegant.

DVD Player

Now you can go to the movies without leaving your Mac. You can watch full screen or just place a small screen in the corner of your monitor (so you can catch the action while you pretend to get work done). You'll surely enjoy the convenience of this booming consumer electronics format.

Apple's DVD Player (see Figure 12-29) can also read CDs, but the remote is primarily for movies.

Figure 12-29: A familiar looking remote allows you to control your DVD player.

If you owned Mac OS X 10.2 (Jaguar), you will find some welcome changes in your new DVD Player:

◆ The DVD Player, used with QuickTime 6.4, adds the ability to play VCDs, or video compact disks.

◆ Even the lowly DVD Player is not without some neat keyboard shortcuts, which are available in a handy list under the Help menu.

♦ You can now set bookmarks in your DVD or videodisc, so that you can stop your movie and restart it right where you left off.

♦ You can set your DVD player to view on a second monitor, so that you can work (or should that be, pretend to work) on your first monitor. Of course, this only works with Macs that can use two monitors.

> **note**
>
> Full screen mode puts a black border around the player window. With this and other large screen settings, you need a fairly fast Mac with a powerful graphics chip to get a clean picture with full frame rates. If the playback stutters a bit, you'll want to reduce the size of the player window and see if things improve.

Stickies

Stickies are the Post-it Notes for your screen. Instead of cluttering up your desk with a thousand little pieces of paper, you can put those notes right into your Stickies. You can color-code the notes (shown in Figure 12-30) or the fonts, change the font, or even add graphics.

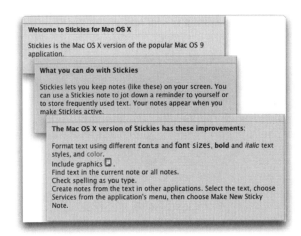

Figure 12-30: When you open Stickies for the first time, you get three notes with instructions and different colors.

System Preferences

Although System Preferences is located in the Applications folder, it's really so much more than an application. It's the main way that you get to change your Mac to suit you and your needs. This simple applicationt replaces much of the headache of pre-OS X systems.

It's important enough that we've given it it's own chapter. Chapter 4 covers everything you need to know about System Preferences, so I won't go into any more depth here.

Summary

The applications folder is chock-full of useful applications, so useful that you may find you don't need to buy another software program for months. Try them all out before you decide to spend another penny, and you may discover that your new Macintosh is a more complete home and office solution than you ever could have imagined. In the next four chapters, you'll discover just how some of these applications are used to fulfill that digital lifestyle you've been longing to live.

"The Beat Goes On" with iTunes, GarageBand, and the iPod

Chapter
13

You know . . . it wasn't all that long ago that Apple made just computers. Yeah. Can you believe it? There was a time that Apple's contribution to the digital world was to build a computer and operating system for which other companies could develop great software.

Some of these developers worked in the arena of digital music for the consumer. I can still remember my copy of SoundJam (by Casady & Greene who is now out of business) that I used to play my favorite music on my first generation iMac. It was great. And then there were those software developers who created a means to download music off the Internet. What a mess that was — and still is to some extent.

And this was just a few years ago. Then Apple decided to get serious with digital music. Within a very short time, they swallowed SoundJam and came out with iTunes. Then they came out with a new digital device called the iPod.

Then they did the unthinkable. They bundled the iPod with some PC software and started selling it to the *enemy*. I thought they were crazy. But in only a few years, they went from a company that didn't sell any MP3 players to selling the number one, best-selling MP3 player on the market.

But Apple wasn't done. They wanted more. They kept improving the iPod. They kept improving iTunes. And then they finally got into the business of music themselves. They launched the Apple Music Store — a place that you can purchase songs for 99 cents apiece after previewing them. They again consorted with the enemy by developing the iTunes software for Windows 2000 and Windows XP. Now, users of Macs or Windows machines can shop for music and get the full range of functionality from the iPod.

So where is Apple today? Well, at the time this was written, 50 million songs had been sold from the online Apple Music Store right through the iTunes interface. Apple continues to sell more than a million songs a week. And everyone is happy. The consumer has a great selection that is updated often and they can pick and choose what they want. The artists and music companies are happy because they are getting their cut. (The last statistic I heard was that 85 percent of all of the legally downloaded music is purchased from the Apple Music Store.)

I think we need to tip our hats to Apple. They've provided a great service for the digital audio consumer — and they did it well. In fact, I don't think they can do it any better. Short of creating software that would allow users to create their own music easily, it's perfect. What? Have I heard about GarageBand? Yeah. Right. Tell me another one.

The next thing you'll be telling me is that I can find music under the caps of soft drinks. . . .

(How gullible do you think I am?)

A Call to Steal Music?

Do you remember the clarion call of Steve Jobs, "Rip, Mix, Burn"? He later clarified that when he said "Rip," he was talking about the audio conversion process and not encouraging people to *rip off* music.

insider insight

Now Apple CEO Steve Jobs is a talented fellow who can change your concept of reality with a few words. So when he first unveiled Apple's music downloading service to the press, he said they got it all wrong about the meaning of "Rip, Mix, Burn." It wasn't meant to be a request for you to pirate music. The word "Rip" is common slang for importing music from an audio CD on your computer. "Mix" the process of creating a custom playlist, just as many used to do with tape cassettes. And the word "Burn" refers to the process of creating a CD. Maybe it is a little revisionist, but I'll take Steve at his word, even if he was rumored to be one of those 1970s phone phreaks who used a device called a "blue box" to, shall we say, borrow access to a phone line to make free long distance calls. Now we just do it on the Internet.

But millions of computer users (PC and Macs) were already busy being digital music pirates. Why use a CD burner just for files, right? After all, isn't music data too, a bunch of ones and zeroes that sounds pretty or however you like your tunes? The same technology that allows you to make legal MP3 conversions of your own CDs also enables the world to share songs without the encumbrance of royalties and other legal considerations.

Now the music industry doesn't take too kindly to any of this stuff. After all, when you download a song from someone else, the artist and the music company don't receive their cut. And I don't blame them. Not only is it illegal, it's immoral.

Fortunately, things got a little better when Apple, creator of the iTunes jukebox software, complemented it with the iTunes Music Store (which we'll talk about more later in this chapter). Now you have a legal way to buy your songs, and do what you will with them, within limits of course.

What do I mean by limits? Well, they're not so bad, really, unless you're in the business of copying music illegally. When you buy a song from Apple, you can burn them onto CDs, transfer them to iPods, and play them on up to three Macs. That's not so bad is it?

note

Even Windows users might be in on the Music Store action (besides the iTunes Music Store) by the time you read this book, but we got it first. And Apple has sizable lead on them. Let them suffer!

Building a Digital Music Library

At a very basic level, iTunes (shown in Figure 13-1) is an application that you use to organize your digital music library and play your songs. If you do nothing else, you can import, organize, and play your music with the iTunes software.

Figure 13-1: You can manage all your music directly from this neat little application.

The Genesis of iTunes

Remember SoundJam, a program from Casady & Greene, publishers of Conflict Catcher, Spell Catcher, and other great stuff? Well, Apple liked SoundJam so much that they bought the product and hired some of the original programmers to work at Apple to develop iTunes. Jeffrey Robbin, who wrote SoundJam on the side, was already working at Apple by then. However, it took a little while for iTunes to match the features of SoundJam and exceed them. Some folks still prefer the original.

The iTunes Interface

Before I get deep into the wide range of iTunes secrets, let me cover the basics of how to use Apple's iTunes software. Consider the following a quick overview to get you acquainted with version 4, the one shipping when this book was written.

Browsing iTunes

The playlists in the Source panel (on the left side of iTunes) is the first way to navigate though your songs. But Apple provides a better method for doing this. In the upper-right corner of iTunes, you can see an eye (you're in the Library or Music Store). This is the Browse button. Clicking on this button gives you an additional Artist and Album panel above the song list in the main panel of iTunes (shown in Figure 13-2).

Figure 13-2: Selecting an artist causes the relevant albums to appear. Selecting the album lists the song (or songs) in the list of songs below.

After you get used to browsing your music like this, you'll probably continue to do so.

Easy Play Controls

Just like your garden variety CD or DVD player, iTunes has a big Play/Pause button, flanked by a Rewind button on the left, and a Forward button to its right.

> **note**
>
> The CD player look of iTunes is no coincidence. Like a regular CD or DVD player, you can easily scan forward or backward through a song while it's playing. Just drag the diamond in the progress bar in the direction you want. Unlike a physical optical disc player, though, you will hear only an occasional blip in your speakers as the diamond is in motion.

Drag-and-Drop Playlist Organization

All your tunes are stored in a folder called Library. To make a new, custom playlist, simply click on the plus icon, which makes a blank playlist folder. Now rename the folder the way you like. Once you get past the preliminaries, you can drag your tunes, either one at a time, or in groups, to the new playlist.

> **note**
>
> Don't despair of messing up your library this way. Dragging a tune to another playlist simply makes a copy of the listing. In fact, if you press Delete to remove an entry, you aren't actually deleting the file itself, just the listing. The original is still stored wherever you left it.

A Quick Way to Rip a Song from a CD to Your iTunes Library

Want to rip a song from a CD to your playlist as fast as possible? With iTunes 4 running, insert the CD in your Mac's optical drive. When the contents of the CD are displayed, drag a song to the playlist. It'll be imported to the Library and added to the playlist in two consecutive actions. This is surely faster than selecting the song and clicking Import, right? Or not!

note If all the songs are from the same artist, your new playlist automatically bears that name. Way to go, Apple!

Control-clicking to Add or Delete Columns

This is worth a secret. You have a wide variety of information columns that can be displayed, aside from the usual song duration, album and artist name, and genre. Just Control-click any column heading (shown in Figure 13-3) and you can add or remove any of the headings.

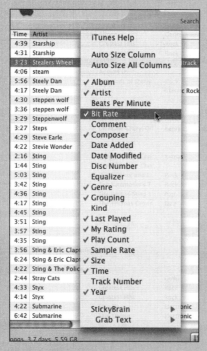

Figure 13-3: Pick a column, any column, and then pick some more.

If you choose more columns just be sure you have a display window and a monitor wide enough to show everything. There are 21 categories in all.

These contextual options are also available from the Show View Options (⌘-J) command in the Edit menu.

Just the Floating Controller

In case you haven't noticed, the maximize button doesn't work the same in iTunes as it does in most other windows and programs. If you click the green (zoom) button, it shrinks to a small window that displays only the controls (see Figure 13-4). Click the button again to restore the window.

Figure 13-4: Sure, sure, it's only a control palette. But what more do you need when your screen is already cluttered with lots of document windows and other junk?

How do you just resize (or maximize) the iTunes window? Option-click the green button.

Secret

Toggling through the Displays

Need a new viewpoint? To toggle through the types of displays in the iTunes control palette, click the time display. Normally you see total time. The other two options are elapsed and remaining time. To switch between display of the artist, title, and album's name, click the song title. All this for a click.

Building Playlists

The great way to organize your music is by building playlists. You can create playlists manually or you can set up rules to build smart playlists.

Manual Playlists

To make a normal playlist manually, click on the Create a playlist button (plus-sign) at the bottom of the Source panel (shown in Figure 13-5). This causes a new playlist, named untitled, to appear in the Source panel. You can then rename the untitled playlist by clicking on the playlist and typing the name you want (shown in Figure 13-6.)

Figure 13-5: The Create a playlist button does the same thing as selecting New Playlist (⌘-N) from the File menu.

Figure 13-6: This manually created playlist is now ready for me to drag music from other playlists or the library.

Drag and Drop to Make a Quick Playlist

You can instantly make a new playlist from an album by selecting and dragging: with the iTunes browser window on display, drag all the songs from a CD to the white area below all the listings in your Source panel. A playlist bearing the name of that album will be created. This is useful, of course, for making copies of a CD. Of course, you're doing it for your own personal entertainment only and nothing more, right?

Smart Playlists

Holding down the Option key (on the keyboard) changes the Create a playlist button (with the plus sign) into a gear-like Create a Smart Playlist button (shown in Figure 13-7). Clicking on this Smart Playlist button causes a Smart Playlist option window to appear (shown in Figure 13-8) where you can enter criteria for iTunes to automatically add songs that conform to those criteria.

Figure 13-7: Option-clicking the playlist button does the same thing as selecting the New Smart Playlist option from the File menu.

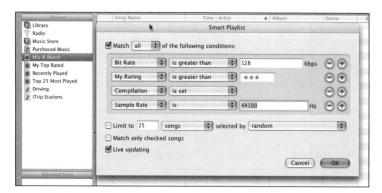

Figure 13-8: Pick and choose your criteria to build your own Smart Playlist.

After you've finished building your Smart Playlist, you can click on it in the Source panel and name it accordingly. If you need to modify the settings you can recall the criteria for editing by selecting the Edit Smart Playlist command in the File menu.

No mater what kind of list you build, you can feel free to do whatever you want with it. Removing songs from a playlist will *not* remove it from the main library.

Making Your Tunes Sound Better

Most store-bought CDs sound pretty good these days. The art and science of recording has gotten pretty good. But that isn't necessarily true for older songs, especially in the early days of CD technology when some songs sounded perfectly awful.

Fortunately, iTunes lets you second-guess the recording engineer and give the sound a tune-up. And even if the sound is great to start with, here you can, within limits of course, give the lows more depth and the highs more sparkle. Let's cover the ways.

Sound Enhancer

This special feature gives your music an extra aura of depth and liveliness. Those are buzzwords for equalizing the sound to a preset level. To make it happen, go to the Preferences dialog box in the iTunes menu. Click on Effects, and select Sound Enhancer. You can, while you're there, adjust the intensity of the enhancing effect, in case it's too much of a good thing, or just not enough.

> **note**
>
> The Effects tab offers other options besides Sound Enhancer. Crossfade playback lets one song begin just before the other ends (great for DJ mixes). Sound Check keeps levels consistent.
>
> The latter feature is especially useful if your musical tastes, like mine, include both Led Zeppelin and John Coltrane.

Equalizer

Click the Equalizer icon at the bottom-right of the iTunes window, and you can tailor the frequencies of the sound spectrum, with the frequency range divided into ten segments (shown in Figure 13-9). By dragging the sliders, you can alter the sound balance to meet your needs, whatever they might be.

Figure 13-9: Reinvent the mix, more or less, in your image.

The best way to start using the Equalizer is to use the presets from the pop-up menu (shown in Figure 13-10), paying attention to how the sound balance is tailored to a song genre.

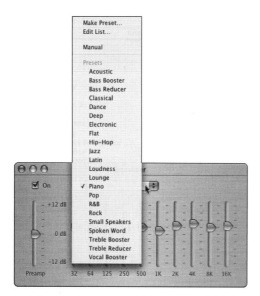

Figure 13-10: You can select from the presets or make your own preset from the pop-up menu.

You'll notice, for example, that when you select Classical or Rock, both the lows and highs are boosted, though to slightly different degrees. With Pop, the mids are boosted, because vocals tend to be in the forefront and you probably don't want to miss the lyrics (or maybe you do). You can use this as a starting point in doing your own acoustic tailoring. If you don't achieve what you want, select Flat and start from scratch.

Secret

Toggling between Approximate and Exact Playlist Times

When the library or a playlist is selected in the Source panel, the number of songs, how much time they will take to play, and how much space they take on your hard drive are displayed at the bottom of the iTunes window. You can switch between the approximate and precise time for all of the songs in the library or an individual playlist. Just click the time display. What's the end result? Well, the exact time shows minutes and seconds, whereas the approximate time shows tenths of an hour (like 6.1, 6.2, etc.). As if you really needed to know.

The Magic and Mystery of the iTunes Info Window

Why did I think of the Beatles *Magical Mystery Tour* when I created that title? Oh well, never mind.

Here's the deal: iTunes knows things about what you are playing. It gathers this information — artist name, album name, and so on — on the music in your library from Gracenote's CDDB, a music database on the Internet. That's one of the reasons, when you first set it up, the program wants you to specify whether to connect to the Internet when it needs to.

If you have a dial-up connection, you can just deselect that option in the General category of the iTunes preferences dialog box.

But when you insert an album, iTunes does not display all this important information; rather, it assumes that you must have it already from the CD. (Not that you can't enter it manually of course, as you'll see when I begin to dissect the information dialog boxes.)

A Workaround for Importing Those Pesky AIFF Files

Do you have a bunch of AIFF music files (with .aiff suffix) at hand? These are the ones you might have acquired before you imported CDs into iTunes; or maybe it's a music file you created with your own music software. (AIFF, in case you're wondering, is the native format of files on a music CD.)

The normal process of opening the File menu and selecting Add to Library or Import won't work. But there is a solution:

1. Drag the folder onto Library in the iTunes window. The songs are now in the library, although they remain AIFF.
2. Scroll to the bottom of the window (the part that contains the songs) and select the tracks.
3. Press ⌘-I and fill in the information about the artist, album, and so on and so forth. You can do this after the conversion process is done, of course.
4. From the Advanced menu, choose Convert Selection to MP3. The originals will remain selected while the songs are converted.
5. When the import process is done, hit backspace. In one fell swoop (is there any other kind), the listing for the original AIFF files are deleted. That is a real time-saver. The files themselves, however, aren't touched. So, you can delete the folder if you wish or just leave it alone if you prefer an uncompressed copy.

As you do with the Finder's famous (or infamous) Get Info window, you can access the iTunes equivalent of this feature by selecting an item and typing ⌘-I. Once you've done that, you have four tabs that display different ways to view and/or change information on a tune.

Summary Tab

The Summary tab (shown in Figure 13-11) shows title and artist information, plus the down-and-dirty details of the file and its encoding. You can also see cover art and any included music rating.

Info Tab

Now we can have some fun. In the Info tab (shown in Figure 13-12) you can actually change such categories as name, artist, and composer, among other things. So, suddenly, you, and not John Kander and Fred Ebb, wrote the song that Richard Gere sang in the movie version of *Chicago*. On a more serious level, if you opt not to connect to the Internet to retrieve this stuff, you can still supply it manually, using the original album artwork as a source for the information.

note   Yes, Richard Gere can indeed sing (although his voice may not be your cup of tea). He got his start in show business performing musicals on stage before he appeared as a male hustler in *American Gigolo*.

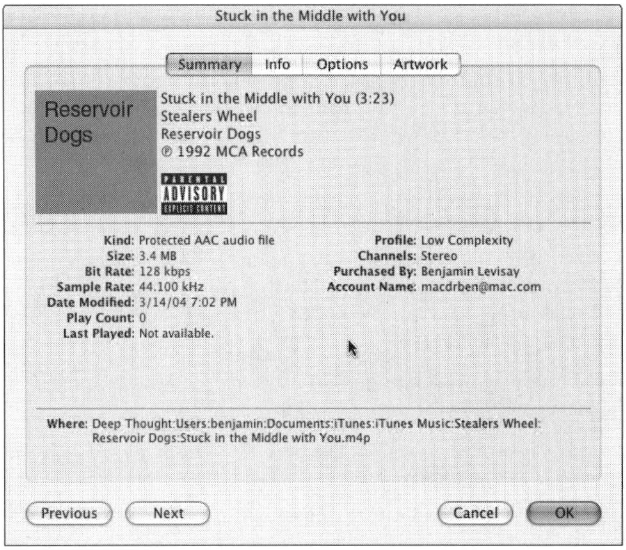

Figure 13-11: This song, purchased from the Apple Music Store, shows the file info and location as well as production information.

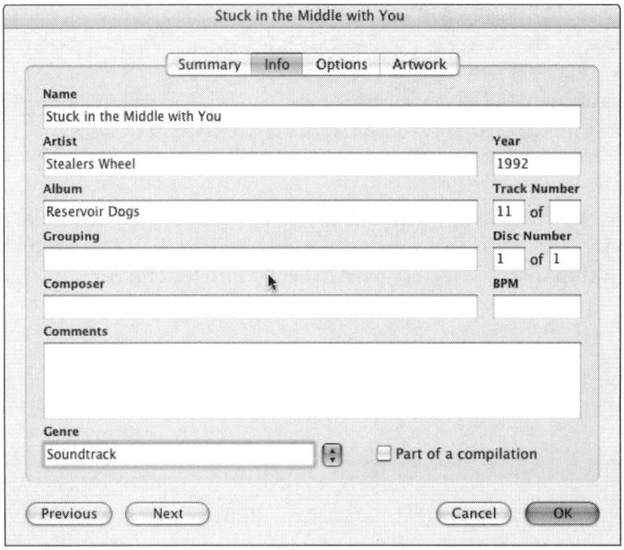

Figure 13-12: If you've purchased a song from a soundtrack on the Apple Music Store, the Genre will show as Soundtrack. You can change that designation (as well as other information) in the Info tab.

Options Tab

This is a neat one, so I'll show it to you (see Figure 13-13). You can adjust the volume setting, choose a custom preset for the equalizer (from the pop-up menu), and give the song a rating, if that's what you want.

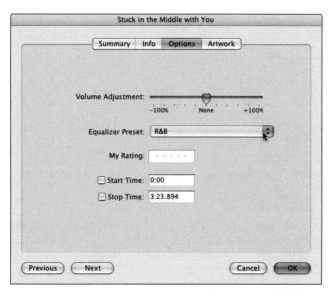

Figure 13-13: Just add a few custom settings to this tune.

No, I wouldn't recommend turning the volume up way high on hard rock songs on a friend's copy of iTunes, because that friend may no longer occupy that status if you try this. But do what ya gotta do. Just don't blame me.

Artwork Tab

For each track, just attach the original album artwork, or whatever you prefer. You can do that by clicking on the Add button or by dragging the image into the Artwork tab window (shown in Figure 13-14).

Album Art

And because we just got done talking about the Artwork tab in the info window, it's probably a good place to show off what that means. If you're ambitious, you might scan and add album cover art to your songs. If you're not, you probably will see album art from only those songs purchased from places like the iTunes Music Store.

Album art can be previewed in the lower-left corner of the iTunes window. Clicking on that artwork will open a larger version of the same art in a new window (both shown in Figure 13-15).

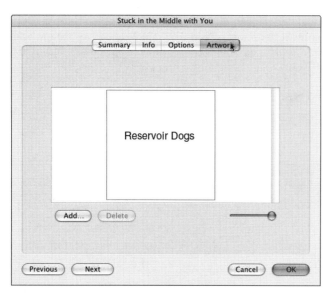

Figure 13-14: You can add, delete, and scale your artwork in this window. So, break out your scanner.

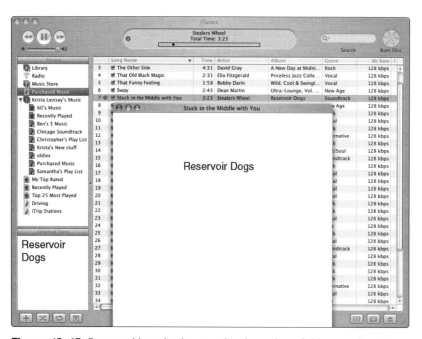

Figure 13-15: Because I bought the soundtrack version of this song, I got the soundtrack album art rather than the original album art from the original recording.

You're not stuck with album art from purchased music. You can change artwork from the Artwork tab in the song info (shown earlier in Figure 13-12).

Understanding iTunes Preferences

There are seven separate sections to the iTunes preferences (shown in Figure 13-16), which you access, as you do most preference sets, from the application menu. Each one of these sections control several items. Rather than going through each of these, I'll list them and give you a little more information about them all.

Figure 13-16: The top row of the iTunes preferences gives you access to all of the controls.

General Preferences

The General tab controls the look of your iTunes. You can change the text sizes, control the way CDs behave, and control the Internet settings in relationship to your iTunes.

Effects Preferences

The Effects tab controls the overall audio preferences in iTunes. You can set the Crossfade playback, the Sound Enhancer, and you can choose to activate the Sound Check capability of iTunes.

Importing Preferences

If mixing and ripping are what you do with iTunes, then you will need to start with the Importing preferences. Here, you choose the encoding model, the kbps settings, and the way songs behave while they are being imported into iTunes.

Burning Preferences

After mixing and ripping comes burning. The Burning tab is where you control the behavior of your burner and the formatting of your burned music CDs.

Sharing Preferences

Thanks to the wonder — Rendezvous — you can share your iTunes with other Mac OS X (10.2 and higher) users with iTunes on your LAN. In the Sharing preference you control how you share and look for music on your network. You can also set a password so that not everyone can get at your shared music.

I discuss iTunes music sharing in more depth later in this chapter.

Store Preferences

A big part of the new iTunes is the iTunes Music Store. And leave it to Apple to help you decide how you want your shopping experience to work right in the preferences. The Store preferences allow you to choose to a 1-Click or a Shopping Cart buying model. (Personally, I like the 1-Click shopping method.)

Advanced Preferences

You find, after collecting music for a while, that it adds up. I have about five-and-a-half gigabytes of MP3s on my hard drive. And I'd rather that they didn't reside in my home folder (which is the default location for music). In order to make that decision, I had to choose to *not* copy my music files to the iTunes Music folder when adding them to the library.

> **note**   Purchased music from the iTunes Music Store is automatically stored in your home folder. If you don't like it there, you'll have to move it manually.

You can also set or change the iTunes Music folder as well as setting the streaming buffer size for iTunes.

Other Stuff about the iTunes Interface

There are a lot of things about the iTunes interface that don't fall into convenient categories. So I thought I'd create this catchall category and talk to you about some of iTunes other functions and capabilities.

Searching for Music

In the upper-right corner of the iTunes window, next to the Browse button, you can see the familiar search field (shown in Figure 13-17). Choosing a playlist or the library and then typing the name of the song or any of the other information will allow you to search by artist, album, composer, song name, or all of them.

Figure 13-17: Clicking and holding the triangle next to the magnifying glass icon gives you a menu to refine your search.

Like all other searches in Panther, you will find that hitting the Return key is not necessary. The results start appearing and changing as you type.

Changing a Song's Rating

Today, you like it and it's five stars, but it grows old really fast, and after five thousand plays, you decide the rating just won't hold up. (I won't mention how many times I've heard the Beatles sing "Yesterday.")

Here's how you alter the rating to address your changing tastes:

1. Select your song (or songs) in the iTunes Library.
2. Control-click on the song and choose the rating in the contextual menu (shown in Figure 13-18).

Figure 13-18: As usual, Apple continues to provide us with great contextual menu support even though they still don't have a two-button mouse.

Sharing Your Music Library

iTunes 4 takes full advantage of Mac OS X's Rendezvous (or zero configuration) networking. What this means is that if another Jaguar user opens iTunes on another computer on your network, that user's playlist(s) appears in your iTunes window too (shown in Figure 13-19). You'll see that list, that is, if they've selected the Share My Music option in the Sharing tab of the iTunes preferences dialog box (see the iTunes Preferences section earlier in this chapter). After that's done, any of the songs in their library can be played.

Figure 13-19: Selected shared playlists will show in a submenu. Sharing an entire library shows only one menu option in the Shared section of the Source panel.

And if you've opted to share your music, you'll be able to open that preference dialog box and actually see how many people are accessing your library.

The feature also gives you bragging rights. If there are some Mac OS 9 holdouts on your network or, perish forbid, Windows users, they won't see the great music library you've created for yourself. It requires Mac OS X 10.2 or later.

Streaming Radio

I work (during the day) in a small office in a section of town where I just don't get great radio reception. And yet, I still like to tune into NPR. So, what's a Panther-running-iTunes-ready-Mac-guy to do? (Wait for it . . .) That's right. You can get and play online radio via iTunes and a decent Internet connection.

Clicking on Radio in the Source panel of iTunes brings up a list of radio subcategories (shown in Figure 13-20). Inside each of those categories are active stations. Selecting one of these stations and clicking on the Play button allows you to listen to simulcast online stations.

Figure 13-20: A radio station is shown here selected and with its info box open. The higher the bit rate, the better the station will sound.

tip   You can drag a radio station into a playlist to create your own short list of your favorite iTunes radio stations.

Speeding Up the CD Burning Process

Get a faster CD burner. Okay, now that all of you are groaning at my temerity or lack of a sense of humor, let me try to get practical and real here. You can't control how fast your optical drive runs, but you can control a few things that'll make the process go smoother, with less intervention on your part.

Here's what I mean:

1. With the iTunes browser window on display, select and drag all the songs you want to the Source panel, the one at the left. This creates a new playlist, and if all the songs are by the same artist, the playlist bears that name by default. Remember to check that the combined size of all the songs in the playlist is not larger than the recording capacity of the CD.

2. Now click the Burn Disk button in the upper-right corner of the iTunes browser window that looks like a little nuclear caution symbol.

note   It's a good idea not to put the CD in the drive before clicking that Burn Disk button. Otherwise, the Finder goes through an initialization process for the CD and annoys you with needless onscreen prompts.

3. When you see the request to insert the CD in the top of the browser window, open the drive and insert it.

4. Now, sit back and wait for the process to complete. You can't speed it up, but like a watched pot, it'll never boil — make that finish — if you stand over it. Just walk away and do something else; it'll finish in its own time.

Getting Groovy with Visuals

Since the very first version of iTunes, you've had the ability to play your music and "get mellow" with Apple's visual effects. To do this, turn the Visualizer on in the Visualizer menu (shown in Figure 13-21) and then choose to have the visual effects displayed in a window or the entire screen.

Figure 13-21: The visual effects are important enough to merit their own menu in iTunes.

What you get are some cool visual effects that are influenced by the music playing. You can also see the song information and album art (if available) at the beginning of the visual session (shown on Figure 13-22).

Figure 13-22: As you can see from this visual, Apple doesn't miss the opportunity to flash its logo in the visual animation.

Toggling the iTunes Info Screen

Speaking of visual effects, you can also change the oval info screen at the top of your iTunes window by clicking on the small triangle to the left of the oval. You usually see the name of the song, the status of the song as it's playing and other such information. This information can be replaced with the dancing digital sound levels (shown in Figure 13-23).

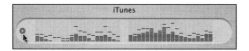

Figure 13-23: Not as informative, but the digital sound level is a little more interesting.

Visiting the iTunes Music Store

Did you ever download a song over Napster or using LimeWire or another file swapping program? Have you thought for a moment whether it's the kosher thing to do? After all, with the likes of Madonna and Mick Jagger living in the lap of luxury, how could you hurt them downloading some of their tunes, right?

I think that this is wrong. And since this is my opinion, let's see if Pieter has anything to say about it.

We Interrupt This Chapter . . .

I have certain moral objections about stealing music. As Steve Jobs said, "It's bad karma." But are there other reasons?

Pieter: Benjamin, not only might the file not be kosher, it could actually be more toxic than that mayonnaise that was left out on the counter during a hot summer day. Hackers have started to seed the major file-sharing networks like Kazaa and LimeWire with viruses and Trojan horses that can infect a computer and cause all sorts of damage. While Mac OS X is largely immune to these little gems, who knows when someone will write one that is as happy destroying your Mac as a vampire in a blood bank. Also, the major record companies have been talking publicly about releasing files that can jam your Mac and they may introduce technologies that, like the anti-counterfeiting technology in Photoshop CS, prevent your Mac from accessing pirated music.

Benjamin: Frankly, I doubt that the record companies are going to convince Apple to open up its architecture enough to be a de facto virus. I believe that kind of talk is alarmist. I don't think there's anything sinister about anti-piracy features. IMHO, this is much ado about nothing!

But if you want another reason (besides the fact that it's wrong and it's bad karma) to buy music rather than downloading it off some peer-to-peer sharing service, how about this . . . you get what you pay for. If you listen to the junk that you download, it's not as good as the purchased music. In my opinion, life is too short to drink cheap beer or listen to low quality music.

This takes us to the Apple Music Store (see Figure 13-24), where you can download any of hundreds of thousands of tunes (or entire albums) for a song, if you'll excuse the pun.

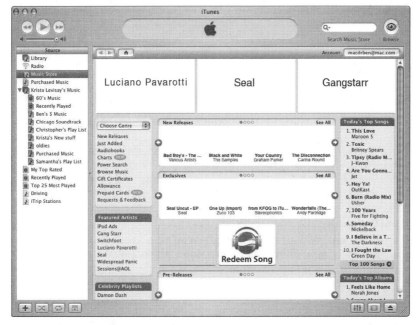

Figure 13-24: Whether you dig classical, jazz, rock or other musical genres, here's a great place to build your music library.

Getting there is so simple, it's hardly worth mentioning. Just get online, launch iTunes 4 or later, click Music Store in the program's browser window, and you're ready to rock.

Let's Go Shopping!

The best way to talk about the iTunes Music Store is to take you through the shopping process. So let's do that together. Ready? Okay.

1. Open iTunes and click on the Music Store in the Source panel. This opens the iTunes Music store in the main window (shown in Figure 13-24).

2. Click on an area, select a genre, or type in a song or selection in the search field. Any of these processes will eventually take you to an album page where you can see information about the music (shown in Figure 13-25).

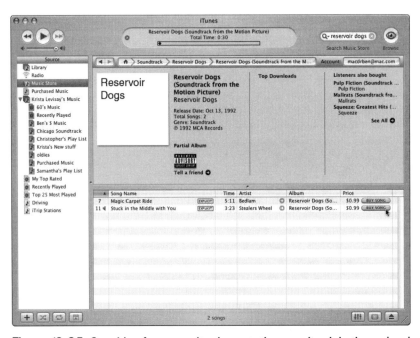

Figure 13-25: Searching for a soundtrack opens the soundtrack in the main window.

3. Once you've navigated to where you want to go, you can double-click on the song to preview 30 seconds of the song. If you like it, and if you've set up your iTunes account for 1-Click shopping, you can buy and download the song by clicking on the Buy Song button to the far right of the listed song.

4. Clicking on the Buy Song button brings a window that prompts you to sign in to purchase the song (shown in Figure 13-26).

5. If your account is Okay, Apple prompts you with another dialog box to confirm your selection and your intent to download it.

Figure 13-26: You can use your .Mac account, your AOL account, or set up a new account to purchase music via the Apple Music Store. All you need is a credit card.

6. Once you've confirmed your intent to purchase the song, your song starts downloading. You see the status of the download in the oval iTunes info window (shown in Figure 13-27).

Figure 13-27: The faster your connection, the less time you have to watch the download status bar.

Enjoy your music. You're done.

Purchased music will be automatically added to a playlist in your Source panel called Purchased Music.

Exploring the iTunes Music Store

What's the best way to discover the huge music library that Apple is assembling for its music download service? I asked the folks at Apple Computer that question and they gave me a few tricks. I won't call them secrets — they are front-and-center for everyone to use — but they can take you a long way towards enhancing the thrill of discovery.

New Music Tuesdays

When you create an account on the iTunes Music Store, which takes just a minute, you can subscribe to a weekly e-mail announcement that highlights the major music and artists that have been added to the store since the previous week (shown in Figure 13-28).

Figure 13-28: See, my e-mail doesn't consist of just, well, questionable offers from questionable companies.

The Thrill of Discovery

Ever heard of the Yeah Yeah Yeahs? Do you care? Listen to free 30-second previews of tracks from their latest album *Fever to Tell* and explore a sound that *Rolling Stone* calls "primal thrust and blare." Now whether or not you're into such things, you can still browse links from the home page for New Releases, Exclusive Tracks, Pre-Releases, Staff Favorites, Up & Coming Artists, and Celebrity Playlists and discover a hot new artist that you can turn all your friends on to.

Why iTunes Skips Purchased Music

Why is iTunes skipping the songs you bought from the Apple Music Store? An antipiracy conspiracy? Not at all. When you listen to songs on a playlist that's being shared, iTunes has a nasty habit of skipping any purchased music on that list. You have to double-click the song to hear it. As that famous newscaster used to say, that's the way it is.

Just Pick a Genre

All you have to do is click on the Browse button and search by musical genre, including Alternative, Holiday, Soundtrack, Children's Music, Alternative, and Rock. I'll pick Rock, for example, since my son wails away to a fare-thee-well on his Fender Strat. You'll see a pretty complete list of your favorite acts, including Aerosmith, Sting, and so on. If you're looking for a band such as Coldplay, press the C-key on your keyboard and the listing will immediately jump to artists that begin with that letter.

Top-10 Lists

What's a music library without a listing of the most popular tunes, right? Well, Apple's Top-10 lists of album and music downloads is right on the home page, and updated regularly. So, if you are always looking for the most popular selections, or you're just curious, you can check the list. If you click on the More Top Songs or More Top Albums links at the bottom of those lists, you can actually consult the full Top 100.

Secret

About the iTunes Web Browser Engine

It is no coincidence that navigating the Music Store is very much like navigating a Web site, because that's what the Music Store is. iTunes 4 incorporates the same Web browser engine that powers Safari. Now you can see that Apple didn't just build that browser just to give it away in a free application. The latest versions of OmniWeb also use the same browser engine, which is freely available to any Apple developer who wants to inject Web-based content into their software.

note Your playlists are permanently related to the songs in your library, just like you are related to your parents or siblings. If you change the way something is listed in the library, or remove it altogether, the playlists spawned from it will change accordingly.

Secret

Previewing Songs with a Dial-up Connection

Bandwidth challenged? You might find that the previews you try to play from the iTunes music store are jittery, because it's streaming at 128 Kbps, and that's entry-level broadband. There's a way around this, although it may slow down your ability to browse the store. Take a fast trip to the iTunes menu and choose Preferences. In the Preferences window, click the Store icon and choose Load complete preview before playing.

iTunes Essentials

You know how you can purchase compilations and collections of genre or theme music from TV? We see short commercials as well as full-blown infomercials about it. Well, Apple has the same thing.

I'm not talking about the Staff Favorites, which is fun to go through. No. Instead, there is a relatively new section called the iTunes Essentials. It contains some great collections put together by what must be some fairly interesting and sophisticated people In fact the first "full album" I ever purchased from the iTunes Music Store was an Essentials album.

AAC and MP3: How Do They Do It?

Ever check the size of an uncompressed audio or video file? When I recorded a 45-minute telephone interview for my weekly radio show, the sound recording software put everything in AIFF format. The entire segment filled 460MB on my Power Mac's drive. At that rate, even a huge 120GB hard drive can get filled up mighty fast.

Now obviously, more data usually takes up a whole lot more space, so how can all of that be squeezed onto a DVD and still include multichannel audio with full surround sound?

How does Apple manage to reduce file sizes so much for the songs you get from its music store? Can StuffIt accomplish this feat of legerdemain or is there another way?

When it comes to music, audio engineers devised something called *perceptual coding* (which is used for both AAC and MP3 files), which means that the music file contains only the stuff you can hear. How this is done is very complicated, but part of this magic is accomplished by the fact that some sounds mask other sounds, so they aren't heard.

When the encoding technique is used properly, and that doesn't always happen, you can barely distinguish the resulting sound from a regular CD, even though the file size is reduced to but a fraction of the original.

Now you might think that these engineers are sitting down with calculators and computers figuring this all out, but they actually use human subjects to test the encoding schemes. The tests are done blind, which means that the sources cannot be identified by sight, only by the sound. When the tests are done properly, and it takes time and dedication on the part of both test administrators and the victims — er, subjects — of the test, you can get a pretty good idea of what works and what doesn't.

MP3 is coding standard for compression of audio data: MPEG-2 Layer 3. This is the most common encoding used on the Internet because of it's high quality. Even if the encoding method is nearly perfect, the level of compression also affects the final sound quality. That means an MP3 file with a bit rate of 256 Kbps should sound better than one at 128 Kbps.

Apple uses 128 Kbps for its music store files, which use the AAC format, created by Dolby, and part of the QuickTime 4 format. The claim is that the sound quality "rivals" that of a regular CD containing the same music.

Can you believe that claim? The only real way to test the theory is with a blind test, same as those scientists and engineers use. If you just listen casually, and you know which is the CD and which is the song from iTunes, your conclusion is tainted. It's human nature. You can't just will your bias away.

And here's my humble view: Both AAC and MP3 sound just great, good enough that it may require a pretty good system to tell them apart from a CD.

iPod: Your Music on the Go

All right, the iPod may seem, at first glance, to be just a music player. You scroll through your playlist, you start a tune, and you stop a tune. You adjust the volume control, and the rest you can explore at your leisure. So why do you need to concern yourself about secrets? Probably because it's not just a music player.

That's the purpose of this book — to explore a few of the more useful secrets and make you wonder how you got along without them.

So, in this section, I tell you things you never knew about the iPod, and maybe a few things you don't want to know. But that's how it goes.

iPod Fundamentals

Whether you have a brand new iPod mini, or one of the larger models (shown in Figure 13-29), they all follow a basic theme. The player is a beautiful package, smaller than a pack of playing cards, on which you can store thousands of tunes.

Figure 13-29: The iPod mini, although smaller, comes in five cool colors. The large iPods come only in white (for now) but hold a lot more music.

Here's an introduction to the iPod, in case you haven't gotten in on the fun.

A Hard Drive and Music Player in One

The iPod uses a hard drive to store your tunes, and its drive can also serve to store your data. In fact, I take my iPod with me on the road with backups to my important data, just in case something happens to my PowerBook and I need a way to get to my files.

When you plug your iPod in to your Mac, it shows up on the desktop as a mounted volume (shown in Figure 13-30). Double-clicking on the iPod icon opens up a Finder window where you can hold your favorite files (shown in Figure 13-31).

Figure 13-30: The Desktop icon doesn't leave much doubt about what this device is.

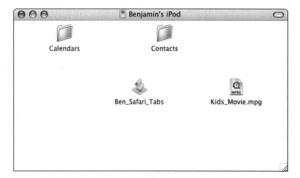

Figure 13-31: Drag and drop. The iPod is also just a FireWire hard drive.

It's important to note that music files uploaded via iTunes take up disk space, but do not show in the Finder window.

Simple Navigation

The iPod has a scroll wheel, a center-mounted select button, and four standard playback controls. So, starting, stopping, and moving forward and back are no big deal. Just twirl the scroll wheel to navigate through the menus on the iPod (shown in Figure 13-32) and pick selections from your music library by such categories as artist or genre. Once you've twirled and pressed a few buttons, you'll find that it all comes naturally, and you can think about listening rather than navigating.

Figure 13-32: Scroll and click is all you need to do to navigate through the iPod screens.

Uses FireWire Port for Power

Although Windows advocates believe in USB-2.0-or-bust, Apple's own invention, FireWire, provides not only a fast peripheral port but also enough power to recharge the iPod while it's connected to your Mac.

note PC users need to know that current iPods do support USB 2.0, with an optional connector. But getting your iPod charged is a bit clumsy, since USB doesn't provide enough power. Your connector has a second port to hook up to a spare FireWire port, or you have to plug it in to the power socket to give the iPod enough juice to operate. But if your Windows PC has the usual four to six USB 2.0 ports and nothing else, and you don't want to invest in a FireWire card, that's the compromise you have to make for using that platform.

Putting the Shine Back on Your iPod

Now this should come as no surprise to you, but the iPod's pretty metallic finish is easily smudged and scratched. That's why there's been such a market for iPod cases; and Apple began to include their own case with some models beginning with the second generation.

But what if the case comes too late? You brushed against it, dropped it, or just carried it around in your pocket or purse along with your car keys. Fortunately, there is salvation, in the form of a product called Brasso Metal Polish. I understand you can get some at your local home improvement superstore. While I don't dabble in such cleaners myself, I suggest you use a soft cloth or paper towel, because you don't want to create new scratches in your quest to remove the old ones.

Store Your Contact List

In some respects, the iPod resembles a handheld computer, so it's natural to think of using the iPod to hold your contacts. To store contacts, simply connect iPod to your Mac and launch your favorite e-mail or contacts application. It doesn't matter whether it's Mac OS X Mail, Microsoft Entourage, or a contact manager such as Now-Up-to-Date. Export your contacts as vCard files and copy them to the Contacts folder on your iPod. In most cases, you can actually drag contacts from the application's address book directly to the iPod's Contacts folder. Next time you unmount and disconnect your iPod, you'll be able to access your contacts within your iPod directly from its menus.

You can also use iSync to upload your contacts and appointments. Launching iSync (from the Applications folder) should show you your iPod as one of your Sync options. If it doesn't, you can add the device from the Devices menu.

Clicking on the iPod in the iSync application gives you synchronization options for your calendars and contacts (shown in Figure 13-33). After you've selected your options, all you need to do is click on the Sync Now button to start the data upload to your iPod (shown in Figure 13-34).

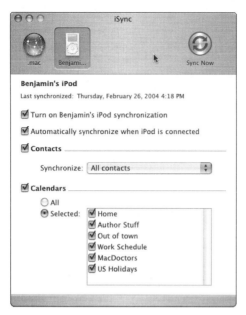

Figure 13-33: Choose your preferences and get ready to sync up.

Figure 13-34: The first time you do this, it takes a while for that blue status bar to move all the way across iSync, especially if you have a lot of information.

You now have your appointments and contacts easily available from the same device that gives you great music.

Unleashing Your iPod for Others to Hear

You've spent a bundle on a fancy home stereo, and you dread the prospect of burn-ing tons of CDs to bring your iTunes music library over, or install your Mac in the same room. (My wife would object.) Wouldn't it be nice just to plug in your iPod to lis-ten to those songs? You can buy an audio adapter to tap the iPod's headphone output, of course. The Apple Store and even Radio Shack have adapter cables, which consist of a ministereo plug at one end, for the headphones, and a pair of phono plugs at the other end, which are compatible with a typical home stereo. (Use one of the auxiliary or line-in jacks.) You will have to adjust the level, so the output doesn't overwhelm your stereo or fry your tweeters. Even better, if you have the third-generation model with the smaller form factor, and are lucky enough to have an iPod dock at hand (an option with the entry-level model), you'll find a real ministereo line-out jack at the rear.

If you want to share the joy with other listeners in your car, there are two ways. One is an FM transmitter, such as the iRock or iTrip. These tiny units plug into your iPod's earphone outlet and send the signal, wirelessly, to your car's FM radio, or one in your home for that matter. The other option consists of a cassette-like module that, at one end, plugs into your iPod or any music player, and, at the other, goes into your car's cassette player. My opinion is that the FM transmitter has somewhat better sound, but you may have problems getting a stable signal if you have lots of FM stations in your city. The cassette adapter has the same limitations as a regular cassette player, and may make the highs seem a little harsh.

iPod Preferences

Remember that in order for you to transfer contacts and other files, the iPod must be enabled for use as a FireWire hard disk. How do you do that? With the iPod connected to your Mac, select the iPod in your iTunes window, and then click the player options button at the lower-right (shown in Figure 13-35). Select Enable disk use (shown in Figure 13-36), and you're done.

Figure 13-35: The little iPod (player options) button is the key to your iPod control.

Figure 13-36: After you've checked the Enable disk use option, you get a warning telling you that you now have to dismount your iPod before putting it away.

By the way, if you've opted to manage your tunes manually in the same preference dialog box, the iPod automatically mounts on your desktop anyway. And don't forget to dismount it before disconnecting, to avoid damaging the drive's directory.

Your iPod and iTunes

I got so caught up about all of the tips and details about the iPod that I almost forgot to show you what it was most intended to do. It's meant to show up in your iTunes window so you can drag songs and/or entire playlists to it so that you can take your music with you.

This is done either by manually dragging your music on the iPod in the Source panel of iTunes or by setting the autoupdate preferences in the iPod preferences (shown in Figure 13-37).

Figure 13-37: If you choose to manually drag playlists to your iPod, you will see those playlists under the main iPod choice in the Source panel.

Although manually dragging music take a little longer, I think it's actually more fun. No matter how you do it, you can monitor the space usage of your iPod at the bottom of the iTunes screen when you select the iPod in the Source panel.

Managing the Space on Your iPod

Is your iPod running out of space? You don't have to toss it out and buy one with a bigger capacity, although Apple would probably love it if you did. I had a customer that ran into just that problem when his 15GB iPod couldn't contain his entire music library.

The solution is simple. With your iPod connected to your Mac, click on the little iPod icon at the bottom right of the iTunes browser window. You have two choices to reduce the number of tunes on your iPod. The first is to update selected playlists, and you can click the ones listed. The other is to update manually, which means you will have to drag songs or playlists into your iPod to copy them over. It's not really a bad idea, as I bet you have lots of songs you don't listen to that often, and others that are beginning to bore you to death.

Hints and Tricks to Make the iPod More Powerful

Before I get to outright secrets, I'm going to summarize some important tips and tricks to help you get the most power out of your iPod. Then we'll get to the really cool stuff, which isn't widely advertised. (Otherwise, why would there be a reason for this book?)

- ◆ **Make your battery last longer.** The third-generation (or 3G) iPod has a smaller battery, hence less battery life. But regardless of the model iPod you have, you can get better longevity from a single charge by following three simple steps. First, make sure you always have the latest iPod software, as Apple is constantly making improvements. Usually it'll show up in your Software Update preference panel, but sometimes it first appears at Apple's Web site. Also, use the Hold switch, which prevents the iPod from accidentally turning on if you press a button by mistake, and third, keep the iPod at room temperature. Very hot is never good for consumer electronics, and a cold climate also cuts short battery life. Apple recommends temperatures from 32 to 95 degrees Fahrenheit, which means they haven't traveled to Las Vegas or Phoenix in the summer. Have you thought of moving lately?

> **note** In case you're wondering, the iPod quickly reaches 80 percent of capacity after about an hour of charging, but can take an additional two hours to finish the process. When the unit as asleep, a small amount of current is used. If you left it that way, it would take two to four weeks to deplete the battery.

- ◆ **Battery life tips in no particular order:** Extra features can consume battery life. The backlight is a big source of power drain. So, keep it off, unless you intend to use your iPod in dim surroundings. Just choose Backlight Timer from the Settings menu and turn it off. While you're at it, you can also turn off the EQ in your iPod and save a bit of battery life, but why hurt sound quality to save a trip to the charging station? You can also increase battery life by keeping your finger off the Previous/Rewind or Next/Fast-Forward buttons. When you use these controls, tracks have to be retrieved from the drive and that requires battery energy. If you just let your iPod play track after track, as stored on the unit, it'll store as many songs as it can in the cache before retrieving more and call its hard drive less frequently.

Checking Your iPod's Hard Drive

You know the score. You want to check the directory of your drive, so you break out a copy of Alsoft DiskWarrior, Norton Utilities, or TechTool Pro. I won't say these programs will certainly damage your iPod's drive directory, but it's better not to take chances.

The best way to check your iPod's disk for health is to follow these steps:

1. Restart your iPod, by holding down the Menu and Play/Pause buttons at the same time. On third-generation models, you have to plug the unit into an AC outlet and toggle the Hold switch on and off before doing this.

2. When you see the Apple logo, hold down the following buttons at the same time: Next, Previous, Menu, and Select (the button in the center). You see an image of a disk and a magnifying glass, and over the next few minutes, the drive is scanned and minor directory problems are fixed.

One iPod Equals One User

The iPod is supposedly designed to mate with a single Mac, so when you hook it up to a second Mac, it wants to update using the second Mac's music library. If that Mac has only those dozen or so tracks that ship with new Macs (or even if it has more music than you have on your iPod), you don't want it destroying that vast library of Classic Rock songs you've created over half a lifetime.

What to do? When you hook up your iPod to that second Mac, just say no. No, this isn't some sort of warning not to steal music or take drugs. Instead, you are telling it not to synchronize that Mac's playlist. Instead, you want to click in the iPod Options button, the little icon at the lower right of iTunes that resembles an iPod. Click the option to manage your playlist Manually, and click OK.

Now you can manually manipulate that playlist however you like, or just play your tracks in the same fashion as any other iTunes playlist.

caution Don't forget that you shouldn't disconnect the iPod until you unmount the iPod's icon. You don't want to damage the drive's directory.

Other Stuff You Can Do with Your iPod

You can play games on a cell phone, so it's natural to expect to be able to play games on anything with a screen. Well, maybe you play games on your cell phone; I always thought they were designed to make and receive calls, but I'm an old fashioned dude (or just an old dude), so I don't know any better.

In any case, there are game(s) on your iPod. On my iPod I have solitaire Here's how to invoke it:

1. Navigate to your iPod's Extra menu.
2. If you want to be practical, you can choose the Alarm Clock (shown in Figure 13-38) and keep yourself on schedule.

Figure 13-38: The practical side of your iPod.

3. But if you're tired of being responsible, maybe you want to select Solitaire (shown in Figure 13-39) or whatever game is on your iPod and play a round or two. Have fun!

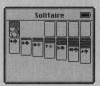

Figure 13-39: On your iPod, no one can hear you cheat. . . .

A Few Last Words about the iPod

The iPod is not just an MP3 player. With add-ons from other hardware companies it can be a fairly good PIM, and audio voice recorder, a radio transmitter, and gosh knows what else in the future. It is more than it was and it continues to grow in functionality and ease of use.

The reason for this is that the same company who makes the *best* computer and computer platform in the world is also at the helm of this digital device. So, when you start comparing the iPod against other MP3 players, keep that in mind.

Getting into GarageBand

"So you want to be a rock 'n' roll star?
Then listen now to what I say
Just get an electric guitar
Then take some time
And learn how to play"

(From "So You Want to Be a Rock 'n' Roll Star" by McGuinn/Hillman)

Sounds pretty simple, no? But that advice is *so* last century. If you want to be a rock 'n' roll star today, you might want to get a Mac, a MIDI keyboard, and iLife '04 with GarageBand to go along with the electric guitar. Then you can be not only a rock 'n' roll star, but an entire rock 'n' roll band! (Of course, you'll still want to take some time and learn how to play. Nothing comes free, kids.)

GarageBand is the flip side to iTunes. Where iTunes is all about storing and playing music, GarageBand is all about making music. And making your own music has never been easier or so much fun. So kick back, tune your axe, and get ready to start jamming.

GarageBand Overture

When Apple released GarageBand in early 2004, tech writers spilled gallons of ink trying to describe just what the heck the program was. It was not as though no software like it had ever been marketed before; it was just that no software like it had been marketed to the general computer-using public before. And what was that software? Essentially, it was a simplified multitrack digital audio recorder/MIDI sequencer/editor/mixer, which included an extensible library of musical loops that users could add to their own compositions. (If your head began to swim while reading that sentence, you can understand why gallons of ink were spilled when GarageBand came out.) But GarageBand is really not as complicated as that description suggests: think of GarageBand as iMovie for music. (Or if you're feeling less charitable, think of it as PowerPoint for music.)

note Many professional musicians, of course, quickly figured out exactly what GarageBand was and, depending on their levels of anxiety, sophistication, and arrogance, variously pronounced it to be extremely cool, uninterestingly trivial, or a gross insult to musicians everywhere — in short, they dealt with it pretty much as professional typesetters and layout artists dealt with the emergence of desktop publishing software twenty years earlier.

Figure 13-40 is a picture of GarageBand in action that's worth at least a thousand words. In it, you can see a few musical *tracks* (a track being all the notes played by one particular instrument over the course of a song), as well as GarageBand's playback controls and a portion of the program's built-in library of musical snippets (called *loops*, which are at the core of most GarageBand musical creations).

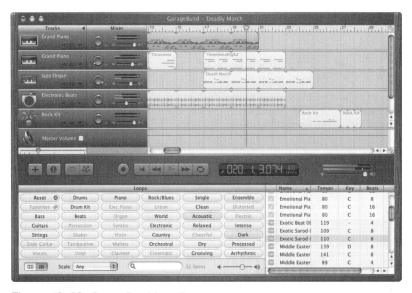

Figure 13-40: GarageBand in action.

Get the picture? GarageBand turns your Mac into a home recording studio. Not the most sophisticated of home recording studios, of course — what do you want for a piece of software that costs less than $10? — but a quite capable one that is really, really, *really* easy to learn and to use. Even if you can't play a note. Even if you're tone deaf.

GarageBand Theme and Exposition

GarageBand is really *big*. About the best I can do here is give you a note-by-note overview of its features. With GarageBand you can do many things, including the following:

- **Record from a MIDI instrument.** *MIDI* stands for *Musical Instrument Digital Interface*, and a MIDI instrument, often called a *MIDI controller,* converts the notes you play (typically on a piano-like keyboard) into a sequence of numbers that indicate the length of a note, its intensity (or *velocity*), its pitch, and so forth. MIDI sequences don't contain any actual audio; they contain the specifications that let a piece of software or hardware generate sound. Think of a MIDI recording as a special kind of musical score that a computer or other device can play back as music.

- **Change the software instrument assigned to a MIDI recording.** Apple calls the audio synthesizers and filters that generate sound from MIDI information *software instruments*. GarageBand comes with about fifty different software instruments. You can buy more instruments from Apple and third-party sources, too.

- **Change the various playback settings of a software instrument.** Aside from the basic instrument sound (such as, say, a piano sound), you can adjust its echo, reverberation, and other audio qualities.

- **Record from a real instrument or microphone.** GarageBand calls such recordings (including vocal recordings) *real instruments*. If your Mac has a built-in microphone, you can record a real instrument track from it. If it has an audio input jack, you can plug in microphones or instruments like electric guitars and record real instrument tracks from them. If your Mac doesn't have an audio input or a microphone, you can still hook up a USB audio converter, such as a Griffin iMic (www.griffintechnology.com), plug a microphone or instrument into the converter, and record real instrument tracks that way.

- **Change the audio characteristics of recorded audio.** GarageBand lets you apply a number of audio filters and effects to audio recordings. Although you can't quite make, say, a guitar sound like a flute with these filters and effects, you can still perform some rather extensive audio manipulation that used to be the province of high-end specialized audio hardware and software: High-pass and low-pass filters, flangers, auto-wah, and tremolo are just a few of the many choices available to you. Rock guitarists will particularly enjoy (and employ) GarageBand's *amp simulation* effects.

- **Edit MIDI notes and other MIDI information.** Among other things, you can manually move a note, change a note, adjust a note's timing, adjust a note's rate of decay (called *sustain*), *bend* a note's pitch (much like bending a string on a guitar), and more. If you have a poor sense of timing and can't quite follow the beat, GarageBand will even fix that for you.

- **Edit digitized sound.** You can cut, copy, and paste sections of recorded audio and move them from track to track.

- **Control volume on a track-by-track basis.** You can adjust the overall volume of any track or change the volume of a track to different levels at different times, making it louder at one point and quieter at another. You can also control how much of the track is played through the left or right stereo speaker (that is, you can adjust its *pan position*).

♦ **Use prerecorded MIDI musical loops.** GarageBand comes with hundreds of short, royalty-free, MIDI recordings, arranged by instrument type, mood, key, tempo, and so on. These *loops* can be dragged into any software instrument track. They are called loops because not only can they be made to repeat, they are *designed* to repeat. When you realize that many songs consist largely of various musical phrases that repeat one or more times, you can see how an extensive library of musical loops can be more than just a minor convenience.

♦ **Use prerecorded audio loops.** A fair number of GarageBand's loops are real instrument recordings rather than MIDI recordings, and you can drag them around and make them repeat, just like you can with software instrument loops.

♦ **Transpose loops to different keys.** *Transposing* means moving all the notes in a musical passage up or down the musical scale by a specific amount. If, for example, you are writing a song in the key of G, and you have a loop in the key of F, GarageBand lets you transpose the loop's notes two *semitones* higher so that it plays back in G. (A semitone is the difference in pitch between two adjacent keys on a piano keyboard or the difference between one fret and the next on a guitar.) And you can do this not only for software instrument loops, but also for real instrument loops (which, let me tell you, is not a trivial exercise in audio engineering).

♦ **Adjust a song's tempo and time signature.** *Tempo* is the number of *beats per minute.* (A beat is, well, a beat, the rhythm that you tap your toes to.) *Time signature* is written like a ratio: the number of beats in each *measure* (measures are the subdivisions into which notes are arranged in a written musical score) over the type of note that a beat represents in the score (for example, a quarter-note is 4, a half-note is 2). Many songs are in *4/4* time: four beats per measure, with each beat being written as a quarter-note. In fact, 4/4 is such a common time signature that it's often called *common time.*

♦ **Mix a song's tracks down to an audio file and store it in your iTunes library.** When you export your song to iTunes, GarageBand renders it as an AIFF file that is in exactly the same format as uncompressed files that you rip from a CD in iTunes: stereo, 16-bit audio sampled at 44kHz. Perfect for burning the demo CD that will launch your trip to the top of the charts.

Concerto for Several Dozen Instruments

In GarageBand, each song consists of a collection of tracks (there's always at least one track in a GarageBand song), and each track consists of the performance of one instrument, either a software instrument or a real instrument. In addition, a song possesses a name, a tempo, a time signature, and a key, all of which you specify when you create a new song (shown in Figure 13-41).

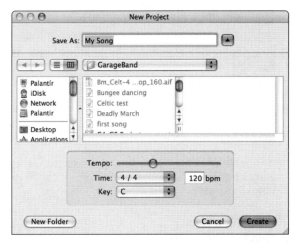

Figure 13-41: Time, tempo, and key are part of each new song.

Although you can play in any key or tempo you like when you record tracks in a song (otherwise, it would be impossible for you to ever play a wrong note [even a *right* wrong note] and GarageBand is neither that smart nor that restrictive), the time signature, tempo, and key you specify are still important: They control the way the timeline is subdivided (shown in Figure 13-42), the readings on the time display (see Figure 13-43), and the rate at which GarageBand's helpful metronome ticks when you record. You can change a song's tempo, key, and time signature at any time, but you can't have multiple tempi, keys, or time signatures in a single GarageBand song. Sorry, Scriabin; condolences, Mr. Copland.

Figure 13-42: The timeline looks like a ruler divided into measures and beats.

Figure 13-43: The time display presents the tempo along with the current measure, beat, and tick.

---

insider
insight

The time display can also show you normal time. Just click the little note at the display's left end to switch between time and tempo displays. You can also change the song's tempo by clicking the Tempo readout on the display's right end and then dragging up or down.

When you create a new song, GarageBand helpfully provides a software instrument track for a grand piano (Figure 13-44).

Figure 13-44: A Grand Piano track header.

But you're not stuck with it: a simple double-click on the track's header opens GarageBand's Track Info window (shown in Figure 13-45) and from there you can switch to any other software instrument GarageBand provides.

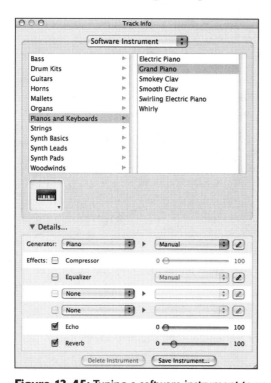

Figure 13-45: Tuning a software instrument to your taste.

You can also use the Details pane in the window to tweak or, for that matter, seriously distort a software instrument's sound by applying various effects to it. This, in itself, can provide hours of fun. You can even save your creation as a new instrument so you can use it in other songs.

Secret

Playing a Software Instrument with a Software Keyboard

Obviously, it's no fun to tweak all the settings of a software instrument if you can't hear what your tweaks sound like. But to hear the instrument, you need to play it, and, as you know (because I've told you), you usually play software instruments with a MIDI keyboard controller. You can pick up one of these wonders at the Apple Store (they sell several models made by third parties that plug right into a USB port on your Mac) — or from any music store. And, because of the genuine intelligence of Panther (which knows a whole lot about MIDI right out of the box), all you usually need to do is plug the USB MIDI keyboard in and start playing.

But if you don't have the bucks to spend (currently these devices are priced starting just below a hundred dollars), you can still play your software instrument with the onscreen keyboard provided by GarageBand itself (see Figure 13-46). Just click a key to hear it play. (Bonus tip: click near the front of a key for a louder sound and near the back for a softer sound.) It's almost like a real keyboard — albeit a keyboard that can only play one note at a time.

Figure 13-46: GarageBand's mouse-clickable keyboard.

If you need more notes at a time than one, you have another free option: Chris Reed's very clever MidiKeys program (http://www.manyetas.com/creed/midikeys_beta.html /) that turns your Mac's keyboard into a MIDI keyboard, so you can play chords just by typing. This program works with other MIDI-enabled programs, too. Sure, it is a little weird to play music on a typewriter-style keyboard, but the price is right.

Creating a new track is easy, too. If you can't be bothered to take a trip to the Track menu and select New Track. (Not that that's, like, hard.) Or, you can just click a big friendly New Track button that lives right below the track list (Figure 13-47).

Figure 13-47: Controls to add a track and to change its settings.

Either method gets you to the New Track window (shown in Figure 13-48) from which you can create a track for a software instrument or a real instrument.

Every track offers controls that let you mute it, play it solo (that is, mute all the other tracks), and adjust its volume and its position between the left and right stereo speakers (see Figure 13-49). And if you need to adjust the volume over time, you can do that, too.

Figure 13-48: Making tracks.

Figure 13-49: Each track comes with its own mute, solo, pan, and volume controls.

GarageBand Demo Files and Tutorials

GarageBand comes with an assortment of demo files. They're on the iLife '04 DVD in a top-level folder called, cunningly, *GarageBand Demo Songs — Copy to your hard drive*. If you have the hard drive space (they take up a few hundred megabytes), you owe it to yourself to take a look at these files. You can quickly get an idea of how much you can do with GarageBand by playing, and playing around with, them. They are broken into those designed for Macs with a G4, G4 and. G5 processors so you don't start something that's hard to finish.

GarageBand also comes with several tutorials in the form of PDF files. You can see these at any time from GarageBand's Help, but if you're the sort of person who doesn't fancy a trip to the Help Viewer (Jaguar users can find this excruciatingly slow), you can locate the PDFs on your hard drive at Library/Documentation/Applications/ GarageBand/English. There are versions of the tutorials in several languages other than English as well, for those of you who want to make beautiful music in, say, Finnish.

All GarageBand songs have one special track in addition to those you create: the Master Track (Figure 13-50). This track, which you can see when you choose Show Master Track (Command + B) from the Tracks menu , lets you control the audio volume for the whole song.

By editing this track's settings, you can also enable or disable various effects in all your song's tracks (turning off, say, all echo and reverb).

Figure 13-50: Now I am the master track.

Expanding Your Instrument Collection

You are not limited to the paltry fifty instruments (and associated effects) that come with GarageBand. Apple's $99 GarageBand Jam Pack supplies an additional hundred instruments, a similar number of effects, and several more guitar amp simulations.

But you don't have to stop with Apple-branded wares. GarageBand's instruments and effects use Mac OS X's Audio Unit format, the company's new standard for audio plug-ins, which it hopes will replace, or, at least become as common as, the existing welter of audio plug-in formats, such as Steinberg's VST, Mark of the Unicorn's MAS, and so on. Audio Units reside in the Library (either your own or the main library, depending on whether you like to share): Library/Audio/Plug-Ins/Components.

If you want to see what's available in the brave new world of Audio Units, one useful place to check is www.audio-units.com. (How *do* they think of these domain names?) You can find many effects and instruments there, some free, some not.

Loop Roundelay

A bunch of tracks is worthless, of course, if there's nothing in them. (As famous musician King Lear said, "Nothing will come of nothing.") GarageBand, though, gives you plenty of music to put in your tracks. In fact, it gives you over a gigabyte of music in the form of *loops.* You have real instrument loops and software loops, loops for drums and loops for piano, loops for happy times and loops for sad. Hundreds and hundreds of them . . . in fact, over a thousand of them.

You can see GarageBand's loop collection by poking the program in the eye: click the big gray button in the GarageBand window that has an eye on it (shown in Figure 13-51) and the loop browser slides up from the bottom of the window.

Figure 13-51: Eye see loops. . . .

The loop browser arranges GarageBand's vast collection of loops into various categories (shown in Figure 13-52). Click a category button and all the loops that match the category become available in the pane along the browser's right side. Click another category button and all the loops that match both selected categories are revealed. (Click a selected category button again to deselect it, or click the Reset button to deselect them all.) Click a loop in the list and GarageBand plays it for you. Again, you can have hours of fun just doing this.

Figure 13-52: Feeling a little bit loopy in the Loop Browser.

---

insider insight

For some reason known only to Apple, the loop browser doesn't show you all the category buttons when it opens up. However, if you click on the dark gray area above the browser and drag your mouse up, the browser area gets taller and more buttons come into view. You'll never be without your bongo loops again.

You may notice that every loop has a tempo associated with it and that most loops have a key as well. (Drum tracks are the exception here.) One of the wonderful things about GarageBand loops, however, is that both timing and pitch are not set in stone: when you click a loop in the browser to hear it, GarageBand automagically plays it in the same tempo and key as your song. Now maybe this is not so magical for software instrument loops (after all, they are mostly just MIDI data, so changing key and tempo only requires changing a few numbers around), but it certainly is for real instrument loops (which are actual audio recordings).

---

note

GarageBand has a preference that makes the loop browser filter loops so that it only shows the ones close to your song's key. If you want to see all the loops and force GarageBand to do serious transposition magic, turn off the Keyword Browsing option in GarageBand's General preferences.

---

insider insight

You can tell real instrument loops from software instrument loops in the loop browser by the colors of their icons (real is blue, software is green) and the images on their icons (real has a waveform, software has a note). You can also tell real and software instrument tracks apart by color: real instrument tracks have a blue header; software instrument tracks have a green header. Of course, if you're colorblind, this scheme doesn't help much.

At this point it might seem that I was being ironic (or lying) when I said that GarageBand was really easy to use — after all, right after I said that I proceeded to bombard you with all sorts of stuff about tempos, time signatures, MIDI, instrument types, and so on. But much of that's background stuff to help you understand what's going on, and you don't need to know most of it to make a song with GarageBand. Here's how you make a GarageBand song: Drag loops into tracks. Even the tracks part is optional: Drag a loop over the light gray area where there *aren't* any tracks (shown in Figure 13-53), and GarageBand makes a track for you and put the loop in it.

Figure 13-53: Drag a loop. Make a track.

tip   If you drag a software instrument loop to a real instrument track, GarageBand converts the loop into a real instrument loop for you, rendering the MIDI information into audio data on the fly. The reverse, however, is not possible: you can't convert a real instrument loop into a software instrument loop.

After that, it's just a matter of stretching loops out by dragging their top-right corners along the timeline so they repeat (that's *why* they're called loops), and moving them around by dragging them from their centers. GarageBand snaps the loops into position to match the beat (unless you turn the Snap to Grid option off in the Control menu) so your song always stays in time. Really easy. So easy you can have even *more* hours of fun randomly dragging, dropping, and stretching loops: no matter what you do, you'll usually end up with something that's at least listenable.

insider
insight   Where are the loops *really* stored? Look in Library/Application Support/GarageBand/ Apple Loops for GarageBand. Feel free to browse; you can play each one right in the Finder using the Finder's Preview feature (QuickTime handles the playback). Just don't rename or move them or you're apt to confuse GarageBand.

By the way, the loop browser brims with cool features. Here's some of what you can do:

◆ Rearrange the loop category buttons by dragging them around.

◆ Flag individual loops as favorites.

◆ Drag loops from other sources into the Loop Browser to add them to your GarageBand loops.

insider insight   To convert any audio file into a GarageBand loop, you need a copy of the Soundtrack Loop Utility. You can download it for free from Apple's Web site: it's part of Apple's AppleLoop Software Development Kit, available at `http://developer.apple.com/sdk/#AppleLoops`. To convert a MIDI file into a loop file, there's another utility developed by Bary Rinaldo: Dent du MIDI. This little freeware application exports each of the instrument tracks in a standard MIDI file as a loop that's suitable for dragging into GarageBand. You can find it at `http://homepage.mac.com/beryrinaldo/ddm/`.

◆ View the loop browser in a column view, similar to the iTunes browse feature.

◆ Search for loops by name.

Soundtrack and GarageBand

Secret

GarageBand may strike some of you Final Cut Pro pros out there as strangely familiar: it seems to have a lot in common with a program that comes with the full Final Cut package, Soundtrack. Well, it should, because the two programs *do* have a lot in common. GarageBand loops *are* Soundtrack loops, and most of the audio wizardry that GarageBand performs comes right out of Soundtrack, too.

Soundtrack was created to give video producers a way to quickly create scratch music tracks for their projects, and it comes with about four times the number of loops that GarageBand does, along with quite a few more features, including the Soundtrack Loop Utility.

Avoiding Processor Overload

Secret

GarageBand is a very hungry program when it comes to using your Mac's PowerPC chip. It really wants a fast one (and lots and lots of memory and hard disk space — but who doesn't?). The more notes GarageBand has to play at once, the more tracks playing, and the more effects being used, the harder the program has to work. Even on a reasonably capable machine, like a 1-GHz G4 iMac, you can quickly hit the wall with just a few tracks playing and see a dialog box telling you that GarageBand is dropping notes. You can tell when you're heading for trouble: the playhead turns from clear to amber to red, and when you see red, you're riding close to the edge.

Effects are particularly hungry for processor power. Turning off echo and reverb in your Master Track can lighten the load a bit, as can turning some tracks off while you're working on others. Using more real instrument loops and fewer software instrument loops can also free up some headroom. In the worst cases, you can mix down and export a bunch of tracks you've completed, delete them, and re-import the audio file into a single track. Or you can buy a dual processor G5 with tons of RAM. (I know what *I'd* do.)

Variations on a Digital Theme

You can edit your tracks with GarageBand's built-in track editor, which you can see by clicking the Track Editor button (shown in Figure 13-54); the track editor appears in the same place in the GarageBand window as the loop browser (which probably explains why the Loop Browser and Track Editor buttons appear side-by-side).

Figure 13-54: The Track Editor button.

The track editor lets you edit the first part (the unrepeated part) of any software instrument loop or any part of a real instrument loop. (GarageBand calls the full area covered by a loop and its attached repetitions *regions*.) Depending on the type of region you have selected, the track editor has one of two appearances: a note-twiddling, parameter-tweaking software region editor (see Figure 13-55) and a waveform-slicing real region editor (see Figure 13-56).

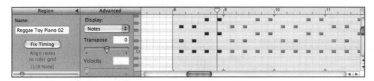

Figure 13-55: Editing a software instrument region.

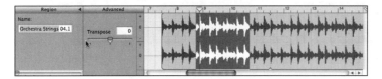

Figure 13-56: Editing a real instrument region.

The real instrument editor offers very basic editing functions. You can select, cut, copy, and paste portions of a region. You can transpose a whole region (if it is a real instrument loop; that is, you can't transpose real instruments you record yourself). And you can change a region's name. That's it. Of course you can also use the track volume controls and all the track filter and effect settings to further modify a real instrument track's sound. So, you may not need much more editing power than the track editor provides anyway.

tip

You can drag any AIFF file or MP3 file into the GarageBand track display to add a real instrument region, which you can then cut, copy, paste, repeat, drag around, and generally mess with. Imported audio regions appear in purple to distinguish them from real instrument loops (just like the real instrument regions you record yourself, which you'll find out about in later in this chapter). For some reason, though, you can't drag and drop AAC files. At least you can't in GarageBand 1.0.2.

The software instrument editor, on the other hand, lets you drag notes around, transpose individually selected notes, lengthen or shorten notes, add new notes, fix the timing of selected notes (that is, make them align with the beat grid), and adjust the loudness of each note; this last is called its *velocity* because it is related to the velocity and force with which the key was pressed on the MIDI keyboard that generated the note. In addition, you can also edit other characteristics that originate from controls that are commonly found on MIDI controllers: the sustain, the pitchbend, and the modulation. As far as software instruments are concerned, you can fix it *all* in the editing — even the sloppiest performance can become a virtuoso piece with some judicious dragging and clicking.

Suite for Recorder

And speaking of performing: you can record your own performances directly into a GarageBand song and mix your riffs with the loops that GarageBand provides. The program supports recording from either an actual audio input on your Mac into a real instrument track (shown in Figure 13-57) or from a MIDI controller into a software instrument track (see Figure 13-58).

Figure 13-57: Recording live audio.

Figure 13-58: Recording from MIDI.

For a live audio recording, plug in your instrument or microphone, select the track, position the playhead, and press the Record button. For a MIDI recording, plug in your instrument, select the track, position the playhead, and press the Record button. Notice any difference? There isn't much.

on the
web
Getting an audio recording to sound right, especially in a live recording, is hard to do, even with all the intelligence and user-friendliness that GarageBand supplies. Much depends on the microphone, the instruments themselves, the room in which they are recorded, and other factors. You can find some very useful tips on live recording (and, in fact, on all matters pertaining to GarageBand) at the Garage Door (`http://www.thegaragedoor.com`).

The Audio MIDI Setup Utility

GarageBand is quite good about taking advantage of whatever audio and MIDI inputs you have available, and you usually do not have to worry about device configuration issues. Just plug something in and you're ready to go.

But you and I both know that Mac folk do all sorts of funky tweaking to their computers, and sometimes you may have to untweak things a bit. Also, not all Macs are created equal, and some of them don't have built-in audio inputs and require some other device (like a USB audio input device or a FireWire audio input device) in order to get sound into the Mac. And, of course, there are those overachievers out there who may have several MIDI devices hooked up.

In such cases, a quick trip to the Audio MIDI Setup program found in Panther's Utilities folder can help you out. This program lets you control how your audio and MIDI inputs behave (shown in Figure 13-59 a and b, respectively). With it, you can specify the sample size, rate, and volume of your various audio input devices; you can also organize and interconnect your various MIDI devices.

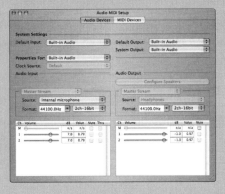

Figure 13-59: The two faces of the Audio MIDI Setup Utility.

GarageBand provides a few nice features that make it even easier to get your recording down. You can have GarageBand play its metronome as you record, so you can keep in time to the song's beat. (You might want to wear headphones if you're recording with a microphone so that it doesn't pick up the tick of the metronome.) You can have GarageBand use a *count-in*, so that it plays the measure just before where you want the recording to start; again, this helps you come in and stay on the beat. Both Metronome and Count In can be found under the Control menu.

> **note**   GarageBand's *cycle region* is also a very useful tool for recording. You can set a cycle region on the timeline so that GarageBand plays and records only over that section; when the playhead gets to the end of the cycle region, it goes back to the region's beginning and continues. For a software instrument recording, you can keep playing and GarageBand keeps recording each time through, letting you layer your perform-ance on top of itself. Real instrument recordings automatically stop at the end of the cycle region, and GarageBand begins playback from the recording's beginning.

> **note**   You may notice a slight delay or offset when you record audio on a slower Mac, espe-cially one requiring a USB audio input converter. This delay is called *latency,* and is caused by all the processing that the Mac must do in order to convert the sound it's recording first into digital format and then back into analog audio so you can hear it. If you experience such latency, just drag the loop you've recorded back a bit to get it to sync up with your other loops. (It helps to turn off GarageBand's Snap to Grid function before you drag so you can get things to line up exactly.)

Summary

We've covered a lot in this chapter. We started with iTunes and finished with GarageBand. And along the way, we found that we can take our music (whether we made it ourselves or not) with us using the iPod.

As one of the early digital hub applications, iTunes made managing a music library so simple, a child could do it. And many a child has taught an adult how to do it. Apple sang the same tune with digital photos, and thus came iPhoto, the topic of our next chapter.

The iPod may not be something that you can "get" without going to a store and picking one up. So if these pages didn't spark your interest, take a trip to your local Apple dealer and you'll quickly see what I mean.

GarageBand opens the door (yes, the garage door) on music composition and recording for the fabled "rest of us." Like the other programs in the iLife package, what it provides is an easy-to-use yet powerful set of functions for working with media and devices (in this case, audio media and devices) in ways that formerly were reserved for experts. You may not be a Mozart or even a Marshall Mathers, but with GarageBand you and your Mac can make beautiful music together.

iPhoto

Chapter
14

◆ ◆

Secrets in This Chapter

◆ ◆

In the beginning, there were film cameras. You had to keep them well fed with consumables to make them do something. After scanners became popular, however, it was inevitable that someone would get the bright idea to stick a digital imaging mechanism behind a camera lens, and store the resulting ones and zeros on some sort of memory medium.

The Origins of Digital Imaging Devices

So where did such digital imaging products first originate? I did a little Internet sleuthing (well, not that little) and ran across a piece describing a cover story from an issue of *Scientific American* way back in 1895. Yes, I said 1895. (I wanted to emphasize that in case one of my editors looks askance at the claim.)

The device in question was known as the Amstutz Electro-Artrograph, and it was designed to scan photos and other artwork and transmit them over a wire. A receiving device was used to reproduce the photo. All right, not quite a scanner, but you didn't need a computer to make it work.

It was inevitable. As soon as high-resolution digital cameras became cheap enough to replace film-based cameras, the digital devices began to take over. After all, why buy film when all you need to do is fill up a memory card, and delete the pictures once they're downloaded to your Mac?

When you used film, you probably wondered what to do with all those pics. Maybe you bought a photo album or two to handle the good ones, but the rest probably ended up in a box that you deposited somewhere in the closet.

With digital photos, your closet is your Mac's hard drive, and it's doubtless become a mess, assuming you're as organized as I am.

While there have been software solutions to bring clutter out of chaos, probably the most elegant solution comes from Apple in the form of iPhoto, which is currently at version 4.

In this chapter, I break iPhoto down into three sections. We look at the organizational side of iPhoto. This will help you understand the mechanics of getting your pictures into iPhoto. After that, we look at the many ways to share your images through iPhoto. This will include printing, online services, and the ever-popular slideshow. And at the end of this chapter, we look at some of the editing features in and out of iPhoto.

iPhoto is compact enough that we can do a very good job of covering most of it. And because, at the time this is being written, Apple has just released its latest version of iPhoto with iLife 4, you can be confident that you are getting the latest information.

Importing and Organizing Your Images in iPhoto

The easiest way to get you into iPhoto is to guide you through the basic process of retrieving files directly from your digital camera. For this exercise, I brought out my trusty Nikon digital camera. (No, this isn't a paid endorsement.)

Getting Files Off Your Camera

The first time you launch iPhoto, you get a message asking if you want to have it open whenever you plug in and turn on your digital camera (shown in Figure 14-1). Just say yes, and move on.

Figure 14-1: The right button is the right answer when it comes to iPhoto.

All right, that was easy enough. Here's what happens next:

1. First, attach your digital camera to the your Mac's USB port or to a USB port on your keyboard or a hub.

2. Before moving further, you'll want to make an important decision. In the Import pane, select whether you want to Erase Camera Contents After Transfer. This means what it says. The memory card is cleared when the pictures are transferred to your Mac.

> **caution**
>
> As you know, my viewpoint here is one of supreme paranoia. That means I prefer to confirm that the picture has been imported *before* I remove it from the camera's memory. This may entail a few extra steps, such as responding to the awkward menu-driven displays offered by some digital cameras, but at least, if something goes wrong, you can import the pictures all over again.

3. You're ready to roll. Click the Import button and watch the action in the progress bar. As the pictures are downloaded to your Mac, you see the progress bar show the number.

caution Don't disconnect the camera till the download process is done. If you decide you don't want to download anything else, click Stop before disconnecting the camera. Also to avoid any problems in transferring data, make sure your camera's Sleep mode is disabled. All this will prevent damaging any of your photos. No, I won't attempt to try to tell you how to handle these features on your camera. They differ from model to model, and your best resource is the manual, if the menus on your camera's display aren't helpful.

The photos you import are placed in their own album, labeled with the date stamped on the pictures by your camera. The filenames bear incomprehensible numbers also inserted by your camera. You can easily edit all this stuff in the Information mode (shown later in this chapter), so you can sort it all out later.

Over time, you will accumulate lots of different images sorted by film rolls and albums (shown in Figure 14-2).

Figure 14-2: Images are shown here in iPhoto's main library by film roll; some open to show the images and some closed to more easily navigate the images.

The library contains all of the images. Film rolls and albums are subsets of the library.

Getting Files from Other Sources

No, the digital camera isn't the only method to get photos into iPhoto. There are other ways to build a photo library, especially if you've got a bunch of pictures stored on your Mac's hard drive, CDs, card readers, and other media. You can even go the whole hog to scan photos and artwork and bring them into iPhoto.

Here's what you do:

1. Launch iPhoto.
2. Go to the File menu and choose Import. A regular Import dialog box appears, like the one you see in Figure 14-3.

Figure 14-3: Select the photos you want to import here.

3. Now it's time to pick the ones you want to copy into iPhoto. You can select a single photo, a bunch, or an entire disk or folder. After they're selected, click Import to bring them into iPhoto.
4. You will know that your images are being imported by looking at the Import area at the bottom of the screen (shown in Figure 14-4).

Figure 14-4: Because you are importing images from a folder, you don't see any camera information when importing images.

note No, I am not forgetting your scanner. All you have to do is scan your artwork in the normal fashion. The pictures you save on your Mac can then be transferred to iPhoto in the same way as any other photo. Easy as that!

Secret

Dragging and Dropping In and Out of iPhoto

If you want to save a couple of steps when you bring pictures into iPhoto, drag them from any folder and drop them into the iPhoto window, and they'll be imported, automatically. Just remember to point them toward a specific album, if that's where you want them to go.

To export photos, just drag them directly to your desktop (any folder will do) and they'll go there automatically, in the same size and format in which they were stored. You still need to use the Export menu, though, if you decide to change the format or size first.

Just remember that you are not actually moving the photos in either direction. They are just copied. That means you get two of each as a result of the import or export operation.

Creating Albums

Having all of your images in the iPhoto library isn't a handy way to organize or work with your images, so Apple has given us virtual albums to help us sort our images out. To create an album you need to select the New Album menu option (⌘-N) from under the File menu in iPhoto or click on the Add button (plus sign) under the Albums panel (shown in Figure 14-5).

Figure 14-5: The New Album menu button adds your new album to the left-hand pane of iPhoto's main screen.

From there, all you have to do is to drag the images you want from the library to the album you want them in. After that, when you select the album, you see only those images in that album (shown in Figure 14-6).

note You'll notice here the growing similarity among Apple's iApps. That Add button performs the same kind of function in both iTunes and Mail.

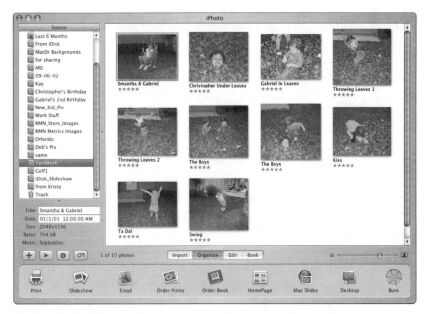

Figure 14-6: Although there were a lot of images on the card from my camera, I moved the ones of my kids in the yard into their own album called Yardwork.

Creating Smart Albums

Smart Albums are new to iPhoto in version 4. The idea of a Smart Album is to allow iPhoto to use other information about your images to organize them in ways that are significant to you. This is especially helpful, if you use iPhoto's rating system or if you add comments or custom names to your imported images.

Assuming that you've added additional information to your images (which we'll talk about a little later in this chapter), here is how you create a Smart Album:

1. Select the New Smart Album menu option from under the File menu or hold down the Option key and click on the Smart Album Button in iPhoto (shown in Figure 14-7).

Figure 14-7: Holding down the Option key turns the Add button into the Smart Album button, which looks like a gear.

2. The Smart Album Options drops down from the top of the iPhoto window (shown in Figure 14-8). Select the options that you want your Smart Album to use as its rules, name the album, and click OK.

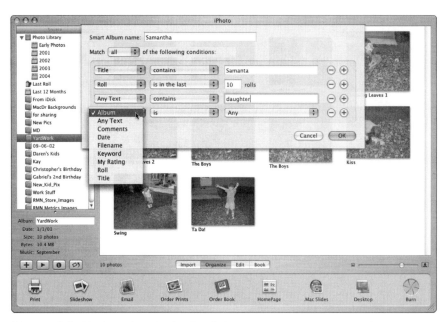

Figure 14-8: There are hundreds of variations you can use to create a Smart Album.

3. What you have is a newly created Smart Album that collects all of those images from within the iPhoto Library that correspond to the rules that you set up in your Smart Album (shown in Figure 14-9).

Figure 14-9: Your Smart Album is done. If you don't like the results you can Control-click on your Smart Album to get at the Edit Smart Album option from a contextual menu.

Viewing Images in iPhoto

As with direct imports from cameras, the collection of photos gets its own library, which you can organize in the same fashion as any other iPhoto album.

You'll be able to view the pictures at high resolution, and the little slider or size control at the right of the window can be used to dynamically resize a picture for better viewing (shown in Figure 14-10).

Figure 14-10: Pick a display size, any size.

By selecting one of the images (in an album or the library) and moving the slider completely to the right, you get the selected image(s) in full panel view (shown in Figure 14-11).

No, the size control slider doesn't actually change the size of the photo. For that, you'd need a dedicated image-editing program.

If you don't like the way that iPhoto displays your images in the main screen, you can modify the display by choosing the Appearance pane (shown in Figure 14-12) in the Preferences, which can be accessed in the iPhoto application menu (Command + comma).

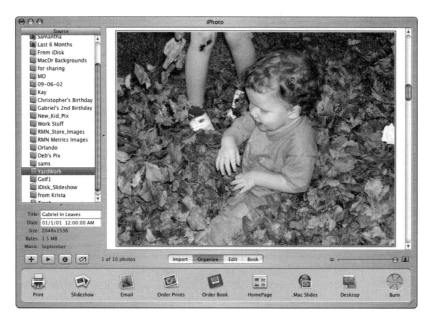

Figure 14-11: My kids get even cuter the closer you get to them.

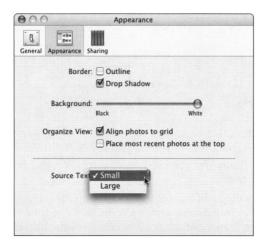

Figure 14-12: Besides changing the size of the text, you can adjust the background and loose the cool drop shadow behind the images.

You will also see in the Source panel that Apple provides you with automatic organization by year (shown in Figure 14-13).

Figure 14-13: Organizing your images by year as well as within the last 12 months is a great feature for those of us who have thousands of images in iPhoto and have been adding images since iPhoto was first released.

This organizational feature makes sense. If you look in your Pictures folder, you can see that iPhoto has been organizing your images by year for several versions now.

Adding Additional Info to Your Image

As I said before, your digital camera may have inserted incomprehensible numbers as the title of your imported images. This information is not the only information that's associated with your photos.

While you can view a lot of image data and/or source information by clicking on an image and then choosing the Show Info menu option from under the Photo menu (⌘-I), this isn't the most useful information in terms of what's going on in the photo. Fortunately, iPhoto gives you the ability to replace the camera's number with a title of your choosing by typing it into the Title field of the info area in the lower-left corner of the main iPhoto pane (shown in Figure 14-14).

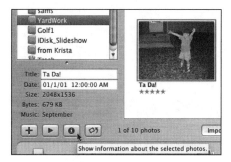

Figure 14-14: Click on an image and tab to or click in the Title field to change the title of an image.

> **caution** There are some limits in adding text comments to an iPhoto. If you stray too far from a basic set of fonts, you risk having the text truncated. So, while it may affect your artistic sensibilities, use these fonts: Baskerville, Brush Script, Century Gothic, Helvetica, Helvetica Neue, Marker Felt, or Papyrus. Don't say I didn't warn you.

Before you forget just why your son is standing over a bunch of leaves with his hands out-stretched, you should make sure that you put that information into iPhoto as Comment text. This information is placed in the Comments field, which appears when you click the information button (with the little *i*) (see Figure 14-15).

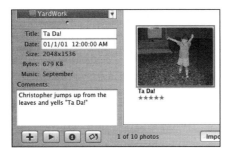

Figure 14-15: This comment "leaves" no room for misunderstanding.

Making Batch Changes in iPhoto

As with many other Apple applications, there are contextual options for your images in iPhoto. Among those options is the ability to change the title or roll information for the images.

With multiple images in iPhoto selected, Control-click and then select the Batch Change option (shown in Figure 14-16). A drop-down dialog box descends from the iPhoto title bar (shown in Figure 14-17).

Figure 14-16: These contextual options are available from images in the Organize and Import modes of iPhoto.

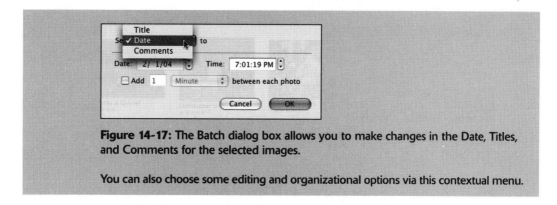

Figure 14-17: The Batch dialog box allows you to make changes in the Date, Titles, and Comments for the selected images.

You can also choose some editing and organizational options via this contextual menu.

There are other kinds of information you can add to your images to help you sort, classify, and prepare for organization in Smart Albums or for other purposes. You can add keywords (shown in 14-18) and/or ratings (shown in Figure 14-19) to your images. Both of these options are available from under the Photo menu in iPhoto.

Figure 14-18: The Keywords palate allows you to add new keywords and then assign them to photos or entire albums.

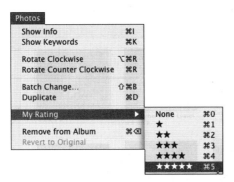

Figure 14-19: The My Rating feature works exactly like the Rating feature in iTunes.

All of this additional data will help you build "Smarter" albums and share your images with more personalized information.

In Case Your Camera Isn't Compatible

So far, I've been assuming that your camera is fully compatible with iPhoto and that you won't run into any trouble trying to download the pictures. Unless it's an early model, downloading shouldn't present any problem at all.

But if you aren't able to get iPhoto to work with your camera, there are other methods to use to bring your pictures into iPhoto.

First, if it has Mac OS X–compatible software, you can install it and then use the software to bring your pictures to your Mac. After they are on your Mac, you can use your favorite method to import them into iPhoto.

Another way to deal with a camera that isn't playing nicely with your Mac may be to take pictures directly off the camera's memory card. For that purpose, you need a Mac-compatible memory card reader. Don't despair at the cost. I've seen them on closeout for as little as $13; and fancy ones with three or four slots run around $40 or $50. Just make sure the one you buy is compatible with the kind of media your camera uses.

After the memory card is placed in the reader, you should be able to open iPhoto and have it import photos directly off the card, without any further intervention — if it doesn't open by itself and ask you import the images for you.

But it would be a bit easier if you just went and bought a camera that functions on your Mac.

True Plug And Play — iPhoto's Worst-Kept Secret

Are you ready to install the software that came with your digital camera? Save your time. Most digital cameras work with iPhoto without any additions. Just plug it in and see.

If you're in the market for a new camera, you might want to consult Apple's iPhoto compatibility page at www.apple.com/iphoto/compatibility/camera.html. Even if the model you want isn't listed, if most or all of the maker's other models are shown, the chances of compatibility are excellent.

Sharing Your Images in iPhoto

Besides holding and arranging your images, iPhoto is a killer app because it provides a lot of great ways to share those images with other people. In this section, I show you how Apple has read our minds and given us almost exactly what we wanted (possibly before we knew we wanted it).

All of the sharing items are represented as icons across the bottom of iPhoto. I'll take you through each of these from left to right.

Printing through iPhoto's Special Printer Features

Printing from many applications, from Microsoft Word for example is relatively simple. You pick the number of copies, which pages to print, and maybe select one of the special options of your printer.

But having photos of different sizes and orientations (I mean portrait and landscape, of course) presents an assortment of printing options for you to choose from.

Before printing, first select the photo or photos you want to print, and then choose Print from the File menu (or click on the printer icon on the bottom of iPhoto). This delivers a very special Print dialog box, which is apt to give you pause (shown in Figure 14-20). There are so many possibilities. Which do you choose? Read on!

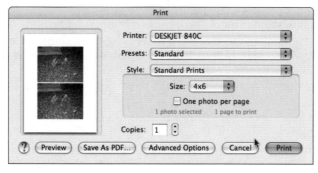

Figure 14-20: You can print one or many photos on a single page. I've selected 4x6 in this Print dialog box.

Style Options

You can format your page in half-a-dozen options (shown in Figure 14-21), and there are a bunch of variations within each. As you select different options, you can see the result in the preview window at the left, so you won't be left wondering what's going to happen. Here's the short list:

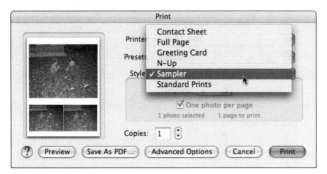

Figure 14-21: So many choices, so little time.

Because you don't need a paragraph about each of the Print dialog box choices, I've listed them below for your benefit:

◆ **Contact Sheet** is what your professional photographer gives you, single sheets with a lot of pictures on it.

◆ **Full Page** means what it says. The picture is scaled up to the size of a full page.

◆ **Greeting Card**, puts the picture right at the top half of the page, so you can custom print your own personal greetings at the bottom.

◆ **N-Up** is a shortcut for putting a fixed number of pictures on a single page. A pop-up menu gives you the numbers of pictures that will appear.

◆ **Sampler** puts, as you see in Figure 14-21, different sizes on a single page, so you can maximize use of that photo paper. I just hope your scissor technique is better than mine, though, as I frequently cut them up rather clumsily.

◆ **Standard Prints** gives you a choice of common photo paper sizes, such as 4x6 and 8x10.

Other Print Options

The other options are straightforward. Specify the margins on the page, and select the number of copies you want to print. You'll notice that the number of photos you selected appear in the dialog, so you can double-check in case you selected too many by mistake. If you are confused by these options, please check out Chapter 22, which tells you a lot more about printing on the Mac.

What's Advanced Options all about? Well, it's not too advanced. It simply delivers the standard Print dialog box, where you can select the special options for your printer, such as output quality, before clicking the Print button.

Making Your Images Fit Standard Sizes in iPhoto

What do you do if the size of your photo doesn't fit into those fixed sizes, such as 4x6? Here's where you'll have to crop the photo to fit properly, and you may want to do that anyway to get rid of extraneous backgrounds or, I hate to say it, extraneous people.

Here's how to handle it with, say, 4x6 perforated paper. Why this size? Because it was the one I had handy when I wrote these instructions:

1. Click the File menu and select Page Setup.
2. Make sure the printer you want to use is the one selected in the Format for: pop-up menu.
3. Choose 4x6 from the Size pop-up menu, and click OK.
4. Choose the photos you want to print.
5. Click the Edit button.
6. Because you want to restrict the printed area to 4x6, select the 4x6 ratio from the Constrain pop-up menu and then click and drag to select the portion of the picture that you wish to print.
7. After you have selected the area you wish to print, click on the Crop icon in the Edit pane.
8. All set? Now click on the File menu and select Print.
9. From the print dialog box, select Full Page from the Style pop-up menu and then click on Print.

Oh, and by the way, you might want to consider using regular paper to print samples until you get used to this routine. Photo paper is not cheap and you don't want to waste it.

Making PDF Contact Sheets for Multiple Photos

Secret

Normally when you e-mail a photo, each is handled as a separate file. But that may not always be convenient, if you want to send a lot of photos to someone. The best way is to save them in PDF form or contact sheet, which means they are all sent in one document.

To make this happen, first bring the pictures into iPhoto, if they haven't been imported. Once that's done, do this:

1. Select the photos you want to convert to PDF.
2. Choose Print from the File menu.
3. In the Print dialog box (see Figure 14-22), click Save as PDF and name your file in the Save dialog box.

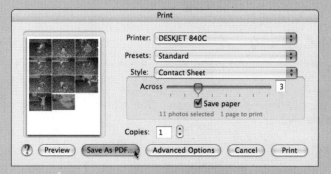

Figure 14-22: Go ahead and click Save as PDF to finish up the operation.

You are prompted to save your PDF document and give it a name.

continues

continued

You can then view and print your PDF in Preview (shown in Figure 14-23).

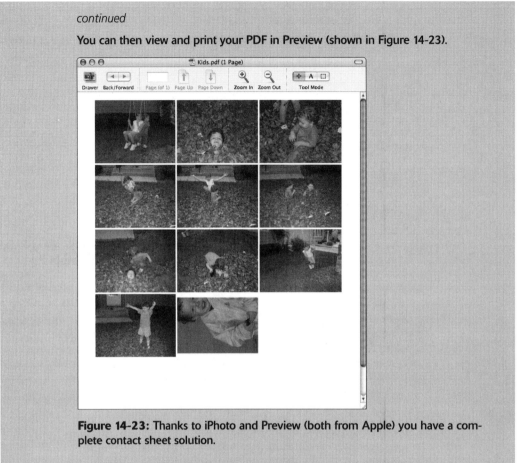

Figure 14-23: Thanks to iPhoto and Preview (both from Apple) you have a complete contact sheet solution.

And that's it. The photos you selected are all placed in a single PDF file, one page per photo, or however you choose to lay them out in the Print dialog. How can you miss?

Make a Slideshow

Making a slideshow in iPhoto is perhaps the easiest and best source of instant gratification if you want to share your images. I showed my wife this feature using images from our wedding and our kids' baby pictures set to Green Day's "Time of Your Life." The result was a shared tearful moment with my wife. (You'd have thought that I just produced a Hallmark commercial.)

With the introduction of iPhoto 4, Apple has added some of the cool Keynote (Apple's pre-sentational software) transitions and expanded iPhoto's slideshow capabilities.

Creating a slideshow is really easy:

1. Create an album of your images. It's best if you think in terms of a theme, as it's easier to find "the song" that captures the images.

2. Select all of the images in that album and then click on the Slideshow icon at the bottom of the iPhoto screen.

3. This brings up the Slideshow dialog box with the settings (shown in Figure 14-24, on the left). In this dialog box, you choose the way your images will appear, including the transitions (shown in Figure 14-24, on the right).

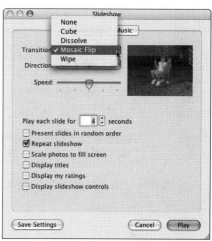

Figure 14-24: The Settings tab (left) of the Slideshow settings enables you to set the Direction, Speed, and other display information for your Slideshow. In this new version of iPhoto, the Slideshow Transitions (right) also include some new transitions, such as Mosaic Flip and Cube, to choose from.

4. Once you've set your Settings, click on the Music tab in the dialog box. This presents you with a listing of the songs in your iTunes library. By pulling down the menu under the Source section of this dialog box, you can choose an album, which then shows you the songs (shown in Figure 14-25).

5. Click on the Play button and dazzle your friends and family.

6. To stop your slideshow, hit the Escape key.

Figure 14-25: Not only can you choose your song, but you can also preview your music from within the Music dialog box by clicking on the Play button.

The only downside to this method of sharing your photos is that it runs only on a Mac. It's not possible (yet, through iPhoto) to export a slideshow onto a CD and have it run on other computers.

It is possible to publish a slideshow without music to the Web to share with other OS X users (10.2 or higher). I cover that option later in this chapter.

> **caution** Slideshows created for loved ones with nostalgic images and emotionally charged songs should be accompanied with an appropriate amount of tissue to accommodate the resulting tearful moments.

E-Mailing Photos Has Never Been Easier

I know that it's common to hear statements like this, but in iPhoto, it's true. There is just enough control in iPhoto's e-mailing features that you have the options you need with the hassles you don't' need.

Just pick your preferred e-mail program in iPhoto's preferences dialog box (shown later in this chapter in Figure 14-52). If you don't set this preference in iPhoto, it chooses your default e-mail reader.

When you select one or more photos in iPhoto and click the Email button (along the bottom of the iPhoto window), a dialog box appears allowing you to choose from four sizes for your e-mailed images (shown in Figure 14-26). When you select the size of the photo, you are shown the estimated size, among other things (shown in Figure 14-27).

Figure 14-26: You have four choices for image/file sizes in the Mail Photo Size pull-down menu.

Figure 14-27: The Mail Photo dialog box allows you to include the images' titles and comments.

Then all you have to do to send is click the Compose button and iPhoto prepares your image as per your size selection (shown in Figure 14-28). After the Progress dialog box disappears, iPhoto launches your e-mail program (set in iPhoto's preferences), opens a blank message, and attaches the photos (shown in Figure 14-29) in one fell swoop.

Figure 14-28: The progress bar indicates that your images are being processed as per your choices.

Figure 14-29: My kids are too cute not to share. And now it's never been easier.

Getting Hard Copies of Your Images without Printing

What's that you say? Hardcopy without printing? (Harrumph! Harrumph!) Well . . . I guess that's not completely accurate. I should have said that, through the Order Prints option in iPhoto, you don't print the images yourself.

Instead, this sharing option allows you to upload your images to Kodak. There, you create an account (if you haven't already), and select images, sizes, and number of copies to be professionally printed, and then they send them to you. You must pay, of course, using a credit card.

To start the process, select the images you want and then click on the Order Prints icon at the bottom of iPhoto. This brings up an Order Prints dialog box (shown in Figure 14-30) that allows you to access (or set up) your account and choose your other print options — just like the options that you'd choose at your local film developer.

Until recently, this service was available only in the United States and Canada. As of iPhoto 4, this feature is available in Japan and several European countries.

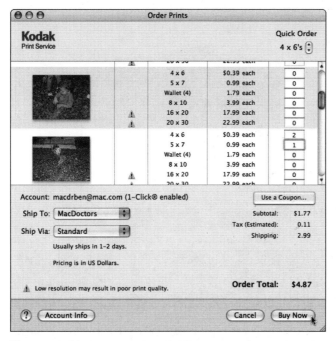

Figure 14-30: Print ordering via iPhoto through the Kodak Printer Service.

Order Hardcover Photo Albums

Another online ordering option through iPhoto is the ability to create and order nice hard-cover photo albums without having a graphic design program (or any graphic arts talent for that matter).

What did it cost in the old days to make a professionally printed photo album? Don't ask. iPhoto makes it easy to select pictures, add descriptive captions in one of several fancy typefaces, and then place an order online direct from Apple's album printer.

Once you select your album, you click on the Order Book option/icon at the bottom of the iPhoto screen and your images are put into a template that you can adjust (shown in Figure 14-31).

As of iPhoto 4, there are now seven different Book themes available. Selecting among those themes and then from the page options within those themes gives you a lot of different layout options. More importantly, the options that you are not permitted keep you from making design mistakes.

And if that wasn't enough variety, you can also choose from among four different cover options for your iBook when you actually order the book (shown in Figure 14-32).

Figure 14-31: Each page of your book can be modified and the text can be changed.

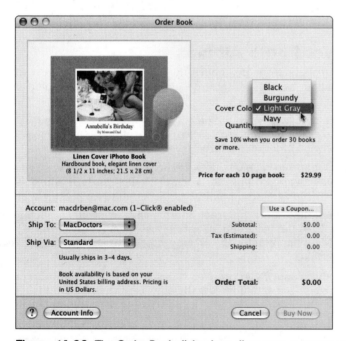

Figure 14-32: The Order Book dialog box allows you to access or set up your account, as well as choose the cover style for your iPhoto book.

Like the basic prints, the albums are now available in Japan and several European countries, as well as the United States and Canada.

---

caution These books are not cheap, so iPhoto puts caution symbols on the images that won't look good when enlarged as per your Book layout instructions. After having had some experience with these options, I'd like to urge you to take those caution symbols seriously. It's better to find an image with more data on it (that doesn't cause iPhoto to display the caution symbol) than it is to pay $30 to $40 for a book with cruddy pictures in it.

HomePage Gets a Boost from iPhoto

HomePage is really a .Mac feature, but it's relevant to this section as well.

Just like the other ways that you share your photos, you select your album or images and then click on the type of sharing you want. In this case, I'm choosing the HomePage icon. Now this doesn't work, of course, unless you have a .Mac account. But, assuming you do, here's what happens.

After clicking on the HomePage icon (at the bottom of iPhoto), a Publish HomePage dialog box appears (shown in Figure 14-33). Here you see your selected images in whatever template you choose.

Figure 14-33: There are now fourteen default choices for photo themes through iPhoto (compared to the previous version's five themes). Those fourteen choices combined with two different layout options give you a quite a few choices.

The themes are available through a theme drawer accessed by clicking on the Hide/Show Theme button in the dialog box. You are also able to change the headline and title text in the Publish HomePage dialog box.

.Mac Slides Extends Your Images to Other OS 10.3 Users

As I said earlier in this chapter when covering slideshows, it is possible with the help of .Mac to publish your images as a silent slideshow on the Web. You can also publish your images via your .Mac account as a screen saver sequence that you can share with other OS X users. Here is the process:

1. Select your album and click on the .Mac Slides icon in the Shared options at the bottom of iPhoto.

2. A dialog box appears asking you to confirm that you want to publish these images to your .Mac account (shown in Figure 14-34).

Figure 14-34: Publishing an album to your .Mac account replaces any previous slideshows on your iDisk.

3. Wait while the .Mac Slides dialog box uploads your images to your iDisk (shown in Figure 14-35).

Figure 14-35: In true Apple fashion, you see the files sizes and previews of your images as they are uploaded to your .Mac account.

4. When this is done, you are given the option of sending out an announcement via e-mail. You can choose this if you wish, as it tells your friends and family how to access your .Mac slideshow.

5. What these instructions tell your friends and family is to open their Screen Saver preferences from the Desktop & Screen Saver preference panel in their System Preferences.

6. Once they are there, it tells them to select the .Mac choice under Screen Savers and then click on the Options button. This brings up the Subscriptions dialog box where they type in the name of .Mac account/iDisk that the slideshow resides on (shown in Figure 14-36).

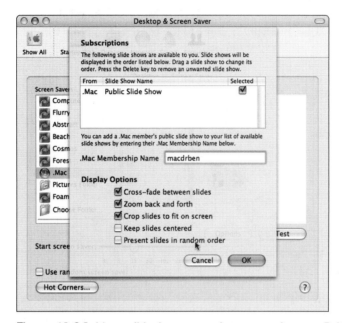

Figure 14-36: It's possible that you can have more than one Public slide show. You have to uncheck the other Public Slide Shows to access the one you want.

7. Click the OK button in the Subscriptions dialog box. If you did everything right, you see the screen saver in the Preview window (shown in Figure 14-37).

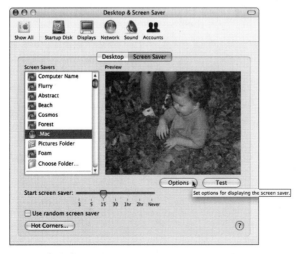

Figure 14-37: If you don't see the right .Mac slideshow, click on the Options button again and check your settings.

This lacks the flavor of a slideshow with music of your choice but, if you're like me, with in-laws (the kids' grandparents) in another country, this is just the ticket to be an online, photo-sharing, hero!

Modify Your Own Desktop from iPhoto

And because you can publish an album to the Internet for access by others (via the Screen Saver preferences), Apple has made it easy access your images for your own desktop and screen saver.

Although you can do this by clicking on the Desktop sharing choice at the bottom of iPhoto, it's actually a lot easier than that. If you open up System Preferences and then open the Desktop & Screen Saver preference panel, you find that your albums are listed as choices in both the Desktop (shown in Figure 14-38) and Screen Saver (shown in Figure 14-39) tabs.

You might as well let your kids run across your desktop as a screen saver. Especially when you're at work, it's a good reminder of why we go there in the first place.

Figure 14-38: An album published from iPhoto is shown at the top of the list. Otherwise, you can scroll to the bottom of the list to see all of the albums in iPhoto.

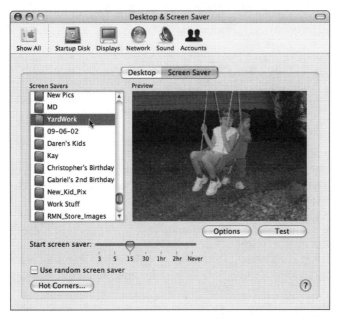

Figure 14-39: Similarly, all iPhoto albums are displayed in the Screen Savers list.

Burn (or Archive) a Picture CD or DVD

The last sharing option in iPhoto is the Burn option. This is very similar to the Burn option in iTunes. (Seeing the trend here?) The Burn option does just that.

If you want to save trees, you can simply burn or archive your albums on optical media. No fading to worry about. You can still organize your pictures by any category you want, exactly the same as they're organized in iPhoto on your Mac.

And the burning process is pretty much the same as burning a disc in iTunes. Select the photos or albums you want to store, pop a CD or DVD blank in your Mac's optical drive, and click Burn. And wait till it's done. What could be easier? You don't even need a manual to figure it all out.

More About Using Picture CDs

And speaking of CDs, have you responded to one of those ads to have your photo lab create CDs of your photos? That's one convenient way of storing the pictures created by your film cameras, and, fortunately, iPhoto (versions 1.1.1 and later) can read those Kodak Picture CDs (and possibly other picture CD formats by other companies).

In order to bring them into iPhoto, simply follow these steps:

1. First, take your Picture CD disc and insert it into your Mac's optical drive.
2. iPhoto should launch automatically, but if it doesn't, don't despair. There are worse things to fret over, so just launch it yourself.
3. When iPhoto opens, it should be in Import mode, and you see the Picture CD listed at the bottom-left. Click Import to download the pictures.

That was pretty painless. Of course, you can't delete the files from the CD after they are acquired by your Mac.

Secret

What to Do When You Have Too Many Photos

If your hard drive is getting, well, a little too filled for comfort, maybe you want to consider transferring your photo library to another drive or a CD. This isn't an obvious feature, but it isn't hard to do. So, follow along with me:

1. Locate your iPhoto Library folder, which is placed in the Pictures folder of your personal directory.

2. Drag the folder to another drive or to a CD to make a copy.

3. This is the part you have to be careful about. Drag the original iPhoto Library folder to your desktop.

4. Go to the library you duplicated on the other drive and make an alias to it. The easiest way is to select the folder, hold down the ⌘-Option keys and drag directly to your Pictures folder (where your iPhoto Library used to be before you dragged it to the desktop). This makes an alias to the one you just copied.

5. Launch iPhoto and make sure it recognizes your photo library just as it did the original.

6. If everything works properly, you can trash the original iPhoto Library, the one you moved to the desktop. But you might want to back it up first, just in case something goes wrong on that other hard drive.

Sharing your Photos via Rendezvous

And yet another new feature in iPhoto4 is the ability to share your photos by sending them to another iPhoto 4 user on your LAN via Rendezvous. Does this sound confusing? If so, let me explain.

By selecting Sharing in iPhoto's preferences pane (shown in Figure 14-40), you can look to other Panther running, iPhoto 4 computers on your LAN for shared iPhoto libraries and albums. Likewise, you can share your own images over the LAN. The participants in this little photofest must have these features enabled — you can't force someone to look at your photos.

Thanks to the magic of Rendezvous (Apple's newest networking and sharing protocol, which you can learn more about in Chapter 29), those shared photo albums show up in your source window (shown in Figure 14-41) allowing others (with Rendezvous-friendly iPhoto versions installed) to view them over your network.

note   This sharing feature is another new feature to iPhoto that you can also see in the newest version of iTunes. The preference panel and the source windows are almost identical.

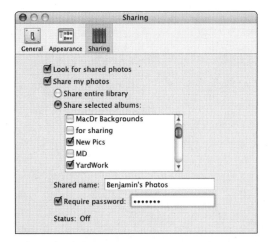

Figure 14-40: You can choose to share your entire library or selected albums. You can also set your shared name and require a password for others to access your shared images.

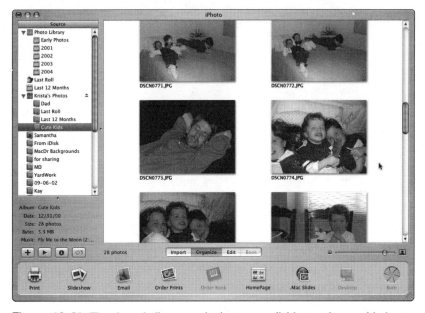

Figure 14-41: The shared albums make images available to other enabled network computers. However, users cannot edit shared images unless they import those images into their own libraries.

Secret

Hot Tips from Apple

You can access some additional tips for use online at Apple by selecting the iPhoto Hot Tips from under the iPhoto application menu (shown in Figure 14-42).

Figure 14-42: The Hot Tips online access is a new feature in iPhoto 4.

Accessing this menu option takes you to www.apple.com/ilife/iphoto/hottips/ where you can find some great instruction on such things as creating Smart Albums and editing your images in iPhoto.

A Fast and Dirty Guide to Photo Retouching in iPhoto

Every time I describe one feature or another on my Mac, I think how it was done before personal computers took over. I have clients who work as photo retouchers. Some of them have been doing it long enough that they started with predigital technology. One in particular talks about using brushes to actually take a photo and paint out the blemishes. As you can imagine, we're talking of a high degree of artistry, as you can't just undo a mistake very easily.

Today it's so much easier, although it still takes talent to do the really complicated stuff. But iPhoto has brought retouching to the masses in a big way. It may not be enough to make you want to remove Adobe Photoshop or Adobe Photoshop Elements, but for most normal retouching purposes, this gets the job done.

Ditching the Red-Eye

This is the most common symptom of taking a photo with a flash. A flash may make the subject's eyes look red even if they don't look that way normally. I suppose even if they were red, you could still blame it on the camera.

---

note

Many cameras with built-in flash attachments use them just to fill in the dark areas, creating a software effect that reduces or eliminates the red eyes. Also, a preliminary flash causes pupils to contract, which reduces exposure of the red retina by the second flash, which is when the shutter opens and closes. No, it doesn't help if your eyes were that way already, so you'll still want to break out the eye drops before you are immortalized on film — er, memory card.

This is how to handle the problem:

1. With your library selected, choose a photo with the problematic red-eye.
2. Click Edit to put iPhoto into its retouching mode.
3. Check to make sure the Constrain pop-up menu is changed to none.
4. Now, move the crosshairs to one corner of your victim's eye, and drag it to enclose the affected eye(s) (shown in Figure 14-43).

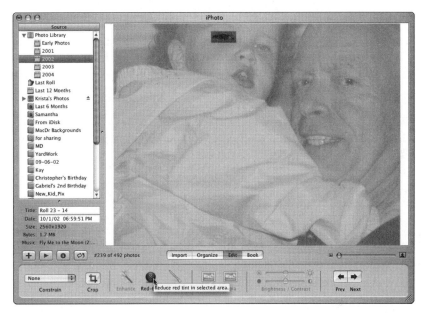

Figure 14-43: When selecting the eye(s) that you want to fix, the rest of the photo is masked out.

5. Drag the size control on the right side of the screen to adjust the image size and make it a bit easier to align those crosshairs.
6. Click the Red-Eye icon in the Edit pane and watch what happens. If you want to compare the edited version with the original, use the Control key to switch back and forth.

Secret

Edit a Duplicate to Safeguard Your Original Images

If you're not sure about some of the changes you want to make and want to have choices, make duplicates of your photos before editing. Just press ⌘-D after selecting a photo to make an extra copy. That way, if your editing techniques bring unintended results, you can revert to the original and start from scratch.

Or you can edit a photo in different ways, and use different photos as a means of comparison before you decide which one to keep.

The other advantage: If you make a duplicate of a photo that appears in several albums, you can edit the duplicate without affecting the way the photo appears in another album.

Quick Picture Enhancements

Before you get involved in any deep-seated photo editing, you might want to try the simplest method, the Enhance function. This modifies color and brightness, using a fixed algorithm. For many photos with the wrong color balance, this method might be more than enough to set things right.

And it involves just a single click.

1. First, select the Photo you want to edit.
2. Click the Edit button to switch into the retouching mode.
3. Click the Enhance button and watch the results.
4. If you feel the picture needs a little more help, try it again. Use the Control key to compare the original with the enhanced version.
5. If the result isn't satisfactory, choose Undo from the Edit menu to clear the changes. If you've gone a little too far in your editing, select Revert to Original in the Edit menu to return the photo to the way it was before you started.

Is Enhance enough to do the trick? Well, for minor exposure blemishes, yes. Otherwise, you'll want to go a little farther in your editing efforts.

And that takes us to. . . .

> **note**
>
> When you edit a picture, it affects what is called the *master photo*. So, if a picture appears in several libraries, each is altered in the same fashion. I just wanted to remind you of that before you wonder whether you have to do the same thing over and over.
>
> This is handy for a user that might want one edited version of the picture in one album and another edited version of that same original in another album.

Fixing Brightness and Contrast

As you notice, the Enhance function adjusts brightness, contrast, and color balance. But it may not be sufficient to get the result you want, so there is another set of editing tools for you to try, and each is simple to try.

With the photo selected, drag the Brightness and Contrast controls to see if it improves the look of your photo. You might want to use the size slider to enlarge the image to get a better feel for how it changes things.

As with the Enhance function, you can undo the change or choose Revert to Original from the Edit menu to bring things back to the way they were.

> **note**
>
> It would be neat if you could alter the brightness and contrast of a selected area, but alas, iPhoto allows you to do just the entire photo, not a portion of it. To move beyond this limited editing capability, you'd have to use another image-editing program. iPhoto is designed to keep it simple.

Making Black-and-White or Sepia Photos

In the old days, if you wanted to shoot a black-and-white photo, you bought the proper film, assuming you could even find it. These days, it's pretty hard to find black-and-white film for sale, unless you can find a specialty dealer.

But when you are converting your pictures to ones and zeros, anything is possible; and if you want to give your picture a vintage look, by converting it to black and white, relief is just a click away:

1. First, select the photo.
2. Click Edit to bring it into the retouching mode.
3. Click the B & W icon (shown in Figure 14-44), and, presto, your color photo has now become black and white.

Figure 14-44: Black and white can give an image a dramatic look.

4. Or click on the Sepia icon (shown in Figure 14-45), and, presto, your color photo is transformed into an old-style copper-like sepia image.

Figure 14-45: Sepia images have the old-style look.

Secret

Making Parts of Images Black and White for Interesting Effects

Remember the movie *Pleasantville?* Two teenagers were suddenly thrust into the pristine black-and-white world of a TV sitcom? It took a lot of careful film editing to make it happen, especially the scenes where people's faces took on a normal flesh color, but the background remained black and white.

But you can create a similar effect, although not with quite the precision.

Just click and select the area you want to convert to black and white and press the B & W icon. Imagine having a red car surrounded by a black and white background. As I said, the precision of the selection area is limited to a rectangular area, but, with a little imagination, you might create some pretty interesting effects, or bizarre ones, depending on your point of view.

Rotating and Cropping

How many times have you shot a photo at a 90-degree angle to make a portrait? Unfortunately, iPhoto doesn't automatically guess at the picture's orientation, so if you happen to take a picture this way, you'll need to rotate the photo first.

To Rotate an image, select the image that needs to be rotated as in Figure 14-46. Then click the Rotate button (which rotates images in 90 degree increments). The image flips in the iPhoto window (shown in Figure 14-47).

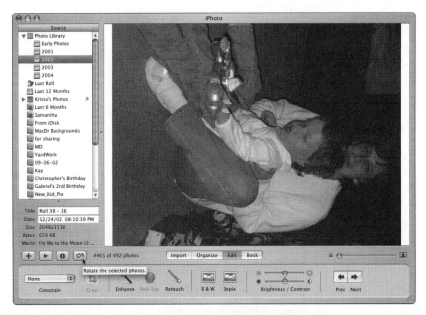

Figure 14-46: Select and click Rotate to turn your landscape to a portrait.

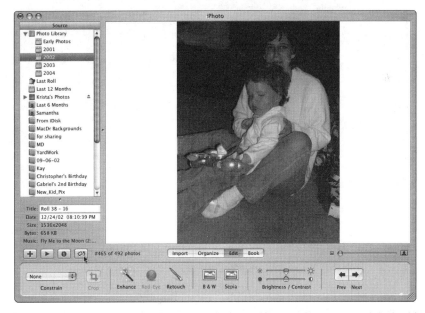

Figure 14-47: Now, maybe it does look better sideways, but you aren't locked in to that choice.

After you've rotated your image, you might find that it also needs to be cropped a little.

If you want to crop a photo so it shows only a specified portion of the image, you follow these steps:

1. First, select the photo.

2. Make sure you're in Edit mode.

3. Click the crosshair cursor at one corner of the photo and drag to cover the area you want to crop.

4. Don't fret if you don't get the area just right. After you've created a selection rectangle, you can click on it and move it around so that it covers the right portion of the photo.

5. If you want to limit or constrain the size to a fixed dimension, such as that of a 4x6 photo, click the Constrain pop-up menu and select the size you want (shown in Figure 14-48).

Figure 14-48: You can select a standard proportion from the Constrain pop-up menu to make sure that the output matches the right physical size.

6. If you already have a crop selection up on the screen, you see it change to the proportions of the selected constrained dimensions (shown in Figure 14-49).

Figure 14-49: The crop area now shows an area that is 4x6 in proportion. Making the area smaller or larger will not change this proportion.

7. After you're certain you've got the right area selected, click the Crop icon to change the photo to its new dimensions (shown in Figure 14-50).

Figure 14-50: And now you have a 4x6 cropped image.

8. Remember that you can press Control to compare the newly cropped photo to the original, and use Undo or Revert to Original from the Edit menu to return things to the way they were.

Choosing Another Image Editor

Are you never satisfied? If fixing red-eyes, enhancing color, brightness, and contrast, and cropping don't do it for you, don't feel you are stuck without the power to do more.

Now maybe a future version of iPhoto will add to its current editing capabilities, but you don't have to wait. All you need is a copy of Adobe Photoshop or Adobe Photoshop Elements, or even GraphicConverter, a cool shareware utility, to extend your abilities to enhance the quality of your photos.

First, you'll want to set up iPhoto to let you edit photos in another application, and to do that, you need to change what happens when you double-click a photo.

To do that:

1. Select an Image from within iPhoto (shown in Figure 14-51).

Figure 14-51: Even with the best of subjects, images like this sometimes need some help.

2. With iPhoto running, choose Preferences from the application menu (see Figure 14-52).
3. Under the double-click category, chose Opens in other and then click Select.
4. In the Open dialog box, click on the Open button to select the application you want to open when you double-click that photo.

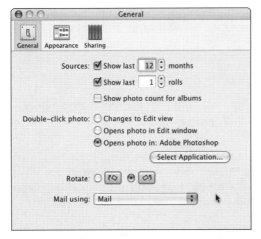

Figure 14-52: Pick a preference, any preference.

5. Dismiss the Preferences dialog box.

6. When you're ready to edit a photo, double-click on it. The application you selected opens, and the photo appears in a new window (shown in Figure 14-53).

Figure 14-53: This shot of my boys is opened in Photoshop CS for further editing.

7. Now fix your photo and, when you're done, save it. That's all there is to it, other than learning how to edit photos in that image-editing program. We talk about that a little more in Chapter 9.

This is something that you should avail yourself of. The image editing features of iPhoto are pretty good, but it's probably a good idea to have something that has some more feature like Photoshop or Photoshop Elements.

We Interrupt This Chapter . . .

Okay. I did it again. I suggested that you spend your hard-earned money buying something that some might think you don't need. But Pieter was here to take up your pocketbook's cause.

Benjamin: While iPhoto does have some very nice features, it's still doesn't have the great editing options that Photoshop or Photoshop Elements does. And at $100, Photoshop Elements is a steal when you start doing more advanced editing and compositing. Besides that, Photoshop Elements has a lot of very cool features for the digital photographer.

Pieter: For most snapshot photographers, especially those with modern digital cameras, there really is not much that you need to do to your pictures. With many modern cameras, the camera does a pretty good job of setting the correct exposure and unless you are shooting in really bad lighting, the chances of you getting a bad picture, from a technical standpoint, are pretty low. So, for most folks, the changes that will need to be made to their snapshots are the common ones like a bit too much light or a bit too little light, red-eye, and so on. Since iPhoto handles all these, I just don't see why it is worth buying a separate application, even one as cool as Photoshop Elements.

A Few Last Things About iPhoto

As you work in iPhoto both in organizing and in editing, you are making changes to your images. It's good to know that you have some options to step back while working in iPhoto.

One of the ways you can do this is by using the Undo command (⌘-Z or Undo from the File menu) to undo what you've just done. When you have gone too far for this to work, say when editing an image, you can always Control-click on your edit image and select the Revert to Original option (shown in 14-54) to take you back to the point before you started messing with your images.

And if you've accidentally deleted an image from your library, you can find those deleted images in the Trash at the bottom of your iPhoto Source pane. If you are really sure you don't need those images any more you can choose to empty your iPhoto Trash (shown in Figure 14-55) under the File menu in iPhoto.

Figure 14-54: Reverting to the original is something to choose when you've made multiple changes and want to step back.

Figure 14-55: There isn't a feature to empty the trash automatically, so make sure that you select and empty your trash as needed.

Secret

iPhoto Keyboard Shortcuts

Because iPhoto makes so many functions available with a single click, you'd be surprised to see that it has a liberal number of keyboard shortcuts you can take advantage of, as well. And if you're a keyboard shortcut person, you're in luck. All of iPhoto's keyboard shortcuts are listed for you from under the Help menu in iPhoto.

Summary

Let me be honest about all this: The only organization you see in my home office is right around my Mac. The rest lies within the realm of systematic disorganization. However, to my wife's amazement, I've managed to keep my photo library in pretty good shape, thanks to iPhoto. After reading this chapter, I trust you'll be able to do it too.

In the next chapter, we'll take pictures to another level, those that move. You'll learn more about iMovie 4 and get a tour of making your own DVDs with iDVD.

Roll camera!

Get Rolling with iMovie 4 and iDVD 4

Chapter
15

◆ ◆

Secrets in This Chapter

◆ ◆

The prices of digital camcorders have steadily dropped in the past few years. This has made it possible for most households to capture holidays and other events in digital format. But a movie is hardly a movie without some form of editing. In the past, editing consisted of fast forwarding and pressing the pause button from the camera, or using large analog editing stations (assuming you had access to one and knew how to use it). Most home movies are unaltered and unedited because the technology to create professional-looking movies didn't exist . . . until now.

Apple's award-winning movie-editing software, Final Cut Pro, is aimed at professionals in the movie and TV business. Although Final Cut Pro can create outstanding movies, it has a high learning curve and costs nearly $1,000 for a full copy. It's probably safe to say that most amateur filmmakers will not want to spend more on the software to edit their movies than they spend on their cameras.

Enter iMovie and iDVD, a home users' dream for turning those home movies into masterpieces. With iMovie and iDVD, you can add titles, create effects, add sound effects, and edit your movie to make it more interesting. And after your masterpiece is finished, you can export it to iDVD to create a professional-looking DVD to watch in your home DVD player. When it comes to fast and easy movie creating, iMovie and iDVD are all you need.

The Nuts and Bolts of Editing Video on a Mac

Editing movies is as easy as telling a story. It's a process of taking the video that you shot and putting it together into a way that is interesting and fun. The addition of titles, filter effects, and sound effects isn't necessary, but it adds a certain feel to your movie; it shows that you put time, effort, and attention to detail while editing.

Making a movie with iMovie boils down to three steps: importing, editing, and exporting. I walk you through these steps in more detail shortly, but first, let's get familiar with the iMovie 4 interface.

The iMovie 4 Interface

iMovie's interface can be summed up in two words: simple and clean. iMovie is simple to use and understand because it doesn't have the many features that you would find in high-end editing software like Final Cut Pro. Instead, iMovie puts just about everything that you need in one window (shown in Figure 15-1). About 90 percent of what iMovie can do, can be done in the main window; this makes it easy and appealing to the amateur videographer.

iMovie's interface is made up of three different parts — the preview window, the elements shelf, and the timeline viewer — all of which live in the one window that makes up iMovie.

The preview window is where you view video. As you will see in a little bit, the preview window can be used to view video that is still on your camera, or used to view your imported movie clips. In high-end editing software, there are usually two windows to view video. One is usually used as a preview window, and the other is used to view rendered video — that is, your final project.

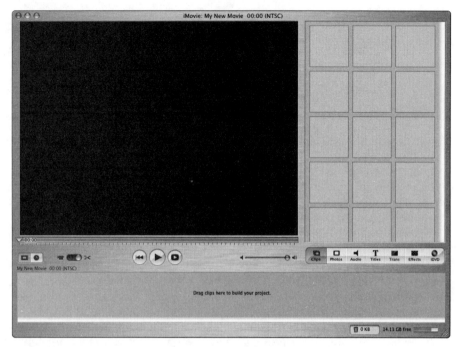

Figure 15-1: The iMovie interface is simple and clean. But don't let this deceive you; iMovie can produce professional-looking movies complete with titles and transition.

---

note

We need to talk about a movie editing vocabulary term — *rendering*.

Rendering a portion or all of your movie is necessary whenever a title or effect is applied to it. Rendering writes in the changes that will appear in the finished movie.

Before processors were as fast as they are today, you would have to render a portion of a movie whenever you wanted to see a preview of each new effect or title. Today, with faster processors, we are able not only to see a preview of an effect or title, but also to continue to edit our movie as the processor is rendering other portions of the movie.

Figure 15-2 shows an example of what the preview window looks like. The preview window has a small timescrubber bar just below it. The playhead indicates where in time the movie is currently at. It can also be dragged along the preview window's timeline to scrub through your video. Scrubbing your video just means manually progressing forward or backward in time quickly to get to the point of the movie you are looking for.

Figure 15-2: The preview window is used to view your video. It has many functions including viewing video still on your camera, viewing individual clips in your movie timeline, and viewing your final project.

The playback controls for the preview window are very simple. There are only three buttons to control your movie. They are rewind to beginning, play, and play full-screen. Notice there is not a rewind or fast-forward button. Those actions are done by scrubbing through your movie via the scrubber bar.

To the right of the preview window controls is the master volume control. As you see later, you can adjust the volume of your video clips or background songs, but they will not be any louder than your master volume level. Think of this control as the volume button on your TV.

Below the preview window is the timeline. The timeline actually has two different views, which are used to organize and edit your movie clips and soundtracks. You use the video track view to put your movie clips in sequence (see Figure 15-3), which is called the sequence view. The Audio track view to adjust the audio levels and timing of the audio (as seen in Figure 15-4) is called the audio adjust view. You can still move and edit your movie clips in the audio adjust view, but often it is just easier to do in the clip sequence view.

Figure 15-3: The first view is best to use when you are organizing your clips. The timeline shows just your movie clips (represented as separate blocks) with your transitions in between.

Now that we've talked a little bit about the three main windows (which include the Elements shelf), let's explore a little more in depth about each of them.

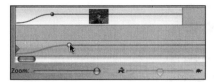

Figure 15-4: The second timeline view is used to edit the volumes and control the speed of your movie. You can still add clips and rearrange them in this view, but you'll find that it's easiest to arrange your clips in the sequence view and edit the level of volume in this view.

Preview Window

I already said much of the features of the preview window, but I left out an important part of editing a movie, and that's importing your video from your camera to the computer.

Notice right below the preview window, in between the timeline view buttons and the preview window controls, is the toggle switch between two icons, one of a video camera and the other, a scissors. The scissors means that you are in edit mode. Plug in your digital camcorder to your computer and flip the switch to the other side and you are ready to import video.

If everything goes right, you see a blue screen that says "Camera Connected."

The next step is to press the Import button (shown in Figure 15-5). Sit back and relax or go get a snack as your video gets transferred from your camera to your computer.

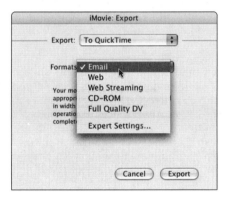

Figure 15-5: When you switch the toggle from the edit mode to the camera mode, the preview window's controls change and a new Import button is added. In the camera mode, the new controls actually control your digital camcorder.

If the import does not go as planned, check to make sure that your digital camcorder is securely plugged into the camera or computer. In some cases, you may need to put the camera into VCR mode (make sure to check your camcorder's manual). If you have connected your camera correctly and turned it on to the VCR setting but for some reason you still can't get it to import video, you may see a widow like that shown in Figure 15-6. You may find it helpful to click on the Connection Help button, which brings up the internal help guide that may have the solution.

Figure 15-6: If all else fails, the Connection Help button may provide some very helpful tips.

The Elements Shelf

Next, you have the elements shelf. The elements shelf is called a shelf because it holds everything from your unused movie clips, to the effects, titles, background music, pictures, and transitions. Let's take a closer look at each button.

Clips

Clicking the Clips button shows you your Clips pane in the elements shelf (shown in Figure 15-7). After importing your movie clips from your digital camcorder, you can find them in the Clips pane of the elements shelf. You can also use the Clips pane for any photos that are not in your iPhoto library, along with any audio files. But remember that any background music you would like that you already have in your iTunes library does not need to be placed in your Clips pane because it can be accessed from a different button. Each separate clip is numbered and displays the time along with the picture of the first frame.

Photos

The Photos button brings up the Photos pane, which includes your iPhoto library (shown in Figure 15-8). From here, you are able to search through all your photos or look through any existing albums. You can adjust the settings of the Ken Burns effect before applying the photos to your timeline. Your iPhoto photo albums can be accessed via the Photo Library drop-down menu.

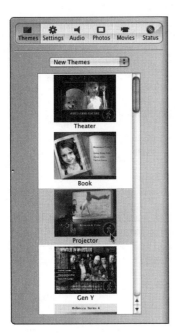

Figure 15-7: The Clips pane. Each clip is represented by its own block, which sits here until you need it.

Figure 15-8: The Photos pane opens and shows you all the pictures in your iPhoto library.

Animate Your Photos with the Ken Burns Effect

Secret

A feature of iMovie 3 and 4 is the use of a great-looking photo effect called the Ken Burns Effect. It's called the Ken Burns Effect after the person who created it. This effect gives your photos a more animated feel by slowly zooming in or out to give emphasis to the subjects in your photos.

The Ken Burns Effect is applied to each photo by default when you place them into your timeline, however you can easily turn this off by unchecking the check box. The Ken Burns Effect can also be configured with a few settings, which mainly set the direction of the zoom (in or out) and the speed at which it does so.

Audio

Most movies have background music, even during the dialog, and what better audio to use then your favorite songs straight from your iTunes library? Like the Photos pane, the Audio pane shows all your songs (shown in Figure 15-9). Easily access your favorite songs in your organized playlists, or search your entire library in seconds for that one song you are looking for with the search field.

Figure 15-9: Your music library and sound effects can be accessed from the Audio pane.

What movie would be complete without sound effects? Apple has included professional sounding sound effect along with iMovie 4. The sound effects are provided by Skywalker Sound. Many of the sound effects are the same used by George Lucas, who is the creator of the *Star Wars* movies and *Indiana Jones* movies. (http://www.skysound.com) If you don't see the sound effects, you can find them by selecting Sound Effects from the drop-down menu above the list of songs.

The Place at Playhead button puts the selected song so that it starts right where the play-head is. This makes it easier than dragging a song to the timeline then having to drag it to the appropriate place.

note With the edition of the iTunes Music Store into iTunes 4, you now have in excess of 400,000 songs to be used in your movies. At just 99 cents per song, you are now saved from buying a whole album for just one track. The iTunes Music Store's 30-second pre-view for every song is also a great way to sample songs before you buy.

You can learn more about the iTunes Music Store in Chapter 13.

You can also create voiceovers from the Audio pane. A *voiceover* is a recording that you can use as a narration, a voice title, or a dubbed voice. Every computer that Apple ships, except the PowerMac G5 and G4, comes with a built-in mic. However, you might want to buy an external microphone as the built-in mics might not meet your satisfaction. Especially on the laptops, the microphones often pick up fan noises and hard drive clicks while recording. Perfect for casual communication, the built-in microphones do not pro-vide satisfactory quality for moviemaking.

Titles

Titles are great to introduce your movie; after all, every movie has a title. Apple provides the user with many different title effects (shown in Figure 15-10). With these effects, you can come up with a simple title in the beginning to caption titles for pictures to a title effect that looks like your movie is a music video.

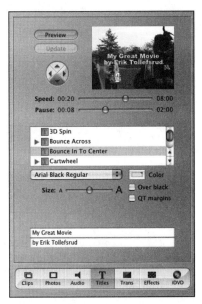

Figure 15-10: Present your movie with fabulous titles, some of which are animated. Just about everything is customizable from the font to the size of text to the direction of animation.

Apple has added more great looking titles in the new version of iMovie that comes with iLife '04. Every title allows you do add your own text and customize its settings. For example, set the speed at which the title enters and exits the movie, or tell it from what direction it should appear. Just place the playhead to the spot you want to apply the title, set the setting, and press the apply button. The preview button is used to get an idea of what the title will look like after you have rendered it into your movie by pressing the Update button. You can tell it's unrendered because of the jerky frame rate when playing back.

Transitions

Use the Trans button to access the Transitions pane where you can pick the transitions for your clips. Transitions are used to give your movie a more fluid feel by making the end of one clip merge with the beginning of another clip. Figure 15-11 shows the Transition pane of the elements shelf. Instead of having one clip end and another clip begin with virtually no pause, adding a nice crossfade moves the viewer from one scene to the next feeling like they were meant to be shown together.

Figure 15-11: Transitions are a great way to give your movie a flowing feeling. There are also a few transitions that are specifically for fading in and fading out.

Effects

The movie effects (shown in Figure 15-12) are a great way to spice up your movie. Adding effects are as easy as selecting the movie clip in the timeline and the effect you wish to use. After you set the appropriate settings, press the Apply button and wait for it to render in the timeline. Depending on the speed of your processor, the amount of RAM your computer has, and the size of the clip the effect is being applied to, it could take several minutes. Luckily, however, a preview of the clip is shown with the effect in the elements shelf. Adding multiple effects is also possible by applying one effect then another to a movie clip. Besides the effects that Apple supplies, you can purchase others from third-party venders. Later in this chapter, you'll find information on where to find other video effects.

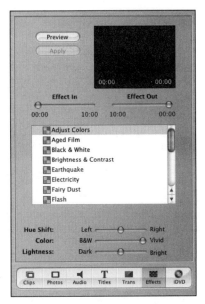

Figure 15-12: Apple provides many effects that you can add to your video.

iDVD

iMovie is tightly integrated with iDVD to help you produce great looking DVDs of the movies you create. The iDVD button allows you to create and remove chapters for when you export your movie to iDVD (as seen in Figure 15-13). For those new to DVDs, chapters are used to quickly skip ahead in time to a certain point in a movie. Skipping to a chapter is easier and quicker than having to fast-forward or rewind to the spot in the movie you are looking for. To add a chapter, simply select the clip where a new chapter should begin and press the Add Chapter button to create a placemark where a new chapter begins.

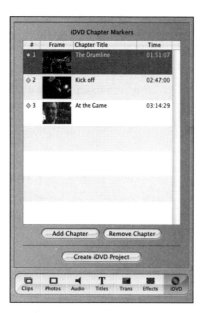

Figure 15-13: It's in iMovie that you already start to create your DVD for when you export the project to iDVD. By telling iMovie where certain chapters begin after you are in iDVD, your work is almost done.

The Timeline

As previously mentioned, the timeline is where your movie is put together. The timeline provides two different views. One is the video track view and the other is to edit the audio which is the audio track view. The video track view is a great way to line up your movie clips from start to finish. Sometimes putting your movie in order first and then going back to edit the volume, add background music, transitions, and effects is an easier and more efficient way than doing it all as you go along, because what happens if you want to change the sequence of the movie? All your transitions would have to be re-rendered and your background music replaced.

The audio track view is used to adjust the volumes of specific clips. Click on the button that looks like a clock to switch to this view; there are a lot more buttons and sliders that appear and the timeline itself splits into three different sections. The top section is where your video clips are and the bottom two are for audio. There are two audio tracks; on one of them, your voices can play and the other plays any background music or additional sounds.

Along the bottom are a few sliders that adjust things such as the volume and speed of the movie clips. The first slider allows you to zoom in on the timeline to get a better view of your movie clips and sound clips in the timeline. The next slider adjusts the speed of the movie. Moving it toward the rabbit makes the movie play faster, and moving it toward the turtle makes it slower. The Edit Volume check box allows you to edit the level of volume of each clip at certain points in the timeline. This is handy if you want the music to flair louder during a more dramatic moment.

Finding Your Way with Bookmarks

Another feature new to iMovie 4 is the use of bookmarks. Bookmarks are used to mark important places in your movie where you would like to skip to quickly. iMovie places a small green dot in the timeline where your playhead is at. To skip to the bookmarks press the Command (⌘) and the left or right bracket ([or]) keys, depending on what direction you want to go. This feature is used to quickly jump to important key frames. The bookmark feature can also be found under the Bookmarks menu.

The picture of the trash can show you how full iMovie's trash is. When you delete a movie clip or picture from the timeline iMovie doesn't really delete it right away. Instead, it gets put into the trash. And that allows you to undo what you did in case you did it by mistake. Clicking on the trash can brings up a dialog box asking if you are sure you want to empty the trash. This option cannot be undone. If you delete something from the trash, you can not get it back.

The green bar on the right indicates how full your hard drive is. This give you an idea about how much more work can be done on your movie before you run out of hard drive space. Editing movies takes a lot of hard drive space, and as mentioned before, it's a good idea to edit your movies on a separate FireWire drive so as not to take up your main partition.

Along the right side are three check boxes. Deselecting these check boxes mutes audio clips of the indicated line.

Preferences

The preferences can be found under the application menu (iMovie menu) in the desktop menu bar (or you could just type ⌘-comma). The Preferences window provides General and Advanced options (shown in Figure 15-14).

The general options control the some basic iMovie display features and timeline behaviors. The Display options toggle the following features on or off: display short time codes, play sound when exporting your movie is complete, automatically start new clip at scene break, and show locked audio when selected.

The Timeline options toggle the following features on or off: show the wavelength of the audio clips (this including sound effects, songs and voiceovers), keep playhead centered while playing, timeline snapping, and play a sound when snapping.

The Advanced section has four different subsections. The first option is to select whether the newly imported clips go to the Clips pane or directly to the timeline. The next option is to choose the broadcast format of your movie. For those who are unfamiliar with the NTSC and PAL broadcasting standards, just know that NTSC is for the United States, Canada, Mexico, Japan, and other countries, whereas the PAL standard is for the United Kingdom, China, Italy, Germany, and many other countries.

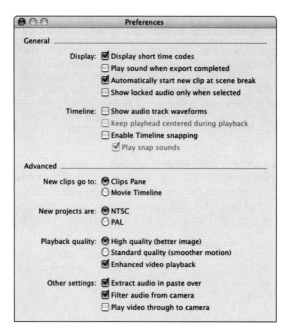

Figure 15-14: There are a few preferences that you can customize to make iMovie run the way you want it to.

on the web **For a full list of what country uses which broadcast standard, visit** www.ihffilm.com/ihf/videostandard.html.

You can set the playback quality by selecting high quality or standard quality. The high quality playback shows a better image, however the frame rate might be a little jerky. The standard quality plays back much smoother, but the image is a little more pixilated.

The other settings are to turn on and off the option to extract audio in paste over, filter video through camera, and play video through camera.

Making a Movie with iMovie

As I said before, the process of making a movie is pretty simple. It starts with the importing of the movie clips that were filmed with the digital camcorder. The next step is to arrange the video in a sequence that tells a story. Add titles, effects, and transitions to give your movie that special look.

Plan Ahead So You Have Enough Hard Drive Space

Before you start importing your movie, make sure that you have enough room on your hard drive. Importing video from your camera can take up a lot of space on your hard drive, anywhere from a few gigs to a few dozen gigs. The amount of space it takes up depends on how long your video clips are. The longer the movie, the more space it's going to take up.

Luckily, external hard drives are getting a lot cheaper these days. It may be a good idea to run out and get a separate hard drive to store your movies on. Make sure that your new hard drive is FireWire 400 or FireWire 800 and has a rpm rate of at least 7200. What's rpm you say? That's revolutions per minute, in this case, how fast the disks inside spin. Typically the faster the disks, the faster your computer is able to read and write to the hard drive, which is important when your computer is reading file sizes of a few gigs while trying to play it back for you.

Importing

The first thing you do when beginning your movie is to import the movie clips from the video camera. Most of the time, this is a matter of plugging the camera into your computer with a FireWire cable. You will probably have to turn the camera on to the VCR setting, however not all cameras operate the same way. It would be a good idea to read your video camera's manual. After the computer recognizes your camera, under the preview window, your controls change to resemble the controls found on a standard video camera — fast forward, rewind, play/pause, and stop — allowing you to find the clips you wish to import. If you do not see these controls, you are probably still in the edit mode. See the discussion in "Preview Window" earlier in this chapter for details.

When you find the place where you would like to start importing, whether it is the beginning of the tape or in the middle, press the Import button. iMovie imports your clips and places them into the Clips pane of the elements shelf or directly into the timeline (depending on how you've set your preferences). A new clip is created for every time the stop and record buttons are pressed on the camera while filming.

Import Additional Video via iSight

Let's say you are finished with the filming of your movie (maybe the holiday is over with and everyone went home), but there was one other thing you needed to say to the camera. Luckily, new in iMovie 4 you are able to import and capture video right from your computer via iSight, a FireWire Web camera. Simply click on the camera icon and when the video feed comes up, click on the button that reads "Record With iSight."

Editing

After your movie clips have been imported from the digital video camera to your computer, the editing process can begin. When I talk about editing video, I don't mean simply putting your clips in a certain order and adding titles, effects, and transitions to them. Editing also involves cutting out the portions of video that you don't need. Think of it as cropping a photo so that the photo is more about the subject and less about the background.

Start by arranging the imported clips on your elements shelf into a sequence that tells a story. Don't worry about the transitions or the effects yet. If your clips are not in the right order, simply click and drag them into the order you want. As mentioned before, organizing your clips is easiest when you are in the sequence mode of the timeline.

To trim a clip, start by placing a movie clip in the timeline or selecting one by clicking on it in the elements shelf. The video loads in the preview window. Suppose you have a movie clip where nothing really happens in the beginning. You'll want to trim out the beginning and leave the last part of the clip. If you move your mouse toward the scrubber bar, a pair of right angle triangles, which are called crop markers, appears on the far left side. Move one of the triangles up to the point there the action starts. The space between, represented in yellow, is deleted when you press the Delete key (as shown in Figure 15-15). Trimming can be done at any time, but it's a good thing to know before you begin to put your movie clips in sequence.

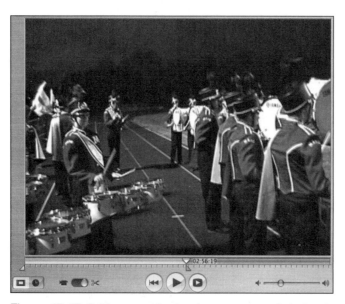

Figure 15-15: Editing your clips involves a process of placing the unwanted material between two triangle markers and pressing the Delete key on your keyboard. The unwanted video is represented in yellow on the scrubber bar below the preview window.

Secret

Sometimes Less Is More — Especially with Transitions

Just a general tip, if you worry about transitions and effects after putting in each clip you may end up applying way more eye-catching effects than you had wanted. Having flashy effects and transitions are great in moderation. You wouldn't want your viewers to be counting how many times they saw that effect used or become bored with a certain transition.

The emphasis should be on the movie, not the additional effects added.

A great movie often has background music or sound effects. To add music or sound effects, click the Audio button in the elements shelf. This loads your music from your iTunes library. A search field is provided to quickly and easily search for the song you want. This can be used for your iTunes library but cannot be used for your sound effects library. After you have chosen a song or sound effect, the fastest way to place it into your timeline is to press the Place at Playhead button right below the search field. This puts the beginning of the song where your playhead is currently located so you may want to place the playhead accordingly. You could also just drag the song or sound file from the library into the timeline. Either way, iMovie converts the song file to AIFF (Audio Interchange File Format) which is the standard Apple audio file format.

As I said before, the timeline has two audio tracks. This is so that one can be occupied by background music while the other is used for additional voices. While background music is playing, it's often a good idea to make the music play quieter so the voices can be heard. You do this by editing the level of the volumes for each audio track. To do this, select the Edit Volume check box. The audio clips are now displayed with lines that indicate at what volume level it is currently playing at, at a certain point.

Let's say you want your volume for your background music to soften as your subject talks but then dramatically fade back up in an attempt to add to the emotional feel. To achieve this effect, click on a point where you want the background volume to start to fade out. This adds a small dot to the timeline, which we'll call a key point. When selected the dot is yellow, otherwise it is purple. Next click the spot on the timeline where the background volume should be at its lowest. This creates another key point to tell the computer that it should be at that level of volume by that point in time in the timeline. This creates a smooth decrease in volume. Now click once again to place another key point in a place where the background volume should increase back to full volume. Figure 15-16 shows an example of what a fade out and fade in of volume looks like in the timeline. You can continue to add key points to your volume lines to your voices, sound effects, and background music.

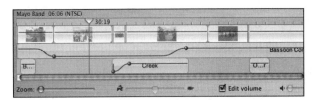

Figure: 15-16: When you add key points while editing the volume of your clips, you can click and drag the key points to a desired level of volume. You can add as many key points as you want to any of the audio files in the timeline.

Effects, Transitions, and Titles

At this point, you are ready to add visual effects and transitions to your movie. The effects are found by clicking on the Effects button in the elements shelf. Every effect has different settings that can be adjusted so we won't go through all of them, but we'll give you the basic idea of how to add them to your movie clips.

To add an effect to a clip, select the desired effect in the elements shelf and press the Apply button. Your computer then starts to render the clip. Rendering is a process of applying an effect to a movie, and depending on the size of the movie, speed of your computer, and the amount of RAM, it could take several minutes. The preview window in the elements shelf gives you a preview of what the effect will look like, however it's a low quality preview. The quality isn't as important at this point as it is to see if the settings on the effect are what is desired.

Transitions are a great way to show off your movie clips. Keep in mind that there is no problem in *not* having a transition, and sometimes it is the best idea. I can't stress enough to be careful in preventing the transitions and effects from stealing the attention from your movie. However, there are many times where an added transition to your movie clips creates a nice effect from one scene to the next. You can find the transitions in your elements shelf after clicking the Trans button.

To add a transition to your movie, it's easiest if you view in the video track view in the timeline. By dragging the desired transition from the elements shelf to the appropriate space between the clips adds the transition and your computer goes to work rendering it into your movie. Adding a transition in the audio track mode can be done the same way, but you have a better view of your entire movie from the video track mode.

Lastly, I'd like to talk about titles. Titles are almost a necessity because they present your movie right from the beginning. Titles can also be used as scene titles or ending credits. iMovie provides many title effects. You can find these under the Titles button in the elements shelf. To add a title, select the desired title effect. After that, add the text of your choice to the provided text areas. Some titles allow you to add more text than others. You can see a preview of what it will look like when applied to the selected clip. Many other titles have settings you can set to say what direction, how fast, and how long the title should be on screen.

Secret

Apple Can Help You Find More Visual Effects

It should also be mentioned that there is an abundance of third-party iMovie plug-ins that give you more video effects. For a large list of places to find them visit Apple's Web site about iMovie at www.apple.com/ilife/imovie/visual_effects.html.

Sharing

The last step is to share your masterpiece with others. The most popular way of viewing a movie is from a DVD. Later, you'll create a DVD with menus using iDVD, but right now I'll show you a few other ways of sharing your new movie.

iMovie allows you to share you movie in many ways. Sharing used to be called exporting. The sharing option can be found under the File menu.

E-mail

The first of six ways to share your movie is by sending your movie via e-mail (see Figure 15-17). Selecting this option compresses your movie and puts it into an e-mail as an attachment. Sometimes, sending your movie via e-mail isn't the best idea because a longer movie could take up several megabytes even after being compressed. It would take several minutes to send and receive that kind of file. For this reason, it's really a bit inconsiderate to send large attachments via e-mail. However, be forewarned that some e-mail services have limit on how large an e-mail size is that you can send out. Most e-mail services have a relatively small limit on the size of e-mail you can receive. Make sure to contact you e-mail service provider before sending a large movie via e-mail.

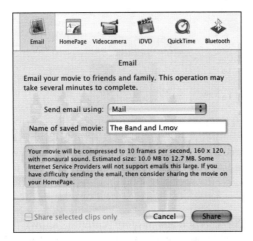

Figure 15-17: You can send your movie via e-mail to anyone you want through Mail and some other e-mail programs.

note
Besides Mail, Eudora, Entourage. and AOL are also compatible e-mail clients that allow direct export.

You can however choose to compress your movie with the QuickTime tab using the e-mail selection. After it's done compressing you are then able to send your movie as an attachment with your e-mail program of choice. Keep in mind that even after compression your movie may still be several megabytes big.

Your only option while choosing to export your movie as an e-mail attachment is your movie's name. Other than that, iMovie chooses the optimal compression methods so you don't have to.

HomePage

If you have a .Mac account, another easy way to share your movie is to publish it to the Internet on to your .Mac HomePage. Figure 15-18 shows the options to publish your movie to your .Mac HomePage. Like choosing the e-mail option, iMovie takes care of the compression settings so you don't have to. Remember that your .Mac site has only 100 megabytes of storage space. This includes your iDisk space that you use for iSync and iPhoto. While iMovie does compress your movie before uploading it to your iDisk, a longer movie can still be a couple dozen megabytes in size. Apple thoughtfully provides a Buy More Space button that takes you to the Apple site so you can buy more iDisk space.

Figure 15-18: A great use of your .Mac account is to upload your movies directly from iMovie to your HomePage. Once complete, iMovie tells you where to find your movie on the Internet.

Back to Camera

Sometimes you will want to export the video back to your camera (shown in Figure 15-19). This is a handy way of sharing your videos if you or the place you are at does not have a DVD player. You can set a few options that control how iMovie acts while playing back the movie so that the camera can record it. These options include the delay time until iMovie starts the movie so that the camera can get ready, and the amount of time a black frame is played before and after the movie starts.

Figure 15-19: After editing your movie, you have the option to export it back to the camera if you decide to store your movie on the media that your camera uses.

QuickTime

The QuickTime export features are similar to some the export features you have already seen. The drop-down menu allows you to select a type of viewing medium (shown in Figure 15-20). iMovie adjusts the level of compression for each of the playback modes. Email compresses the movie the most, because e-mail services tend to limit the size of the mail box. The Full Quality DV setting provides no compression at all. Be careful when using Full Quality DV, which copies your whole movie into another file. This means you end up with a movie file that can be several hundred megabytes to a few gigs large. The Expert setting allows you to control the compression settings a little more. If you know what settings are appropriate for a type of playback, you may use this option. However, if you are new to video editing or creation, choosing between the predefined settings is the better idea.

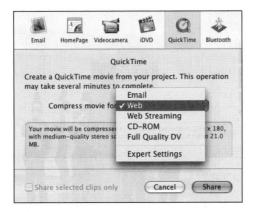

Figure 15-20: You have many options to choose from when exporting your movie as a QuickTime file. The different settings determine how much compression is used while exporting.

Bluetooth

The Bluetooth option is new to iMovie 4 (shown in Figure 15-21). This setting is much like the Back to Camera option. iMovie compresses your movie and exports it to a device where it is recorded. Only this time the device is not a digital video camera, but rather a cell phone or PDA that has Bluetooth capabilities. This process can take several minutes to complete.

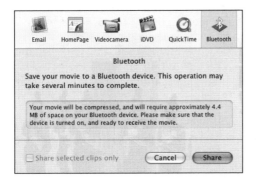

Figure 15-21: If you have a Bluetooth phone or PDA that allows you to view movies, you can export your movie directly to your Bluetooth device right from iMovie.

The Nuts and Bolts of DVD Creation

Part of the new iLife '04 suite of programs, iDVD 4 is Apple's beginner DVD authoring program, intended for those that are new to the DVD creation world. You need almost no experience with movie creation to make a wonderful looking movie and publish it to a DVD with menus and chapter selections.

Getting Your iDVD Project Ready

First thing to remember when creating a DVD is that you must have a SuperDrive installed in your Mac. If your not sure if you have a SuperDrive, it's a good possibility that if you have iDVD installed on your computer that you also have a SuperDrive for iDVD will not install on a computer that does not have a working SuperDrive. Also, in the new iDVD, Apple has added support for third-party DVD-R burners.

Remember back in the iMovie sections, I talked about creating chapters for iDVD. Once your movie is edited and all your chapters are marked, your next step is to press the Create iDVD Project button. This is the same as selecting the iDVD option from the Share command in the File menu.

Once iDVD has loaded, your project is almost complete.

The iDVD Interface

The iDVD interface is relatively simple, however, it has more to it than iMovie. In the main window there are seven buttons: Burn, Preview, Map, Motion, Slideshow, Folder, and Customize.

The Burn button starts the burning process of your DVD. You won't use this button until the very end. The Preview button loads your movie with a mock-up version of your DVD menus. With a DVD remote present, you can test the interface you have created to make sure there aren't any errors. You can exit out of the preview mode by pressing the stop button on the remote.

A new button was added in iDVD 4. The Map button allows you to look at a visual map of your DVD menu (example provided in Figure 15-22). This enables you to see without having to test every button, that your clips and chapters are organized to your satisfaction. You can see how your menu works and make sure you didn't forget anything.

A DVD menu is typically made up of a theme. A theme is a combined set of background pictures, button styles, fonts, music, and animations that give a DVD menu style. A few themes offer animated motion, such as the moving of the background in the Road Trip One theme. The Motion button stops these motions as they can be a bit of an annoyance while trying to edit your main menu screen (see Figure 15-23). You may also find that not having the motion turned on while you are configuring your menus saves on processor performance.

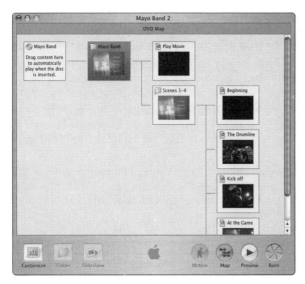

Figure 15-22: The Map button shows you a visual map on your DVD menu.

Figure 15-23: The Motion button stops or starts motions while you are editing.

The Slideshow button creates a slideshow out of any pictures you may have. It places a file on your main DVD application menu called My Slideshow. Select it and you can add any photos, including photos from your iPhoto library, into this slideshow.

The Folder button creates a new folder on your application menu that can be renamed to whatever you want simply by selecting the name from the menu. Folders can be placed inside of folders just like in the Mac OS Finder. Adding folders can help organize your media and make it easier to find what you are looking for in the DVD menu.

The last button is the Customize button, which opens a side window of even more buttons and controls. Along the top of the side window are tabs labeled Themes, Settings, Media, and Status.

The Themes button shows you the different themes you can choose from your iDVD menu (shown in Figure 15-24). The drop-down menu allows you to select all of the themes present in iDVD 3 and iDVD 4. Choose a theme simply by clicking on one. You may have to wait a few seconds for the theme to load.

Figure 15-24: Apple has added a lot of new great looking themes in iDVD 4, however you can still use the old iDVD 3 themes by selecting from the drop-down menu to view them all.

The second button is Settings (as seen in Figure 15-25). The Settings button provides additional controls for each theme. These settings include the duration of the menu (the default works very well). Eventually there is a point where the DVD menu has to restart itself from the beginning. Often this is after several seconds.

Figure 15-25: Although Apple provides great looking themes, you have the ability to customize them to fit your preference. You can change the font, add your own menu music, or even change the size of the buttons.

You can set the transition of one menu to the next by selecting a transition from the drop-down menu. Below the drop-down menu is a place where you can add your own picture and music to the currently selected theme.

Just below the menu settings is where you can set the font, size, and color of the menu text. In most themes, a different font is used based on the theme; however, nothing is stopping you from changing this. Last is the setting to change the style of the buttons. Not only can you change the shape, but you can also change the way they sit on the menus and even the size.

The Media tab is where you find your photos, extra movies, and music (shown in Figure 15-26). The drop-down menu at the top allows you to select audio, photos, and movies. Select Audio to access your iTunes library much the same way you do in iMovie. Once you find a song, simply press the Apply button. Select Photos to load the photos that are in your iPhoto library. Use the search field provided at the bottom to find the photo you want. Use the Movies selection to see the different QuickTime movies you have in your Movies folder in your home directory. To use a movie in your menu items, click and drag one into the desired spot on the menu.

Figure 15-26: The media tab takes on three different jobs. This is where you can access your music from your iTunes library, your photos from your iPhoto library, and your extra movies from your Movies folder in your home directory.

The Status tab shows you various limits that you will encounter when burning a DVD. DVD Capacity shows you how much space you have left for burning your movie onto your DVD. For example, the Motion Menus bar shows that you have 15 minutes of movie menus available, and so on and so forth.

iDVD Preferences

iDVD preferences include three different sections which resemble iMovie's preferences. You can find the preferences under the File menu. Under the General tab (shown in Figure 15-27), you can customize the project settings. These options include show drop zones, show apple logo watermark, and delete rendered files on closing a project. Maybe the most useful of these options is the ability to leave out the Apple logo watermark. While we all might be thrilled with Apple for creating such a great piece of software, we may not want them to be showing up on our family moments like some sort of advertisement.

The encoder settings are either best quality or best performance. By default, Enable background encoding is selected.

Like in iMovie, iDVD also allows you to select the PAL standard. You may want to keep it on the NTSC standard unless you are planning on sending a copy of your DVD to the UK or other European countries. You may find that video playback using the PAL standard does not work or does not work correctly with U.S.-made DVD players and TVs.

Figure 15-27: You can customize the encoder settings under the General tab.

The Slideshow preferences (shown in Figure 15-28) allow you to control whether the original photos are added to the DVD or not. Using this option requires more space when burning your DVD. You can also select to always scale slides to fit the TV aspect ratio.

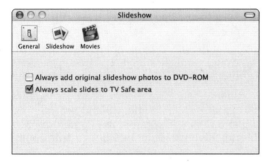

Figure 15-28: The slideshow preferences give you the on/off options to add original photos that were used in the slideshow onto the DVD, and to scale your slideshow to TV safe area which makes sure that your slideshow fits on the TV screen.

Using the Movies tab (shown in Figure 15-29) you specify whether chapter marker submenus are created when importing movies, or if you should be asked at the time of importing whether they should be created. Of course, you may have movies located on other drives or in folders other than the Movies folder in your home directory. To tell iDVD where to look for other folders (while you are choosing movies in the Media tab), you specify the path to these folders here. This is a handy option if you store most of your movies on a separate drive.

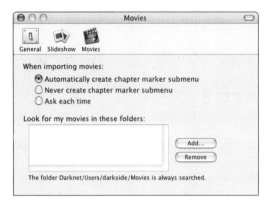

Figure 15-29: The Movies tab; you can have iDVD look into folders other than just your Movies folder in your home directory for your extra movies.

Creating a Quick DVD

As mentioned before, after creating the chapters in iMovie and pressing the Create iDVD Project, the hard part and almost 75 percent of your job is done. iMovie creates a project for iDVD that says how many chapters there are and the only thing iDVD needs to know is what theme you want to apply to it.

Press the Customize button on the bottom of the iDVD menu if you cannot see the options drawer. Select a theme from the options drawer and click on it. The theme loads all the necessary fonts and menu items. These menu items can be customized under the Settings tab.

Most themes have a place where you can add your own picture or movie to make it seem like the theme was made just for you. Click on the Media tab and browse your movies folder or your iPhoto library to find a photo or two to place in the menu drop zones of the specific theme. Remember, not all themes have the same number of drop zones to place photos and movies.

Most of the themes come with music, others do not. Either way, you can change or add your own music to any theme. Browse your iTunes library under the Media tab. Once you have found the music you would like to accompany your menu, press the Apply button.

Secret

Royalty Free, Better Background DVD Music

FreePlay (at www.freeplaymusic.com) has a lot of music that you can use as background music for your DVD menus. The best part? They are free, legal, and royalty free. Available in the audio formats of MP3 or .wav.

One thing that you should know is that you have to set the theme of every submenu. The reason for this is that there are some instances where each submenu could be a separate theme with different background pictures/movies and music. This flexibility allows you to be very creative when putting your DVD together. It's always a good idea to preview your entire DVD menu before going on to burning it.

Last, you may want to look at the DVD menu map, accessed by pressing the Map button at the bottom of the main window. Always make sure to preview your DVD menu by pressing the Preview button. After you are completely satisfied with your iDVD project, press the Burn button. The computer prompts you to insert a blank DVD. Once you have done this, press Burn Disk. The burning process takes one, two, or more hours to complete so go have a snack or watch TV. Congratulations, you have created a home movie complete with DVD menus to share with the rest of the family.

Breaking the DVD Burning Rules

iDVD says that it will only burn DVD-R disks. In fact, if you try to give it a DVD-RW when it asks for blank DVD, it won't take it! But to trick iDVD into burning a DVD-RW, place a DVD-R disk into the drive when iDVD asks for it and while iDVD is processing and encoding your movie (which takes a long time), press the eject button on your SuperDrive. Eject the DVD-R and pop in a DVD-RW. iDVD burns the disk thinking it's a DVD-R. Now, just use Disk Utility to erase the DVD-RW when you no longer want the movie!

Summary

In this chapter, I covered making a movie in iMovie 4 and then sharing that movie in a variety of mediums, including the creating a DVD using iDVD 4. Both of these programs are part of Apple's newest iLife offering and represent a major step forward in home movie making.

Along the way, we accessed your iTunes 4 and your iPhoto 4 libraries. If we had thrown GarageBand into the mix, we would have touched on all of the new iLife '04 applications. (If you're interested, you can find more on GarageBand in Chapter 13.)

In the next chapter, we'll look at how you can sync your life with your Mac.

Syncing Your Life with Your Mac

Chapter

16

◆ ◆

Secrets in This Chapter

◆ ◆

I f you're lucky, you have one computer only at home that you use from time to time to send e-mails and keep track of dates and contacts. If you're unlucky you have to do all of that on two or three computers (one at home, one at the office, and a laptop for on the road), a PDA (Personal Digital Assistant), and a cell phone. The nightmare comes from trying to keep up with what computer has what calendar event or what PDA device has what contact information for whom. Looking through your address books on your cell phone and your computer to see who's who, and then adding/editing those that are not in one or the other device can give you a big headache.

Yikes, what a hassle. Luckily, there is an easier way to say organized and have your life free of headaches by keeping everything synced up with everything else. Apple's iCal, iSync, and Address Book make it easy, when combined with a .Mac account, to almost automatically keep everything up-to-date with the same information. Some third-party applications have comparable features to Apple's software.

As computers and computer devices such as cell phones and PDAs drop in price and grow in numbers, the complexity of staying organized and consistent will grow. We won't have time to learn confusing and complicated software. Having information sync up with all your devices with little to no effort is important, and Apple makes it easy to do.

Using iCal

iCal is Apple's answer to the call for a powerful and easy-to-use calendar application. Currently at version 1.5.1, iCal has many great features that not only allow you to stay organized, but also make it so that you and your friends and family can stay connected no matter how busy your schedules.

The Elements of iCal

While iCal just doesn't cut it as the top choice for office use, it goes above and beyond the needs for home users and their personal lives. iCal has a friendly and simple interface. Everything you need to do can be done in the main window. Extended outlook and personal calendars are located on the left side. The main window can display three different views: the day view, the week view, and the month view (shown in Figure 16-1). You can switch your different views by pressing the corresponding buttons at the bottom-left of the window. Located at the bottom center is a power search field. As soon as you start typing a key word, a portion of window pops up and dynamically narrows down your appointments as you type more letters (shown in Figure 16-2). This makes it easy to quickly recall events with out having to remember what day it was, or even how it was spelled.

To keep yourself completely organized, iCal allows you to create as many customized calendars as you need. All your calendars are listed in the top left portion of the window. Each calendar has a corresponding color.

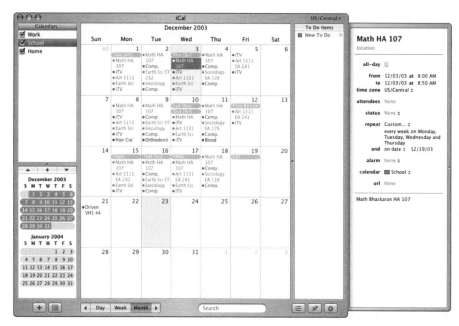

Figure 16-1: iCal has a simple interface that requires little to no additional information to understand.

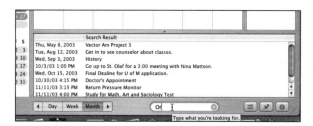

Figure 16-2: iCal has a quick and powerful search tool at the bottom of the main screen.

Secret

Custom Calendar Colors

You can choose a custom color for your calendars by selecting a calendar. Make sure you have the info side panel open by clicking on Info button (the little button that has an *i* in it). This opens the side info panel if it isn't already open. On the top, the name of the selected calendar is displayed. Next to the name and above the description is a color field. Clicking on it, you are able to select a preset color or choose Custom to create a custom color.

True, the color of your calendars isn't that important, but, after you have used up all the preset colors, you will start to have two or more calendars that are the same color and that tends to get a little confusing.

The ability to create different calendars for different events or for different occasions has a huge unique benefit. Create calendars for your work, school, home, birthdays, and daily events and hide or show them in combinations that allow you to see your availability at any given time (as shown in Figure 16-3). With iCal you are able to publish your calendar events to the Internet so that other iCal users can subscribe to them. What this does is allow you to create a calendar for your friends and family that can automatically be updated on their computers whenever you update it on yours.

Figure 16-3: You can have as many calendars as you need. It's a good idea to keep different calendars so that you can hide and show just the ones you need to see at any given time. This eliminates any potential confusion in the schedule.

Publishing Your Calendar Online

The reason a lot of people don't use iCal is because they don't know how to get the most out of it. This is done by sharing calendars with other people. To publish a calendar, follow these steps.

1. Simply create a new calendar and add events to it. You can also use an existing calendar.
2. When your events have been entered, go to the Calendar menu and pull down to Publish (shown in Figure 16-4).
3. A dialog box drops down with a few options (shown in Figure 16-5). Give your shared calendar a name, check all the boxes that apply, and press Publish! If you have a .Mac account and the information is already entered in your System Preferences, you're good to go. If not, you'll have to give iCal more information.

on the
web

You don't need a .Mac account to publish your calendars. You can try iCal World (www.icalworld.com/) and iCalShare (http://icalshare.com/) among other Web sites.

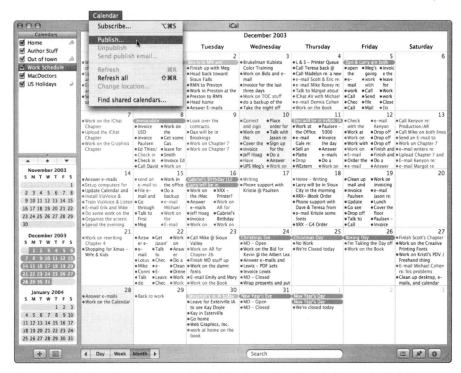

Figure 16-4: The Calendar menu in iCal is where all of the sharing and publishing options are located.

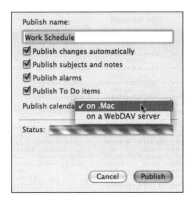

Figure 16-5: You do have some control over what you want to share in your Calendar; as well as how you want to publish it.

4. If the process is successful, you get a dialog box telling you so (shown in Figure 16-6).

Figure 16-6: The confirmation dialog box also gives you the options of viewing the shared calendar online or sending an e-mail to people you want to share your calendar with.

5. To help in notifying people that you have a newly shared calendar, click the Send Mail button on this Calendar Published dialog box and iCal launches your e-mail program and sets up an e-mail message that tells your contacts that the calendar has been published online (shown in Figure 16-7). All you have to do is address the e-mail, and add a few personal lines of text.

Figure 16-7: The highlighted text is what iCal puts in the new e-mail. You add the recipient and a few personal lines.

6. When the recipient of your e-mail receives it, clicking on the second link (the one starting with `webcal`) causes their iCal program to launch and a subscribe dialog box drops down from the iCal window (shown in Figure 16-8). To subscribe to the calendar so that they can access it via iCal, they click on the Subscribe button and the Calendar is added to their Calendar list.

Figure 16-8: On the other side of the Calendar, subscribing to a shared iCal Calendar gives you some choices about how much info you want to deal with.

7. If the recipient isn't on a Mac or doesn't have iCal, clicking on the first link (that starts with `http`) launches their browser and allows them to see the calendar online (shown in Figure 16-9).

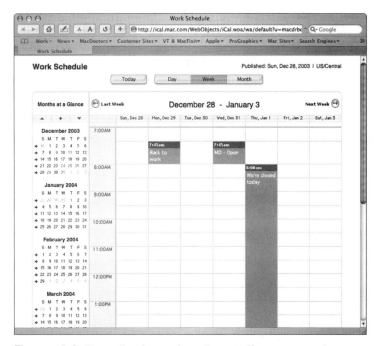

Figure 16-9: The online feature is really great if you want to share your schedule with a friend on a PC. (Although friends don't let friends use PCs.)

After you have a calendar published, a small broadcast icon appears next to the calendar name in the calendar list, letting you know that it is a published calendar and that any changes will be uploaded (shown in Figure 16-10). If you were sharing a calendar from someone else, you would see a little curved arrow next to the calendar name in your iCal list (shown in Figure 16-10).

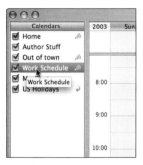

Figure 16-10: Your calendars appear in your iCal list. A calendar with a speaker icon next to it indicates that you have shared that Calendar. A Calendar with an arrow icon next to it indicates that you have subscribed to that calendar from someone or somewhere else.

Another Way to Share an Event without Publishing It

If you don't want to publish an event, but you want to give someone with iCal the event, you can e-mail it directly to them with the power of contextual menus.

Simply Control-click on the event you want to share. The contextual menu offers the option to Mail event (shown in Figure 16-11).

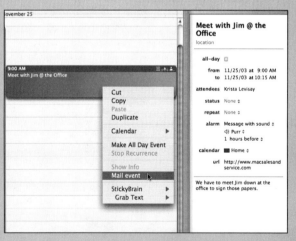

Figure 16-11: All of the information in the event (on the right) is included when you select the Mail event contextual option.

This option opens your mail program and attaches the event as an iCal file along with enough text to explain the event (shown in Figure 16-12).

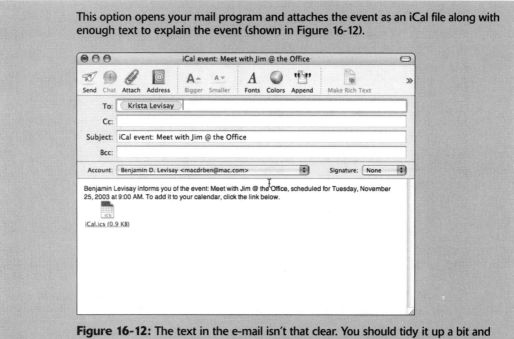

Figure 16-12: The text in the e-mail isn't that clear. You should tidy it up a bit and address the e-mail before you send it out with the attached iCal event.

A Few Last Things About iCal

Adding an event to a calendar is simple. Choose the calendar the event belongs to. After that, just double-click on the appropriate day and or the approximate time of the event depending upon your current calendar view, or select the day you want to add a new event to and choose New Event from the File menu (or press ⌘-N). Realize that further editing of the event's details can be done in the info panel. Everything from fine-tuning the exact start and stop time to the URL for the event can be added or edited (shown in Figure 16-13).

iCal also has a To Do list for daily chores or errands. The To Do list is hidden, unless you press the show/hide button that looks like a push pin in the bottom-right of the main window. This creates a To Do items panel in the main window. To add a new To Do item, select the calendar that the event has to do with, then select New To Do from the File menu (or press ⌘-K). Like adding a new calendar event, the new To Do event's information can be edited in the info pane. You can specify the priority of the event and whether it has been completed.

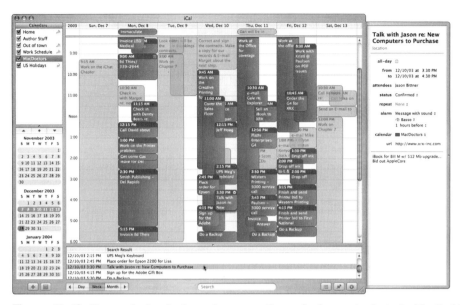

Figure 16-13: The week view is shown here as well as a single event selected with all of the options used inside the detail panel on the right.

Fast Selecting of Priority

If you haven't noticed, you can select the priority of the event simply by clicking on the icon that looks like three parallel bars next to the event name. One bar filled means not important, two bars filled means important, and three bars filled means very important.

Let's say you have a party planned and you want to let your friends know exactly what time and where it will be. You can e-mail invitations from iCal (shown in Figure 16-14). But these aren't your typical e-mailed invitations. If your friends have iCal, they can accept or decline your invitation. When they do this, you are alerted of their decision automatically. Type the e-mail addresses of your friends in the attendees field, the invitations are e-mailed to everyone. It's like a modern-day RSVP.

One last very useful feature is the ability to find shared calendars. These are like published calendars, but they are really meant for more universal events such as holidays. There are an abundant amount of shared calendars on the Web. You can find many that you are looking for just by selecting Find Shared Calendars under the Calendar menu. This takes you to Apple's iCal portal at www.apple.com/ical/library/. You'll find U.S. Holidays, sports and entertainment schedules, and more.

Figure 16-14: iCal works with Address Book by searching for the e-mail address of the name you start typing. If a match is found the e-mail address is automatically finished, ready to be mailed. If not, you can simply type in the e-mail addresses manually.

Secret

Another Resource for Sharing Calendars

Besides Apple's iCal portal, there are others. Most notably, you can find more iCal Calendar to subscribe to at iCalShare at www.icalshare.com/. Here you can find almost any calendar you want to subscribe to as well as a way to publish your iCal Calendar online. Compared to Apple's library, this is by far the more interesting resource: 1,565 calendars in 37 categories!

The iCal preferences are few. Some things you can set are whether you would like iCal to display a seven-or five-day week and what day to start with or at what time your day starts and stops (shown in Figure 16-15). A great feature for those that travel is the time zone feature. Enabling this feature places a drop-down menu in the upper-right corner of the main window that lets you switch your times simply by selecting different times zones. Other options change the way your To Do list is displayed.

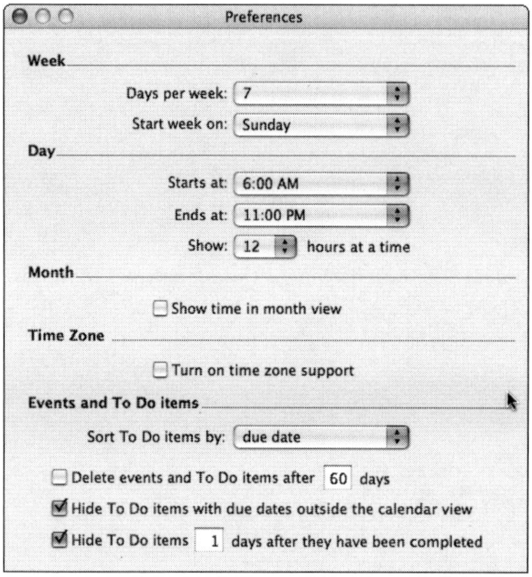

Figure 16-15: The iCal preferences are simple, the way preferences should be.

iCal can be summed up as a small but mighty calendar program. While it has features that would suit even the toughest office environments, its place is in the home and for people's personal lives and events.

Syncing Without a Fuss

How many times have you been at a meeting or out and about, and was given new contact information from a friend or coworker, so you put their information into your PDA. But then, later, you wish to call them so you find their number in your PDA only to enter it into you cell phone by awkwardly pushing those small number keys that somehow type letters and numbers. Finally, you get home and find that you wish to send that person an e-mail, but their e-mail address is in the PDA. Wouldn't it be great to enter a person's contact information once and have it sync up with all your devices? iSync (located in the Applications folder) does this and more!

iSync Preferences

Let's first look at the iSync preferences located under the iSync menu. The preferences are very simple, offering only three options (shown in Figure 16-16). (Only two are active as the third option requires that you have a Palm OS–based PDA for it to become active.) If you select show iSync in the menu bar, a little icon is placed in the upper-left of your screen. This allows fast and easy control over starting an iSync session. The other preference option is to specify an alert message if a certain percentage will be changed during a sync. This prevents any unwanted changes to your data.

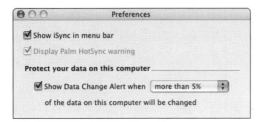

Figure 16-16: iSync has very few preferences. One that you might find helpful is to display iSync in the menu bar so that you can start an iSync session right from the Finder.

One of the things that the iSync preferences allow you to do is to add one more menu to the menu bar of your desktop (shown in Figure 16-17).

Figure 16-17: The iSync menu provides a quick way to see the last time you "Sync'd," as well as a way to start a Sync or open iSync.

iSync with Devices

iSync was designed to help those who have more than one computer or electronic device at home and the office. But iSync does more than sync your address book with your Mac, Palm and cell phone, it also syncs your iPod by adding your iCal events and address book contacts. Plus, you can sync your iCal events with multiple computers with a .Mac account. This is a great solution for those who spend all day at work adding new events to iCal; they can come home, launch iCal, and see the same things that were added during the day — and vice versa.

iSync works by adding Devices that are to be synced together. These can be a .Mac account, an iPod, a PDA, a cell phone, and even another computer. Start by adding your devices to iSync by selecting Add Device or by pressing ⌘-N. Make sure that your devices are hooked up to your computer before searching for them in the Add Device dialog box (shown in Figure 16-18). If there is a device that can be added to iSync, it shows up as a found device.

iSync connects to PDAs, including Palm, Handspring, and Sony Clié. (For a complete list of compatible devices, see Apple's iSync Web page at www.apple.com/isync/.) While Palm provides a program called Palm Desktop that allows you to sync your Palm device with a calendar application and address book, it just doesn't match the intuitiveness of iCal and Address Book, which are built into Mac OS X.

Getting your Palm device to sync with iSync is a little trickier than plug-and-play simplicity. However, if you know that your Palm works with the Palm HotSync, then you know it will work with iSync.

Figure 16-18: After your computer has found a peripheral that can be used with iSync, it shows up in this dialog box. Double-click on the device to add it to iSync.

First, you need to install the Palm Desktop software. Then download and install the iSync Palm Conduit (available as a download link at http://www.apple.com/isync/download/) so that HotSync knows that you want to sync your calendar events with iCal, rather then the Palm Calendar, and sync your addresses with the built-in Mac OS X Address Book rather then the Palm address book.

Apple's iPod also includes the ability to display your contacts from Address Book and your calendar events from iCal. While you can't edit the events or contacts, iSync can be used to move them on to your iPod for future display when you are out and about without your PDA, cell phone, or laptop.

Cell phones are a little easier to get set up. You might first want to check the iSync Web site to see if your cell phone is compatible. While there are a lot of models listed, there are still many more cell phones that are not compatible. Most cell phones with built-in Bluetooth are compatible with iSync. Bluetooth is discussed a little later in this chapter, for now, know that it's a way to connect devices wirelessly. Some phones can be connected via USB, in which case adding it as a device is similar to adding it if it was a Bluetooth device.

Again, realize that not all cell phones have the capability to sync your address book on your phone with the address book on your computer. If this is an important feature you are looking for in a phone, a good place to start is the iSync Web site for a complete list of compatible phones.

You can use iSync to sync your iCal and address book contacts with your home and office computer. This is handy because it's like using one calendar for two different computers. After a day at the office, you come home and use iSync to move any changes you have made to the other computer.

iSync with Your .Mac Account

iSync also has the option to sync your Address Book and your Safari bookmarks with your .Mac account (shown in Figure 16-19) so you can have online access to that information from any online computer in the world.

What you'll end up with is an online version of your address book as well as your bookmarks. To get your addresses to work correctly with your .Mac account, you have to log in (as yourself) and select Turn On .Mac Address Book synchronization (shown in Figure 16-20).

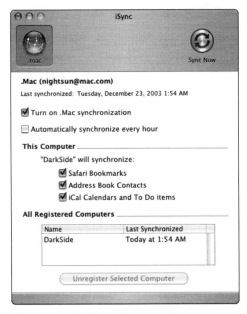

Figure 16-19: You can set up iSync to sync your iCal calendars, Address Book contacts, and even your Safari bookmarks if you have a .Mac account.

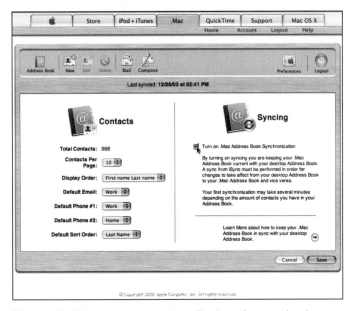

Figure 16-20: Your online Address Book preferences is where you turn on address synchronization and specify how you want your addresses to display in your browser.

This also acts as a handy backup of your address book — one more way to protect your data.

To Sync up your Safari bookmarks, you'll also have to log in to your .Mac account, and select Turn on .Mac Bookmarks Synchronization (shown in Figure 16-21). From there on in, a small browser window displays your bookmarks (shown in Figure 16-22).

Figure 16-21: Your bookmarks also need to have the synchronization turned on in the online preferences. You also see (in the preference window) the last time the bookmarks were synchronized.

Your bookmarks and your addresses, combined with your schedule published online and your .Mac e-mail account, which is accessible online, make the core of your desktop available to you from any online computer — Mac, Windows, Linux, or whatever. And the ability to synchronize more than one computer gives you the option to sync another computer up and then go offline. What a great way to truly bring your office and home computer closer together, eliminating the confusion of multiple entries in iCal, Safari, and Address Book.

Figure 16-22: If you're successful, your bookmarks show up in this window. Clicking on the Preferences button takes you back to the screen shown in the previous figure.

The Nuts and Bolts of Bluetooth

Because iSync is able to handle Bluetooth-enabled phones and PDAs, we need to spend a few words talking about it.

You can think of Bluetooth as wireless USB. Bluetooth operates on the 2.4-GHz frequency band, which is a worldwide standard. You might be wondering why someone would need Bluetooth if they already have AirPort. To answer this question, you need to think of AirPort as a networking tool (like Ethernet is to networking a home or office) and Bluetooth as a way to connect peripherals (like USB when connecting a keyboard or mouse to your computer).

While Bluetooth isn't a new technology, it's taken a while for it to show up in many devices. Just recently, Apple announced their own Bluetooth-enabled keyboard and optical mouse. And it wasn't too long ago when Apple made Bluetooth a standard in their 12" and 17" G4 laptops. Now you can get Bluetooth as a built-to-order option on every Macintosh. If you missed out on getting Bluetooth for your computer, D-Link (online at http://dlink.com/) sells a Bluetooth module that plugs into a USB port on your computer.

Bluetooth works in much the same way as AirPort does. In fact, it can do many of the same things, but Bluetooth's connectivity range is about 30 feet, whereas AirPort has a range of about 200 yards. Another difference is that Bluetooth transfers data at about 1.1 Mbps, whereas AirPort (802.11b) transfers data at a faster 11 Mbps and AirPort Extreme (802.11g) transfers at a blazing 54 Mbps. However, some cell phone services allow you to use your cell phone as a type of modem to the Internet. Imagine connecting through your cell phone that is in your pocket or backpack to the Internet with your laptop on your table or lap in the park.

Not only are we seeing Bluetooth in mice and keyboards, but also cell phones and PDAs. This allows easy close-range connectivity with other devices. For example, in the past, if you wanted to transfer data from your Palm device to your friend's, you would have to point the infrared port at each other and keep a clear view while the data was sending. But now, because Bluetooth operates on radio waves much like a cordless phone, you are able to be more flexible with how you send your data.

If you're interested in more "Bluetooth goodness" on the Mac please see the Bluetooth section in the Utilities chapter (Chapter 5).

Third-Party Programs and iSync

There are many other calendar and address book programs on the market besides iCal and Address Book. And if you find that what Apple has to offer doesn't meet your needs, then you can probably find something to spend your money on that will suit you. We're going to talk very briefly about two very popular programs.

Microsoft Entourage

Entourage is like Mail, Address Book, and iCal all rolled into one only more powerful. Offering a one-window interface, Entourage is for the professional that needs more options then what iCal and Mail have to offer. With Entourage, you feel as if you are in a more professional environment, where certain events marked on the calendar, like meetings, can be linked to the people's contact information in the address book.

Entourage also has a Task list much like iCal's To Do list. The address book in Entourage is like a beefier version of Apple's Address Book. Some experts have said that Entourage creates truer v-Cards than Apple's Address Book. This is another good reason Entourage may be a better address book solution.

Now Up-to-Date and Now Contact

Yeah, Entourage is great, but it cost $499.00 bundled with the rest of the Microsoft Office Suite. Apple's iCal is cool, but you need a $99.00-per-year subscription just so you can publish noneditable calendars. For those that have grown out of the "free organizer software" phase, like small businesses and power users, Now Software's Up-to-Date and Contact is their solution.

At a low cost of $119.95, Now Up-to-Date wants to be the best organizer application available. It has many long-time devoted fans, because, unlike iCal and Entourage, Now Up-to-Date has been around for over 10 years, so Now Software has had a while to add some fantastic features that you can't find in any other organizer application.

For businesses that have more than one computer platform, it would be nice if a scheduling program was available for both platforms. Now Up-to-Date and Contact run on both Windows machines and Macs and can share calendars, schedules, and address books over the network or over the Internet, something iCal with iSync or even Entourage (unless you have a Microsoft Exchange Server to plug it into) can't do.

For those that need a beefier, more flexible solution than iCal or Entourage, Now Up-to-Date and Contact is the perfect choice. iCal is free software that isn't nearly powerful enough for the business environment. Entourage is just another program in an office bundle suite, but Now Up-to-Date was meant to do one thing and do it well. It was made to be the best organizer application on both the Windows and Macintosh platform.

Summary

As we become busier and busier and the simplicity of software organizers becomes easier and easier, we will eventually want to trade in our archaic paper organizers with built-in calendars and address books for a small PDA or cell phone or even a laptop. But by doing so we will all need to be able to sync our devices to make sure we are truly up-to-date with our busy lives.

We have looked over a few possible solutions — from the free and easy-to-use iCal and iSync to the midrange yet expensive Entourage and finally to the ultimate in organization, Now Up-to-Date and Contact for the Mac and Windows.

In the next chapter, we look at some online options — part of the synchronized digital hub equation.

Part IV

Getting Online and Staying Safe and Sane

Part IV features several chapters covering the "killer app" of computing today: getting online while staying safe and sane. Here you'll make sense of email options (including combating spam), learn how to get more out of instant messaging, learn the ins and outs of Safari and other popular Web browsers, get more out of Apple's .Mac and iDisk services, and even how to build your own Web page usingt the best Mac tools available.

In This Part

An Overview of Online Options

Chapter
17

◆ ◆

Secrets in This Chapter

◆ ◆

Panther is not just an Internet-ready operating system — Panther is almost Internet-hungry. It's true you can use Panther without an Internet connection, but so many of its features, from Sherlock to Safari, from Software Update to iChat AV, are pointless without one, and, let's face it: no Mac is an island . . . or, at least, no Mac should be. The decision you have to make is not *whether* you will connect to the Internet but *how*. After all, you do want to keep your Panther well-fed and purring, don't you?

Choosing How (Not If) to Be Connected

Panther can connect to the Internet in many ways. It can use all of the following connection types:

◆ Modem connection

◆ Ethernet connection

◆ Airport (which requires that the Airport Base Station have an Internet connection)

◆ Bluetooth

Chapter 29 explores the secrets of the Network System preferences that you let control and fine-tune your Internet connection, but first you have to have one. The kind of connection you chose will depend on several factors, including cost, service availability, and your own preferences and needs.

> **note** You won't need to choose a connection method if where you live (such as, say, a networked college residence building) or where you work already has Internet service because the choice will have been made for you. But you may want to consider setting up an account with an Internet service provider anyway. Establishing an account with a national Internet service provider, for example, means that you can still connect when you travel. Even if you don't travel, having your own account means that you'll have an e-mail address independent of your workplace or school.

Modem Connections

It wasn't very long ago that even a modem connection to the Internet was considered so high-tech and geeky that most mere mortals could only stand in shocked awe at the prodigy who had such a setup. (At least, that's what the prodigy imagined those blank stares meant.) Today, though, a modem connection is considered the lowest common denominator of Internet connection methods, and modems themselves have changed from pricey add-on boxes to a bit of circuitry and software already built into your Mac, complete with phone jack.

> **note** What's a modem? A modem is a device that does two basic, related things: it converts a digital stream of information into the analog electrical signals that a normal telephone line (often called *POTS*, for *Plain Old Telephone System*) can carry, and it converts such an analog signal back to a digital stream of information. Going from digital to analog involves turning the information into a complex sound waveform — this process is called *modulation*. Converting this waveform into digital information is called, not surprisingly, *demodulation*. The word *modem* is short for *modulator/demodulator*.

Today's modems can handle data-transfer speeds of between 5 and 6 kilobytes (or 5 KB) a second. This is blazingly fast if you're dealing with plain text information — fast enough to transmit or receive a page's worth of unadulterated text every second, faster than most of us can read. On the other hand, if you're dealing with, say, a typical MP3 file, it's fast enough to transmit, at best, only a half-second's worth of music each second — slower than most of us can listen.

Modem connections are fast enough to handle basic Web browsing — especially if you tend to look at pages that are relatively light on graphics and other nontextual features — and e-mail — especially if you don't get or send much e-mail, and if you and your correspondents avoid adding all sorts of attachments and graphic fripperies to your epistolary endeavors. But for transferring any but the smallest files, or for experiencing the full range of multimedia available on the Web, a modem connection may be as satisfying as filling your SUV's gas tank through a soda straw: you may be able to do it, but you'll spend a lot of time waiting.

So why go that way?

- ◆ **It's convenient.** Most Macs have a built-in modem port, and you can probably find a phone-jack almost anywhere.

- ◆ **It's cheap.** You don't need any extra equipment. (Macs even come packaged with a phone cable these days.) Most Internet providers charge between $10 and $25 a month for a *dialup* connection.

Secret

A Baudy Tale of Modems

When you read some spec sheet that tells you that you have a 56-K modem, that doesn't mean that your modem can send or receive 56 KB of data each second. (Though wouldn't it be pretty to think so.) It may not even mean that the modem can handle 56 Kilobits — rather, it means that the modem handles a speed of 56-K *baud* per second.

The *baud rate* is named after Jean Maurice-Émile Baudot, who, in 1874, patented a method for transmitting character information over electrical lines, building upon the work of Samuel Morse (inventor of the Morse code). The full version of his scheme could transmit 7 or 8 simultaneous signals, useful for character transmission, and even more useful when computers came along and text began to be encoded into 7- or 8-bit sequences. Although Baudot's code system is not used in today's computer systems, the underlying ideas — multiple simultaneous signals, including error-correcting signals, being transmitted over an electrical connection — are still used, and the signaling rate has come to be called the *baud* rate.

Some manufacturers equate one bit-per-second to one baud. That is marketing. One baud can equal anywhere from one to sixteen bits sent in each signaling cycle, depending on the modulation method used. However, one baud *does* roughly equal one bit per second in most common implementations, so it's not completely inaccurate to say that a 56-K modem theoretically can handle 56 Kilobits a second. But the truth of the matter is more complex, and might win you a few bar bets if you're into that sort of thing.

In many cases, when you purchase a high-speed (a.k.a. *broadband*) account from your Internet service provider, you are also given access to a dialup network as part of the deal. Don't scoff at the deal — if your provider has a regional, national, or international presence, that modem connection can get you online when you are traveling, and such a connection can be very useful should your high-speed connection equipment ever stop working.

note   A modem's actual speed for any connection depends on the quality of the phone connection; on noisy phone lines the rate will drop until the modems at each end of the connection can maintain a reliable connection. Therefore, don't be surprised if your 56K modem ends up communicating at 33K or even 28K (or less) from time to time.

DSL Connection

DSL (*Digital Subscriber Line*) has become an increasingly popular way for sophisticated urbanites to connect to the Internet over their phone lines at speeds much faster than a normal modem can handle. Why sophisticated urbanites? Actually, sophistication is not required, but an urban setting is generally required. DSL connections require proximity to the telephone company's central office, or *exchange*, to be effective. The further you are from the nearest telephone company exchange, the less speedy the connection; beyond, say, a distance of three miles, DSL connections are usually not practical.

Secret

DSL Details

DSL connections work by transmitting high-frequency signals over the same telephone line that you use for voice communication; these high-frequency signals are beyond the ability of the typical telephone handset to produce, so it is possible — and, in fact, quite common — to use the same phone line for both voice and data transmission at the same time.

At each end of the DSL connection is a special device: at your end is a DSL *transceiver* (commonly, though inaccurately, called a DSL modem) that handles the high frequency data transmission and conversion from your computer; at the phone company's exchange is a DSL *Access Multiplexer* (DSLAM) that handles, and keeps separate, the multiple connections from you and other phone company DSL customers. It is also common for DSL connections to require you to put *line filters* on your home phone jacks to further reduce the chance of interference between your voice calls and your data transmissions. When everything is working right, a DSL connection can transmit data at more than ten times the speed of a typical dialup modem connection.

Nonetheless, the existing phone system's wiring was never really intended to support high-frequency signals, which get weaker *(attenuate)* over distance much more quickly than the lower-frequency voice signals. That's why DSL is seldom practical for rural telephone company users.

One final caveat: most DSL connections are actually ADSL — the *A* stands for *asymmetrical* and means that the speed of transmission is faster in one direction than another. Typically, the fast direction is from the phone company's exchange to you (great for Web browsing); the data-rate of signals originating from your Mac (or Windows PC; DSL is platform agnostic) is usually only twice as fast as a dialup modem connection.

With a DSL connection you can expect to see download speeds ranging from 380 Kbps to as much as 1500 Kbps. What's more, a DSL connection tends to be always on. Although you can disconnect and reconnect (using the Point-To-Point-Protocol-over-Ethernet, or PPPoE, described more fully in Chapter 29), you seldom need to — once connected, you tend to stay connected for hours, days, or weeks at a time.

Arranging for a DSL connection to be installed at your home or office can sometimes be tricky, because it involves coordination between your Internet service provider, your telephone company, and you, and because at least one of the players in this game likely will be a large corporate bureaucracy, getting everything arranged and working may take some patience. On the other hand, more local phone companies are becoming Internet service providers themselves, and in these cases, the coordination problem may be reduced.

And what does it cost? Prices vary, but expect to see costs running in the $40-to-$60 per month range for most residential DSL installations. Competition in this part of the broadband service market is brisk, though, so you may see lower prices and attractive sign-up deals when you go looking for a service provider.

Cable Modem Connections

Internet connections over cable modem let you use the same cable television connection for Internet access that you use to feed your inner couch potato. As more and more cable companies convert from providing analog to digital cable services (and, in the process, renting you a newer, more expensive cable box, and supplying you with many more channels that you probably won't watch), cable access to the Internet becomes that much more available.

You don't connect your Mac to your set-top cable box, though. Instead, a separate cable line is run to a special cable modem, which connects to your Mac by way of an Ethernet connection. Like DSL, cable modem connections are usually asymmetrical: upload data-transfer rates are slower than download rates. Even more than DSL, cable modem connections are always on. Once the modem is hooked up, the connection is there. Cable modem connections tend to be a faster than DSL connections, too, often twice as fast. Also, unlike DSL, the distance from the cable service provider's main office is not an issue for cable modem customers.

Secret

Cable Modem Details

A cable modem truly is a kind of modem, unlike a DSL transceiver. It usually contains a modulator and demodulator. In addition, a cable modem contains network circuitry and even a CPU — in fact, in many cases the CPU is a PowerPC, similar to the one inside your Mac. The network circuitry and CPU make it possible for the cable modem to eliminate much of the configuration set-up that other kinds of connections may require. From the point of view of your Mac, you are simply connected to a local network and using the cable company's DHCP server to get an IP address. (For more about DHCP and IP addresses, see Chapter 29.)

Digital cable systems dedicate a 6-MHz frequency range to each cable channel, a range that is sufficient to handle a typical television transmission. Cable modems simply use one of the many available 6-MHz channels to transmit and receive data One 6-MHz channel is usually sufficient to handle the Internet traffic of up to a thousand cable customers at a time, and given that there are many hundreds of 6MHz channels available on a typical digital cable system, just a few dedicated channels are sufficient to handle the Internet traffic for a large number of customers.

continues

continued

But, although cable modems may be faster than DSL in many cases, the speed of each customer's transmissions can be affected by the number of customers using the same channel at any given time — the more customers, the less bandwidth each customer has available. On crowded systems, therefore, congestion can create discernible slow-downs. Also, because each cable modem user is, in essence, on the same local network as other customers, there are security risks — if you have file sharing enabled on your Mac, your files may be available, or, at least, visible, to all your neighbors. So take heed. In a cable modem environment, the use of secure passwords and firewalls (again, see Chapter 29) is highly recommended.

Most cable modem Internet services are handled directly by your local cable company (although they may partner with a separate Internet service provider), and costs tend to be comparable with DSL connections. Cable companies may also bundle Internet access with many of their programming bundles, lowering the connection costs if you agree to some of their premium cable programming services. As with DSL, competition is fierce in this market.

Satellite Connections

If you live far enough out in the hinterlands that neither DSL nor cable modem service is available to you, look to the skies: you might be able to connect with a satellite dish.

What you need is a south-facing view of the sky (if you are living north of the equator; if you're living in New Zealand, for example, you'll need a north-facing view) and electricity. Satellite Internet access uses the same communication satellites that satellite TV does, so if you can get one, you can get the other.

Satellite Internet Details

Satellite access requires a satellite dish (obviously) and, usually, two special modems connected to it: one for *uplink* (sending your information into the heavens) and one for *downlink* (for receiving heaven-sent data). The uplink speed seldom exceeds normal dialup modem speeds, but the download speeds tend to be as much as ten times faster, roughly 500 kilobits per second. Two-way satellite Internet traffic uses a technology called *IP multicasting* that combines and compresses the data streams so that as many as 5000 channels can be handled by a single satellite. Note that some satellite access providers provide downlink service only and use regular telephone modem connections to handle the data that you send.

Because you're dealing with the skies, it shouldn't surprise you that weather can affect the performance of satellite Internet connections. Rain, especially heavy rain, can temporarily block reception and transmission of satellite signals. Strong winds can move satellite dishes out of alignment, which will affect not only *your* signal, but, because of the magic of IP multicasting, the signals of others who use the same satellite.

Keep in mind, too, that satellites orbit 22,500 miles above equator, meaning that it takes a signal traveling at the speed of light about a quarter of a second to get to the satellite and back. This delay, though seemingly small, makes satellite Internet access less than ideal for things like interactive Internet "shooter" games and iChat AV. In addition, IP multicasting means that applications using protocols other than TCP/IP won't work with it.

The monthly cost of satellite Internet service is comparable to the cost of DSL or cable modem service. However, you also have to pay for the equipment and dish installation, which can cost $500 or more.

Bluetooth Cell Phone Connections

Some models of digital cell phones come with Bluetooth capability, which means your Bluetooth-equipped Mac can communicate with them. This, in turn, means that you may be able to set up an Internet connection wirelessly: your Mac talks to the cell phone via Bluetooth, and the cell phone talks to the Internet, passing the information back to your Mac.

There are two ways to connect to the Internet with a Bluetooth cell phone.

   ◆ **You use the phone as a Bluetooth modem.** With this method, you need to have a dialup account with an Internet service provider. Your phone establishes the connection by dialing the provider's access number and then acts like a modem, converting the analog signals into digital ones before sending them on to your Mac.

   ◆ **You use your cell phone provider's GPRS** (General Packet Radio Service) data network to access their WAP (Wireless Application Protocol) services. In other words, your cell service provider acts as your Internet service provider.

The first method is slow and less reliable, tending to be no faster than about 9 kilobits a second. The advantage, though, is that it will only cost you for the dialup account and for the cell phone minutes that you use, which, depending on your service plan, might not be that costly.

The second method is faster (around 30 kilobits per second) and more reliable because GPRS is a digital service. However, cell phone service providers usually charge by the amount of data traffic when using their WAP services; for downloading mailboxes that get large quantities of spam, or for extensive Web browsing, the costs can quickly pile up, and pile up high. The WAP rate structures offered by cell providers tend to assume that you are using the cell phone for transmitting very small items (like text messages), not for feeding big, meaty Web pages and buckets of spam to your Pantherized Mac.

In short, getting to the Internet from your Bluetooth cell phone is useful for those situations when you can't connect any other way, but the price (for WAP service) or slow speed (for Bluetooth modem service) make it an option of last resort. You'll want to have another connection option that you use most of the time. On the other hand, connecting from your laptop while sailing on the lake is just *so cool!*

Choosing an Internet Service Provider

Choosing an ISP isn't just about connection speed or even whether you need a persistent connection, though both can be major considerations. The menu of services provided is also something to consider. How many e-mail addresses do you receive with your account and how large are the mailboxes? How much personal Web space is provided and is it cumulative or so much per e-mail address? How many simultaneous connections are you allowed? (This comes up in multi-computer households with broadband connections a lot.) Does the service include Usenet newsgroup access and, if so, how many groups does the server offer, how good is the completion, and how long are messages retained? If this seems something like ordering from a Chinese restaurant menu (two from column A, three from column B, with four you get egg roll, etc.), you definitely recognize the situation.

Choosing an ISP can present something like a chicken-and-egg problem. Sometimes, you need an Internet connection to sign up for an ISP or get the information on how to sign up when your connection is going to be via modem. You might need to sign up with Earthlink or AOL temporarily so that you can get to the point of finding and contracting with the provider of your choice. If you're going broadband (DSL, cable, or even ISDN), you've got it a lot easier. Just contact your telephone (DSL/ISDN) or cable operator via telephone and let them do the heavy lifting.

All ISP choices have one thing in common. You get an Internet connection for your base location (whether that is at home, office, school, or wherever). Dialup ISPs, at least the major ones like Earthlink, offer local access numbers just about anywhere in the United States. Smaller ISPs are often local and you will need some other method of accessing the Internet when you're traveling. If you're on the road a lot, the additional monthly cost of a nationwide ISP can be well worth the investment. For broadband connections, the situation is far more problematic. Local access when away from home is almost never a part of your service, so you might want to consider a basic backup (dialup) ISP if you're going to want to connect to the Internet when away from home base. One inexpensive solution (currently $9.95/month for their Platinum service) is NetZero (www.netzero. net), which includes local access numbers almost everywhere in the United States and free access if you are willing to be limited to a 10-hour per month connection maximum. NetZero offers only connectivity and an e-mail box, but the e-mail can also be accessed via a Web interface.

E-Mail Options

Most ISPs offer multiple e-mail accounts as part of their service agreement with you. In the olden days (before OS 9's Multiuser or OS X), this almost always meant multiple family members sharing a household computer, but wanting personal e-mail addresses. Now, it is more likely to mean that multiple family members have accounts on a single Mac. (We're going to ignore the Dark Side during this discussion, but most of the coverage is platform-agnostic.)

Whether you get three accounts, five accounts, seven accounts, or whatever, having multiple accounts is useful even for a single individual. You can use one for personal and one for business, for example, or dedicate one as your while-I'm-on-the-Internet address, set to catch all the spam that Internet activity generates.

Each e-mail address has a *mailbox* (collection point) associated with it. Mailboxes might support either *Post Office Protocol* (POP) or *Internet Message Access Protocol* (IMAP) or both. POP and IMAP are the methods most commonly used for accessing your electronic mail.

What Are IMAP and POP?

POP servers have been around much longer than IMAP. Generally, when you access a POP server, the mail is downloaded directly to your computer and deleted from the server. You can tell a POP server not to delete messages after downloading, but there is no indication on the server that the message has been read and your next connection to the server will still treat it as "new mail." POPs main strengths are that server message space (mailbox size) requirements are lower and that POP is designed for offline use where users only need an Internet connection when downloading or sending mail and don't need to be as diligent about managing their mailbox space.

IMAP servers act as if they were local to the computer from which they're accessed — sort of like a remote disk. Thus, regardless of whether you're accessing your e-mail from your office, home, or laptop computer, your mail is there for you and you don't have to synchronize the mail databases on the different computers. Messages are marked as read, filed in folders, or otherwise manipulated just as though they were on your local computer. Further, they'll remain there until you delete them. IMAP is designed for online use, where (almost) all your mail activity takes place while connected to the server, because that's where the messages actually reside.

While the location indicates a possible bias, you can find pretty good online comparisons of IMAP and POP at www.imap.org/papers/imap.vs.pop.html and at www.imap.org/papers/imap.vs.pop.brief.html.

There's actually a third protocol, Distributed Mail System Protocol (DMSP). The only application implementing this protocol is PCMAIL. DMSP is designed for *disconnected* use — where messages are left on the server, but copies are cached on the local computer.

Unlike packaged services, such as AOL and MSN (described later in this chapter), with a conventional ISP, you use a dedicated e-mail client and you need to configure it properly. This means that you have to know the URL of your incoming mail server, whether it is POP or IMAP and you have to know the URL of your Simple Mail Transport Protocol (SMTP), or outgoing, mail server — yes, incoming and outgoing mail are handled by different software.

Web-based interfaces to mail servers are increasingly popular. This means that in addition to, or instead of, a dedicated e-mail client, you can use a Web browser to read, respond to, and manage your e-mail. As you can surmise, Web-based interfaces are another advantage of IMAP.

note

Apple's .Mac service is not an ISP, simply because Apple doesn't provide the Internet connectivity portion. You get e-mail addresses, remote storage, Web hosting, and many other amenities considered perks of an ISP account, though, and most of the ISP discussion pertains to .Mac for those reasons.

You can find a much more detailed discussion of .Mac in Chapter 20.

Web Hosting

The World Wide Web is not just a tourist destination. It is also a place to express yourself. Most ISPs dedicate space for each user ID (e-mail account name) to post Web pages, but these allotments are typically pretty small (usually between 2MB and 6MB), especially in today's world of digital photography and video. Additionally, many of the Web authoring tools the services provide are biased far more toward Windows users. This isn't to say that Mac users can't host their Web pages; it's just that we usually have to work a little harder and know a little (or a lot) more than our Windows-using cohorts to do so.

Secret

Why You Might Not Need Web Space

You, fortunate soul, are running Mac OS X and that means that you have the Apache Web server running right there on your Mac. Apache is, arguably, the dominant commercial Web serving software in use.

As long as it is not a violation of the service agreement with your ISP, you can host the Web pages right there on your Mac. (That's what the Sites folder within your Home directory is for — shown in Figure 17-1.)

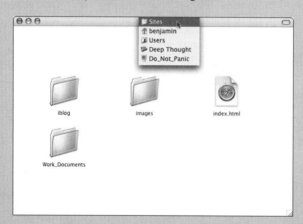

Figure 17-1: The hierarchy of your site is stored and organized in the Sites folder in your Home folder on your computer.

A little consideration will show, though, that serving your own Web site from your Mac is not the best idea unless you have a high-speed, always-on connection such as DSL or cable. For one thing, if you have a constantly changing IP address, people are going to find it difficult to locate your site. Secondly, if you have a low-speed connection, people are going to be frustrated by how long it takes to load a page from your site — even worse is if they are also on a dialup connection. And, unless your connection is persistent, visitors will be frustrated by messages that the URL couldn't be located when you're offline.

The first problem, changing dynamic IP addresses has spawned a cottage industry — Dynamic DNS services. If you set up an account with one of these services, your IP address is communicated to them when you're online and they redirect from your static IP address on their server to your current IP address. This way, they don't have the overhead of maintaining all the disk space necessary to host Web sites and you avoid the hassles of having to manage your site remotely. Some of the companies providing redirecting services for folks with dynamic IP addresses are DNS2Go (http://dns2go.deerfield.com), **DynDNS.org** (www.dyndns.org), **No-IP** (www.no-ip.com), **and TZO** (www.tzo.com).

Unfortunately, most ISP-hosted Web sites include a little built-in ISP advertisement because when someone wants to access your site, they don't type in a cool name like www.thetwains.com, but a name similar to www.earthlink.com/~twain635. Fortunately, if you're willing to spring for a few more dollars, plus an annual or biannual fee, you can register your own domain name and most ISPs will host the site for you. Some ISPs, like Earthlink, will even (again for a fee) handle the paperwork for you of registering your domain name with Internic (the clearing-house for domain name registration). Once again, though, the paltry amount of Web space that comes with an ISP service agreement probably won't please you if you're willing to expend the extra cash to get your own domain. You can often get additional space (for yet another fee) from your ISP or you can contract with a Web-hosting service like Dotster (www.dotster.com).

insider insight Regardless of what you may believe, there really isn't such a thing as a WYSIWYG Web page editor. There are visual editors and text-based editors. Oh, some of the really good visual editors like Adobe GoLive or Macromedia's Dreamweaver will come close, but unless the page is just one big graphic, your pages' displays are going to depend upon the browsers used by your visitors and, to some extent, the preference settings your visitors have established for their browsers. Link underlines could be different colors or nonexistent, fonts you use might or might not be present, font-sizes and spacing could be different, and a wide assortment of browser-specific features (such as the level of style sheet support) can also affect the display. This is one reason you should check your pages in multiple browsers, maybe even on multiple platforms.

After you have created your Web pages, using whatever tool you find convenient, you still have the task of uploading the Web pages to your Web server. In some cases, your ISP (like AOL) will provide tools to assist you in getting your pages uploaded into your Web space. Most of the time, though, you're going to need to deal with File Transfer Protocol (FTP). In some cases, Dreamweaver, GoLive, and BBEdit, for example, your HTML editing application will have FTP capabilities built in and you can just give it the location, user-id, and password to synchronize your Web site with the pages you have on your hard disk. If your editor doesn't include this functionality or you're the do-it-yourself type, the easiest way to accomplish the upload is to use a visual FTP client such as Robert Vasvari's RBrowser Lite (www.rbrowser.com), Panic Software's Transmit 2 (www.panic.com), Fetch (fetchsoftworks.com), or Interarchy (www.interarchy.com) to connect to your Web server and then just drag the files to their destination.

note This is another place where .Mac can make life a lot easier for you. You can either use the HomePage tools or just mount your iDisk and drag your Web pages into the iDisk's Sites folder — no FTP hassle at all.

A lot of the nice features you might want to add to your Web site are things like counters, guest books, and forms. All of these amenities require external code on your server. The external mechanism is Common Gateway Interface (cgi) scripting. For a great introduction to cgi as well as numerous cgi-related tutorials and resources, check out http://hoohoo.ncsa.uiuc.edu/cgi/.

Usenet

FAQS.ORG (www.faqs.org) describes Usenet as "a world-wide distributed discussion system." So far as this goes, it is a good and accurate description. Usenet is a hierarchic organization of subject categories (called *newsgroups*) containing *articles* (messages) *posted* (uploaded) to the newsgroups by people using Network News Transmission Protocol (nntp) client software. The articles uploaded to a news server then *propagate* (spread) to all the other news servers with which the first server communicates. Getting past the jargon, Usenet is an unsupervised global community with all the beauty and blemishes you might expect from such an entity. Usenet is verbal anarchy and much more. If you want to discuss dogs, your favorite TV show, virtually any form of government or politics, software, computers, philosophy, photography, religion, or just about anything else, you can find one or more newsgroups in which to hold the discussion. There are binary newsgroups where pictures (licit and illicit), music, TV broadcasts, or movies are available for download.

Usenet is one of the oldest parts of the Internet, much older than the World Wide Web. Further, until very recently, its articles were pure 7-bit text. Even binaries had to be encoded in a 7-bit form for transmission, which occasioned many formats and protocols you might have encountered, like BinHex, uuencode, and Base64, a lot of which show up in the history of e-mail. With over 60,000 newsgroups, a huge number of which are heavily trafficked (articles per day in the tens of thousands, with article sizes up to 1MB or even more), carrying a relatively full slate of newsgroups is a costly proposition, especially if your customer base wants the messages to be around long enough so they can check in every day or even once a week and not miss anything. We're talking about disk storage in the tens or even hundreds of terabytes and a lot of bandwidth and processing power to handle both the incoming articles and posts as well as the article requests from you, the interested browser.

Due to the expense, many ISPs don't provide news servers of their own, either contracting to a commercial provider like GigaNews (what Comcast contracts in many of its service areas) or leaving you to find your own commercial news server. If, however, your ISP provides a news server, you have found a valuable additional benefit. Earthlink, Road Runner, and AOL are among the service providers offering Usenet newsgroups, as does Comcast in some locales (where they inherited ATTBI's existing infrastructure).

NNTP Clients — The Right Tool for the Job

Just as you require a Web browser (http client) to access Web pages, you need a News program (nntp client) to access Usenet newsgroups. No graphical news client ships with OS X, but there are a number available. Hardcore and heavy Mac Usenet users tend to employ Thoth, MT-Newswatcher, Hogwasher, or MacSoup; however, other clients such as Panic Software's Unison (a new client at this time) and Microsoft's Entourage are available, as well as many from the Unix world that you can use from the command line in Terminal or under X11. Check out Version Tracker, searching for Usenet to get a sampling.

The choice of news client is almost as much a religious issue as whether to use a Mac or PC. Check a few out and see what works for you. Just one tip, though. If you're going to frequent the binary groups, you're going to require one that understands both the traditional uuencode and new(er) yEnc encodings, and you're probably going to need to acquire some tools to handle Windows formats, because that's what the majority of folks use. (MacPAR deLuxe will help you deal with RAR archives and both PAR and PAR2 parity recovery files.)

Choosing an ISP

Face it, as a Mac OS X user you are both privileged to be using the best hardware and operating system currently available. And you'll likely experience discrimination. The mere fact that 95%+ users are using Windows (and not using Macs) means that a lot of ISP technical support personnel are going to be clueless when it comes to helping you. Some of them have probably never even used a Mac or seen one other than on a TV or movie screen or a store shelf. Training resources are allocated to handle the most common problems, and that means that Windows training takes precedence over Mac training. Besides, everyone knows that Windows users have more problems than Mac users, so they need more attention and resources from the beginning.

From the perspective of a Mac user, ISPs fall into three categories: Mac-hostile, Mac-indifferent, and Mac-friendly. Ideally, you'll want a Mac-friendly ISP, which means that the ISP's staff not only knows and understands Macs, but the ISP has ancillary support in their Web-hosting or e-mail services that cater to Mac users. Failing to find a Mac-friendly service provider, you should be okay with a Mac-indifferent ISP. Mac-indifferent means that they support the Mac, though their support might not always be current and you might have to bounce through a few support people before you find one with a clue when a problem arises. You will also need to do a lot more work yourself to keep your Internet life running smoothly. You probably don't need to worry about a Mac-hostile provider, since as soon as they hear that you have a Mac, they start to ridicule you or just flat-out tell you that they don't support the Mac.

Secret

There Are Some Mac-Friendly ISPs

Earthlink is an example of a Mac-friendly major ISP. They almost have to be because Apple and Earthlink have a business relationship and Apple sets them up as the recommended ISP for new OS X users who are setting up their Macs. Look in your Applications folder's Utilities folder and you'll see an Earthlink icon and an Earthlink Connect icon. Apple and Earthlink try to make your Mac-Earthlink experience as pleasant as possible.

Comcast, probably the nation's largest cable ISP, is a prime example of Mac-indifference. They have some support staff that know the Mac, but the majority can only operate on Mac questions from canned scripts. If working from a script isn't bad enough, the scripts aren't always current. For example, I recently had a problem where their DNS decided to stop recognizing one of my Mac's IP address, even though their DHCP server assigned the address. (I was testing a Web page before uploading it to a client's server.) The support person told me to look for the Network Control Panel in the Apple menu, even after I told him that I was running OS X 10.3.2 (Panther). He insisted that they only supported OS 9. Fortunately, asking for a supervisor got me rerouted to someone who actually was able to help.

Until very recently, ISPs such as Juno and ISP.com were Windows-only and definitely Mac-hostile. Even today, though, they're a lot closer to hostile than indifferent. For example, the free version of Juno still doesn't support the Mac at all and the Platinum version provides limited functionality to Mac users as compared to Windows users. (Windows users can access multiple accounts while Mac users can only access one.) With the advent of OS X and its Unix heritage, rabidly Mac-hostile ISPs are fading from existence or morphing into Mac-indifferent providers.

Looking at AOL and MSN

The two biggest names in the online connectivity world are, coincidentally, both TLAs (Three-Letter Acronyms) based on two-word names: AOL (America Online) and MSN (Microsoft Network). For the past few years, these two behemoths have been playing Godzilla versus King Kong, wrestling for the hearts, minds, and pocketbooks of the Internet-hungry masses.

Both services provide a virtual gated-community approach to the online experience, offering security and assistance to the Internet-anxious first-time user, and augmenting basic Internet services with special features and content. But because both services are aimed at the mass consumer market, both tend to offer their latest features and services to the vast number of Windows users before they come to the smaller (but infinitely more tasteful) Mac community. The questions arise: Which is better? Is either worth it? Unsatisfactorily, the answer to both is "it depends."

America Online

AOL is by far the senior of the two online services and it has, by far, the largest customer base. As the oldest and the largest online service, AOL has set the standard for what an online service should offer, and everyone, including Microsoft, compares their offerings to AOL's.

Secret

A Brief History of AOL

AOL started life in November of 1985 as a service offered by Quantum Computer Services called Q-Link. On its first day, it had 24 users; within three months it had 10,000.

In 1988, Quantum hooked up with Apple to produce AppleLink Personal Edition, an online consumer service for Apple similar to the AppleLink service used internally by Apple developers and retailers. AppleLink Personal Edition became the genesis of the AOL look-and-feel, with its multiple windows, mail services, message boards, and online content. Within two years, Apple and Quantum went their separate ways, and AppleLink Personal Edition was renamed America Online, debuting on the Mac and the Apple II in 1989. The DOS version of AOL came out in 1991, around the same time that Quantum officially renamed itself America Online.

As online fever spread in the early 1990s, AOL quickly grew. Microsoft tried to buy the company in 1992, but when that attempt failed, Bill Gates gave the go-ahead to build a rival service, and the earliest seeds of Microsoft Network were sown.

The Internet continued to become more popular throughout the decade. Though it ran a proprietary network that did not adhere to Internet standards internally, AOL capitalized on its preeminent position in the online world to establish gateways between its network and the Internet. Providing Internet connectivity through a dialup service was so successful a tactic that AOL's popularity surged faster than the company could handle for a while, and customers attempting to connect were met with endless busy signals and network congestion. Those problems, though, only cemented the idea in the minds of the public that AOL was the preeminent dialup Internet service provider; in a sense, it had become the Microsoft of the online world.

By the end of the decade, with AOL's growth propelled by the Internet boom, the company was in the position of being able to absorb numerous content and online service companies, most prominently Netscape and CompuServe. By 2000, AOL was in a position to merge with Time Warner, an event that was looked upon as the marriage of two equals — in fact, the new company was called AOL Time Warner. But the Internet bubble deflated within months of the merger, and AOL's position of influence in the Time Warner empire rapidly declined. Time Warner dropped the AOL part of its name in 2003, but AOL still remains an important part of the company . . . how could it not be, with 30 + million active AOL subscribers?

AOL's Specialties

And what is it that AOL offers?

First and foremost, ubiquity. True to its roots as a dialup service, AOL has local modem access phone numbers almost everywhere you go in the United States. (The exact number is hard to find, but it seems to be in the thousands.) And, its name notwithstanding, the service is available in many countries around the world, from Paris to Bangkok.

Second, community. AOL has not forgotten that it began as a bulletin board system, hosting some of the earliest discussion groups for those online pioneers who roamed the Internet before the Web was born. The service still maintains an enormous number of message boards and chat rooms that let you discuss just about any topic you'd like — within limits. Message board topics and posts that are generally considered grossly indecent or offensive are forbidden: The AOL communities all must abide by the service's reasonable but strict Terms of Service (TOS), and the TOS *are* enforced.

Third, content, and plenty of it. AOL has both accrued and offered access to online content from the earliest days, and although the amount of free content on the Web today may dwarf AOL's proprietary holdings, the amount of edited, high-quality exclusive content the service provides is huge. As a subsidiary of the Time Warner multimedia conglomerate, AOL gets first dibs on movie, television, music, book, magazine, and other content that its corporate siblings produce.

The AOL Experience

The AOL software has been totally revamped for Mac OS X and it is harder to avoid getting the software than it is to obtain it. AOL has been mailing out promotional floppy disks and CD-ROMs for years, and though the packaging usually touts the featured Windows version of the software, the latest Mac versions are almost always included.

The forty or more megabytes that comprise the software provide a completely self-contained online environment, including all of AOL's proprietary features, such as its instant messaging client, its mail client (which can send to and receive from Internet addresses as well as AOL addresses), its Web browser (built upon the Gecko browser engine developed by AOL's Netscape subsidiary), its toolbar, and so on.

The interface tends to take over the screen (Figure 17-2); when you click an AOL link, you usually get a new window containing the link's destination: either an AOL proprietary content window or an AOL Web browser window. Your screen, which when you first log in contains AOL's toolbar channels palette, and welcome window, will quickly fill up — it's almost as though Panther's Exposé was made just to tame AOL window proliferation.

Figure 17-2: AOL loves to fill your screen with windows.

You know the famous "You've got mail!" sound identified so strongly with AOL? It was recorded in 1989 by Elwood Edwards, who was also responsible for "File's done," "Welcome," and "Goodbye."

Mr. Edwards even has a Web site (`http://members.aol.com/voicepro/custom.html`) where you can commision a customized alert.

AOL provides online storage for mail you've read or sent in the past three to five days, an address book, and a variety of ways to filter mail for spam or indecent content. It offers 20MB of storage for user-developed Web pages, along with tools for creating and managing those pages. Each member account can have up to seven screen names associated with it, so that one account can provide mail and access service for a typical family.

Speaking of families, parents have a good deal of control over how their kids use AOL: there are various age level settings for screen names that block access to inappropriate sites, for example. Parents can also set AOL to keep records of a child's online activities and e-mail a report to the parent's account.

In addition, AOL members can set up online calendars, use digital photography services, receive customized news and weather information, track stock portfolios, and enjoy a range of other benefits.

note   Although AOL does cater more to Windows than Mac users, the company's long-standing rivalry with Microsoft has helped keep AOL from being a bastion of Windows-only technology. Multimedia, for example, is often available in QuickTime as well as Real formats, and links to music in AOL-delivered content connect AOL users directly to the iTunes Music Store, where their screen names function as Music Store accounts. And, of course, Apple's iChat program uses AOL's Instant Messenger network for text chatting.

MSN

Ever since America Online refused Microsoft's buyout offer in the early 1990s, Microsoft has been waging a campaign not only to get a piece of the online pie, but also to take over the bakery. With its typical trademark persistence, the software company has released and reinvented its Microsoft Network repeatedly, incrementally improving it, leveraging its formidable operating system base to enhance the service's value for Windows users, and capitalizing on every misstep that AOL has made. The result has been an MSN that in many ways rivals AOL's offerings, and at a price that is always just slightly below what AOL charges.

The Frankenstein Service

Not having the advantage of having grown up along with the Internet, MSN has not so much developed as accreted. As Microsoft has acquired various technologies, services, and sources of content over the years, it has welded them, sometimes successfully, sometimes not, to its online service.

For example, Microsoft's deal with NBC in the mid-1990s, which gave birth to the MSNBC cable channel, served to provide MSN with a variety of digital media content. Microsoft's Encarta project, begun to compete with the new media encyclopedias developed for CD-ROM by companies such as Grolier, and originally based on content acquired from Funk & Wagnall's, eventually formed the basis for the Encarta reference service in MSN. Microsoft Money, a personal finance management application, developed to compete with programs such as Quicken, also became a feature of MSN. Microsoft's early forays into digital multimedia eventually led to the latest versions of Microsoft Media Player, the software platform that powers MSN's multimedia offerings. And, of course, a specialized and feature-rich version of Microsoft's Internet Explorer is the foundation of the MSN user experience.

What Does MSN Offers for Mac Users?

There's no denying it: MSN's real target audience is the millions of Windows users who belong to AOL. Nonetheless, Microsoft's Business Unit knows that there's money to be made in the Macintosh market, and that it just doesn't make good business sense to ignore millions of potential customers. The MSN software, built atop Microsoft's now-discontinued Internet Explorer platform for the Mac, provides an AOL-like experience that is more streamlined than its competition, though with somewhat less content and community.

MSN offers nine user account names, as opposed to AOL's seven, and those accounts can be simultaneously logged in when MSN is accessed via broadband connections. The e-mail client will be familiar to Mac users who employ Entourage, including color-coded messages and offline mailboxes, and MSN's junk mail filtering is quite powerful. And, as with AOL, parents have a great deal of control over their kids use of the Web; the way that restrictions are set differ slightly between the two services but the overall effect is comparable.

The MSN interface is much less window-hungry: almost everything happens either within the confines of the Explorer window that forms the core of the software, or in a Dashboard panel that floats off to the side of the main window (Figure 17-3). The underlying software is as not quite as compatible with its Windows equivalent as Microsoft could have made it, though. MSN's Explorer, albeit improved over the free version, still doesn't (and probably never will) handle the Windows-native ActiveX controls that make some sites unusable on a Mac, and the Mac version of the included Windows Media Player does not support all the Windows-only digital-rights-management (DRM) features of its counterpart, making some media inaccessible to Panther users.

Pricing

MSN charges just slightly less than AOL for its dialup service at $21.95 a month, and its bring-your-own-access model is only $9.95 a month. MSN doesn't directly provide high-speed connectivity; instead, it works with local high-speed access providers. There are also reduced costs for yearly subscriptions, and sign-up offers to reduce the initial cost of the service.

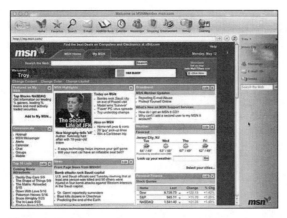

Figure 17-3: The MSN experience.

The Bottom Line

Both services are more focused on the Windows market than the Mac, but both of them have quite useful and appealing features for those of us who think different. Both services provide an easy way for novice users to find their way around the Internet, both help parents protect their children from some of the nastier aspects of the online world, and both provide exclusive content and online communities.

Which one? Either? Neither? Finally, it all comes down to a matter of taste, and *de gustibus non est disputandum*, ya know?

Troubleshooting Connection Problems

One of the first rules of modern computing should be, "Just when you think you have the world by the tail, that Internet tiger is going to turn around and bite you on the butt." Murphy would have loved the Internet. In addition to all the things that can go wrong in everyday computing, you now get to add your physical Internet connection and your ISP's software and hardware to the mix.

What You Need to Know Before Calling Your ISP

When your Internet connection disappears into the ether, you have a problem . . . well, at least one. The first thing to do is to determine whether it is something simple. Did your modem hang up? If so, redial and see if you can get back online. Is your cable modem or DSL modem functioning properly (all the little lights blinking the way they do when things are going well)? If not, unplug it, let it sit about 30 seconds, and plug it back in — this is the first thing that the support person at your cable provider is going to suggest anyway, so you might as well get it out of the way. Check your Network preferences pane and determine whether your IP address looks good. (This is a good reason to know what numeric form your IP address takes when things are going well.) If it doesn't, the problem might be with the DHCP server at your provider.

Secret

Know Who's Responsible for Your Connection Problems

This is not really a Secret, but it's important enough that I'm going to put it here and hope that you really read this text and take it to heart.

When you have connection problems, it is usually not the fault of your Mac. Calling Apple or your Apple reseller (the person who sold you your Mac) is almost always a waste of time and effort. Apple is usually too far away to be of real help. And your reseller can't make the ISP fix your account problems. And to put it more bluntly, your connection problems are really not their responsibility to fix.

Calling your reseller or Apple should be the last resort, after you've done your own troubleshooting, talked with your ISP, and checked with the vendor of any particular software that's causing a problem (your e-mail program, if you aren't using Apple's Mail, for example).

You may well find that contacting your local reseller/Mac service center yields good results. But you also should expect a bill for that consultation. After all, the company who sold you your Mac probably isn't making a monthly fee off of your connection to the Internet. Your ISP, on the other hand, is!

Additionally, your ISP wants to keep its customers content because that means money in its coffers, month after month and year after year. Between wanting to maintain the ongoing relationship and the very high probability that the problem is either on their end or pilot error on your part, the ISP should be your first external point of contact.

Check your service agreement to make sure that you know your account number and the telephone number for technical support, have the information you've gathered above at hand, grab a book or magazine, settle in for a (possibly) long wait, call your ISP, and navigate the maze of telephone switches to get put in the wait queue for the next available support person. When you finally get an operator, take a deep, calming breath and tell them how they can help you.

tip
You'll get a lot better support if you are both calm and polite. Remember, the support folks are dealing only with folks having problems. They didn't cause the problem, their job is to try and help you, and they have feelings, too.

Preparing for Disaster

There will be occasions when bad luck, weather, or other natural disasters take your ISP out of the picture for a while. If you're on cable, but your phone still works, use your backup ISP for traveling (see earlier in this chapter) to try and connect. A major ISP will almost never be unavailable for very long, but having a backup ISP is a good fallback position. If your ISP is a small, local provider, you need a backup plan even more, unless you're willing to forego your Internet fix for a while; let's face it, once we're connected, it's a lot like an addiction.

Summary

With a little luck, this chapter didn't burst your bubble about putting your Mac online. If it did, please read between the lines. If it still did, then ignore it and jump online anyway.

In this chapter, we looked at some of the ISP options available to you as well as some of the issues that surround connecting to and maintaining a relationship with them. I have expressed some strong opinions that are part experience and part personal opinion. If you find that you have different luck than I do with some of these providers, then good for you!

In the next chapter, we'll look at e-mail and Web browsing the Apple way. Between these two chapters, I hope you will feel well prepared to get yourself online.

E-Mailing and Web Browsing the Apple Way

◆ ◆

Secrets in This Chapter

◆ ◆

irst things first. I am not going to waste your time giving you a bunch of platitudes about the importance of e-mail. You know the answers.

Writing e-mail has become a substitute for the telephone, which is often relegated to providing complicated recycling voice menus. Why talk when you can write?

To go one further, some even prefer instant messaging, but that's the province of another chapter.

As you might expect, this chapter has lots of information about the most popular Mac e-mail programs, but you'll learn about a few programs that you may not yet know.

Rather than repeat the same information about all the programs and bore you to death, I give you a single tutorial covering the basics of setup involving all e-mail programs.

You'll find they are more similar than different when it comes to the basics. That way, as new programs and new versions come along, you'll be able to perform these tasks without having to pore through help menus, read manuals (when there are manuals to be read of course), or pull out your hair (in whatever order you wish).

The Nuts and Bolts of E-Mail

Ready? All right, let's get cracking. Most e-mail applications (a.k.a. e-mail clients) work in a similar fashion. They simply retrieve messages to you from the servers hosting your account and dispatch your messages to others using that server, or one run by your Internet service provider (ISP) if they're different.

That sounds pretty simple, although what's happening behind the scenes is incredibly complicated, because e-mail by the billions is transferred daily around the world. That it works at all is amazing, and that very few messages go astray and fail to reach their intended recipients is also pretty amazing.

Of course, things can and do go wrong, and the friendly face of e-mail (shown in Figure 18-1) has changed lots since the system was originally set up as a means for university professors to communicate with each other.

Account Creation and Other Shenanigans

So, to get those programs running, the first thing you need to do is set up your account information. Otherwise, you'll have a neat piece of software with nothing to do but hang out and look pretty; that is, if it sports a nice interface. Here's how to proceed:

note
I wish I could say that this section covers all e-mail possibilities, but it doesn't. AOL and Microsoft's MSN go their own way and require their own software to get e-mail, unless you use one of their WebMail systems, which can be dreadfully slow. The major exception to the rule is AOL Communicator, which can handle all your accounts (except for MSN and Microsoft Hotmail, of course), and Claris Emailer, a long-discontinued product that supported both standard and AOL mail.

1. Find the setting. It may be under Accounts, Personalities, or Tools, but whatever it is called, it's a place where you can insert your user or account information. For the sake of lessening confusion, I'll use Apple's own application, Mail, to illustrate the standard procedure.

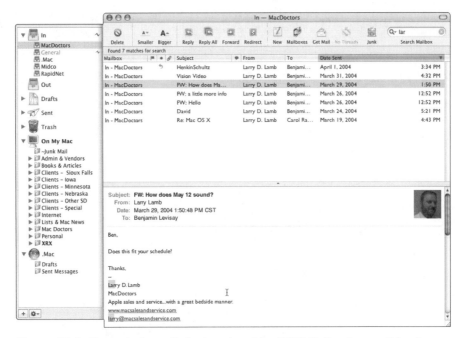

Figure 18-1: The typical e-mail client, such as Mac OS X Mail, puts everything in a convenient three-paned interface.

Mail Is a Smart Program

Mac OS X Mail is smarter than the average program, because it can read the e-mail settings you made when you first set up Panther and incorporate them automatically in its preferences. If you opt for a .Mac account, that information will be set up in your Mail as well.

2. Choose the account type, which is usually POP or IMAP.

insider insight

I'll keep the technical stuff brief. IMAP, short for Internet Message Access Protocol, is a system that keeps your incoming mail on the ISP's server until it is deleted. You can decide whether the messages will be stored on your e-mail server, downloaded only when read, or whatever you want. Although not supported by all ISPs, keeping a message on the server is a useful choice if you intend to check the same messages on different Macs. That might happen if, for example, you see an important message from a business contact at home and need to get it again once you go to the office.

The other e-mail delivery agent or protocol is POP. POP (for Post Office Protocol) is the one used by the majority of ISPs. Here messages are transferred from the mail server to your Mac when retrieved. You can, however, opt to leave messages on your ISP's POP server, using the preference settings in Mail and other programs. This gives you some of the flexibility of IMAP. Obviously, you'll want to check with your ISP before you make a choice.

3. Next, it's a good idea to give the account a name or description (see Figure 18-2). Why? Well, maybe it doesn't make any difference if you have a single online account and don't plan to have any more.

Figure 18-2: Give your account a unique name if you have more than one. Otherwise, any old thing will do.

4. Next on the agenda is, of course, your e-mail address.

> **note**
>
> Don't forget the standard Mac technique to jump through hoops — no, make that text fields. Press Tab to jump to the next field and press Shift Tab to jump to the previous field. With Mac OS X Mail, you'll see the fields filled out with sample text, to get a better handle on what you need.

5. After your e-mail address, you move on to your full name. You are not forced to fill this in, and nobody can stop you from calling yourself by a nickname or another name. (But don't impersonate anyone of course.) This is your decision.

6. Here comes the hard part. You will need to specify the name of your ISP's incoming mail server, such as `mail.earthlink.net`.

> **note**
>
> Every single ISP has a different naming scheme for its mail servers. One might refer to its server as `pop.mailorbust.com`, or whatever; others, like EarthLink, prefix everything with the word `mail`. The only real source of information is your ISP. Sometimes it comes on a CD. Sometimes it's in some sort of printed documentation. Sometimes you have to go to the ISP's Web site, but then you are faced with the prospect of having to be online to learn how to get online.

7. The next settings are your garden-variety login information. Put your username and password in the appropriate spots.

note Depending on the setup, some ISPs require that you enter just a username, whereas others require that you enter your complete e-mail address as your username, such as `whosit@mailorbust.com`. It's important to check your ISP connection settings carefully to make sure you are entering things as per their specifications.

8. The final setting is the SMTP (or sending mail) setting. This is much like the POP setting, and again you need to contact your ISP about what to put here, as logic doesn't always prevail.

Using AppleScript to Change SMTP Servers

Secret

One of the most irritating things about using a mail client program like Mail on a PowerBook is that you may have to change your SMTP settings depending on where you are and from what service you are accessing your e-mail from. If you have browser-based mail (like .Mac) you can access it via a browser and then you don't have to worry about it. But if you don't or if you just like using an e-mail client, you will have to deal with different SMTP settings — which is kind of a pain.

Andreas Amann has provided us with a free set of scripts for Mail (found at `http://homepage.mac.com/aamann`) and among these scripts is a very useful one for changing SMTP addresses. The Mail Script pack has a nice little installer so you won't be forced to drag items around your OS.

After you install it, you can access it from the Script menu at the top of the screen (shown in Figure 18-3).

Figure 18-3: You may find these other Mail scripts useful as well.

continues

continued

Choosing this option brings up a Change SMTP Server dialog box (shown in Figure 18-4). All you need to do then is choose the accounts and then select the SMTP server from the pop-up menu under the account list.

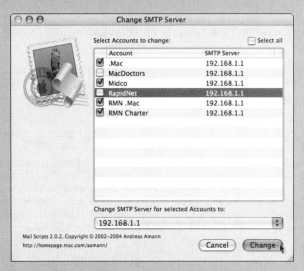

Figure 18-4: You can select individual accounts or click the check box at the top of the window to select all the accounts.

When you have chosen your SMTP setting, you then have to click on the Change button. If everything goes well, you get a drop-down window telling you that everything changed according to your choices. You then have to click on the OK button to proceed back to Mail.

Aside from typing these settings directly into the location management of a PowerBook's network settings, it couldn't get much easier.

---

note

Before you cry "uncle" about all these notes, let me explain. There's yet another option, Server Settings, which you might need for an ISP or e-mail that requires authentication. When you click this option, click the Authentication pop-up menu to select the method your ISP requires, then enter the user name and password and click OK.

Yes, it's true that some e-mail programs will have variations on the theme, such as calling your accounts *personalities*, but the type of information they need is exactly the same.

Using AppleScript to Set Up a New Account

Want to automate the process of account setup in Mail? Go for AppleScript. There's an AppleScript menu in Mail, with a bunch of standard scripts. They reduce setups to simple assistants. So, for example, the Create New Mail Account script asks you a few simple questions, and as you answer and OK the dialog boxes, all of the information is filled in for you automatically.

Another script, Count Messages in All Mailboxes, informed me I had thousands and thousands of stored messages. Maybe I'm becoming a pack rat in my old age.

A Few E-Mail Pointers

This shouldn't be a big deal. Click Reply, type your response, and click Send. But there are a few things you can do to make life easier for your intended recipient:

◆ **Quote the original message:** I get lots of mail, and when someone simply replies "Yes," I have no clue what they're talking about. If you exchange only a few messages with friends, this is okay. But if you are a busy correspondent, you want to know the context of the reply, so you don't have to fish out your original message to figure out what's going on. How to do this depends on the program. With Mail, for example, you click Reply and the message is automatically quoted (see Figure 18-5). AOL does the reverse. Nothing is quoted unless you select part of the message before the Reply button is pushed.

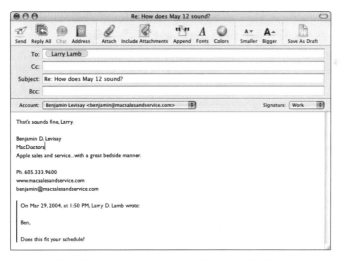

Figure 18-5: The material you quoted automatically shows up in the return message.

◆ **But don't quote the entire message:** I mean it. If the message is really, really long, just select the portion that sums it up before clicking Reply. That way your recipient doesn't have to be overburdened poring through a lot of unnecessary text to get to your response. Quoting should merely serve as a reminder of what the writer said to you originally, so your answer makes sense.

◆ **Type your reply at the top:** There's a guy that I work with who replies to my e-mails and puts his response at the bottom of the quoted text. This is due to the way that his e-mail program deals with replies and quoted text. Regardless of the reason, it's inconvenient for the sendee.

◆ **Be nice:** I know that you are probably upset at that online merchant because the toaster oven you ordered was used for a Frisbee game by the delivery service, but try to avoid the nasty language, or at least wait till they are nasty to you. Sarcasm is also something you should avoid. The reader cannot hear what you are saying, so they are left with the text, which can look much worse than you meant it.

◆ **Run the spell check:** Mail has built-in spell checking. So, if you are on Panther and you send someone an e-mail (in Mail or Entourage) that is full of spelling errors, you are telling the recipient that you don't care enough to run an easy-to-use, built-in feature. It shows courtesy and it keeps you from looking stupid.

◆ **No caps please:** Some of you think of your Mac as a Teletype machine . . . stop . . . AND THUS TYPE IN ALL CAPS! This is a big no-no on the Internet, because caps are meant to show emphasis or, if an entire sentence, shouting or anger. Now you don't yell at people, right? And you don't want them to yell at you, so keep the caps to a minimum, or when grammatically proper.

About the Humble Origins of E-Mail

So how did it all begin? Like lots of Internet features that today are taken for granted, it all began as a method for university professors on the original Unix computers to talk to one another.

Originally, you couldn't even send a message to another computer. Professor Frankenstein, for example, would be able to send a message to Dr. Dracula if both were using the same computer. And we assume Dr. Dracula did his stint at night, of course.

Finally, a method was created to allow you to exchange messages between computers, and thus was born the POP and SMTP protocols we use today to shoot messages across the Internet.

Of course, in those days, you didn't have fancy e-mail clients with pretty interfaces, powerful rules, HTML displays, and spam filters. No, you had to do it all via the command line. While Panther's Terminal application allows you to revisit the old days and bypass the graphical interfaces, most of you would, like me, prefer to point and click.

Panther's Mail Application

If you've used previous versions of Mac OS X, no doubt you regard Mail as a serviceable, reasonably reliable e-mail program. (That's my polite way of saying that it was nothing to e-mail home about.) But the version that comes with Panther has grown by leaps and bounds over what previous versions offered. Some of the original features were great and so Apple kept them. But they added a whole lot more cool features as well. Here's the short list of the best Mail features (IMHO):

♦ **Message threads:** You don't have to be a seamstress to appreciate this feature. When you turn on the Organize By Thread command in the View menu, all messages with a single topic or thread will be grouped together. Click the arrow next to the thread (see Figure 18-6) to see all the messages (or click again to collapse the whole thing). What's the value? If you're involved in a long string of communications with friends or business contacts, this allows you to keep tabs on them a lot easier. No more searching for the message about that change in the shoe store ad that you got last Thursday, which you forgot because the message went to the bottom of the list.

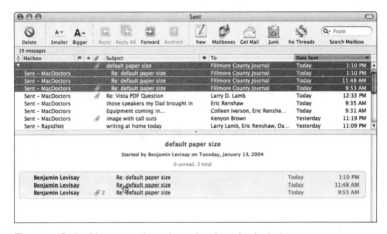

Figure 18-6: Give your thread a color, but don't do buttons.

We Interrupt This Chapter . . .

And thus, a short conversation about threads was born between Pieter and myself.

Pieter: Benjamin, threading has been around for years and originated in the Internet newsgroups that still offer a huge wealth of information and opinion on all subjects under the sun. Threading is a great tool for helping organize correspondence as it lets you see the whole thread and comments that have been made. While it is useful when digging through correspondence with one person, it really shines when you are digging through the messages that you get from a mailing list like many of the ones that I read every day.

Benjamin: You are correct, Pieter. And I agree with you about the usefulness of threading. I use Mail for my e-mail client. And I use the threading feature. The fact that Apple didn't invent this idea doesn't detract from the great implementation of the feature in their e-mail client. Like most good things from Apple, it's simple and easy to understand.

♦ **Drag-and-drop addressing:** Just what it implies. Open Apple's Address Book, select a name or group of names, and drag them to your new mail message. You can also drag e-mail address between the To, CC (carbon copy), and/or BCC (blind carbon copy) fields. There's yet another option. If you need a constant reminder that joeboxer@whizbang.com is really Fred Flintstone with a silly name, you can opt to view addresses by just the real name. No more confusing Fred with julieboxer@fizbang.com. She doesn't appreciate your off-color jokes.

Secret

What to Do When You're Tired of Keychain Prompts

As if your day isn't busy enough, why do you get those irritating messages about your Keychain password? Why do you have to answer those silly dialog boxes, when you already set up your passwords?

These are pressing questions, because more and more applications use Mac OS X's Keychain as a repository for all your login information. Here's why such problems might occur:

You may have set your keychain to lock after a period. The setting is down in the Keychain Access application (spirited away in the Utilities folder). You go to the Edit menu and choose Change Settings for Keychain Login (shown in Figure 18-7). The check box is off by default and if you're the sort that never visits preferences beyond the basics, you don't have to be concerned. But if you did make this change, you will want to open this preference, and deselect Lock after [number] minutes of activity and Lock when sleeping. You should never be bothered by these messages anymore.

Figure 18-7: Alter your keychain settings here.

If that doesn't help, there's one more solution. There's a command called Keychain First Aid in the Window menu of Keychain Access. When you invoke this account, select the mail account that's still asking for the password and click Verify. You'll see a list of errors, if any exist. (Don't try to translate what they are as they're not important.) Now click Repair and the Start button and that should, as they say, be that.

If you still get the message, click the option to Always Remember. And it will; at least that's the hope and the dream.

♦ **Messages on steroids:** No weightlifting jokes, please. But Mail used to be rather poky retrieving messages, particularly on a dialup connection. I remember waiting a full hour getting my mail on a PowerBook, when I visited my sister-in-law's home. With the new version of Mail, you won't get broadband speeds, but things will move a whole lot faster. Maybe that hour will drop down to 20 minutes. All right, you know I get an awful lot of mail.

Secret

What to Do When Good E-Mails Go Bad or Missing

No, no, no, you can't believe it, but you deleted your client's message about a change in Thursday's appointment. It has slipped your memory bank, and you don't want to embarrass yourself (as I've done often) asking what it was. Well, I suppose you could always say that your e-mail got messed up. I hear that often, but they are probably using someone else's application.

First, make sure you haven't emptied the trash mailbox or used the Rebuild command to fix a mail database. Once you do that, the messages are gone, kaput.

If you haven't done that, there's hope for you. First, if Mail has been set up to move your deleted messages to another folder, go to that folder. Normally it's the Trash folder, unless you've fiddled with the preference settings.

Once you're there, just drag the message back to another mailbox, and it's back, arisen from the ashes.

There's yet another option, and that is to mark the deleted messages, and leave them be. If you've turned off the option to Move Deleted Messages to the Trash Mailbox in your Accounts setting pane, just go to the View menu, and select Show Deleted Messages and select the message you want to undelete.

Still can't find that message. Maybe it's in a different mailbox. This happens when you're using more than one account, and haven't combined the display. Beyond that, I can't think of much, unless you just made a mistake as to the name on the message.

♦ **Junk filtering on steroids:** With the Panther version of Mail, the automatic method of filtering junk e-mail is on by default. But there are two preference panels you'll want to consult to make it even more powerful. First, when you click the Junk Mail icon in the preferences box (see Figure 18-8), you'll find a bunch of options that allows you to customize the way it works. The default setting I've shown is really the best, because it depends on the filtering your ISP provides (assuming it does provide something) and accounts for your correspondents who shouldn't be filtered. You can also edit the actual rule that Mail uses to flag junk by clicking the Advanced button (see Figure 18-9). Most of this is self-explanatory — the rules are spelled out in English. They are pretty much what the regular preference panel sets. You can, however, set different options, such as just tossing the junk messages into the Trash, by switching to that folder in the "to mailbox" pop-up menu, if that's what you want to do.

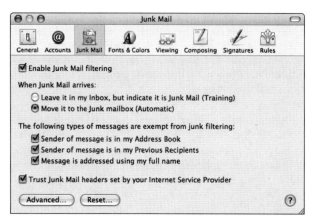

Figure 18-8: Activate or deactivate junk mail filtering. But why?

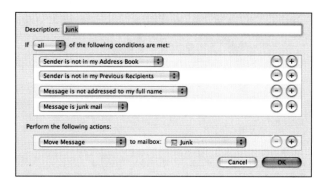

Figure 18-9: Customize the rule Mail uses to process your junk mail in this dialog box.

> **caution**
>
> It's your Mac, and I can't tell you what to do. Or at least I can tell you, but you are free to ignore me. But Mail sometimes goofs, and labels a message you want as junk by mistake. It's better to leave things be, and just inspect your Junk folder every so often to see that all the messages really are spam. If you see a mistake, just open the message (or select it in the folder), click **Not Junk**, and Mail will remember. Well, usually.

♦ **Safari-bred HTML display:** Using the same rendering engine as Safari, Mail can deliver HTML content lickety-split. That is, of course, if you have a reasonably fast connection to your ISP. It looks great too.

Speeding Up Mail Dialup Users

Is your e-mail display dragging? If you have a dialup connection, even the fastest browser in the world (the claim Apple makes about Safari) may seem to be slogging through quicksand. If you can't tolerate the delay, go to Mail's Preferences. Click the Viewing icon and deselect Display images and embedded objects in HTML messages.

Don't fret about not being able to see Aunt Jenny's dogs and cats. Just click Load Images on the mail you wish to view, and they'll be displayed in a few seconds, or whatever speed your ISP allows.

Now that we've looked through the features, let's look at some of the logistics of Mail and how to make it work for you.

Importing E-Mail

If you don't really care to retain old messages and contacts, you don't have to worry about this. But if you want to have your new mail software store all the messages and contacts you've laboriously built over the years, you'll want to check out just what your software can do to import messages.

Mail, for example, is as complete as it gets. The list of programs it can import from (see Figure 18-10) includes Entourage, Outlook Express, Claris Emailer, Mozilla and Netscape, Eudora, and previous versions of Mail.

Figure 18-10: Here are Mail's import options, front and center.

There's also an Other category that allows you to import messages from other programs, so long as they are saved in such formats as MBOX, which is an industry standard.

Reading It Back

This isn't a secret, but it's a neat way to let your computer do the work for you, rather than the other way around. And, if you can tolerate the limitations, it helps give your tired eyes a rest, by taking advantage of Mac OS X's text-to-speech feature.

To take advantage of this feature, which may be appealing or not, depending on your point of view, just do this:

1. With the message open, select the text you want read back.
2. Choose Speech from the Edit menu and select Start Speaking.
3. When you're finished, or just sick and tired of the mechanical sounding computer voice, return to the Edit menu and select Stop Speaking.

Secret

Control-Click to Get Your Mail to Read to You

A secret for text-to-speech — just one. Control-click the text you want your Mac to read to you, and choose Start Speaking from the Speech menu.

4. If the standard voice doesn't inspire confidence or is intolerable, open System Preferences from the Apple menu or the Dock. Click Speech Preferences icon, and change the voice in the Default Voice pane.

I'll avoid the editorial comments about the benefits or lack thereof of Apple's speech technology. But I do want to remind you that not every word is pronounced correctly. However, the Panther version is fairly smart and it did manage to handle such common oddities as "AOL", "MacDoctors", and "Call me Ishmael." without missing a beat.

However, if robotic voices are not your thing, you'll have to wait for the arrival of a better technology.

Some Third-Party E-Mail Clients

I won't spend a lot of time on this section, but it is important to recognize that Apple's Mail program isn't the only choice. Let's look at a few of the choices.

Microsoft's Entourage X . . .

. . . marks the spot! All right, I couldn't resist. But Microsoft's combo e-mail program and contact manager is a first-rate application, even if you're not a fan of the great giant from Redmond, Washington. For one thing, it is a real Mac application through and through despite its source, and doesn't owe anything to the Windows variations of Outlook.

Entourage is usually sold as part of Office X (www.microsoft.com/mac/) which also contains Word X, PowerPoint X, and Excel X. So, if you purchase this suite of programs (for the obvious reasons), you'll find that you also have another choice for e-mail clients.

It's actually based on the Mac Outlook Express, which was a decent e-mail application. Unlike the other e-mail programs in this chapter, it can even parse newsgroups, those online discussion boards that are so fascinating to read and participate in.

Making a Junk Rule in Entourage

Although Entourage X has a passable spam filter, it's not easy to customize. The Junk Mail Filter dialog box is located under the Tools menu. A slider in the Junk preference pane helps you adjust its strength, but you cannot, for example, tell the filter to automatically recognize a given message as spam, unless you create a custom rule. And if you did that for all the junk mail you receive, you might not have much time to get anything else done.

But if you perform this little trick (which also works on the Mac OS 9 version of Entourage and Outlook Express), you can actually make it behave, more or less, just like the one in Apple Mail.

1. With Entourage running, go to the File menu and choose Folder from the New submenu (or just type ⌘-Shift-N).
2. Name your untitled folder Junk.
3. Now it's rule time. Go to the Tools menu and select Rules.
4. Click New and give your filter a name. I call it Junk just to keep it simple.
5. Next on the agenda is to set the kind of rules you want.
6. Under Execute, choose "if any criteria are met."
7. Under Add Criterion, click on the pop-up menus, choosing Category Is Junk as the basis on which the rule acts.
8. Under Add Action, specify Move Message and Junk as the name of the folder.
9. Click OK to make it all happen.

Once you've done this, it'll work like Mail and move Junk messages to another location. And don't forget to make sure Enabled is selected; otherwise, nothing will happen to all those messages you hoped were moved.

One more thing: Entourage X's Junk Mail Filter is adjusted by moving the sensitivity slider in the Junk Mail Filter dialog box (available from your handy-dandy Tools menu). The best way to make it transparent is to turn it all the way up. Of course that means you'll have to spend a few days clicking on messages, and selecting This Is Not Junk mail if it flags the wrong stuff. But after a few days, it shouldn't make too many mistakes.

---

note I'm not spending much time on newsgroups, as they aren't quite as popular as they used to be, especially with the growth of simple-to-manage message board systems that you find on many Web sites. Originally known as UseNet (for Users Network), there are tens of thousands of them, covering every subject from autos to beliefs in alien visitors. They can be fun, they can be wild and woolly, but a discussion about the ins and outs is probably worth a whole book. Maybe some day. . . .

Eudora

When I first began to use an e-mail program other than AOL's, I set up an account with a local ISP, and got a copy of Eudora Lite, the free version.

Version 6.0 of the program is now published by Qualcomm (www.eudora.com/), best known for supplying chips for the mobile phone industry. To this day, many regard it as the e-mail program of choice because of its intriguing, powerful features.

Some of Eudora's Features

Of course, it does all the basics as far as setting up multiple addresses and filtering spam. But there are a few advanced features worth noting:

- **Drag-and-drop nicknames:** Give your contacts a name to identify themselves, such as "my brother the fat slob," and you can quickly open a new message window already addressed. And please don't tell your brother I called him a "fat slob." I have enough trouble dealing with my own relatives.

- **MoodWatch:** You are mad at someone, and you can't take it anymore. So, you write a nasty letter of complaint. MoodWatch gives you a bit of a cooling off period, because it will flag words that might be considered offensive, such as "jerk," "crook," or whatever. Some of us prefer to just count to 10, but this is a pretty unique feature and definitely helpful in keeping you out of trouble.

- **Syncing:** No, it's not iSync, but the Eudora Sharing Protocol (or ESP, which has nothing to do with extra mental powers) lets you synchronize your files to keep your family and friends up to date.

- **Usage stats:** How many messages do you send every day and how many do you receive? Eudora wants to keep you well informed.

- **Import capabilities:** Like most e-mail clients other than AOL, you can import your stored messages from Claris Emailer or Outlook Express. Not a whole lot, but it may be all that you need.

- **Labels:** In a fashion similar to the Mac OS X Finder, you can attach a color label to messages automatically or manually, to make them easier to find later on.

- **Interactive spell checking:** You may not appreciate the reminder, but Eudora can be configured to highlight your mistakes as you type, just like Entourage and Mail. This way you can fix your spelling errors before you inflict them on your friends or business contacts.

- **Animated GIFs:** See the action within an HTML message, without having to save the attachment and open it up in your Web browser.

---

caution　Before you decide whether to enjoy Eudora's animated playback, you ought to consider whether you really want to turn on HTML display. Some think it increases spam (as I'll explain later). But if you opt to open images manually, you can pick and choose which ones you'll get to see. You may prefer the dancing girls or the dancing guys, but do you really want to have ten thousand other junk mailers send such things to you?

Eudora's Unique Marketing Scheme

Eudora is marketed in a unique fashion among e-mail clients. There is a Paid Mode, which you get by ordering a user license. If you don't want to pay, opt for the Sponsored Mode, which inflicts a small ad banner on your screen. All right, it's not all that bad. The ad is subtle, and free of the usual Internet-based scams. And because Qualcomm is a respectable company, you don't have to worry about it.

If your objections to ads are paramount, however, you can accept the Lite Mode, which deprives you of a bunch of powerful features, such as spell checking, junk mail filtering, and multiple signatures. You still get the basics, and maybe that's enough for you, especially if your ISP does its own junk mail filtering and you have only one or two accounts.

note   If you want to get a complete picture of how Eudora changes depending on which mode you want, click on the Payment and Registration window, and select the mode you want to examine. You'll see a text window that gives you the option of activating (or canceling) that mode. By default, you get the Sponsored scheme.

Secret

A Few Eudora Secrets

No powerful e-mail application would be complete without a selection of neat secrets and Eudora has its share. Here's what I mean:

- Customize the interface: ⌘-click between two toolbar buttons to insert a new button between them.
- If you want to open the folder that contains an attachment, hold down Control and Command while clicking on the attachment in the mail message.
- If you're sick and tired of keeping some messages in your Eudora mailboxes, select the messages you want to zap and hold down the Shift, Option, and Delete keys. They don't make it easy, but they do make it safe; I can't imagine anyone but my technical editor remembering this shortcut without some careful thinking.
- If you want to highlight or open the mail folder where a specific message is stored, ⌘-click on the Title bar of the open message.
- If you'd like to forward a message in its original shape, sans the quotes, select a message and then hold down the Option key while selecting Forward from the Message menu. Wish I could do that in Mail.
- If you want to change the sending preferences for a message, press Option when you click the Send button in a message. This delivers a Changing Queuing dialog box where you can alter the settings.

Bare Bone's Mailsmith (Not Jones)

You make think the name is some kind of play on a very common name, but Bare Bones Software (www.barebones.com/), publishers of the popular text editing tool, BBEdit, clearly had another motive in mind for its e-mail client.

In the spirit of such traditional occupations that reflect a master of a certain craft, such as a blacksmith, Mailsmith is meant to be the master of your messages. And, unlike other applications, the second syllable isn't preceded by a second capital, and that's unique.

Because it comes from a company that specializes in developing a world-class text engine, Mailsmith is closer in concept to the original Claris Emailer, which means Mailsmith presents messages strictly as plain text. That means no HTML and no pictures.

Despite these differences, and they are differences that you may appreciate or not, depending on your point of view, Mailsmith has some useful features that will help you get up and running in no time.

For example:

◆ **Efficient importing:** Right out of the box, Mailsmith puts up a message offering to import your messages from another client. Predictably, it includes Claris Emailer, but also includes Eudora Pro 4.0 or later and Apple Mail. If you consult the Bare Bones Web site, you'll also learn how to grab messages from Pegasus Mail, a popular Unix e-mail application.

note   Rather than keep you in suspense, let me tell you that, when I first set up Mailsmith, I had it import my messages from Mac OS X Mail. It put up a warning that I had to quit that application first, and when I did so, it proceeded without further response on my part. The whole process, involving over 10,000 stored messages, took only a few minutes to complete.

◆ **Database-based:** Getting out e-mail stored in Mailsmith is a tad harder as Bare Bones Software uses its own mail database to store your messages. However, Mailsmith does let you export mail to a MBOX format file and that format can be read by many other mail clients, including, of course, Apple Mail.

note   One of the limitations of Mailsmith is that it does not support IMAP (unlike many other e-mail programs), so if you are using an e-mail server that requires the use of IMAP, like Hotmail does for some accounts, you may be out of luck.

◆ **Security:** Under Mac OS X, Mailsmith 2.0 works with PGP 8.0 or later, allowing you to encrypt and sign e-mails, as well as verify incoming mail that is signed. This proves to the recipient that you are really, for example, James Kirk rather than Mr. Spock, or whatever.

Secret

Setting Keys in Mailsmith

Here's a way to speed up access to your favorite features in Mailsmith: You can create keyboard shortcuts for your scripts, plug-ins, and glossary items that aren't available in the Set Menu Keys dialog box, by using the various floating palettes, located in the Window menu, under the Palettes submenu.

First, select the item that you want to make a shortcut for; then, click on the Set Key button and you're in like Flint (with apologies to the late actor, James Coburn, who starred in a popular spy spoof by that name).

CTM Development's PowerMail, the Unique Alternative

When a program has the temerity to use the word "Power" in the job description, you expect something to make it smarter than the average e-mail program.

Can that possibly be true?

PowerMail, from Geneva, Switzerland's CTM Development (www.ctmdev.com/), does have possibilities. Based on a powerful cross-platform e-mail engine, it promises speedy performance and a wide range of import and export options. And if you must reboot in the Classic Mac OS from time to time, you'll be pleased to know PowerMail still runs in the older operating system, so you can retrieve your messages without the hassle and drudgery of dealing with separate programs.

In addition, PowerMail boasts that it uses Apple's Sherlock search technology for mail database indexing, and multithreading to allow you to read and write mail while downloading from your various online accounts. Then again, Apple's Mail application can use multithreading in the same fashion.

---

note

Everything has plusses and minuses, and PowerMail has a few of each. One is the lack of a spell checker. However, as with other things, there's another way.

One is a third-party spell checker, such as Spell Catcher X from Rainmaker Research Inc. (www.rainmakerinc.com/products/spellcatcherx/), that will work with any Mac OS X program. Other possibilities include Grammarian Pro X from Linguisoft (www.linguisoft.com/), a grammar-checking application, of course, and Excalibur written by Rick Zaccone (www.eg.bucknell.edu/~excalibr/), a freeware spell checker.

Which do you choose? My major experience is with Spell Catcher X, which I've followed through the years through various names and publishers. Once it was called Thunder 7, symbolic of the lightning icon.

By default, PowerMail does not delete mail that is stored on the mail server. This can be a problem if you have a small amount of storage on your mail server and get many messages, especially with attachments. Here's how to get PowerMail to delete or stop deleting the mail stored on your mail server after it has been retrieved by PowerMail:

1. Click on the Setup Menu and then choose Mail Account.
2. Choose the account you want to modify from the list of accounts on the left. Selecting a given user account displays all of its current settings.
3. Click the Receiving button.
4. Look for the Delete from server options and then choose the setting you want.

Compacting PowerMail's Mail

Secret

When you delete a message in PowerMail, is it really, well, gone? Worse, what happens when you delete a mail message that you really wanted? Well, like Entourage X, PowerMail keeps all its messages in a database file and only marks those messages that you have slated for deletion as being expendable when you compact the database, which is designed to clear out the cobwebs, reduce the size and increase the program's performance.

If you are like me and rarely compress your mail database, you should be able to retrieve messages that you deleted long ago. Of course that means someone else can, as well. However, if you have compacted the database between when you deleted the message and when you want to recover it, there is not much hope.

But if you want a reasonably secure way to dump the messages you don't want outsiders to see, use the Compact Database tool. Just go to the File menu, choose Database, and select the command from the submenu.

MSN for Mac OS X

The words "MSN for Mac OS X" may seem an oxymoron, but with a saturated market on the Windows platform, Microsoft had to do *something* to take on number one, AOL.

Now I don't pretend to be able to read the minds of Microsoft's marketing people, but expanding to the Mac platform surely widens its horizons and helps it compete with AOL. Thus begat a true Mac OS X version of MSN that incorporates most of the features of the Windows version. The top bar of the MSN interface shows all of the features (shown in Figure 18-11).

Figure 18-11: These services are the same as the Windows version.

If you're familiar with MSN for Windows, you'll find the layout comfortable and familiar. Everything, including e-mail, instant messaging, and access to the forums, happens in a single browser window. This makes a sharp contrast to AOL, which puts up lots of windows when you access its various features.

A Few Things to Get You Started in MSN

Secret

To make MSN simple for novice users, you have to rely on methods that aren't always visible. Here are a few examples of what I mean:

◆ If you want to export your contacts or mail, simply drag them from the message window to the desktop. Contacts will be saved in vCard format, and the contents of your mailboxes in the MBOX format, same as Apple's Mail.

◆ Importing contacts and mail involves the reverse procedure. Just drag them into your message window.

◆ This drag-and-drop scheme also extends to file attachments. Just drag them to the MSN icon in the Dock and it'll open up a blank mail message containing that attachment (or attachments).

Combating Spam and Online Scams and Viruses

Before I get down and dirty into this section, let me clarify something. There is spam and then there is SPAM. The latter is a lunchmeat of mixed composition that hails from the folks at Hormel. (If you're curious you can visit the SPAM Museum in Austin, MN as I have — more than once.) The former is the bane of the existence of every computer user.

Way back when, your mailbox was filled with bogus offers of one sort or another. Earn money while working at home stuffing envelopes, and all that.

Well, those offers no longer fill the mailbox on the corner. Instead, they fill your mailbox on your Mac (or PC if you must). On a typical day, you might encounter not just the work-at-home scheme, but offers to enhance your virility, increase the size of . . . well, you know, or find fame and fortune.

The list goes on. Sad to say, some of it comes from legitimate companies who use this sleazy method to increase business, not caring, I suppose, that one doesn't grow a business by upsetting its potential customers. Or maybe I'm out of touch.

Secret

A Pyramid Scheme by Any Other Name

So what the real skinny on that envelope addressing scheme you read about? How does it work?

Well, it's something that has been going on for years. You see print ads for it in the supermarket tabloids too. When you respond to the ad, you receive an offer to purchase some sort of information kit.

If you fall for this scheme, you impatiently open the package when it arrives, and sit down and read the short booklet (usually amateurishly printed), and your jaw drops in amazement!

What did you fall for? The information pack tells you that in order to make money, you contact others offering the same deal, and send them the same sort of reading material.

And it goes on and on and on, just this way. You can only make money by making others fall for the same pyramid scheme you did. Now you know.

Do's and Don'ts About Making E-Mail Safe from Spammers

To be perfectly blunt, when I wrote the first draft of this manuscript, I was getting a grand total of 400 junk mail messages a day. I'm quite sure this is a whole lot more than you receive. (At least I hope it is.)

What did I do to be so lucky?

Well, one thing that makes me vulnerable to receiving such garbage is that I have chosen, partly because of my profession, to ignore the cardinal rule and use e-mail addresses that are prominently displayed and easy to remember.

I accept the fact that my ego is partly satisfied by possessing the screen name macdrben@mac.com, even if I must suffer the slings and arrows of a constant bombardment of messages.

The Origins of the Word Spam

So how did a name of a meat product become identified with junk e-mail? Well, I had to spend a little time exploring the history of the word and I got up close and personal with a famous skit by the British comedy quartet, Monty Python's Flying Circus. When an unwary diner tried to place an order at a restaurant, everything they offered had SPAM in it.

Even quoting the skit wouldn't convey the madcap humor. You'd have to see the actual sketch, often broadcast on cable TV, to really appreciate those comic geniuses. Now let me go and make a SPAM pie for dessert.

So, do as I say, not as I do, and consider the following ways to keep your mailbox clean:

♦ **Don't publish your e-mail address.** Just as many of you tell the phone company not to put your number in the telephone directory, try to avoid giving out your e-mail address to strangers. What should you do if the company you deal with needs a valid address? In addition to using a different address (see the next suggestion), check the company's privacy policy, which is often posted at the site in very fine print. A reputable company would either pledge not to give out your name to others, or only with your approval, so watch the check boxes about such things to make sure you don't sign up for spam by error.

A Trick to Avoid E-Mail-Harvesting Spam Bots

Here's another way to post your address if you must, and that is to spell out "at," and not use @, if possible. So, I might give "macdrben at mac.com" instead of the regular alternative, because it won't be detected as easily by the spam bots that harvest names. On the other hand, one supposes those bots will eventually get the message and guess it anyway, but every little bit helps.

♦ **Get a temporary e-mail address.** If you must post your name to third parties, set up a special address for the purpose, perhaps a free address from Hotmail or Yahoo. (And the Google mail service will probably be live by the time this book is published.) That way you can ditch it when the load of junk gets too much for you to take, and you won't have to keep sending out change of address notices to your regular contacts, because they will have your regular address instead.

♦ **Don't ask to be taken off a mailing list.** It will usually have the opposite effect, because it merely confirms your address is real and makes you a target for even more spam. The spammers merely use that information to separate the legitimate addresses from the fake ones.

> **note** There's one condition in which it is safe to request the removal of an address from a mailing list. If you are receiving messages from a mailing list or a company that you originally requested, there's nothing wrong with following instructions to get off the list, if you change your mind. Often it'll be in the message itself, or at a company Web site. This is a perfectly reasonable way of doing business.

♦ **Don't respond to the offers.** Many are bogus; some can cost you a lot of money for products and services that aren't worth it; others allow someone to steal from you.

An Introduction to Challenge-Response

If you have lots of online contacts, no doubt you've received one. You write to someone and you get back a letter saying you can't get your message through unless you prove you're for real.

What gives?

The process involves clicking a link to log onto a Web site, where you usually have to enter the number you see to demonstrate that you are a real person and not a spam bot. What is this world coming too?

This system, known as the challenge-response, is just one method devised to protect folks against getting unwanted messages.

Does it work? Depends on who you ask. If you have a short list of e-mail contacts, mostly family and friends, and you don't receive a lot of mail from businesses, it's a useful technique to reduce the level of unwanted messages.

But it has a caveat, as so many of these systems do. And that is when a company you patronize needs to send you information about a product or service you've ordered. The automated message systems they use can't respond to the challenge — and the message is blocked.

> **note** The worst possible scenario of a challenge-response gone wrong is a situation where you send an important document to a business contact to meet a deadline. Your contact uses challenge-response and the system sends a message that you must answer right away to get that document through. Unfortunately, you just went on your lunch hour, so you miss the message and the deadline.

Some systems, though, promise to handle this dilemma more efficiently. The e-mail managing service Mailblocks, for example, uses a system called Trackers to help you manage the messages you get from legitimate mailings, say from commerce sites and mailing lists. The technique involves setting up a series of disposable addresses that you can use for such purposes.

If the spam-meisters find you out, you ditch the address, but at least you get the sales receipts and other material you need before you change the address. This doesn't affect your regular e-mail address, which you never have to give out except to a trusted few.

So, if you want to give a fascinating variation of challenge-response a try, go to `www.mail blocks.com` and see what it's all about.

---

insider insight   A few words about the CEO of Mailblocks, Phil Goldman. If you are a follower of Mac OS lore, the name is going to be significant to you.

You see, Phil once worked at Apple, where he was one of the two developers of the original MultiFinder, the method used to run more than one application at the same time on your Mac.

The way Phil tells it, they made it perform this miracle by fooling the operating system into believing the other application is really a desk accessory, which, of course, was allowed to run in tandem with another application.

Phil was also the man who brought virtual memory to the Mac OS, and they said it couldn't be done. (Although Connectix managed the feat way before it became part of the operating system.)

What did Phil do after leaving Apple? Well, he did work on Microsoft's WebTV among other things, but nobody's perfect.

Is HTML a Spam Trigger?

You just love getting those beautiful photos of Aunt Jenny's dog, all fluffy and happy. Most e-mail applications have built-in Web browsers, so they can put the pictures in place. But you also get all those ads that you don't want that create pictures of the sort you'd really rather not have inflicted on you.

And it just gets worse.

Well, here is something you might try to lessen the junk mail load. Turn off your mail program's HTML feature.

With the Panther version of Mail, you can do it this way:

1. Choose Preferences from the Mail menu.
2. Click on the Viewing icon (shown in Figure 18-12).
3. Deselect the Display images and embedded objects in HTML messages option.
4. Click the close box.

Figure 18-12: Deselect the option to display HTML in your mail in this dialog box.

Now what's this all about? Why set aside those pretty pictures? What does this have to do with anything?

Here's what it's all about: You see, when your e-mail software retrieves those graphics from the Internet, the sender of that spam gets confirmation your address is real. So, it just sends some more. It's a vicious circle.

But if you turn off the feature, the message isn't transmitted, and you should, the theory goes, see fewer junk messages over time. Another great feature is that you are also no longer subjected to the images you do not want to see.

Does it work? Well, as I wrote this chapter, I turned off the HTML feature. As you recall from earlier in this section, I was getting over 400 junk messages every single day. The first day, it went down to 300 messages. Then it increased to 430 and was, within another day, over 450 messages and then some, and the upward climb continues.

After two weeks, I wasn't able to see a dime's worth of difference, yet others claim that disabling HTML display is a magic bullet. Now perhaps my online visibility makes me a target for junk mail, and I'm an exception to the rule. So, when it comes to this prospective solution, I'm really on the fence. But it doesn't hurt to try. I welcome your cards and letters about the results.

note   Another way to help reduce spam is the Bounce to Sender feature in Apple's Mail. You'll find it in the Message menu, or just type ⌘-Shift-B after selecting the messages you want to return. After you accept the requisite warning, the mail will be returned to the sender. Unfortunately, like the HTML scheme, it's not always successful. The reason is this: Most junk mail contains a phony return address. The result is that half of the messages you return will, themselves, be returned to you. And the likelihood that it'll lessen your junk mail load is slim to none, at least in my experience. But desperation sometimes breeds extraordinary solutions and, sometimes, inventive ones.

You can still see pictures in your messages if you want. Just click the Load Images button in Mail, for example, and they'll appear. Just make sure you don't do it with a message you really didn't want to see, or you will just bring yourself some more aggravation. So, try to resist the temptation.

We Interrupt This Chapter . . .

Pieter has decided he has to weigh in on the growing spam problem, so let's give him his due:

Pieter: Spam has become the bane of almost every user who has an e-mail address accessible over the Internet. From the very first spam that was posted years ago to the early newsgroups by Gene "Spamford" Wallace, who posted notices advertising his immigration law firm, folks have been using the Internet as a cheap way of advertising.

These days, whenever you open your e-mail inbox you will likely be inundated with offers to increase the size of things best left unsaid in a family book, drugs, vitamins, free software, and quick techniques to have a portfolio bigger than Bill Gates Jr.

The reality is that all of these are scams designed to separate you from your money. Alas, unlike the old three-card Monty scam of yesteryear, there is not even a chance of you ever getting what you paid for. Spammers gain your e-mail address from a variety of sources. They can harvest them from newsgroups where you may have posted a message, or they might have grabbed them by hacking into a company's Web site and stealing their list of customers. Sometimes, some less-than-scrupulous companies actually sell your private information to the spammers.

These days, spammers are getting craftier and sleazier by creating viruses that access your PC (and I suspect it'll happen on the Mac before long), to feed them your e-mail and passwords. Some spammers are also sending out viruses that turn your computer into a remailer that sends and retrieves spam from the mailer and feeds it to others.

For Macs with Mac OS X's SendMail feature configured and running, a common scenario under Panther Server, you should make sure that it is set up so that it will not relay messages from outside your home network. If you do not, spammers will quickly locate your Mac and start using it to relay their messages to people all over the world — and get your ISP very, very angry with you.

Benjamin: I might add, angry enough to cause you to lose your Internet access. So, be cautious.

Secret

Customizing a Mailto Link

Before you send me cards and letters about the fact that this is a browser tip and not a mail tip, let's call it a toss-up because it does involve e-mail. And we are looking at Safari at the end of this chapter anyway . . .

In any case, the version of Safari I reviewed for this book doesn't have a Mail button, so I thought I'd let you know how to add one, all by yourself. The great thing about Apple's development environment is that you can do these things without knowing a lick about programming. (I know even less than a lick and I managed to perform these tricks.)

This particular secret allows you to add a Mail link in Safari. When you click on that link, it'll open up an e-mail message containing the name of the Web site in the subject line and the address in the message.

Just follow these simple directions:

1. Paste the following line into the URL address box, all in one line (this is critical):

```
javascript:location.href='mailto:?SUBJECT='+document.title+
'&BODY='+escape(location.href)
```

2. When it has been pasted into the address box, a little blue icon appears in front of it. Grab the icon and drag it to the bookmark bar. As with regular bookmarks, you'll be asked give it a name. Feel free to be inventive, but Mail ought to be sufficient for jazz.

3. When you've named your fledgling bookmark, press the Return or Enter key and the bookmark appears in its appointed locale on the bookmark bar.

E-Mail Viruses

Can it happen on a Mac, or is it just a Windows problem? Well, it doesn't matter, because if you forward a file or message that contains a virus or Trojan horse to a Windows user, you are the Typhoid Mary that will infect the unsuspecting user. So, be careful.

In addition, it is possible to make e-mail viruses that affect Mac users. The reason we haven't seen so many is not because the Mac is less vulnerable to viruses, but because, to the virus writer, our favorite computing platform is just a blip in the sky. Such are the advantages of being a smaller player in a larger universe.

However, that doesn't mean Macs are totally immune. It is possible for viruses to affect your e-mail software. Those of you who recall that infamous Simpsons virus of a few years back know that other software, in that case AppleScript, can be attacked.

There are a few things you can do to avoid contributing to the problem, especially if your Windows contacts are your friends:

◆ **Don't open unsolicited attachments.** You get a message from someone you don't know, saying "Here's that file I promised you." Don't open it, and certainly don't forward it to anyone else. After all, why would a total stranger send you a file?

◆ **Don't open unexpected attachments.** Your friend Mary sends you something, and you trust her, so you open the file or forward it to Jane, so she can look at it too. Only you don't remember Mary promising you to send a file. You didn't expect it, so you should ask Mary what this is all about. It's possible a virus infected her computer, especially if it's a PC, and that the offending message is simply being propagated to more unwary recipients.

caution If you're using AOL, be careful. By default, AOL's Automatic feature can be set to open attachments automatically when you do a scheduled mail session. Obviously, this isn't a very good idea. So, make sure the option labeled Download Files That Are Attached to Unread Email remains unchecked. You can always manually download those files when you're online, once you're sure they are on the up and up.

Solving E-Mail Problems

Like Web site issues, e-mail problems can sometimes be troublesome. Servers get overloaded, or simply go down. It's not reserved for the big players, small servers sometimes go down too, although they do often manage to provide better control of their network resources.

Here follow two common problems and their solutions. Just bear in mind that it's not necessarily your fault, in fact it's usually not your fault.

Solving Full Mailbox Issues

You check your e-mail daily, or many times a day. So why are you getting constant messages that your mailbox is filled? Is someone sending you a virus or just a big attachment that you didn't expect?

Usually the answer is none of the above. It simply means that your read messages are all being kept on your ISP's server, and you need to purge them and change the settings of your e-mail software to delete them automatically.

Here's how to make it happen, using Mail as the guide:

1. Launch Mail.
2. Choose Preferences from the Mail (application) menu.
3. Select the Accounts and then account you want to change from the list.
4. Click the Advanced button.
5. Select "Remove copy from server after retrieving a message." This means that your mailbox will be cleared of a message once you receive it.

note This pop-up menu is not present in accounts set up for .mac, only for POP and IMAP.

Authentication Failure

What's this, you get a message asking you to reinsert your password? What happened? Well, maybe the setting got, as the techies say, messed up. Go ahead and put in the password, and see what happens.

If that doesn't work, you should verify whether you're actually online. If you have a dialup connection, look at the light on your phone, or open Internet Connect and see the connection status. It's very easy to lose such connections and not notice.

If it does show that you are connected, try to access a Web site and see if it works. If you're offline, log on again. If not, quit and relaunch your e-mail software and see if it works. You may also want to redo the settings, just in case the preferences got mangled somehow (maybe when you were forced to restart your Mac the other day).

If your connection is via cable modem (or DSL or any broadband connection), the usual gambit is to unplug the power cord from the cable modem, wait a minute, then plug it in again. AirPort users will also want to unplug the base station, if it's attached to the cable modem, and wait for it to reboot itself once you see the cable modem is working.

If all else fails, call your ISP. That may not be encouraging if your provider isn't friendly to Macs, but if things don't work, that's the remaining choice.

Safari — The Best Web Browser

When this book was originally outlined, this chapter was slated to be an e-mail chapter. About two-thirds through the book, I realized that we hadn't allotted anywhere to talk about Safari. So even though this section sticks out a bit like a sore thumb, I'm going to take a little space in this chapter to give it a better overview than I did in the Mac OS X applications chapter (Chapter 12).

About Safari

Apple unveiled it's new browser, Safari, at the Macworld Expo, San Francisco, January 7, 2003. It has gone through two generations of public betas, and in July, 2003, was released as a finished product.

Apple calls Safari "The Fastest Web Browser Ever Created for the Mac." Third-party benchmark tests back this claim up. Safari's highly tuned rendering engine loads pages over three times faster than Microsoft's Internet Explorer for the Mac and runs JavaScript over twice as fast. Safari also uses the advanced interface technologies underlying Mac OS X to offer you an all-new view of the Web, one that's much easier to use. These break-throughs don't come as much of a surprise — if you think about it. The Safari development team (a department at Apple) enjoys unprecedented access to the rest of Apple's software engineering resources — making the browser and Panther work almost as one.

It was probably for that reason that on June 13, 2003, Microsoft announced that they will be dropping the development of Microsoft Internet Explorer (IE) — the browser that has been bundled with the Mac OS for the last three years. And although there are other browsers that can be downloaded and used on the Mac OS, I think we can safely say that Safari is here to stay.

Safari is now Apple's default Web browser and can be found in your Dock. Clicking on this Dock icon launches Safari and starts you on your way to Apple's take on the World Wide Web.

Safari's Interface

The Safari interface is not that different that from Netscape Navigator or IE, as you can see from Figure 18-13. It has the same kinds of controls and features. We'll go into more depth on some of the features later on in this chapter. For now let's look at the features you see with the main window up.

At the top-left corner below the window controls you see two arrows. These are the Back and Forward buttons that allow you to move back and forth between visited Web pages — one page at a time.

To the right of those buttons, is an icon that looks like a house. This is your Home button. Pressing this button takes you to the page that you have designated (in your preferences) as your default or home page.

To the right of your Home button you can see the AutoFill button. Using your preferences and your Address Book, you can set up Safari to autofill online forms with your information. Your Address Book card is the one that you set as yourself in the Address Book. It is shown in the Name list with a different icon (shown in Figure 18-14).

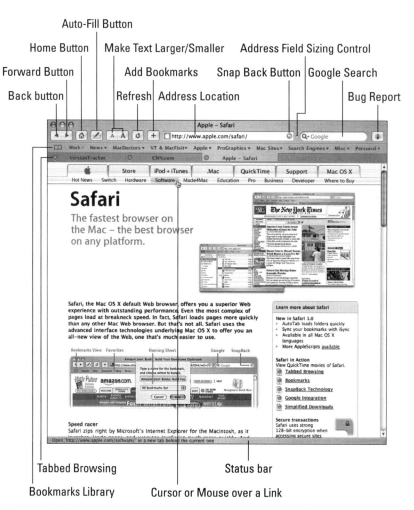

Figure 18-13: The main Safari interface.

To the right of the AutoFill button are the Text Control buttons. The smaller *A* button makes the nongraphic type on a Web page smaller. The larger *A* button makes the non-graphic type on a Web page larger.

The button to the right of the Text Controls is the Refresh button. This button, when pushed, instructs Safari to reload the current Web page — updating the Web page contents.

The Add Bookmark button (plus symbol) to the right of the Refresh button allows you to add the current page to your bookmarks. We'll go into a lot more detail about bookmarks later on in this chapter.

The Address Location field is directly to the right of the Refresh button. This the area where the you type a Universal Resource Locator (URL) or Web page address into to go directly to that Web page.

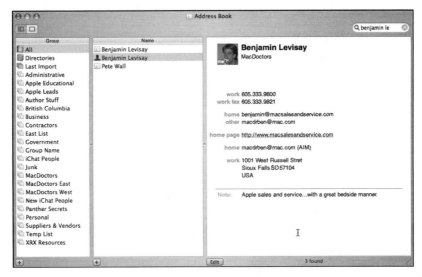

Figure 18-14: You can also tell who you are by looking at the picture. It should say "me" on the picture if it's specified as "you" in the Address Book.

At the right end of the Address field, is a small orange button with a white arrow in it. This is the SnapBack button. This is a new feature in almost any browser. SnapBack gives you the ability to thread your way back to the beginning of a search or from a point of origin. The SnapBack button returns you to the point where you last typed a URL or selected a bookmark.

On the far-right side of Safari, you see a built-in Google Search field.

To the right of the SnapBack button is a control that lets you adjust the size of the location field and the Google Search field.

Directly below these buttons and fields, you can see an area that can store bookmarks and/or bookmark folders called the Bookmarks bar. Clicking on single bookmarks on the Bookmarks bar instructs Safari to go to that site/Web page. Clicking on a folder placed in this bar will cause a menu to drop down showing all the bookmarks in that folder.

Directly below the Bookmarks bar you can see the tabs. Each of these tabs represents an open tabbed Web page. Tabbed browsing is one of the most popular features in Safari. Tabs give you the option of having more than one page open within a single browser window. This feature, released in Safari Beta 2, lets you see and switch between multiple Web pages in a single window, using tabs. You can even open a folder of bookmarks with a single click. Tabs resize themselves based on number open and the available space. There is also a Close button on each tab. We will go into more depth on this subject later on in this chapter.

The cursor appears as an arrow on the screen when moving over regular graphics and text. It appears as small gloved pointing hand when it passes over links.

And at the bottom of the Safari window, you see the Status bar. The Status bar displays the link or URL information of any link that the cursor/mouse is over. It also displays information on loading pages. Clicking on the link takes you to the address that the Status bar indicates.

Breaking Out Safari's Features

Safari's features are well documented by Apple. Here is an overview and brief description of Safari's features (that I have not covered yet) to get you started.

Open Source

Safari uses open source software at its core. For its Web page rendering engine, Safari draws on KHTML and KJS software from the KDE open source project. As an open source participant, Apple shares its enhancements with the open source community.

Browsing with Tabs

My favorite feature of Safari is tabbed browsing. To use this you have to turn that feature on in the preferences. And once you do, you find that Apple has given you a way to have multiple pages open in one window (shown in Figure 18-15).

Figure 18-15: Flipping through open pages is as easy as clicking on the tabs.

The other cool thing you can do is to open an entire folder's bookmarks into separate tabs. One of the easiest ways to do this is from under the Bookmarks menu or from the Bookmarks bar by selecting Open in Tabs after the bookmarks (shown in Figure 18-16).

Figure 18-16: Choosing Open in Tabs causes all of the listed bookmarks to open in separate tabs within the same browser window.

Bookmarks

Bookmarks work differently in Safari than they do in IE or Navigator.

When you add a bookmark in Safari (by clicking on the Add Bookmark button on the Safari button bar), a naming sheet (shown in Figure 18-17) gives you the opportunity to edit the bookmark name and file it away immediately in just the right folder. No more bookmark menus a mile wide — and deep.

Figure 18-17: The Naming sheet lets you change the name and choose where to store a bookmark.

You can also drag a Web address directly into the bookmarks bar, giving you one-click access to that site. As you move an address to the bar, the other addresses rearrange themselves automatically.

Managing bookmarks have been, in the past, very difficult. With Safari, it's not difficult at all. In Safari's Bookmarks library (shown in Figure 18-18), you'll see a two-pane interface, like that of iTunes, which lets you edit bookmark names and addresses in place as though you were renaming an icon on your desktop.

You can create any number of folders in your library, and keep them in the Bookmarks bar or menu, like the preinstalled News folder. Safari offers a host of bookmarks to get you started — and some should be very recognizable, as Safari automatically imports your Internet Explorer, Navigator, and Mozilla favorites.

Moving Sites from Your History to Your Bookmarks

Secret

The History folder is also available from the Bookmarks Manager. The History keeps track of sites you've visited recently, so you can go back a day or even a week later to see where you've been. You can then drag items from the history to your bookmarks folders.

Safari also takes advantage of Rendezvous to find any Web addresses on your local network. This is especially hand for setting up network devices like Rendezvous-enabled printers or for accessing local Internet pages on your LAN.

Figure 18-18: Clicking the small Open Book icon under the Forward and Back buttons opens the Bookmarks Manager.

note Now, with iSync 1.1, you can also use your .Mac account to keep your Safari bookmarks synchronized (see Chapter 20 for more information about using your .Mac account) across multiple Macs, in addition to your Address Book and iCal info. Perfect for when you've done a lot of weekend research but need to make actual phone calls during business hours.

Porting Your Navigator and IE Bookmarks to Safari

Secret

If you've used Netscape Navigator or Internet Explorer for years, as I have, you probably don't relish the though of starting over and losing all your bookmarks. I know I sure as heck didn't want to lose the over-organized (compulsively so) collection of URLs that are my bookmarks.

But soon after I started using Safari, I found a small utility that helped me make the move from IE to Safari. It seems that a guy named Gordon Byrnes from Alaska created a cool little utility called Safari Enhancer (www.lordofthecows.com/safari_enhancer.php) that, among other things, transfers bookmarks from your other browser to Safari. And Gordon has done a good job at keeping the software updated there is now a version for both Jaguar and Panther.

It should be noted that this is donation ware and that if you do use this utility, it would be good karma to send Gordon a few $s. Select Donate under the Help menu (while in Safari Enhancer) if you want to support this great little utility's developer.

Integrated Address Book with AutoFill for Forms

If you've used Internet Explorer or Netscape, you've probably used the Auto Fill feature. Safari also has a very good AutoFill feature. But unlike other browsers, this one is tied to the Address book — giving you even more integration between your OS integrated applications. But you're not stuck with just the information on your Address Book (ME) card. You can set other sources for Auto Fill in the Safari Preferences. Safari also gives you a separate option to automatically enter your accounts and passwords, stored securely in the Mac OS X Keychain.

Secret

Access Web Sites from Your Address Book

A little-known feature of Safari is its ability to access any URLs from your Address Book to give you fast access to the Web sites associated with any person or company address card. The person(s) or company(s) will show up under the Address Book submenu under the Bookmarks menu in Safari.

Downloads

The thing that I like best about the Downloads window in Safar is that it's simple. But that doesn't mean that it doesn't have some great features. You can even install an application through the Download window without switching to the Finder.

Precision Layout

I know this sounds silly, but one of the great things about Safari is that it does a very good job of what it's supposed to do — which is to render online content. It uses the latest Internet standards to make sure that not only regular old HTML looks "right" but more advanced Web pages containing things like HTML, XML, XHTML, DOM, CSS, JavaScript, and Java specifications the way they are supposed to.

And because Apple is the maker of QuickTime, you can expect their browser to do a killer job at displaying QuickTime content. Not to fear, Safari supports Flash, and Shockwave plug-ins.

One of the reasons that the pages in Safari look so good is that the text looks better than other browser. The reason for this is that text in Safar is automatically anti-aliased. And because Safari understands Unicode, you can view sites in different languages and different writing systems.

New Java Support

Safari harnesses the built-in Java 1.4.2 (in the OS) to give you more speed and power for Java Web sites than ever before. This is not a clumsy stab at Java support. This is the real deal. And if you're worried about security, you should know that any certificates used in signed applets are now shored directly into the Mac OS X Keychain.

Blocking Pop-Ups

This feature doesn't need a lot of explanation. If you hate pop-up ads while you're surfing the Web, all you need to do is to set your preferences to deal with those annoying pop-ups for you. This feature alone might make Safari the reason to leave Navigator or IE in the trash.

AppleScript Support

Safari is fully AppleScriptable. You can well imagine that with Tabbed browsing, built-in Google searching, Rendezvous support, and Address Book support there are a lot of different automations you can choose from. The one that I use the most is one that was developed by me and a friend to launch Safari and then open a collection of addresses in tabs. If you're interested in this script, e-mail me directly (macdrben@mac.com) and I'll send it to you.

Favicon Support

The Windows world knows all about favicons. Those are the little custom icons that you see in a browser address field just to the left of the URL (shown in Figure 18-19).

Figure 18-19: These little graphics are also saved in your history and your bookmarks.

There isn't that much to say about favicons. If you're site has one, Safari will see it.

SnapBack Feature

At the far-right of the address field you can see (if you've visited a few pages in your session) an orange curved arrow. This is the SnapBack indicator. The idea here is that Safari is remembering the page where you started from so that any time you want to get back to the beginning of your Web journey, all you have to do is click on the orange arrow and presto you're back to the beginning. If you've visited a lot of pages, it's simpler than hitting the back button 20 or 30 times.

Secret

Another Way of Navigating in Safari

If you've visited several sites and you want to see where you are in the hierarchy of the site, you can hold down the Command key and click on the top of Safari (shown in Figure 18-20). This gives you the most direct location from the top level of the site.

Figure 18-20: Click, pull, and let go to get back to the top level of the site you're on.

Google Search

Safari also remembers your most recent searches in a pop-up menu and tracks your Google SnapBack point separately (shown in Figure 18-21).

Figure 18-21: The Google search allows you to access the last ten Google searches made using this feature.

note

The menu that records the last ten Google searches only remembers searches done from the Google search field next to the address bar. Searches done in the main panel of the browser, while on Google.com are not recorded in Google search menu.

Secret

A More Powerful Search Using Sherlock

Although you have the Google search feature built right into Safari, you shouldn't forget about Sherlock. Besides the ability to run a search on general information to normal search sites (like Google) Sherlock combines different search features and search sets called channels. Choosing a channel allows you very specific search criteria and results.

Searching for a movie in an area not only gives you theater choices but also play times, ratings, and even a QuickTime trailer, if one is available (shown in Figure 18-22).

The Yellow Pages is even more fun. If you provide your address, all you have to do is decide that you want pizza and click on the Search button. This gives you all of the pizza places in your area. You will be given driving instructions as well as a map to the pizza place, if it's available (shown in Figure 18-23).

continues

continued

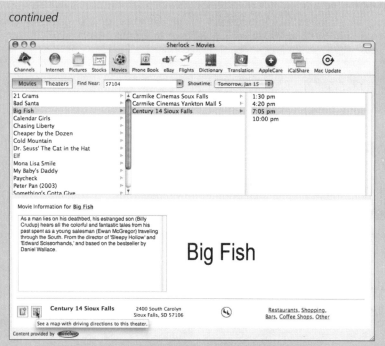

Figure 18-22: Not only can you find a movie and play time, but you can also ask Sherlock to give you driving instructions.

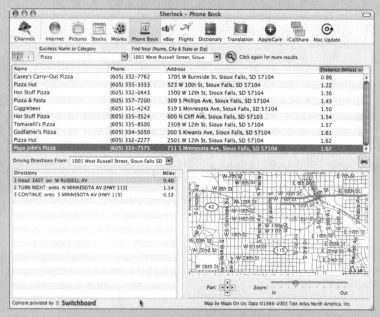

Figure 18-23: It's everything you need to know about the local pizza places except who's offering two-for-one deals.

Secret

And of course, you can use Sherlock to shop, get news, translate words, and even look up and check your stocks. You will also find that you can download channels for new Sherlock searches.

Once you get used to Sherlock as the way you look for things, you may never dial up a search page in Safari again.

A Few Last Words about Safari

When people get confused about Safari, there's really only one reason — they're over-thinking it. It is as simple as it looks. If the mouse turns into a hand, click on it. It will take you somewhere. If you want to find a bookmark, try the Bookmarks menu. You will probably find that your first instinct with Safari is the right one.

But if something seems buggy, click on the Bug icon at the upper-right corner of the Safari window and let Apple know that something isn't working the way you think it should. So, use the browser and don't be shy about expressing yourself if you see things that should be better.

Summary

For heaven's sake, is nothing safe anymore? It's dangerous in the streets and on the high-ways; and your e-mail seems to be a candidate for vandals and spammers too. But e-mail is also one of the most important methods of communication, and if you take the proper precautions, you'll be able to survive the pitfalls and get the maximum value out of it.

There is a lot more that we could say about Safari, but space constraints won't allow it. (Besides that, I'm on a very tight deadline.) So we'll stop (for now) talking about both Mail and Safari and move on to something even more interactive.

In the next chapter, I'll tell you more about online communication, in the form of instant messaging. I'll even cover Apple's iChat AV and its iSight video camera. No, I'm not going to start using smoke signals — at least not yet.

The Secrets of Instant Messaging and iChat AV

Chapter
19

♦ ♦

Secrets in This Chapter

♦ ♦

I got into instant messaging a few years ago with the advent of AOL Instant Messenger (AIM) for the Mac. And at the time, I thought it was the greatest thing since sliced bread. I came to AIM from e-mail as a way to talk to my really geeky friends. And I thought it was great how I could type to my friends in real time.

A few generations of the AIM client later, it incorporated voice chat — sort of. It didn't work all of the time, but it showed us all the promise of the Internet for more-than-text communication.

About that same time, other chat clients started to have enough features and stability to get the Mac community talking to each other. So there we all were, on different OS's with different hardware all talking to each other. And it was perfect.

Well . . okay. It wasn't perfect. If you didn't have the same version of the same kind of Chat software, it didn't work very well. Also with things like AIM you found yourself dealing with stock market reports and news tickers before you could exchange recipes with your friends in Alaska. And most of all, the programs weren't all that stable.

What we needed was something for the chat world that was more Mac-like. And almost as if Apple read our minds, when it released Jaguar we got an Apple-made chat client: iChat. And now with Panther, we've been given iChat AV (which we get into later in this chapter).

And while it's still not perfect, it's getting better all the time.

In this chapter, we will cover the three major instant messaging services and a few applications used to chat with them. Not all services offer the same features. And you might find that most of your friends are able to use one type of service only (depending on their OS, ISP, and so on).

Also, we look at how you can protect your children from potential danger while chatting on the Internet.

The Instant Messaging Subculture

Communication has become both critical and a pastime in the office and home. The need to communicate quickly is shared by all in this day and age. Luckily, there are many different ways to talk to friends and family over the Internet. Some services offer not only text chatting but also voice chat. For example, Apple's iChat AV offers voice and video-conferencing.

Communication Potential

The Internet can be thought of as a whole other universe where you can be whoever you want to be. Many life-long friendships have been made that could have only been done by instant messaging. Everyday, millions of computer users log on to chat with friends and family for virtually no cost. No expensive phone bills, no money spent on stamps, people are communicating like never before in history. While there are many advantages to communicating over the Internet, there is also a darker side.

Potential Problems

With the plethora of ways to communicate to so many people, it is easy for predators to seek out new victims. While there will never be a completely safe way to be on Internet, there are many ways to protect yourself and your children. It's not practical to say just stay out of chat rooms, because that's what makes up the majority of instant messaging activity. That would be like telling you not to put your car in drive while trying to get somewhere!

Chat rooms are virtual places where people with the same interests can talk with each other about the same topics. The trickiest part is finding the right room to be in. Most instant messaging services host their own chat rooms, however, more often than not, these chat rooms fill up with lots of people and just trying to have a conversation turns in to a nightmare!

Emoticons

The chatting community has evolved over the years and has adapted an almost new language with which to communicate. Through the use of *emoticons*, users are able to express emotions through symbols or icons. This probably started in usenet newsgroups, but has evolved into an almost standard way of showing emotions; programmers now put in actual visual icons that show up when sent.

Just as there are many languages in the real world, there are many different forms of emoticons. An example such as the happy face displayed :-) in one community on the Internet might be differently displayed as ^_^ in the next. There are even some people who actually just spell out what they are feeling, between two symbols. An example would be ::frowns:: I just got an F on my math test.

While there isn't a set way to show emotion on the Internet, I say you should express how you feel however you want. After all, you are talking to someone through emotionless text. Anyway to show emotion is fair game. Until everyone gets a Web cam and starts using videochat to talk with friends and family, we are stuck using archaic ways to express feelings.

Choosing an Instant Messaging Client

There are many different instant messaging programs, which are called *clients*, out there; most of them are free to download and use. This chapter only covers the three main instant messaging services: AOL, MSM, and Yahoo!. While there are a few more, we stick with these three because they are the most popular and you are more likely to find more people than with a lesser-known messaging service. I'll also tell you about a few different programs you can use with each of the different services. Not all programs are the same. You might find that one program is easier to understand or maybe it runs faster. It's up to you to try different programs if the one you use first just doesn't seem to fit your personal preference. The fundamental concept, however, is the same; select your buddy, type your message, and press enter. It's pretty easy.

But over the years, each messaging service has added its own special features, such as the ability to send and receive files, and the option to have a voice chat or even a videoconference. But not every service or even the programs that allow you to use the services are exactly the same. What it really comes down to in the end is using the services and programs that best fit you and your friends.

AOL

The advantage of using AOL is that it has the most subscribed members to its service, which is a community of millions of AOL users. You won't have any trouble finding a person to talk to with AOL. It's also the oldest of the three services. However, just recently with the introduction of iChat from Apple and its .Mac service, Mac users with a .Mac account can use their user name (`username@mac.com`) as a screen name on the AOL service. This is unlike the usual format of AOL screen names, which just consist of a single screen name with no suffix.

AIM & iChat AV

AIM is AOL's own version of its instant messaging client. While providing the same feature of text messaging, AIM does not offer voice or videoconference options. Oddly enough, however, the Windows version has had these features for a long time. As of the current Mac version, which is Version 4.7b, these features are still absent.

AIM (from AOL) is free to download and use. You can find AIM at `www.aim.com`. AIM supports not only the Macintosh platform but also Windows and Linux. Make sure you download the Mac OS X version to install.

iChat, on the other hand is only for Mac OS X. I put it here because iChat AV uses the AIM protocols. Just recently, Apple updated iChat to iChat AV. Many improvements were made to iChat, such as the ability to do voice chat or videoconference, and Apple has decided to start charging those who want iChat AV without upgrading to Panther. Fortunately, those who do upgrade from Jaguar to Panther receive iChat AV free with the installation. You're reading this book, so I think we can assume you're using Panther. Otherwise, you can purchase it for $29.95 at the Apple Store online (`www.apple.com/store`).

AIM works about the same way as iChat AV (covered in more depth later in this chapter) does. The basic idea of double-clicking on a buddy in your Buddy List, typing your message, and hitting the Send button still applies.

One thing you might notice that is different in iChat AV is the advertisement on the top portion of your Buddy List. Also along the bottom is a stock ticker. I'm guessing that these are relatively pointless to the average users, who are teenagers. However, adults might find these somewhat useful.

As mentioned before, .Mac users are able to use their .Mac e-mail addresses. It's important to remember when telling other AIM users about your screen name that they must use your whole .Mac e-mail address when adding you to their Buddy List. They might get a little confused as to why they are entering a full e-mail address as a screen name, because a typical AOL screen name does not end with an e-mail-like suffix.

Other than the slight interface differences, AIM works like iChat in many ways.

MSN

Moving along, you have the MSN service. MSN Messenger is similar to iChat in the fact that your screen name also indicates your e-mail address. While you can even use your .Mac e-mail address as your screen name, it's not quite the same as using it with iChat and AIM.

Like AIM, the MSN service offers both voice and video chatting among the Windows community and nothing of the sort for the rest of us. Also, like AIM, the MSN interface has advertising displayed along the bottom of the window. This doesn't cause any problems, but in a world full of advertising, any break from it is welcomed. Alas, it's not meant to be for MSN Messenger.

A positive feature of MSN Messenger is that if your buddy is currently offline, you can still double-click on his or her screen name. This brings up a dialog box stating that the current user is offline, but offers the option to e-mail that person instead. This saves time from having to go into a separate e-mail client just to send them a quick e-mail.

Overall, MSN Messenger is an okay instant messenger client for the Macintosh. It's disappointing that MSN Messenger for the Mac lacks the features of its Windows counterpart, but it stands as a solid chat client that delivers what it promises — but nothing more.

Yahoo!

The last service is the Yahoo! service. Standing in as the main application for the Yahoo! service is the Yahoo! Messenger. Yahoo! is unique in that Mac and Windows clients have many of the same capabilities. While still not treating the Macintosh community with full fairness, Yahoo! has at least come through with some of its good features.

To use Yahoo!, you will need to sign up for a free Yahoo! account. This means that when you sign up you also get a small e-mail account with the Yahoo! suffix.

Yahoo!'s method of sending and receiving messages is similar to other clients. One cool feature of the Yahoo service is that you can send messages to a offline yahoo messenger user and the other person will receive it when they log in.However, one feature that does stand out in Yahoo! is the ability to use a Web cam. Unlike MSN Messenger and AIM, Yahoo! actually allows you to connect to your friends by inviting them to view a silent view of you through a Web cam. Unlike iChat, Yahoo! doesn't disable the use of USB cameras. While this feature doesn't compare to iChat AV's ability to do live videoconferencing with sounds, this feature holds more true to the Web cam premise that often people just want to watch what you are doing and not necessarily interact with you.

Yahoo! does a good job at being an instant messaging client for the Macintosh. Yahoo! Messenger is one of the better-supported applications on the Macintosh. USB Web cam users are going to like the fact that they can use their Web cams with this program and allow their PC friends to see what they are up too. However, Yahoo! just does not match iChat AV's abilities when it comes communication via voice and videoconferencing.

Hybrid Instant Messaging Clients

Typically, all your friends and family do not share a common interest in just one instant messaging client. Worst case scenario is that you have friends on all of the three different instant messaging services that we've discussed. Acting like the hub in a communication network, you might think you will need to download and install all three of these applications, however, using a hybrid instant messaging client could cut down the need for separate applications.

The top two hybrid instant messaging clients are Fire (www.epicware.com) and Proteus (www.indigofield.com/). These powerhouse programs not only support AIM, Yahoo!, and MSN, but also other services, such as IRC (Internet Relay Chat), ICQ (I Seek You), and Jabber. This makes it easy for a person with friends on many different services to chat using only one application. Buddies will show up with an icon of the service they are on next to their screen name so you know what service they are using.

While there are many advantages to using a hybrid client such as Fire or Proteus, there are some disadvantages. Because each service has its own unique features, when using a hybrid client those special features are stripped away. That means, no more using your Web cam to show your Yahoo! buddies what you look like, and no more voice chatting with those on AIM. Yet, if chatting is all you are interested in, then using Fire or Proteus is the way to go.

> **note**
>
> The biggest disadvantage, of using clients like Fire or Proteus is that they are not supported by the folks who run the network, so the clients will stop working from time to time when the network changes its client protocols. This was most evident in the AIM versus MSIM wars a few years back.

Getting into iChat AV

So if AIM is free to download and use, and iChat AV costs $29.95 to own if you haven't updated to Jaguar, why bother with iChat AV at all? While iChat AV does cost money now, Apple is planning that the majority of their customers will upgrade to Panther.

Beyond that, iChat AV provides features that exist in iChat AV only, like the ability to do voice chats and videoconferencing if you own a FireWire Web camera.

> **insider insight**
>
> Because of the higher requirements of doing live streaming video. the CPU limits of iChat AV, and to boost the sales of Apple's own Web camera called the iSight, Apple has decided to disable the ability to use USB Web cameras.

Main Interface

Let's look at the main interface of iChat AV. Your window will look different than the one pictured here, because you have different buddies and obviously a different name. Across the top of the Buddy List window, you see your name, status, whether you are available to do a voice chat or video chat, and your icon picture (shown in Figure 19-1). Setting an away or available message is as easy as clicking on the Available menu below your name and changing it to another message. You can even customize an away message by choosing custom. Likewise, clicking on your icon in the center of the window is where your buddies' name and icon is displayed.

Add a Buddy

At the bottom, you see four buttons. One looks like a plus sign. This button is where you click to add a new person to your Buddy List. You can select from your Address Book (shown later in this chapter) or add new buddies directly in this dialog box.

Figure 19-1: The iChat window displays mainly your online and offline buddies, but you can set your away status and change your icon, also.

Select Chat Names in the Address Book

When you click on the plus symbol, you get your Address Book application.

The Address book allows you to include Chat client names for most of the major Chat clients. If the person in your Address Book has a .Mac e-mail address (that they are using for both their e-mail and iChat username), you can select the user and it will understand that the .Mac address is the iChat username (shown later in this chapter in Figure 19-27).

Start a Text Chat

The button with a capital *A* is the Start a Text Chat button. Normally this button is kind of useless because double-clicking does the same job.

However this little button does come in handy with you want to start a group chat with several persons by Command-clicking on people then pressing the button. The Phone and Camera buttons do the same thing as pressing the Phone or Camera button next to a person who is able to do voice and video chat.

Select two or more users (⌘-clicking both users) in your Buddy list and then click the Start a Text Chat button (A) to invite those participants to a multiparty text chat (shown in Figure 19-2).

Figure 19-2: As long as the users are available to you, you can add them to a text chat.

Once you've gotten the text chat going, your participants appear in a side window next to the multiple text chat window (shown in Figure 19-3). A multiple chat window always reads "Chatting with <Name of the first buddy> et al" to indicate a multiple-person chat.

Figure 19-3: Participants of a multiple person text chat see each other in the window even if they are not included in each others' Buddy Lists.

Additional people can be added to the chat by clicking on the plus button below the participants and adding them.

> **note** You can have a text chat only with multiple buddies. When you select more than one user in your Buddy list, the Start a Text Chat button (A) is the only one that isn't grayed out. Currently only the text chat option is available for multiple users.

Start an Audio Chat

When you click on the Start an Audio Chat button (phone icon) at the bottom of your Buddy List (shown in Figure 19-4) while selecting a person in your Buddy List, a new window pops up saying that it is connecting to your buddy (shown in Figure 19-5). As this is happening, your buddy gets a window telling them that they are being invited to a voice chat. They can cancel, accept, or reply with text instead of accepting.

Figure 19-4: When a person on iChat is able to do a voice or video chat, a phone or camera icon shows next to that person's screen name. Shown here is a person able to do a videoconference.

Figure 19-5: The wheel spins as we wait for a reply to hear from our friends.

When that person accepts the chat invitation, the window changes and you can now start talking (shown in Figure 19-6). The advantage of voice chatting over the Internet is that it's almost as clear as a phone call and doesn't cost anything, no matter if it's a call to your friend's house a few blocks down, to your family across the states, or to that good friend you know on the opposite side of the world.

Figure 19-6: During a voice chat you can adjust the volume of the incoming voice. You also have the option of muting your microphone by pressing the button that looks like a microphone with a slash through it.

The only requirement is that your computer is running Mac OS 10.2.5 or later and has a microphone. No need to worry about having a fast computer or fast connection to the Internet, for any G3 or better computer with a 56K modem connection can handle a voice chat just fine.

The disadvantage to voice chatting is that you are at the mercy of the Internet, which tends to be unpredictable at times. Don't be surprised if there are blips or cut outs of voice when you are talking. This, of course, can be improved with a faster connection.

If you "have what you have" for hardware and bandwidth, you can do a little detective work on your audio connection by enlisting the help of Apple's Connection Doctor, built right into iChat AV. You can select the Connection Doctor from the Audio (or Video) menu in iChat. You get a new window that displays connection information to help you figure out what the problem(s) may be (shown in Figure 19-7).

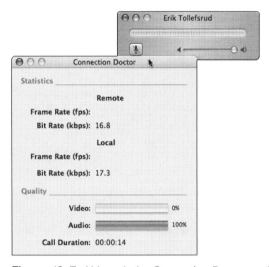

Figure 19-7: Although the Connection Doctor can't fix much, sometimes it can be useful to see where you're having the problem. If the signal and the bandwidth look good, you may need a System tune up.

Also, as of right now, even though Windows users of AIM can do voice chats with each other, iChat AV only voice chats with other iChat AV users. Another downside is that the Macintosh version of AIM doesn't even have the voice chat feature. For now, you are stuck with iChat AV and talking to Mac users only.

Start a Video Chat

Starting a video chat is a similar process. If you have a FireWire Web camera or a FireWire DV camcorder, and a 600-MHz G3 processor or better, you can start a video chat.

First, you might want to set up your Web cam preferences. Do this by selecting Preferences in the iChat application menu (⌘-comma), selecting the video camera and clicking on the Video button. You will see a similar window to the one shown in Figure 19-8 (although you may not see such a devastatingly handsome face :)).

Figure 19-8: The video preferences in iChat is where you make sure your Web cam is working, and set the microphone source if you choose to use a different microphone. You are also able to cap the bandwidth, but it's probably a good idea to leave it set to None as your video will be a lot smoother with no limit.

You can also access your video chat preferences by clicking on the Video camera next to your picture at the top of your Buddy List.

tip

What you see in the Video preferences is what others see in their windows when you start your video chat. This is the time to decide if you need to run a comb through your hair or clean up the laundry on the floor behind you.

After you're satisfied with the settings (and how you look), you can close the preferences and get back to your Buddy List.

Upon pressing the video camera icon next to your buddy's screen name or the Start a Video Chat button (shown in Figure 19-9), you are presented with a preview window as the connection is made. This way you are able to adjust your image before connecting (shown in Figure 19-10).

Figure 19-9: The icon next to the picture of your buddy lets you know what they are capable of. If there is a camera icon there, then the buddy is capable of all three kinds of chats.

Figure 19-10: To provide you with a quick glance of what you look like, a preview window displays what you look like before a connection is made with your buddy.

After starting the video chat, the message window remains the same but the message at the top changes to "Waiting for response from" to indicate that the user has received the invitation but that you are waiting for the invitation to be accepted and the connection to be established.

That invitation, if sent to you would look just like the screen in Figure 19-10, but the message at the top would show the name of the user that's initiating the video chat (shown in Figure 19-11).

Figure 19-11: When you receive an invitation you can choose Accept to start the video chat; if you haven't had a chance to run a comb through your hair yet or if you're busy, you can hit Text Reply or Decline.

Once a connection is made, the image of you shrinks to reveal your buddy with a little box with the video you are sending. Your videoconference window has two buttons on the bottom (shown in Figure 19-12). One (that looks like a microphone with a slash through it) is used to mute your microphone so no sound is sent. The other button is to enable full screen mode. Once in full screen mode, only the video of your buddy is displayed on your computer screen. To exit full screen, press the Escape key on your keyboard.

Figure 19-12: Your video chat window is clean and simple with few controls to confuse or complicate your video chatting experience.

A Great Way to Capture Your Image and Your Buddy's

Once you have yourself up or your buddy up in the window you can capture that window to use as a background or as a new picture in your Buddy List (shown later in this chapter). To do this, you just need to select Take Snapshot in the Video menu (shown in Figure 19-13).

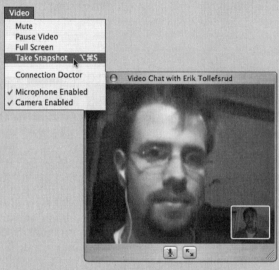

Figure 19-13: You should ask your friends before you take their snapshots and/or post them to the Internet if you want them to remain your friends.

A picture is created and placed on your desktop in TIFF format (shown in Figure 19-14) for you to use in what ever way you want.

Figure 19-14: You may want to remove the preview of yourself before you take a snapshot of your friends. If you forget you'll probably want to crop yourself out later.

Using the video chat window is as easy as talking and keeping your eyes open. It's important to remember that when you look at the screen, you are not necessarily looking at the camera. This also applies to the person who you are talking to. So, it may seem like the person you are talking to is not meeting your eyes.

Pushing Your Own Video Image Around

The little window in the videoconference of you can be moved around or even resized. In case your window is blocking something of the incoming video, drag it to a new location (shown in Figure 19-15).

Figure 19-15: Your little preview window can be resized using the slider below the image or moved around your video chat screen. In this figure, you can see it has been moved from the right corner to the left corner.

One-Way Video Chat

As much as we all would love to do nothing but video chats with everyone, Web cameras are not yet in every household. Luckily, you can start a one-way video (or audio) chat with another user. Click on the buddy you would like to make a connection with in your Buddy List. Then go up to the Buddies menu and select Invite To One-Way Video Chat (shown in Figure 19-16).

Now that we've looked at the basic features of iChat, let's look at some of the less well-known features.

Figure 19-16: Sometimes your buddies will not have a Web cam. Fortunately, this won't stop you from starting a one-way video chat, which allows your buddy to see you and talk to you, but you won't be able to see them.

Monitor Levels and Error Messages with Connection Doctor

As with the voice chat, you can diagnose your video connection issues with the Connection Doctor. Although you can't effect much change with this window, don't underestimate the importance of the Connection Doctor in iChat AV. This little window can be found under the Audio menu (or Video menu if you have a Web camera connected). This window can monitor the levels of sending and receiving video and audio data and is a helpful troubleshooting tool if a connection can not be made (shown in Figure 19-17).

Figure 19-17: The Connection Doctor can be a helpful troubleshooting tool if connections cannot be made successfully.

Rendezvous Chats

In the modern business world, information is passed almost constantly. In the old days, this meant calling your colleagues, or worse, getting up and going out of your office to find them in order to speak with them. Collaboration would be done in an all-too-often meeting that took more time to schedule than to actually have. But not anymore — thanks to instant messaging programs.

AIM, MSN, and Yahoo! do a good job at being instant messaging programs, but the problem with using them in the corporate environment is that they are too much of a hassle to set up. Everyone would have to sign up for an account and then enter everyone else's name into the Buddy List. That's too much work. Luckily, the Rendezvous technology built into OS 10.2 and higher makes iChat a great candidate for the corporate environment.

Rendezvous provides what is known as *zero-configuration networking*. What it does is recognize all rendezvous enabled computers (with the right software) on a network (that are on the same local area network) automatically. (We'll go into Rendezvous in more depth in Chapter 29.) In iChat, if your Rendezvous Buddy List doesn't show, you can find it under the Window menu. Once enabled, a new buddy window similar to your other one shows up. In this new Buddy List are all the computers that have Rendezvous iChat enabled (shown in Figure 19-18). This is great because now you can text, voice, or video chat with everyone on the network. And it's all zero-configuration, so there is no need to add people to your list.

This cuts back the need to get up from your desk to talk with other employees, or try to find them if they are not at their desk. Just leave them a quick message. A quick meeting could be held in a virtual chat room instead of around a coffee table in the break room, all thanks to iChat AV and the ease of Rendezvous technology.

Figure 19-18: The buttons not grayed out at the bottom of your Rendezvous list indicate what kinds of sessions are available to the selected user.

To start a Rendezvous text chat, follow these steps:

1. Click on the buddy you want to talk to in the Rendezvous list and then click the Start a Text Chat button (shown in Figure 19-19).

2. The iChat text window comes up and you can start typing. Hit the Return key to send your first text and invite your buddy to the chat (shown in Figure 19-20).

3. Go ahead and type away. Your buddy's and text will show up with their picture using a different colored text balloons (shown in Figure 19-21). If you want to change the fonts and colors of the text windows, please refer to iChat Messages Preferences shown in Figure 19-31 later in this chapter.

Figure 19-19: Starting a text chat in Rendezvous is the same as starting a text chat from your Buddy List.

Figure 19-20: The invitation will not be delivered until you type something and hit the Return key.

Figure 19-21: The text appears in both participant's windows each time one of the participants hits the Return key. You can also scroll up to see previous text or enlarge the window to see more of the text.

Using iChat AV for Transferring Files

Another not-so-well-known feature of iChat AV is that it is a very good tool for transferring large files over a local area network or even over the Internet.

You may (or may not) have tried to e-mail a very large file (over 5MB) to someone only to find out that that person is on dialup connection or that their service provider doesn't allow for files that large to be transferred via their e-mail servers. And even if you did manage to make it work, you may have encountered problems using the file(s) after they were e-mailed because of MIME translations and encoding issues that are inherent to e-mail protocols.

The reason for these kinds of problems is that e-mail is not the ideal protocol to send files to one another.

We Interrupt This Chapter . . .

Okay. Now I've done it. I went out on a limb and said what I thought about e-mail and attachments. You may have a problem with this, so I'll make my argument and let Pieter take your position on this.

Benjamin: E-mail was created as a way of sending and receiving text messages. Mostly it works on POP (Post Office Protocols) to ensure that text can be sent, delivered, and read by almost any e-mail client on almost any platform. That's a really great thing. And we all use e-mail a lot. But e-mail and e-mail servers were never meant to be used to send and store large file. Protocols like FTP (File Transfer Protocol) and FTP clients are what the professional world uses to transfer large files around. The reasons for this is that it's more reliable, it's done in real time, and you don't have all of the strange file corruption issues that can occur when sending files via e-mail.

Pieter: Actually, I agree with Benjamin (mark the date and time). I never send large files by e-mail because of the problems that ISPs and companies have with viruses and spam. Besides SMTP really is very poor at handling large mail attachments and mail servers are simply not designed to store large files in the mail queue. Using a .Mac account or storing files that you want to transfer on a FTP or Web site and then e-mailing a link to the file is the proper way of doing things. There are few things ruder than clogging up someone's e-mail server with a large file. Besides, many companies no longer allow their employees to receive attachments due to the threat of Trojan horse e-mails and other dangerous payloads that can infect entire networks, costing untold work hours to clean up.

The professional world uses FTP sites as a WAN (Wide Area Network) storage place to send, store, and retrieve files that other people need. In fact, during the production of this book, I moved the Word document chapters and all the figures to Wiley's FTP site each time I worked on them.

But what do you do if you don't have your own FTP site, have a file that's too large to e-mail, and still need to get it to someone? Well, if that someone is also on a Mac using iChat, you can move that file directly to them using the iChat client.

note   You can also transfer files using AIM, ICQ, MSIM, and Yahoo messenger.

Let me take you through this, step by step:

1. Select your Buddy from either the Buddy List or the Rendezvous list and initiate a text chat (shown in the previous section).
2. Before you send a file, you should use a little common sense as well as a little courtesy and ask permission from your buddy to send them a file.
3. Once you get permission from your buddy, select the Attach File option from the Edit menu (shown in Figure 19-22) and then navigate your system until you find the file you want.

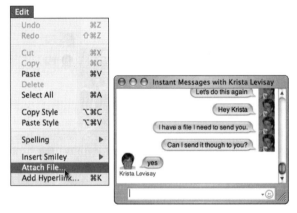

Figure 19-22: As with all things on the Internet, courtesy is key. You should also let your buddy know if the file is exceptionally large and will tie up their bandwidth for a long time before you send a file.

4. Choose the file and click the Open button to select the file for transfer. You are taken back to your chat screen where the icon of the file is shown at the left side of the text field (shown in Figure 19-23).

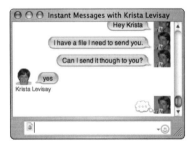

Figure 19-23: The icon in the text input field means that the file is ready to be sent. It has not been sent yet.

Another Way to Select a File to Send via iChat AV

Because you're on a Mac, you can also drag a file you want to send into the input text menu from the Finder or a Finder window.

5. Click on the Return key (on the keyboard) to start sending the file.

6. A window comes up showing the name of the file and indicating the status of the transfer process (shown in Figure 19-24).

Figure 19-24: The file shows up in the text message with an icon and the name of the file as a link that indicates that your buddy needs to click on that link.

7. The waiting message in the status window remains until your buddy clicks on the file in her text window to start the download.

8. After the transfer has been accepted, the status window changes to show a status bar, the size of the file, and the time remaining (shown in Figure 19-25).

Figure 19-25: Besides showing the status of the file you are sending, you can also choose to stop the transfer by clicking the Stop button.

9. Once the file has been transferred, the status window disappears indicating that the file has been successfully sent. You're done. Make sure you thank your buddy (shown in Figure 19-26).

Figure 19-26: A little courtesy can be helped with Apple's built-in emoticons. This is my wife, so it's appropriate for me to give her a quick wink.

Secret

Image Files Sometimes Display Rather Than Transfer

Not only is OS X graphically inclined, but so is iChat. For that reason some files transfer slightly differently than others.

When you send installer files or stuffed files that aren't graphic in nature, they transfer much the way shown in the steps above.

But files such as some PDFs, TIFFs, or JPEG files won't necessarily transfer. Instead, they may display in preview in the iChat text window itself. To actually complete a transfer, your buddy must drag the preview out of his chat window and onto his desktop.

That's all there is to transferring files via iChat AV. If I can give you any advice with this, I'd tell you to know how big your files are, know what kind of connection you and your buddy have, and be courteous with your buddies.

Tweaking Your iChat Preferences

I've decided that although we've gone through iChat AV in quite a bit of depth that you need to look at some of the settings and ancillary information that will make your iChat experience more "yours." This little section of the book is dedicated to the more advanced ins and outs of iChat.

The *main* advantage of iChat AV is that it was developed and made by Apple. This makes it extremely easy and simple to use. It's so simple and easy at times that there are a few cool features that you might not even realize.

Quickly Add Buddies from Address Book

For example, iChat makes it really simple to add your favorite buddies to your Buddy List through the help of the Address Book. Typically, the Address Book application located in your Applications folder is where you would store all your information about your buddies. Notice that in the address field, there is an entry for an AIM screen name (shown in Figure 19-27).

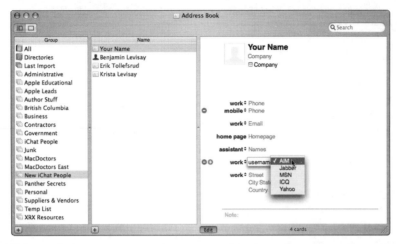

Figure 19-27: AIM is the section where AIM addresses are kept. .Mac addresses don't need to be stored in the chat field in the Address Book for iChat to understand them.

The chat name field (in the address panel) isn't just so that you can remember the person's screen name you can actually drag the address (or vCards) straight into the iChat window. Add all your buddies by pressing ⌘-A to select all your vCards and drag them into your iChat buddy window.

Use Your Picture as Your Buddy Icon

There are two ways you could add your picture to your buddy icon. The first way requires a Web camera that is compatible with iChat; the second way involves using an existing photo of yourself that is on your computer.

Notice in the upper-right corner where your icon is. If you click on that picture, a new window drops down (shown in Figure 19-28). This is where you can store many pictures for you to use as an icon. But the last item on that list is an Edit Picture button. Select this and you are presented with a window that allows you to add and edit any picture on your hard drive. Simply select the picture you want by pressing the Choose button and finding it on your hard drive. From there, you can zoom in and position the picture (shown in Figure 19-29) however you want in the window.

Figure 19-28: You can select recent pictures shown in this pull-down menu as well as the options to edit or clear those pictures.

Figure 19-29: You can also drag images into this window and then size them using the slider.

Or, if you have a Web cam, press the Take Video SnapShot button to have your camera take a quick picture of you, which you can place as your icon. It's that easy.

A Tip for Getting USB Cameras to Work with iChat AV

I know I've said that only FireWire cameras work with iChat AV, however, I'll clue you in on a secret that proves me wrong. The folks at Ecamm provide a great shareware program by the name of iChatUSBcam (www.ecamm.com/mac/ichatusbcam/) can enable the use of most USB cameras with iChat. All you need is an OS X driver for your camera — and Ecamm gives suggestions on where to find these — and in no time you'll be chatting away with your USB Web cam on iChat AV.

Animate Your Buddy Icon

If you have a Web cam, you are in luck. While using your picture as your buddy icon is a cool idea, it would be even better if you could stream a live video feed from your camera *as* your buddy icon!

Thanks to a great shareware program called iChat Streaming Icon (http:// ichat.twosailors.com/), your friends that have you in their Buddy List can see your image through your camera animated as you work in front of your computer.

If you have a slow Internet connection or older hardware, this can bog down your speed because this is a continuous stream from the camera to your computer.

Protecting Your Kids from Online Predators

Now on to a serious topic. With the growing number of people on the Internet, there is a very real threat to not only your kids, but to you too. The reality is that anyone can be whoever he or she wants to be on the Internet. This means that predators can easily trick unsuspecting people over the Internet, and I'm not talking about just child molesters. There have been reported cases of even rapists becoming close to their victims over the Internet until the time comes to strike. Fortunately, there are ways to protect yourself and your children from these types of predators.

The first and foremost thing to do is trust your instincts. Avoid anyone that you just don't trust. It just isn't worth risking your safety with someone who claims they are nice and offers things that sound too good to be true.

Also, remember that every instant messaging program comes with the ability to block other users. Don't hesitate to block someone who is being offensive or acting shady. iChat AV and other instant messaging programs enable you to block a new person's message by adding them to a list in the preferences. Although AIM and a few other clients have a warn feature, this doesn't do much other than mark a person with a percentage that eventually goes away. The warn feature should not be used as a tool to avoid potentially bad people because it does nothing to protect you from them talking to you more. The best idea is to block that person altogether.

If privacy and security matters most to you, most instant messaging programs come with the ability to block everyone and accept only the desired people that you enter. This way you are invisible to everyone except the people you wish to talk to (shown in Figure 19-30).

Figure 19-30: Shown here in the iChat AV preferences, you are able to block everyone except the people you authorize. While this example just shows iChat AV, other IM clients have this ability too.

If you are a parent that is worried about who your children are talking to online, there is a feature in iChat and in the other instant messaging services that allows you to record all chat sessions. This feature is turned off by default in iChat AV. Turn it on in the iChat preferences under the Messages section. You can choose what folder you would like to save the chat sessions in (shown in Figure 19-31).

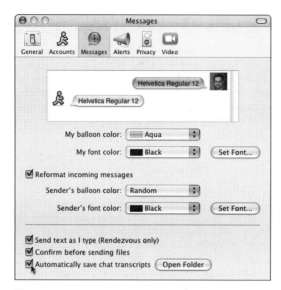

Figure 19-31: iChat does not record text conversations by default, but you can turn this feature on in the iChat Preferences.

Remember that no matter how many software/firewall-type programs or procedures you put into effect, you are never going to be completely safe. The best way you are going to be able to keep safe on the Internet is to watch what you are getting into. Never completely trust someone on the Internet, because nothing is stopping someone from saying that they really are your best friend.

Summary

Instant messaging has become a very popular way of communicating over the Internet. With advancements in technology, communication is moving from text messages to full-blown voice and video conversations.

In this chapter, we looked at some different chat services and chat clients.

We also took a good look at iChat AV and all of its capabilities. After reading this chapter, you should have no trouble getting the most out of iChat AV.

Whether at work or at home, instant messaging can be used for fun and profit. So use this technology, but be wary of online predators by blocking everyone except your buddies. Chatting online should be a fun experience. AIM, MSN, and Yahoo! are just a few choices of programs that will get you up and chatting on the Internet with friends and family around the world.

Using .Mac and Your iDisk

Chapter
20

♦ ♦

Secrets in This Chapter

♦ ♦

What's in an e-mail address? Does it really make a difference if the domain is aol.com, msn.com, or earthlink.net? Well, let me amend that: To some people, anything with the letters *a-o-l* in them is a badge of dishonor. But for the rest of us who don't really regard those things as anything more than some letters we have to make sure are appended to the end of our username, it is nothing to fret over — once the arcane characters are committed to memory, of course.

However, when Apple first introduced iTools as a free set of Web services, one particular address imparted an air of exclusivity. When you tell everyone your e-mail is your-name@mac.com, it carries a lot more prestige than, to be blunt, yourname@aol.com.

But iTools was a lot more than mac.com. It also included the ability to make your personal home page, send and receive greeting cards, and store up to 20MB worth of files on an online iDisk.

Not that 20MB is much, but it's okay for family photos and smaller documents and such, and your Quicken and QuickBooks financial files, to name a few possibilities.

Best of all, it was free as a perk of paying for an upgrade to Apple's then new OS. But all good things come to an end, and no doubt Apple's bean counters decided that receiving money for paid services was better than spending money to manage free services. And thus was begat .Mac (as you see in Figure 20-1).

Figure 20-1: In all its glory, a recent iteration of .Mac and the services it offers.

In moving from free to paid, Apple expanded the list of features and included a free backup utility, a copy of Virex, a well-known virus protection application, and an expanded version of iDisk, boosted to 100MB.

> **tip**
>
> If you dig online storage, you can buy some more, up to 1GB worth. Apple's .Mac Web site has the particulars. Such a deal!

Dissecting .Mac

I didn't write this chapter to get involved in the politics of Apple charging for a service that was once free. It's not that I am reluctant to get into a good debate, but I'm here to help you get the best value out of .Mac. It's up to you to decide whether you need it.

Instead, Pieter, our friendly, neighborhood technical editor — threatens to chime in a bit later in this chapter.

The Nuts and Bolts of .Mac

So the first thing I'm going to do is review the features of the current version. But be fore-warned that the feature set is always changing, and Apple is constantly packing on extras to make .Mac a better value for the money. So please don't complain if I missed something. I'd be surprised if I didn't. I'd much prefer that you send me your cards and letters on other subjects.

All right, here's the short list of what .Mac offers, circa early 2004:

- ◆ **Exclusive mac.com e-mail account:** This may be the deal-maker for some of you. Having that e-mail address gives you something Windows doesn't have. You can use it with most any ISP.

> **note**
>
> You can't use your AOL or MSN software to reach your mac.com e-mail account, because of their proprietary systems; but you can arrange to have those messages for-warded, or you can access the account via your Web browser, using the WebMail feature. What's more, you can buy extra e-mail addresses if you need them for home or office.

- ◆ **iDisk:** This may be the best feature of all. When you subscribe, you get 100MB of storage space for your stuff (more if you are willing to pay extra). You can use it for transferring large files to your friends and clients, backup storage, and other stuff. It's not platform-specific; so, if you do have a Windows friend who needs a file, they can, as you'll learn later on in this chapter, access your iDisk too. (The process is a little more complicated with Windows than on your Mac.)
- ◆ **Virus software:** The latest version of McAfee's Virex is offered for free download. Even though Mac viruses are nowhere near as ubiquitous as on that other plat-form, they still occur from time to time, so you'll want to be protected.

◆ **Backup software:** Apple's Backup can be used to save your files to your iDisk, or to a CD or DVD. It may not be quite as flexible as such programs as Dantz Retrospect, which supports lots of storage devices, including tape drives, but if you use your Mac at home or with a small business, it may be more than sufficient to make sure you are protected in case something happens to your original files.

◆ **HomePage Web site:** For a personal page, a place to share family photos, newsletters, or even your resume, this is an ideal and simple way to make a site. Apple's HomePage builder gets the job done in just a few minutes, and soon you're up and running.

> **note**
>
> All right, there's some fine print in all this: HomePage is, as the name implies, a personal site. It's not really suited for business use and certainly you can't use it if you order up a custom domain name, such as macsalesandservice.com or some such.

◆ **iCards:** Yes indeed, send a greeting card to your friends and business associates via .Mac (see Figure 20-2). You have a choice of existing artwork, or you can easily upload your own and use the simple tools to customize the message the way you want. Hey, maybe even Hallmark will like your work so much, they'll come calling with a job offer. Or maybe not, but it's fun to try.

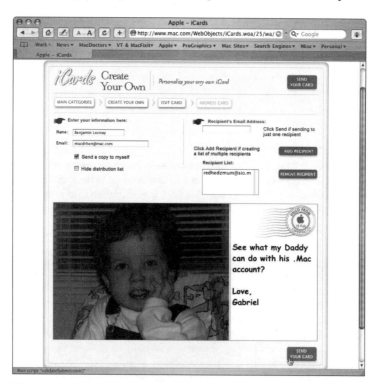

Figure 20-2: Fun and frolic with a genuine .Mac greeting card.

- ◆ **iCal and iSync support:** This partly repeats a previously listed item, but you can also use iSync to synchronize your contacts with your cell phone and handheld, assuming both support Bluetooth or USB hookups (or both if you're really lucky).
- ◆ **.Mac online bookmarks:** You've spent months or years building up a set of bookmarks on your Mac, and down you've got all that stuff set up in Safari. From news sites, to your favorite online stores and maybe a few Mac sites, everything is organized just right. But you have both a desktop and a laptop Mac, or you want to get those bookmarks to be available on your office Mac. (This feature doesn't work under Windows, sorry folks!) With .Mac Bookmarks, plus Safari and iSync, you can do the impossible and that is to synchronize your bookmarks among all these computers. I'll tell you how later on in this chapter.
- ◆ **??????:** Apple calls it ".Mac exclusives," but since I can't tell you what they will be when you read this book, you'll have to check for yourself. In the past, these special perks have included free compression software from Aladdin Systems, publisher of StuffIt, free games, online tutorials for Mac OS X, product discounts and other stuff, which probably depends on the member renewal rate that month over at .Mac.

caution Having your own virtual hard drive on the Internet can be a great convenience, but it also has some risks, one of which is security. So if you have documents you want to keep private, keep them out of the Public folder, a location that makes them available to anyone on the Internet. Also, you can turn on password protection, although I have to admit the protection level isn't super robust and you may want to supplement it. But I'll get into that in more detail a little later in this chapter.

Joining .Mac

If you're ready to explore the possibilities, don't feel you have to shell out 100 bucks right away. Apple will give you 60 days to decide if .Mac is your cup of tea.

You get your first crack at .Mac when you set up your new Mac or Mac OS X. But don't feel that you are being coerced to make a decision. It doesn't matter if it's now or later. But if you decide that you want to give it a whirl, here's the simplest way:

1. Launch System Preferences and click on the .Mac pane.

note If you're already online, you can simply point your browser to www.mac.com, and, on the .Mac home page, click the Sign Up for a Free Trial link.

2. Click Sign Up, which launches your default Web browser.

3. Fill in your name, address, and other requested information (shown in Figure 20-3).

note Bear in mind that things change rapidly over at .Mac, so if the signup screen you see is a little different from this one, don't freak or write me nasty letters. It's Apple's fault, not mine.

.mac   Sign up for a 60 day free trial

Please provide the following information to sign up for a .Mac 60 trial account.
.Mac is available to those who are 13 years of age or older.

Personal Information

First Name
Yelnick

Last Name
McWowa

Current Email Address
yelnick@yoyoyoyoyo.com

Country
United States

Select your preferred language for communications
English

Password

Member Name and .Mac Mail Address (3-20 characters)
yelnickman   @mac.com
Your member name becomes the unique part of your .Mac Mail address as
well as your HomePage URL. You cannot change your member name after
your account is established.

Password (6-32 characters)
••••••

Password (confirm)
••••••

Verification Information

This is required to reset your password should you forget it.

Date of Birth
January (01)   10

Password Question (e.g. What is my mother's maiden name?)
What is my cat's name?

Password Answer (e.g. Smith)
Sassy

Referral Information

Referral Program (optional)
If you were referred by a .Mac member, please enter his or her full .Mac email address below (ie .steve@mac.com).

macdrben@mac.com

Additional Information

☑ I acknowledge that I must accept the Terms and Conditions to get my free .Mac trial, and so by checking this box, I acknowledge and accept
the Terms and Conditions. The personal information that I provide when signing up for my 60 day .Mac trial will only be used to inform me how I can
get the most out of .Mac during my trial period, and to remind me when my trial period is going to end, and from time to time inform me about
great .Mac offerings in the future. The free trial program is not subject to Apple's Privacy Policy.

What is your level of experience with Macs?
Choose...

Continue

Figure 20-3: Here's the fast track to a simple .Mac signup.

4. You will be asked to give yourself a username, which is of course, the name that will precede your mac.com address. It would be nice to be able to get the name you really want, but common names are pretty much taken. I tried to get benjamin@mac.com within an hour after the original iTools service was announced, and I was unsuccessful. No doubt Apple's employees all got there ahead, and there was never any home for steve@mac.com. I finally settled for macdrben@ mac.com. But if you are willing to be patient, and want to try a few alternatives, I'm sure you'll find something that works.

Now that wasn't so hard, right? Once you set up your trial membership, you'll get your address plus 20MB storage on iDisk. If you like what you see and want to go the whole hog, you can give Apple your billing information and get set up at any time.

note   If you miss the 60-day trial membership deadline, no fear. You should be able to reclaim your mac.com address even a few weeks or months later. If you need more .mac addresses on your account for the rest of the clan, it's $10 per account per year.

One thing that you should think about with regards to the trial account is that you may get busy and use your .Mac account for things like e-mailing, your iChat AV account, or your user ID for the iTunes Music Store. And at the end of 60 days you may find that you have entrenched yourself in an identity that you use for enough other services that it's difficult to disentangle yourself.

So, think it through as you use your trial .Mac account. Don't send an e-mail to 100 of your closest friends to show them you have a new e-mail address. You may find that some of them update their address books and continue to send e-mail to you at your .Mac account after the 60-day trial period.

Using Your iDisk

If you're running Panther, Apple has made your iDisk so transparent and so convenient that it may seem strange that there's anything secret about it. But a few features aren't quite front and center, and took a while to detect.

So in this section, I'll show you how you can make your iDisk do lots of things you didn't expect, and even appear on a Windows PC (running XP or later).

Sharing Your iDisk

Here's the dilemma: Your iDisk has lots of files you need to provide links for, so visitors can reach them via a browser rather than mess with file sharing techniques, which can get particularly troublesome and unreliable under Windows. Perhaps you want to send a URL to friend or colleague so they can access a file via a browser. Well, I have put on my Sherlock Holmes hat and done a little sleuthing; and my trusty magnifying glass has found an answer for you.

You see, your iDisk can be accessed if you know the exact URL and you do a little preparation; and that may get a little complicated when you need to access a specific folder.

Here's a method that you can use to get to what links to use. But first, you need to know that some folders just won't allow this sort of access, and no Unix Terminal tricks will work. (At least that's what they tell me; so write me if you manage the trick.)

To begin, you have to share your stuff. To do that, simply follow these steps:

1. Go to www.mac.com and click on HomePage.
2. When you're there, simply click the File Sharing option among the list of theme categories.
3. Click on a theme for your My iDisk, which brings up the iDisk File Sharing Web interface (shown in Figure 20-4).
4. In order to give a description of the library, click on the Edit button at the upper-right corner of the screen. On the next page, you have two fields that can be changed: Your name and the description of the files.

All done? Click the Publish icon to activate the site.

Figure 20-4: It's not my dark mood that encouraged me to make this choice. I just like gray textures.

note

It's important to note that only files that you have stored in your Public folder of your iDisk can be shared with the public. You have to upload those files to the iDisk before you do anything else.

Secret

Protecting Your .Mac Site

I just want to emphasize this point: Your Public folder can be accessed by anyone with Internet access, even if you password-protected the folder. And if you protect your site, the Public folder can still be accessed by others, so you have to use the .Mac preference panel or iDisk Utility to protect the folder. I know that's confusing, but that's Apple.

Anyway, here's what to do with your Web page and the public folder once it's published:

1. On the .Mac Web site, click HomePage in the menu bar on the page.
2. Click on Protect This Site. Should you have more than one site, you will be able to select the one you want to protect from the Sites listing and then select Edit.

3. Click the check box labeled, coincidentally, On, and enter a password in the entry field. I won't belabor the point about choosing a strong password, because I cover that stuff in the networking chapters. Let me just say that you should try a mix of upper- and lowercase letters and numbers, so they can't be easily guessed. Don't forget to write down the password, just in case your mind, like mine, doesn't like to remember complicated sequences. Only my tech editor, Pieter, can manage that task.

4. Once your password has been selected, click Apply Changes to make it happen.

Anything else? Yes, if your intended recipients are Windows users, be sure any documents you provide are properly named. That means, for example, that a Word document would be called, for example, poetry.doc, and all that stuff. Otherwise, they simply won't know how to access the file. Fortunately, some programs are smart enough to save files in a way that a Windows operating system can understand.

We Interrupt This Chapter . . .

Pieter: I'd like to chime on with my take on .Mac. All right, in my not-so-humble opinion, .Mac is one of those things that you will either love or hate. I like the idea of being able to easily upload and share files from a easily accessible site and the ease with which it allows you to share information, such as your calendar, and to access your stored information from just about anywhere.

The downsides of course are a fairly high price, $100 per year, the fact that only Macs and now PCs running Windows XP can easily access your files on iDisk, and the lack of really good security when uploading and downloading files if you don't have a Mac. Also, Apple has built the iSync software to work with its applications only, so you cannot easily share this information between Macs and PCs.

I like the idea of backing up your data to a system that is accessible from all over. However, it still makes me nervous when folks are backing up critical information, like their Quicken data, to iDisk, as there is the possibility of that data being read by folks that you would rather not have access to it.

Benjamin: Well, you can always password protect your Public folder and post valuable files as encrypted disk images. The feature is available in Apple's Disk Utility.

Pieter: Point taken. If you feel you can afford it, .Mac offers a lot of great features in a well-integrated suite. If you are working in an all-Mac environment or working with just a few PCs, then the limitations of .Mac will not really affect you. However if you need to share files and information with a variety of operating systems, then you might find that .Mac is not quite right for you, unless you want to go through the drudgery of making those disk image files.

Panther's iDisk Access Tricks

Your .Mac membership (or prospective membership) becomes even better integrated in Mac OS 10.3 Panther. Not only do you have the ability to bring up your iDisk quickly (if you haven't opted to leave a copy on your desktop, which we'll talk about later), but you can easily get to other iDisks as well.

Here's a roundup of the techniques:

✦ To bring up your iDisk from your trusty keyboard (or untrusty, if you've poured a little too much java and Diet Coke on it over the years), use ⌘-Shift-I.

✦ Use the My iDisk command from the iDisk submenu in Panther's Go menu to bring up your iDisk.

✦ If you want to access someone else's iDisk, you can pick either Other User's iDisk (see Figure 20-5) or Other User's Public Folder. For the first, you need to know the member's name and password. (Let's assume they are giving you the password voluntarily.)

Figure 20-5: Type the user's name and password to connect to their iDisk.

---

note

If someone has password-protected their Public folder, you'll need to use the Other User's iDisk command instead, so you can enter the proper password to open the door. This is the method if you are going to mount the iDisk Public folder on the desktop via the Finder. If you connect via a browser, you have to use both the username and password.

Mounting an iDisk Without Panther

If a fellow Mac user isn't lucky enough to use Panther, they aren't cut out of the loop.

Mounting iDisks in Pre-Panther OS X Systems

If the other Mac user is running Mac OS 10.1 or 10.2 or one of the derivatives, there are two simple ways to get to your iDisk.

All that's necessary is to select Connect To Server from the Finder's Go menu and, once it's there (see Figure 20-6), enter the following in the Server text field: `http://idisk.mac.com/`*memberid*`-Public` (The word *memberid* is the .Mac address).

In the event the folder is protected by a password, you'll have to enter the username (again, sigh!) and password in a prompt. Either way, it'll appear as a special iDisk icon on your desktop and/or in the Finder windows.

Figure 20-6: You have to enter a few bits of information to bring up your friend's Public folder.

Mounting an iDisk in Classic

What's more, even Mac OS 9 users can get in on the act. I mean, if a Windows user can get there, Apple really had no choice. In any case, the process is similar to file sharing and involves the following steps:

1. Go to the Apple menu and select the famous (or infamous) Chooser.
2. Select AppleShare (shown in Figure 20-7).

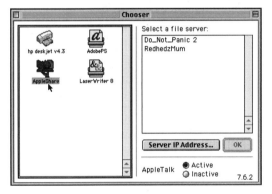

Figure 20-7: Yes, none other than the Chooser for your viewing pleasure.

3. Click the Server IP Address button and enter `idisk.mac.com`.
4. Now click Connect, which produces a prompt for the username and password. No password? No problem. Just leave the password field blank.
5. Click Connect. I know, this feels a little redundant, but I don't write the user interfaces, I just try to make sense of them.
6. On the next screen, click the name of your friend's iDisk's Public folder, and then OK.

Naming Conventions and Your iDisk

All right, you read that you can create files under Mac OS X containing up to 256 characters. But when you are typing the name of your file on iDisk, you get an error saying that the name is too long, yet the same filename works great in Mac OS X.

Why do you have to endure such aggravation? Why can't life be simple?

Well, the problem is that on iDisk filenames are limited to a maximum of 31 characters. Part of the reason is that they need to be accessible to users of older Mac OS operating systems that do not support the extended filenames. Such is backwards compatibility.

Accessing Your iDisk via Windows

All right, it's a lot more fun to do it from a Mac, but, let's face it, you may have to call up your iDisk from a Windows PC from time to time, or give access to a Windows user.

Apple is realistic enough to enable you to get there from most any Windows PC through a fairly simple process; well, as simple as it gets on the other side of the computing aisles.

If you are running Windows XP, you'll find the process is the easiest of all. Just download the iDisk Utility (shown in Figure 20-8) from the .Mac Web site. You'll find it behind the iDisk icon.

Figure 20-8: The Windows iDisk Utility is just that, a utility — not a compromise.

Once you've downloaded it and set it up, the rest of the process is butter smooth:

Launch the application, and pick your poison. The options are clear, iDisk and Public Folder. Click the icon you want and enter the login information.

Now there is actually one feature the Windows version lacks, and that's the ability to password-protect your Public folder. See they do have a reason to switch to a Mac.

As to users of older Windows operating systems, the situation is not quite as seamless. Here's what I mean:

♦ **Windows 98:** To get to the Public folder, open My Computer. Now double-click on the icon labeled Web Folders and then double-click Add Web Folder. Now you just have to enter that handy-dandy iDisk access URL: `http://idisk.mac.com/memberid-Public?`). All right, it really wasn't that bad.

♦ **Windows 2000:** Welcome to the land of interface inconsistencies. To open the Public folder: Open My Computer. Okay, it seems similar. The next step, though, is to choose Map Network Drive from the Tools menu, and choose Web Folder or FTP site. Once you've done that, choose this location to add: `http://idisk.mac.com/memberid-Public?`. Usually when I want a map, it's to avoid getting lost on the highway, but that's me.

Secret

Creating a Local Copy of Your iDisk

If you have a slow Internet connection and you're tired of having to wait for things to upload or download, or if you just want access to your iDisk without any delay at all, Panther gives you a cool new option. You can actually have the contents mirrored right on your Mac's hard drive, and synchronized with the online version whenever you're online; it'll even be done in the background so your Mac doesn't hang up waiting for the process to complete.

The biggest benefit is the fact that performance is as good as your hard drive, none of the annoying waits to download a file or back up some data. (But remember, the files still have to be synchronized with your iDisk at .Mac when you get online again.)

Here's how it's done:

1. Launch System Preferences, and click on the .Mac preference panel.
2. Now click the iDisk button (see Figure 20-9), and select Create a local copy of Your iDisk.

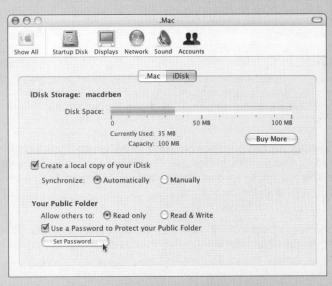

Figure 20-9: You can set most of your iDisk options here.

The first time you do this, you'll see a prompt that says the contents of your iDisk are being transferred. You've got to be online for this to happen, and with a bandwidth-challenged dialup connection, it can take hours to complete, the first time at least. After that, your online connection is only tied up long enough to store the changes.

Other Cool Stuff to Do with .Mac

This chapter wouldn't be complete until I tell you about all the other coolest stuff you can do with your .Mac account.

To get started, I'll tell you about a feature that was added right when I was in the middle of this chapter. Now why do they do that?

Using .Mac Bookmarks

Here's Apple's smart solution to the eternal dilemma of having all your bookmarks out of sync. With .Mac Bookmarks, you can have the same carefully chosen list on all the Macs you use.

In addition to your .Mac membership, of course, there are just two additional ingredients in this stew and that's the Safari browser and iSync 1.1 or later.

> **note** iSync does what the name implies, and that is to match up your contact lists, iCal calendars, and bookmarks among the appropriate products, such as other Macs. Contacts can also be synced with cell phones and handhelds. You'll learn more about this no-fuss, intuitive application in Chapter 16. Here I'm only going to try to get one part of your busy life organized. (The rest will come.)

Here's the simple technique to get those bookmarks to match up. (It seems almost too easy, doesn't it?):

1. First launch iSync and click the icon labeled .Mac (naturally).
2. The first time you launch the iSync, you need to register your Mac with the program.
3. In order to include a Mac in the synchronization scheme, you'll need to register all the other Macs you're using. Once they are registered, they'll show up in the All Registered Computers panel (shown in Figure 20-10).

> **note** When you sync for the first time, don't forget to check whether you want to merge your various Safari bookmarks, or have one set become the master for updating on the other Macs. This process, by the way, should make your Windows-using friends jealous, assuming they are hip to the possibilities.

4. When you're all set, click Sync. Over the next few moments, you see a progress display in the iSync window (shown in Figure 20-11).

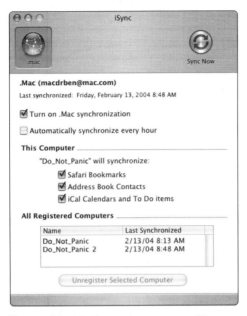

Figure 20-10: First make sure your Macs are all registered in iSync.

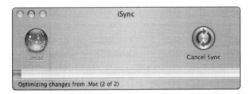

Figure 20-11: As the progress bar moves across iSync, your data is being synchronized with your .Mac account.

5. After iSync has done its thing, you have to login to your .Mac account via a browser. Clicking on the Bookmarks link opens a Welcome to .Mac Bookmarks screen. This is where Apple tells you a little about using .Mac Bookmarks.

6. When you've read your fill on this screen, click the Open Bookmarks button and your bookmarks are now available to you (as shown in Figure 20-12).

If you have followed all of these steps and you don't see your bookmarks, then you should click on the Preferences icon in the Bookmarks window. This gives you your online options as well as the option to Turn on .Mac Bookmarks Synchronization (shown in Figure 20-13).

Figure 20-12: Aren't my bookmarks tidy?

Figure 20-13: The Synchronization option is set to On by default.

That's all there is to it.

.Mac Addresses

If you've done a good job with iSync in the previous section, you will also have synchronized your address book with your .Mac account. If you haven't, repeat all the steps in the previous section taking care to set the Address in the iSync application. Then, instead of clicking on the Bookmarks icon in your main .Mac screen, click on the Addresses.

If you did it all right, you see your address. And if you didn't, you'll have to click on the Preferences button in the address screen (in .Mac) and click on the Turn on .Mac Address Book Synchronization option (shown in Figure 20-14).

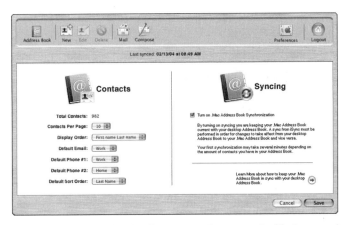

Figure 20-14: This is also the screen where you decide how to view your address in the browser.

And More

.Mac includes some other great offers that change from time to time. Some of these, like the free online training in the .Mac Learning center, enhance your .Mac experience. Some of the options utilities, like the Virus software or the Backup software, are intended to give you some added security. Some of these are standard, unchanging features and some of these are special offers that change over time.

The features of your .Mac account can be seen in the main navigation panel of your .Mac screen (shown in Figure 20-15). The special offers that change are best tracked in the What's New section of the .Mac screen (shown in Figure 20-16).

This doesn't mean that you shouldn't look at the rest of the screen. Apple tries to get your attention by highlighting features in the main body of the screen. And if you missed it, don't worry. Apple will probably send you an e-mail to let you know about new stuff.

Figure 20-15: This is the core of your .Mac functionality. Get to know these.

Figure 20-16: Some of these offers are for free software and some are for discounts.

The Learning Center May Be the Reason to Purchase .Mac

If you are a brand new Mac or OS X user, the files at the learning center may be just the ticket. I know it doesn't sound all that exciting, but the goal here is to get the most out of your Mac. And these can really help you.

These are not boring help files. Nor are they just for .Mac services. There is training for the OS itself as well as for the iLife applications. They are excellent instruction that you'd pay hundreds of dollars per course to take at a computer instruction center. They are a great value-added feature of a .Mac account.

I went through the iMovie training prior to doing the iMovie chapter in this book just to bring myself up to speed.

Extending the Power of .Mac E-Mail

Once you've set up your .Mac account, no doubt you're ready to tell your friends, contacts, and anyone else who'll listen about your new digs.

One of the simplest ways to get this done is to use an iCard to let them in on the fun.

caution

But before I tell you all the things you can do with your .Mac e-mail service, I'd like to talk to you about a common misconception about .Mac.

.Mac isn't an ISP. What this means is that if you want to join and use the service, you have to sign up with an ISP. Remember, too, the limitations of AOL and MSN when it comes to lack of support for third-party mail systems. But if you can live with WebMail, this may only be a small inconvenience. Otherwise, it'll work with any ISP that uses standard POP or IMAP e-mail protocols. That gives you a choice of thousands.

note

One really inexpensive way to get connected is with a Juno or NetZero account. At $9.95, these are among the best bargains on the Internet. The services have some limits (such as having to pay for live technical support), but they may be worth the sacrifice if all you need is a single address and a solid connection with access numbers liberally sprinkled throughout the United States. I cover these and other online options in more detail in Chapter 17.

Here are some of the most commonly used .Mac e-mail features:

- **Store your .Mac e-mail.** When you sign up for a trial account, you receive only 5MB of storage space. This expands to 15MB when you opt for the whole megillah. If that's not enough for you, you can upgrade to a larger mailbox, like upgrading your iDisk storage space, for an additional fee at the .Mac Web site. You can also order up to ten additional addresses for $10 per new e-mail address per year.
- **Forward messages automatically.** If you'd prefer to have your .Mac mail sent to another address (say to an AOL or MSN account because you aren't in tune with WebMail), this feature is available as part of your WebMail settings (shown in Figure 20-17). You can also leave an away message in case you got a big enough tax refund to support that long-postponed trip to Maui.
- **Check your other e-mail.** As you just saw, you can also set your WebMail preferences to retrieve e-mails from another POP-enabled e-mail server by importing them into your .Mac account. This is a boon for travelers, especially if you can get online, but not with your regular ISP.

Figure 20-17: Use this preference page to forward messages, buy more storage space, and set up other preferences.

◆ **Make it your permanent address.** Lots of Mac users jump from one ISP to another, and have to go through the drudgery of sending change-of-address notices. This is particularly true if you've finally had the good fortune to move from a dialup connection to broadband — a move I heartily recommend, if you can find one with good technical support (not always a certainty). Because your mac.com address follows you wherever you go (with the AOL and MSN limitations cited previously), you don't have to fret over having to make your friends remember a new address.

Your .Mac E-Mail Address Includes Spam Filtering

Did you know that Apple has spam filters in place at .Mac? It's not widely advertised, but it's true. I got the information right from the mother ship. However, Apple is coy about the type of filtering and its strength. I have heard reports of some folks being unable to send legitimate e-mail as a result, but it doesn't happen too often. The nice thing about the feature is that it's all done behind the scenes, seamlessly, and fewer messages will pollute your Junk folder under Mac OS X Mail.

This may be one strong argument in favor of a mac.com address, aside from the prestigious name of course.

A Tale of Lost Access

My client was frustrated. He'd been trying to send e-mail via his mac.com account for days, without success. Finally, he called up the resident genius at a local Apple store, and was told to change his outgoing e-mail server to that of his ISP, rather than the one normally used for .Mac, smtp.mac.com.

Surprise, surprise, it worked! The mail went through without a hiccup.

Strange as it seems, I use the same broadband ISP and never had a problem. Finally, I asked someone in authority from Apple to explain, and this is the answer they gave me:

"The reason that this guy can't use .Mac's SMTP server is that his ISP is blocking the SMTP port globally for all of their ISP customers. This is an increasingly common practice and it's fine to be able to use their SMTP server to send mail (depending on the configuration, users may also have to enter their username and password for their SMTP settings)."

Now why would an ISP block the SMTP port for third-party servers? Spam. Relaying messages from server to server is a common technique to spread junk mail while hiding its source; so, it makes sense that many of these services are cracking down. If it happens to you, just change the outgoing server to the one used by your ISP (in the SMTP section of your Accounts preferences). This will have no impact whatever on your ability to get your mac.com mail; nor will it change the return address your recipients use.

And now you know!

Secret

Setting Pictures in Your .Mac E-Mail

When you get a message from someone, do you ever wonder what he or she looks like, or would you rather not know. Well, if you can stand looking at your mug in the mirror every morning, maybe you do want to add a picture with your mac.com messages. Or maybe you'll share a family photo, so the focus isn't on you directly.

To add a picture with your mac.com messages, you can do the following:

1. First log in to .Mac, go to the WebMail page, and click Preferences.

2. On the preferences page, click on the Choose File button under Step 1 (shown in Figure 20-18).

3. Now, click on the Browse button to select the proper photo to include with your mail messages. (The usual place for such things is the Pictures folder on your Mac's hard drive.)

4. After you have selected the picture that sets you or your family off in the most complimentary fashion, click on Upload. You should then be returned to the Preferences page where you click on Save to make sure that .Mac remembers your choice.

continues

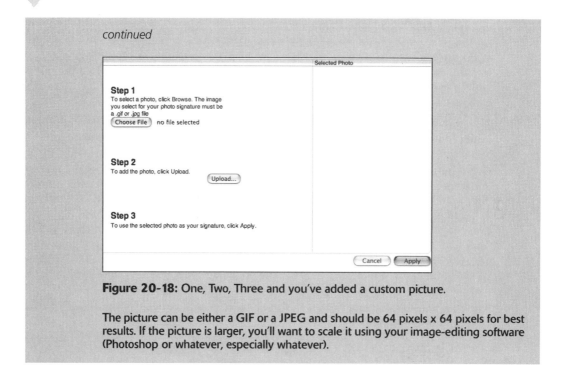

continued

Figure 20-18: One, Two, Three and you've added a custom picture.

The picture can be either a GIF or a JPEG and should be 64 pixels x 64 pixels for best results. If the picture is larger, you'll want to scale it using your image-editing software (Photoshop or whatever, especially whatever).

Summary

All right, so maybe you don't want to pay for another e-mail address, even if it's the famous mac.com. On the other hand, the other features of .Mac, such as the online storage, virus software, and all the rest, might be immensely appealing. If you have comments or questions about it, just write me at macdrben@mac.com.

In the next chapter, we'll look at the other end of a Web site, the cold, hard details of how you can build your own. But, as you'll see from that chapter, they aren't all that cold or hard, if you use one of those fast builder-upper tools to get the job done. There will even be a section on harnessing the power of Apple's HomePage, which makes a great segue from this chapter.

A Crash Course on Building Your Own Web Site

Chapter
21

♦ ♦

Secrets in This Chapter

♦ ♦

Your Mac is not just a tool to access the Internet. Although you probably bought your Mac to, among other things, access the Internet, you aren't relegated to simply accessing the words and images of others. You can build and share your own Web pages full of your own ideas and images.

Putting up your own Web page has become increasingly easier. In the past, a Web page was hard-coded into a text file and uploaded to a server. You no longer need to know the architecture of a Hyper Text Markup Language (HTML) document or structure of a Web site to create your own online presence. Now, software programs are used to visually create a Web page without typing one line of code.

I'm not going to go into a great deal of depth about Web site construction. And I'm not going to talk overly much about design or service providers. If you're interested in this subject, there are lot of good books on the market that will help you bring your inner Webmaster to the surface. Instead, in this chapter, I talk about two programs (as well as using .Mac) that make it easy to create a Web page, and one other way that doesn't require software at all to create a Web page in 15 minutes flat. No joke!

Don't be afraid of this process. It's not too much for you to get into. Hey . . . you're on a Mac. You're supposed to be using it to express yourself.

The New Ways to Build a Web Site

Web pages used to be coded (typed in) almost exclusively in a descriptive language called HTML, which stands for Hypertext Markup Language. While being a very simple and easy-to-understand language, the majority of computer users just don't have time or don't want to learn a computer language to display a little information and a few photos of their family. This is where a WYSIWYG program helps.

note   Wait a second, WYSI-Wha?? WYSIWYG (pronounced wizzy-wig) stands for *What You See Is What You Get*. This means that instead of typing HTML code to create a green background for your Web page, you would select the color green from a fill color palette and place it as your background in a computer program. So, simply put, what you see as your background in the program you use to create your Web site is what you will get when you upload it to the server. This cuts out the need to learn computer syntax, and makes it easier to pick up a program and learn it quickly.

Later on in this chapter, we're going to look at a few excellent professional WYSIWYG programs: GoLive by Adobe and Dreamweaver by Macromedia. They both are a part of their own suite of programs that help in aiding the design and deployment of a Web site. Adobe sells the Adobe CS suite of applications that includes Illustrator for vector design, Photoshop for bitmap editing, and Image Ready, which makes it easy to create animated gifs for button rollovers.

Macromedia provides similar programs in their Macromedia Studio MX. At the heart of the suite is Flash. Flash has been around for some time on the Internet, but it wasn't until recently that it has become almost a standard part of almost every Web page. (More about this later.) Macromedia Studio also includes other programs aimed at helping you produce topnotch Web sites, such as Freehand, which is much like Illustrator; Fireworks, which is used to optimize bitmap pictures and create animated GIFs; and, finally, Dreamweaver to bring everything together to generate your Web site.

Both Dreamweaver and GoLive cost hundreds of dollars, which most home users are not ready to spend to just create a basic Web page. Luckily, and oddly enough, the Web can help you build a Web page. If you are a .Mac subscriber (which I recommend), building and customizing a simple Web page is fast and easy through the .Mac Web interface.

Using .Mac to Create a Simple Web Page

I know that .Mac has its very own chapter in this book (Chapter 20), but it has its place here too. In fact, I think it's fair to say if you're a novice user that wants to get a personal Web site up on the Web, there is no easer way to do it than with a .Mac account.

Here's How

The basic process for creating a Web page through .Mac is threefold: choose a template, edit the text and photos, and then publish the Web page to the Internet. It's pretty simple. Let's walk through the steps visually.

Apple has provided many great-looking, ready-made, templates that can be used as a starting point in building a Web site. Not only are there many themes to choose from, but also there are different styles for your different needs. For example, a teacher might want to choose a Homework template to show what homework is due for his or her students. Those templates would be found under the Educational tab when choosing a theme. There are general-purpose themes and others for special days like holidays (shown in Figure 21-1).

Figure 21-1: Apple offers some great-looking templates for many occasions. Everything from fun holiday themes to templates for teachers can be found under specific tabs.

After you have selected a template, you can edit the content of the page by clicking the Edit button at the top of the page. Add a fun title and your own pictures. Remember that some templates are better suited for other content. For example, you wouldn't want to choose a File Sharing template if you want to display pictures.

One of the best parts about using a template is that you don't have to think too hard about what you want to say in a certain field. For example, when filling out a resume, the template suggests what should go in each field (as seen in Figure 21-2).

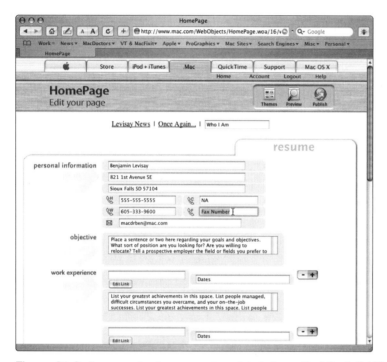

Figure 21-2: An example of a resume template being edited. Each field has a suggestion of what text to be filled in, however it can be used for anything you want.

After you finish editing your content, go back up to the top of the page and press the Publish button. Remember that any fields you have left unedited will retain the suggested text comments. Obviously, you won't want a text field to be saying "Insert Text Here", so it's a good idea to just add something or delete the suggested text so it doesn't show up when published to the Web.

When you press the Publish button it will display the address of your newly made Web page. You might want to write this address down just for reference, however you can later find out the address by going back to the homepage of your .Mac account and selecting the page from the list of Web pages you've created.

Another good idea to do after you've created a few single Web pages with templates is to create a site menu Web page. You can find a few site menu templates in the same place as the other templates. The difference between the site menu template and the other templates is that the site menu will bring all the other Web pages you've made together.

A Web site is pleasing to be at when navigating is easy to do. You wouldn't want to spend a lot of time trying to figure out how to view the other pages on the site; it just wouldn't be worth your time. What the site menu template will do will look at the Web pages you have already made and create links to them. That way your user can easily get to each of your pages from that one main page.

Using iLife to Publish to Your .Mac Account

Okay. This isn't so much a secret as a new feature of Panther and the new iLife programs.

If you have a .Mac account and are using iPhoto and iMovie, you will see features inside those programs to upload your pictures and movie clips (respectively) to your .Mac account after choosing templates from within the programs themselves.

These integrated online publishing features make Panther, your .Mac account, and your new iLife programs the fastest way to share your stuff with the rest of the world via the World Wide Web.

Where Your .Mac Pages Are Kept

The templates provided to a .Mac user are all good. And there are a decent number of them, but you have to expect that you may find other .Mac users whose pages look a lot like yours. So if you're the kind of person that doesn't like to own a car or wear the same clothes as anyone else, my guess is that you won't be happy with Apple's .Mac templates.

Fortunately for you, you're not bound by the templates just because you want to use your .Mac account to publish your files. If you decide to invest in more professional Web authoring software, you can create and upload your images to the Sites folder in your iDisk (shown in Figure 21-3). From there your files can be accessed via your home page address: http://homepage.mac.com/<username>/<webpagename.html>.

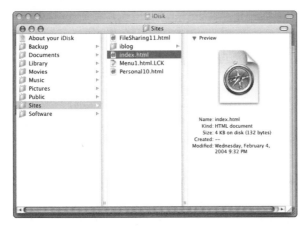

Figure 21-3: The Sites folder is where you would keep your entire site if you want. If you want to use Apple's templates, you may want to put your images and film clips in the Pictures folder and the Movies folder (respectively) to take advantage of Apple's HomePage features.

And because you're running your Mac in Panther, it's possible to create a local copy of your iDisk on your desktop. That will allow you to work on your .Mac HomePage Web site without having to wait to copy files up to the Internet.

> **note** When modifying Web files on your desktop, you're working on a copy of your iDisk; you will have to wait until your iDisk is completely synchronized with your local copy until your Web pages can be viewed by others.

I talk more to you about publishing your files to your iDisk and other places later on in this chapter.

Other Web Service Providers

It should be mentioned that .Mac isn't the only online service that allows you to create your own Web site with templates. Two other very popular sites are Earthlink and AOL. Both of these services allow you create little Web sites if you are a member of their services. Like .Mac, you create your Web site by filling out and editing templates.

AOL isn't like Earthlink in that AOL is more like a portal service or shopping mall rather then a true Internet service provider (ISP). With Earthlink, you don't have to start up a program to connect to the Internet like you do with AOL. It's a pretty good service for those that don't poke around on the net that much, but most of us would rather feel more free rather then feeling tied down or on a ball and chain with a particular program.

Migrating to Professional Web Software

Using .Mac is a great way to create a fast and simple Web page, however, some people and businesses need more power and more flexibility when creating Web pages. And as I said before, using ready-made templates doesn't always cut it, especially in the professional world. With .Mac templates, you choose to make the background look a certain way, or add a text field where one is needed. This is where professional Web software would be the right tool.

As mentioned before, Dreamweaver and GoLive are two the best tools on the market for delivering great looking Web sites. Both programs do similar things, yet because they integrate so tightly with the other programs in their suite, each of them have to do things that the other does not.

Adobe GoLive

GoLive is Adobe's powerhouse Web application. It was originally made by a company named CyberStudio and then bought by Adobe. And when it first came out, it was the best WYSIWIG Web site editor on the market. It sells, by itself, for about $400. You can find out more about it on Adobe's Web site (www.adobe.com/products/golive/main.html).

And before we get too far into this, I should admit that it's the one that I use and prefer. And unless you're a professional Web developer I would probably recommend this product over its main competitor, Macromedia's Dreamweaver (which we will cover in the next section).

We Interrupt This Chapter . . .

The shoot out between GoLive and Dreamweaver is a hotly contested issue. Fortunately for you, Pieter has different thoughts on this that I do. So, you'll get to see two perspectives.

Benjamin: The reason that I like Adobe's GoLive is that it fits so tightly with the other Adobe products in its Creative Suite. Unless Web development is your full-time gig, you won't miss some of the things that Dreamweaver can do that GoLive doesn't do as well. And no matter what level of Web site creation you are in, you are most likely using Adobe Photoshop or Photoshop Elements. And if you're slightly more advanced, you're probably using at least one of the Acrobat versions as well. The ability of GoLive to utilize and leverage data with and from those applications alone is why I would recommend GoLive over Dreamweaver. And if you work in the print world with programs like Illustrator and/or InDesign, then choosing GoLive is a no-brainer.

Pieter: For me Dreamweaver is a better fit because it is tightly integrated with Flash and Cold Fusion. Because I like my sites to have lots of scripting and some snazzy Flash animation, I want a tool that can work closely with my scripting tools and with the animation creation software that I use. Wickedly cool Flash animations allow you to create Web sites that really stand out. Dreamweaver has all these options and more; it really does an excellent job of supporting all sorts of scripting. The tight linkage between Dreamweaver and Cold Fusion makes the integration of Cold Fusion scripts into my Web sites very simple. Additionally, it, like GoLive, is tightly integrated into the many graphics tools produced by Macromedia, including one of my favorites, FreeHand.

While GoLive has a relatively steep learning curve (like Photoshop), just about anyone can produce a basic Web site with its tools.

When you open GoLive (we are using GoLive version 7 of the Adobe CS Premier Suite), you are presented with a dialog box asking if you would like to create a new page, a new site, or open an existing site (as shown in Figure 21-4). The difference between creating a new site, as apposed to a new page, is that creating a new site will define where your home page is and all the pages that branch off from it. Creating a new page will give you just a plain HTML file that is not apart of a Web site yet.

You will be asked a few questions from the GoLive Site Wizard. Because GoLive is a professional program, it has the option of working on a Web site that is also being worked on by other Web site developers. Selecting Version Cue allows you to set up a new site that more than one developer can work on, or connect to an existing site.

Besides working on individual Web pages, both GoLive and Dreamweaver enable you to manage an entire Web site — a great feature. When working on a page you not only have the ability to drag items into a new document, but also to drag links and source information from the controlling palettes directly on the elements in the Web document itself (shown in Figure 21-5).

Figure 21-4: The first screen you will see when you start Adobe GoLive is a dialog box asking if you would like to create a new site, a new page, or open an existing site.

Figure 21-5: The source information from the Inspector palette is shown here as changed after I drag the field to the new image on the document.

GoLive is a very large and complex program; so we won't go over everything, but we will describe a little bit about the interface to get you started. On the left side (see Figure 21-5) is your tools palette. Here, you can find things like the text box tool, the picture box tool, and more.

One the right side are several additional palettes. Each of these modifies things like the color of objects, the parameters of a movie, the alignment of text and or picture boxes, and much more. They will come in handy when you want to tweak an object. Across the top is the tool bar where you can edit the size and style of text, and also change your preferences.

Secret

Looking at Your Site Graphically in GoLive

One of the really cool features of GoLive is accessed by selecting In & Out Links from under the Window menu. This brings up an In & Out Links dialog box (shown in Figure 21-6) that allows you to see how all of the HTML pages and images connect to each other.

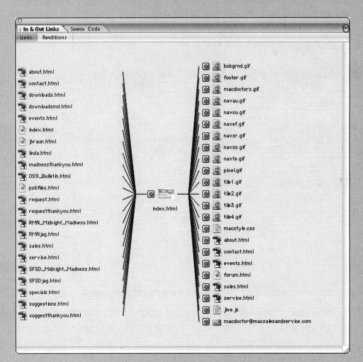

Figure 21-6: Clicking on any document in the In & Out Links dialog box will put that document at the center showing the connections to any other document (connected to it in some way).

Dreamweaver has a similar feature as part of its Web site management.

On the bottom is your site window. This window not only shows you what Web pages are in your site but also any files associated with it. Any pictures, movies, or music you will use should be put into your site window or it will not be uploaded to the server when the time comes. You can create folders in the site window to organize your material. This is not necessary, but it's probably a good idea when you have many pictures or multiple sites to work with.

And while it's handy to be able to drag from a document to the inspector to create and edit links, that's nothing compared to linking documents by dragging from the Inspector palette to a document in the Site window (shown in Figure 21-7), thus creating a new link between documents and/or images.

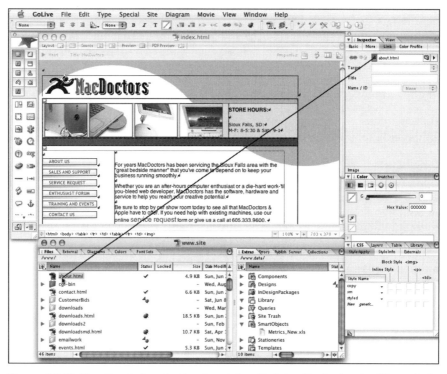

Figure 21-7: The site window (bottom) contains all of the files in the site. Through the Inspector, you can create links between documents and/or images by dragging.

---

caution

In the center of Figure 21-7 is the Web page that will be edited. Notice how it is titled as index.html. It's important that you don't change this title to anything else. The reason for this is that when you go to a Web site, your browser looks for that special index file to display first. This is typically your homepage. Some Servers look for different names, but usually, index.html will work.

Depending on your site architecture, you probably don't have to worry about the naming of all of the other pages.

After you've finished creating or editing your page in GoLive, you can open the page in a browser or you can click on the Preview tab on the page itself to see how it's going to look and behave (shown in Figure 21-8).

Figure 21-8: The Preview view is handy. And if you're in a hurry, it's a quick way to check your site. But the best thing to do is to check your site in a few browsers.

> **note**   This Preview feature is also available in Dreamweaver and many online services as well.

Another great feature of GoLive has to do with image editing. Once your images are imported and placed into your Web page, you can double-click on them to launch Photoshop or Illustrator for editing. Once saved, the images are automatically updated in your Web page. Typically, this would require you to find and open the original picture, save, and then re-import and relink the images in your Web site. This feature, however, will only work with GoLive and Photoshop.

Dreamweaver

Dreamweaver is much like GoLive in its capabilities. Dreamweaver MX is made by Macromedia and sells, by itself, for about $400. You can find out more about this product from Macromedia online (www.macromedia.com/software/dreamweaver/).

Like GoLive, Dreamweaver integrates with its other programs to be a powerhouse suite. Because Fireworks is a great program to compress and edit bitmap images, you are sure to find great ways to edit and use those digital photos on your hard drive. Where

Dreamweaver shines (as Pieter said before) is that it uses Flash for many of its built-in options, such as rollover buttons.

Flash has become so popular that most of the killer sites on the Internet rely on at least some Flash technology. Usually you see it in the typical introductory movie at the beginning of such large company sites as Ford Motors (http://ford.com/) and Coca-Cola (http://coke.com/).

Flash is a vector-based animation. It's also scriptable. This means that you can actually write animated programs like games or applications. But really, what you are doing when you are scripting is controlling the movie.

The main Dreamweaver interface kind of resembles GoLive (see Figure 21-9). On the top is your tool bar where all the objects such as text boxes and image boxes are. On the right side are your windows to hold, store, and organize your files. Along the bottom is your properties window. This is where, for example, you can edit the size, font, and color of your text.

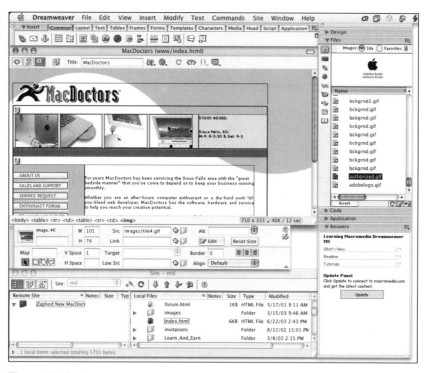

Figure 21-9: Dreamweaver looks a lot like GoLive at first. Typically, your Web page is in the center of your tool bar, your property editor, and your inspector windows.

And just like GoLive, Dreamweaver has a Site Manager, shown in Figure 21-9 at the bottom of the window. All of the site's documents, images, and assets are controlled from this indexed site. Unlike GoLive, Dreamweaver's site dialog box (shown in Figure 21-10) does the work of the In & Out links dialog box and the Site window in GoLive. But you can still drag between documents and/or images to create new connections from within the Dreamweaver site window.

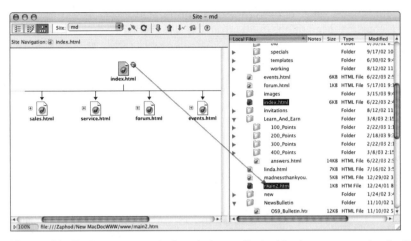

Figure 21-10: Dreamweaver's site window pulls double duty compared to its GoLive counterpart. But you can still click, drag, and drop.

Dreamweaver also has a separate Files window (shown in Figure 21-11) where other assets can be indexed by site and used in the creation of Web pages.

Figure 21-11: The separate Files window allows for not only control of a site's active digital assets, but also of the assets used to create the site, as well as the site documents themselves.

Using Contribute 2

If GoLive and Dreamweaver are just too much program or money, there are some programs and/or options that cost a little less but give more choices than normal online templates. Some of them cost very little. And some of those that cost next to nothing are truly worth what you'd pay for them.

A notable exception to that rule comes from the same people that make Dreamweaver. Yes. Macromedia makes a product for $99.00 called Contribute 2 (which you can find on Macromedia's Web site; www.macromedia.com/software/contribute/) that gives a surprising amount of user-friendly versatility to a new Web site creator.

Another great feature of Contribute 2 is that there are also .Mac templates available for Contribute 2; so, you can preserve that .Mac look but still stand apart from the regular .Mac users.

One thing that I found very easy to do with Contribute 2 was to access my .Mac account and have it copy my .Mac pages (made from the .Mac templates) to my hard drive so that I could edit and add to my home pages. This allows for more manipulation of the .Mac templates than are available via editing them through the browser.

The Contribute 2 interface (shown in Figure 21-12) is a little simpler than GoLive or Dreamweaver. You have your editing controls at the top of the browser, the page itself in the middle, and helpful tutorial links along the left side. Instead of a separate site window, you have a Pages area in the upper-left part of the screen.

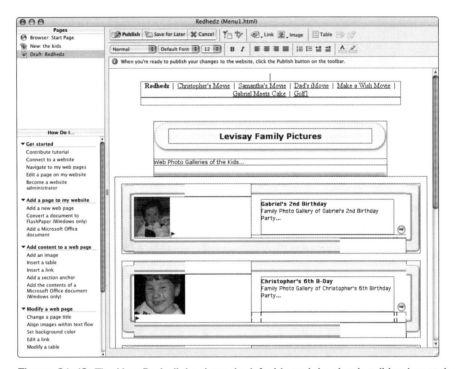

Figure 21-12: The How Do I... links along the left side and the simple editing bar at the top of the browser make Contribute 2 a perfect choice for a beginner Webmaster.

And because Contribute is more of a consumer Web editor, the good folks at Macromedia have made it easy for you to integrate it with a .Mac account. If you set your .Mac preferences up in the Contribute 2 preferences, all you have to do is hit the Publish button to upload your site directly to your iDisk. What you will get can then be seen in your browser (shown in Figure 21-13).

If there's a simpler way than that, I don't know about it.

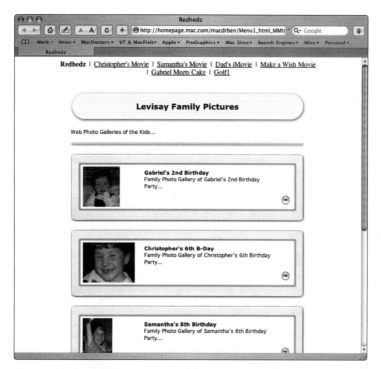

Figure 21-13: Safari shows my .Mac home page made from Contribute 2 editor and published to my iDisk by clicking on one button (Publish).

Bloggin' It

The Weblog, now shortened to the commonly used "blog," is the newest form of the electronic journal or diary. Just like the traditional diary, it's based on a timeline. Entries are made by date and then published to the Web. And because the format of these screens is pretty much static, the templates used are simple enough not to need traditional Web site editors (like those we've covered earlier in this book).

Notable Blogs and Blog Sites

The blog has become quite a phenomenon. During the 2004 Democratic primary race, John Edwards (http://blog.johnedwards2004.com/index.shtml) and John Kerry (http://blog.johnkerry.com/) used blogs very successfully (although obviously one was more successful than the other). Even the Bush/Cheney campaign found themselves "bloggin' it" (www.georgebush.com/blog/blogstuff.html).

If politics aren't your bag, you may enjoy one of the hundreds of sports blogs at `http://sportsblog.org/`. And if you're you're not looking for a specific kind of blog, you could check out `www.ibloggers.net/` or `www.blogger.com/` from among the thousands of blog site listings.

One of my own favorite blogs is Dave Barry's Unofficial Blog site (`http://davebarry.blogspot.com/`). It's always good for a chuckle during a bad day at the Mac.

Using iBlog

There are a couple of Weblog software clients for the Mac. The one that I like the best is called simply iBlog. It comes from Lifli Software (`www.lifli.com/`) and sells for $19.95 for a two-client license.

The iBlog interface and entry screen (shown in Figure 21-14) look more like an e-mail program and new message (respectively) than a Web editor.

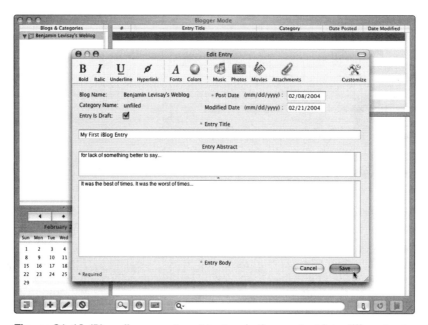

Figure 21-14: iBlog allows you to put text and other content into different categories before publishing them. The Edit Entry window gives you the same kinds of options that a good e-mail editor would give you.

After you make your iBlog entry, you save it by clicking on the Save button. But before you can publish it, you need to make a connection to where you're going to host your iBlog. One of the things that got me working with iBlog was its ability to integrate with my iLife applications as well as my .Mac account. In the preferences under the Publish option (see Figure 21-15) you can set your iBlog to be hosted and published to your iDisk (shown in Figure 21-16).

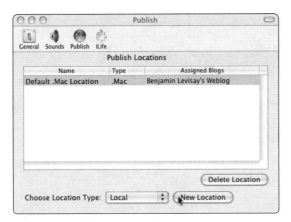

Figure 21-15: The iBlog preferences allow for multiple locations as well as the ability to choose the iDisk itself or a local copy of the iDisk.

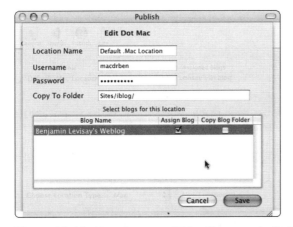

Figure 21-16: Choosing your iDisk will automatically fill in your .Mac settings for the iBlog Publish preferences.

After you set your preferences, all you have to do click on the Publish button (⌘-Shift-P) and you've shared your entry with the world (shown in Figure 21-17).

This is a very simple process, but if you find yourself having problems with using iBlog, you should know that the folks at Lifli Software did a very good job with iBlog's help (shown in Figure 21-18).

Figure 21-17: Once the iBlog entry has been made, saved, and published it will update your main iBlog page with the newest entry information.

Figure 21-18: iBlog's help uses the Macintosh Help Viewer application.

You will find that the help is complete, easy to read, and very useful. You'll probably even get some ideas on how you want to use iBlog. Kudos to Lifli on good support documentation.

Using iBlog as a Blog Reader

At the bottom-right corner of the iBlog window there are three buttons. The one that looks like a light switch (see Figure 21-19) turns the iBlog Editor into an iBlog Reader.

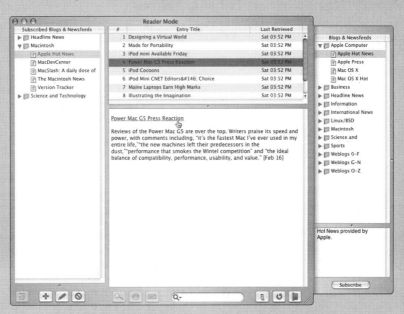

Figure 21-19: Even Apple Hot News (usually viewed online at `www.apple.com/hotnews/`) can be viewed through your iBlog reader window.

The button at the far right-bottom corner of the iBlog window shows blogs and news feeds that you can subscribe to and read through your iBlog software.

Using iBlog is a nice fast way of getting at news information without waiting for graphics and advertising to download. This is not limiting at all. The content within iBlog still contains links that will allow you to launch your browser to a Web page with more information (graphic or otherwise) than your iBlog presents.

If you're one of those people that believes that what you have to say is more important that how it looks on a Web page, then this is the way for you to get yourself online. If you also feel challenged by organizational ability, site management, and technophobia, then bloggin' was made for you.

Other Programs as HTML Editors

If you've used word processors (and some other programs) in Panther, you've probably noticed that you have the ability to save your documents as HTML pages. So the question naturally presents itself; "Can I use my word processor (or other program) as a Web site editor. The short answer is "Yes." But the idea that "results may vary" is an understatement.

AppleWorks as an HTML Editor

AppleWorks comes with iMacs, eMacs, and iBooks. And it boasts the ability to make Web site pages. Let's go through the process and see how it works.

1. I created a two-column document in AppleWorks with some text and two images (see Figure 21-20).

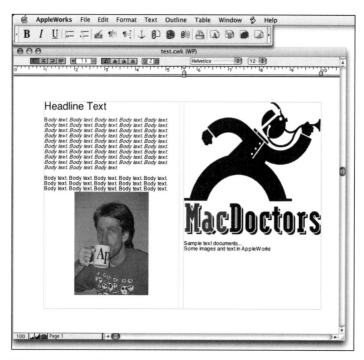

Figure 21-20: Different size text, a picture of me, and my company's logo are used in this example document saved as an AppleWorks document.

2. Choosing Save As from the File menu brings up a Save dialog box with the option to save the document in HTML format (see Figure 21-21).

Figure 21-21: Saving a document in HTML format in the AppleWorks Save dialog box automatically appends the document with the .html suffix.

3. Because there are placed graphics in the document, the page is saved as an HTML document and the graphics are named variations of the document name and placed in the same folder as the HTML document (shown in Figure 21-22).

Figure 21-22: The HTML document and the newly renamed and converted JPEG images are saved at the same level. Removing one of the images or changing the name of one of the images will cause the HTML document not to see that image.

4. Opening the new HTML document in a Web browser (see Figure 21-23) shows the content but not the same two-column formatting.

It's not bad, but it doesn't come close to the layout precision of even a basic HTML editor.

Figure 21-23: What you see is sort of what you get. Going from an AppleWorks document to HTML via AppleWorks is not a perfect transition.

Word as an HTML Editor

Microsoft Word didn't do any better than AppleWorks. The same document was successfully converted from an AppleWorks document to a Word document. And Word X does have a Save as Web Page option in the File menu (shown in Figure 21-24).

The process from here is almost the same. The Save As dialog box gives the ability to save in HTML format and the file is appended with an .html suffix.

As you can see in Figure 21-25, the text style and font remained true to the document, unlike the document converted by AppleWorks. You will also see that Word ignored the two-column layout just like AppleWorks.

Figure 21-24: Save as Web Page is an option for any document in Word X.

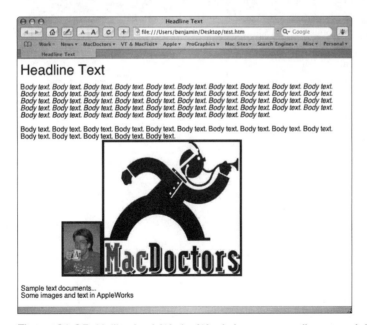

Figure 21-25: Unlike AppleWorks, Word also put an outline around the converted images in the new HTML page.

Dreamweaver Can Clean Up Word HTML Documents

If you already have HTML work done in Word and you want to "move up" to a professional Web site editor, you should consider Dreamweaver. The reason for this is that Dreamweaver has a feature to help clean up your Word documents.

After opening a Word HTML document in Dreamweaver MX, you choose the Clean UP Word HTML option from the Commands menu (shown in Figure 21-26).

Figure 21-26: Dreamweaver provides the ability to clean up the special HTML compatibility issues that Word HTML documents have.

Choosing this command brings up a Clean Up Word HTML dialog box with Basic (see Figure 21-27a) and Detailed (see Figure 21-27b) options for the clean up.

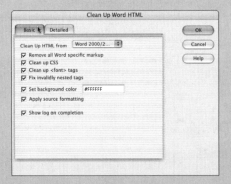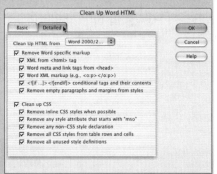

Figure 21-27: The Basic (a) clean-up options allow for fixing most problems while the Detailed (b) clean up tab gives more CSS- and Word-specific fixing options.

Getting to the Source of a Web Page

Besides seeing HTML in your Word Processor or WYSIWYG editor, you should know that there is also another layer to the Web pages themselves that can be viewed in both, as well as in a browser. I'm talking, of course, of the HTLM *source code* itself.

If you're interested in seeing the source code of an HTML document (which is a great way to learn HTML), open that page in a browser and choose the View Source option (see Figure 21-28).

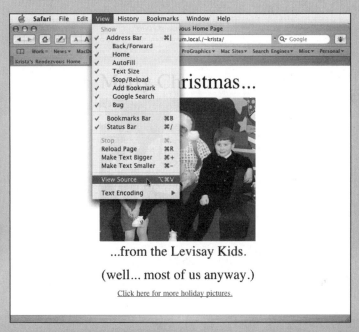

Figure 21-28: Safari's View Source option is in the View menu. Most browsers have this option.

What you will get is a new window with a lot of text (shown in Figure 21-29) that may or may not mean much to you.

continues

continued

Figure 21-29: The source information for this page shows us, among other things, that it was created in GoLive 6 and that it was built as a Rendezvous home page.

If you're ever interested, try this on your favorite page online. If you find it interesting, you may be a sleeping Webmaster.

InDesign Works with GoLive

As I said before, Adobe's Creative Suite products work very well with each other. In fact, you will see options from within these products to hand off or repurpose the document for other programs to make your work easier for you.

This book isn't really about page layout, so I won't go into too much depth, but I did want to show you that if you have a print document open in Adobe InDesign, you can choose to Package for GoLive the assets and converted styles (shown in Figure 21-30) to preserve the overall look and feel of the layout between InDesign and GoLive.

This packaging, rather than saving as, allows InDesign to be a layout program and GoLive to be a Web editor but to use each other's completed work.

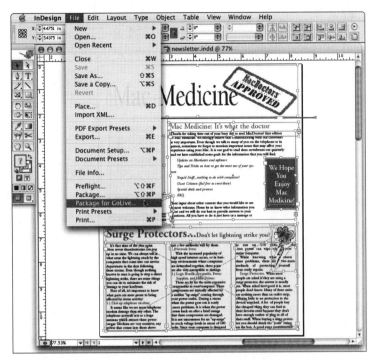

Figure 21-30: Choosing the Package for GoLive command from within InDesign CS converts the images to JPEG format and creates an XML page to be used by GoLive.

Photoshop and Photoshop Elements

I know what you're thinking. Here goes Benjamin getting into the whole world of working on your graphics for a Web site. Right? Wrong. Although it's not widely known or used, Adobe Photoshop (www.adobe.com/products/photoshop/) and Adobe Photoshop Elements (www.adobe.com/products/photoshopel/) are both Web editors, in their own limited way.

And because you probably should have at least Photoshop Elements if not Photoshop itself to do custom Web pages, I though we should include these features here.

In the File menu in Photoshop Elements you will see the Create a Web Photo Gallery command (shown in Figure 21-31).

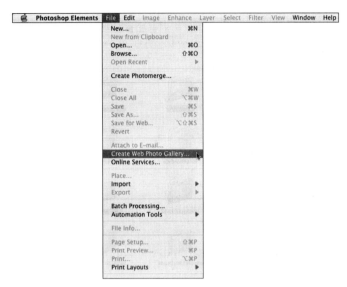

Figure 21-31: In Photoshop Elements, the Create Web Photo Gallery option is the same as the Automate submenu in the File menu in Photoshop.

This brings up the Web Photo Gallery dialog box (shown in Figure 21-32) that allows you to select a template, a location for the original files, a location for the destination files, and some other Web site options.

> **note** The source or original images do not have to be in JPEG or GIF format. Photoshop and Photoshop Elements are also image editors, so they will convert as well as size and index the images before they are put in the destination folder.

Clicking on the OK button (in the Web Photo Gallery dialog box) starts the program repurposing your images and saving them out in different sizes (depending on the Style/Template chosen) to the destination folder.

If you have quite a few images in the source folder, you may want to walk away and get a cup of coffee. If you have hundreds, you might consider taking in a movie. When it's all done, you'll find that Photoshop Elements (or Photoshop) has created HTML pages, images in an Images folder, and images in a Thumbnails folder (shown in Figure 21-33).

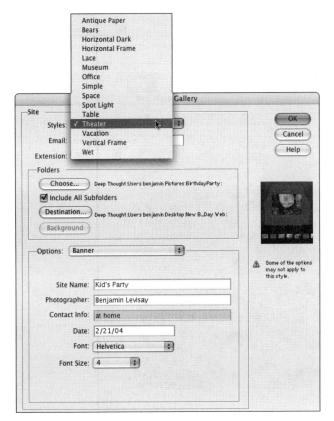

Figure 21-32: A small preview of the Style (template) choice can be seen at the right of the dialog box.

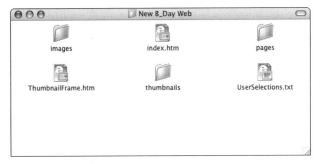

Figure 21-33: The entire site — HTML pages and images were created by Photoshop Elements.

Opening the index.html file (in this folder created by Photoshop Elements) in a browser shows a site created with frames that allow you to click on a small image in the bottom frame to see a larger version of that image in the top part of the browser window (shown in Figure 21-34).

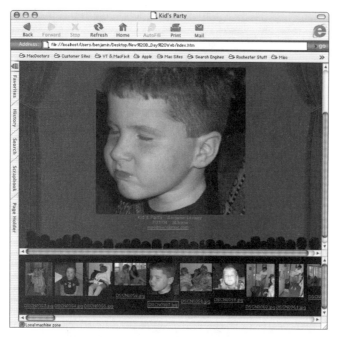

Figure 21-34: This good-looking kid is brought to you courtesy of Dad and a Web Photo Gallery created by Photoshop Elements in Microsoft Internet Explorer in OS 10.3.3.

Obviously Photoshop Element's or Photoshop's Web Photo Gallery features are best suited for just that — a Web Photo Gallery. They're not well suited for a lot of text or custom content. But if you need to quickly process four hundred images from a long trip, this is an easy way to get at and view them all.

The Process of Publishing Your Files

Creating some Web pages has been covered in this chapter, but I wanted to take some time to cover the actual publishing of your documents. We went through the iBlog publishing, but we haven't looked at the other issues in other programs.

Publishing Files via .Mac

If you haven't made a local copy of your iDisk on your computer and you want to upload your newly created files (from any editor), you will have to mount your iDisk and then copy your files to the iDisk.

To do this, get in the Finder's Go menu and select the My iDisk (⌘-Shift-I) option in the iDisk submenu (shown in Figure 21-35).

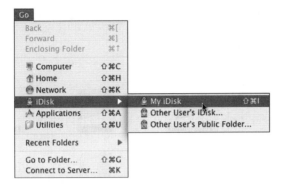

Figure 21-35: If you don't have an alias for your iDisk, Apple included this submenu connection option for you.

> **note** The Go submenu option mounts the iDisk set in your .Mac preferences. If you have more than one iDisk, you will need to use the iDisk Utility. You can download that utility from the Apple Web site at www.mac.com/1/idiskutility_download.html.

After you've mounted your iDisk, you need only open it up and drag your files to the Sites folder (shown in 21-36) in your iDisk.

Figure 21-36: A Finder copy to your iDisk Sites folder is all it takes to publish your files to your iDisk.

After that you just need to add the HTML page to your .Mac address and your site is live.

Publishing Files through Web Editors

Many of the more professional Web editors have synchronizing or FTP services built in to the program itself. For most of them, a setup assistant usually asks you to plug in the server information for your Web site (as shown in Figure 21-37).

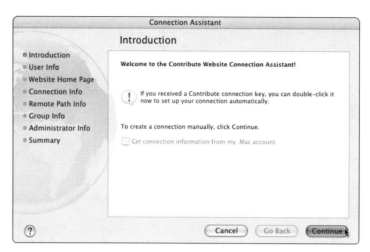

Figure 21-37: Macromedia's Contribute 2's Connection Assistant makes FTP connection to a Web site directory easier than any of the other Web editors shown in this chapter.

Some programs, like GoLive give you access to the FTP settings through the Preferences (shown in Figure 21-38).

Figure 21-38: GoLive's server publishing preferences allows for multiple sites as well as variations of the FTP protocol.

Macromedia's Dreamweaver MX combines some of the higher-level features of GoLive with the slightly friendlier interface of Contribute 2 (shown in Figure 21-39).

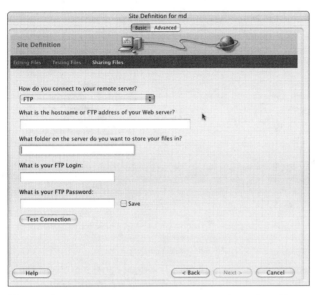

Figure 21-39: Dreamweaver MX's connection wizard is part of the Site Definition wizard.

It should be noted that both Dreamweaver and GoLive provide not only FTP service, but also synchronization between your local files (on your computer) and the published site (on the Internet server). This is a great feature because it allows you to not have to keep track of what you've done; instead, you can let the program(s) take care of updating the public (online) site.

FTPing Files via FTP Client Software

And last but not least, you can use a FTP client to publish your pages to the Internet. The idea here is that you create a site locally (on your hard drive) and then FTP those file(s) to the online folder(s) that mirror your local site using an FTP client software like Transmit from the good folks at Panic Inc (www.panic.com/transmit/) (shown in Figure 21-40).

Some FTP clients show you a preview or file type information as well as creation and modification date information. Because synchronization is not possible with an FTP client like this, you will need this info to help you figure out which file(s) are the newest ones.

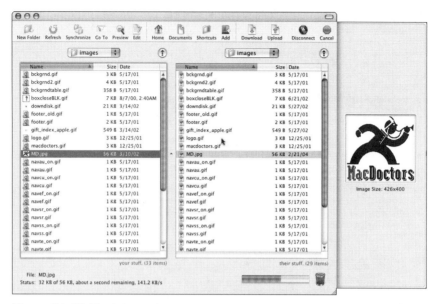

Figure 21-40: The left panel represents the local files. The right panel represents the online files. To move files up or down, click and drag them from one place to another.

Testing Your Site for Compatibility

One thing any Web designer must keep in mind is that not all Web pages are displayed the same on every computer. Not only is there the obvious PC-versus-Mac difference, but there are also compatibility issues in the browsers themselves.

Currently there are three (possibly four depending how you look at it) major browsers in use today. They are Internet Explorer, Safari, Netscape, and Mozilla.

What we mean by checking for compatibility is to preview your Web site in at least the four major browsers to make sure they look right. Sometimes the different browsers interpret HTML code differently. This is often the reason why you might see a message to the effect that "Internet Explorer needed to view this Web site." This just means that the other browsers are not able to render the page correctly. Usually when a page does not render something correctly, it's because the browser is out of date. The web standards are always changing. This means that if your browser if too old, it will not know how to display what it's being told.

Also, while you are making sure each browser displays your Web site correctly, take the time to view your Web page in many different resolutions. Set your monitor to display 640x480, 800x600, and 1024x768 resolution. You might find that a smaller resolution takes away from what you truly meant the viewers to see.

In both Adobe GoLive and Macromedia Dreamweaver, you are able to preview your Web page with different browsers that are available on your system. It's a good idea to keep at least Safari, Internet Explorer, and Mozilla on your computer system to test your Web pages, but if you are a hardcore Web designer, you might want to also download, install, and test your pages on other browsers like Opera, Omni Web, and AOL. It would also be a good idea to test your pages on Linux, Wintel, and other computer platforms.

A Few Do's and Don'ts to Web Design

Good Web design is very important to every Web page. The design of the Web page could determine how much time a person spends at your Web site. For example, if a Web site is too confusing to navigate, the user might just give up and go to a different Web site. But if you have a clear and simple layout, the user will gladly spend more time on your site, or even better, come back later. Here is a list of Do's and Don'ts when it comes to good Web design.

Do's

Make your site easy to understand. People who visit your Web site should be able to understand what it's all about from the title page. Not only that, but they should also be able to understand what the site is about just by looking at the top 25 percent of the homepage. This means putting the most important information at the top because some people have monitors that can only view 600x400 resolution.

Remember that sometimes the best use of space is to not use it at all. The fact is that if a Web site has too much going on — perhaps pictures lined up one after another with large flashing text or glowing/throbbing buttons — the viewer might feel overwhelmed. Use *white space*, that is, space without text or images, to emphasize what you are trying to communicate. This will give the viewer a chance to soak up all your information.

Update regularly. There are a few cases when updating isn't necessary, but normally when you are trying to get lots of people to view your Web site, you have a better chance of people coming back if they think or know that something has changed. There is nothing more annoying then to become attached to a Web site only to find out that it never gets updated.

Use your own original images. It's encouraged that you find, make, or use your own original images for your site. It's not necessary, but the fact is that if everyone uses the same library of images all Web sites will start looking the same.

Secret

Optimizing Your Images Is a Quick and Easy Thing to Do

Both Photoshop and Photoshop Elements have Save for Web options that enable you to play with file format and compression settings. This is a good thing to do because it saves bandwidth. Not only do your images load quicker for your viewers, but most of the time every server has a file size limit.

Make sure you know the difference between JPEG, GIF, and PNG images (covered in more depth in Chapter 9) before you start messing with your images.

Remember that each Web site is meant to serve a different purpose. Good design of an online store will look different than good design for a standard home page. Likewise, Web sites having to do with a band or something more personal tend to have a more lax standard of what is good design.

Don'ts

While good design is really in the eye of the beholder, there is almost a universal feeling of annoyance toward looping animated gif images. The worst thing you could do is place a few dozen gifs on your home page to just dance around. This is just plain annoying and typically turns any viewer off.

Don't have what is called *mystery meat navigation*. Sometimes you might see nonintuitive symbols or pictures used as links to express navigation. This is not a good idea because your viewer will be left feeling lost or wondering where they are being taken if they click on a link. This also includes rollover buttons that only display words like "Home" or "About Me" when the mouse is over the button. Again, you feel lost or like you are searching for a way out when you have mystery meat navigation.

Plagiarism is an issue on the Internet, just as it is in print. The Internet is full of copyrighted material, including words, images, music, and video, that you must acknowledge, get permission, and/or pay for when using.

If you are going to have a little music loop for background music on your site, make sure there is a way for the viewer to either turn down the volume or turn it off completely. Normally, if a song that I can't turn off is starting to get stuck in my head I find the quickest way off the site. Even if it's your favorite song, remember that it isn't going to appeal to everyone.

Introductory movies are okay in some situations. However, it's a good idea to have a way to skip the intro or a way to only see it once only. Typically, an intro movie is a little too long for the average viewer to want to sit and watch each and every time they go to your site.

Summary

While HTML is the language used to describe (or generate) Web pages in a browser, advances in technology have provided us with ever easier ways to place our own personal Web page on the Internet; you don't need to be a Webmaster to make your own Web site. All you need to know is a few good design concepts and put your ideas on the Internet for everyone to see.

Best of all, because the Web doesn't use paper or ink, if you don't get it right the first time, you can do it again without being out anything but your time.

Part V

Connection Secrets: Peripherals and Networking

Part V delves deeply into connection secrets—printing, using digital cameras and scanners, getting the most out of CD and DVD drives, hooking up your own network (yes!), and even dipping your feet (just slightly...don't worry) into the powerful world of UNIX for even more productivity. This part also contains a professional troubleshooting chapter, which could save you a great deal of time and money when things go wrong.

In This Part

Printing and Faxing

Chapter

22

♦ ♦

Secrets in This Chapter

♦ ♦

Click Print, press ⌘-P, and cross your fingers. So what's so secret about that? It's a basic function and you want to take it for granted.

And most times, you can; but what good is a printing chapter in a computer book if I don't help you figure out the exceptions. Alas, there are exceptions, and sometimes your document, if it prints, takes forever to complete the process or just doesn't look the way it should.

So why should such a basic, fundamental process be so flawed that you can't depend on it 100 percent of the time? No, it's not a conspiracy to keep book writers and support people employed helping you sidestep the landmines. You see, when there was only an Apple LaserWriter and an ImageWriter, things were very simple.

Now that you have a gazillion printers out there, with the number growing almost every day, the support issues get crazy. Each ink jet printer requires its own drivers, which are updated on a regular basis. That means loads of chances for things to go wrong.

Each time Apple updates its operating system, and that even means those minor updates that only fill a mere 40 or 50MB of disk space (yes, that's small for Mac OS X), something becomes incompatible. The printer that sings and dances under Mac OS X 10.3 may suffer arthritic pains under 10.3.1, and so it goes.

But it's not just driver updates that can drive you distraction. As you'll see in this chapter, even with the proper software, your printer may not deliver all that you expected. Before you toss it out and buy yourself something new, take stock of the situation. You will find ways to get the most out of that printer.

And if you do decide it's time to replace it, you'll learn how to set up your new printer and have it work out of the box with as little fuss as possible.

How to Handle Printing in Two Operating Systems

You've just about given the Chooser its walking papers, secure in the knowledge that Panther's simple printer setup routines will get the job done. But then you launch a Classic application and all bets are off.

Suddenly you are thrust into an uncertain universe where the laws of physics don't seem to operate, and your efforts to print a document bring uncertain results. You see, as soon as you use an older application, you must operate by Mac OS 9's rules.

And that means using the infamous Chooser (or famous Chooser if you're so inclined).

But it's not all that hard to print from the joint operating system environments. You just have to be aware that you are dealing with two different methods of setting up your printer; after that's done, the Print command will do its thing for you regardless of whether your application is Mac OS X–native or not. Here are points to keep in mind:

♦ **Install both Mac OS 9 and X drivers.** Some printer driver installers are smart about setting things up in both environments, but don't bet on it. Check the installation CD for evidence of separate installers for each operating system.

♦ **If you can, reboot under Mac OS 9 before installing Classic drivers.** Normal installers should work okay regardless of the OS you have booted, and if you have a Mac without dual boot capability, there's no choice. But if you can boot in OS 9, the installation might go better. While in theory, this shouldn't matter, theories don't always work on personal computers, regardless of operating system.

◆ **Use both the Print & Fax preference panel and the Chooser.** Because a printer is selected in one environment, doesn't mean it is set up in another. Double-check both settings to make you chose the right printer.

A Quick Way to Get to the Printer List

Secret

The print function can be flaky, even under Panther. Seems to be the nature of the beast . . . One common symptom is the loss of the ability to use a printer. So what do you do?

The first and most common remedy is to remove the printer. Not physically, but from the Printer Setup application. You can access it in several ways. Perhaps the fastest route from your application is the Print dialog box. Choose Edit Printer List from the Printer pop-up menu (shown in Figure 22-1). This beats going to the Utilities folder or opening the Print/Fax pane in System Preferences (unless no application is running of course).

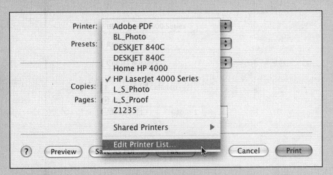

Figure 22-1: This is an alternate route to bring up the Printer Setup application.

After you've done that, click on the name of the printer that's gone astray (or wherever it went to) and click Delete. Bye-bye printer . . . well not quite.

Next, press Add, and then follow the dialog boxes (which I'll talk you through in a bit) to add your printer once again. That ought to do the trick. And if it doesn't, try reinstalling your printer software.

◆ **Try to avoid printing in both environments at the same time.** It should work, of course, but you want to be safe rather than sorry. (Feel free to substitute your favorite cliché.) Officially, the print queue is prioritized on a first-in, first-out basis. Gee, I sound like an accountant. Now if I could learn how to balance my checkbook. . . .

---

tip

This isn't a secret, but I just wanted to remind you. There is no need to fret over which environment you're in. When you jump to a Classic application, the spiffy Panther interface disappears, and is replaced by the one you knew and loved under Mac OS 9. Your Apple menu will be altered too, to one that contains the Chooser, control panels, and other stuff. Confusion is not an option.

Using the PDF Workflow

The usual way to control PDF workflow is to create a PDF Services folder in your home directory's Library folder. After you do that, you can put an alias to an application in that folder and that application will control how the PDF is handled. So, if you want to send an electronic document to a client, put an alias to your e-mail software in the PDF Services folder.

Next time you make a PDF file, it'll automatically be attached to a new message in that program, assuming it is, like Mac OS X Mail, scriptable.

Using PDF U to Print Better PDFs

Remember when you save a document or Web page as PDF, it'll normally make a file containing the entire document. But if you need just a specific page, don't fret. Like any normal printed document, you can restrict the number of pages the way you do with printed documents, on the Copies & Pages screen of your Print dialog box. Like a regular print job, only the designated pages will be included in the PDF file.

If you want to extend the power of Mac OS X's PDF print capabilities, download a utility called PDF U from If Then Software (http://www.ifthensoft.com/). What does it do? Well, to simplify the complicated, it turns on a hidden PDF Services menu that lets you customize the workflow, or how the PDF feature is handled.

Now PDF U simply lets you access this extra feature automatically, without having to create the special folder. And the prefab scripts that come with it are really useful as well.

Selecting and Setting Up a New Printer

Choices, choices . . . The old printer has had its day and now you want a new one, or you're setting up a new Mac and you want everything that goes with it to be pristine.

But how do you trudge through the quicksand of multiple choices to find the product that suits your needs? Laser printers, ink jets, bubble jets, photo printers, seven-color . . . a bewildering array of choices and nowhere to turn but to the bottle of (your headache remedy of choice here) . . . or maybe a different sort of bottle. . . .

Why should it be thus? Why can't you just open a catalog or visit a store and figure out what's the right product for your home or business?

note   If you have the right reseller, you can visit a store and get the help you need to pick out the right printer to fit your needs. If you want this, look for a reseller you can trust and then support it by purchasing your products from there. Sometimes it can be simple.

It's worse than the old days when you couldn't separate Mac models without a scorecard. Even printers from the same maker often bear model designations that make absolutely no sense in any earthly tongue.

Your Printing Hardware Options

Rather than explain why printer makes befuddle you with diversity, let me paint a clearer picture of the choices:

♦ **Laser printer:** When you and I were young(er), a laser printer was an expensive commodity. I paid $3500 for an Apple LaserWriter II NT, but today's $299 printer is faster, with superior print quality. A laser printer uses something called the electro-Xerographic process, in which an electrostatic image of the printed image is created, inked with the powdered toner, and then the image is transferred to the printed page. Consider a laser printer to be essentially half a copier, because it doesn't have a mechanism or optics to copy and then duplicate a printed page. There are multifunction devices that do it all. I'll get to those shortly.

♦ **Color laser printer:** It uses the same principle as the black-and-white laser printer, with the addition of extra toner cartridges for each of the primary colors, which consist of black, cyan, magenta, and yellow. However, many models require a separate pass to place each color on a page, which means, basically, that the print process is slower. Obviously, color models are more expensive than the black-and-whites, but these days the color models do not cost any more than noncolor lasers of a few years ago.

♦ **Ink jet printer:** Possibly the closest thing to old dot matrix printers, such printers use print heads that spray tiny droplets of ink as they travel across the page on a carriage. There are variations of the theme, bearing such trade names as bubble jet, but you get the idea.

♦ **Color ink jets — four-colors, six-colors, and whatever:** The normal version has four colors, but extras are added, the better to provide a realistic printout of a photograph. In practice, the quality of ink jets vary from model to model, even from the same manufacturer, so a great four-color printer may blow the socks off a mediocre six-color model.

I get the to whys and wherefores of selecting a printer next.

Advantages and Disadvantages

Now that you know what's out there, how do you pick the right printer. Or does it really matter so long as it runs reasonably fast and the pages don't jam?

Here are a few givens and a few personal observations on making a choice:

♦ **Get an ink jet** if you want to print color photos and graphics and don't want to spend a lot of money. Getting a color laser printer with good enough output to match even a $100 ink jet is mighty expensive, and is best left to a company's graphics department, unless you have deep pockets.

♦ **Get a laser printer** if you want to print lots of copies, don't care about color, and want to save money on consumables. Bear in mind, however, that a color laser printer can cost a lot more per page because you have four toner cartridges to buy, and each one gets used unless you stick with black.

♦ **Budget for consumables.** Ink jet cartridges can cost anywhere from $10 to $35, on average, and you'll usually need at least two every few hundred copies or so. If you print color photos, the ink will bleed you dry (financially) a lot faster because the page is filled with solid color. Figure on each printed page of text costing from a little over three cents to as much as three times that amount, depending on the model. Photos can cost 20 times more. If you opt for a laser printer, figure on spending anywhere from $50 to $250 for a toner cartridge and sometimes a drum. But you get thousands of copies for your dollars, and a per-page cost of a penny or two is quite normal.

♦ **Look seriously at a printer using four or more cartridges.** In lower cost printers, you buy one cartridge with ink for three colors. If only one color is spent, you still pay the same dollar for the other two colors you don't need. But if you get a printer with a separate ink cartridge for each color, you'll only have to replace the color that's used up.

Secret

Show Me the Money — Consumables Are It!

You see those offers for color printers that handle a dozen pages a minute or more, yet cost only $99, plus a $99 rebate. How does a company make a profit by giving things away? Is this a new economic plan we need to learn more about?

Nope. It's a plan, affectionately known as the Gillette razor approach, which is already being used in other industries. You give away the product, but charge a bundle for the things needed to make it work. So if you follow the razor metaphor, you have to keep your ink jet printer well fed with ink cartridges. Because these products can cost anywhere from $10 to $35, you can see where things add up.

If you print a lot of documents, you may find yourself spending a lot more on ink than you'd spend on gas to keep your car running. I'm serious. Are there alternatives? There are few, but there are no guarantees. Some third-party companies sell cheaper replacement cartridges, but test reports show quality isn't always as good as the real thing.

One of my clients uses bulk ink, and that seems to be okay, but you have to do a little jury-rigging to make it work. You have to refill the cartridge, giving it something like a doctor's injection. It can be messy, but it works for some.

Another problem is that some printer makers use custom chips in their cartridges, so third-party companies can't get in on the act. That, however, is the stuff of lawsuits and beyond the scope of this book.

My best suggestion is that if you intend to print a lot of copies, and can live with black and white, consider a laser printer. You still have to buy consumables, in the form of toner cartridges, or perhaps a drum. But the per page costs are much, much less. We're talking of maybe 1 or 2 cents a page compared to 3.5 to 6 cents for regular pages and up to $1.00 or more per page for photos.

Wow! I'm in the wrong business.

♦ **If you don't care about quality,** print less than 100 pages a month, and just want something that runs fast enough to make sense, go for the free or low-cost ink jet sometimes offered with the purchase of a new Mac. You won't go broke on ink cartridges.

♦ **If you do care about quality,** check the product reviews in your favorite Mac magazine or Web site. In fact, look at a PC magazine too, as most printers work in both platforms. If you visit your favorite computer dealer, expect to find printers with a special demo feature, which allows you to print a sample page. Understand that these pages are optimized to show off the printer to its best advantage, but you'll get a good indication of the quality levels you can achieve.

◆ **Choose paper wisely.** Yes, I know it's tempting to pay $2.99 at the supermarket for copier paper, and, frankly, it'll work just dandy on a laser printer. But when it comes to ink jets, text may smear, colors may look off. Ink jets are quite sensitive, and if you want the best quality prints, test different papers and see what looks best.

Fast Printer Setup Advice

Unpack it, plug it in, turn it on. Are you missing anything? Maybe. Or maybe not.

Before you conclude that I've taken leave of my senses (which goes without saying), let me clue you in on why I say such a silly thing.

As I explain in the next secret, the software for that printer may already be installed, so test it first.

Secret

Plug and Play or Plug and Pray?

Do you know that you may be able to make your new printer work just fine on your Mac without having to install new software? How can that possibly be?

Well, it seems Apple has taken a few hints from the Windows universe (yes, it does happen on occasion) and worked with manufacturers to incorporate lots of drivers for common ink jet and laser printers with Panther. And, courtesy of an open source set of printer drivers known as Gimp-Print that's part of the regular Panther installation, even many older models are supported, including products that the manufacturers themselves have long abandoned.

So, before you do install anything new, go ahead and attach the printer to your Mac or network interface. After the printer is running with ink cartridges or toner installed, open a document, go the Print dialog box, and see if the Printer is listed. If it is, take the printer through all its functions. Most ink jets will be listed, unless they are very new models.

If something doesn't work, you should go to the maker's Web site and look for a newer version. Yes, you could install the software from the CD, but it may have been sitting in the warehouse for months, which means it'll be an older version.

On the other hand, if the CD contains extra stuff, such as picture editing software, you may want to at least install that stuff.

Before you concern yourself about print drivers, though, there are a few things you should do before you begin to use your new printer. Some of this is basic, common sense stuff, and some of it may require a careful checking of the setup information the manufacturer gives you.

Don't read manuals or setup guides? Well, maybe the following will guide you:

◆ **Don't buy the cheapest printer you can find.** Printers that cost $20 are usually not worth that. You can occasionally get a deal on a $79 or $89 printer when you purchase a new computer so that, with a rebate, the printer costs you nothing. When you do this, and it doesn't work well, please keep in mind that you are probably getting what you paid for. If you don't want to be disappointed, aim a little higher in the price range. In our store, the base (low-end) model that we sell is a printer for $149.00. We do this because we don't have hassles from customers when we sell it. How much is hassle-free printing worth to you?

◆ **Don't buy the unit with the crushed box.** Even if the dealer swears the printer is okay, you have to wonder how that box got so damaged in the first place. Did the dealer play soccer with it, or did something happen during its long passage from plant to distributor to dealer? And obviously if you receive a package in this condition via a package delivery service, it may be a good idea to refuse it and ask the dealer to send a replacement. If in doubt, check with the dealer first about what to do with damaged goods.

◆ **Remove the packing stuff.** Tape, cardboard, and other inserts are put inside the printer to keep it safe and sound during its trip from plant to distributor to dealer and finally to your home or office. Most printers these days may, in fact, travel half way around the world before you've placed your order. So, open everything that can be opened to make sure there is no tape left around. If you fail to do this, the printer may jam big time before you are able to print a document.

◆ **Make sure you have the right cables.** Batteries are extra on most toys, and cables are extra on just about every printer I've used. Why? Well, one printer maker gave me what seems a logical response. Most models have at least two ports. Ink jets, for example, may have USB and parallel (for Windows PCs). Laser printers might come with USB and Ethernet. Rather than raise the cost of the printer with cables you don't need, they supply none. So, factor in $10 to $20 extra to cover the cost of a cable, if you don't have a spare. And you may want to order it at the same time unless you want to look at your printer for a week while you wait for your cable.

◆ **Use the right paper.** All right, that $2.50 package of copy paper you bought at the local supermarket may seem find and dandy, and it'll work fine on a laser printer. But ink jets are more finicky. Text may smear, graphics will look washed out, even on the models that tout lab-level photo quality. While the manufacturer's own papers may yield the best quality, I always suggest you begin with multifunction paper, which is supposed to be okay for ink jet and laser printers. If you must have real photo quality, go for the expensive stuff, but for most of your work, it's not necessary. You can use the money you save to buy more ink cartridges.

Secret

Take a Good Look at the Printer Specifications

I believe in truth in advertising and I always wondered about those incredible claims of printing speed. Can you believe, for example, that a $150 ink jet printer can print 20 pages a minute? Are advertisers just playing a numbers game?

The truth is somewhere in between, as usual. The numbers are real, but there's a fudge factor. They are rating the speed in the draft or lowest quality mode, and only counting the time from the moment the paper drops into the paper path. In fairness to HP, I've seen that they provide speed ratings for various quality modes, so you get a truer picture of how long it takes to get printed pages into your hands.

As to laser printers, there's a fudge factor there too. The manufacturer is rating how long it takes to print simple text pages, one after the other, once the first starts to feed through the printer. But with complicated pages, with a heavy dose of graphics and lots of fonts, the printer may spend long minutes processing a page before it spits it out. And it may often run in fits and starts, a page or two at a time, interrupted by a little extra time to think.

So how do you figure out which printer is fastest? The best thing to do is read the product reviews at your favorite Mac Web site or magazine. In fact, because all those printers also work under Windows, feel free to check out PC sources as well, because they actually rate far more printers, and you'll get a better idea of a model's real performance.

Also, remember that speed isn't everything, unless you really aren't picky about print quality. A slower printer that delivers better text and graphics may still be the better buy. But also pay attention to the cost per page, because you still don't want to go broke keeping it well fed.

Setting Up and Using a Printer

Before we get lost, let's take a minute to set up and use a printer. I know this sounds basic, but there are some dialog boxes that would be good to go through together.

Printer Setup

If your printer doesn't automatically configure itself, then you will have to set it up yourself. I think the best way to explain this is to go through the process with you. Here is how you would set-up a network PostScript laser printer:

1. Open up the Printer List by double-clicking the Printer Setup Utility (in the Utilities folder) or by clicking on the Set Up Printers button in the Printing pane of System Preferences.
2. Click on the Add button at the top of the Printer List.
3. The Add Printer dialog sheet drops down from the top of the Printer List window. Here you need to choose the port/protocol from the pop-up menu (shown in Figure 22-2).

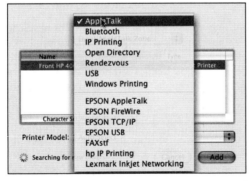

Figure 22-2: AppleTalk (which is set up to use Ethernet in the Network Preferences).

4. After a brief pause while the Printer Setup Utility looks for AppleTalk printers, you see the AppleTalk printers on your network show up in the window below the protocol selection. Choose that printer by clicking on it.

5. If it's a common printer, you should be able to choose the AutoSelect option and then click the Add button. If not, you'll have to configure the printer to the correct PPD manually. To do that you select the Other option from the Printer Model pop-up menu (shown in Figure 22-3).

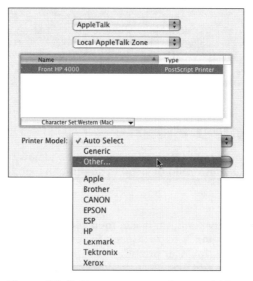

Figure 22-3: If you want to navigate quickly to the right printer drivers, you can try selecting the brand. Otherwise, you'll have to manually navigate to the right PPD by selecting Other.

> **note**
>
> There are a lot of functions available for laser printers. You can get them to do duplexing, as well as handle different paper sizes and trays. How does Mac OS X sort this all out? Or does it have a spare Ouija board on hand to divine the information?
>
> The secret lies in a little text file, known as a PPD, which is short for PostScript Printer Description. This file tells Apple's laser printer driver just what your printer can do, and it can get quite intricate. For example, in addition to special paper sizes and duplexing, it defines the various print resolutions and graphics settings that your printer can do. There are pages and pages of these definitions, all so that you can access the features your printer offers.

6. If the PPD has been loaded on your system by an installer, you have to navigate to your en.lproj folder, which is in the Resources folder in the Contents folder in the PPDs folder in the Printers folder in the Library folder on the top level of your hard drive (Hard Drive/Library/Printers/PPDs/Contents/Resources/en.lproj) (shown in Figure 22-4). When you find the correct PPD for your printer, select it and click the Choose button.

7. This takes you back to the Printer Add dialog sheet where you can see your choice listed in the Printer Model pop-up menu (shown in Figure 22-5). Click on the Add button to finish adding the printer.

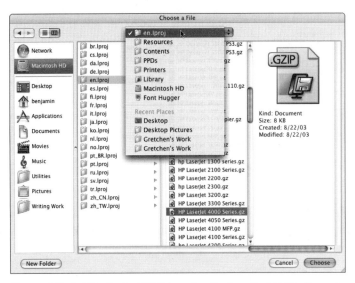

Figure 22-4: This is the OS X location for installed PPDs. If you have them stored elsewhere on your computer (copied from another computer), you have to find and then navigate to that location.

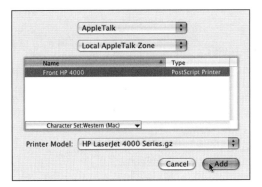

Figure 22-5: On your mark. Set. Ready. Add.

Printer Info

After you finish adding your printer, select your printer from the Printer List and choose the Show Info option. This allows you to rename and set up additional configurations for your printer.

The Name & Location Printer Info screen allows you to change the name of the printer and change the location if you have more than one zone (shown in Figure 22-6a). The Printer Model Printer Info screen allows you to change the PPD information that you previously set up (shown in Figure 22-6b). And the Installable Options Printer Into screen allow you to set optional preferences like additional trays and more RAM (shown in Figure 22-6c).

Figure 22-6: A local printer can always be modified in the Printer Info dialog boxes.

Printing, Actually

And I know that this is a radical idea, but after you set up a printer, you can actually print to it. You can see your printed jobs in both the printer queue and in the Printer List (shown in Figure 22-7).

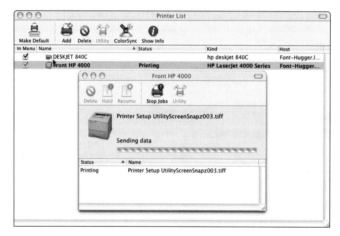

Figure 22-7: Double-clicking on the printer in the Printer List opens the selected printer's printer queue.

From the printer queue, you can stop the job, hold the job, or even delete the job.

Optimizing Printing Performance

Click-Print, and wait . . . and wait . . . and why does it take so long? You have a Mac with processor power to die for and yet the printer's light just flashes and flashes and nothing happens. What's going on here?

To be fair, sometimes a printer goes in a loop and nothing happens, but that's fodder for another section of this chapter, or rather, peerless prose. Here I just want to tell you what you need to do to make your printer sing, dance, and be merry.

Here's a list of ways to make your printer do more, separated by ink jet and laser printers because the demands are different.

Ink Jet Printers

To be blunt, although ink jets may have their own processors and memory banks, it is your Mac that does the raw number crunching. As pages slide out the tray, your Mac is doing the processing and feeding it to the printer in a language it understands.

While Mac OS X and a fast Mac can make the process happen almost invisibly in the background, this isn't always the case, especially if you're using some resource-hogging software at the same time. Panther's preemptive multitasking can do wonders, but it cannot make miracles. Something's gotta give.

Is there any solution to making your printer deliver the goods with more alacrity?

Maybe a few:

- ♦ **Take a rest.** Maybe not what your employer ordered, but you don't have to fret over reduced performance on your Mac if you're doing something else. If you are feeding a big multipage document to the trusty ink jet, see if a coffee break or lunch break is called for.

- ♦ **Recruit another Mac.** You can share your personal printer across a network; so, if you have an older Mac around that's gathering dust, see if it can serve duty as a print server or maybe, with a third-party program, as a true RIP (short for Raster Image Processor). Because most printers support Mac OS 9, you don't even have to install Panther on the older Mac if it's too slow or not compatible with OS X. That way, you don't have to fret over speed slowdowns. Unfortunately, you do run out of excuses as to why you are taking too many breaks.

- ♦ **Trade off quality with speed.** Do you just want to have a printout of an online sales receipt or a story from your favorite Web site? You just need a readable copy, so go to your printer's draft mode.

It's important to note that most ink jet printers are not PostScript printers. That is they do not rasterize the way a Raster Image Processor would) data from your files into flattened dots from different kinds of vector, raster, and type information.

If you're working with graphics programs, you may not like your printed results if you send your jobs directly to an ink jet printer out of a program like Illustrator or QuarkXPress. You may find that your type and other graphic elements look bitmapped or choppy. If this is the case, you didn't buy the wrong ink jet printer, you probably just bought the wrong kind of printer.

Using PDF to Make Your Files Print Better on Your Ink Jet Printer

Secret

If you do find that your files don't look all that good you can always try printing to PDF. You can then print the PDF file as a rasterized image directly out of Preview or Acrobat Reader.

There are some downsides to this. The color might change. And the file will be bigger and the printing time will be longer, but it's a nice free workaround if all you have is an ink jet printer.

Using Third-Party Software to Turn Your Ink Jet Printer into a PostScript Device

As I said earlier, most ink jet printers, even the high-end ones, aren't PostScript devices capable of RIPping (rastering using a Raster Image Processor) jobs the way even a simple/cheap laser printer (with PostScript support) can. The results from your printing can be bitmapped graphics and unpredictable color. But there are third-party products that can help.

One such product that I have had a lot of luck with is an OS X–friendly PostScript software package(s) from ProofMaster (www.proofmaster.net) that allows a host computer to act as the RIP mechanism that then sends the RIPped information to the ink jet printer.

The way that this works is that the printer queue is set up on the host computer. The queue is then either printed to directly (on the same Mac) or the queue is shared (via Print Sharing) across the network. Users then print to the software queue as if it were a real print device (shown in Figure 22-8). The queue, in turn, rasterizes and handles the color information and sends the information directly to the attached ink jet printer.

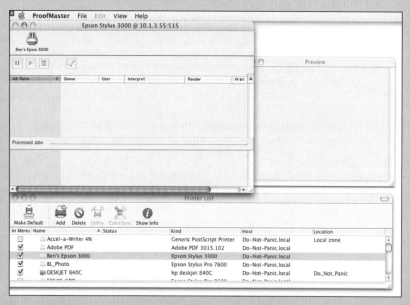

Figure 22-8: My Epson 3000 is set up with the ProofMaster software. The software queue shows as a printer choice in the Printer List.

The good news about this kind of software is that there is probably a version to suit your ink jet printer. And the results are pretty great. And if you need to have accurate, controllable color, this is really the way to go. The bad news is that this kind of software runs anywhere from $500 for a smaller printer to $3800 and more for a large format color printer. So, this kind of solution isn't for someone who wants to print out e-mail and Web pages.

And speaking of PostScript. . . .

PostScript Laser Printers

The average PostScript printer has its own computer and memory bank, so all your Mac needs to do is feed the data across the USB or Ethernet port, and the printer does its thing. After it gets to the printer, things can bog down for a variety of reasons.

Let's see what they might be:

◆ **Document is too complicated.** Too much artwork, too many fonts, all conspire to give you headaches. Before they can actually print, PostScript printers need to take all the data in your document and convert it to a form that can be imaged on paper. The more complicated the file, the longer this takes. If the processor isn't fast enough, or if memory is tight, it may take even longer, and the printer just chugs and chugs away. What to do? Use fewer fonts (multiple sizes don't count). Chapter 23 gives you some of my handy-dandy font advice based on many years of suffering through the font wars on old-fashioned typesetting machines (some of which would only manage one or two fonts at a time). You may also want to see if you can reduce the complexity of your graphics.

> **tip**
>
> If you are using a pro-grade drawing program, such as Adobe Illustrator or Macromedia FreeHand, see if you have some unneeded content on a layer that's being covered up by something visible. Unless you need it for another version of the drawing, get rid of it or flatten layers prior to printing. Also, check the corners of the page for little bits and pieces of artwork you might have forgotten about. It's easy to insert or place an image into your favorite page layout program, then crop it so you don't see the extraneous stuff.

◆ **Printer needs more RAM.** Some jobs that take forever to print. You may even get some inscrutable messages about why (such as "limitcheck"). No need for a translation book. Your printer is telling you that your document may be too complicated to process. If you can't make it simpler, turn the printer off and then on again and see if that helps. If not, check your printer's manual and see if more RAM makes sense.

> **note**
>
> Most printers PostScript laser printers can be upgraded with extra memory. When the manufacturer, such as Brother or HP, uses standard RAM that can be purchased from most computer dealers or dedicated memory suppliers, it'll be pretty cheap to double or triple the allotment. If the manufacturer (you know their names) uses some proprietary kind of RAM, you may end up spending a lot extra for the privilege, but short of buying a new printer, this may be your only option.

◆ **Printer has a slowish interface.** Some lower-cost PostScript printers have USB interfaces, and adding an Ethernet networking port may cost you $100 or lots more. Does it make sense? Well, if your Mac and the printer support the new USB 2.0 standard (which is faster than Ethernet), probably not, unless you want to share your printer across a network without using Print Sharing (covered later in this chapter). But otherwise, Ethernet support means that the data gets to the printer faster, and that can shave a few seconds off print times. Whatever it takes.

◆ **Your Mac doesn't like to share.** On the same subject, being able to share a personal printer is a great feature of Mac OS X. But don't forget that such printers often use your Mac as the brains, which means your computer's performance can suffer if the printer is working on documents from other computers on the network. If you don't want to spend a bundle on a network adapter, you might see if you can dig up a spare, older Mac and make it your print server. That way, it can chug away to its heart's content, and you don't have to give up speed, RAM, and CPU power to make it work.

note
Even if your printer doesn't come with built-in Ethernet, you may be able to get by with an adapter. Most printer makers, such as Epson, HP, and Lexmark, make their own proprietary adapters designed for easy installation; but such adapters may not work with all the printer models in the manufacturer's line. You'll want to check for compatibility. Also, don't expect the network upgrade to be cheap. They can sometimes cost over $200, a lot more than you may have paid for your printer. When you add it all up, maybe you can give up a little performance and let the thing hang out on the USB port after all.

About Shared Printers

I hate to say it, but Windows supported the idea before it turned up in Mac OS 9, and then it took a couple of releases to Mac OS X to resurrect the idea. But it doesn't matter. Being able to share a personal printer is a real plus and definitely cheaper than buying a printer with a network card — even if that printer sets you back only $50 or so, plus the rebate of course. (And isn't there always a rebate?)

Under Panther, the option is front and center in the Print & Fax preference panel (shown in Figure 22-9). Check Share My Printers With Other Computers to automatically turn on Printer Sharing in the Sharing preference panel, which is also another way to attack the problem.

note
Printer Sharing in Panther isn't a free ride. Your shared printer will only be available to Mac OS X users on your local network, or subnet if you have a large network. If you want to share with Mac OS 9 users, the USB Printer Sharing control panel must be set up on the Mac that's opening its printer to network use. However, you can also let Windows users on the network in on the fun by turning on Windows Sharing in the Sharing preference panel. But remember that your Mac must be on whenever someone else needs to use that printer.

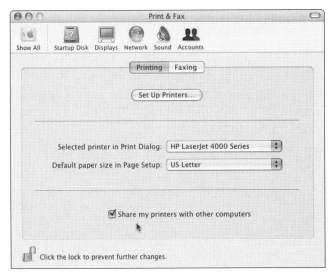

Figure 22-9: Panther finally moved the printing controls to the System Preferences.

After that's done, your Mac becomes, in effect, a printer server (although not necessarily a PostScript print server). Whenever someone on the network sends a job to you, your Mac's processor or processors go to work crunching the files to ship off to the printer. On a slower Mac, this may cause a noticeable drag in performance, and I suppose it can get irritating if the printer is getting lots of attention.

Connecting to the shared printer across the network is no big deal. The first time you do it, open the Print dialog box, and, in the Printers pop-up menu, locate the Shared Printers submenu and select the name of the printer (see Figure 22-10).

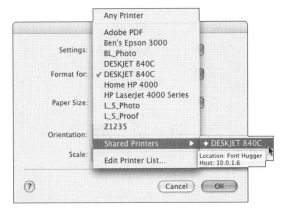

Figure 22-10: You need to select that shared printer just once for it to migrate to the top portion of the Print dialog box.

Your Mac lists only those printers that it can see on the network. Usually this is just those that are on its subnet, but it may also be those that are configured in your LDAP (Lightweight

Directory Access Protocol) profile. It's important to note, also, that you may not have access to all the printers that you can see on the network.

Now you can print to it normally, as if it were the same as any other network device. Even better, the next time you want to contact that printer, it'll be right at the top portion of the Printer pop-up menu, along with any other printer on your network.

You can see shared printers at the bottom of the Printer List (shown in Figure 22-11) by opening up the Printer Setup Utility (located in the Utilities folder in the Applications folder).

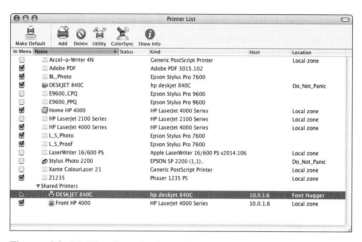

Figure 22-11: The shared printers in the Shared Printer section of the Printer List show the model, the host IP, and the location name of the computer when applicable.

Choosing the Printer Info option shows you additional information about the shared printer (shown in Figure 22-12).

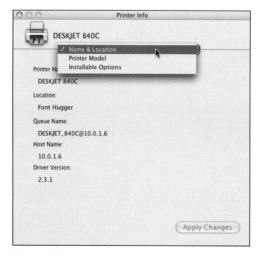

Figure 22-12: Because this is a shared printer, the options are not editable the way a local printer would be.

Printing to a Shared Printer works exactly like a regular printer. Both the queue and the Printer List indicate that the printer is in the process of printing (shown in Figure 22-13).

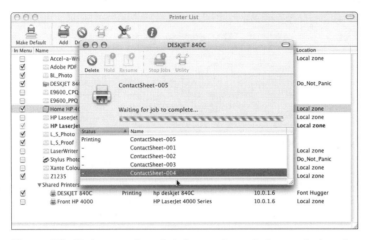

Figure 22-13: It may take a little longer, but printing works just the same with a shared printer.

Secret

Using an Airport Extreme Base Station for Print Sharing

If you're thinking of going wireless, this may be another incentive for you. The new Airport Extreme Base station has a USB port on it. That port is used to plug in a USB ink jet printer. The base station itself can be configured as the print server — effectively turning your ink jet printer into a network device.

Understanding the Print Dialog Box

The first time my tech editor looked at this line, he said, "What's the big deal? Everything is front and center. Just pop up a few menus and it's all clear as a bell."

Indeed, but why resort to guesswork, when you can read this book and find out the purpose of all those options? Besides, I have pages to fill to earn my advance.

In any case, here's a fast tour of the various options the Print dialog box affords you, other than the sharing feature, of course, which we covered in the previous section. To get going, choose Print from the File menu in almost any application, or just type ⌘-P (my preferred weapon), and you see something approaching the dialog box shown in Figure 22-14.

note

I'm covering the standard Print dialog boxes here. Some applications customize the Print dialog box in their own image and have additional options. It's not to confuse you (well, I don't think it is), but to allow you to harness that program's power, or at the very least make the dialog box longer and wider.

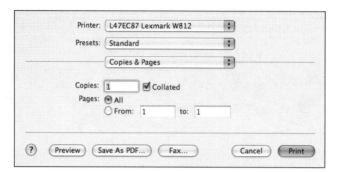

Figure 22-14: Unless the application has changed the Print dialog box substantially, here's what it normally looks like.

◆ **Printer Menu:** Select the printer you want to use in the pop-up menu. If the printer is not listed there, and it's being shared on another Mac on your network, just click on Shared Printers and choose the one you want. The Edit Printer List feature allows you to bring up the Printer Setup application to configure new models. The Check For Printer Updates feature is strictly limited to those made available via the Software Update preference panel.

◆ **Presets:** Store settings for different printers. This is dealt with in exquisite detail in the next section.

◆ **Copies & Pages:** This pop-up menu deserves a label, because you're missing out on all the custom capabilities of your printer (shown in Figure 22-15). Depending on the model you have, you'll be able to adjust print quality, color settings, printing on both sides of the paper, how error handling messages are displayed, and even if you want a cover page. Why a cover page? It helps to direct the job to a specific department in your company. There's even a prebuilt cover page labeled Confidential. I'm serious.

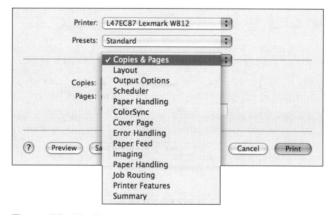

Figure 22-15: Choose your printer's special setup features in this dialog box.

◆ **Pages:** One copy or more. If you click Collated, and print several copies, all the pages are organized neatly, so you can just staple or clip each copy without having to collate the pages by yourself. You can also select individual pages to print, if you don't want to output the entire document.

◆ **Special Features:** The bottom part of the dialog box lets you see your document in Preview before you print it, or save it as a PDF or as a Fax. (We'll cover the Fax options later in this chapter.)

Saving Print Presets

With a zillion possibilities to configure your printer, do you really have to remember the one you tested and found perfect for your needs every time you want to print a document? Is there no way your Mac can do the work for you?

Now maybe you and my tech editor have memories that are perfect enough to do that. But your aging author still has to be reminded when it's time to take out the trash (not the trash on my Mac, but the trash that goes in that big, black container in the garage).

It's nice to know that Panther (as well as previous versions of OS X) has a way to do this, once you've settled on the best ways to get maximum printer performance, and here's how it's done:

1. Choose your optimum setting for your printer in the various setup dialog boxes under Print.

note It's not a bad idea to test the results, just to make sure that the printouts look all right. Just because the quality label in the settings for your ink jet say it provides the best printout doesn't mean it'll look best to you, or different from the lower-quality setting.

2. Click the Presets pop-up menu and choose Save As (shown in Figure 22-16).

Figure 22-16: Store your favorite printer settings for quick recall.

3. Give your preset a name that makes it clear when you need to figure it out later, such as Picture Perfect Photos or Low-Grade Text.
4. Click OK to store the setting. Repeat the process for all printer settings you need to preserve. From here on, whenever that preset is selected, your printer delivers exactly the quality level you choose.

Default Page Setup Settings

What does "Format for Any Printer" mean? When you click the Page Setup command, that's what the dialog box tells you, but it may not be what you need.

The short answer is that different printers support different page sizes and probably have different maximum margins. Your printer may support larger page sizes, such as tabloid or 11x17, but if you don't format for that printer, you won't be able to print that huge document, because support for larger size pages is available in specially designed printers only.

The best way around this is super simple:

1. With the Page Setup box open, select the name of your default printer from the Format For pop-up menu.
2. Click Settings and choose Save As Default, and that's all there is to it. The result will look very much like the screen shown in Figure 22-17, which displays a Lexmark wide format printer.

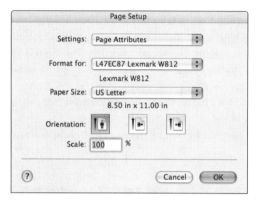

Figure 22-17: This is a default setup for a printer that can use all those large paper sizes.

> **note**
>
> The limitation of this default Page Setup scheme is that you can set it up for a single printer only. If you want to change it for a second printer, you either have to pick a new default, or just select that printer on a one-time-only basis. Fortunately, this really doesn't matter unless you have more than one printer with the capability of handling unusually large pages. Also, if you're using a page layout program, such as Adobe InDesign or QuarkXPress, you can use the printer setup features in the programs themselves, which allow you to set up as many presets as you need.

After you've got your presets and other options set, all you have to do is hit the OK button. After that, your Page Setup options are used for your jobs unless otherwise specified.

Understanding CUPS

I will avoid such obvious jokes as my cups runneth over and that sort of thing. (All right I said it anyway.) CUPS is a acronym for Common UNIX Printing System, and it is, as the name implies, an open, cross-platform printing solution that has really put Mac OS X's printing capabilities on the map.

It first premiered in Jaguar and those of you who, like me, labored with incessant, irritating, and downright slow printing performance under the original version of Mac OS X will be grateful that improvements have come fast and furious since then.

Now rather than simply fix the broken printing function of the early releases of Mac OS X, Apple simply licensed CUPS and adapted it for use in its operating system. In the old days, when Apple believed that the words "not invented here" were dirty, it would never have considered such a thing. Instead, its programmers would have attempted to develop their own system, however long it took.

Configuring CUPs via a Web Browser

Would you like to configure your Mac's printing capabilities from a Web-based interface? Do you care? Well, if you want to really explore the awesome power of what CUPS can do, just point your Web browser to `http://127.0.0.1:631/` and you'll see a result very much like the one displayed in Figure 22-18.

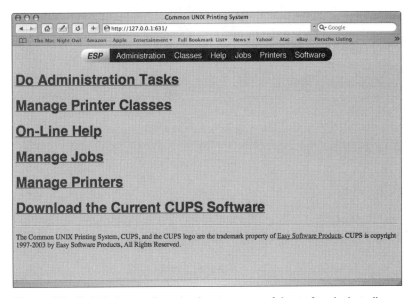

Figure 22-18: This is your introduction to a powerful set of tools that allows you to configure the guts of your Mac's printing system.

All set? You can use it to configure your printers and manage your jobs, just as you do in the standard print queue. But you can also harness some special features that aren't available anywhere else.

CUPS Basics

Once you start combing through Web pages to set up your printer, it may all seem a little complicated, but it's not. Most of the CUPS features are pretty straightforward, even if the CUPS jargon can be confusing and intimidating.

Let's start with a Printer Class. What's that? It's a little misleading, because the term isn't referring to the type of printer, but to the queue. It's actually a virtual print queue and it's used to balance print jobs across several printers. It's great for a larger business, where you may have several office laser printers, and you want to make sure that one doesn't get all the attention.

It's not even all that hard to set up. This is what I mean:

1. First, you have to establish a separate queue for each printer with your CUPS tools. To do that, open your Web browser, and as mentioned above, access the CUPS administration site at `http://127.0.0.1:631/`.

2. Click Do Administration Tasks (see Figure 22-19).

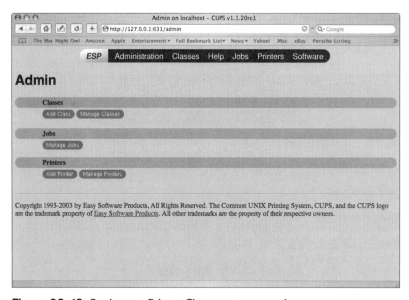

Figure 22-19: Begin your Printer Class setup process here.

3. Next click Classes, and choose Add Class. This brings up the Class administration page, which is shown in Figure 22-20.

4. Give your class a name. This should be no big deal. Let's use My_Kids_Junky_Ink_Jet_Printer_That_Just_Will_Not_Die, okay? That's a little long. But you get the idea.

> **note**
> The underlines are in the class name because UNIX doesn't dig spaces. Also, I have exaggerated a lot in Step 4. You should be specifying the location of the printer as it appears in Printer Setup, and remember that the name you give for your printer here is the one used in the queue, so don't get carried away.

5. Finished? Click Continue to produce the Class members page, which is simply a list of the printers that you have set up on your network.

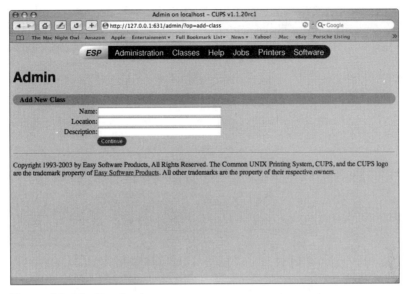

Figure 22-20: Class begins.

6. Choose one or more printers from the list and add them to the class and click Continue.

7. This produces a status page that shows if the class was added properly. If not, review your settings, or start from scratch.

8. To finalize the setup, use the Server Settings page to start up sharing in a printer class. The result is that the class you've created appears as just another printer queue in your Print dialog box. It's that simple. Behind the scenes, the jobs is spread among the printers in the class, so they all share equally in the load.

Troubleshooting Printer Problems

If you ever read the famous nineteenth-century science fiction novel, *The Invisible Man,* by H.G. Wells, you have an appreciation of what it means to click Print and see nothing. Did your job just vanish, or did Scotty, the crusty engineer from *Star Trek,* beam it up?

Fortunately, the real reasons for that and other printing ills don't lie in the science fiction world, but in the here and now.

Poor Quality Printing

The printer seems to chug away all right, but don't ask about the quality. Pages are light, smeared, or there are big splotches from one end to the other. You see your investment in buying and setting up that printer go up in smoke.

Should you just toss it away or is there a better solution?

Usually it's a matter of simple maintenance, so let's look over the possibilities and solutions.

Light Printouts

Start with the obvious for a laser printer. Make sure you didn't turn the density way down to save toner. While older printers had a knob to make this adjustment, sometimes it's done via the setup menu or as an option in the Print dialog box (usually under the Imaging category).

♦ **Toner is spent.** Whether it's 5,000 copies or 20,000 copies, the toner cartridge isn't a horn of plenty. It runs out. But you can sometimes stretch the life by removing the cartridge and gently rocking it from side to side. This redistributes the toner and you can sometimes eke out a few hundred more copies before it runs out.

♦ **Ink is running out.** Usually it's all or nothing, but with an ink jet printer, you might see gaps in the printing before the ink is gone. One quick thing to test, first, is whether the print heads are clogged. So invoke Printer Setup, select your printer, and choose Utility. This brings up the printer maker's own configuration software (shown in Figure 22-21). You can use this to clean the cartridges. It uses up a some ink, but may, if you haven't run out, give it a bit more life. But first, check the ink levels, just to be sure.

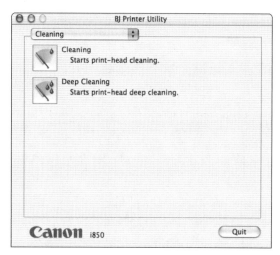

Figure 22-21: This Printer Utility screen is used for a Canon i850 printer.

♦ **You used draft mode by mistake.** With some ink jets, the highest speed, or draft setting, produces not just poorer quality prints but lighter ones as well. The setting can usually be changed in the Print dialog box, under the Quality category in the Copies & Pages pop-up menu.

Uneven Printing

The cause may indeed be spent consumables (check out the previous section), but sometimes there are other answers, and you have to probe a bit more deeply if the density varies, or you see streaks in the printouts.

Here are a few of the more common possibilities:

- **Ink or toner is defective.** If the problem happens as soon as you replace your printer's consumables, pop the appropriate cover, and remove and replace the cartridge or toner. If it still won't print properly, get in touch with your dealer about a replacement.

- **Printing heads are clogged.** Follow the cartridge cleaning procedure I described in the previous section (refer to Figure 22-21). Run your ink jet's setup utility and clean the print heads. If several runs don't fix the problem, consider replacing the ink. After that, see if there's a separate set of print heads that require replacement. Some models from Canon and HP use separate print heads, rather than having them embedded within the ink cartridge. I hate to say this, but your manual may be the best source of information.

note
Rather than running the clean and then running a test, I have found that running the cleaning cycle three times works best for my HP and Epson ink jet printers. Of course you should know that running cleaning cycles uses a lot of ink, so it's a good idea to have a couple of spare cartridges at home just in case.

- **Laser fuser is defective.** The heating element that operates in the image transfer process may be damaged or defective. If you can view the fuser, see if it has streaks or uneven sections. While fusers can sometimes be cleaned, they might be delicate enough to sustain damage if you try. Be guided by what your manufacturer tells you.

caution
This is no secret. The internal workings of a laser printer can get mighty hot. Before you futz around with the fuser assembly, make sure the printer has enough time to cool down. You can really risk a nasty burn if you put your fingers in the wrong spots. Your printer repair may even require a dealer visit to fix or clean.

caution
Unless you are highly skilled at removing the many delicate mechanical parts found in printers (some of which might be made of flimsy plastics, even on expensive models), it's worth the money to have an expert take on the responsibility to set things right.

Paper Jams

Ouch! You hear that horrible crunching sound, or a few snaps and crackles and pops, and you wonder if your printer is toast after the paper gets stuck inside.

It's fair to say that most paper jams are easily fixed, and, if you're careful, they do not really damage anything.

There's no mystery about a paper jam. Open the various compartments of the printer and gently remove the pages or scraps of paper. Some of this will be obvious when you examine the printer. Sometimes the mechanical parts are well hidden and you have to look at the manual to figure out what's what and where it might be.

When All Else Fails, Refer to the Printer Manual

Secret

Where's the manual? Most printers come with a printed setup guide and not much more. The actual documentation is usually on the installation CD. At least that saves a few trees, but you might want to make printouts of the troubleshooting section, so you can refer to it easily without having to figure out where the CD went. Instead, all you have to do is figure out where the printouts went. A loose leaf binder, the kind used in schools, may be the best place to put this stuff.

caution Be doubly careful messing around with a printer's rollers and other internal workings. Even expensive models may use simple plastic pulleys and levers to direct paper transport. So, pull torn pages out gently. Otherwise, you might face a nasty repair bill.

Printer Errors and Other Nasty Stuff

This is the hardest nut to crack, and it happens more often than not on a PostScript laser printer. After shelling out a bundle on your printer, you want to be able to count on it for clear printouts at any time. Usually you can, but the exceptions are far too numerous to be taken for granted.

Over the years, as we've moved to Mac OS X and the Unix-based CUPS printing software, the problems have lessened considerably. So, I can make this section shorter than previous editions, but there's plenty of meat to cover.

Let us begin:

♦ **Text and graphics are jagged.** What gives? Mac OS X is supposed to have built-in PDF rendering, a subset of the PostScript page language. So why isn't everything sharp and clear? If you're still using a Mac OS 9 application, which runs in the Classic environment, you're still forced to use Adobe Type Manager for screen rendering. Adobe has a free Lite version for download at its Web site. You also have to make sure you follow the proper precautions in installing a PostScript font, by making sure both printer and screen fonts are installed, and both in the same folder. This is true regardless of whether you're using Mac OS 9 or Mac OS X.

You may also need some kind of a third-party RIP solution (covered earlier in this chapter) to completely resolve this kind of issue with a normal ink jet printer.

Check the Links in Your Documents

An all-too-common mistake is omitting the linked graphics. You see, when you import or place a graphic in many word processing or desktop publishing programs, the actual contents of that file remains separate. The program forms a link to it. If you move the file, the link is lost. So, don't forget to make sure the graphics are in the right place. Such programs as Adobe InDesign and QuarkXPress are smart enough to put up a warning message so you can locate and relink the files.

A good rule to follow, based on my experience with such things, is simply to put the original document and graphics in the same folder, or put the graphics inside a sub-folder labeled graphics or artwork so you can easily find it.

♦ **Printer starts and returns to ready.** Assuming the printer queue hasn't stopped for some reason, maybe the job is too complicated for your printer. Sometimes, it'll flash an error message, which you'll probably have to check the manual to decipher, but usually it won't. To remedy, simply turn the printer off and then on again. Try printing the document and see if it works. If it still fails, recheck the printer setup, and perhaps delete and add the printer again in Printer Setup. Beyond this, if you have a laser printer, it may simply be a case of giving the printer too much to swallow. Simplify the document, user fewer fonts and complicated graphics, or get the printer more memory, if that's possible. Better yet try sending another, very simple, document to the printer. This will let you know if you have printer problem or a file problem.

The printer may also go gaga, so to speak, and seem to be processing the same file forever. If that happens you may need to reboot the printer. You may need to delete the printer job from the queue so that it does not end up getting sent to the printer over and over again each time you reboot the printer.

♦ **Font printouts look different.** You print in Times and it comes out in Courier. This isn't your day. The solution may be a simple font conflict. Perhaps you have two versions of the same font or one is damaged. Try removing the duplicate, or just replace the font itself if you have only the one set. For more information, go check out the next chapter for some hard-earned font advice.

♦ **Oddball PostScript errors returned.** They bear such strange names, seeming from faraway places, as VMerror or –8133. What's it all mean? Usually such messages simply mean your printer's memory bank has been overwhelmed and it needs some help. If you turn off the printer and turn it on again, the memory is cleared and this often solves the problem. Failing that, go back to simplifying the document with fewer fonts and graphics. Or buy a memory upgrade, if that's possible.

Getting a Hard Copy of Your Errors

Sometimes a printer error doesn't appear long enough for you to get a grip on it. But you can make the printer actually output the specific error (such as it is) that caused the problem. Just swoop over to the Print dialog box, choose Error Handling (which is only available for PostScript printers) from the Copies & Pages pop-up menu (shown in Figure 22-22) and select the Print detailed report option. Next time you will see the reason for your the printer's failure, or maybe not.

continues

continued

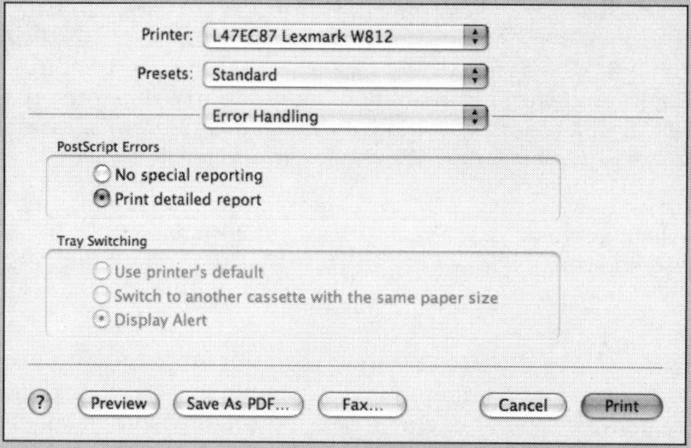

Printer: L47EC87 Lexmark W812

Presets: Standard

Error Handling

PostScript Errors
○ No special reporting
◉ Print detailed report

Tray Switching
○ Use printer's default
○ Switch to another cassette with the same paper size
◉ Display Alert

(?) (Preview) (Save As PDF...) (Fax...)   (Cancel) (Print)

Figure 22-22: Engage the printer's error messaging for your edification or confusion, depending on your point of view.

All right, I know you can usually enable this feature via a printer's setup menu, but the Print dialog box is a shorter reach, and I'm getting lazy in my old age.

◆ **Margins are clipped.** Did you specify the proper page size in the Page Setup box? Look again and at the Paper Size pop-up menu. Some printers, such as HP LaserJets, specify two letter-sized options. The first, labeled small, may speed up printing but leaves a larger margin. Regardless, unless the printer allows for full bleed, which is edge to edge and then some, there will always be a small print-free area around all sizes. How much? The easiest way to find out is to check the Page Setup box and make sure your printer is chosen in the Format For pop-up menu. That can make the difference, as maximum margins vary from one model to another. Now choose Summary from the Settings pop-up menu (see Figure 22-23). You may have to scroll down a bit to find it, but you should see a clear display of the actual printed page dimensions your printer supports, and you can adjust your document accordingly, or reduce its printout size.

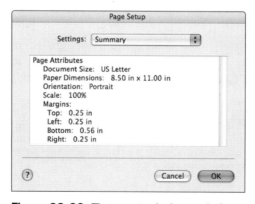

Page Setup

Settings: Summary

Page Attributes
Document Size: US Letter
Paper Dimensions: 8.50 in x 11.00 in
Orientation: Portrait
Scale: 100%
Margins:
  Top: 0.25 in
  Left: 0.25 in
  Bottom: 0.56 in
  Right: 0.25 in

(?)   (Cancel) (OK)

Figure 22-23: That quarter-inch margin is not quite enough, I fear.

Time to Toss Out That Printer?

I still know people who have a vintage Apple LaserWriter in daily production, churning out hundreds of pages per day. I also know people who buy an ink jet printer, and have it go bad before the first ink cartridge is gone.

Welcome to the age of disposable hardware. Today, you buy something cheap, but when it comes time to fix it, you'll find the cost of replacing even a simple part is twice as much as the product originally cost you.

Why should this be so?

For the most part, cheap, overseas labor and automated production systems have caused this strange set of circumstances. Add to that the fact that some printer makers will sell products on little or no profit margin, hoping to make big profits on the ink, toner, and paper.

If the printer happens to fail during the warranty period, then you're fine and dandy. The manufacturer will replace it free of charge. After that, see if the company will give you a replacement at a special price, and if it's reasonably less than the cost of a new one, go for it, unless you tire of the model and want something better.

A big, washing machine–sized workgroup printer should go on chugging for years without anything but standard maintenance. I've put tens of thousands of copies on my HP 4MV (with the extra tray), a big printer that my wife hates because it clutters up my home office. I bought years ago, and have never done anything but replace the toner and run a dust spray on the interior. It looks and works like new, and that's what you should expect from these devices.

Secret

Printer Warranties and Service Contracts

Ready for a service contract? At the checkout counter with your new printer, the cashier gives you the last pitch. Wouldn't you rather have a service contract? You'll extend the warranty for two years or three years or what-not. What's it worth to you for peace of mind?

First, don't forget that most printers come with a standard one-year warranty, which means the manufacturer itself is taking on the obligation of replacing it in case it bites the dust. Some even offer overnight exchange, which means, if you give a credit card number to secure the shipment, they'll send you a replacement before you even send back your old printer. Of course, it has to be returned in a reasonable period, for otherwise you pay for the exchange.

More to the point, if one of these products is going to fail, it'll probably happen early in its lifecycle or after it's worn out, and not often between those extremes.

Past that, it depends on the price and who is carrying the paper. If it comes from the manufacturer, and costs, say, a quarter or a third of what you paid for the printer, maybe it's worth the peace of mind, at least for an ink jet because they are sometimes cheaply built and not made for the long haul.

But dealers make big profits from selling those service policies, so watch out and read the fine print. For more expensive products, such as a big workgroup laser printer, it's not necessarily a bad idea.

The Case of the Stalled Printer Queue

This problem happens so often, you'd think there'd be a better way to fix it. Maybe some day. . . . The symptom is always the same. You print a document, and the print icon pops up in the Dock and then disappears just as quickly.

Well, maybe your printer took a dose of steroids when you weren't looking and is suddenly operating in the fast lane, except that nothing comes out of your printer. It doesn't seem aware that you printed anything at all. Frustrating? You bet.

Fortunately, there is a way that will, at the very least, tell you what went wrong, and maybe lead you on the road to setting things right:

♦ **Check print queue.** All right, it disappeared, right? So where did it go? The best way to access it is to launch Printer Setup. As you recall from earlier in this chapter, you'll find it in the Print dialog box, when you choose Edit Printer List in the Printers pop-up menu. The application can also be found courtesy of the Utilities folder, or via the Print/Fax preference panel. Once Printer Setup is open, double-click the name of the printer, and it delivers its queue window (shown in Figure 22-24). Click Start Jobs and it should work, well, mostly.

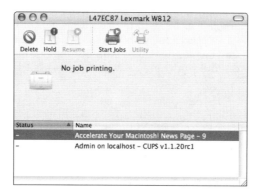

Figure 22-24: This print queue is stopped.

♦ **Check media or consumables.** A printer should put up a proper message that it's out of paper or ink or toner is low. But that doesn't always happen. If the print queue simply stops again, go ahead and check the printer and see if it is putting up a flashing light display or, with a laser printer, some warning message in its print queue. If you don't know what the message means, check the manual and see. It may simply indicate that you are out of consumables. Also, look for an empty paper tray or a paper jam. Even after you fix the problem, you may have to shut the printer off and turn it on again for the fix to be recognized. If it still doesn't work, stop the printer queue and restart it.

♦ **Check power button and cables.** When you turn off your Mac for the night, you may next shut off the power strip. No problem, but when you turn it on, the printer may not go on automatically. Just check for the power light. If it still doesn't work, remove and reconnect the cables. Maybe that last spring-cleaning attempt resulted in a few cables being unplugged. It's happened to me more often than I care to admit, but at least my home office got cleaner in the process.

Printer Disappears from Network

Where did it go? No, it wasn't thrown out with the trash last night. It's still sitting there, looking perfectly normal. But when you try to add it using Printer Setup or via the Chooser in the Classic mode, it's missing in action.

What went wrong?

First, you want to make sure that the proper printer software is installed. Now most laser printers just appear in the network, but an ink jet with a network adapter still requires the proper drivers. It never hurts to check. You'll also want to look over the printer for indications of spent consumables, a paper jam, or other factors that may cause it to shut down or fail to talk to your network properly ("hello network").

This may be your first exposure to a network problem, but it's usually simple to manage. With printers connected via Ethernet, look at the hub or switch of your network. Trace the wire to the port to which it's connected, or should be connected, and see if the LED light for that port is lit. If not, make sure the printer is on, and the cable is attached. Yes, sometimes Ethernet cables and hardware go bad. Not often, but it's worth checking.

Secret

Check Your AppleTalk Preferences

What ever happened to AppleTalk? When you install Mac OS X for the first time, AppleTalk may be turned off by default. It has to be turned on via the AppleTalk option in the Network preference panel to see those network printers. While some printers can talk to your Mac via IP numbers (the language of TCP/IP), that's not always the case, so double-check.

One more thing: If you have AppleTalk turned on for an AirPort or Wi-Fi network, it may be turned off via the Built-in Ethernet option. Doesn't hurt to double-check.

You can find your AppleTalk preferences in the Network pane of your System Preferences.

Solving the Exasperating Problem of Tiny Print

To show you how current this book really is, let me tell you about a problem that I faced writing the section on customizing the Print dialog boxes.

After writing what I thought was a particularly clever sentence, I stopped to do a little Web research and decided I needed a printout for reference. All right, I'm not terribly good when it comes to saving trees, but I promise to do better.

To my shock and awe, the printout was tiny. What should have been a full-sized page of text and pictures ended up fitting a tiny area about two inches high and one inch wide stuck at the bottom left of the page.

All right, crazy things can happen, even in an industrial-strength operating system. So I restarted, which meant I couldn't fulfill my boast of a two-week's uptime without a having to reboot or shut down. Oh well, maybe next time.

Alas, it didn't do a bit of good and a quick look at the Panther Help menus and Apple's Knowledge Base didn't turn up any solutions, so I decided to do what I always do when something strange happens, and that is to gnaw at the problem until I find a solution.

This time, I didn't have to skip any meals or field any complaints from Mrs. Levisay about why I was staying up so late. The solution was at hand in a little item deposited in my personal Library folder. Inside a folder labeled, conveniently enough, Printers, I found a file bearing an icon for my chosen laser printer.

I trashed the file, and to be certain that it didn't stick in memory, I restarted.

Sure enough, the next time I printed a document, everything was back to normal size. The file, by the way, is an application built by Panther to display a Dock-based printer queue. You'll find one for every printer you have and you don't have to fret about losing it. Next time you print a document, a new one will be created. That system can be pretty smart sometimes.

Classic QuarkXPress Hangs Up Printing Queue

When I wrote this chapter, I had been using QuarkXPress 6.0 for Mac OS X for several weeks, and it seems relatively free of the ills that plague dot-zero releases from Quark Inc. But if you're sticking with the Classic QuarkXPress version until the dust settles, you might encounter weird troubles when trying to print your document.

You send a print job or two and then . . . and then . . . well you get the picture.

Fortunately, this is not a terribly difficult problem to solve. You see, with some printers, the queue simply stops dead in its tracks. Forget about why, because all you want to do is print your document.

Here's the ultra speedy solution:

1. Locate your print spooler. This shouldn't be a big deal. Just go to System Folder, the Mac OS 9 version.

2. Open the Extensions folder and look for PrintMonitor (for most PostScript printers) or something with the word "Monitor" in it that conforms to the kind of printer you have, such as Epson.

3. Double-click on this application to launch it (see Figure 22-25).

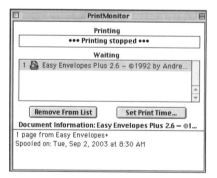

Figure 22-25: Whoops! The print queue has stopped.

4. If the print queue is stopped, click the File menu and choose Start Printing. At this point, remaining jobs should be sped to your printer.

Anticipating More Trouble with Your Classic Print Queue

Even if you free the Classic print queue, don't expect it not to get stuck again. So here's what you do: Make an alias to your PrintMonitor or other print spooler and place it on your desktop.

When it stops again, simply launch PrintMonitor or whatever it is you're using and restart the print queue. Of course the final solution is to update to a Mac OS X version of QuarkXPress or whatever program is killing the queue, and that, as they say, will be that.

Hard-Earned Advice for Visiting the Service Bureau

Is your document destined for a printing press? For graphic artists, publishers, and others, laser printers and ink jets are strictly for test or proofing purposes. It's not the final test. You want to see that everything is all right before spending a bundle on getting 10,000 copies made of that 400-page research report. Rerunning a job is a costly thing to do.

You do not want to encounter an unhappy surprise and be forced to rerun the job at your expense. In the old days, of course, the printer did it all, including the typesetting from your written or printed manuscript. Today's world of desktop publishing forces you to shoulder the responsibility. If there's a typo, it's your fautl . . . I mean fault.

Points to Remember

I work with clients who are and use service bureaus. And over the years of talking to them, I've picked up a few things that I'd like to share with you:

- **Choose a printing company or service bureau with care.** Does it have the same applications you used to make your original document? Can it supply special services, such as last-minute corrections and perhaps high-resolution scanning and color proofing? Don't be afraid to shop around till you find the right place to ship your work. You'll also want to make sure that you and the companies you work with are all on the same page, and you can get the help you need promptly, without rudeness or enduring long phone menus when you need assistance.

- **Read it and read it again.** The printer or service bureau may furnish a proof of your job for your inspection, but it doesn't have time to read it. You must expect that the copy that comes out of your own printer to be what you see in the version that comes off the printing press. If you wrote and edited it yourself, it's a good idea to have someone else look at it. You may read it ten times and miss the same error every time, because your mind corrects the mistake automatically. A fresh view is best.

Secret

Print It Out and Check It Again

Even if you have a second or third pair of eyes to help you edit, don't assume it's perfect. There are always mistakes. What's more, it's not a bad idea to use a printed page, rather than your Mac's screen to examine the job. No matter how big and clear your screen might be, and Apple's 23-inch HD Cinema Display is simply gorgeous, you still will suffer more eye fatigue. The old-fashioned printed page is not obsolete. In fact, many fiction publishers often still review manuscripts with pen and ink on printed pages rather than onscreen, because they want to see it the same way as the reader of the printed book will see it.

♦ **Supply your own fonts.** Yes, they have Helvetica, but maybe they used Adobe's version, and you got a neat knockoff from Bitstream. The license agreement that is supplied with your commercial font library will usually allow you to submit copies of the fonts to the service bureau or printer, so long as it does not use them for anyone else's work. Such programs as Adobe InDesign and QuarkXPress have special collect-for-output features that allow you to create a job ticket complete with a list of all the fonts and graphics used.

♦ **Don't forget the graphic files.** It's so easy to do. You're in a rush, and you send the actual document and maybe even the fonts. But you forget the illustrations. I already mentioned this in passing in the section on dealing with jaggy printouts. But even if the printout looks perfect on your printer, that doesn't mean it'll be perfect on the high-end output device your printer uses. Remember, if it has to be done again, you are the one that has to pay the piper.

♦ **Use the right application.** A relatively unsophisticated application such as AppleWorks is just fine if your destination is your ink jet or laser printer, or a quick-print shop, but it doesn't offer the precision color handling that is needed for high quality work. The pros use such programs as Adobe Illustrator, InDesign, and Photoshop, Macromedia FreeHand, and QuarkXPress to build their documents, because these programs provide the precision and color support required. While this may seem rather daunting if you're not a graphics artist, managing the basics may not require a terribly long learning curve. If you're willing to devote a few hours of time to the purpose, you should be able to make simple newsletters, brochures, and even large text documents in both InDesign and QuarkXPress. I tell you more about it in Chapter 8.

♦ **Be careful about color matching.** It looks great on the screen, but the printout is terrible. Blue looks like green, and forget about the flesh tones. Apple's ColorSync software can help, because it lets you synchronize your onscreen color to your printer, assuming, that is, that your printer supports the feature. But that doesn't mean that your printout will match the one your printer users. For a multicolor job, it pays to ask your printer or service bureau for advice on how to set up the files. Don't take anything for granted. A good firm will have experts on staff to handle color output. Unless you really know your stuff here, don't be afraid to ask questions to make sure you get what you want.

♦ **Check and recheck your material.** If the service bureau has a job ticket, fill it out. Most use Web-based ordering systems, but, however it's done, double-check to make sure all the information is entered. Make sure all the files are in place before you send them along.

Searching for the Ideal File Format for Your Service Bureau

I keep talking about the good old days, but I saw it from the beginning, so I like to think I've got a bit of perspective here. Then, you simply sent the original document you used to the service bureau along with your fonts and graphics and that was it, assuming they had the same application you used to create your document, of course.

Today, though, there's another way, and that's PDF, or portable document format. Using the very same format Apple harnesses to display text on your screen, you can prepare your documents so anyone can read them, without having to have the same software you do.

This doesn't mean, of course, that this is a perfect method. Not everyone is 100 percent behind PDF, because it may be more difficult to set up for ideal color settings. In addition, various settings may be needed for your PDF to print properly, such as whether images are compressed and how fonts are embedded, and those settings are not part of the Save As PDF feature in Panther.

Fortunately, the applications, such as InDesign and QuarkXPress, that you will likely use to prepare your materials for print have built-in PDF creation tools that you can use to match the service bureau's needs. If not, you might consider buying a copy of Adobe Acrobat; or just ask the firm if they can accept your documents in their native format.

Faxing

Brand new to Panther is the ability to Fax via the Print dialog boxes. In older versions of the OS, you had to purchase third-party software to send and receive faxes. This is something that we use in our office. And if you like the idea of not having a hard copy of every junk fax that you get, you might consider this as an option.

Faxing Preferences

Faxing from and to your Mac starts in your System Preferences in the Print & Fax preference pane. Choose this preference pane and then click on the Faxing Tab (shown in Figure 22-26). All you need is Panther, a modem, and an active phone line.

Not only do you set up the number (probably of the phone line connected to your computer) but you can also set your computer to automatically print the incoming faxes and/or e-mail it to you when you get a new fax.

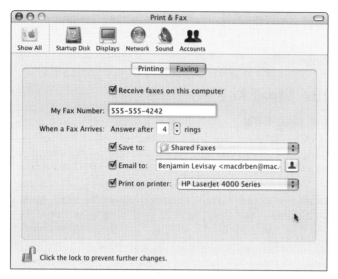

Figure 22-26: You set your computer's faxing identity in the Faxing preferences.

Faxing Dialog Boxes

After you've finished with your Faxing settings, you're ready to fax. You fax just like you print. Select Print from under the File menu (in almost any application) and then click on the Fax button in the Print dialog box (shown in Figure 22-27).

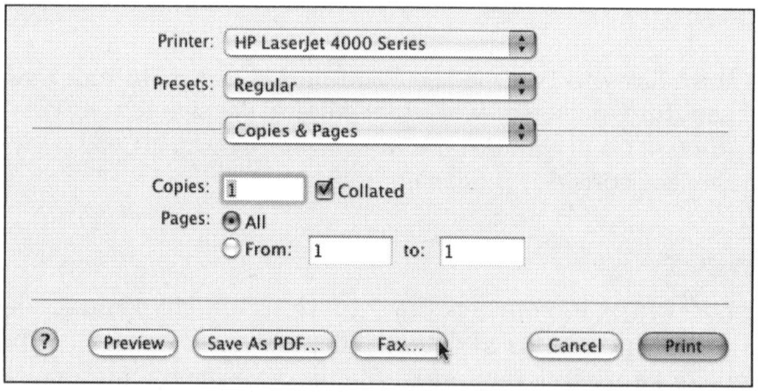

Figure 22-27: Sometimes Print doesn't mean Print.

A series of dialog boxes lets you tell your computer who and what to fax. The first page is the Cover Page (shown in Figure 22-28). Besides selecting the recipients from your Address Book or typing the fax numbers, you can also enter a subject, choose your modem, and specify the type to be used on the cover page of your fax.

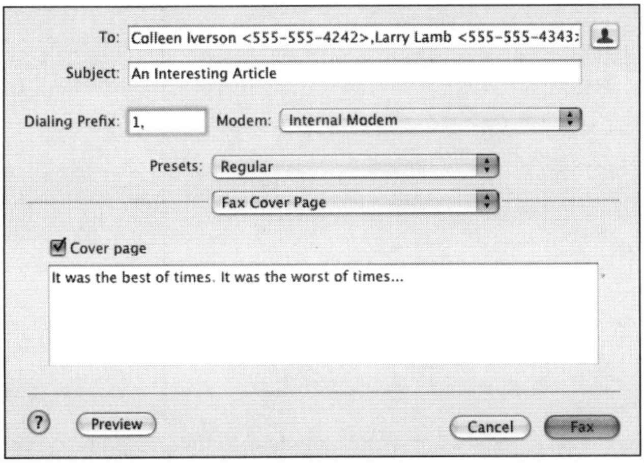

Figure 22-28: You don't have to have a cover page. By deselecting the Cover page option, the first page of your document will be your first faxed page.

In the same pop-up menu as the Fax Cover Page you can also select more modem settings (shown in Figure 22-29) and the number of Copies and/or Pages (shown in Figure 22-30). These will probably be the main settings that you will check and change when using your Mac to fax documents.

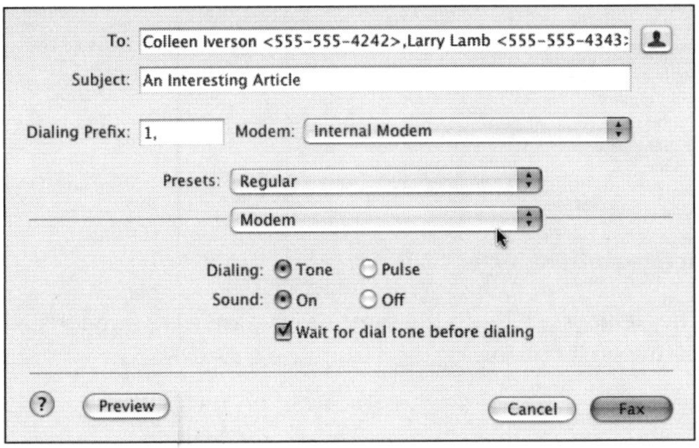

Please 22-29: If you have more than one modem, here is where you set your modem to be used for your fax.

All of the other fax options are pretty much the same as the print options. You can access those dialog boxes from the same pop-up menu as the Modem and Copies & Pages menu (shown in Figure 22-31).

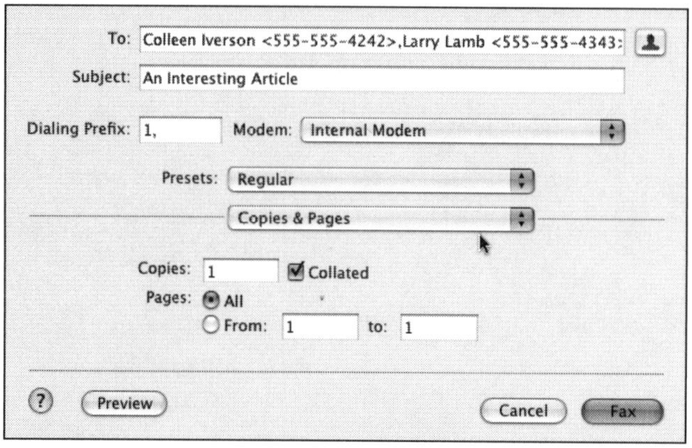

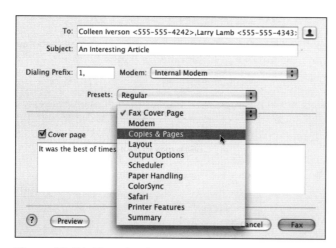

Figure 22-30: The Copies & Pages options are almost identical to those used when printing a normal document.

Figure 22-31: The other fax settings are much the same as what we went through earlier in this chapter when I covered the print options.

Your Faxing Queue

And just like a printer, your fax queue is just like a printer queue (shown in Figure 22-32) right from your desktop.

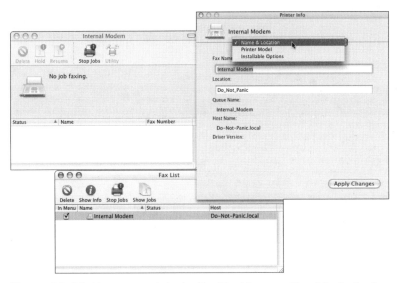

Figure 22-32: You can see it in the Fax List. You can affect jobs in the fax queue, and you can access queue info.

While I wouldn't set up my personal computer to be a faxing computer, this is another great place to use/recycle an older Panther-compatible computer. You may need to do some configuring to make it a network fax computer, but it is possible.

Summary

Why should something so easy be complicated? No, I'm not about to get into the psychology of printing. Everything has an answer and I hope you find plenty here to make your printing as seamless as possible.

Now that you've made sense of printing and faxing, the next chapter is designed to make sense of something you need when you print, and that's fonts. With multiple fonts folders under Panther, it can get mighty aggravating. But there are solutions to those dilemmas as well, as you'll find out when you turn the pages.

Making Sense of Mac OS X Fonts

♦ ♦

Secrets in This Chapter

♦ ♦

When I told my partners that I was going to work on the font chapter of the book, it brought about some snickers. You see, I have a bit of a reputation about fonts. I've even earned the geeky nickname "font hugger" for the way that I talk and deal with fonts for our customers. In fact, once you get me started about fonts and font management, it's hard to get me to stop. I could write a whole book about it (hint, hint, Wiley).

And what's not to like? ASCII (American Standard Code for Information Interchange) becomes vector images. In every font, we have a small art gallery of images — usually hand drawn with attention to ligatures, descenders, and so on. When you peel back the top layer, you see that there is some pretty cool math associated with the spaces between (kerning) each combination of letters. (How cool is that?)

My interest in fonts is my father's fault. When I was a kid, way back in the 1970s, which is ancient history for most of you, my family started a magazine here in the Midwest. The Mac wasn't even a gleam in the eye of Steve Jobs and Steve Wozniak back then, so we bought (at considerable expense) a Compugraphic typesetter. It was a big blue monster of a computer and desk with a tiny little two-color screen. We generated type in justified columns using this interface, and then output those columns to a developer (a device) using photosensitive paper.

Many of these machines used fonts that consisted of filmstrips placed upon a narrow drum. As the drum spun around, a little light flashed through a letter and exposed the character onto the paper. Now this all happened in fractions of a second, and the machines seldom made a spelling mistake. It looked pretty good too, when done right, and some say that desktop publishing has rarely, if ever, achieved similar levels of quality.

I remember that we sprang for something like eight additional font faces/strips so that we could have some variety and offer our advertisers some diversity. And considering the expense of these fonts/strips, this was a major investment at the time.

> **note**   Purists will remind me that some machines put the characters on a disk rather than a filmstrip. Yes, I used some of those devices too. But the results were the same.

Now all these machines were set up the same way. The characters were on the filmstrip or disk. But there was one more essential step. Unlike a typewriter, and such standby monospace fonts as Courier, a typesetting machine (and the fonts you use on a personal computer) has different space values for each character. Those values were programmed onto a punch tape, printed circuit card, or floppy disk. For example, when the letter M was accessed, wider space values were used. Obviously, the letter I gets a much narrower spacing.

When Adobe created PostScript fonts for computers in the 1980s, the company actually used a similar technique, except that the spacing values were inserted in the screen font file. But the result was the same. The second part of the package was the outline or printer font file used to provide the visual output on the printer.

Aha! Two files. One is used for printing; the other specifies the width values. How little things have changed.

As I said . . . I can (and probably will) go on about fonts for a great many pages if not checked. Before we talk about controlling them, let's just start, at the beginning, with the fonts themselves.

Fonts Come in Different Flavors

As I alluded before, the main font format that has been the standard for years consists of a font suitcase and a printer font. However, not all fonts consist of two separate files. Here, I briefly list the Mac font formats, and later in this chapter, I tell you why you'd want to use one over another.

◆ **Bitmap fonts:** This format dates back to the very first Macintosh. A bitmap font and a screen font are one and the same, designed to provide a font's width and kerning settings, and to provide screen display and printing in a single size. As I explain shortly, after you move away from the native size, the image quality deteriorates sharply.

◆ **PostScript fonts (or Type 1):** The standard for the publishing industry, this format was created by Adobe in the 1980s. As you just read a moment ago, the font packages consist of screen fonts and the printer fonts. What this means is that you can get clear output in all available sizes, with a few conditions, as I explain in more detail later in the section on Adobe Type Manager.

◆ **Scalable fonts:** In part, I'm repeating myself here, but it's my book and that's my inalienable right. As explained above, scalable fonts can be used at any size, and are available in PostScript, TrueType, and the new OpenType formats.

◆ **Multiple Master:** This special type of PostScript font allows variation of one or more font parameters (such as weight) to create a large number of custom styles, also known as instances. Depending on whom you ask, publishers either love or hate these.

◆ **TrueType fonts:** Although the situation wasn't as bad as it used to be, Adobe used to exact a fairly hefty license fee for use of its PostScript technology. So, Apple worked with Microsoft to come up with a new font format that would sidestep those requirements, and save some money. The result was TrueType, introduced in 1990. The advantage of TrueType was that both screen and printer font were in the same file, and the rasterizing software was part of the Mac OS. Hence, there is no need for an Adobe Type Manager (see below) to handle TrueType. But it never really took off in the professional printing industry, and the expensive output devices used by the printing industry would often choke on TrueType, unless expensive hardware updates were purchased.

note The situation isn't nearly as bad as it used to be, but I recall a local printer who was forced to pay $10,000 to update his expensive output device, known as an imagesetter, to work with TrueType. So, Apple didn't have to pay. But others did.

◆ **OpenType fonts:** If you thought you were already inundated with font formats, here's another. OpenType (a cooperative project from Apple, Microsoft, and Adobe) can combine PostScript and TrueType in a single file. In addition, you get larger character sets, including special characters, such as swashes (little flourishes surrounding a letter — you'll recognize it when you see it!) and other goodies. Adobe was converting its fonts to the new format as this book was written.

◆ **System fonts (dfonts):** These fonts are specially designed TrueType fonts that pack everything in the data fork. To be slightly technical, Mac files usually consist of two elements. One is the resource fork and the other is a data fork (as opposed to the salad fork I suppose).

This is actually an over-simplified breakdown of the font types. Without opening FontLab and looking at encoding options, I thought it would be best to keep this simple for now. Maybe someday you'll see on the shelves a book with my name on it about fonts and you can continue to read my ramblings on the subject.

The Nuts and Bolts of Mac OS X Font Handling

The best way to explain where to find your fonts is to compare it to the way it was done in the old days, under the Classic Mac OS. And therein lies a tale.

Back in ancient times, meaning before Mac OS X existed, you only had one location for fonts, and that was the Fonts folder inside the System Folder.

> **note** For those who are concerned with precision, let me put an asterisk to that, before my technical editor interrupts this chapter too. (He has a habit of doing that!) This font installation technique first came about beginning in Mac System 7.1. In System 7.0 and 7.0.1, screen fonts actually resided in the System file. Before that, everything was placed in the System file, and managed via a program known as Font/DA Mover, a program some affectionately called a "buggy mess."

However, because Mac OS X is a multiple-user operating system, the theory is that each user can have his or her own fonts. That sounds great in practice, but it also gets very complicated because now you have several places to place fonts. After you get used to the new order, however, it's not so bad. Trust me.

Where Your Fonts Live Natively

First, here's a brief list of where you can place your fonts with Mac OS X and my basic advice on how each location should be used:

> **tip** Later in this chapter, I will tell you ways to bypass all this clutter by using a font management program, either Apple's Font Book or one from another company, to sort out the whole mess. But it may not be worth the effort unless your font library exceeds a couple of hundred or so. Otherwise, the standard organizational scheme will probably be all right.

 ◆ **Classic Fonts folder:** Yes indeed, right where they used to be. These fonts are automatically recognized by your Classic Mac applications. If you must run older software, you'll want to place extra fonts here.

> **note** Sorry to be the harbinger of bad tidings, but, without the help of a third-party font manager program, your Classic applications will see these fonts only, not the ones installed elsewhere under Mac OS X.

◆ **Fonts folder inside Mac OS X System folder** (as opposed to the Mac OS 9 System Folder): How do you tell the difference? The OS X System folder has the X icon on it, and bears just the single word, "System" (shown in Figure 23-1). The fonts are actually stored in a folder called Fonts in the Library folder in the folder called System. This is where the fonts your Mac needs for dialog boxes, menus, and title bars are stored. Under normal circumstances you can't add or remove anything here without gaining root access, something best left for emergencies. If you do try to drag something out of one of these folders, it's just copied, and the original stays put. The best thing to do is leave well enough alone unless you really know your Mac OS X lore.

> **note**
>
> Some of the font management utilities I'll tell you about later on in this chapter do let you manage system fonts directly. Even then, I don't think it's worth the bother, except, perhaps, for graphic artists who might need to use a different version of some of those fonts, but the choice is yours.

◆ **Fonts folder in the Library folder:** There's one at the top or root level of your hard drive (which is not like root access to your Mac, which is the same as being king of the world in Mac OS X parlance). This folder's icon is four books, just like any of the other Library folders (shown in Figure 23-1). Here you can place fonts that are available to anyone who uses your Mac. Just drag them into this particular Fonts folder and they will be recognized by all the Mac OS X applications you launch.

◆ **Fonts folder in your personal Library folder:** Everyone with a separate user account on your Mac has their own personal Fonts folder in the Library folder in their home directory (shown in Figure 23-1). The fonts you put here are only recognized for a single user account. So, you can have 100 fonts earmarked for a special job, but if a coworker doesn't want you to inflict your choices on them, they can have their own personal font collection. It works the same as the system-wide Fonts folder. Drag your fonts into this folder, and they are recognized by the programs you run while logged onto this account.

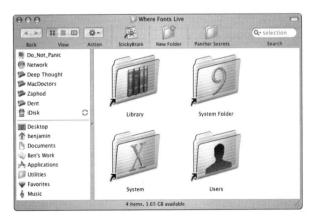

Figure 23-1: The System folder and the System Folder. You can see the difference by the version number embedded in the folder icon.

♦ **Fonts folder in your Network/Library folder:** What is that Network globe all about? Well, if you're lucky enough to be connected to a network using Mac OS X Server, your font library can be placed on the server. Anyone on the network with proper access can subscribe to these fonts, all at the same time.

note I should also mention, even if you didn't ask, that there are network versions of some of the font managers, and that they provide a similar set of services, along with powerful font management capabilities. But I'm getting ahead of myself, as I usually do. This is all available later on in this chapter.

♦ **Fonts folder inside an application's folder.** This happens to be a location that isn't always available, simply because many applications are offered as *packages*, which means that all the files are hidden behind a single icon. But some Mac OS X applications have their own Fonts folder, in which you can place fonts that only run for those programs and nowhere else. One example is Adobe InDesign 2.

Cross-Platform Fonts

Secret

Did you know you can actually use Windows fonts on a Mac with Mac OS X? Not all, of course, but you can use TrueType fonts with the file extension .ttf and .ttc. (The latter is for font collections.) You can also use Windows OpenType fonts, which bear the extension .otf.

Any limitations to all this font handling power? Yes, you'd have to convert Windows-based PostScript fonts to Mac format and the Windows fonts won't work in a Classic application. Now ask your Windows friends to see if they can run a Mac font without conversion.

Classic and Mac OS X Font Installation Differences

Do you remember the time when you installed a font in the old Fonts folder and, for some reason, it never showed up in the font menu? That was probably the result of a common mistake we all made. Instead of dragging the actual fonts to the System Folder icon or the Fonts folder, you moved a folder instead.

The solution was to get the fonts out of the folder and install them directly.

Under Mac OS X, the system is smarter. It doesn't matter whether you put your fonts or the folders that contain them in the Fonts folder. It'll sort things out for you.

But as you'll see shortly, there are far better ways to organize your fonts, if you have a large library to contend with.

Transferring Macintosh TrueType Fonts to the PC

All right, the Mac uses TrueType fonts, and so does Windows. But does the twain meet or not? Well, it's not quite a matter of just moving the fonts from one machine to another, because the resulting fonts may not work.

Now why is that? Well, it's all because of the way Mac files are constructed. They consist of two elements, the data fork and the resource fork. And the difference is a lot more significant than just the way you handle dinner and salad forks when you go to a fancy restaurant.

Windows is only designed to use the data fork. Hence the font is, basically, not usable. So how do you get around this? The best way is a font conversion utility.

Secret

Converting Fonts with TransType 2

The folks at FontLab (famous for the FontLab application) make a utility called TransType 2 (www.fontlab.com/html/transtype.html) for about $97.00. They have developed this program for Mac OS X, Mac Classic, and even Windows. This great little utility lets you convert almost any type of font from any platform to any other type in the same or other platform. It's very simple and easy to use. And it doesn't require advanced knowledge of font construction and encoding that its big brother FontLab needs in order to manipulate fonts.

For the average user, this is too much money to spend. But if the alternative is spending thousands of dollars on an imagesetter upgrade, then $97 probably isn't too much money.

TrueType fonts, contained in single-font files or in font suitcases, are copied to the PC in individual TTF files. Those files can then be installed in the usual way (that is through the Fonts item of the Control Panel or with a font management tool like Adobe Type Manager).

Bitmap fonts and TrueType fonts both appear in suitcases. On the Macintosh, the bitmap fonts are displayed with an icon bearing a single *A*. TrueType fonts use an icon bearing three *A*s.

Because TrueType font files contain all the elements needed to display and print the text, this all-in-one feature is really powerful and should not bring any of the usual corruption problems.

Avoiding Font Conflicts

Hevetica is not Hevetica is not Helvitica. Here's Helvetica and there's Helvetica[NLR1], and maybe you have a TrueType and a PostScript version. Does it make a difference if you use them all? Absolutely. Applications recognize fonts by name, and if there is more than one of each face, things can get mighty screwy.

What do I mean? Let's say you are using a certain font in a document. And let's say that when you display or print that document that the letters look weird — the letters are widely spaced, or too tight. Screen display doesn't match the output. That's a problem.

Life even gets more complicated if you handle jobs from clients, each of which may use a different version of a font (and consider themselves designers without equal).

My partner Larry, who also works with a lot of print and design customers, is fond of saying, "Some people design and some people use a lot of fonts." Unsaid is that these people are not usually the same person. And it should be noted that due to my fondness for different font faces and my tendency to use them as I see fit in my own documents that he occasionally is referring to me (smile).

A common mistake that young or inexperienced designers make — as well as people who think that they are designers but aren't — is that they use too many fonts. If this applies to you, check your work. If it makes you tired to look at the list of fonts used in a single document, my guess is that you have just such a problem.

Here's a brief tutorial about how to sort things out:

◆ **Ask clients to send you copies of the fonts they are using.** Fonts are licensed by the number of output devices you use, not the number of computers. So, you could have 100 copies of a font and one printer, and still comply with a license that restricted you to one output device. Font makers don't complain if you send fonts to a printer or graphic designer to make sure your work is done properly.

◆ **Create a separate set for each version.** Don't confuse yourself. Label a set in some fashion to allow you to separate Adobe fonts from Bitstream fonts. That way you don't activate the wrong one by mistake.

◆ **Turn off the fonts you aren't using.** If you're using one version of Times, disable the other versions.

Secret

Understanding the Way Panther Chooses Fonts

Mac OS X has set up its own pecking order for choosing one font over another in the event of duplication. First, it looks at the fonts in an application's Fonts folder, then the ones in your personal or Users Fonts folder. From here, it moves on, in this order, to your main font library, in the Fonts folder within the Library folder at the top level of your hard drive. Next up are network fonts, followed by System fonts and Classic fonts. If you don't use a font manager, just keep this sequence in mind.

The Need for a Font Manager

From the very first, organizing your fonts on a Mac proved to be a chore. From the inability to handle huge font libraries, to the fact that font menus could become so big, you'd waste precious seconds or minutes trying to pick the one you needed.

In addition, in those early days, removing and adding the fonts you wanted was a chore. The infamous Font/DA Mover would crash at unexpected moments, so you'd end up having to restart your Mac several times just to add a bunch of fonts. In those days, I'd usually add a handful at a time to keep things running, but even a few of those steps would often be enough to bring the Mover down.

Another irritating issue was the inane way some fonts were named in those days. While just having Times and Times Bold would seem logical, Adobe used to call it Times and B Times Bold. And the printer font component would be known as TimesBol. Of course, Adobe eventually realized that this naming scheme made no sense, but there are lots of those old fonts still in use.

Now none of these font organization hassles made much of a difference if you installed, say, a few dozen fonts, and went on with your life.

But graphic artists can't survive on a few dozen fonts. Some have libraries in the thousands, often with half a dozen versions of the same type family.

Now why would anyone want to have more than one copy of Times? Well, in the type business, each foundry or publisher of fonts has its own design criteria. So, the Times from one maker may be a tiny bit different from the Times made by another maker. Letters may be a little thicker or wider, or a little taller. Believe me, it may take real careful checking to confirm this, but it can mean a lot when you use the wrong version of a font, and all the line endings in a document change. In addition, due to copyright restrictions, the name of the font may even be changed, but the letterforms are almost the same. It's not just a purist who builds a big font collection. Adobe Illustrator, CorelDraw, and Deneba Canvas all come with decent font bundles. You get a few of these over the years, and suddenly you are overflowing with fonts, and ready to cry uncle, or font manager, depending on your point of view.

Why Does Panther Need Font Management?

OS X has added new problems to the font front. In addition to the problems that you used to have in Classic, you may now find that fonts that you've used successfully for years no longer work in OS X with your new OS X applications. Some of this is due to the new applications and some of this is due to a little-known feature of OS X that actually checks the font prior to allowing it to be used by an application. Yes. Some of this is Apple's fault.

This is part of the stability that Mac OS X is now so famous for. So in a way this is a good thing. The bad thing is that you may well find that moving from OS 9 to OS X, especially if you're a designer that has a large font library can be a true nightmare. This nightmare is best handled in advance by cleaning and sorting your fonts as well as implementing a third-party font management program.

The basic function of a font management program is to help you organize everything from a single, simple interface. By clicking a simple button, for example, you can also turn fonts on and off. Why not keep them all on? Imagine if you had 10,000 fonts installed, and they all showed up in your font menu. How long would it take to scroll from top to bottom, even with one of those fancy 23-inch Apple Cinema Display monitors?

note
The length of your font menu is not the only (or even the main) reason to have a font manager. Another is the fact that applications load font menus when you launch them. More fonts, longer launch times.

Programs such as Illustrator 10 will die a quick death if you try to load thousands of active fonts as it starts up. You will also probably notice that your computer (even a new, fast computer) runs at a crawl.

Now if you put fonts in one of the various Fonts folders (hopefully you've chosen the one in the User's font folder), how do you turn them on and off? The answer is you don't. If they are in that folder, then they are on. And that's part of the problem.

Here's how you'd organize a font library with a font manager in place:

- ◆ **Leave the System fonts alone.** Messing with these could get you in trouble.
- ◆ **Lighten the Classic System Fonts.** The Fonts folder in the Classic System folder should be lightened to the few that you are going to need for your leftover classic applications (if you aren't using a font manager that crosses the classic barrier). You should consider keeping the list of fonts in the Classic System folder down the minimum.
- ◆ **Move the Library Fonts.** The fonts in the Fonts folder of the Library folder as well as the fonts in the Fonts folder in the Library folder in each user's home folder cannot be turned off. So if you want control over these fonts as well, they need to be moved out of those folders so that they can be managed by a third-party font manager.

note
If you choose Suitcase X1 or FontAgent Pro 2.1, you don't have to move your fonts out of any of the System/Library fonts folders. These programs move and manage these folders for you. In fact allowing programs like these to handle those System/Library fonts folders is safer than moving them yourself. I recommend this. Things are complicated enough as it is.

- ◆ **Create a special Fonts or Resources folder.** Use this brand new folder to store your nonsystem fonts. This is what your font management program uses for handling big font libraries.
- ◆ **Subdivide.** How you organize your Resources folder is up to you. If you have a couple of hundred fonts or so, you can pack them all in. Just remember to keep the screen and printer font files of PostScript fonts in the same folder, not separated by another folder. Otherwise, the font manager won't know they're there. (Only the operating system manages to sort this out.) With bigger font libraries, you can set up separate folders for each letter of the alphabet, or even divide by font foundry. One folder might suit for Adobe fonts, another for Bitstream, and so on.

tip
If you choose the right font management program, such as FontAgent Pro 2.1 or FontReserve 3.1.2, your font management program organizes your fonts into a new folder as part of the font management process.

Secret

Even More Font Grouping and Organization

Graphic artists even go further with font organization. They might divvy up fonts by the job. So one ad has its own collection, a book has its, and so on. Font managers let you organize fonts by sets (and some by libraries), so all the fonts for a single task would be accessed by a single step, and turned off when they are no longer needed.

This means that the same font can be in multiple sets for different jobs and/or clients. Because a set is usually treated as a subset of the entire library, these fonts don't take up any extra room by being in multiple sets. (This is not, however, the case for fonts in different libraries.)

The Obligatory History Lesson

One of the most popular font management programs these days is Extensis Suitcase (`www.extensis.com/suitcase`), but it has a long and checkered history. Rather than force you to have to deal with Font/DA Mover to mangle, I mean manage your fonts, programmer Steve Brecher begat Suitcase. The program in those days relied on, shall we say, unadvertised hooks to the operating system that allowed you to turn fonts and off like a light switch.

The key was that you didn't have to use Font/DA Mover to install fonts inside your System Folder. Instead, you put them anywhere on an available hard drive, using Suitcase to activate and deactivate them as needed. While you'd still have to quit an application and relaunch it to recognize the new font layout, over time, some applications, such as QuarkXPress, were upgraded to recognize immediate changes in the font setup.

The program worked so well, it got a competitor, in the form of Alsoft's MasterJuggler (`www.alsoft.com/MasterJuggler/`) and then another in the form of Adobe Type Manager Deluxe (no longer sold or supported by Adobe).

Like many programs that were produced by small software publishers, Suitcase had to experience a bit of a nomadic lifestyle. When its publisher, Fifth Generation Systems, was acquired by Symantec, who produces such software as Norton Anti-Virus and Norton Utilities, Suitcase came along for the ride.

It's clear, however, that Suitcase's presence in the Symantec line up was oil and water, the oddball out. It finally ended up in the hands of Extensis, a publisher of add-ons for graphics and desktop publishing software, such as Adobe Photoshop and QuarkXPress.

The Third-Party Font Management Choices

There is a good selection of third party-font management choices. And in this section we're going to look at most of the top contenders as well as a little more on the whys and wherefores along the way.

The Legend of Adobe Type Manager

With programs to manage fonts, there was one more equation not yet solved on Macs, and that was font display. As you recall, PostScript fonts came in two files, with the bitmap font providing the screen display. Usually font makers included a handful of sizes with their fonts. And there's the rub. If you called for a type size that matched the one on the screen font, things looked pretty good on the screen.

But if you chose a size that had no screen font, the operating system would make a good guess — well, a guess at any rate — and make the display smaller or larger as needed. The more the size differed from the screen font, the worse it got. The blotchy, bitmapped look of big fonts made it almost impossible to get a good fix on what a document with a variety of text sizes would look like, but at least you could take a break while it printed out. No doubt, the manufacturers of laser printers sold lots of toner in those days.

Worse, if you didn't have a real (or fake) PostScript laser printer, the screen fonts couldn't scale the output to provide clear printing, so you'd get whatever you saw on the screen, for better or worse. So of course, you didn't buy a printer that didn't support PostScript if you were a graphic artist or desktop publisher, and you probably remember how expense such printers were way back when.

note   So what do I mean by a *fake* PostScript printer? Funny you should ask. Some printer makers emulate PostScript, rather than license it and paying a fee to Adobe. It means you might save a few bucks on your printer, but it also means that compatibility, while good, may not be 100 percent.

Finally, Adobe got a better idea, and in the fall of 1989, it released Adobe Type Manager. ATM, as I'll refer to it from here on, was, in essence, a mini-PostScript font processor. If there was no screen font available in a particular size, ATM would grab the data from the printer font and use that, so everything on the screen looked relatively crisp.

There was another useful side effect. If you didn't have a PostScript printer, ATM would handle the processing (or rasterizing, to use the proper term) of the font for your printer too, so you'd be able to get clear text. Of course, all this depended on installing both the screen and printer fonts correctly.

The Difference between ATM Light and ATM Deluxe

In the 1990s, Adobe finally had an epiphany and realized that ATM was half a loaf. Adobe had already perfected a technology to use generic substitute fonts when the actual ones weren't present in a document, so why not manage your regular fonts too? And thus came Adobe Type Manager Deluxe.

In my humble opinion ATM Deluxe is still the standard by which all other third-party font managers need to measure themselves. I used it exclusively. You could drag and drop by sets and manage your fonts in a two-paneled window (shown in Figure 23-2) that was simple and powerful.

Its greatest strength was the ability to autoactivate fonts, on the fly, whenever you opened or printed a document that contained them. And it include the ability to mange your fonts by verifying them for various kinds of conflicts, sorting for damaged fonts (to remove them), and managing duplicates — all from the Tools menu (shown in Figure 23-3).

Figure 23-2: Sets & Fonts. You could drag fonts in to add them and Option-drag them out to collect them for output.

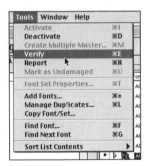

Figure 23-3: You could verify your fonts, manage duplicates, and even sort your fonts in ATM Deluxe.

> **note**
> All right, the other font managers can autoactivate fonts too, for the most part. It just seemed that ATM managed the task more seamlessly than the rest.

Unlike many of the other font managers, autoactivation in ATM was done with a simple trip to the Preferences dialog box, by clicking Global in the Auto-activation section of General options (shown in Figure 23-4).

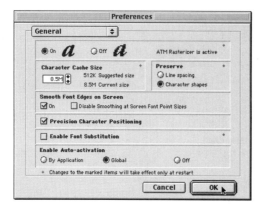

Figure 23-4: Global activation, font substitution, and character cache controls were all part of the ATM Deluxe Preferences.

It could even activate fonts when required for printing a document, regardless of whether the application was open.

But when Mac OS X arrived, with its built-in support for PDF rendering, one of the needs for ATM was eliminated. Yes, a good font manager was still required by some Mac users, but Adobe decided not to move to Apple's new operating system (despite the many times I signed the petition to Adobe).

But that doesn't mean that ATM Deluxe is dead. No sir/ma'am! My customers who still run in OS 9.2.x still find that ATM Deluxe suits their needs just fine. And for those customers who moved to OS X and purchased font management software that doesn't manage fonts in Classic as well as OS X, they use ATM Deluxe to do the font management work in the Classic environment — a good choice at that.

Besides Classic support, ATM is not unneeded (a proper use of a double negative). It's the Classic environment, where you see need for a special free version of ATM, known as ATM Light (shown in Figure 23-5), to handle font rendering chores.

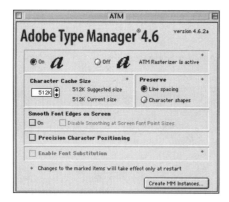

Figure 23-5: Lighter, but not out, here's ATM.

Except for the autoactivation feature, the ATM Light control panel does exactly the same things as ATM Deluxe.

Common to Font Management Programs

Font-management programs all do their thing in a similar fashion. You're free to put your fonts on any available hard drive. You aren't restricted to the folders Mac OS X assigns to such duties, because the program can be set to store the locations in its database.

> **note** A major exception to the rule is Apple's Font Book application. When you use it to open a font, it will immediately store it in your Fonts folder in your home Library folder. When it's turned off, it goes into another folder in your Library folder called Fonts (Disabled). In that sense, it works somewhat like the Classic Mac's Extensions Manager.

A Fast, Extremely Dirty Look at Font Book

Now some might debate Apple's reasoning to make Font Book (www.apple.com/macosx/features/fontbook/) part of Panther, what with so many great programs already around. But all these programs are around because efficient font handling was missing in action for years in the Mac OS.

And Apple has finally gotten the message. Apple's response is Font Book (see Figure 23-6).

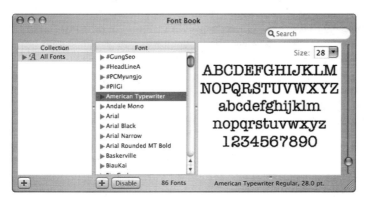

Figure 23-6: Apple's Font Book makes font management butter smooth, with a familiar three-pane interface.

Using a brushed metal, Finder-like look, you can quickly preview your font library, search for fonts, and turn them on or off as needed. Assuming your applications are fully compliant with Apple's own font programming guidelines, your font menus update as the font libraries are changed.

I'm going to spend a good chunk of time in Font Book because it's new and because it's part of Panther.

What Font Book Can't Do

All right, here are some reasons why you might want to go out and buy a commercial font manager. First, you can't print a font sample sheet in Font Book; everything is visual. Second, it doesn't work with Classic Mac OS applications.

In addition, the fonts you add within the program are placed in your personal Fonts folder; they aren't added system-wide. This may be a convenience or a disadvantage, depending on your setup, but it is a limitation.

Moreover, some of the retail alternatives can make fonts available directly from your Mac OS X Server; or they can even manage multiple libraries at the same time. They also load fonts dynamically as required in a specific document.

We Interrupt This Chapter . . .

As you can probably tell from the way that I've been qualifying most of my remarks about Font Book, I'm not a fan. That has prompted a small exchange between me and my technical editor, Pieter.

Benjamin: Now it's perfectly true that the version of Font Book I'm covering here is 1.0. As the program matures, it's likely it'll grow some of these missing features, further lessening the need for commercial products. But that's the future. For right now, I find this program extremely limited and without many of the options and diagnostic capabilities that make a font manager worth having. In my opinion, Font Book is a glorified font-viewing utility. That's what it seems to do best.

Pieter: Hey Ben, while I miss the ability to scan for damaged fonts, for all my needs as a editor and a systems administrator, Font Book does everything I could want. For those of us without the huge font libraries of a prepress expert like you, Font Book is more than adequate to manage a limited number of fonts. Likewise, as someone who used to work for a company that made Macintosh utility software, I am glad that Apple did not make Font Book into a Suitcase killer; they should help support the legions of developers that support the Mac instead of competing with them.

What Font Book Can Do

Here's a brief primer on using Font Book. I cover a few secrets as we go.

To install a font:

1. Double-click on an uninstalled TrueType font or PostScript font suitcase. The action launches Font Book, displays a preview of the font, and gives you an Install button (see Figure 23-7).

Figure 23-7: You are one click away from installation.

2. Click Install to add it to your list of fonts.

How to Add Multiple Fonts in Font Book

With Panther, there are always alternatives, and here's one if you want to add more than a single font at the same time. Just choose Open from the File menu, and it'll bring up the standard, garden-variety Mac OS X Open dialog box. Clicking the plus symbol in the Font pane produces the same result. Now just select the folder or font suitcase you want to install, or Open as the dialog box states. (There is no difference as far as Font Book is concerned.)

If you want to open more than a single font, just use the standard Finder shortcuts, such as Shift-clicking to select a range, ⌘-clicking to choose separate fonts, and ⌘-A to select them all. Piece of cake.

Other Font Book Features Described

Now that I've whetted your appetite for more, let me give you a brief highlight of the short list of capabilities of Font Book:

- **One click to Disable or Enable:** Select a font family, an individual font, or a group of fonts, click the Disable button and they are turned off. The font menus in most Mac OS X applications update to reflect the change. Clicking Enable turns them on again.

- **Dynamic font resizing:** Clicking and dragging the resize bar automatically resizes the font displayed in the sample window. You can also manually enter a size or select from a default list in the Size menu, or click the slider at the left to switch the sizes (by 10ths of a point).

Font Preview and Information via Font Book

Just double-click on a font's name in Font Book and it not only brings up a preview of the face in a separate window, but also displays the maker of the font (shown in Figure 23-7).

- **Dynamic font searching:** Just like iTunes and the Finder, as you type the name of a font in the Search field, Font Book's lightning-fast search tool goes to work locating it from your listing of installed fonts.

- **Font Collection:** The commercial font managers call them sets, but it's a distinction without a difference. When you click the plus sign in the Collection window, it makes a new folder or collection. Name it, and drag in individual fonts or groups of fonts to form a special set that you can set up for specific jobs, or just to organize your library more easily.

note

When you create a collection, or click the disclosure triangle next to the All Fonts category, you will see the Disable/Enable buttons, as needed, to turn off entire sets — er, collections as needed. Once again, the font menus of cooperating Mac OS X applications update to reflect the change.

A Fast, Extremely Dirty Look at the Font Panel

To use your existing font library, expanded or otherwise, the Font panel (shown in Figure 23-8) does the trick.

Figure 23-8: As simple as it looks at first glance, you'll find hidden treasures when you click the Action (sprocket) menu of the Font panel, as I did here.

The Difference between Font Book and the Font Panel

So, what's the real, secret difference between Font Book and the Font panel, since both handle collections? There is actually more than one. Font Book can turn fonts on and off, and you can use it to install new fonts. The Font panel can't do any of these things. In addition, the Font panel is available from the menus of most Mac OS X applications, while Font Book is simply a separate application. Of course, you can drag it or keep it in the Dock so it'll be at your beck and call when needed.

On the other side of the coin, the Font panel can be used to activate special typographic features, such as character kerning, and display a palette of the characters available in a font, so you can take advantage of special symbols.

Let's sit down and check off what Font Panel can do:

♦ **You can invoke it from most Mac OS X applications.** Simply type ⌘-T or choose Show Fonts from the Format menu.

♦ **As with Font Book, click the plus symbol to make a new font collection.** Name it what you want, and then drag individual fonts or groups to the collection. The minus symbol is used to delete a collection.

♦ **Use the Search window to locate fonts installed on your Mac.**

♦ **Click the submenu under A to select the extra features** that I've shown previously in Figure 23-8. They are all described next:

• **Add to Favorites:** A step short of a collection, because you don't have to make a new category in which to add fonts, but it's still available from the Collections pane.

• **Show Preview:** Choose this command (see Figure 23-9) to put a small preview pane atop the Font panel window.

Figure 23-9: Now, you can see what that font really looks like.

• **Color:** This option brings up the famous Mac OS Color Wheel, which you can use to apply any available color to a font.

note I don't want to interfere with your artistic judgment, but you don't want to pick a color that looks too faint, as it just makes your material that much harder to read.

- **Characters:** Sorry, no jokes about what kind of character I am. But this may be one of your most-used features. Just where do you find that copyright symbol or square root symbol? When you choose Characters from the Font panel (shown in Figure 23-10), you see a Character Palette where you can double-click a character or click the Insert button to put it in your text wherever the cursor is pointing.

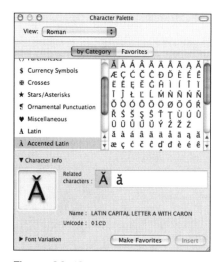

Figure 23-10: Pick a character, any character.

- **Typography:** You can set some default type settings with this palette, including whether to turn on ligatures, those special characters that combine the *f* and the *i* and other combinations, swashes, which put flourishes around letters, default character casing (all caps, small letters, etc.), and other stuff. Why would you want to do this? Well, unlike the expensive page layout program I'm using, not all software can handle special features by default. This way, even a bare bones word processor, such as TextEdit, can do a lot more.
- **Edit Sizes:** You really need 26.5 point? No problem. Just click Edit Sizes, then drag the slider or enter the custom size you want to use.

note If you tire of 26.5 point or whatever, just click Reset Sizes to set things back the way they were.

- **Manage Fonts:** What can I say? It simply invokes Font Book. End of story.

Font Family and WYSIWYG Menus in Panther

Secret

What about those fancy font menus that you had under the Classic OS? You know the ones I mean. Adobe Type Reunion, Action WYSIWYG, or Menu Fonts. All of these handy utilities would group fonts into families and display a font in its real face.

Well, some of that's already in Mac OS X Panther. Such programs as Microsoft Word, for example, display fonts in their proper face, via a Preference option. Others, such as Adobe Illustrator 10 and QuarkXPress 6, group font families. If that's not enough for you, there's yet another solution.

Unsanity makes a haxie called FontCard (www.unsanity.com/haxies/fontcard) that can be installed in the System preferences that allows for selected applications to sort fonts into families as well as display them in their own typefaces (shown in Figure 23-11).

Figure 23-11: With FontCard, individual applications can be selected or you can choose to give all applications WYSIWYG font menus.

Because some programs do a very good job of font menus, you will probably select only those applications where you can use it. When you do enable those kinds of options for an application (like StickyBrain, a great program from Chronos which can be found at http://chronos.iserver.net/&/products/index.html), **you get** a font menu that gives you the options you choose (shown in Figure 23-12).

continues

continued

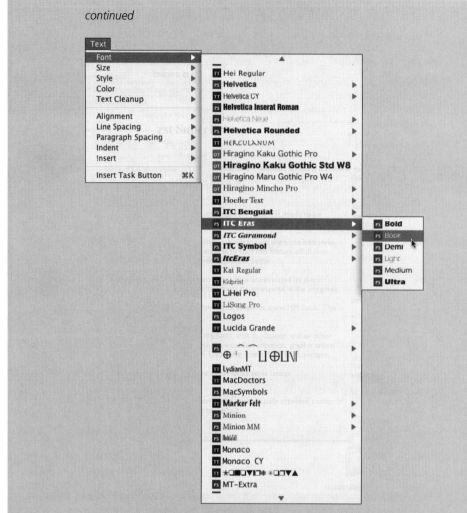

Figure 23-12: The fonts are shown here grouped in families with the kind indicated as well as the names shown in the font's own face.

A WYSIWYG display for fonts (both in a window or in a font menu) takes up a lot of memory and slows applications down, so it's a good idea to turn that feature off if you have a lot of fonts or an older computer.

A Look at Other Font Options

Something missing? Well, yes. At one time, you checked for special characters with Key Caps, a little utility that existed from the very early days of the Mac OS. With Panther, it's no longer a separate application. It's not needed, simply because the Character Palette is so much better.

However, Key Caps does live on, more or less, but finding it is not the easiest thing in the world. What you have to do is turn on the Input Menu in the International preferences and then turn on the Keyboard Layout option. This gives you access to the same old Key Caps.

But wait there's more, and that's Silk (see Figure 23-13). What is Silk? It's another useful haxie from Unsanity Software (www.unsanity.com/haxies/silk) that is used to provide what is called Quartz text rendering and smoothing for Carbon applications, something introduced to the Mac OS way back in 10.1.5.

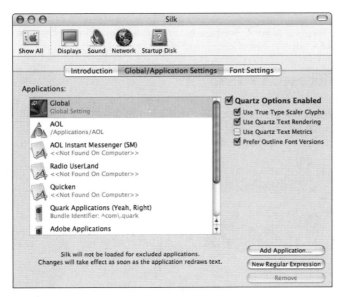

Figure 23-13: Silk makes fonts appear silky smooth in some applications that otherwise don't do such a good job at it.

Now why would anyone need to activate a feature that has been available for so long? Well, unfortunately, not all software publishers have gotten the message, and so their efforts at font smoothing, well, stink.

That brings us back to Silk, which enables Quartz rendering and smoothing for programs that don't already support it. But a single feature like this is a diminishing asset, so as more and more Carbon programs get proper updates, Unsanity decided to do a bit more to make the program useful. In addition to smoothing text display, you can use it to substitute default fonts in applications and to change the theme font, which is used to display such widgets as menus and titles. So if you need any of this stuff, give Silk a try. It works, as you might have noticed in Figure 23-13, as an add-on to your System Preferences panel, so you can easily customize it for the applications that are still behind the times.

---

tip

I don't want to lull you into a sense of security that I've covered everything. Another way to view special characters is PopChar X. This program from Ergonis (`www.macility.com/products/popcharx/`) gives you one-screen access to all the special characters in a font. Like its predecessor, which was a popular standby with graphic artists over the years under the Classic Mac OS, PopChar X puts up a tiny box with a *P* inside at the top-left corner of your screen. Click on it and, presto, you'll see the characters that are available in the font you're using, even better than the Character Palette, to my way of thinking, but this is one program you have to pay for.

The Main Third-Party Font Managers

So far we've covered ATM and Font Book. Because ATM is no longer a current font management program, and because Font Book is made by Apple, it occurs to me that we haven't really covered the third-party choices that you have yet. So let's get to it . . .

An Extensis Suitcase X1 Primer

I have used Extensis (`www.extensis.com/suitcase/`) Suitcase (shown in Figure 23-14) off and on for so many years, I feel I've grown up with the program, so I'll give it first crack here. Although its interface went through an overhaul some years back, the basic layout, with a three-pane window (now with a side drawer), forms the basis for the programs that followed it.

Figure 23-14: Still around after all these years, but with a face lift.

Here's how you set up Suitcase after a simple installation process.

1. First, create a special folder for the fonts you want to leave out of the Mac OS X Fonts folders. These are the fonts you want to set up for part-time use, to turn on and off as needed. Some folks call it a Resources folder; others call it Fonts, but remember to keep this folder outside of the various Library folders, or you'll end up replacing another Fonts folder by mistake.

2. Launch Suitcase and then open the Suitcase preferences and make sure that you aren't activating the fonts as you add them to the application (shown in Figure 23-15). Do this by making sure that the option to Activate fonts when added to Suitcase is deselected.

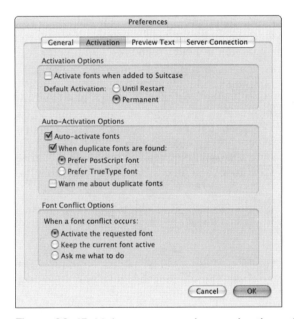

Figure 23-15: It's important to make sure that the option to Activate fonts when added to Suitcase is deselected when you add fonts to Suitcase.

3. After you close the preferences, click the Add (plus sign) button in Suitcase's toolbar, which brings up a simple Open dialog box that you can use to locate the fonts you want the program to recognize. Once the fonts are added, information about them is stored in the program's database, but the fonts themselves are not actually moved or copied.

Secret

Drag and Drop in Suitcase to Add Fonts

Here's an even faster way to add your fonts. All you have to do is drag the actual fonts or the fonts folder(s) that encase them to the bottom pane of the Suitcase window. Presto! They are now indexed in the program's database.

If you drag a folder of fonts to the sets panel (at the top), you create a set that is the same name as the folder of fonts you are adding.

Let's cover the rest of the features quickly:

- ⬥ **Classic application support:** Suitcase also supports your older applications. As part of the installation, it pops a handful of system extensions into your Mac OS 9 System Folder to accomplish this magic. That way your older programs can benefit from the enhanced library under Mac OS X.

- ⬥ **Printing of font samples:** Yes, you can preview them on screen, but wouldn't it be nice to print out sample pages for your own reference or for your clients? Just choose Print Sample Pages from the File menu to get hard copy of your favorites.

- ⬥ **Sets:** What's in a name? They're called collections in Font Book and sets in Suitcase and other programs. But it's all about the same thing, the ability to set aside a group of fonts for specific purposes.

- ⬥ **Activation of a font for temporary use:** When you click on the name of a font, an amber bullet suddenly appears. Next time you restart, the font is turned off, so you don't have to remember to switch it off when you don't need it.

- ⬥ **Activation plug-ins:** While some Mac OS X programs automatically update their font menus, others require special plug-ins. So, Suitcase comes with the add-ons for such applications as Adobe Illustrator, InDesign, and QuarkXPress.

- ⬥ **Fonts for your server:** There's yet another version of Suitcase, bearing the name Server, which puts your font libraries in a central database on a network server. This is quite useful for a larger company, especially if you have an active art department that needs convenient access to lots of fonts.

- ⬥ **New management features:** From under the Tools menu in Suitcase you have the options to Scan & Repair Selected Fonts as well as to Manage Duplicates and/or the System Fonts (shown in Figure 23-16).

Figure 23-16: Suitcase has been pumped up with lots of new features for scanning and controlling your fonts as well as the System fonts.

- ⬥ **System font control:** As I said in the last point, you can manage your system fonts. The newest version of Suitcase not only allows you to see the fonts in the various system folders, but also allows you to move them so you can turn them off.

note You probably know the score. When you buy software, it is licensed to one computer unless you have a special site license. The exception is laptops; you can sometimes use it on a portable, so long as the desktop doesn't use the same software at the same time.

But fonts usually work differently. They are usually licensed per output device — a high-falutin' word for a printer. That means you can use fonts on a large number of Macs, so long as you only have the number of output devices specified in the user license, usually two.

In addition, you are usually allowed to package your fonts and send them to the printer, so long as they're only used for your documents. Then the printer is supposed to either archive them or delete them, but you and I both know that some companies pay only a nodding acquaintance with these limits. From personal experience, I can tell you that a few of you have some fonts of unknown origin around, but the law's the law, and you should do your best to make sure you follow the user licensing requirements specified for the fonts you buy.

A Diamond Soft Extensis Font Reserve Primer

Taking another approach to font storage is Font Reserve (see Figure 23-17). Rather than simply store information about your font library, this application creates a single "Vault," or database, that actually contains all your fonts, or at least the ones you add to it.

Figure 23-17: Font Reserve's browser window is familiar territory for Suitcase users. It's shown here with one of the fonts in a separate preview window.

When I started writing the book, Font Reserve (`http://www.extensis.com/fontreserve/`) still belonged to Diamond Soft. Somewhere along the way, it was absorbed by Extensis. Because Extensis also makes Suitcase (its leading competitor), it makes one question the long-term availability of Font Reserve. To date, there have been no public statements about discontinuing either for the other. But common sense would suggest that in the end there will be only one.

You can opt to just copy the fonts rather than move them. This can be done to be more flexible, or simply because you're paranoid that the fonts might up and disappear for good if something happens to that database. This isn't anything you should worry about if you follow a good backup regimen. These options are accessed in the Preferences dialog box (shown in Figure 23-18).

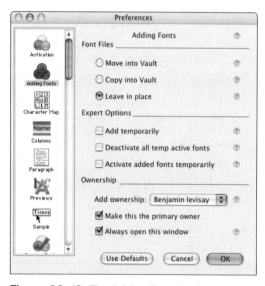

Figure 23-18: The Adding Fonts Preferences pane is where you choose where and how to add fonts to Font Reserve.

Font Reserve goes a little crazy with Preferences. Besides the adding fonts prefs, there are export prefs and ownership prefs. IMHO, there are too many prefs to make this a user-friendly font manager. But if you must know, when I have used Font Reserve, I do opt for the copy option, and I back up, so call me what you will, but I never flinch at the *p* word.

Here's a few Font Reserve pointers to get you up and running:

♦ **It has to be activated after installation.** Just installing the thing isn't enough. Until you activate it, it just sits there and does nothing, which isn't very productive. So to get started, you have to launch the Font Reserve Settings (displayed in Figure 23-19) program, where you can activate its features, which include becoming a startup application and working with Classic applications.

Figure 23-19: First you have to select On to make it all happen.

> **note** As with Suitcase, you'll need to install programs for the major graphics applications from Adobe and Quark to support font autoactivation. Other programs manage the feat without any outside help, but don't get me started.

♦ **Use the browser.** After Font Reserve starts doing its thing, you'll see the Font Reserve Browser application (look again at Figure 23-17 if you must). You can, as with Suitcase, drag to add fonts to the Fonts pane. This program's unique aspect is its ability to purchase fonts from major foundries (a buzzword for a font maker), such as Adobe and Bitstream.

Dealing with a Quirk of Font Reserve

All programs have a quirk or two or three, and Font Reserve is no exception. On occasion, the On button in the Settings application won't stay on, so fonts can't be activated. If this happens to you, don't run for shelter. Rebuild the font database.

Here's how you do it, if you had the forethought to make a backup copy of your database:

1. Launch Font Reserve Settings and turn the program off.
2. Locate the Font Reserve Database folder, which goes in your Users/Shared folder.
3. Rename the folder, so it's not replaced. Yes, you can trash it if you want, but I'd do that after you are certain the new folder works.
4. Dig out the backup copy of the Font Reserve Database folder and bring it on over to this directory.
5. Now launch Font Reserve Settings, click Select, and locate the replaced folder. Remember to select the folder; don't open it, okay?
6. If you see a request to check system fonts, let it do so, to complete the job of recognizing your backup database.

No backup? Okay, the process is a bit more involved because the database must be rebuilt, so let's get started:

1. Locate the Font Reserve Database folder on the Users/Shared folder on your Mac's drive.
2. Select the folder, and bring up the Get Info pane, by choosing that command from the File menu or by typing ⌘-I.
3. Write down the size of the folder, and double-check the available space at the bottom of a Finder window when your hard drive is selected. You need to make sure that you have enough space to make a copy. I don't want to make a big deal of this, but you really should always make sure that at least 20 percent of your hard drive is empty for best performance.
4. Launch the Font Reserve Settings utility and switch the program off.
5. Now, click New, and switch the default name of your font database to something different, such as Font Reserve Database Copy or perhaps something a bit more inventive.
6. Navigate to the very same folder the original copy is located, and click Save. This process makes a brand new font database, which will be listed in the Folder pop-up menu. Now you can reactivate the program and quit.
7. Next, you'll launch Font Reserve Browser, and give it a chance to examine your system fonts, if you've chosen to recognize them.
8. This next step is necessary only if you opted to move rather than copy your fonts into the database (which is why I take the paranoid approach myself). Locate and drag the original Font Reserve Database folder to the Fonts pane.

♦ **Don't use the option to support system fonts.** If you find you'd rather cut back on some of the system fonts not needed for font display, you do have the option to have Font Reserve handle the whole shebang. My recommendation is don't! For one thing, some Mac OS X applications are a little finicky about what fonts they look for and where, and might not run properly. So, at the very least, leave the fonts in the System/Library/Fonts folder alone.

♦ **Print font samples.** Build a sample book, waste some trees, or just print on both sides of the paper . . . your choice.

An Alsoft MasterJuggler Pro Primer

Earlier in this chapter, I told you that Alsoft's MasterJuggler (www.alsoft.com/Master Juggler/) came along to compete with Suitcase. What I didn't tell you that it did a very good job. Originally, it was better than Suitcase. For a time I worked for a magazine, and I can remember that we used this until ATM Deluxe came out.

Alsoft does a good job with their products and MasterJuggler is no exception. The interface is simple and elegant. It's not the program I use any more, but it has its advocates.

The interface is broken into two panels (shown in Figure 23-20). The far-left panel is the sets and fonts. The main panel shows tabs that give you the various ways you look at your fonts.

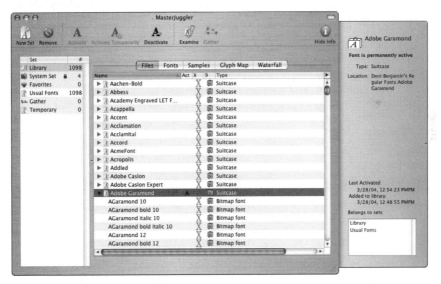

Figure 23-20: To switch from the font lists to the viewing options, you just click on the tabs above the main window pane.

The info drawer shows additional information about whatever is selected in either of the two other window panes.

One of its main strengths is the Font Guardian feature, which can be accessed in the Preferences dialog box (shown in Figure 23-21). These options allow MasterJuggler to prevent problems in your fonts before you use them.

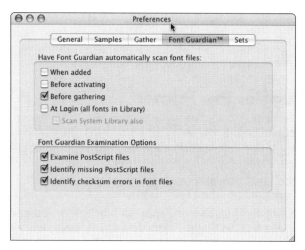

Figure 23-21: The Font Guardian features can be set to work when you add or when you activate fonts.

As I used MasterJuggler, I found it a little slow and unwieldy. Some of this is probably from being used to other programs. But I'm as guilty as anyone else for displaying what I call the Macintosh mentality. If you haven't heard this one, it goes like this, "If you walk up to a program and it doesn't do exactly what you want it to do right away intuitively the very first time without any learning curve, then it must not work well or be broken." That's the Macintosh mentality. That being said, I still think that it's not as clean as some of the other font management programs that I have used.

I don't use MasterJuggler myself right now, but I'm going to keep my eye on it.

An Insider Software FontAgent Pro Primer

For years, graphic artists depended on Insider Software's FontAgent to unearth damaged fonts. The smart people at Insider finally decided that they had a better answer to complete font management, and thus FontAgent Pro (www.fontagent.com/) was born (shown in Figure 23-22).

My confession is that I'm a big fan of FontAgent Pro (v. 2.1) and the great folks at Insider Software. I use it and have switched our little company to selling this product as our font management program for our pro and prosumer[NLR2] clientele. The program is not only great, but the people at Insider Software truly care about listening to their customers to develop features that are useful and powerful.

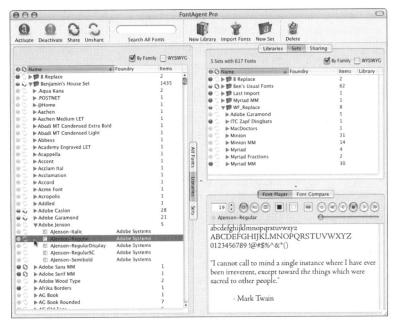

Figure 23-22: FontAgent Pro 2.1 gives you that famous three-pane interface with some new icons and without that brushed metal look.

With FontAgent Pro, not only are fonts examined for damage, and fixed, but also the optimized versions are all moved to a special folder. This means that if your fonts are a mess and you need to organize them you can do that through the program rather than before you get to the program.

Secret

Using FontAgent Pro Trial to Clean Your Fonts for Free

If your font library is as messy as my desk, here's one great feature of FontAgent Pro you may not notice. As part of its font fixer-upper process, the application will organize your fonts into families. So, finally, you can get all those Helveticas and Futuras together.

You can download FontAgent Pro for a free 30-day trial version. This trial version is a fully functional version of the program. You can then use this trial version to organize your fonts. Regardless of what you do after 30 days, you will have an organized font library (shown in Figure 23-23).

New in the latest version of FontAgent Pro is a feature that fixes an old problem. If you have homemade (or bloated) font suitcases that contain a whole bunch of fonts, like an A-font suitcase that contains 40 different fonts, this new version splits these fonts apart and creates new suitcases for each style and then organize them into folders in your new font folder. This leaves you with a converted library of fonts that contain font suitcases that contain only one font each.

continues

continued

Name	Date Modified	Size	Kind
▶ A	Mar 20, 2004, 1:22 PM	--	Folder
▶ B	Mar 20, 2004, 1:22 PM	--	Folder
▶ C	Mar 20, 2004, 1:22 PM	--	Folder
▶ D	Mar 20, 2004, 1:22 PM	--	Folder
▶ E	Mar 20, 2004, 1:22 PM	--	Folder
▶ F	Mar 20, 2004, 1:22 PM	--	Folder
▶ G	Mar 20, 2004, 1:22 PM	--	Folder
▶ H	Mar 20, 2004, 1:22 PM	--	Folder
▶ I	Mar 20, 2004, 1:22 PM	--	Folder
▶ J	Mar 20, 2004, 1:22 PM	--	Folder
▶ K	Mar 20, 2004, 1:22 PM	--	Folder
▶ L	Mar 20, 2004, 1:22 PM	--	Folder
Last Import.plist	Yesterday, 1:42 PM	4 KB	XML file
Log.txt	Yesterday, 1:42 PM	Zero KB	Plain t...ument
▶ M	Mar 20, 2004, 1:22 PM	--	Folder
▶ N	Mar 20, 2004, 1:22 PM	--	Folder
▶ O	Mar 20, 2004, 1:22 PM	--	Folder
▶ P	Mar 20, 2004, 1:22 PM	--	Folder
▶ Problem fonts	Yesterday, 1:42 PM	--	Folder
▶ Q	Mar 20, 2004, 1:22 PM	--	Folder
▶ R	Mar 20, 2004, 1:22 PM	--	Folder
▶ S	Mar 20, 2004, 1:22 PM	--	Folder
▶ T	Mar 20, 2004, 1:22 PM	--	Folder
▶ U	Mar 20, 2004, 1:22 PM	--	Folder
▶ V	Mar 20, 2004, 1:22 PM	--	Folder
▶ W	Mar 26, 2004, 3:36 PM	--	Folder
▶ Z	Mar 20, 2004, 1:22 PM	--	Folder

Figure 23-23: Your newly FontAgent Pro–sorted fonts will look like this.

The rub on this is that you now have a whole lot more font suitcases than you started with. Not to worry, if you decide to purchase the program you can get the program to group the single font suitcases back into families for ease of use.

Now if it could do the same for my office floor, my wife would buy stock in the company.

Here's a brief look at how FontAgent Pro works:

◆ **Setting activation and Classic preferences:** Before you import any fonts, you need to set your preferences (shown in Figure 23-24). One of the cool new preferences is to activate the fonts for Classic applications. This means that you can use just this one program to manage fonts in both OS X and Classic. And thanks to the autoactivation plug-ins, the classic programs will autoactivate fonts in FontAgent Pro.

◆ **Setting general preferences:** All you can do in this preference panel is to enable multiple libraries and choose to manage the System fonts. If you choose to manage the System fonts, the fonts are moved (except the fonts in the System folder), so you can turn them off and on at will.

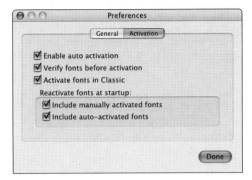

Figure 23-24: FontAgent Pro preferences are as simple as preferences get.

♦ **Importing fonts:** When you run FontAgent Pro for the first time after installation, you see a dialog box asking you to specify the location of the fonts to import. Here you'll want to, as I suggested previously, put your spare fonts in a separate folder, and specify that location. You can also drag a folder of fonts on the program interface or click on the Import button at the top of the FontAgent Pro window.

If you click on the Import button, you get a dialog box that asks you for your choices (shown in Figure 23-25). You can move or copy the fonts. And you can choose the diagnostic options as well as the destination of your newly organized font library.

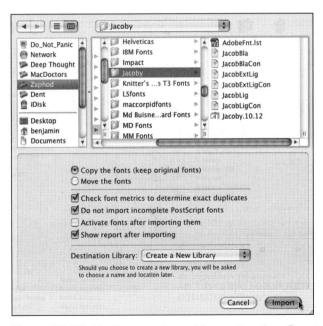

Figure 23-25: You have to choose Move rather than Copy to get the most out of the diagnostic and fix-it-up features.

caution

> If you choose Move rather than Copy, you should have another copy of your fonts somewhere else. FontAgent may do things to your set that you may not like, if you choose to use another font management program besides FontAgent Pro.

◆ **Check the report:** After you import your fonts, you should look at the Report dialog box (shown in Figure 23-26). You will see what went wrong. You can also look at the what's wrong in the destination folder in a folder called Problems Fonts (shown earlier in Figure 23-23). You can also find a copy of the last FontAgent Pro report in the destination library font folder.

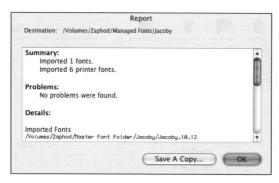

Figure 23-26: The report varies depending on the options you've chosen when importing fonts.

Secret

Using Libraries for More Control in FontAgent Pro

FontAgent Pro, unlike the other font management programs, can actually handle more than one font library at the same time. This allows you to add and subtract by something that is similar to sets.

This way, your own fonts can be put in one place, and the fonts you may receive from clients for special purposes can go in another. Then when you're done, you just remove the customer's library.

◆ **Playing back your fonts.** A unique feature of FontAgent pro is the ability to play back font samples in slide show fashion, using its Font Player. This way, you or your clients can watch the show and select the best styles for a particular job. It may also be a unique alternative if you can't find anything good to watch among those 250 channels your cable or satellite TV offers. But that's another story.

◆ **Printing font samples:** Just like the others, FontAgent Pro can produce printed samples. But even better, you can save them as PDF files and e-mail them to your clients, so they can see your font library at their leisure.

◆ **Displaying fonts — WYSIWYG:** Click on the WYSIWYG button that is active when you click on your Fonts pane, and you'll see them in their actual styles.

♦ **Searching fonts:** If you have a huge library like I do and it contains some interestingly named fonts, it's handy to be able to search your library (or libraries) for a single word (shown in Figure 23-27). What you get is all fonts that contain that word.

Figure 23-27: A fast way to get at your Garamonds when they don't all start with *G*.

♦ **Sharing fonts:** New in FontAgent is the ability to utilize Rendezvous to share fonts with FontAgent users running Panther on your network. This can be done in a peer-to-peer fashion or in some future workgroup edition. You have to choose which fonts you want to share and then subscribe to those fonts that are being shared.

A Few Last Words about FontAgent Pro

It isn't perfect, but what is. It's simple and it's powerful. I use a font library of about 35 hundred fonts in five different programs. FontAgent Pro does the best with them. It adds them more quickly than the others. It finds more problems than the others, and it starts up more quickly than the others.

So, until I see one of the other programs gear up with some significant new features, it's going to be FontAgent for me.

Secret

Avoiding Font Problems in OS X and Classic Using Target Disk Mode

Did you know that a damaged Classic font may prevent your Mac OS X system from working? Strange, but true. I know of a couple of situations where that damaged font resulted in a stagnant blue screen every time the affected Macs were booted. Solution? In these cases, the Macs could still restart from Mac OS 9. Once booted in OS 9, the Fonts folder was moved to the desktop. When the Macs were rebooted under Mac OS X, all was right in the world. FontAgent Pro should be able to fix those damaged fonts.

continues

continued

This kind of fix isn't so easy when you have a Mac that can't boot under Mac OS 9. There a suggested workaround is to hook that Mac up to another Mac via the FireWire ports. Then restart the affected Mac, holding down the T key till you see a FireWire icon on its display. Now its drive will mount on the desktop of the other Mac as a regular hard drive, and you can do your Fonts folder removal surgery. After that's done, press and hold the affected Mac's power key till it shuts down, disconnect the FireWire cables, and restart normally.

Don't have another Mac or at least another with FireWire? Time to call your friends.

Summary

I'll take Times, you take Helvetica, and with a little organization, we'll be on our way to font bliss. And don't ignore those font managers, because they can make the work of font mavens far, far easier.

You shouldn't get the sense that an $89 font management program will fix your whole world. It won't. In fact, if you use a font management program correctly you will probably find that you have a bunch of new problems with your document not finding the fonts that you originally used. But of the font-related problems that you *can* have — like poor stability or documents that won't print without postscript errors — missing fonts are the lesser of your font management evils.

In the next chapter, we'll leave behind the world of the kerned pair and move into the world of Apple hardware. (Not to worry . . . fonts won't cause hard drives to fail.)

Macintosh Hardware Part by Part

♦ ♦

Secrets in This Chapter

♦ ♦

This book is really about OS X — specifically Panther — but the powers that be thought it might be a good idea to throw in a hardware chapter. As a Macintosh hardware sales and service provider, I have to admit some discomfort with the idea of wrapping all-things-hardware into a single chapter. If you've ever looked at Apple's Service Source (hardware resources for Authorized Service Providers), you can easily see that there are volumes of information that require quite a bit of skill to use.

The original idea behind this chapter was to give you some good tips and techniques for basic hardware repair. But, due to the volume and problematic nature of the topic, I'm limiting this discussion to an overview of the basics. We look at the typical Mac, from keyboard, to mouse, to motherboard to see how they work together to provide the Mac's marvelous user experience.

And despite some of my reservations, I show you how to open a Mac to add memory, drives, and maybe even an expansion card or two.

What Makes a Mac a Mac?

The short answer to this is that the hardware and operating system are both made by Apple. This is very different from the PC world where a manufacturer, like Dell, builds a box and then goes to Bill Gates and asks for an OS to run on it.

The Biggest Difference between Macs and PCs

This is probably a harder thing for Microsoft than it is for the hardware manufacturer. They have to try to develop and sell an OS that runs on a wide range of boxes with processors, logic boards, and other components from gosh knows where. (Did you notice my little dig at the PC hardware manufacturers there?)

Apple doesn't have this problem. They only have to write an OS to work on their own computers. And because Apple doesn't allow (anymore) anyone to make clones, they have a significantly easier task. Of course, it doesn't hurt to have a superior OS to start with. (And there's my little dig at Microsoft. I didn't want them to feel left out.)

Macintosh computers typically contain components that have to meet Apple specifications; this sounds obvious, but most manufacturers send out bids for a particular component and whatever component manufacturer has the cheapest bid gets the order (providing that the specifications are met). If all components were of the same quality, it would make sense to always go with the cheapest components. In the computer world, throwing a group of the cheapest components into a box and calling it a computer is a mixture for failure. Manufacturer defect rates vary greatly and Apple continually has one of the lowest defect rates.

The Hardware Expense Myth

A myth that still exists to this day is that Apple computers are substantially more expensive than Windows-based computers. If a true comparison is done of the individual features, Apple computers typically cost less. All Apple computers include FireWire, Ethernet, CD burners, and more as standard features. A number of these features are add-ons and the user typically pays a premium price from other manufacturers.

Remember, it is not only the hardware that makes a computer. Software bundles are very important when comparing computers. What are Apple's iApplications worth? What price do you put on an operating system that rarely crashes? How much is it worth to know that your data is secure and the fear of a virus is minimal?

There's also the cost of ownership. If you buy a PC for $600 and then spend $200 a year (which isn't much in the PC world) for the next three years for things like component failure and virus problems, then you're PC deal starts to look like not such a great deal. On the other hand, if you spend a few hundred dollars up front and buy a Mac and you don't have to worry about viruses and the usual component failure, then maybe that is a better deal. (It certainly sounds like less aggravation.)

Why It Pays to Have AppleCare

AppleCare is Apple's extended hardware warranty offering. And usually, as a consumer, when I hear the words "extended warranty," I immediately think that a pushy commissioned sales person is trying to up his commission by selling me a useless piece of paper that I won't use.

Having said that, I can tell you that Apple's AppleCare is not a useless piece of paper. I'm a fan of AppleCare not only as a service provider but also as a consumer.

AppleCare is available on all of Apple's new computers, and now even on its iPod line. The terms and conditions vary a little, but usually your hardware's warranty is extended an additional two years. That gives you three years total hardware support on a new computer. This means that Apple pays your service provider to fix or replace your logic board, modem, and so on if they go down.

Planned obsolescence is the model for all computer manufacturers. No one builds a computer to last forever because software changes too quickly and the market needs computers to be cheaper. This translates into computers (from all manufacturers) that breakdown more frequently than they used to (another example of "they don't make 'em like they used to").

If you do the math on what it costs (which varies depending on the model), you'll probably have your AppleCare paid for if you use your extended warranty once or twice within a three-year period (which is more likely these days).

If you want to learn more about AppleCare, you can check it out online at `www.apple.com/support/products/`.

It should be noted that AppleCare does not cover you if you mess up the software on your computer. If the problem you are having on your computer can be fixed by wiping out your hard drive and reinstalling, you won't be able to get Apple to cover this under AppleCare. Sorry.

Esthetic Value

Apple's design and style need to be considered as well. The elegance of the iMac dating back to the first generation and now to the latest revision with a 20" flat panel display are very appealing to the eye.

Apple's form factors have that classy look that PC manufacturers have tried to copy for years. All of the computers in Apple's current line have a style that is unrivaled and true feel of quality.

My wife has a 17" flat panel iMac downstairs just off the dining room and everyone who comes over stops and looks at it. I don't know that has value for you or not. But I thought it was worth mentioning.

Apple's Current Line of Computers

One of the things that we can do in this chapter is to talk about computers that Apple is offering to the world right now. Please keep in mind that by the time this book is published, these models and features will probably have changed.

iMac

Apple's current lineup of computers includes the iMac, which is comprised of a computer base that resembles half of volleyball. This portion houses all of the computers components (hard drive, logic board, CD/DVD drive, modem, etc.) and connections (FireWire, USB, Ethernet, etc.). An adjustable neck comes out of the top of the base and holds the LCD flat panel display. The LCD displays vary on the iMac in size and include a 15", 17", or 20" version. The individual models also vary in processor speed, amount of RAM, hard drive size, and other options. The iMac is typically marketed to home and small business users.

eMac

The eMac was originally introduced strictly for Apple's education channel. It wasn't until public demand for the units rose that Apple decided to make them available to everyone. The eMac has a G4 processor and has many similar features as the iMac but uses a 17" standard tube monitor instead of the LCD flat panel. The eMac currently consists of two models that vary in the amount of RAM, hard drive size, and type of optical drive (Super Drive or Combo Drive). It resembles a big brother version of the original iMac. The eMac is marketed to schools and home and small business users.

iBook G4

The iBook is Apple's consumer portable. The latest revision includes a G4 processor. The three models vary in processor speed, hard drive size, and screen size. All of the iBook models come with Apple's Combo drive allowing you to burn CD's and play DVD's. The iBook is not currently available with Apple's SuperDrive, which allows you to burn DVDs. The iBook is marketed to mobile consumers who desire portability in a small, inexpensive package.

PowerBook G4

The PowerBook is Apple's prosumer portable. *Prosumer* refers to a person who makes a living using the computer. This includes graphic designers who work with large files and need the additional processor speed and typically desire the SuperDrive mechanism and a larger screen. All of the PowerBooks use the G4 processor. Apple's current line of PowerBook's vary in screen size 12", 15", and 17", processor speed, amount of RAM, hard drive size, optical drive (Combo drive versus SuperDrive), and video cards.

PowerMac G5

Apple's tower model consists of the PowerMac G5. The tower model's market focus is to prosumers who need every bit of speed they can get to manipulate the large files or video production they are involved with. The tower chassis allows future internal expansion of RAM memory and hard drives as well as the addition of expansion cards. The current line of G5s varies by processor speed (including two models that use dual processors), amount of RAM, number of available RAM slots for expansion, hard drive size, and video cards. All G5 models come standard with the SuperDrive mechanism.

Xserve & Xserve RAID

Apple also has its own line of IU server with a G5 processor in a rack mounted form factor called the Xserve. This has been a big breakthrough for Apple. They now have a high powered, cross-platform server that boasts unlimited clients and killer speed. The internal drives can be striped or mirrored for speed or security. And it's designed to run headless (without a monitor).

With the addition of a fiber channel card, the Xserve can be hooked up to Apple's Xserve RAID, which gives you up to 3.5 terabytes of data storage in 14 separate drive bays.

Other Stuff

Besides Apple's separate flat panel displays that are designed to be used with the pro line of PowerMac and PowerBook, a few other hardware products don't fall into the computer category.

The iPod is the Apple best-selling MP3 player and the portable jukebox for your iTunes library. It can be used on both the Mac and the PC. And because it works with Apple's iTunes (running on either the Mac or PC platform), you're still assured of a relatively easy experience, even if you're on the PC. If you're interested in iTunes, it has its own chapter (Chapter 13) in this book.

The iSight is designed to be the digital eye for Panther's iChat AV. Like the iPod, it connects to your computer via FireWire (although the iPod can also be connected via USB 2.0 as well). And just like iTunes, iChat AV has its own chapter (Chapter 19) in this book.

The AirPort Base Station and the AirPort card (by Apple) use the 802.11 protocols for wireless networking. These are used a great deal in portables, but they can also be used in desktop units in environments that make running traditional cable (for networking) difficult.

Some of these devices can be used on computers other than the Mac. But all of them are designed to be installed and used by the average consumer with a minimum of fuss.

Secret

Finding a Place to Buy and/or Service Your Mac Hardware

One of the problems with being a Mac owner is that you sometimes have to look pretty hard for a place to take your Mac. There are always a few Mac guys around, but are they authorized to service your in-warranty Mac?

A great place to find that out is at http://wheretobuy.apple.com/locator/ on the Apple Web site. All you have to do is to type in your location in the browser (shown in Figure 24-1), the kind of customer you are, and Apple helps you find the authorized Macintosh resource nearest you.

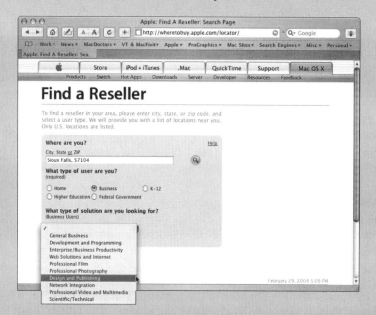

Figure 24-1: Enter your city, zip code, and kind of service and then click on the green spy glass to get your listing of Apple resellers.

The Apple resource locater is a good place to start. At least you'll know what you have available in your area.

If you what you're looking for is someone that deals either primarily (if not exclusively) in Macintosh hardware and software, you'll want to find yourself an Apple Specialist. An Apple Specialist is both an Authorized Apple Reseller and an Authorize Apple Service Provider (like yours truly). We (Specialists) also have a Web site (www.applespecialist.us/) that helps you find one of *us* near you (shown in Figure 24-2).

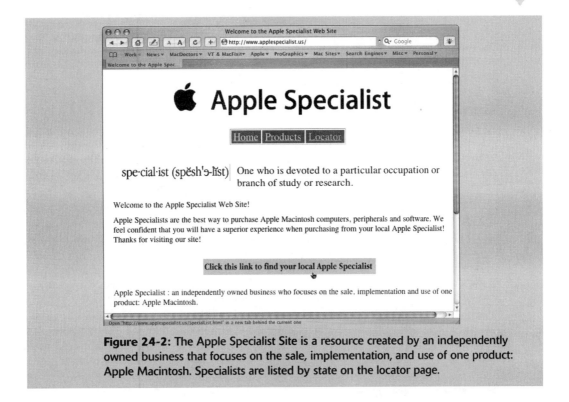

Figure 24-2: The Apple Specialist Site is a resource created by an independently owned business that focuses on the sale, implementation, and use of one product: Apple Macintosh. Specialists are listed by state on the locator page.

Differences between a Desktop Unit and a Laptop Unit

Portable computers (laptops) are the fastest growing segment of Apple's computer sales. For the right user, the laptops make a lot of sense. Early models of laptops lacked many of the features of their desktop counterparts, but that is no longer the case. The newest laptops give you portability and are feature laden. Many users including myself use a laptop for their main computer. I like the portability and the ability to watch a DVD anywhere and still have the computing power that I crave. When I come into my office, I connect a standard keyboard and mouse, 17" monitor, and network connection.

The downside of laptops is the lack of expandability and in some cases computing power relative to their tower counterparts. The tower models give you room on the inside to add bigger or different drives and RAM. Given the memory overhead of many of the graphic arts programs, a graphic designer may find the RAM limitations in laptops a hindrance. And it's not just professionals. Some games (and gamers) require (or at least like) much more Ram than someone who use Microsoft Word all day long. Laptops typically don't have the latest and fastest processors. The reasons for this are two-fold. First, the newest fastest processors run too hot to be adequately cooled inside of the small laptop case.

Second, the newest processors are usually inefficient when it comes to power consumption. These items are not factors in a tower unit that has adequate cooling and is always tethered to an AC outlet. But in a laptop, the efficiency and cooling of the processor is critical. It does no good to have the fastest processor in a laptop if it operates on battery power for less than one hour only.

Battery

Battery consumption on laptops also varies greatly depending on how it is used. Want to use the laptop to play DVDs while traveling in the car? Be sure to have an extra battery — or better yet a DC adapter. The constant spinning that a DVD requires while playing cuts the battery rating in half and may leave you with a car full of screaming kids while you try to explain why the laptop quit ten minutes before the movie ended.

Expansion

Expansion is another consideration when considering a laptop. If you need to work on extremely large files, 2 gigabytes of RAM is not out of line. The top-of-the-line G5 tower allows RAM expansion to 8 gigs, while some of Apple's Pro PowerBooks currently have a 2-gig limit. Similarly, a G5 tower allows for the addition of video cards, SCSI cards, and real time video processing cards for professional video production.

The only expansion that the pro line of PowerBooks has is the PCMCIA (Personal Computer Memory Card International Association) card slot (not counting the 12" G4 PowerBook, which doesn't have that option) to allow you to add new (future port technology) to your laptop.

Processor Power

Tower computers allow dual processors for the power hungry users. This enables the computer to manipulate files much faster than a single processor machine. Panther takes full advantage of dual processing power, as do most applications running natively in Panther. For example, Photoshop is written to use dual processors. The video cards in a tower computer usually have more RAM (or at least upgrade options) and redraw large images at a much faster pace than their PowerBook counterparts.

Secret

Online Resources for Apple Hardware

Although you can get a lot of information from Apple's Web site, there is also a great site by Glen Sanford for more hardware information as well as some great photos of Apple's hardware at www.apple-history.com/.

If you're looking to know more about your hardware or the history of Apple's hardware, this is a great site to start with.

Input Devices

Universal Serial Bus (USB) keyboards and mice ship standard with every Mac. USB enables you to connect multiple devices. Currently, scanners, printers, joysticks, and removable media drives are just a few of the devices using USB technology. Unlike previous Apple Desktop Bus (ADB) technology, USB is expandable and is the recognized universal standard in the computer industry. Two versions of USB currently exist. USB 1.1, which is used for most input devices including keyboards, mice, printers, and scanners, runs at a slow 11 megabits per second. USB 2.0 runs at 480 megabits per second and is typically reserved for some hard drives, CD/DVD burners, and backup mechanisms, which require high throughput.

While USB 2.0 ships on most of the new Macs, USB 1.1 is on every new Mac. USB 2.0 is not catching on in the Mac platform as rapidly as it is in the Windows environment. The main reason for this is every Mac comes with FireWire technology. FireWire also has two versions. The original FireWire 1.0, which runs at 400 Mbps and FireWire 2.0 (more commonly know as FireWire 400 and FireWire 800), which pushed the speed up to 800 Mbps.

Why a Single-Button Mouse?

The mouse that comes with every Mac is a USB, single-button optical mouse that uses a LED on the bottom of the mouse for tracking. Prior to that, the mouse was an ADB, single-button mouse that used a roller ball for the tracking mechanism. The optical mouse is much more efficient and easy to use, and does not require the cleaning and maintenance of the original mouse.

Why it has only a single button is something that you'd have to ask Apple about. The OS understands and works very well with two (or more)-button mice. But so far Apple hasn't created any of its own.

Third-Party Mice

Other third-party input devices exist that can enhance your computing experience. Third-party mice often have two buttons and a scroll wheel. While the second button is not a necessity, in most cases, the button can be programmed for a specific function. The scroll wheel is very handy when viewing a lengthy document or a Web page. The wheel allows you to scroll through the document without having to move the mouse to the scroll arrows on the window.

Wireless Input Devices

Wireless keyboards and mice exist, and the latest use Bluetooth technology. Bluetooth broadcasts a short-range radio frequency from the computer to Bluetooth devices. Once recognized, a Bluetooth device can be used anywhere within the range of the frequency regardless if the device is aimed at the computer or not. Wireless devices have been around for years, but the older devices used a line of sight technology and worked well while stationary but poorly when moved or if the sensor was blocked. To use Bluetooth technology, both the computer and the input device must be Bluetooth-enabled. Bluetooth adaptors may be purchased to allow older computers to use Bluetooth devices.

Trackballs and Tablets

Trackballs are another alternative to mice. The trackball works on the reverse process of the mouse. If you visualize a mouse turned upside down, this is the trackball principle. With the trackball, you move the roller ball while the base of the trackball is stationary. While the trackball is not as popular as the standard mouse, people who have switched to a trackball rarely go back to using a mouse –sometimes to relieve wrist trouble associated with using a regular mouse.. Trackballs are also available in multiple-button varieties.

Another less popular input device is the drawing tablet. The tablet allows graphic designers the ability to draw free hand as if the tablet was the computer screen. Drawing tablets can be very precise. Some models react to the amount of pressure exerted on the tablet, drawing darker or wider lines according to touch. Some designers draw a sketch on paper and the place the sketch on the tablet and trace it with the pen. This allows designers the ability to take a precise drawing and import it into the computer.

Expanding Your Mac

Earlier, I used the terms *consumer* and *prosumer* to refer to Apple's current line of computers. Consumer is a general term meant to refer to the user who has a computer but does not need it to make a living. Prosumer is the user who makes a living using the computer. Prosumer computers typically provide the maximum processor speeds and the highest level of expandability. Consumer computers typically come with software bundles such as AppleWorks and a game or two. Prosumer computers usually provide the operating system, Apple's iApplications, and little else, because Apple knows these computers are going to be loaded with the latest applications.

Expansion of both consumer and prosumer computers is always an issue. Prosumer computers are generally easier to expand, more expandable, and the expandability is usually done internally. Consumer computer have maximum RAM limitations far below that of their prosumer counterparts. Similarly, adding internal hard drives is not an option with consumer computers. In some cases, such as the iBooks, the SuperDrive mechanism is not an option, whereas the SuperDrive can be added or comes with any PowerBook.

Secret

A Small Utility to Give You Apple Hardware Information

There's great little piece of donate ware called Mactracker, written by Ian Page, that you can get on the Internet at www.mactracker.ca. This little utility gives you access to the basic hardware information to Apple's products.

To use Mactracker, launch the application and choose a computer kind and model from the application menus (shown in Figure 24-3).

After you have selected a model, you are presented with a new tabbed dialog box, which gives you even more information about the selected computer (shown in Figure 24-4).

This is exactly the kind of information you would need to know before you order more RAM or a new video card for your computer.

Figure 24-3: The computer kinds are shown across the top of the Mactracker's interface and the subcategories give you menus to select specific models.

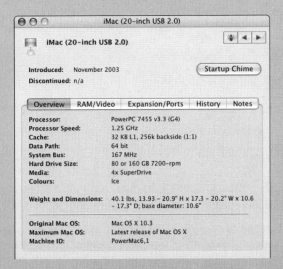

Figure 24-4: This dialog box shows you more information about the video, RAM, expansion, history, and even a picture of the selected hardware.

Knowing about Your Mac and Adding RAM

One of the things that you can do to rev your Mac up is to install more memory. And the way you install RAM is dependent on what kind of Mac you have. This information can be located in the Apple System Profiler. The easiest way to open the profiler is to open the About This Mac window and click the More Info button.

1. Check the amount of memory by clicking on the Apple in the upper-left corner and scrolling down to About This Mac (shown in Figure 24-5).

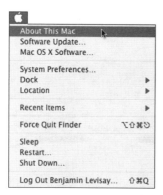

Figure 24-5: The first thing in the Apple menu is a way to find out more about your Mac.

2. This opens the About This Mac information dialog box (shown in Figure 24-6). Click on the More Info button to open the Apple System Profile applications (found in your Utility folder located in your Applications folder).

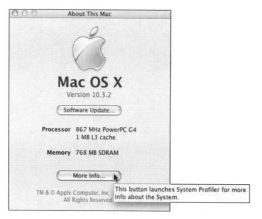

Figure 24-6: A handy info dialog box, the About This Mac window shows you your software version, your processor speed, and the amount of physical RAM read by your computer, and then provide you with buttons to access the System Profiler and the Software Update System Preference.

3. The System Profile gives you options to look at your hardware and software. Clicking on the Hardware section in the Contents panel shows you a Hardware overview (shown in Figure 24-7).

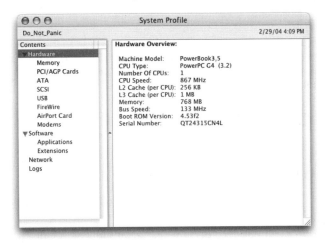

Figure 24-7: The System Profiler application shows the contents in the left panel and information for the selected contents in the right panel.

4. Selecting the Memory line (in the Contents panel) of the System Profiler shows you the amount of RAM installed in your computer (shown in Figure 24-8).

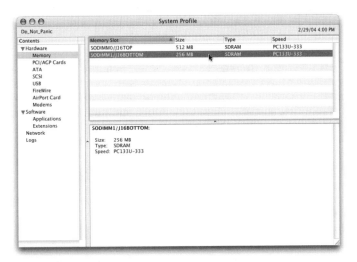

Figure 24-8: Click on Memory and the profiler displays the number of RAM slots, whether they are empty or full, what size chip is in each slot, and, most importantly, what type of memory.

Different Chips for Different Macs

All Mac's vary some in the number of slots, type of memory, speed of the memory, and the ease at which you can get to the memory.

PowerMac RAM

Apple's tower computers typically provide the easiest access to the memory slots. To add memory to a G4 tower, make sure the computer is shut down. Unplug the tower from AC power and pull the release ring on the side of the G4. The side of the G4 swings down and the memory slots are accessible. Locate an empty slot and push down on the levers at both ends of the slot. If you look closely at the memory slot, you notice two notches; simply align the notches on the memory chip with the slot and press down firmly. The levers return to their upright position when the memory is properly seated.

iBook Ram

The current iBooks have 128 MB of RAM permanently attached to the logic board and one user-accessible memory slot. In some instances, this slot is filled with a 128-MB memory chip. In order to expand the memory past 256 MB of RAM, this 128-MB chip must be removed.

With iBook shut down, unplugged, and the battery removed, locate the user-accessible slot by lifting the keyboard. To remove the keyboard, locate the two release tabs. One is next to the F1 function key and the other is by the F12 function key. Pull the release tabs towards the front of the computer and lift slightly on the tabs. The back of the keyboard lifts and can be placed face down over the trackpad. One cable remains attached and it is not necessary to unplug this cable to access the memory slot.

Depending on the model of iBook, a visual reference is on the back of the keyboard or next to the memory slot. The slot is located under the AirPort card (if you have one installed) and the AirPort card needs to be removed by disconnecting the antenna cable, lifting the retaining wire, and removing the AirPort card.

Remove the small screws that hold the memory cover in place and remove the cover. The memory slot is now visible. To remove the existing memory card, push out the retaining clips on either side of the card. Lift the memory card slightly to a 45-degree angle and remove the memory card. Install the new memory card by aligning the notch in the card with the slot. Place the card at a 45-degree angle and push it into the memory slot. The gold connectors disappear when the card is properly installed. Then press down until the retaining clips are in place. Install the memory cover and screws, reinstall the AirPort card if necessary, and reseat the keyboard.

To check the memory installation, go the Apple menu and down to About This Mac. The memory line should reflect your additional memory.

PowerBook RAM

The current PowerBooks have two memory slots with one that is usually empty depending on how you have ordered it from Apple or another reseller. To access this memory slot unplug the PowerBook and remove the battery. Close the PowerBook and place it upside down on a soft cloth. Remove the four screws that retain the memory cover. Align the notch in the memory chip with the slot and hold the memory chip at a 45-degree angle. Push the memory into the slot until the gold connectors disappear and press the chip down until the retaining clips grab the chip. Reinstall the memory cover, battery, and AC power. Start the PowerBook and check the memory line in the About This Mac window.

iMac RAM

iMacs have two memory slots, but the bottom slot is the user-accessible one. Shut down the iMac and disconnect all of the cables from the back of the iMac. Place the iMac on its side on a soft cloth so its bottom is visible. The memory cover is the entire metal plate on the bottom of the iMac. To remove the cover, unscrew the four screws and set the cover to the side. Two items are accessible from the bottom, the AirPort card slot and the memory slot. Align the notch in the memory chip with the slot and hold the memory chip at a 45-degree angle. Push the memory into the slot until the gold connectors disappear and press the chip down until the retaining clips grab the chip. Reinstall the memory cover, stand up the iMac, and connect the cables. Start up the iMac and check the memory line in the About This Mac window.

eMac RAM

eMacs have two memory slots that are both user accessible. To install memory into the eMac, disconnect all cables and place the eMac face down on a soft cloth. Remove the single Phillips screw on the white plate that covers the memory slots. Like the G4 tower, you must press the retaining clips to open them for the memory chip. Align the notch in the slot with the one in the memory chip and press firmly. When the retaining clips return to their upright position the memory chip is properly installed.

G5 PowerMac RAM

I know that G5s are also PowerMacs, but I thought I'd let them have their own section just to be clear.

To access the G5 memory slots, locate the release lever on the back of the G5 and pull it away from the computer. The side of the G5 can then be removed and set aside. Now remove the clear plastic shield and set it aside. Then, grasp the fan module by its handle and pull towards you. While it is not necessary to disconnect all cables when installing G5 memory, the computer must be shut down. The memory slots are located right behind the fan module that was just removed.

Memory chips in G5s must be added in pairs. If you want to add 512 MB of RAM you need to purchase two 256-MB modules. Look closely at the logic board right next to the memory slots and you see the slots are numbered. Factory memory is installed in slot one on the top and bottom memory slots. Locate two like-numbered available slots, align the notches in the memory chip with the notches in the slots, and press firmly. Be sure to reinstall the fan module, clear plastic cover, and outer case of the G5 before starting the computer.

Adding Expansion Cards to a PowerMac

To add an expansion card to your G5, shut down the G5, pull the lever on the back, and remove the metal the side panel of the G5. Next, remove the plastic cover and set it aside. Locate the PCI or PCI-X expansion slots and remove the metal cover for one of the slots. Align the notch in the card with the notch in the slot and press firmly. Install the retaining screw into the card, reinstall the plastic cover and metal side, and start up the G5.

note   Some expansion cards require additional software to function. You should check out the manufacturer's Web site for the most up-to-date drives as well as any known issues for any card you install in your PowerMac.

Installing Hard Drives without Bruising Your Fingers

How you install additional hard drives varies from Mac to Mac, but here are some general rules you need to follow. Find out if your computer is using SCSI or IDE hard drives by using the System Profiler. You can do this by selecting the ATA listing (shown in Figure 24-9) and the SCSI listing (shown in Figure 24-10) under the Hardware section of the Contents in the System Profiler.

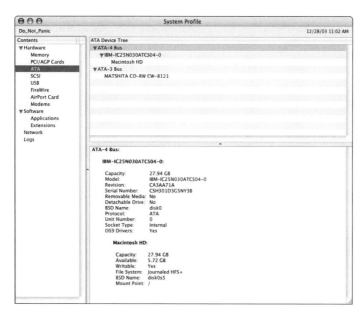

Figure 24-9: IDE, ATA, and Serial ATA devices are shown under the ATA contents. The internal hard drive and the Combo drive on my PowerBook are shown here.

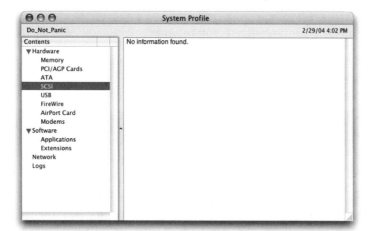

Figure 24-10: You can see both internal and external SCSI devices, their IDs, and termination information. As you can see here, I have no SCSI hardware attached to my PowerBook.

IDE Hard Drives

You can have only two drives on each IDE (ATA) bus. One of those drives needs to be set to master — the default setting for factory installed drives — and the second drive must be set to slave using a jumper on the jumper pins on the hard drive. Some computers have the option to set both drives to cable select, in which case the computer determines which drive is master and which is slave. It should be noted that in some cases, setting cable select can cause IDE conflicts – some of which can be serious.

SCSI Hard Drives

SCSI hard drives are a completely different matter. The nice thing about normal SCSI hard drives is that they allow for up to seven devices to be connected to a single SCSI controller. The downside is you have to manually set an ID number for every drive. SCSI drives have ID numbers from 0 to 6 and are set by installing jumpers across the SCSI ID pins. Termination is also an issue with SCSI drives. In theory, every SCSI bus, whether internal or external, has to be terminated.

With that said, SCSI is closer to black magic than science; so, go with what works. I have had computers that would not start up with termination installed and others that required termination to function properly. This is one of the reasons that SCSI seems to be going by the wayside.

Serial ATA Hard Drives

To add an additional hard drive to your G5 you must first purchase the correct drive. The G5 uses a serial ATA hard drive that is unique to the G5 Macintosh in Apple's line. The serial ATA drive has a small data cable connector and either the special SATA power connector or the standard 4-pin power connector. To install into the G5, shut down the computer, locate the release lever on the back of the G5, and pull it away from the computer. The side of the G5 can then be removed and set aside. The hard drive location is in the upper-right corner and has two drive bays. One is occupied by the factory-installed drive; the other is empty. Apple has provided the screws necessary to mount the drive and they are located just to the left of the hard drive bay. Unscrew these and mount them onto your new drive. Slide the drive into the available bay until it latches in place. Connect the data and power cables, flip the lever labeled *B* so that it locks the drive in place, and reinstall the outer cover. Start up the G5. If the hard drive was already initialized, it mounts on the desktop. If it was not initialized, you need to launch Disk Utility to initialize the drive.

The G5 Compared to Earlier Models

You need to make note of the G5 architecture. The G5 is a complete redesign of Apple's popular G4 tower, and many of the internal components have changed. Specifically, the hard drives in the G5 are serial ATA and are used solely in the G5. Similarly, the memory situation is unique. G5s accept 184-pin DDR SDRAMM (PC2700 or PC3200 depending on the processor) type of RAM and the RAM must be added in pairs.

Currently, the basic, single-processor G5 has four RAM slots, which sounds like enough. But keep in mind that the factory-installed RAM occupies two of these slots and when you add memory, you fill the other available two slots. With this in mind, it is a good idea to purchase more memory than you think you need. If you purchase RAM and later decide you need more, you will have to remove two of the existing modules to install more. This should be a consideration when deciding which G5 to purchase, as the dual-processor 1.8Ghz and 2Ghz G5s have eight RAM slots with six of those available for additional memory.

If you are moving from a G3 or G4 tower and need to move expansion cards that are PCI compliant, you may need to purchase new cards for the dual 1.8 or 2Ghz G5s, because the expansion slots are now PCI-X. The single 1.6Ghz G5 still accepts the PCI cards but does not accept the new PCI-X cards.

note

PCI-X is a superset of PCI and as such does support PCI cards, but with a few limitations. PCI cards will work in PCI-X slots, however they will decrease the PCI-X performance as the PCI-X bus will slow down to the maximum speed supported by the PCI card. Apple details this at `http://developer.apple.com/documentation/Hardware/ Developer_Notes/Macintosh_CPUs-G5/PowerMacG5/4Expansion/ chapter_5_section_3.html`.

Secret

Utilizing Your Reseller

If you purchase additional RAM, a new hard drive, or an expansion card from a place that you can't call when you have a problem with it, then you have made a bad purchase. Do yourself a favor and buy from (and support) a company that can not only help you determine what you need, but also help you if something doesn't work well. You may even find that the installation (of RAM or a PCI card) is included in the price of the purchase.

And if you didn't purchase it from your local reseller or service provider, you should be prepared for a bill if you take your problem to them. Ask yourself "who is responsible for making this work?"

Apple supplies a quick look at its hardware at `www.info.apple.com/support/ applespec.html`. Before you do anything with your hardware, you might want to check you computer's specs out on this site.

Summary

Messing around with your hardware can be a lot of fun — if you know what you're doing. This chapter *does not* qualify as enough information to make you a hardware expert. I hope it gives you, if nothing else, direction to find out more information about your Apple hardware.

In this chapter, we looked at some great online resources and third-party products. You also learned about Apple hardware as well as a built-in application. This information should make a more discerning Apple consumer of you.

In the next chapter, we'll give your computer eyes and expand the hardware arena to include scanners and digital cameras.

Digital Cameras and Scanners

Chapter

25

◆ ◆

Secrets in This Chapter

◆ ◆

If your Mac is a digital hub, it needs digital eyes; and that is where scanners and digital cameras come in. In this chapter, we're going to compare digital cameras and scanners, and look at how to use them . . . a bit.

Charge-Coupled Devices

Digital cameras and scanners are essentially the same technology used in two different ways. Both devices are made possible by a mechanism called a *charge-coupled device*. It sounds complicated but it is actually very simple. A charge-coupled device uses a measurement of electrical charge to represent a variable amount, such as how bright or dark a light is. Charge-coupled devices can be used for all types of things, including memory for answering machines. In a scanner, the charge-coupled device is a row of sensors that take samples of a picture at regular intervals. Then, you use scanning software to assemble the information collected and create an image that should closely resemble the one you scanned.

If scanners and digital cameras essentially use the same technology, why have scanners been around so much longer than digital cameras? The reason for this is the demands required to capture the different types of subjects each device is geared for. A scanner captures an image that can remain motionless almost indefinitely. The scanning device can take all the time it needs to move across the image and collect each bit of data it needs.

A digital camera, on the other hand, has to capture all of its data rather quickly. Even a shot of something as sedentary as a tree can be a challenge. A slight breeze can blow and make the leaves move, leaving a great green blur where a tree should be. And if that isn't challenging enough, no matter how steady the photographer is, the camera never remains completely still. So, a digital cameras sensor needs to collect all of its data in an instant, whereas a scanner can take its sweet time.

Secret

The Origins of the Charge-Coupled Device

The charge-coupled device was invented in the late sixties by Bell Labs' George Smith and Willard Boyle, who were working toward creating a new type of semiconductor memory for computers. Bell Labs later used their technology to create the first video still cameras, which were the precursors to today's digital cameras.

What Is a Pixel?

Pixel is an abbreviation of the expression *picture element or picture sample*. A pixel is the smallest bit of information in a digital image. Take a whole bunch of pixels and arrange them in the right manner and you have picture. And if it is done right you don't notice the pixels but see a gorgeous continuous-tone image.

So what it boils down to is a pixel is a square of color, no more, no less. This square can be any size, and that can be confusing. All pixels are not the same size, and different output devices can represent pixels in different ways. Before you can understand how pixels behave, we should review how pixels are measured.

Pixels are commonly measured in *dots per inch,* abbreviated as *dpi.* Sometimes this number is abbreviated as ppi, or pixels per inch, or spi, samples per inch. Dots per inch is the most common term for measuring pixels because printers use dots to make up a halftone image, and when you look at a picture in a newspaper or magazine with a magnifying glass you can see a pattern of dots make up the image. Hence, dots per inch. Pixels per inch is probably the most accurate way to describe your digital image, and this is the expression used with most image-editing programs, including Adobe Photoshop (see Figure 25-1). But because I like to kick it old school style, I will use the term dots per inch.

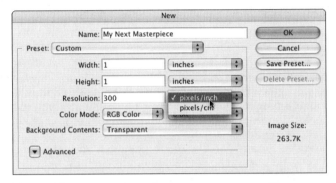

Figure 25-1: Photoshop allows you to set a new file to any resolution you want. And you can set how it is measured to whatever system you are familiar with. In this case, if you are used to using the metric system, you can set the image to pixels per centimeter.

You can determine the dpi of your image by adding the number of pixels in a horizontal row across an inch of image. So, if your image is one inch square and there are 72 pixels across that inch, your image is 72 dpi. This resolution is acceptable for display on the Web.

Now if you can take another one-inch by one-inch image that is 266 pixels across, you can determine that this image is 266 dpi. This resolution is acceptable for printing in a magazine format.

Now the two images we just discussed are the same exact physical size, one inch by one inch, but the 266 dip images has many more picture samples than the 72 dpi image.

And this brings up another concern with high-resolution images. They take up more space on your hard drive. Each pixel, no matter how small, takes the same amount of data to define it. So, while each of your images is one inch across, the 266-dpi image requires almost 14 times as much memory to store its data information.

So, How Many Pixels Do I Need?

The answer is it depends on your output device. If your image is bound for the Internet, 72 dpi is the standard. If you are going to print it on your ink jet printer 150 dpi should be enough. If you consider your work fine art, fine art prints usually run about 350 dpi. 400 dpi images are considered photographic quality.

Secret

The Truth about Printer Resolution

So, now you are a pixel pro and a dpi expert. But you have a printer that says it can print 1200 dpi. Well it can, and it can't. When it says it can print at 1200 dpi, it is telling you how large its smallest dot is across. This dot is either a dot of full color or nothing, just plain white paper. So, when you are trying to build an image full of subtle changes in tone, all or nothing doesn't cut it. What your printer is bragging about when it says it can reach that high resolution is how smooth vector art will look. (Look to Chapter 9 for more about vector art.) A 1200-dpi printer can print some very smooth type, but that doesn't mean it can print a 1200-dpi photo.

So, What Is Lpi?

This term also comes from the print world, and is an abbreviation for lines per inch. Lines per inch are the frequency or screen ruling for a halftone. A halftone, another term from the wide world of printing, is a printed reproduction of a photo using evenly spaced dots of varying diameters to produce different shades. The darker parts of your image will be populated with larger dots, the lighter portions will consist mainly of small dots. The higher the lpi of your halftone, the greater the image quality. If you take your dpi and divide it by two, you get your lines per inch.

Choosing and Using a Digital Camera

When looking for a digital camera you must keep in mind what you are using it for. Are you just using it to take family photos or do you want to be able to take shots on the sidelines of a sports events? Or do you want to be able to enlarge these photos so you can proudly place your image on the face of the Hoover Dam?

The first thing to consider is the size of image you want to output. As covered earlier, there are many destinations for your digital images. If you are just trying to put some pictures on the Web, most any camera will have the resolution you need. If you are hoping to use your digital camera as a replacement for your current 35-mm camera for recording family memories, then a two- to three-megapixel camera is probably enough. If you are taking photos destined for print production in a magazine or newspaper, you probably want as many megapixels as you can get your hands on, just so you have the flexibility to crop and enlarge your images in any manner you wish.

Secret

What's a Megapixel?

But what exactly is a megapixel? A megapixel is a million pixels (actually 1,048,576, but who's counting). So, in theory, your one-megapixel camera gives you one million pixels of information to build an image. Well, not exactly. There are a million sensors in a megapixel camera, but those sensors see in black-and-white. Your camera uses a set of filters so its sensors can see red, green, and blue, but it has to divide that information up between the sensors. In order to fill in the gaps, your camera interpolates the information. So, basically, it comes up with a pixel map of as much information as it can, and guesses (usually by averaging against a neighboring pixel) the rest. That is why your photos, at full size, can look a little mushy. But you can overcome this limitation — by buying more megapixels!

But, as things generally go, the more megapixels you want, the more money you are going to have to spend, which is the bad news. The good news is megapixels are getting cheaper all the time. The price per megapixel is hovering right around $60 these days, and it is certain to drop more.

So, you should be able to get a six-megapixel camera for $360 dollars right? That $60-a-megapixel figure comes from a camera with hardly any features at all — no optical zoom, nothing, the digital equivalent to a pinhole camera. If you want a digital camera that better emulates a film camera, you have to pay more for those features. And if you want to zoom in to get closer to your subject, you are going to spend more money on lenses than you are on the actual camera box.

But you say your camera has zoom? You have to check this closely. Some cameras say they come with 2x digital zoom and 2x optical zoom. The 2x *optical zoom* changes the way the image your sensors see through a lens and is thus a true 2x zoom. The 2x *digital zoom* works differently. It essentially takes the image the your camera's sensors read, crops out the outer part of your image, and enlarges the cropped image 200 percent. So all it has done is taken each pixel its sensors have collected and stretched them to be twice as big as they were before. If you have ever seen an image taken in this manner, the image looks like it is made of little blocks. This is called *pixelization*.

So Where Does the Film Go?

This is the digital world, so your image doesn't get stored on film. It is sent into the magical realm of zeros and ones inside your camera's storage device. But what is the storage device? Most often, the storage device is flash memory. Flash memory is used for fast and easy storage of information. Think of it as a little hard drive with no moving parts.

The most popular form of flash memory used for digital cameras is the CompactFlash card. These little cards are about an inch-and-a-quarter square and about as thick as a quarter. They are available in 8 megabyte to 512 megabytes in memory. And like anything, the more memory, the more it will cost.

Next in lines is the Memory Stick. Memory Sticks were developed by Sony and have similar storage capabilities to the CompactFlash card. This form of memory is tiny as well (about the size of a stick of gum), and costs a little more than CompactFlash cards, but it is more versatile. MP3 players and other mobile devices use this type of memory as well.

There are cameras that use different storage media. Some cameras even use compact disks for storage. If you are a studio photographer that uses a digital back for a traditional camera (an expensive traditional camera), you probably use an actual computer as memory. Images collected from a digital back are in the 16-megapixel range and would fill up smaller memory devices too quickly. But for the average user, CompactFlash and Memory Sticks should be up to the task.

The great thing about CompactFlash and Memory Sticks is that they are relatively cheap and can be easily popped in and out of your digital camera. Think of your memory cards or sticks as rolls of film you can use over and over again.

But what do you need to do to get this information on your Mac? Most cameras have a USB cable you can connect right to your computer. Barring that, there are inexpensive media card readers that connect to your Mac via your USB port. Most drivers for these types of readers are already in Panther's deep collection of drivers it ships with. If your computer doesn't recognize your flash card reader, your can contact the creator of the product and get a driver so you can get at your images. This is usually as easy as going on the Internet, typing the name of your product and the word "driver."

note A great place to compare digital cameras (and hence find the right one for you) is www.megapixel.net. This monthly Web magazine features over 270 published reviews of cameras of all capabilities and prices. The site has quick reference scores for each camera on a scale of one to ten, and in-depth analysis of features and costs.

Reusing Lenses in the Digital World

A new trend as of late in the world of digital cameras is for manufacturers to create digital camera bodies that mimic the traditional cameras they build. The main benefit of this practice is if you are already an avid photographer and have a collection of lenses, you can use these lenses on your new digital camera. Prices for these types of cameras are also dropping, with Canon offering a six-megapixel model for right around $1000.

I have a friend who is a photographer and it took him about two seconds to drop the coin for that item. He had a small collection of lenses for his Canon SLR camera (which he spent a small fortune on) and when he could move to digital without having to spend any more money on new lenses he was ecstatic. The camera does not have the same customizable capabilities as his traditional camera, but the savings on film and the ability to plug into his Mac and go more than outweighs the limitations of his digital camera.

Golly, I Wish Apple Had an Easy Way to Deal with My Photos

Well, wish no more. For those of you who have read this book sequentially, you already read the chapter on iPhoto, so you already know that Panther brings you the free program to import, organize, and display your photos.

But there is also a lesser-known predecessor to iPhoto that is included in Panther (as well as earlier versions of OS X) called Image Capture. Image Capture is a great program because, if you don't want to use iPhoto to organize your photo assets, this utility works well with whatever method you are using. Image Capture, unlike iPhoto (which does not permit your to select/import individual photos), allows you to download only the photos you want off of your camera or video card (see Figure 25-2). When you are ready, click Download and Image Capture saves the files to your hard drive. If you want to select a specific folder, click the Download Folder button at the top of the window and select Other. Image Capture lets you browse your hard drive to find the folder where you want your images to go. If you want to download only a few of your images off your digital camera, open Image Capture and click on the Download Some button to open up a browser that shows all the images on your camera.

Figure 25-2: After you have selected to photos you want to save to your hard drive (option-click to select the ones you want) you can download your images to the default file by hitting the download button in the lower-right corner of your camera's dialog box (the Picture folder in your user To change the default target file, select a new destination by clicking the Download Folder tab on near the top of the box.

Getting Around iPhoto and Image Capture

Secret

For those of you that do not want to use any of Apple's digital asset management offerings with your digital camera, you can plug your digital camera or card reader into your Mac and it will recognize the memory in your camera or reader as another drive. Your Mac mounts the camera or memory card reader as it would any external USB memory storage device. Just open the drive and drag your files into a folder on your hard drive. You can open them with an image-editing program as you would any image file.

With the Panther version of Image Capture, you can share your camera's files over a local network using Rendezvous, essentially turning your digital camera into an image server (as shown in Figure 25-3). In Image Capture Preferences, select the Sharing tab. Click in the Share my devices check box, and then select your camera. Then click in the Enable Web-Sharing check box. Hit OK. Now your digital camera is a Web server.

Using Your Camera to Spy on Others

Secret

For those of you who think using your camera as a Web server is cool, you can also use Image Capture to remotely monitor an area, but it only works with certain cameras. On the Web page where you view the photos, you can select Remote Monitor; the camera takes a new photo every sixty seconds. The photos are not saved on the camera. To change how often your remote camera takes a photo, click on the preferences button (which looks like a little light switch) but remember, this doesn't work on all cameras, and if yours is not one of those certain cameras, the Remote Monitor option is grayed out.

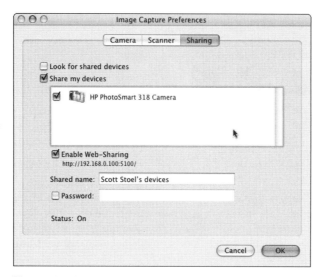

Figure 25-3: To view you images in your Web browser, just type in the URL below the Enable Web-Sharing check box. If you are using Safari, just click on the Bookmarks button on your Bookmarks Bar and select Rendezvous. Double-click on your camera's name and view your photos.

Taking Good Shots with Your Camera

Getting the best results from you digital camera isn't very difficult, and you will get better with a little practice and a little experimentation.

First, make sure your camera is set to its highest resolution setting. Digital cameras offer many different capture resolutions. On the camera's lowest setting, you can often take hundreds of shots before you fill your memory card, but these are low resolutions shots, and there is little you can do in the area of enlarging them. If your shots are going to stay on your computer, however, and you will only view them on a monitor screen, this lowest setting can be enough.

The next most important thing you can do to insure a good digital photo is to hold the camera still. This might sound obvious, but keeping the camera motionless is particularly a concern with digital cameras because they can take longer to capture an image than a traditional camera. The easiest way to do this is get a tripod. Most digital cameras come ready to mount on a tripod, and even the cheapest tripod holds your camera much more still than you can.

Also, make sure your digital zoom is off. Remember this is only using the center portion of the captured image and interpolating the image to a larger size, usually with poor results.

Take lots of shots and toss the ones you don't want. Most digicams have a small LCD screen that allows you to preview your images right on your camera. If you take a family shot and little Billy is making a face or Jenny has her eyes closed, you can dump that shot and take another.

Also, memory cards and sticks are relatively cheap. Just swap out your memory and take more pictures. You can pick the ones you want and throw away the rest when you upload them to your Mac.

Editing Your Images

Getting a good shot is just the beginning of getting good images. Once you have them on your Mac you can edit your pictures so they look even better.

iPhoto comes with a few editing tools that can help make your images more pleasing and also help you tackle some of the common problems you will encounter with your digital images.

Saving an Original Image in iPhoto

When you edit your photos on your computer, edit a copy of your file and save the original someplace safe. You might think you are improving the photo one day and the next day get attacked by a case of what-the-$%#&-was-I-thinking! You never know if you will need to get something back from that original image. In iPhoto, you can duplicate your image by selecting Duplicate under the File menu, or by typing ⌘-D (shown in Figure 25-4).

Figure 25-4: Make sure you save a copy of the photos you edit. That way you still have the original pixel information if you want to edit a photo in a different manner later. When you want to edit your photos just click the Edit button below the image to have access to iPhoto's image editing tools.

Let's look at a few of the editing tools iPhoto offers.

Listed at the bottom of the iPhoto window is the Enhance tool. It claims to enhance the colors of a photo, but it is not a very subtle tool. If you click this tool and you like the picture better, then consider it a success, but there isn't much you can do to adjust the colors in your images. If you don't like what you did, you can always select Undo from the Edit menu.

Secret

Compare iPhoto Edits Using the Command Key

If you want a quick way to compare your enhanced image with your original image in iPhoto (or any edit you perform for that matter), just hit the Command (⌘) key, and iPhoto shows you what your image looked like before you edited it.

The next tool, Red-Eye, takes care of that condition which is caused when your camera's flash passes directly into a person's eye and is reflected back to your camera. (Yes, that is the blood in your retina you are seeing.) Red-Eye reduces this spooky appearance, drawing the red out of your subject's pupil. Just drag your selection tool over the pupil and click the Red-Eye button (shown in Figure 25-5).

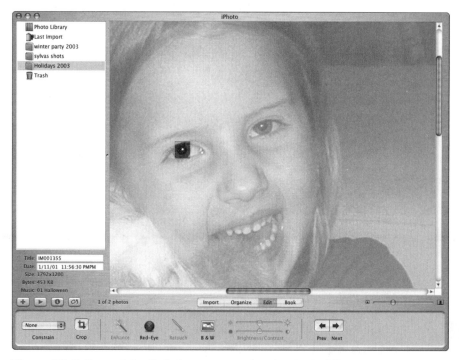

Figure 25-5: Be careful to limit the area you select for the Red-Eye tool to just the eyes. Red-Eye affects all the reds in an image, so your favorite red sweater can be converted to charcoal black with the click on a button.

iPhoto's Retouch tool is intended to remove blemishes or small marks from a photo. This is a godsend for scanned images, which often have creases, pits, or scratches on them. Suppose you shot a photo of Aunt Gertrude just when a fly landed on her forehead; you can use this tool to eliminate all traces of the pesky beast. Just select the Retouch tool and position the crosshair over the blemish you want removed, then, using short strokes drag the colors in from the surrounding area to blend.

If you want to remove unwanted parts of your image, or change the focus of interest on your picture, iPhoto offers the Crop tool. Just select the photo you want to crop and click the Edit button. Place your crosshair at one corner of the area you want to select, and then drag diagonally until the area you desire is selected (shown in Figure 25-6). Then click the Crop tool. Your image is trimmed of all the unwieldy parts and your masterpiece is ready to go.

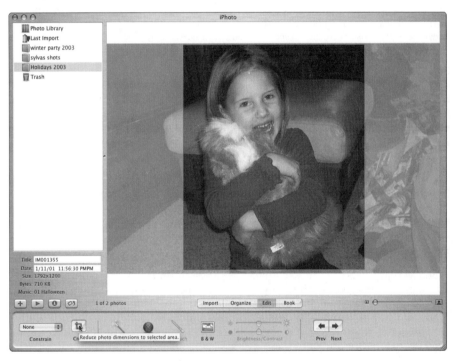

Figure 25-6: When you use the Crop tool, the area that is faded is the part of the image that is trimmed.

Secret

Shoot High, Save Low for a Better Image

Another way to enhance the quality of your photos is to shoot at a higher resolution than you need and then size the image down. This helps remove some of the interpolation artifacts, especially in older and more inexpensive digital cameras. Your images end up smaller, but they appear sharper.

Choosing the Right Scanner

Digital cameras have not been around long, so chances are if you are a shutterbug of any rank, you probably have a collection of old analog photos lying around. But how are you going to get them on your computer? Well this is where the scanner comes in. And scanners come with even more capabilities and kinds than digital cameras do. How do you find the right one for you?

Well, like its technological cousin, the digital camera, you have to carefully consider what you plan on using the scanner for. Do you just want to archive your snapshots? Or are you a professional photographer with a huge collection of 35-mm slides? Or do you just want something to scan documents or line drawings? Or do you want your scanner to do all of the above?

Scanners can be broken down into two basic categories: reflective or transparency scanners. *Reflective scanners* can take your standard photo or artwork and create a digital representation of the image. Scanners do this by shining a light *on* the image and measuring the reflected light. You can usually get a good letter-sized reflective scanner for less than $500.

Transparency scanners work on the same principle, but the scanner has to shine a light *through* the image medium. The most common transparent medium is the 35-mm slide. But there are transparency scanners that scan film negatives and even larger format slides.

But these scanners can get expensive. If you want a good one, you can expect to spend over a $1000 dollars.

There are flatbed scanners that have transparency adapters, so if you need a scanner that is versatile, this may be the way to go. But with this sort of scanner it is important to do your homework. In theory, the transparency adapter is a good idea, but in practice, these adapters often fall short in the area of quality.

Resolution versus Interpolation, or Good versus Evil?

When you are looking for a scanner, you have to find one that is going to take enough information from your original so you can enlarge it without losing too much detail. If you have an 8-inch by 10-inch image and you want to be able to enlarge it to a 16 by 20 for output at 300 dpi, you need a device that can scan at least 600 dpi. Fortunately, most scanners have this capability, but what about scanners that advertise themselves as 600 dpi by 1200 dpi?

So let me explain these numbers a bit. A scanner such as this can scan natively at 600 dpi. The other number (1200 dpi) describes the capability of its *stepping engine*, the motor that moves the scanner's row of sensors across the image being scanned. The motor can move in such a manner that its sensor array picks up the extra 600-dpi worth of info, just by moving in tinier steps.

So how can your scanner come up with those missing pixels so you can get a 1200-dpi scan? Well, to explain this we have to look a little closer at interpolation.

We talked about this earlier with digital cameras, and how they come up with their number for megapixels, but with scanners, it takes on a whole new meaning. *Interpolation* is the process your scanning software uses to increase the perceived resolution of an image. It does this by creating extra pixels between each pixel actually read by your scanner's sensors. Your software arrives at the value these pixels by guessing. Most software arrives at the value of these pixels by simply finding an average between the neighboring pixels. So, when your scan an image on a 600-by-1200 scanner, at its highest resolution, two out of every four pixels is generated by interpolation, which is a guess on what the value could be. An educated guess, to be sure, but still it is not a true representation of your original image.

For the bottom-line resolution capabilities of your potential purchase, always look to the lower number. That is your scanner's native capability. Now, can a 600-by-1200 dpi scanner get a better scan than a 600-by-600 scanner? Probably, but it is not going to be as high a resolution as a scan from a 1200-by-1200 dpi native scanner. But then, will that be as good as the 1200-by-2400 scanner? The vicious cycle continues . . .

So . . . How Do We Hook Up My Scanner?

Scanners can connect to your computer in any number of ways. The main difference between the methods is speed and cost. Most consumer scanners come with a USB connector, which is the least expensive, but is also the slowest. FireWire connectivity is not much more expensive, but is much faster than USB. SCSI (Small Computer Systems Interface), pronounced "skuzzy," is the fastest mode of connection, but it is also the most expensive.

And SCSI is the most problematic. For those of you with SCSI external devices, troubleshooting SCSI chains is one of the first things you do whenever your Mac starts to act up. Apple used SCSI for years but has dropped it, opting for FireWire. You can still get SCSI cards for your computer, and for those who bought a scanner more than just a few years ago, you will probably keep migrating your SCSI cards to your new Mac purchases for years to come.

Software and Drivers

In the good old days, it was very difficult to get a scanner to communicate with a computer and vice versa. So, developers came up with TWAIN, a public standard that links your computer's applications and scanners. A TWAIN driver translates information from the scanner into something your Mac's programs can understand. You can get these drivers by contacting your scanner's manufacturer, which usually means going to their Web site and downloading the driver to your hard drive.

Scanners usually come with their own scanning software and a TWAIN driver that makes it possible to scan from various image editing programs. Some graphic professionals never use scanning software, preferring to bring their images directly into Adobe Photoshop and start editing there (shown in Figure 25-7).

Figure 25-7: In Photoshop, you can access your scanner's TWAIN driver in Import under the File menu. Here I have selected the TWAIN driver for the Epson Perfection 1650.

The Truth about TWAIN

Secret

There has been a lot of speculation about what TWAIN means. Some claim it is an acronym for "Technology Without An Interesting Name," but those close to the source (i.e., the people who developed TWAIN technology), say it comes from Rudyard Kipling's "The Ballad of East and West" which features the statement ". . . and never the twain shall meet . . .," which aptly describes the difficulty, early on, of getting scanners and computers to work together. The technology was presented in all uppercase letters to make it stand out, which led people to believe it was an acronym. I, however, find the acronym version of the story more interesting, and will continue to spread it until the more literary origin of the term is stomped from our collective memory forever. I'd rather be known as cheeky than well read.

What to Look for in Scanning Software

It depends on what tools you need, but there are different capabilities you should look for in finding the right scanning software for your scanning needs.

As we just talked about, if you have a specialized workflow and use one program for your image editing, look for a scanning solution that offers a TWAIN driver that works with your program. When OS X first arrived, people in graphics were slow to move to the new platform because of the lack of support for drivers that were compatible with the new Unix-based operating system.

But with Panther, most scanning manufactures have successfully played catch-up and have posted drivers that make their machines work flawlessly (as flawlessly as can be expected). As we mentioned earlier, you can download these installers for most of these drivers from the manufacturers' Web sites.

48- or 24-Bit?

If you are doing some heavy-duty image editing you might want to go for a scanner that can obtain a 48-bit image. Most scanners are capable of collecting a 24-bit image, but some can scan a 48-bit image.

Why does this matter? After all, most output devices only accept 24-bit information. Well, it matters because with all that extra information, you can make some fairly radical alterations to an image because you will later sample down the image to a 24-bit image for output. It's like scanning at a higher resolution. You get more information to work with, so when it gets sized down, it can take the information and interpolate it to a nicer-looking file. (I mean, in this instance, interpolation in a good way.)

A Bit about Bits

What does all this bit stuff mean? Well, an RGB image defines a pixel with three different numbers, which represent how much red, green, and blue is in the color that makes up the pixel. Each number is an 8-bit number and describes 2^8, or 256 levels of color. You have 8 bits for each channel, and you have three channels (red, green, and blue), which adds up 24 bits of information for an RGB pixel. A 48-bit image has three channels with 16 bits for each channel, or 577,536 levels for each color. Now that's a lot of information.

If you have to scan images from printed materials, especially halftones, it would be highly beneficial for your scanning software to have a descreening feature. Often, when you scan photos from magazines or newsletters, you can see a moiré pattern (shown in Figure 25-8). Descreening software eliminates or reduces the different patterns (the pattern of the halftone and the pattern your scanner wants to use) and gives you a scan that looks more like a continuous tone.

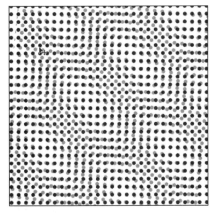

Figure 25-8: When you have two similar line screens, and the results are obscene — that's a moiré! Here is an example of a moiré pattern.

Back to the Future with the Line-Screen Determiner

Secret

If you have to scan a lot of halftones, you should arm yourself with a nifty little tool called a screen determiner from Arthur H. Gabel, Inc. It costs about four dollars and you can use it to find out the line screen of the image you need to scan. It's made out of clear plastic with a pattern of black lines. You lay it over your halftone and rotate it slowly until a four-pointed star appears. Two opposite points of a star indicate the number of your line screen. All this without a single microchip! It's a super low-tech solution (unchanged since it was copyrighted in 1953) to a high tech problem.

Another thing to consider when looking for scanner software is batch processing. If you have a couple dozen 2-by-2 pictures you want to scan, you certainly don't want to have to do them one at a time. If your scanner has batch processing, your can select multiple live areas on your scanner bed to scan. Sometimes this takes a little while for your scanner to go through each area, but it makes for a great excuse for a coffee break.

The Secrets of Making a Good Scan

There are a few things you can do to give your image a leg up toward making a good scan. First, and this might sound obvious, make sure your scanner and the image being scanned are clean and free of dust. Anything foreign in the image area will be scanned, and then you will have to eliminate it from the scan in what can be a very time-consuming process.

We Interrupt This Chapter . . .

As we started talking about scanning and image correction, two of us found ourselves in a small debate. Let me share it with you . . .

Scott: One hard and fast rule to getting good scans is "the better the photo the better the scan." If you have a small fuzzy image with bad color, there is little you can do to improve the quality of the image. You cannot create details that are not there. You cannot create focus where there is none. Like Grandma used to say, and this applies to scanning as much as her cooking, "garbage in, garbage out."

Benjamin: I guess I'd agree with that, to a point. But it's not really a "hard and fast rule." Newer versions of Photoshop, as well as third-party plug-ins, are designed to get the most out of smaller files that have problems. Those features, as well as a little talent, can get some really poor images (that were unsalvageable in years past) to look good enough for a lot of uses, and may just let you recycle that garbage.

After you capture your scan, you should decide what format you want to save it as. If you don't have to worry about drive space, your can save your files in TIFF format. Most scanning programs allow you to use LZW compression to save your image. This is a good choice because it is lossless, and your image, when it is opened for editing, will look the same as when you saved it.

If drive space is a premium, you may save your files in JPEG format. If you make sure the image is saved as at high quality or maximum quality setting, the compression will appear lossless, and you will be able to save many more photos to your hard drive. But remember, this is the first and last time you should save your image as a JPEG (unless it is bound for the Web). Each time you save as a JPEG, it compresses the image on top of the previous application of JPEG compression. Do this a few times and your image will be full of arti-facts and there will be no rescuing it.

Scanning software often offers color correction and sharpening controls. Some of these programs offer sophisticated tools, but for most part, using this software to edit your images is not a good idea. They are just not as subtle, flexible, or powerful as the tools found in an image-editing program like Adobe Photoshop. But if you don't have an image editing program, these tools are a good way to get your scan closer to where you want it to be.

Third-Party Software to Help

There are several third-party tools you can use to help you with your scanning. If you have an older scanner and are looking for some software to run it, there is an inexpensive and very capable utility from Hamrick Software called VueScan. It is so capable that many pros swear by it. It has color balance capabilities, filters, and options for saving in either TIFF or JPEG format (as shown in Figure 52-9). You can make your scanner act like a copier and send your image right to your printer. VueScan also supports batch scanning.

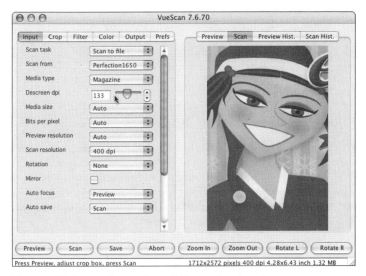

Figure 25-9: VueScan offers all kinds of options for you to tweak your scans. One of my favorites is the Descreen option, which helps you avoid some (not all) of the moiré pattern that results from scanning halftones.

All in all, there are over 200 different options and over 120 different scanners types of scanners VueScan supports. If you are not sure VueScan will work with your scanner, you can download a free trial version (www.hamrick.com) of the program and test it yourself.

You can't talk about scanners without talking about that pixel powerhouse, that raster master, Adobe Photoshop. Most scanner manufacturers offer TWAIN modules so you can scan your image directly into Photoshop (or programs like it), and some of the modules offer dozens of options so you can customize your scanning environment (shown in Figure 25-10).

Figure 25-10: Epson offers robust TWAIN modules for their line of scanners.

For most scanners, you will have to make some adjustments to an image-editing program for you to get the results you want, but if you see something's wrong (too dark, too bright, too red, anything) with the scan from the get-go, you can make adjustment so you scan looks more like the final product you are aiming for. These settings are made from the preview, and will be applied in the scanning process. So, tweak away (within reason), because you haven't degraded the information from the scan, because you haven't made the scan yet.

The Photo Retoucher's Friend: The Dust and Scratches Filter

Photoshop has a bunch of tools for the photo retoucher, but one of the most helpful ones is the Dust and Scratches filter. You can find this Filter in the Noise section under your Filters menu. This filter reduces noise (posterization or image artifacts that can appear in images) in your image by changing dissimilar pixels. This is especially helpful in background areas of an image that have a lot of constant color. Don't go crazy with this filter though, you can lose a lot of detail and make your image appear soft and mushy.

Photoshop is a tool that professionals use for photo manipulation, and they pay a professional price for the product ($649). But if you are looking for the power of Photoshop without the epic price tag, you might want to consider Adobe's Photoshop Elements. Adobe sells their stripped-down version of Photoshop for $99. It has most of the tool set for image manipulation that Photoshop does. It does, however, lack some of the important capabilities, such as being able to save to CMYK format.

Optical Character Recognition

When you scan a page of text, you have a picture of the text, and you can print the page out again and have others read it. But what if you want to take that text and edit it or place it into another program? That is where optical character recognition, or OCR, comes in.

What OCR programs do is take the text off a piece of paper with the aid of a scanner and convert it to editable text you can place in a word processing program and then edit it. There are several commercially available programs, and they can get very expensive. OmniPage Pro for the Mac is nearly $500.

And the results you can get from these program is mixed. If you have a clean sheet of paper with crisp text, generally you will get text that is ready to go with little editing. But if you have a photocopy of a fax of a typewritten document, you better be prepared to go in and check the document. So if you need to convert many pages of text and you definitely don't want to retype them, a good OCR program is the way to go.

Summary

If your Mac is the heart of your digital hub, then scanners and digital cameras are its eyes. And with Panther, the Mac has managed to make almost every form of image capture welcome. Macs can scan your old analog images, can receive your digital images, and if need be, can read your documents for you. And it all is easier than ever before. Now, if your Mac could whip up a tall vanilla latte at the drop of the hat, it would be perfect.

And speaking of eyes — in the next chapter we go optical and look at CD-ROMs, DVD-ROMs, and the world of optical drives on your computer.

CD-ROM and DVD: The World of Optical Drives

Chapter 26

♦ ♦

Secrets in This Chapter

♦ ♦

No matter what the platform, optical drives have become standard configuration for a home or office computer. Gone (for several years now) is the internal floppy disk drive. Everything from games to word processor applications to the operating system itself comes on a small disc (or sometime several discs), whether it is a CD (Compact Disc) or a DVD (either Digital Video Disc or Digital Versatile Disc — depending on whom you ask). With sales of DVDs surpassing VHS tapes in the movie sector, it's becoming more and more of a needed feature on a computer to be able to play those DVDs, and with the prices of digital video cameras dropping, making home movies to watch on your DVD player on your TV has become more practical.

The only thing stopping you is the technical jargon found on the labels of DVD players. Computer technical specifications and even the CD and DVD labels themselves make it seem like there are a thousand different formats out there, each one incompatible with the next. Some of this is marketing by the manufacturers and some of it isn't.

This chapter is going to try to clear up the format confusion and tell you how to check what your computer is capable of doing. Whether it is installing your favorite games, watching DVD movies on your computer, or making movies to burn to a DVD, we'll have this confusion all cleared up and offer you an alternative to the built-in Apple burning software.

The Magic and Mystery of Optical Drives

The compact disc has been around since 1981, but it wasn't until 1984 that it was extended to the computer environment as the CD-ROM. CD-ROM stands for compact disc-read only memory. Likewise, the DVD, which stands for digital versatile disc, was developed in Japan in 1996 but wasn't introduced in the US until 1997. In the past, the CD and DVD recorders used to be separate from the readers.

Apple has included a variety of optical drives in its computers over the years. Nowadays, Apple has reduced the options to two, and sells only Combo drives and SuperDrives in their computers.

If you don't know what type of optical drive you have, you can easily check by going into the System Profiler (found in the Utilities folder in the Applications folder on your hard drive). Select ATA in the left side of the window. This will show you any ATA devices it found, such as your hard drive and optical drive shown in Figure 26-1. If your optical drive is a SCSI drive, you'll find it under the SCSI devices list.

Secret

A Shortcut to the System Profiler

A quick way to get into the Apple System Profiler is to select "About This Mac" in the Apple menu. Then click on the More Info button to launch the System Profiler.

CD and DVD drives are also sold as external devices. They are usually connected via FireWire or USB 2.0 because of the amount of data being transferred.

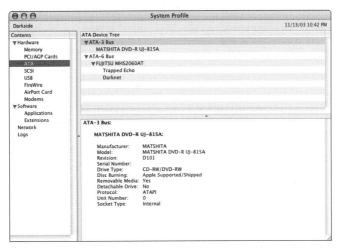

Figure 26-1: You can see that I have a CD-RW/DVD-R, which means that my drive is a SuperDrive.

Sorting out the CD and DVD Read/Write Mess

For most of us, understanding optical drives means understanding the different formatting capabilities and speeds of drives and media. Let's look at both, right now.

Media Formats and Normal Optical Drives

Giving an optical drive names like Combo drive or SuperDrive can be a little unclear. Just remember that the Combo drive is a CD-ROM, CD-RW, and DVD-ROM. The SuperDrive does all that *and* is a DVD-R.

Here is a list of the optical disc drives, the formats, and what they do. Looking at the format and/or optical drive options is important because some optical drives can deal with more than one kind of media.

CD-ROM

CD-ROM designates both a drive that can read only what is on a CD and the media itself. Most third-party applications are installed from a CD-ROM.

A music CD is still a CD-ROM that has data on it in AIF format so that audio CD-ROM drives (that is, CD players) can read and play music. CD-ROM drives on most computers can also play music CD-ROMs.

CD-R

A CD-R is a media type more than a drive specification. Although there were CD-R drives, they were not as prevalent as CD-RW drives. However, you will find that CD-R media is the most prevalent and popular media used in almost all the optical drives in computers. You can write, or burn, data to a CD-R once using a CD-RW drive, a Combo drive, or a SuperDrive. You can read a CD-R (with data burned on it) on almost all optical drives.

---

note   The terms *write* or *rewrite* are most often expressed as *burn*. The terms *recorded* or *written to* are most often expressed as *burned*.

CD-RW

A CD-RW is a special type of drive that will do exactly what a CD-R drive does but can also erase and reburn data to special kind of media called CD-RW discs. CD-RW drives are much more prevalent in the computer world. They can read CD-ROMs, CD-R media with data burned on them, and CD-RW media with data burned on them.

CD-RW media is common enough but not quite as common as CD-R. CD-RW media can be erased using a CD-RW drive, Combo drive, or SuperDrive and written over again.

Secret

CD-R Media is More Compatible than CD-RW Media

It seems logical that the CD-RW (or DVD-RW) would be the best option. However, CD-RWs come at a cost (literally). Not only are CD-RW discs more expensive, they will not work with older computers with other CD-ROM drives. While those older CD-ROM drives are becoming scarce, you just know you will encounter one at an important time. Another thing about CD-RW discs is that although they can be rewritten, they are less reliable because of the way they are made to be reburnable. The cheap price of a CD-R, although they can only be burned once, seems to outweigh the reusability of the CD-RW.

DVD-ROM

A DVD-ROM drive can read only what is on a DVD (or DVD-ROM disc) or a CD. Most DVD-ROM drives can read both CD-R and CD-RW media.

DVD-R

A DVD-R drive is much like the CD-R drive, but it can burn DVD-R discs (once). Besides being able to read DVD-R media with data burned on it, the DVD-R drive can usually read CD-ROM, CD-R, and CD-RW media with data burned on them.

The DVD-R media is the most common DVD-R media in use. DVD-R media is most likely the media you would purchase to burn a movie using movie-authoring software. DVD-R media can also be used to store data.

DVD-RW

A DVD-RW drive is like its CD-RW counterpart. With a DVD-RW, you will be able to erase and reuse the DVD-RW again and again. DVD-RW drives can also burn to DVD-R media as well as to DVD-RW media. DVD-RWs can most times read CD-ROM, CD-R, and CD-RW with data burned on them.

The DVD-RW media is probably the second-most common DVD media in use. The DVD-RW media is probably not the media you would purchase to burn a movie. You would probably use DVD-RW media for burning (and possibly reburning) data that you want to back up or store for archiving.

DVD+R and DVD+RW

When we talk about DVD+R and DVD+RW it starts to get complicated. Notice the difference between DVD-R and DVD+R. This is to distinguish the different formats of DVD although they act the same as DVD-R and DVD-RW. They are competing formats and you should be careful to note what type of blank DVD media you buy.

note Apple added support for many of the additional DVD+/-R/W media types in Panther.

DVD+R and DVD+RW media formats can be used by some optical drives and not others. Some programs can burn data and/or movies to these formats of media. But it's important to note that not all DVD players can read movie data burned on some of these kinds of media types.

The simple rule about using these media types is to know your optical drive, know your software, and know your DVD player.

DVD-RAM

The DVD-RAM drive is a drive that writes to DVD-RAM discs. DVD-RAMs are written to, not burned. A DVD-RAM drive can sometimes read DVD-ROMs and can usually read CD-ROMs, CD-Rs, and CD-RW media with data burned on them.

When a DVD-RAM drive reads and writes to a DVD-RAM disc, it acts as if it's an actual hard drive or Zip drive by reading and writing, as it needs to. This is a very slow process. Because the DVD-RAM media has moving pieces, DVD-RAM media is not an idea media form for archiving data the way the other media I cover is.

It's important to note that there are several different sizes of DVD-RAM media. Usually drives that can read the larger media can read the smaller media as well, but that's not a hard rule.

DVD-RAM Drives were popular for a while, but they are not widely used any more.

Hybrid Optical Drives

Hybrid optical drives are drives that can read, write, and rewrite a variety of different medias. Apple's Combo drive and SuperDrive are both hybrid optical drives.

Combo drive

The Combo drive is a hybrid optical drive that is a CD-RW/DVD-ROM. That means that this drive can read CD-ROMs, CD-Rs, and DVD-ROMs with data on them. It also means that this drive can burn to CD-Rs and CD-RWs.

The only differences between different Combo drives are the manufacturer and the speed that they write (CD-R) and rewrite (CD-RW) media.

SuperDrive

The SuperDrive is a hybrid optical drive that is a CD-RW/DVD-R. That means that this drive can read CD-ROMs, CD-Rs, and DVD-ROMs with data on them. It also means that this drive can burn to CD-Rs, CD-RWs, and DVD-R media.

Secret

Apple Started the SuperDrive Craze

On February 19, 2001, Apple announced it had begun shipping its new 733 MHz Power Mac G4 with the SuperDrive. Apple unveiled the SuperDrive at the Macworld Expo in San Francisco the previous month. The SuperDrive was launched in conjunction with the new iDVD application that enabled users to easily create professional quality DVDs for playback on consumer DVD players.

"The new Power Mac G4 with SuperDrive is the industry's first complete solution for CD and DVD authoring," said Philip Schiller, Apple's vice president of Worldwide Product Marketing. "The combination of Apple's amazing SuperDrive, super-fast MPEG2 encoding software and easy-to-use iDVD application is a real breakthrough."

The only differences between different kinds of SuperDrives are the manufacturer and speed that they write (CD-R and DVD-R) and rewrite (CD-RW) media.

note   Even though Apple introduced the SuperDrive into the market, they don't manufacture the drive.

Third-Party Hybrid Drives

Third-party manufacturers not only make Combo drives and SuperDrives, they also make other hybrid drives with even more reading and writing capabilities. Far more such drives are available than be covered here. We'll look at one such drive as an example.

LaCie makes a MultiDrive in an external FireWire case that can read and write to a great many media formats. Here are the specifications:

- Supports DVD-R, DVD-RW, DVD-RAM, CD-R, and CD-RW media
- Supports CD-ROM, CD-ROM XA, CD-DA, Photo CD, CD-R, CD-RW, CD-Extra, CD-Text formats
- Supports DVD-ROM, DVD-RAM, DVD-R (General Use only), DVD-RW, DVD-Video formats

caution   SuperDrives can be used with applications like iDVD, iTunes, DVD Studio Pro, and Toast. And you can purchase external SuperDrives (like the LaCie MultiDrive) that can be connected to your Mac via USB, USB2, FireWire, and SCSI to give your Mac some more versatility.

It's important to note, however, that iDVD (which spawned the popularity of the consumer SuperDrive) can only be used by an *internal* DVD-R or DVD-R hybrid drive. If you want to make movies with your Mac and you can't upgrade the internal optical drive to a SuperDrive, you will probably have to purchase DVD Studio Pro to make movies.

Speed

The speed of the optical drive, whether it is a CD or DVD will determine how fast you will be able to write, rewrite, and read your files. It's especially important to understand an optical drive's speeds when you are shopping for a new drive or comparing feature sets.

CD-RW speeds are usually shown as (Write, Rewrite, Read). For instance, you might see the specifications as 12x/8x/32x. What this means to you is that the drive can burn a CD-R at 12x. It can rewrite to a CD-RW at 8x. And it can read a CD-ROM at 32x. DVD-R speeds don't list an RW speed because they don't have an RW option.

DVD-RW and hybrid drives can be hard to understand because they have so many options. The easiest thing to know here is what all of the different media do. This will help you figure out what media has what speed. Here are the speed specifications for the LaCie MultiDrive that we talked about in the last section:

♦ DVD Speeds: DVD-R: 2x (write) / DVD-RW: 1x (rewrite) / DVD-RAM: 2x (read) / DVD-ROM: 12x (read)

♦ CD Speeds: CD-R: 12x (write) / CD-RW: 8x (rewrite) / CD-ROM: 32x (read)

You will find that CD-RW drive will usually have a faster write and rewrite speed rating than the same features inside a hybrid optical drive. That's one of the trade-offs that you make for having a hybrid drive.

CDs and DVDs (media) also have speed limits. These limits can be broken, however, I don't recommend it. Although there are few reported cases of CDs shattering inside an optical drive this likely won't happen if you burn a 24x CD-R at 56x speed. The only bad thing that might happen is that the data will be corrupted because the disc just couldn't take that much speed. You should burn at the recommended rated speed on the disc for the most reliable outcome.

Secrets of Apple's Disc-Burning Software

The biggest secret about Apple's disc-burning software is that there is no secret to it! Apple's disc-burning software is generally invisible to the user, popping up only when needed.

Burning a CD with the OS Software

Suppose you want to burn a data CD or DVD to back up your files. Follow these steps and you can't go wrong:

1. Simply insert a blank CD or DVD into your disc drive. A dialog box will pop up asking you what application you would like to use to read the disc.
2. Because you will be making a back up copy of files that are in the Finder, select Finder.
3. A CD or DVD icon will show up on your desktop. Now, simply drag any files you would like to put on the disc to the icon. This will make a copy of the original files and put it into a temporary storage file. The storage file will eventually be like the template to what will be burned onto the disc itself. You can open the disc and make folders to organize your files; they will also be burned onto the disc just as you see it.
4. Name your CD or DVD in the Finder if you haven't already.
5. When you are satisfied with the files on your disc, either drag it to the Trash (shown in Figure 26-2), which changes to a Burn icon, or select Burn Disk from the File menu.

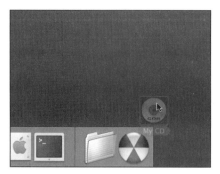

Figure 26-2: Dragging a recordable media disc to the trash will turn the Trash icon to a Burn icon.

note Dragging a disc to the Trash came from the old OS 9 (and earlier) days when doing this action would eject a CD or floppy. In OS X, this still holds true, but now dragging a CD-ROM to the Trash makes the Trash icon change to an Eject button. Likewise dragging a recordable media will trigger the Trash icon to show as a Burn icon.

Secret

Burning by Dragging Your Data to the Burn Icon

Another, maybe quicker, way of burning a CD with Apple's CD-burning software is to place the Burn icon into your toolbar of the Finder Window (shown in Figure 26-3). This will allow you to burn a folder to a CD. This is great if you have one specific file you keep all your backups in. Select the file, press the Burn button, insert a CD and, boom! You've burned a backup copy of your files. It's quick and easy.

Figure 26-3: You can add other things to your toolbar for your Finder windows, like the Burn icon. This will allow you to burn a folder with one click.

Setting Your Burning Preferences

But the Apple disc-burning option is in other applications too, like iTunes, iPhoto, and iDVD. When you insert a blank DVD or CD the Finder will ask you what application to use it with (shown in Figure 26-4).

If you want to make a music CD, select iTunes. This will prompt iTunes to prepare to burn a CD. Likewise, if you want to make a backup copy of your digital pictures in iPhoto, select iPhoto. You could choose iDVD to make a DVD of your movies.

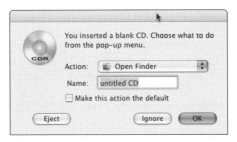

Figure 26-4: This dialog box prompts you to decide if you want to make a data, photo, music, or movie CD/DVD.

You also have the option in this dialog box (shown in Figure 26-4) to name the blank media and/or set the application you choose as the default preference for that media.

You can set CD and DVD default methods for handling a blank CD-R, CD-RW, or DVD-R. If you have specific software that you want to handle specific kinds of blank media this is a good idea. Here's how:

1. Open up System Preferences (in your Dock or under the Apple menu).
2. Click on the CDs & DVDs icon in the Hardware section of System Preferences to bring up the preference panel that allows you to set actions for different kinds of media (shown in Figure 26-5).

Figure 26-5: You can set actions for blank media as well as media with different kinds of data on it in the CDs & DVDs preference panel.

3. Use the appropriate pull-down menus to choose your action (shown in Figure 26-6).

Figure 26-6: You can choose an application or run a script to handle blank media. You can also choose to have the OS ask you what to do or to ignore blank media.

4. Close the CDs & DVDs panel to save the changes you have made and then burn away.

Using Disk Copy to Duplicate CDs

So let's say you want to make a backup copy of a CD. This is a good idea to do with *any* important disc you can't afford to lose. You don't need two different CD drives to make an exact copy of a CD to a blank CD; instead, you will use Disk Copy to do it all.

> **note** In the past, Apple had a separate disk copier program called Disk Copy. With the release of Panther (OS X 10.3), Apple seems to have decided to slim the number of applications by adding the Disk Copy application to the Disk Utility application (shown in Figure 26-7).

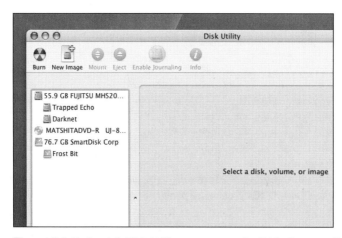

Figure 26-7: Apple's Disk Utility now sports the Disk Copy application with a built-in Burn button.

There really is only one good way to make a direct copy of a CD with the Disk Copy utility. Follow these steps to do so:

1. Put the CD into your CD drive.
2. Start the Disk Utility program located in the Applications/Utilities folder.
3. Select the CD you would like to make an image of. This usually requires selecting the middle image representing the CD as a whole (shown in Figure 26-8).

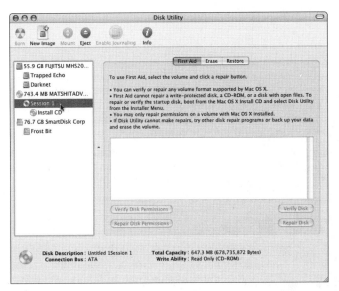

Figure 26-8: Selecting the middle image will tell the Disk Copy program you would like to make an image of the whole CD, not just a partition. If a CD had more than one session, more images would show up under this image.

4. With the CD image selected go to the Image menu, pull down to New and select Image from [name of CD]. This will bring up a dialog box asking you to give a name to your new image file. You can name it whatever you want, but naming it the same as the CD you are copying would probably be a good idea. When finished, press Save and Disk Copy will make an image file of the CD.

> **note**
>
> Some of you might be wondering what exactly an image file is. Isn't that a picture? Well, yes, it is, and for the most part you are right! But what Disk Copy does is create an *image* of everything that is on the CD. In other words, it's taking a snapshot of everything on the CD exactly how it's laid out, thus taking a picture of the data and saving it to a file that in the case of these figures ends in .dmg.

5. After the image file is created, it will show up in the left panel of the DiscUtility window , if not locate the new image file and drag it into the Disk Utility window. Click on the image file and click the Burn button (shown in Figure 26-9).

Figure 26-9: The Burn button is located in the upper-left corner of the application window. You can't miss it.

This process of copying a CD (using the Disk Copy utility) is unnecessarily long. Although Apple makes it very easy to burn data, it almost seems like Apple doesn't want its users to know how to make copies of CDs. Perhaps they don't want to contribute to piracy. Perhaps they just haven't gotten around to making this part of the OS friendlier.

What would really be great would be if copying a CD could be a matter of pressing one button then sitting back to relax as the computer does all the necessary steps for you. Luckily, there is a program that does just that: Roxio's Toast.

Roxio's Toast Secrets

Apple's built-in disc burning software may be good, but Roxio's Toast takes the cake in my book as the best burning software yet. Not only does Toast make it easier to make copies of CDs and DVDs, but it's actually faster than Apple's disc-burning software.

Toast will also allow you to burn *true* PC-formatted CDs. While Apple says it can burn PC-formatted CDs, sometimes folders do not show up like they should. If you live in a mixed PC and Mac environment, Toast will save you the headache of having PC/Mac compatible CDs.

Secret

Getting Contextual with Toast Titanium

Burning with Toast can just be easier than with Apple's disc-burning software. If you read Chapter 1, then you're familiar with third-party contextual menu items. Toast adds a contextual menu of its own to the OS.

To burn a folder or file with Toast, Control-click on a file and select Toast It in the contextual menu.

Toast's interface is simple and straightforward. Data, Music, Video, and Copy tabs sport the related options (shown in Figure 26-10).

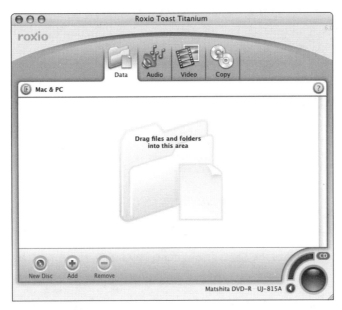

Figure 26-10: The Toast interface is simple and elegant. You will find options for the different types of media you would like to burn.

The Data Tab

The Data tab is the one you are most likely to use if you are creating new CDs or DVDs of your data. Under the Data tab, you can map out and organize your files by placing them in different folders.

Okay, this is cool, but Apple's software can do that too. What else has Toast got? It has a lot actually. When you click on the Disk Options icon next to the format on the upper-left corner of the Toast interface, a drawer pops out of the side giving you more options for formatting your CD or DVD (shown in Figure 26-11).

As you can see in Figure 26-11, there are more disc-formatting options that you may use. Burning a CD in Mac & PC format is probably your best bet to make sure your CD is able to be read by most computers. But it's good to have them there in case you need them. It's important to know your media when you are using Toast Titanium. In the upper-right corner (shown in Figure 26-11) you will see the number of items as well how many MB the data adds up to. If you surpass the data storage for the media you are burning, you will be prompted to remove items or create multiple CDs.

After you've got your data ready to go and you've selected the burner and chosen whether you are burning to a DVD-R or CD-R(W), you only have to click on the big red button to start your burn.

> **tip**
> To let Toast Titanium know if you want to use a DVD or CD, click on the little CD icon above the big red Burn button to switch back and forth (shown in Figure 26-11).

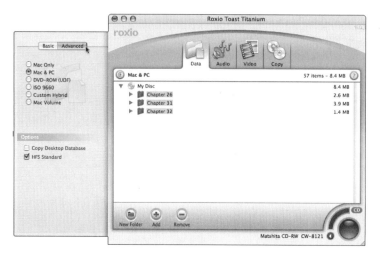

Figure 26-11: The Basic options in the Disk Options drawer is for kids. Use the Advanced settings.

Use Toast to Make Multisession CDs and DVDs

A not-so-well-known feature of Toast is the ability to make multisession CDs or DVDs. This is a handy thing to do if you are making incremental backups of data.

Unlike a CD-RW, where you erase and then burn over the data, this is done with a CD-R. You insert a blank CD-R and burn some data to it, naming it a date or session number. When you want to burn this data again (perhaps as an update) you insert that same CD-R and burn another session onto that CD-R with another session name.

The CD-R will show up on the desktop as multiple CDs.

You can continue to do this until you run out of room on your CD-R.

The Music Tab

Under the Music tab, you can organize the songs in the order you want and listen to a preview of it right from the Toast interface. To match this option with Apple's software, you have to use iTunes.

We Interrupt This Chapter . . .

This is one of those rare times where I consider Apple's audio solution better than the third-party alternatives. I find that there are differing opinions about this.

Pieter: Toast is a great program and part of that greatness is its ability to take a bunch of your MP3 files and turn them into the AIFF format files that audio CD players read. This lets you create CDs that can be read on just about any audio CD player as well as almost any DVD player on the market. This is especially useful if you have recorded a bunch of MP3 files of your own voice or music and want to create a master CD that you can use to make copies for all of your friends and fans. Toast also lets you work with the enhanced audio CD format if you want to add special features to your CD or to just dump your MP3 files to the disk in a way that CD players that can read MP3 files will find palatable.

Benjamin: To be honest, I don't often use Toast to burn music CDs. I much prefer organizing and burning my music CDs right out of iTunes.

Toast will give you some more formatting options for your music CDs (or DVDs) that are not quite as apparent in iTunes. Toast allows you to make an audio CD, an MP3 disc, and enhanced audio CD, and a mixed mode CD from the Disk Options pop out drawer (shown in Figure 26-12).

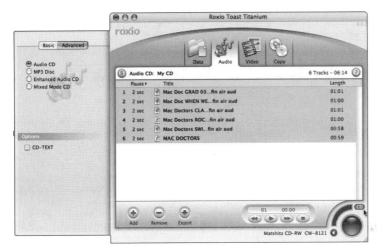

Figure 26-12: The Audio tab shows you the number of tracks and the time rather than the number of files and size in MBs.

But who needs these options to make music CDs for themselves? Apple nailed every-thing we need right in iTunes.

> **tip**   Toast allows you to export your songs as AIFF files. To do this, drag your songs into a play list and press the Export button next to the Add and Remove buttons.

The Video Tab

Under the Video tab, you can make video CDs or photo slide shows. The Advanced tab gives you options for Super Video CDs and Video DVDs.

When you drag in your photos and movies, you are able to edit them by clicking the edit button (shown in Figure 26-13). This is a pretty cool feature.

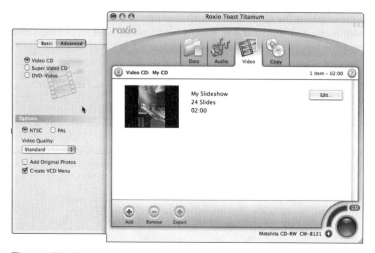

Figure 26-13: Like a music CD or DVD, you are shown items and time rather than files and MBs.

The Advanced options pop out-tray allows you to control the Video Quality and format options.

The Copy Tab

Remember how I said that Apple should have put a one-button way to make a copy of a CD into their Disk Copy application? With Toast, a one-button click is all you need.

When the Copy tab is selected, you are able to drag a CD or an image of a CD to the window and then by clicking the red Burn button you will start a copy of the CD shown in the main Toast window (shown in Figure 26-14).

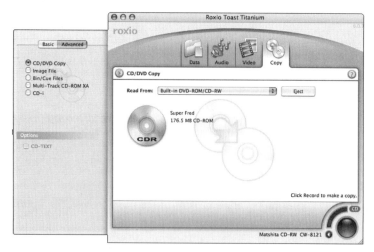

Figure 26-14: One-click disc copy is realized with Toast Titanium.

Once the original CD is copied, Toast will eject the original CD and prompt you to insert a blank CD so that it can finish the copy. It's just that simple.

Toast Titanium 6 Can Burn via Rendezvous across a Network

Here is a *great* feature of the new Toast 6. This version sports Rendezvous burning. By selecting the network burner in Recorder Settings under the Recorder menu, you have access to network burners (shown in Figure 26-15).

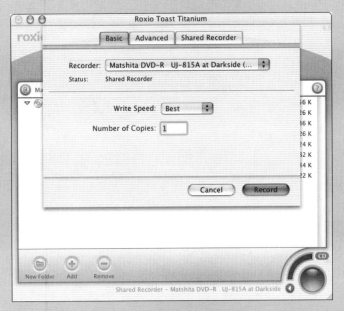

Figure 26-15: Toast 6 does Rendezvous burning over the network. Now it's possible to burn a CD or DVD on that old computer.

This means if you had an old iMac with no CD burner on the same network as a new PowerMac G5, the iMac could use the G5's SuperDrive over the network.

Clicking the burn button on the iMac would prompt you to put a CD in the G5 with the burner. That computer is then alerted to put in a CD to be burned.

And that's the highlights of Toast Titanium. There is a fairly large book that accompanies Toast Titanium when you purchase it, and obviously, I can't cover all of its options here. Suffice it to say that if you need burning options, Toast Titanium is the way to go.

I consider it a must-have program.

Summary

And that's a pretty good look at the world of optical drives and media that you are likely to use. Hopefully you have a better understanding of the differences between drive and media types.

We covered what can be done by the OS (both with the Apple burning software and with Disk Copy) and what can be done better by Toast Titanium.

In the next chapter, we look at newer hardware protocols such as FireWire, USB, and ATA. And we'll see if we can't give SCSI the old heave-ho.

FireWire, USB, and IDE: Do We Still Need SCSI?

Chapter
27

◆ ◆

Secrets in This Chapter

◆ ◆

V arious Mac models, such as the iMac or eMac, have been called *all-in-one* models. *Mostly-in-one* would be a more accurate description. After all, none of them includes such necessary items as printers; and even the keyboards and mice are separate devices except on laptop models. Because of this "mostly" situation, Mac users need to concern themselves with cables, ports, and so forth for connecting their printers, scanners, mice, keyboards, trackballs, external hard drives, iPods/MP3 players, digital cameras, digital camcorders, microphones, and myriad other peripheral devices.

Mac Peripheral Standards Evolution

In the Mac's infancy, there were very few peripherals and connecting them was easy. Either it was a floppy disk (or the original HD20 hard disk) and you connected it to the floppy connector at the back, a kind of *parallel* connector called a DB 15, similar to the ones used on IBM PCs to connect various devices, or it was a serial device like a dot-matrix printer or modem and you connected it to one of the Mac's serial ports.

Things got a little more interesting when the Mac Plus was introduced, with its new Small Computer Systems Interface (*SCSI*, pronounced "scuzzy") connector. Now known as SCSI-1, this interface allowed a blazing 5 megabits per second of transfer rate and you could connect up to seven devices in series. Printers and modems were still connected via the serial ports and scanners were usually serial, but SCSI models started to appear on the market.

When the Mac II and the SE rode onto the scene, things got a little more interesting, because the Mac SE was the first model to include expansion capabilities with its NuBus slots. Not only could you connect hard drives externally via SCSI, but there were also internal hard drives for the first time, also on SCSI. These models also introduced Apple Desktop Bus (*ADB*) connectors for such low-bandwidth devices as keyboards and mice.

note   Don't think that Apple was alone in this hubris, creating a proprietary desktop bus "standard." IBM was doing the same thing with their PS2 connectors.

And ADB is actually a close relative of what USB has become in that it was a intelligent peripheral bus. PS/2 connectors are basically simple serial connectors, like the old DB9 mouse connector and the old AT keyboard connector shrunk down so that they could reduce the size of the PC.

Except for minor tweaks, such as support for Wide- and Ultra-SCSI, things really didn't change much for a decade. Then came the iMac in 1997. Not only did the iMac begin the elimination of the floppy disk from the Apple product line, but it also replaced ADB and serial connectors with USB, and became the first Mac shipped since the 512Ke that did not provide SCSI support. In fact, it was the first Mac (other than the PowerBook Duo) in a decade that did not have a SCSI connector. The late 1990s provided a sea-change in connection protocols for the Mac; and the iMac was the model that also introduced FireWire for high-speed peripherals with the iMac DV. Apple had, for reasons of economy, shipped various Performa models (consumer Macs) during the 1990s with internal IDE drives, but they all had SCSI for external devices. The Blue & White G3 became the first desktop model that not only used an internal IDE bus, but also made SCSI an option, available on a PCI card. But FireWire was the standard way to connect external hard drives, digital camcorders, and other high-bandwidth devices.

note USB actually appeared as an optional connection protocol on some PC models before the iMac's appearance, but there were few USB devices and no one was pushing the USB standard. Like the Sony 3.5" floppy that predated the original Mac and mouse-driven windowing technology (Xerox), the technology was there, but it was brought it to popular use when Windows 98 was realized in 1998.

note In 2002, Apple tried eliminating the audio-in port from all their models, leaving audio input to USB and such devices as the Griffin iMic. Fortunately for anyone interested in using a microphone with a Mac, that decision has been reversed. After all, recording one's voice for annotation in iMovie is one of that program's nicer features; if the user doesn't have a built-in mic, the situation becomes a lot more complicated.

Today, we're seeing the appearance of USB 2.0 and FireWire 800, allowing even faster transfer rates and higher-speed devices.

Dissecting Peripheral Standards

We're only going to discuss those standards shipping on or readily available for current Macs, but that isn't a small set. It includes USB 1.1 and USB 2.0, FireWire and FireWire 800, as well as the venerable SCSI.

USB

For those who have been living in a vacuum, USB is the acronym for *Universal Serial Bus*. Currently at revision 2.0, also known as *Hi-Speed USB*, the protocol supports data rates of up to 480 megabits per second (Mbps). The previous 1.1 and 1.0 specifications supported speeds of 12 Mbps and 1.5 Mbps, respectively.

The original iMac and all models predating the G5 introduced in the latter half of 2003 implemented the 1.1 standard, although you could use PCI cards supporting USB 2.0 in many desktop G4 models. Currently shipping G5 models have three 2.0 ports (supporting both USB 1.1 and USB 2.0). These two protocols are represented by USB and USB Hi-Speed logos (shown in Figure 27-1).

Figure 27-1: These registered trademarks represent USB 1.1 and 1.0 (left) and USB 2.0 (right).

Prior to adding USB 2.0 support, modern Macs relied exclusively on FireWire for high-speed connections and USB for low-speed connections. Low-speed connections include devices like floppy disk drives, (slow) CD burners, keyboards, mice, scanners, and inkjet printer. You can have as many as 127 USB devices on a single bus.

caution   In particular, external USB CD burners are susceptible to the drastically reduced bandwidth supported by USB 1.1. These burners are supposed to be able to support up to 4× burning speeds, but I am unaware of anyone successfully burning a relatively full CD at 4× over USB. In fact, 2× is pushing things. A 4× burning speed means that approximately 800MB of data would be transferred and burned to disc in 20 minutes — 40 MB/minute. While 12 Mbps is 1.5 MBps (90 MB/min), that is sustained throughput with no other bus activity taking place, since the 12 Mbps is shared between all the activity on that bus. Reality is that two-way communication between the drive and the computer takes place and the necessary throughput is just not sustainable to support 4×. For successful 2× burning, you should make the burner the only device on that USB bus.

Keyboards, mice, inkjet printers, and floppy drives are the most commonly found USB peripherals. Initially, you could also find USB Zip drives and hard disks, but the slow performance of these peripherals in dealing with the quantity of data they held rapidly dropped them from favor. In fact, today the Zip drive (even in its large-capacity versions) is a dying technology, replaced by flash memory devices (usually called *thumb drives*, *keychain drives*, or *flash drives*) that hold as much or more data than a Zip disk and are very compact and much sturdier than a Zip cartridge. When FireWire became standard on all Mac models, the USB hard drives all but disappeared from the scene.

Today, digital cameras, media readers, and scanners are commonly found attached to USB, in addition to the typical devices listed here.

To be sure that a USB device is going to be compatible with your Mac, make sure that the USB logo is accompanied with a Mac logo (shown in Figure 27-2).

Figure 27-2: These trademark logos indicate Mac compatibility.

If you want to make sure that your device is not only Mac compatible but also OS X–compatible, look for the OS X logo as well.

Most Macs come with two USB ports, though some boast three or more (as shown in Figure 27-3). You have two major considerations when it comes to discussing USB connections. The first is how many connectors you have, as that determines how many devices you can attach before you need to acquire a USB hub. The second is how many USB buses you have, as that determines what sort of bandwidth you can support on an individual bus.

Figure 27-3: The 1 GHz 17" iMac has three USB 2.0 ports on the back of the CPU.

To make things even more complicated, hubs come in both powered (you plug them into an electrical outlet) and unpowered flavors. Your Mac keyboard, with its two connectors, is an unpowered hub.

Secret

We Need More Power (Or Do We?)

Like ADB, USB carries some electrical current, allowing various unpowered devices like keyboards and mice to draw their minimal required electrical power from the bus itself, reducing the number of batteries or power cords required for your Mac's operation. In fact, Apple's USB Fact Sheet (www.apple.com/usb) touts being able to power your USB devices (up to 2.5 watts) from the cable rather than requiring an electrical outlet as one of the major features favoring USB over other serial protocols. While this is truly a real advantage, it comes with a few limitations that Apple (and other manufacturers) fails to mention.

If you have a number of devices that draw their power from the USB cable, either plug them directly into one of your Mac's USB ports or into a powered hub. If you are using an unpowered hub, connect only devices that have their own power sources (either batteries or plugs you insert into an outlet) unless you want to risk overdrawing on the power carried by the bus. For example, you could attach an inkjet printer to the connector on your keyboard without encountering difficulty, but connecting an unpowered floppy drive/media reader (like my VST TriMedia) will often cause USB lockups.

While you're less likely to encounter lockups at startup today, as compared in the early days of USB (both pre–OS X and with OS X), one of the techniques recommended for troubleshooting these lockups is to disconnect any USB devices other than your keyboard and mouse and then reconnect them once your Mac is running. Some of the problems arose from poorly written USB drivers or badly implemented USB firmware in the devices; inadequate power on the bus was another major culprit.

While Apple, Sony, and others promote FireWire for high-speed peripherals, the required licensing fees provide a barrier to entry for a wide range of PC manufacturers, fighting to save every nickel they can on their commodity Windows boxes. One result of this quandary was USB 2.0's development with a maximum throughput threshold of 480 Mbps (60 MB/sec). The Wintel market is a 400-pound gorilla; anything that becomes standard or even common in that market tends to be relatively inexpensive due to economies of scale. Thus, USB 2.0 devices are often less expensive than the FireWire equivalent device. In fact, though, many devices, such as the Maxtor high-capacity hard drives, support both USB 2.0 and FireWire connections.

Theoretically, USB 2.0 is up to 20 percent faster than the original FireWire 400 specification. In practice, the speed difference is not noticeable.

USB is a backward-compatible technology. You can connect USB 1.1 devices to USB 2.0 ports and continue to use them (at USB 1.1 speeds). For example, the currently shipping iMac models sport three USB 2.0 ports on the base unit. You connect your USB 1.1 keyboard to one, which makes your keyboard an unpowered USB 1.1 hub with two USB 1.1 ports. If you connect a USB 2.0 device to a USB 1.1 port, you can use it at the lower speed (usually).

FireWire

FireWire is the Apple-trademarked name for the IEEE 1394 specification. Sony calls it iLink. You might see any of those three names on cables or hardware supporting FireWire. You can also look for the distinctive FireWire logo (shown in Figure 27-4).

Figure 27-4: This trademarked logo stands for both the FireWire 400 and the FireWire 800 protocols (covered later in this chapter).

Ports identified as FireWire 400 or IEEE 1394 are the same. On a Mac, these ports look like rounded rectangles (shown in Figure 27-5).

Figure 27-5: The iMac has two FireWire 400 6-pin ports.

FireWire 800 is the Apple name for the IEEE 1394b standard revision, supporting speeds of up to 800 Mbps. These ports are square-like ports (shown in Figure 27-6).

Figure 27-6: The FireWire 800 port is Apple's newest connectivity option.

Both of these protocols are hot-pluggable.

Like USB, FireWire is a serial data transfer bus. Also like USB, FireWire devices are hot-swappable, meaning that you can connect or disconnect them without having to shut down your Mac first. You will need to tell your Mac to unmount any mounted devices, such as a hard disk like the iPod. The IEEE 1394 standard supports up to 63 devices on a single bus.

Secret

And the Winner Is . . .

The Television Academy of Arts & Sciences awarded FireWire a primetime Emmy in 2001 for its impact on the TV industry.

Apple's first major promotion of FireWire was in the iMac DV, when they introduced iMovie. Virtually all digital video cameras include IEEE 1394 ports; and iMovie lets you control your camcorder from your Mac when it is placed in VTR (or VCR) mode rather than camera mode.

> **note** Closely related to the digital video camera is the analog-to-digital video converter. These converters are extremely useful to individuals with large libraries of analog video (e.g., VHS, VHS-C, Hi-8, or Beta) that they wish to archive to digital media. You might do that to avoid quality loss during editing or subsequent duplication.

FireWire 400 cables come in flavors, based upon the connectors at either end. You can have 6-pin connectors (such as plug into your Mac) or 4-pin connectors (like the ones that plug into camcorders). Therefore, you might have 6-pin on both ends, like the one that comes with an iPod to connect it to your Mac; 6-pin on one end and 4-pin on the other, like the ones usually used to connect a digital camcorder to your Mac; or 4-pin on either end, to connect two devices with 4-pin ports (which is probably the most seldom-seen of all FireWire cables). FireWire 800 cables use a 9-pin connector and you need to use an adapter to connect a FireWire 400 device to a FireWire 800 connector. FireWire 400 cables can be up to 4.5 meters in length and FireWire 800 cables can be as long as 100 meters.

> **note** Like FireWire 400, USB 2.0 allows only short cable lengths — less than 5 meters. So, if you wish to hook up devices in a separate room, FireWire 800 is your optimum cabling solution.

Unlike USB, but like SCSI, FireWire devices can be chained (often called *daisy-chained*) to connect one device to the next. Alternatively, you can employ a FireWire hub and chain multiple devices off the hub. A similarity between ADB and USB is that the FireWire bus provides power to devices, but unlike the munificent amounts available on those buses, FireWire (6 pin, not 4 pin) carries up to 45 watts. This is how FireWire supports free-standing hard disks and recharging an iPod.

> **tip**
> I recommend use of a FireWire hub over daisy chaining, particularly as your collection of FireWire devices grows. While FireWire is a hot-pluggable standard, if an intermediate device is powered off, you might not get signal or power pass-through to subsequent devices in the chain. Additionally, many common FireWire devices such as digital camcorders, the iSight digital video camera, and the iPod have only one FireWire port and must be the last device on the chain.

Not only is FireWire fast enough for high-speed devices like digital camcorders and hard disks, but it is also fast and versatile enough for high-speed networking. Mac OS X (Jaguar and Panther) support *IP over FireWire* — the ability to use one Mac as a DHCP server and your main connection to the Internet, with another Mac connected to this central Mac via FireWire for file sharing, Internet access, and any other networking operation.

> **tip**
> IP over FireWire comes in particularly handy for folks with a cable-modem or DSL connection where the ISP doesn't support routers (my Comcast account is a prime example).

> **caution**
> There are some incomplete implementations of the FireWire 800 standard in the Oxford 922 bridge (which you can learn more about at `www.oxsemi.com/products/IEEE1394/oxfw900.html`), used primarily for connecting high-speed hard disks. Make sure that your drive's firmware has been upgraded to version 1.05 or later before attempting to use the disk with Panther. Data loss on restart is extremely likely if you're using an early version of the firmware. More detail can be found at `http://maccentral.macworld.com/news/2003/10/30/firewireissue/index.php`.

In addition to the aforementioned, obvious candidates for FireWire use, you'll also find a variety of high-end scanners that attach via FireWire as well as FireWire CD and DVD burners.

IDE (or EIDE or ATA)

IDE (Integrated Drive Electronics), EIDE (Enhanced Integrated Drive Electronics), and ATA (Advanced Technology Attachment) are all acronyms that are used almost interchangeably. IDE is the original specification and is synonymous with ATA. EIDE is *fast IDE* and is sometimes called ATA-2. Subsequent versions of ATA include ATA-3, Ultra-ATA (a.k.a. Ultra-DMA, ATA-33, and DMA-33), ATA/66 (developed by Quantum Corp.), ATA/100, and now, ATA/133.

ATA is a relatively simple specification and that simplicity made it much less expensive to implement in the commodity world of IBM-compatible, now called Wintel, computing. Becoming the de facto standard of the Wintel world drove prices even lower as economies of scale took hold.

The cost difference between ATA and SCSI continued to grow, but Moore's Law holds that computers will continue getting faster and that means that the peripherals need to handle more data more quickly as well; and SCSI *was* significantly faster. At first, that meant only that high-end users required SCSI. However, each of the above iterations of ATA specification allowed for faster and faster devices.

> **note** An ATA bus (also called a *channel*) can have only two devices, and only one can be active at a given time. So, if you have a hard drive and CD-R drive, and wish to add another drive, you'll need to add another EIDE controller to your computer.

For those of you old enough to remember, price disparity was the biggest hammer used by the DOS/Windows crowd to pound on the Mac community. For a basic unit, the cost of SCSI versus ATA was a significant factor. Apple, though, wasn't totally oblivious to the cost argument. In fact, they first started using ATA drives in many of the Performa (lower-priced consumer) models in the 1990s. But, they still included SCSI as a standard interface, so they didn't reduce cost as much as they might have. That important change occurred with Steve Jobs's return and the iMac's release. Not only was it an attractive unit, but the iMac was much less expensive than other Mac models. Part (maybe a large part) of the cost disparity was due to the adoption of industry-standard interfaces like ATA and USB combined with the complete removal of expensive SCSI and proprietary ADB support.

> **note** Price disparity and open architecture are not to be scoffed at: They are the reasons that VHS is now dominant in videotape over the technically superior Beta format. JVC and RCA partnered with everyone they could to promote VHS, driving down component costs. They also got the cost-per-hour down by getting more video, even though at a reduced quality, on a single tape. Sony kept Beta close, licensing only a very few other companies and not really supporting their efforts. For the historically inclined among you, this might resonate with the PC-Mac situation of the mid-1990s and Apple's licensing of Mac-compatible units.

As hard drive capacities continue to increase, some problems will arise. For example, drives larger than 128GB are now fairly common. But, you can't swap in a 250GB drive and access all its space unless you have at least an ATA/133 controller. Stick it in one of the many Mac (or Wintel) computers with the ATA/100 controller that was standard until just recently and you'll only be able to address the first 128GB. Note that this problem doesn't occur with FireWire, so you could put the drive in a FireWire enclosure and use it externally.

SCSI

As we noted earlier, SCSI is the great-granddaddy of Mac high-speed peripheral connectivity. SCSI has been used for everything from hard disks, through printers like the Apple LaserWriter IISC, to scanners. Until very recently, with the advent of such products as Apple's XServe RAID (Redundant Array of Independent Disks), SCSI still had a niche for high-performance, high-capacity hard disk solutions, particularly RAID solutions. Now, though, the need for SCSI revolves mainly around those who have legacy hardware that they wish to continue employing.

Apple's OS X scanner support took a long time to make its appearance, and it still doesn't support SCSI. If you have a SCSI scanner, check out Hamrick Software's VueScan package (www.hamrick.com).

Unlike most everything in computing (excepting the human factor), where there are iron-clad operational rules on which you can rely, SCSI's rules are merely guidelines. They work most of the time, but if you work with SCSI very much, you'll encounter situations where you have to do the exact opposite of what the rules tell you if you want the system to function. "SCSI Voodoo" is the phrase long used to describe managing chains of SCSI devices in the hope of creating a stable operating environment. The rules for managing a SCSI chain revolve primarily around two points. First, both ends (and only the ends) of the chain must be terminated. Second, each device on the bus must have a different SCSI ID (address) in the range 1 through 6 (although you can go up to 15 devices with UltraSCSI), as 0 is reserved for the Mac, itself. Unfortunately, some devices were sold with internal termination or switchable internal termination and you had to know which device did what and to whom. Sometimes, the order of devices on the bus affected the bus's stability, for reasons no one was ever able to forecast or explain. I've even experienced SCSI chains that had performed beautifully for months suddenly develop problems where switching the devices around fixed the problem. For a particularly trenchant, albeit a bit dated, coverage of SCSI on the Mac you should check out www.mactech.com/articles/mactech/Vol.15/15.10/WellConnectedMac. If this article doesn't give you a feeling of just how chaotic the SCSI world is and make you glad that SCSI is no longer the principle method of Mac high-speed device connectivity, you're more intrepid than I am.

A discussion of SCSI's capabilities, foibles, folklore, and operation could easily fill a book (and it has). Check out http://fieldhome.net:9080/scsi_faq for a wealth of information and links to even more.

Summary

Peripheral connectivity is not an interesting subject. Basic knowledge is necessary, but this stuff is supposed to *just work*. Besides, hooking hardware up is, hopefully, a one-time operation. For a really detailed discussion of troubleshooting connectivity as well as other problems, I recommend *Mac Upgrade Bible*, 3rd Edition (Todd Stauffer & Kirk McElhearn, Wiley 2003).

PCI and Other Slots

Chapter
28

◆ ◆

Secrets in This Chapter

◆ ◆

I remember when the Blue and White G3 was first released. Not only was it not beige and boxy, but it was (as Apple stated in its commercials) the most "Open Minded" computer on the market. As they said this, you could see the side of the computer open up, showing you easy access to all of the internal components. For guys in my line of work, this new design was very cool. (If you've ever taken apart an 8100 you'd know why.)

Not all Macintosh models allow you to expand the computer internally, beyond memory. Of course, that doesn't matter if you don't need expandability.

> **insider insight** It should be noted here as well that Apple really did invent the expandable personal computer with the Apple II back in 1976, everyone has copied them since then

But slots are the name of the game in this chapter, and I'll concentrate on the models that have internal expansion slots. I'll lay out the best way to expand your Mac and stay out of trouble, well at least stay out of the trouble that might come from trying to expand your Mac and having an unsavory result. As far as any other trouble you're apt to get into, all I can say is that I'm able to help you with Mac-related problems only. For the rest, it'll be up to you to work it out.

A Brief History of The Mac's Expansion Slots

Now I'm sure most Mac users have come to regard Intel as the enemy, because of that chip that's "inside" most Windows boxes. However, those same Mac users don't know — or just don't like to admit — that Apple uses Intel-invented technologies in its computers. In addition to USB (also found on most Windows boxes), these are the standards for the expansion options in present-day Macs.

Of course, this isn't the only area in which Apple's competitors are present and accounted for on the Mac platform. There's Microsoft, naturally, with which Apple has had a long love/hate relationship and Hewlett-Packard, which produces lots of Mac-compatible printers and scanners, but also makes some very popular PC boxes.

However, politics isn't the subject of this chapter. It's expansion slots.

The first one I'm going to cover is Peripheral Component Interconnect (commonly called PCI), which is a high-performance bus developed by Intel in the 1990s to replace the slower and hard-to-configure interfaces that were used in existing PC designs of the time. PCI not only greatly increased the speed of the connection, but also greatly lessened the configuration options that the user had to set and tweak to get their new card to work with the other cards already in their system.

PCI is designed to be plug-and-play, which means that, like NuBus, Apple's former slot standard, PCI cards are automatically recognized by the computer when you boot with one installed. However, you still need to install the proper drivers for the card to communicate with the operating system. Still, for jaded PC users who never enjoyed such an easy setup process, it all came as a revelation.

Apple Thinks Different about the Battle of the Busses

Apple has always had the rap of preferring to go its own way when it came to using or setting standards. Back in the early days of the Mac, the company's engineers looked at the ISA and EISA busses that were being used on the PC and saw that they were very hard for the user to work with. While ISA was cheap, most cards required the user to set jumpers or switches to customize them for the PCs that they were installed in. EISA was easier to configure, but it was very expensive and still required more expertise and tweaking than Apple liked. "The computer for the rest of us" shouldn't saddle users with such problems.

So, the first expandable Mac, the venerable Macintosh II, released in 1987, used a technology called NuBus, which had been developed back in the 1970s in MIT's labs, and later perfected by Texas Instruments for high-end computer systems. Using NuBus at the time made perfect sense and it worked quite well in practice.

This was all well and good, and the Mac benefited from the superior performance of NuBus. What wasn't so good was the fact that, like other technologies Apple adopted over the years, the rest of the PC industry didn't quite jump on the NuBus bandwagon. One consequence was that Mac peripheral cards had low production runs and were hideously expensive. Instead of spending a few hundred dollars for a decent graphics card, you'd sometimes spend thousands.

note

Here's how card prices have changed over the years: When I bought a Mac in 1993, the graphics card I wanted listed for $2500, and it wasn't even a top-of-the-line product. Fortunately, I found a dealer with an overstock and managed to save hundreds of dollars on my purchase. Now if you believe Mac peripherals are expensive today, this was only one example. A fully outfitted system from Apple in those days cost as much as a new car. (And I'm not talking about a Yugo.)

It took a while for Apple to get the message that there had to be a better and cheaper way to expand your Mac. In 1995, it adopted PCI for its second-generation Power Macs. PCI didn't just give Mac users access to cheaper expansion cards, which often required a new driver and firmware to become Mac-compatible. Performance also took a sizeable boost.

PCI originally ran at 33 MHz, in contrast to the NuBus speed of 10 MHz. It wasn't just another megahertz myth in the making. Data throughput was more than twice as fast as NuBus, based on a figure of 20 to 40MB per second, compared to 10 to 16MB per second. That, in itself, was sufficient reason to make the switch, even if you didn't factor in the greatly decreased price of admission for the new cards.

It also attracted new players to the Mac marketplace, such as ATI Technologies and, later, NVIDIA, which gave you a chance to buy those super-snazzy gaming cards and enjoy three-figure frame rates in Quake and other 3D games.

Graphics Gets a Slot All Its Own

Yes, perhaps adopting an Intel standard was strange for Apple, because it was, in effect, playing nice with the enemy. And let's not forget another Intel bus, USB that languished until Windows 98 was released which offered native USB support.

The next Intel standard I'll talk about is Accelerated Graphics Port (AGP) invented by Intel in the mid-1990s to address the problems that they were having delivering enough data to the video card. As PCs got faster and faster, it soon became evident that PCI-based video cards were unable to receive and transmit the needed amounts of data over the PCI bus. It wasn't just a matter of getting 3D game frame-rates exceeding 100 or 200, sophisticated 3D rendering programs also required even speedier graphics processing units (GPUs) to strut their stuff.

> **note**   Mac OS X's Quartz Extreme feature exploits AGP and then some. But you have to have lots of power available, and even the basic AGP cards aren't up to the task. Apple wants a GeForce2 or later card from nVidia to properly support Quartz in OS 10.2 or later.

As a result, Intel designed a new slot standard dedicated to supporting the video cards of the future and this is what developed into AGP. Here Apple was late to the game. AGP first appeared on PC boxes in the latter part of 1997, but didn't get widespread use on the Mac until 2000. After it was introduced, however, use of AGP spread through Apple products like wildfire. Today every single desktop model has an AGP port of one sort or another, even the cheapest eMac.

AGP addresses two of the limitations of PCI: performance and the demands on video memory. You see, AGP permits the GPU to access system memory as needed, if its built-in memory is filled. The sharing process is dynamic, depending on the requirements of the particular system. AGP delivers a direct connection between the video chipset and the main processor, so there's no performance hit when different expansion cards vie for bandwidth.

AGP is designed strictly for video hardware, so it's easier for graphics chipmakers to boost performance as needed for new games and 3D software.

> **insider insight**   AGP ports are rated at speed multiples, such as 2x and 4x, the ratings commonly applied to the bus on your Mac. Like a CD drive, the figures indicate how much the bus is accelerated, but it doesn't mean that a graphics card will magically become faster if you move it from a 2x AGP port to a 4x. Card speed depends on the performance capability of the card itself, and the slower cards may run no faster even if faster throughput is available.

Making Sense of Slot Confusion

I know. They look the almost the same. But AGP and PCI are designed for different purposes. PCI is an all-purpose expansion port that can handle, as I said, an extensive range of expansion cards. These might include, in addition to graphics cards of course, a faster network card, a SCSI card (particularly important since Apple ditched SCSI support), or even a dedicated audio or video capture board.

All right, AGP and PCI both look a lot alike in person (although they are not identical, especially on many of the G5 PowerMacs using PCI-X), but how do you tell them apart? I never thought this would be an issue, until I attempted to install a graphics card on a client's computer, and found the box was mislabeled. His Mac had an AGP port, and that's how the box was labeled. But the card itself was PCI.

note   PCI-X Runs at 133 MHz, you need to mention the PCI-X bus that was developed by Compaq/HP and is now used by Apple in some G5 models.

The best way to tell the difference between a PCI card and an AGP card is to examine the connector. On an AGP card, there is a small *L* to the right of the main connector. The PCI connector has a large number of connectors on the edge that run from the top to the bottom of the connector. AGP connectors consist of what appear to be two rows stacked one atop of the other.

Secret

Slot Problems, or Dust in the Wind

If you live in the Midwest as I do, you'll appreciate this one. Sometimes a PCI or AGP card can act up if it's been in storage for a while or if you have a really dirty Mac. Yes, a familiar scenario. The problem is that both PCI and AGP cards have very dense connectors that allow them to talk to the Mac that they are plugged into. When you leave one of these cards out of your Mac or the original packaging for a while, these connectors can get dirty and this dirt interferes with the communication between the Mac and the card. Likewise, if you have a dirty Mac, that dirt can work its way down into the PCI or AGP slot and interfere with the proper operation of the card.

Unless it's "caked on," this kind of dirt can be removed with a can of compressed air. I recommend that anyone who works inside a Mac keep a can of compressed air on hand for just such situations.

caution   Many new AGP cards, equipped with the most powerful graphics processors, come with their own heat sinks and fans to help cool themselves. On the latest GPUs, there are heat sinks on the cards that will extend nearly the entire length of the board. As these cards generate a lot of heat, you may run into problems where your graphics card overheat and start acting weird. If this is the case, make sure that the fan(s) on the video card, if it has one, of course, is running properly; you can just open up your Mac and take a quick look while the Mac is on. If it is not, call the maker of your video board and see about getting a new fan. If there is no fan or the fan is working, try moving any other cards in your Mac away from the video card. If the problem persists, especially on hot humid days, look at moving your Mac someplace cooler so that it does not overheat.

Some Cold, Hard Advice on Installing an Expansion Card

Plug-and-play. So simple. So why do I need to write a section on installing one of these cards, except to meet my publisher's word count, or for the fact that I just adore foaming at the mouth. Well, there is a practical reason.

For one thing, there are a few gotchas when you install an expansion card on your Mac, and if you don't follow things carefully, you could easily fry the computer, and I know you'd rather fry some chicken breasts instead, right?

So, if you take the following steps literally, you should be able to get through the process without serious damage to your psyche and without damage to your Mac. I haven't lost a patient yet, and I've done lots of installations of this sort over the years.

note   First and foremost, don't believe someone who says you could void your warranty if you install an expansion card on your Power Mac. This *was* true in the old days, when a compact Mac had some readily accessible high voltage video hardware inside. Apple just wanted to keep your hair from standing on end. But today, there are a number of user installable parts on a Mac, so you don't need fret over this. Except for one thing: If you do manage to fry your Mac because you did something wrong, Apple won't cover the damage. That, my friends, is the way it is, as the TV newscaster said.

Installing Your Card

There are a number of reasons that I could give you for not installing a card on your own. Because I do this for a living, my motives could be questioned. While it is true that I (we) prefer to do this work for our customers and then present them a bill, it's not all about money. There are also other considerations. When people in my profession do that kind of work, we take some responsibility, not only for the selection of the card, but the installation of the card. That peace of mind may be worth the bill to you. If it isn't and you're ready to go it alone, I thought the best thing to do would be to talk you through the process.

If you are lucky enough not to have tossed out your Mac's manual, go ahead and check the section on expanding your computer. It is well illustrated, and contains information more closely in tune with your model. Best I can do here is give you general advice.

So, without further ado, let's install a card:

Secret

Using Apple's Knowledge Base Online

If you can't find your user guide, pay a visit to Apple's support Web site at www. info.apple.com/. You should be able to use the Knowledge Base search feature to locate the instructions you need, along with illustrations, to guide you. Hint: clicking the Manuals link helps speed your search. But that's all I'm going to say about reading the "friendly" manual.

1. **Prepare your parts for the installation and prepare yourself.** If you're going to be doing this on a carpeted surface, you want to make sure you don't have to get up and leave in the middle of the process for a restroom visit, because walking across a carpet can produce static electricity that can be death to an expansion card or the internal workings of your Mac.

note Get yourself a Phillips head screwdriver, the one with four sides. A normal sized one should be adequate to the task. If your expansion card comes with a wrist strap, attach it to your wrist before going further; unfortunately, few of these products include wrist straps. Also, prepare to endure the jokes from family and coworkers about you finally being wired.

note When installing a card you should always touch a piece of metal on the Mac you are installing the card into before unplugging it to equalize their electric charge potential between yourself and the Mac. However you probably shouldn't open a plugged-in Mac. And while you're working you should avoid moving (shuffling) your feet, especially on a carpeted surface.

2. **Before shutting down your Mac, check to see if you need to install new drivers.** I can't tell you if you will need to do so, as it depends. Mac OS X supports the common ATI and NVIDIA cards out of the box, but you may find a later version in the box, and in the case of ATI products, some additional configuration features. If you need to install new drivers, do it before adding the card, so you don't run into a problem with video display because of an unavailable driver.

We Interrupt This Chapter . . .

Pieter has a few words about my last point.

Pieter: Benjamin, if you install the new driver first and then shut down your Mac, you are basically committed to the upgrade. Should the new video card be bad, you may have problems reinstalling the old card with the new driver present. I always recommend that you install the new card and boot up your Mac. Then download and install the latest driver from the manufacturer's Web site.

Benjamin: I see what you're saying, Pieter. But there are situations where you *must* install the driver first. Because these cases are the exception and not the rule, I'd say that the reader should consider your advice on one condition. The installer should read the card's installation instructions to see what they're dealing with . . . the rule or the exception.

note Is there really a danger of having a black screen if you don't have the required drivers? Well, I haven't run into this problem so far, but I am highly cautious about such things, so I always double-check the driver situation before venturing into the great unknown.

3. Shut down your Mac and open the case. On the newest graphite and silver Power Macs, or the Blue & White Power Mac G3, just pull the latch at the top of the right end of the case, and pull it down (shown in Figure 28-1). Here you see the insides, ready to receive your card.

Figure 28-1: Slot, slot, give me a slot, and set me free.

> **note** On the new G5 PowerMacs you pull out a lever from the back to remove the metal side panel. Once you've removed that, you pull out the clear plastic cover to get at the insides of your G5.

4. If you have a wrist strip, attach the other end to the power supply. Otherwise, touch the power supply once to ground yourself and drain static electricity. If there's a slight electrical pop, don't be afraid. Just be grateful that the static charge didn't destroy your Mac's motherboard or your new expansion card.

> **note** If your ground strap had a an alligator clip, attaching the alligator clip to a metal part of the case is a tad safer than attaching it to the power supply as there are capacitors in the power supply that can discharge at the wrong moment. However, you must attach it to some metal so as to ground yourself. In any case, the power cord must be plugged in to provide a ground. Once you are grounded, unplug the power cord. You can always attach the grounding strap alligator clip to a known ground and then touch the power supply, while wearing the grounding strap, to equalize the potential between the Mac and yourself.

5. Remove the screw from the top of the slot that's earmarked for your installation and place the screw on a soft, visible surface.

How to Avoid Losing Your Screws While You Work

Secret

When you do work on a computer, there can be a lot of screws and/or pieces that can easily be lost under the work bench (or dining room table).

A plastic bag or, perish the thought, an ash tray is a great place to put the tiny screw that anchors your expansion card in place. If you have neither, you could use some cellophane tape to hold the screw in place while you proceed.

If you're doing a lot of work inside a computer you could use what we use to keep things sorted — an ice cube tray.

6. If the slot is unoccupied, there will probably be a small metallic cover covering the hole at the rear of your Mac. Remove this cover and place it in a safe place. (I usually put them in the box the expansion card came in.)

7. Is there a card in there now? No problem. Just wiggle it back and forth gently to pry it out. If the card is in the AGP slot (shown in Figure 28-2), you have to do this with two hands, by first pulling back the little clip that holds it in place, and then lifting it out with your other hand. You may also have to unscrew the retaining screw that holds the card rigid with the back of the case. Just remember not to be too rough. You don't want to snap it off.

Figure 28-2: Carefully lift the card up and away from the slot.

8. Gently place the card into the slots, making sure the pin layouts line up (after all, you don't want to wreck the slot). As with removal, you may have to rock it back and forth. Again, with an AGP card, you must move back the clip (if your Mac has a clip — not all do) gently (but not enough to break it of course).

9. Push the card down until it snaps into place, and I don't mean that too literally. You just want to make sure that the card is in tight, so it doesn't pop out and wreak havoc while your Mac is running.

10. Reinsert that tiny screw, and hand tighten. You don't want to have to struggle to get it off.

Secret

How to Avoid Losing Screws Inside Your Mac

Place the screw in its hole carefully. It's very easy to drop it, and it doesn't take clumsy fingers to have an accident. I have long, thin fingers, as I've said before, and I have often found myself searching through the nooks and crannies of the chassis with a flashlight trying to find the missing screw. I suppose if you're really adept with tools, a long-nosed pliers could be used to hold the screw while you use the screwdriver with your other hand to lock it down.

Some tape or rubber cement on the tip of the screwdriver can be very useful in holding the screw to the screwdriver. A screw driver with a magnetized head can be useful as well.

11. Double-check to make sure the card is fully seated in position, and then close your Mac's case.

12. Hook up your display to the graphics card, drive to a SCSI card, or whatever you have to connect to it.

13. Plug the power cord back into your Mac.

14. Turn your Mac on and verify that everything is working properly.

If everything went according to plan, then the card and the attached device should be humming along, but if something goes awry, read on; I give you some advice on how to solve the problem.

Any Slots Missing?

Indeed there are. But some of those slots are passé as well. Take for example, the Processor Direct Slot (a.k.a. PDS slot), used on a number of expandable Macs, such as the famous LC, in the early days. The PDS slot is attached directly to your Mac's logic board, and it was used for cache cards in the days when the processor didn't have an integrated cache. You could also use it for a processor upgrade or accelerator card, which would take over the number crunching chores from your Mac's built-in processor.

note In some cases, the PDS slot was also able to do double duty as a NuBus slot with the appropriate adapter. Those were the days, my friends, and I'm glad they finally ended.

Beginning with the first PCI Power Macs, the processor was actually placed on a module that loaded into a separate slot. This had the added advantage of making them easy to upgrade, no harder than plugging in an AGP or PCI card.

insider insight In fact the PM7500, 8500, and 9500 had the processor on a card. The PM 7200 still had the processor glued into the socket.

More recently, Macs used Zero Insertion Force (ZIF) sockets for replacing processors, and even today's Power Macs have processor cards (beneath huge heat sinks) that can be removed and replaced.

We Interrupt This Chapter . . .

Should you replace your Mac's processor? Depends. On an older Mac, it can really boost performance tremendously, and some of the basic processor upgrade cards are downright affordable. Even better, most are fully compatible with Mac OS X without need of special drivers.

Pieter feels that it makes perfect sense to upgrade the processor to get your Mac a healthy speed boost without having to pay a bundle. "I mean," He says, "applications never require less power, and you can't afford to buy a new Mac every year unless you make a lot more money than I do."

I agree, in part, but I have to qualify that. A new processor only replaces one part of your Mac's system. Your Mac's motherboard doesn't get any faster, nor do the graphics card, hard drive, and optical drive. Computer speed depends on the interaction of all your hardware components, and if you begin to add up the cost of replacing everything, suddenly you've bought a new Mac. So, upgrade judiciously, unless you're absolutely in love with your Mac and can't bear to see it go.

If Something Goes Wrong

You checked and rechecked and your Mac still won't restart, or the monitor or other peripheral fails to function. Now you're in a pickle. Did you fry your Mac or that costly graphics card that was supposed to deliver gaming bliss?

Don't panic. Take stock, look over your options, and make sure that you did everything properly.

Just check these possibilities:

◆ **The card isn't compatible with your Mac.** You did make sure you bought a Mac-compatible card, right? Yes, there is an ATI Radeon and an ATI Radeon, but the firmware for Windows and Macs are different. While some manufacturers manage to flash (or update) the firmware to induce such cards to work on a Mac, there are no guarantees. You may just end up with something that doesn't work. So be certain to check the product's label to be sure you have the right card. If not, return it to your dealer.

> **note**
> What do you mean you ignored my advice and failed to install the drivers? It's bad enough that my wife and kids ignore me, so please try not to make me feel inadequate. In fact, this may be the source of your problem. But with a graphics card, you'll have to restore the original, first, so you can get a picture and run the software installation.

♦ **The card is defective.** It happens. Although I've not encountered any problem in many years of pulling these installation stunts, the fact is that others aren't so lucky. The best thing to do here is to shut down, remove the card, and, if it's a graphics card, put the old one back. If the display lights up, you can be sure where the blame lies.

> **caution**
> Try to avoid pulling the plug on your Mac if you must shut down. The usual method is to press and hold the power button, and, after a few seconds, it should shut down. The plug-pulling gambit is only done as a last resort.

♦ **Reset the motherboard.** What's that? Pushing a reset switch on a Mac? Yes, when you shut down your Mac and reopen the case, you will find a tiny amber or black button that is usually situated near the battery. Press and hold this button, known in the vernacular as a Cuda chip, for about twenty seconds. This is equivalent to a super PRAM zap (you can read more about zapping PRAM in Chapter 32), which clears up everything that needs to be cleared up. When other methods fail, this one often works to restore your Mac to full functionality. By the way, I've also seen this fix work if your Mac is turned off because of a power failure. (I would never suggest the power went off simply because you forgot to pay the bill.) In any case, it's not terribly likely you fried your Mac if you followed my advice and took proper precautions.

♦ **Find an expert.** There is no shame here. You get points for trying it yourself. But you shouldn't expect to be as good at the inner workings of your Mac as someone who does just that as a living. I've said it before in this book, if you don't know an Apple Specialist or certified Apple technician, then you should go out and find one. Then when you really need one, you'll know where to go.

Summary

Slot confusion doesn't have to be your curse. As you saw in this chapter, it's very possible to figure out what hooks to what and how to avoid getting stuck with the wrong card for the wrong slot.

The image of the Mac as a device for ultra simple networking is mostly true, that is if you compare the other options in the personal computer universe. But that doesn't mean that everything is easy or that there are no pitfalls. You'll learn more in the next chapter.

Networking

" **I** understand you're looking for a business gonnegtion."

(Wolfsheim to Carraway in *The Great Gatsby*, F. Scott Fitzgerald)

Networks are all about connections: to other Macs, to printers, to local file servers, to remote file servers, to e-mail systems, to Web sites. Almost from the start, the Mac was designed to connect to networks. Today, a Macintosh without a network connection seems as uncomfortable and out of place as a Beverly Hills socialite on an Arkansas farm. In fact, one network per Mac is often not enough — a Pantherized Mac is comfortable with multiple network connections of multiple types. Ethernet, AirPort, Bluetooth, fiber channel, USB, FireWire, even the lowly but still proud modem can all handle network traffic coming in and out of your Mac.

Apple proclaims that Panther features "automatic networking." In many cases, that is true enough — out of the box, Panther's defaults allow a Mac to connect to many common network setups with almost no fuss or fiddling. But not always. . . . Luckily, Panther provides access to a huge number of network settings and options that you can use to get your Mac onto all but the most arcane and idiosyncratic networks.

So, sit back and pop open a cold one (or, if you'd rather, brew yourself a nice cup of tea) while we look at how all this networking stuff works.

Protocols and Standards

Here's the first check: what *is* a network? What's the difference between a Mac connected to a printer with a crossover Ethernet cable, say, and a Mac connected to a printer with a USB cable?

Not much, actually. You could make the case that these are both networks of a sort. After all, at its most basic level, a network simply consists of a bunch of devices hooked together so they can exchange information. Yet, Those-Who-Decide-What-Things-Are-Called (a shadowy group of indeterminate membership who meet every Thursday for malai kofta and nomenclatural discussions) have decreed that one is a *network* and one is a *bus*.

Part of the reason for deciding what is a network and what isn't has to do with the *way* that the information is exchanged, with the standards and protocols that impose order on the gangrel bits roaming between all the devices on the network.

The OSI Model and Network Stacks

For all practical purposes (which is to say, so that we can all agree that we are talking about more-or-less the same thing) a network consists of devices that communicate following the Open System Interconnection (OSI) model, a model created by the International Standards Organization (ISO) back in the late 1970s in order to define a standard way that disparate devices, with possibly quite different operating systems, could communicate together. (It is only a coincidence that *ISO - OSI* forms a palindrome . . . or is it?)

The Birth of the OSI Model

Secret

The OSI model began in the depths of Honeywell Information Systems in the mid-1970s as part of an attempt to create a standard set of protocols — that is, formats for exchanging information — for distributed database systems. The working group studied similar sets of protocols, including the protocols being used on the ARPANET (the Advanced Research Project Agency's network, funded by the Department of Defense, which grew up to become the Internet that we all know and love to browse), IBM's SNA (System Network Architecture) protocols, and some other work in the database field. Meanwhile, folk in Britain (to be specific, the British Standards Institute) were trying to crack a similar nut and prodded ISO to come up with generalizable standards for supporting distributed processing. ISO, doing what large organizations do when prodded, formed a committee (actually a subcommittee to a committee — Subcommittee 16 of Technical Committee 97) to look at Open Systems Interconnection. This subcommittee then asked the American National Standards Institute (ANSI) to develop proposals for the subcommittee's first meeting.

At this point, the Honeywell group, who participated in ANSI's discussions on this whole interconnectedness issue/problem/thingie, presented the seven-layer interconnection model they'd been devising, which ANSI asked them to present to ISO when Subcommittee 16 of Technical Committee 97 met in March 1978, in Washington, D.C. The Honeywell folk must have wowed them, because the model was adopted as the basis for the provisional model that ISO published the same month, and slightly refined the following year.

Just in time to give the people working under the pirate flag in Cupertino one more thing to think about as they began to devise the Macintosh . . . but that's another story.

What makes the OSI model important is that is doesn't describe *how* to design any kind of network but how to *think* about designing networks. Using the OSI model, all sorts of different networks with all sorts of different hardware and software can be built. The model breaks the whole connection problem into levels, from the most machine-specific hardware level (for example, what kind of cabling or electrical system is used between devices), up to the most abstract user-interface level (how a user mounts a remote hard disk on the desktop). Each level of the model is where various individual protocols live, and devices on the network are compatible when the protocols implemented on each of the devices, at each level, are compatible. The whole collection of protocols, as implemented on various operating systems, is sometimes called a *network stack*.

The OSI Model to Go

Secret

You don't *need* to know this in all of its rich, zesty detail, but a general understanding of the layers that constitute the OSI model can help you understand what the various network-related System Preference panes and utility programs are managing.

Here are the layers, from lowest to highest, along with what things happen or are implemented at that layer.

1. **Physical**. Signals on cables or wireless transceivers.
2. **Datalink**. Switches, hubs, routers, and driver software.

continues

continued

3. **Network**. Addressing schemes (such as IP numbers).

4. **Transport**. Package and send data.

5. **Session**. Set up and maintain connections between two entities.

6. **Presentation**. Convert data to formats that the OS expects.

7. **Application**. Make sure the right program gets the data.

If you use the first letter of each layer to build the mnemonic, *Please do not throw sausage pizza away,* you'll always remember the OSI layers.

One Network, Many Flavors

The OSI model is why you can have AppleTalk or TCP/IP function on your Mac over various physical kinds of connections, such as AirPort or Ethernet, and why you can have both, and possibly other network protocols as well, active at the same time. AppleTalk and TCP/IP are merely two ways of packaging, addressing, and transmitting digital data, ways that involve only a couple of the levels of the OSI model. The physical connection level (AirPort transmission, Ethernet, LocalTalk cabling, etc.) is irrelevant to the packaging, addressing, and transmitting problem. AppleTalk and TCP/IP are protocols at one level of the model, the hardware protocols are at a different, lower level.

insider
insight

In fact, TCP/IP is really two protocols, not one, but they are protocols that like to hang out together. The *P*'s in TCP/IP actually stand for *protocol*: IP is the Internet Protocol and it handles the packaging and addressing of data; TCP is the Transmission Control Protocol and it handles the reliability of the data exchange, making sure that the sender knows that the receiver got each of the IP-wrapped packages of data (called *packets*), and in the right order. It's been a great pairing: together, these two protocols helped build the Internet.

If you're curious (and you must be or you wouldn't be reading this book), you can check out the details concerning the workings of some of the various network protocols running on your Mac. Just fire up Network Utility, an informative program found in your Utilities folder (just head down to near the bottom of your Applications folder and turn right), and you can see how many TCP/IP and AppleTalk packets your Mac has been sending since the last time you rebooted (and much, much else). The AppleTalk tab shows you the AppleTalk statistics (see Figure 29-1), while the obscurely named Netstat tab shows you the TCP/IP and related statistics (see Figure 29-2).

insider
insight

Netstat is not all that obscure a name if you've been a longtime Unix and Internet geek. The Netstat tab and its associated buttons in the Network utility simply provide a GUI for the venerable netstat Unix terminal command, which has been around for many years and which came to Mac OS X along with all the other Unix goodies. The command's purpose is simply to display *net*work activity *stat*istics, which on Unix machines generally tend to be more or less synonymous with TCP/IP and related activity. For a real thrill, open a Terminal window and type `man netstat` to find out all that the command-line version of netstat can do.

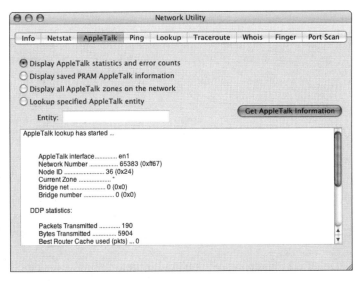

Figure 29-1: Network Utility reveals your AppleTalk activity.

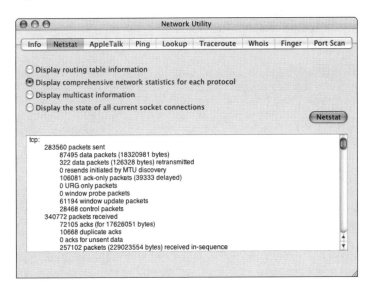

Figure 29-2: That's a lot of TCP/IP packets. . . .

AppleTalk or TCP/IP?

As you've probably guessed by now, the two most common network data protocols you'll be using in Panther are TCP/IP and AppleTalk. Both come built into the system. What's the difference, and what are they for?

♦ **TCP/IP** is common on networks that contain mixed platforms, such as Windows, Linux, and Unix workstations (including Mac OS X boxes). The Internet relies on this protocol, so you pretty much have to use it if you want to use the Web. TCP/IP is not quite as plug-and-playish as AppleTalk, but Apple's implementation of it in Panther gets you much closer to that digital nirvana than most users on other platforms.

Some Enchanted Rendezvous

Secret

Apple has worked hard to bring some of the same kind of plug-and-play power to TCP/IP networks that AppleTalk has had all along, and the result of that work is Rendezvous, which has been a part of OS X since 10.2 and has been improved in Panther.

Like AppleTalk, Rendezvous enables you to connect a printer, computer, or other device to your local network and it will just work — no configuration required. Unlike AppleTalk, Rendezvous is built upon open standards and uses TCP/IP, which means there's a chance that other computer vendors will support it. Rendezvous, in fact, is simply the name Apple has given to its implementation of the Zeroconf standard developed by the Internet Engineering Task Force (IETF), a group that oversees a number of standard Internet protocols. Apple is not just hitching a free ride, here; they've been regular contributors to the Zeroconf standard's development. If you really want to know all the gory details of how Zeroconf works, check out `www.zeroconf.org/`.

♦ **AppleTalk** is typically used for networks that are all, or mostly, Mac-based, especially those that mix Macs running Mac OS X with Macs running Mac OS 9 or earlier. If the network also hosts older printers and AppleShare servers, AppleTalk is pretty much de rigueur. AppleTalk, as is typical of Apple products, tends to require little in the way of technical configuration from a user's point of view. Turn it on, and presto: It just seems to work.

As noted previously, using one protocol doesn't mean that you can't also use the other at the same time. In fact, you probably are.

Turning on AppleTalk Server Browsing

Secret

In a break with Apple tradition, Panther by default has AppleTalk server browsing disabled . . . at least for some users. This means that when you click the Network icon in a Finder window, it won't show you any AppleTalk servers on your network. Whether this is a sign of Things to Come (see the sidebar, "W(h)ither AppleTalk"), or just the result of a braincloud affecting the folk who built the Panther installer is not clear.

But not to worry. You can fix this oversight (if oversight it was) pretty quickly. Take a trip to your Utilities folder and launch Directory Access (see Figure 29-3). Click the Services tab and you see a check box that lets you enable AppleTalk. Then, click the lock at the bottom of the window to authenticate with an administrator name and password, click the AppleTalk check box, and you're good to go.

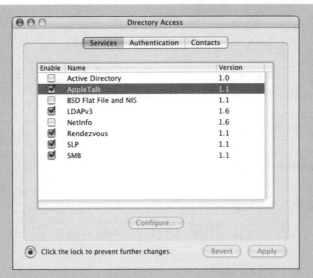

Figure 29-3: Here's where you can turn on AppleTalk server browsing, and a whole lot more.

W(h)ither AppleTalk

Secret

Back in the day (that day being sometime in the mid-1980s), the Mac was just about the only right-out-of-the-box network-ready desktop computer you could buy. The reason? Apple had a laser printer they wanted to sell, and a business market they wanted to crack. But because a laser printer was significantly more expensive than Apple's dot-matrix ImageWriter (the only other printer that worked with the early Mac), Apple figured that businesses would buy a laser printer only if it could be shared among computers. So, the LaserWriter was designed to communicate using network technology, and Apple developed a network protocol to let the LaserWriter and the Mac talk. Thus was born AppleTalk, along with something called desktop publishing. And they're still with us today.

The original AppleTalk protocol was designed for small workgroups only; at the time, its limit of a few hundred devices on a single network seemed next to limitless. However, limitless turned out to be not what it was cracked up to be, and the AppleTalk protocol evolved to be able to handle many more users and to span individual local networks.

But there were other network protocols out in the world, and they worked with all sorts of (non-Apple) devices and computers. AppleTalk, instead of conquering the network world, remained standard only for Macs and for the publishing industry. In fact, one of AppleTalk's best advantages — that it just worked when you turned it on — was also a drawback: every AppleTalk device was responsible for sending information out on the network periodically to announce its presence so that other devices on the network would know about it. (This was how you could "see" printers pop-up in the old Mac OS Chooser just as soon as they were turned on.) On a large, busy, network,

continues

continued

these announcements took up enough bandwidth to affect the network's efficiency. The rap on AppleTalk was that it was "too chatty."

Other protocols became dominant in the non-Apple world, among them TCP/IP, which was wildly popular in the Unix world, was flexible enough to handle most networking tasks, and was anything but chatty. When Apple bought NeXT, it bought the seeds of OS X, the whole Unix mindset, and a development team that felt about AppleTalk as most non-Apple folk felt about it. Apple's network direction was clear: AppleTalk was the past, interoperable standards like TCP/IP were the future. Except AppleTalk wouldn't die. It couldn't . . . not with all those AppleTalk printers and desktop publishing bureaus out there in the world.

Today, AppleTalk is something of a second-class citizen on the Mac: in some cases, Panther even comes with it turned off. And, eventually, it may go away completely. But don't count on it.

Network Preferences

You would think that Panther's System Preference pane for Network settings would provide one-stop shopping for all your networking needs. Although it doesn't, it does come close, providing a rather startling number of settings and information displays for its size. With it, you can adjust settings at various layers of the OSI model, from the physical layer (such as which devices you're using) all the way up to the application layer (such as which proxy server your Web browser uses to obtain pages). If you don't know what a proxy server is, don't worry, you'll find out soon enough.

> **tip** You can get to the Network preferences right from your Apple menu in Panther: just choose it from the Locations sub-menu.

Network Status Pane

When you first open it, the Network preference pane displays basic network status information (see Figure 29-4). Here's where you can see at a glance the *ports* that are connected to, or set up to connect to, a network.

Ports, Real and Imaginary

Secret

The *ports* referred to in the Network status display are physical ports (in the OSI model, they exist on layer 1). They either can be removable devices, such as a USB Bluetooth adapter or an AirPort card, or they can be built-in devices that physically *look* like what you'd ordinarily call ports, such as Ethernet ports or modem ports.

Don't confuse these ports with the ports in the Firewall pane of the Sharing preferences described later in this chapter; those are conceptual rather than physical (they exist at the higher levels of the OSI model) and are used for communicating with different Internet services (such as Web browsers or iChat AV).

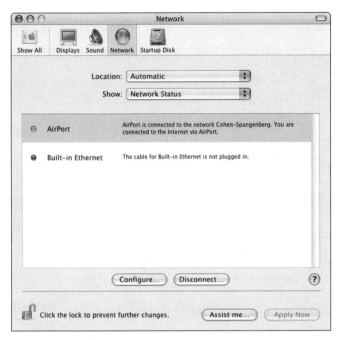

Figure 29-4: The Network preference pane in System Preferences reveals your network's current status.

Getting at Settings for Network Ports

To get at the individual settings panes for each of your available network ports you select it from the Show menu (shown in Figure 29-5) — or you can just double-click on one of the ports shown in the Network Status display.

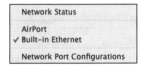

Figure 29-5: Network preferences' Show pop-up menu.

Each port's settings pane gives you tabs along its top that let you get at the all the settings panes associated with the port. Figure 29-6 shows the settings pane for an AirPort network connection (what the Show menu is showing), and for that network connection's device-related settings (what the highlighted AirPort tab is showing).

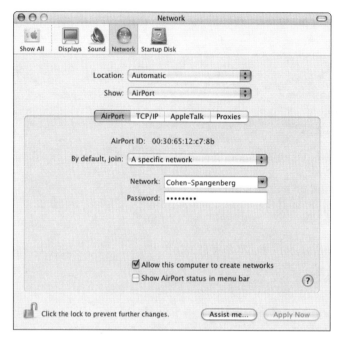

Figure 29-6: The AirPort settings pane for an AirPort network connection.

The AirPort Tab

Here's what you can do from the AirPort tab:

♦ **See your AirPort card's ID** (which some network administrators may ask you for if your Mac is connected to a business or school network).

---

insider insight

The AirPort ID is also known as its MAC ID, but in this case MAC is not short for Macintosh — it actually means *media access control,* and is a unique number that your AirPort card, and no other, has. Your Mac's Ethernet port also has a MAC ID that is unique to it and no other Ethernet port. MACs are used on the datalink layer of the OSI model. If you were wondering.

♦ **Control the way your AirPort software looks for base stations.** You can have your Mac look for a specific base station, or for the nearest base station (that is, the one with the strongest signal). In an environment with several base stations (like, say a college dorm where several students nearby may each have their own base stations), specifying a particular base station is handy — especially because you can still choose another available base station from your AirPort menu if you need to.

♦ **Control whether your Mac can create a separate AirPort network.** You set this option if you want to use a wireless connection to connect directly with another nearby computer, like a friend's iBook, so you can share files or play network-enabled games. No separate base station is required for this: The two AirPort-equipped Macs talk directly to each other.

◆ **Choose whether to show the AirPort status menu in the menu bar.** (And, trust me, if you are using your AirPort card at all, you probably want that menu where you can get to it.)

The TCP/IP Tab

If a network port's connection can handle TCP/IP traffic, a TCP/IP tab for that connection appears in the connection's Network preferences. Figure 29-7 shows the TCP/IP settings pane for the AirPort connection shown in Figure 29-6.

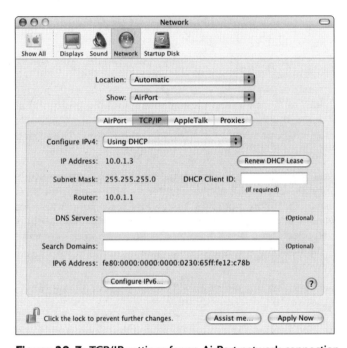

Figure 29-7: TCP/IP settings for an AirPort network connection.

You'll see pretty much the same sort of TCP/IP pane for any network connection using any device, although the settings *in* the TCP/IP pane might differ from device to device. The TCP/IP settings control the network connection at the transport and network layers in the OSI model.

On a TCP/IP network, each connection has one TCP/IP address associated with it. This pane lets you set that address information. Refer to Figure 29-8 for the discussion that follows:

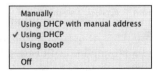

Figure 29-8: The Configure IPv4 pop-up menu.

◆ **The Configure IPv4 pop-up menu** (Figure 29-8) lets you select how the TCP/IP address is set.

- **Using DHCP** (which stands for Dynamic Host Configuration Protocol) is what you'll usually select if you have a home connection from an Internet Service Provider (ISP); it automatically sets the IP address, the Subnet Mask, and the Router fields, getting them all from a DHCP server, and makes those fields uneditable. (You may need to fill in the DHCP Client ID field if your ISP tells you to, but I've never had to, and you probably won't either.)

- **Manually**, not surprisingly, lets you set those three fields and ignores the DHCP server; you'll choose it if you have a *static* IP address and you know, or your friendly neighborhood network administrator or ISP can tell you, what these fields should contain.

- **Using DHCP with manual address** works like Manually, except that only the IP address field is unlocked.

- **Using BootP** is probably not for you, unless your network administrator or service provider tells you to select it, because it's an old protocol that DHCP replaced and improved.

- **Off** disables the network connection from handling any TCP/IP traffic.

---

note   DHCP servers assign you TCP/IP addresses for a limited time; usually an hour or two. (That's what the *Dynamic* part of DHCP is all about.) After the time expires, the server either renews your lease on that address or takes it away (which can happen on a local network with fewer available addresses than users). The **Renew DHCP Lease** button, which appears when you select Using DHCP from the Configure IPv4 pop-up menu, asks the server to start the clock running again.

◆ **The DNS Servers** field lets you specify the TCP/IP address of any Domain Name System servers that you'd like to use for the network connection. You can specify several, one, or none at all, in which case you'll probably be using DHCP and have a DNS provided by your ISP (your ISP can tell you if you need to add a DNS address, and, if so, which one(s)).

Masters of the Domain

Secret

TCP/IP addresses are long and hard to memorize (and are even longer and harder to memorize in the IPv6 scheme [see the The Configure IPv6 bullet in the "TCP/IP Tab" section]). That's what the Domain Name System is all about: it associates names like www.example.com with those pesky numeric addresses.

The naming system breaks the Internet down into nested hierarchical *domains* (domains within domains within domains . . . you get the idea). The top-level domain names are the names like .com and .net and .edu; second-level-domain names are names like example.com, and so on down through as many levels as you can wrap your mind around (like freesongs.freegoodies.freeserver.example.com).

DNS servers are regularly updated so that if the numeric address associated with any domain name changes (which can happen, for example, when a Web site is moved to a different server), the rest of the system finds out within a few hours or so.

◆ **The Search Domains** field is there to save you some typing. The domain names you enter there (such as `example.edu`) will be added to the end of any incomplete domain names you enter in your Internet programs, such as a Web browser or e-mail program.

◆ **The Configure IPv6** button brings up a sheet that lets you enter an IP address in the form used by version 6 of the Internet Protocol. If you need to use it, your network administrator will tell you.

Secret

IPv4 and IPv6

The Internet, including the World Wide Web that we've all grown to know and love and spend countless hours prowling, is built on version 4 of the Internet Protocol. This version breaks network addresses into four groups of three-digit numbers that can range from 0 to 255. This provides, theoretically, over four billion unique addresses.

Even with all sorts of clever tricks that can hide rather extensive local networks behind a single IPv4 address, however, four billion addresses is proving to be inadequate to the growing Internet's need. Internet Protocol version 6 solves that problem by using a new addressing scheme that can provide more than 340,282,366,920,938, 463,463,374,607,431,770,000,000 unique addresses.

At this time, most of the Internet is still running on IPv4, but Panther is ready to prowl an IPv6 Internet if you need to.

The PPPoE Tab

Most home and many small businesses that connect to the Internet using a high-speed modem (such as a cable modem or DSL modem) physically connect to that modem with an Ethernet cable, either directly or via a local Ethernet network. Figure 29-9 shows the PPPoE tab (Point-To-Point Protocol over Ethernet) that appears when you look at any Ethernet port settings in Network preferences; the tab allows you to configure a high-speed modem to establish an Internet connection.

cross ref

The Point-To-Point Protocol means what it says: it connects one machine (like your Mac) to one network access point (like your ISP's cable modem bank). You can't have two Macs connecting directly to the Internet (or any other network) through the same cable modem. What you can do is set up *one* Mac to share the connection that it gets from PPPoE with any other Macs on the same network. This essentially turns the Mac both into a *router* and a DHCP server. The section on sharing an Internet connection, later in this chapter, shows you how this works.

cross ref

When your Mac connects to the Internet using an AirPort network connection, the AirPort base station handles the PPPoE connection for you, so you don't see the PPPoE tab in an AirPort connection's settings. However, you will see PPPoE settings in the AirPort Admin Utility program that you use to set up an AirPort Base Station. "AirPort Base Station," later in this chapter describes AirPort Admin Utility.

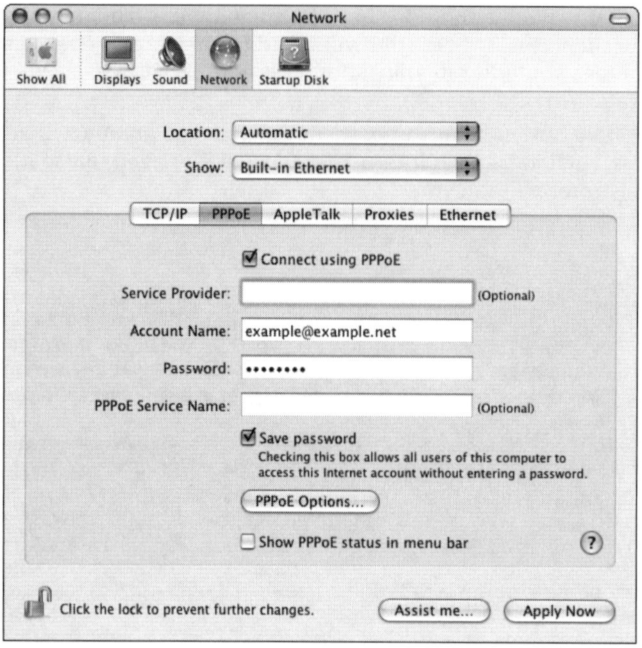

Figure 29-9: PPPoE settings for Cable and DSL modems connections.

To set up a PPPoE connection to the Internet, click the Connect using PPPoE check box.

> **caution** Checking the Connect using PPPoE check box will alter some or all of TCP/IP settings you've made in the TCP/IP pane.

Most PPPoE connections usually require you to enter only an Account Name and a Password in the appropriate fields of this pane, although some ISPs may require you to enter a PPPoE Service Name and Service Provider, as well. Your ISP will tell you how to fill out the fields on this pane.

The Show PPPoE status in menu bar places a small menu on your menu bar (see Figure 29-10) that lets you see whether you have an active PPPoE connection and control that connection.

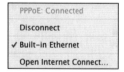

Figure 29-10: The PPPoE menu in the menu bar.

Finally, the PPPoE pane provides a PPPoE Options button that produces a sheet with which you can set, well, your PPPoE options (Figure 29-11).

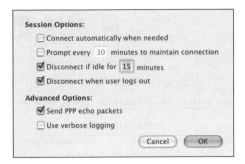

Figure 29-11: The PPPoE Options sheet.

Most of the PPPoE Options control when your Mac will ask the high-speed modem to establish or end an Internet connection; you can set those as you wish.

The Send PPP echo packets advanced option should be set according to your ISP's instructions; it is usually on.

One last option, Use verbose logging, is useful if you have a troublesome PPPoE connection and want to find out all the technical details you can about what is going on. This command records detailed information about the connection in your system logs. (You can read these with the Console program in your Utilities folder.)

> **caution**
>
> Don't turn Use verbose logging on and then forget to turn it off after you solve your problem. Verbose logging of PPPoE connections will increase the size of your log files substantially, and could cause problems if you are running short of disk space.

The AppleTalk Tab

The AppleTalk tab appears for every network port that is capable of handling AppleTalk communications. Click the tab to see the AppleTalk settings pane (shown in Figure 29-12).

AppleTalk networks, as we've seen, are designed to be almost completely self-configuring, so in most cases the only thing you need to decide is whether your Mac wants to participate in an AppleTalk network — that's what the Make AppleTalk Active check box is for.

The Computer Name appears in this pane solely for your reference; as the field says, you can change it in the Sharing Preferences, described later in this chapter.

> **note**
>
> On an AppleTalk network, all devices have names. They also have numeric network addresses, similar to TCP/IP addresses, under the hood, but AppleTalk employs a *name binding protocol* that connects user-defined, human-readable names, with the underlying numeric network address. Unlike the DNS client-server model used in TCP/IP networks, AppleTalk's name-binding is a cooperative effort that takes place among all the network's connected devices.

Figure 29-12: The AppleTalk pane with the Configure pop-up menu open.

The AppleTalk Zone menu is inactive on small local networks; it appears only on larger AppleTalk networks that a network administrator has divided into *zones* (which have names, just like devices). When it is active, it lets you choose the AppleTalk zone to which your Mac belongs, which, in turn, controls the other network devices you can readily access, such as printers and (older) AppleShare file servers (newer AppleShare servers use TCP/IP). Zones reduce the amount of network traffic by keeping any communication between devices in separate zones from intruding into any other zones as it goes on its way. Zones are similar, but not necessarily identical, to TCP/IP *subnets*.

The Configure menu gives you two choices (see Figure 29-12). You'll rarely need the Manually choice (AppleTalk really was designed to be simple), but if you do select it you'll get two fields, Node ID and Network ID, to fill in with information that your network administrator provides.

The PPP Tab

The PPP tab appears for every network port that supports Point-to-Point Protocol: this protocol was developed for modem connections, either with a Mac's internal modem, or an external modem, such as a wireless Bluetooth modem, so you'll usually see it when you look at Bluetooth or modem network ports. Like its Ethernet brother, PPPoE, PPP connects one device to one network access point. Your Mac uses the PPP settings (see Figure 29-13) to make a modem dial your ISP and to establish an Internet connection.

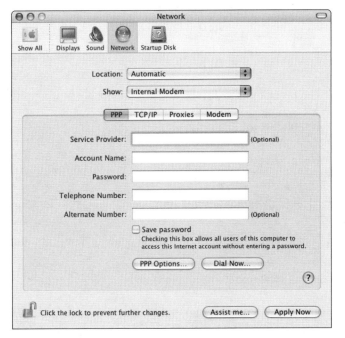

Figure 29-13: Network preferences' PPP pane.

Click the PPP tab to see the PPP settings pane (shown in Figure 29-14). This pane lets you enter the information necessary to connect to a dialup account provided by an ISP: an Account Name, a Password for the account, a Telephone Number to dial (along with an Alternate Number in case of busy signals).

> **caution** Do not click the Save password check box if your Mac is accessible to anyone you don't want using your dialup account. If the box is unchecked, you'll have to enter the dialup account's password each time you make an Internet connection; but that's a small price to pay to avoid, say, an evil roommate downloading illegal MP3s onto your Mac and leaving you prey to the RIAA's lawyers.

Click Dial Now to have your Mac instruct the modem to dial the ISP and make an Internet connection.

Click PPP Options to see the Options sheet (shown in Figure 29-14).

The PPP Options sheet looks like an expanded version of the PPPoE Options sheet (see Figure 29-11), and, in fact, the first four items are the same on each.

The group of boxes labeled Session Options lets you control how long, and under which circumstances, your Mac will tie up your phone line with a network connection, and how persistent it should be if the modem encounters a busy signal when dialing.

Session Options:

☐ Connect automatically when needed

☐ Prompt every 30 minutes to maintain connection

☑ Disconnect if idle for 15 minutes

☑ Disconnect when user logs out

☑ Redial if busy

Redial 1 times

Wait 30 seconds before redialing

Advanced Options:

Terminal Script: None

☑ Send PPP echo packets

☑ Use TCP header compression

☐ Connect using a terminal window (command line)

☐ Prompt for password after dialing

☐ Use verbose logging

Cancel   OK

Figure 29-14: The PPP options sheet from Network preferences.

Secret

Secrets of Automatic Dialing

Connect automatically when needed will cause your Mac to dial your modem whenever any program needs to establish an Internet connection and there isn't a connection already in place. This can happen at what may seem like surprising moments. Aside from the usual suspects, such as Safari or Mail, a number of other programs and services (such as Personal Web Sharing or Personal File Sharing) can require Internet connections and, thus, can trigger your Mac to dial.

Sometimes your Mac's modem won't dial the phone automatically even when the Connect automatically when needed box is checked. This can happen if you've canceled an automatic connection while the modem was dialing, or if you've manually disconnected after an automatic connection attempt. To fix this, Apple suggests you simply put your Mac to sleep and wake it up or make any change in the PPP settings.

Also, the Connect automatically when needed check box will uncheck itself automatically if your Mac has made three automatic dial-in attempts in a row that have failed. Not only that, the Mac attempts to use the next available network connection (such as Ethernet). Successive failed dial-in attempts usually indicate a problem with the ISP's phone number, a problem with the account information your Mac is sending, or a phone line problem, and, once you've fixed the problem you'll need to check that your Network preferences settings are still set to use PPP.

The group labeled Advanced Options are just that: advanced. They're available to let your Mac be compatible with various idiosyncrasies that your ISP's modem set-up might possess, so you'll usually set them in whichever way your ISP instructs you to set them.

> **tip**
>
> The *terminal scripts* and the *terminal window* PPP options help you connect to *very* idiosyncratic networks. For example, a network may require you to issue a number of commands beyond a standard login account name and password to create a successful connection: with a *terminal script* (a text file containing commands and responses to prompts) your Mac can automatically when it attempts to make a connection. You can also have a terminal window appear when a connection is being made so you can enter commands and respond to prompts manually if the network connection requires it. (This often is done to ensure network security.)

The Modem Tab

The Modem tab, as you'd expect, appears for those network ports that connect to a modem, which usually means the internal modem that is built into most Macs. This tab brings up the Modem settings pane (shown in Figure 29-15).

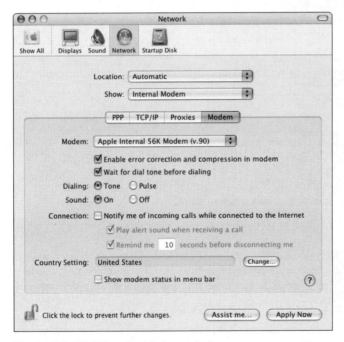

Figure 29-15: What the Modem tab shows.

The Modem settings let you choose from an extensive menu of *modem scripts* — these contain the modem control commands for a range of commercially available modems (see Figure 29-16). For most Macs, the default Apple Internal 56K Modem script is the one you want, but it's nice to have a choice.

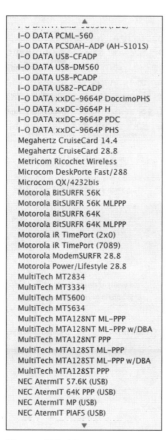

```
I-O DATA PCMB-560
I-O DATA PCML-560
I-O DATA PCSDAH-ADP (AH-S101S)
I-O DATA USB-CFADP
I-O DATA USB-DM560
I-O DATA USB-PCADP
I-O DATA USB2-PCADP
I-O DATA xxDC-9664P DoccimoPHS
I-O DATA xxDC-9664P H
I-O DATA xxDC-9664P PDC
I-O DATA xxDC-9664P PHS
Megahertz CruiseCard 14.4
Megahertz CruiseCard 28.8
Metricom Ricochet Wireless
Microcom DeskPorte Fast/288
Microcom QX/4232bis
Motorola BitSURFR 56K
Motorola BitSURFR 56K MLPPP
Motorola BitSURFR 64K
Motorola BitSURFR 64K MLPPP
Motorola iR TimePort (2x0)
Motorola iR TimePort (7089)
Motorola ModemSURFR 28.8
Motorola Power/Lifestyle 28.8
MultiTech MT2834
MultiTech MT3334
MultiTech MT5600
MultiTech MT5634
MultiTech MTA128NT ML-PPP
MultiTech MTA128NT ML-PPP w/DBA
MultiTech MTA128NT PPP
MultiTech MTA128ST ML-PPP
MultiTech MTA128ST ML-PPP w/DBA
MultiTech MTA128ST PPP
NEC AtermIT 57.6K (USB)
NEC AtermIT 64K PPP (USB)
NEC AtermIT MP (USB)
NEC AtermIT PIAFS (USB)
```

Figure 29-16: Brother, can you spare a modem script?

note
: The Apple Internal 56K Modem (v.90) script allows for the fastest connection with your internal modem, but it may be incompatible with some ISPs or unreliable if your phone line quality isn't quite up to snuff. In that case, you should choose the Apple Internal 56K Modem (v.34) script.

Secret

Hayes and the AT Codes

The plethora of modem scripts demonstrates what can result when "standards" just happen by accident. Back in the early 1980s, every modem had its own command language that let a connected computer control it. A company called Hayes was one of those modem manufacturers, and it produced a modem that could handle an astounding 1.2kbit connection speed. When Hayes produced that modem's successor, one that could handle twice the data rate (2.4kbits — kool!), the modem used the same command set as its predecessor, making Hayes the first modem producer to produce different speed modems that could understand the same commands.

Other modem makers saw that Hayes had figured out a *good thing* and they began to emulate Hayes, even going so far as to copy the Hayes command set. At first they called these modems "Hayes-compatible," but Hayes threatened to sue and so they began referring to their wares as "AT Command Set compatible" because most of Hayes's commands began with the letters AT.

Unfortunately, this de facto standardization was incomplete, because different modem makers offered different features on their modems, which required them to add modem-specific commands to each modem's version of the AT set. That's why you see all those modem scripts listed on your Modem menu even though most of their commands are identical.

To see your modem scripts, just take a trip to your Mac's Library⇨Modem Scripts folder.

The setting check boxes and buttons on this pane control features that are standard for most modems: turning on error correction and compression, choosing to dial with a pulse or a tone, detecting and handling incoming calls (essential if you have Call Waiting on your phone line). You can also put a modem status menu on your menu bar from this pane, which lets you control modem connections without a trip to the Network preferences.

note Just because the settings pane has a check box or button for a modem feature doesn't always mean that the control for that feature actually does anything. For example, not every modem is designed to detect incoming calls, and checking that check box in the Modem settings pane won't suddenly give the modem that ability.

The Bluetooth Modem Tab

If your Mac has a Bluetooth adapter (either built-in or external), Panther's Network preferences provide a Bluetooth Modem settings pane (shown in Figure 29-17) that lets you choose a modem script to work with a Bluetooth-equipped cellphone. Yes, that's right, your Mac can connect to the Internet wirelessly using a Bluetooth cellphone: perfect for the traveler with a laptop, a cellphone, and the urge to go online.

The process of connecting with a Bluetooth modem is similar to using the Mac's internal modem with PPP. In addition, you must have Bluetooth active and paired with your cellphone, your cellphone has to be on and within range, you need a modem script that is compatible with your phone (check your Bluetooth cellphone provider's Web site for this if you don't have one), and, of course, you need an account with an ISP.

insider insight Setting up a Bluetooth network connection can involve various trips to different panes in the System Preferences, including the Network preferences and the Bluetooth preferences. You can certainly do it that way, but it is far easier to launch Applications⇨Utilities⇨Bluetooth Setup Assistant and let that program do most of the configuring for you. You can always examine and alter the individual Network and Bluetooth preferences.

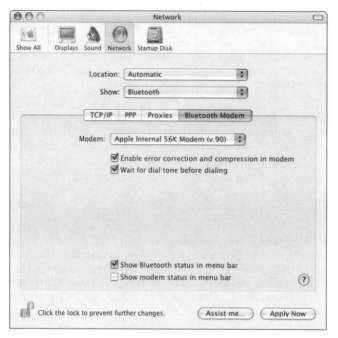

Figure 29-17: The Bluetooth Modem settings.

Secret

The Medieval King in Your Pocket

Bluetooth is a low-speed (roughly one megabit a second) wireless protocol that works across short distances, typically a couple dozen feet (or around ten meters).

It is named after the tenth-century king of Denmark, Harald Blåtand, known to the English-speaking world as Harald Bluetooth. Harald united all of Denmark and Norway into a single kingdom, which, after his death in 985, his son Sweyn expanded to include parts of Sweden and England. The Bluetooth protocol was developed by a consortium of companies, chief among them the Scandinavian companies, Ericsson and Nokia, who gave the protocol its name in recognition of their hopes that Bluetooth would unite the computer and mobile communication industry much as King Harald did for Scandinavia.

The Ethernet Tab

You'll see the tab that reveals this pane (shown in Figure 29-18) for each network port that connects using Ethernet. You seldom have to see it at all, though: Panther is smart about detecting and configuring itself to match the sort of traffic it finds coming in through your Mac's Ethernet port.

But if you do check it out, all you'll probably see is the Ethernet port's Ethernet ID (also known as a MAC ID — defined earlier in this chapter) and a Configure menu set to Automatically. If a network administrator asks you to provide her with the Ethernet ID before you are allowed to connect your Mac to the network, this pane is where you can find it.

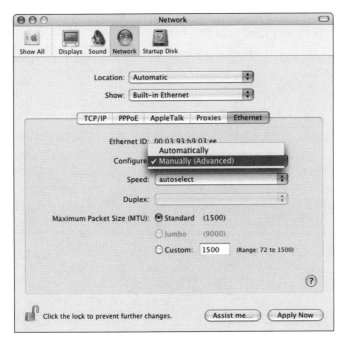

Figure 29-18: The Ethernet panel with its Configure pop-up menu showing.

> **note** You can also find your Ethernet ID by using the System Profile application: Click Network in System Profile's left pane and choose the Ethernet port about which you're interested from the top pane on the right.

Select Manually (Advanced) from the Configure menu to reveal additional settings. And Panther isn't lying: These manual settings *are* advanced, and they require detailed knowledge of your network environment's configuration that most Mac users neither care nor know about. You'll select it if

- ♦ Your Mac is connected to a network that has specific Ethernet communication requirements, and your network administrator tells you to make specific setting changes.
- ♦ You have an additional Ethernet network card in your Mac, and you need to adjust *its* settings (almost certainly in consultation with your network administrator).

Otherwise, the Automatically choice on this menu is the way to go. Panther is pretty smart about such things as a rule.

The 6 to 4 Tab

The 6 to 4 tab appears when you have created a 6 to 4 network port configuration (shown in Figure 29-19). A 6 to 4 configuration is the rare network port available in Panther's Network preferences that isn't really a physical device or closely associated with one. (That is, it lives at a slightly higher level in the OSI model.) It is a *virtual* network port that lets a Mac using IPv4 communicate with a site that uses IPv6 addressing (see the "IPv4 and IPv6" Secret, earlier in this chapter). You'll rarely encounter a site that uses IPv6 unless you are part of the scientific research community, but, if you are, Panther is ready to help you out.

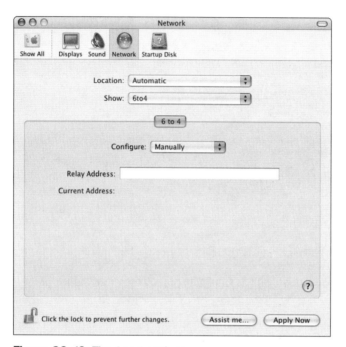

Figure 29-19: The 6 to 4 settings pane.

6 to 4 settings (see Figure 29-19) are quite basic, consisting of just a Configure pop-up menu that lets you choose either Automatically or Manually. If you choose Manually, you see an additional field that lets you specify a Relay Address that you can fill out if your network administrator tells you that you should. Otherwise, go with Automatically. Panther takes care of the rest.

The Proxies Tab

A *proxy server* is a server that stands between your Mac and the server that your Mac is trying to contact, intercepting all the communications between them. But why do such a heinous thing? Two reasons: speed and security.

 ♦ **Speed:** Suppose two different computers on the same local area network want to look at a Web page. The first computer makes the request for the page, the Web site's server returns the page's data, and the proxy server saves a copy of that data. When the next computer asks for the same page, the proxy server intercepts the call and returns the copy of the page that it saved. This can reduce global network traffic, take the load off of heavily accessed sites, and increase responsiveness.

◆ **Security:** Proxy servers can provide security by *filtering* network requests and stopping transmissions that can be dangerous or flawed. For example, suppose you have a file that contains a virus. (Yes, I know that is rare on a Mac, but Mac users have friends that don't use Macs and these less-enlightened friends can supply you with such files in ways that neither you nor they may suspect, so stop looking so smug.) If you attempt to upload that file to a Web server, a proxy server sitting between your Mac and the Web server can intercept the upload, detect the virus, and take appropriate action. Proxy servers can also provide security by hiding information that normally accompanies network communications, such as your Mac's IP address, from possibly malicious servers that might want to use this information for nefarious purposes.

Each of your network ports has a Proxies tab that lets you specify proxy servers for various network services (shown in Figure 29-20).

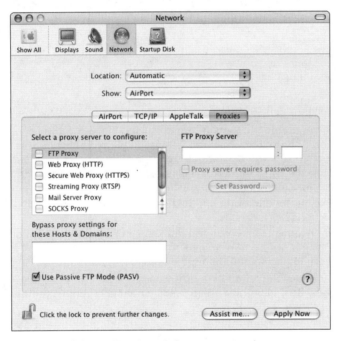

Figure 29-20: The Proxies tab for your protection.

The Proxies settings pane provides a list of proxy server types you can use. For each server, you specify an IP address and a port number; you can also supply a password that the proxy server may require.

Ports of Call

Port numbers have nothing to do with the network ports shown in Panther's Network preferences: *network ports* refer, more or less, to physical ports, and they live near the bottom of the OSI model. *Port numbers* are denizens of the session layer of the OSI model; they are conceptual rather than physical. Think of them as being something like extension numbers on a telephone or mailbox numbers at a mailing address.

Different port numbers are customarily assigned to different network services at the same network address; for example, the HTTP protocol used for Web pages usually occurs over port 80. There are over 65,000 port numbers available to be used by various services at each IP address.

Some port numbers are considered standard, others are not. The Internet Assigned Numbers Authority (IANA) keeps track of them and you can find out which ports go with which services, and much more, at `www.iana.org/assignments/port-numbers`.

You'll come across port numbers again when you use the Firewall pane of the Sharing Preferences.

Here are the proxy types that Panther offers you:

- **FTP:** This is the venerable file transfer protocol used to send and receive files over the Internet. FTP predates the Web by a good many years and was the way files were (and often still are) exchanged from the Unix terminal command line. (We're talking old school.) Programs such as Fetch, most Web browsers, and even the Finder can handle the FTP protocol to some extent.
- **Web:** Your Web browser and other applications that can handle the Hypertext Transport Protocol (HTTP) use this.
- **Secure Web:** Your browser and other programs use this secure variant of HTTP, known as HTTPS, for secure transactions so that you can protect credit card information when buying something online, for example.
- **Streaming:** QuickTime Player and your browser's QuickTime plug-in use this for streaming movies. Real Player may also use it. Streaming servers use the Real Time Streaming Protocol (RTSP).
- **Mail:** Used by e-mail programs.
- **SOCKS:** A type of generic proxy server that can handle all sorts of TCP/IP traffic, including Web and FTP programs.
- **Gopher:** Before the World Wide Web, there was Gopher (named for the Golden Gophers of the University of Minnesota) to provide the disparate variety of information that today's Web handles, presented as a set of hierarchical file lists. (Some people called moving down the various hierarchies "going down a gopher hole.) Some people still use Gopher. You probably won't, but who knows?

The last choice in the scrolling list is Automatic Proxy Configuration, which lets you provide the address of an automatic proxy configuration file that your network administrator may give you. When you select this choice, Panther helpfully tells you what it is all about right in the settings pane.

Below the list, there is a field into which you can enter domain names and addresses that you don't want to pass through the proxy servers you've selected.

Finally, below that is a check box that lets you choose PASV (i.e., passive) mode for FTP transactions; Panther sets this by default. Unchecking it lets you use the older, less firewall-friendly active FTP mode, known as PORT.

> **note** What's up with PORT versus PASV? It's the difference between which end of the FTP connection is acting as the server and which is acting as the client for data exchanges. In PORT mode the client (that is, the program on your Mac) is initiating all data transactions. In PASV mode, the FTP server is doing it. Of course, it's more complicated than that, but you can find out more at `http://slacksite.com/other/ftp.html`.

Managing Network Port Configurations

Panther lets you create, delete, and organize the network ports that your Mac uses to connect to that big wide wonderful world out there. Figure 29-21 shows you this pane, which you can get to by selecting Network Port Configurations from the Network preferences' Show pop-up menu.

Figure 29-21: Here's where you can manage your various network ports.

note   The network ports that you see are the ones for the location you have specified in the Location pop-up menu. Network locations are described in the next section.

Panther, helpful cat that it is, provides some basic information right in the pane that explains what is going on here:

♦ Each of the checked network ports listed is active; unchecked ports are not.

♦ You can drag the listed ports up or down to change the order in which Panther will check them when attempting to make a network connection.

The buttons beside the port list let you modify the list. Starting from the bottom and working our way up, here's what the buttons do:

♦ **Duplicate** lets you duplicate a selected port; the button becomes inactive for any port that can't be duplicated (such as an AirPort). Duplicating a port lets you create alternate settings for a particular network connection, such as a having a static TCP/IP address in one Ethernet port configuration and a DHCP-derived address in another.

♦ **Delete** lets you delete the selected configuration. If you delete a configuration that you added to the list, it vanishes from the list completely, but Panther won't let you completely delete some configurations: specifically, configurations tied to devices that Panther has detected are installed on your Mac (like the Ethernet or internal modem devices). For those configurations, clicking the Delete button simply unchecks the configuration and moves it to the bottom of the list.

♦ **Edit** simply selects the configuration's name so you can rename it. You can also select the configuration's name by double-clicking the name.

♦ **New** lets you create a new port configuration and choose the device to which it will be assigned. Figure 29-22 shows the sheet that drops down from the top of the pane when you click the New button. Type a name for the configuration, choose a port from the Port menu, and click OK. The Port menu, by the way, will list all the configurable network devices that Panther has detected.

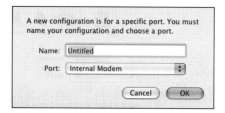

Figure 29-22: New port configuration sheet lets you name and assign a port.

Network Locations

Panther, like Jaguar before it, provides the ability to create network *locations*, which are groups of network settings collected together under one name. Panther comes with one location already prepared for you; it's called Automatic.

What are locations good for? For a firmly ensconced desktop Mac, not much, other than for their curiosity value. But for a portable Mac, network locations make moving between a variety of places, each with different networks and connection requirements, a much simpler affair — after you create locations for these places.

> **note**
>
> You might confuse the Network preferences' location management abilities with Mac OS 9's Location Manager control panel, but the locations provided by Network Preferences apply *only* to networking, while the Mac OS 9 Location Manager can let you create locations that control network settings, QuickTime streaming speed, auto-open items, extension sets, sound level, and more. Though sometimes confusing to use, the Location Manager control panel is quite powerful indeed, and is one of the items that many long-time Mac users who have moved up to OS X still miss. Maybe we'll see the return of the king of location managers in OS X 10.4.

Creating and Editing a Network Location

The Network preferences pane makes access to your locations easy to find: The Location pop-up menu is the first item in the Network preferences, it is centered on a line by itself, and it is always visible in Network preferences (shown in Figure 29-23).

Figure 29-23: The Location menu in the Network preferences pane.

Each location listed on the menu gives you access to the settings for all the Mac's network ports (Ethernet, AirPort, modem, Bluetooth, and so on). For each location you can choose which network ports are enabled, and you can specify the order in which Panther tries each port to establish a network connection. (See previous sections, "Getting at Settings for Network Ports" and "Managing Network Port Configurations.") The changes you make to each network port's numerous settings apply only to those ports *for that location*. For example, you can create a location where Panther uses the modem port as the first network port to try, and then create a different location where AirPort is the first port that is tried and the modem second. (And you can even have the second location use a different phone number and account than the first location's modem setting.)

To change the settings for a particular location, the process is quite simple:

1. Choose a location from the Location pop-up menu.
2. Make a bunch of changes.
3. Apply the changes using the Apply Now button.

And even Step 3 is optional: If you forget to click the Apply Now button, Network preferences displays an alert asking if you want to apply the changes when you close the window or switch to a different system preference display.

tip

Sometimes you want to make changes to one location's settings while continuing to use the settings for another location. If so, make the changes as above and then simply switch back to the location you want to continue using from the Location pop-up menu before you click Apply Now. The changes to all locations' settings are saved whenever you click Apply Now and not just the settings for the currently active location.

note

If you are not administrator, you must click the Network preference pane's lock icon and enter an administrator's name and password to make changes to any Network preferences settings. The Network preferences pane is even kind enough to tell you so.

To create a new network location, choose New Location from the Location pop-up menu. A sheet appears that lets you give the location a name (see Figure 29-24). It also tips you off to one very important piece of information about locations: *every* user account on your machine can choose *any* location; you can't limit access to specific locations to specific users.

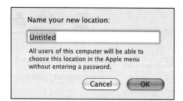

Figure 29-24: New locations are available to all users.

The Location pop-up menu also has an Edit Locations command, but you don't use it to change your locations' network settings. The Edit Locations menu command produces a dialog box that lets you duplicate, rename, or delete locations (shown in Figure 29-25).

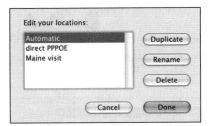

Figure 29-25: The Edit Locations dialog box in Network Preferences.

caution

The Delete button in the Edit Locations dialog box does not ask you to confirm a location's removal, so don't press Done until you have taken time to pause and reflect upon your actions. If you do erroneously delete a location, you should click Cancel.

Choosing a Network Location

One obvious way to change the network location that your Mac is using is by opening up System Preferences, selecting Network, and choosing a new location from the Location pop-up menu, which was discussed previously in "Creating and Editing a Network Location." But Panther makes it much faster: you can choose a location at any time, from within any application, by simply selecting it from the Location submenu in the Apple menu (shown in Figure 29-26) — your Mac starts using the new location's network settings immediately.

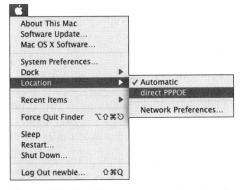

Figure 29-26: Choose network locations from the Apple menu.

Secret

Network Locations and Multiple Users

Unlike previous versions of Mac OS X, Panther allows several user accounts to be active at one time on the same Mac. So, what happens when User A allows User B to switch to her account and she chooses a new network location? What happens is that User B changes the network location for *all* logged-in users, not just User B. Network locations are not user-specific; they apply to the whole Mac.

Almost any user on a Mac can change the Mac's network location — no authentication required. That makes some sense: you don't want to restrict people running non-administrative user accounts to be unable to change locations on their laptops as they move from place to place and network to network. However, user accounts that are limited to the Simple Finder don't have a Location item on their Apple menus, which means, say, that if you give little Billy an iBook (lucky Billy!) and set him up with Simple Finder before you send him off to school, he won't be able switch locations to use the school's network without help from someone who can log into a non-Simple Finder account. If you're a parent or a teacher, that's probably a Good Thing. (Though Billy may have his own thoughts on the matter.)

Connecting and Sharing

After you've made all your network settings, you often don't have to do anything else (other than, say, plug in the appropriate cables) to get connected: Panther will try to do the right thing. But it's nice to know what Panther is up to when it tries to do the right thing, and even nicer to know enough to be able to help Panther out when it can't figure out what the right thing is.

Connecting Locally and Globally

Panther wants to be connected to any available networks it can find, and if the Network preferences settings provide any way for it to do so, Panther will make a connection as soon as it boots up. That's what the list of network ports in the Network Configuration display of Network preferences is all about: Panther prowls down that list of active network ports trying to find at least one that will gratify the jungle cat's hunger for connectivity.

Panther will not connect to a network if any one of the following conditions is true:

♦ **There is no active network port.**

♦ **None of the active ports have been set up to establish a network connection.** (For example, an Ethernet port that has not been given a proper TCP/IP address manually nor been set to obtain a TCP/IP address from a local DHCP server.)

♦ **The only available network ports that can connect to a network have been explicitly set not to establish a connection without the user's intervention.** (For example, the Mac's internal modem, which you can set *not* to dial automatically.)

Otherwise, Panther will connect to a network as soon as it finds a network port that will let it. What's more, Panther will connect over *all* the active network ports that will allow a connection. This means, for example, your Mac can be connected to the Internet both via an Ethernet cable and an AirPort card at the same time and any application that needs Internet access will simply use the first available connection (which is usually the first one in the list of active ports that has a connection).

And, if any of the ports is connected to a network that is part of the Internet, Panther will have an Internet connection as well. And Panther likes to have an Internet connection as much as it likes any other type of network connection.

Using Internet Connect

In some cases, Panther can't make an Internet connection without your help. That's where the Internet Connect application, located in the Applications folder, comes in handy (shown in Figure 29-27).

Figure 29-27: Internet Connect helps you establish connections.

Internet Connect serves two main purposes.

♦ **It shows you the status of all your active Internet connections.** Click the Summary icon on the toolbar to see them.

♦ **It allows you to establish or terminate Internet connections manually.** Click any of the connection method icons on the toolbar to see the appropriate settings needed to establish an Internet connection.

> **tip** Internet Connect also gives you the ability to put connection menus on the menu bar for several of its connection methods (such as modem, AirPort, or PPPoE), thus obviating a need to open Internet Connect to make or end a connection (shown in Figure 29-28). And it can show you exactly how strong your AirPort's signal is with a real-time meter as well as providing other important information about the connection (shown in Figure 29-29).

Figure 29-28: The AirPort menu bar icon provided by Internet Connect.

Figure 29-29: How strong is your AirPort Connection?

Secrets of VPN and 802.1x

Secret

In the Panther version of Internet Connect, the File menu provides commands that establish VPN and 802.1X connections (shown in Figure 29-30). Both VPN and 802.1X connections make your Mac more compatible with all the hitherto Mac-hostile corporate networks in the world.

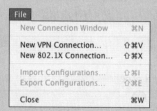

Figure 29-30: Secure corporate connections courtesy of Internet Connect.

VPN stands for Virtual Private Network. It lets two widely separated private networks, or a remote user and a private network, connect over the public Internet while maintaining the security and protocols used by the private network(s). You often use VPN to connect your Mac to a corporate network over modem, DSL, or cable modem connections from home or on the road. Internet Connect gives you two widely used connection options for VPN connections: L2TP over IPSec and PPTP.

- L2TP is Layer 2 Tunneling Protocol. Tunneling is a process that wraps a network packet inside an Internet packet; at each end of the connection, the VPN software (down in the OSI model's network and transport layers) removes the Internet packet wrapper and passes the original network packet along to the local network.

- IPSec is the Internet Protocol Security Protocol and it handles encrypting the wrapped network packet and its header information while it is traveling over the public Internet.

- PPTP is Point-To-Point Tunneling Protocol and is quite commonly used between Microsoft networks (not surprising, given that Microsoft was a prominent member of the PPTP Forum that promulgated the standard).

802.1X is an authentication standard used for protected networks. It supports a variety of authentication methods (such as one-time passwords, public keys, certificates). Like VPN, you can use it to establish a secure connection to a protected network.

Sharing an Internet Connection

If you have a broadband Internet connection via DSL or cable modem at home, and if you live in a two-computer household, you don't have to have family feuds over who gets to use the fast connection, because Panther lets you share an Internet connection among users on a local network.

The secret to connection nirvana is found under the Internet tab of System Preferences' Sharing preference pane (shown in Figure 29-31). What Internet Sharing does is make your Mac into a router between your local network and your Mac's Internet connection.

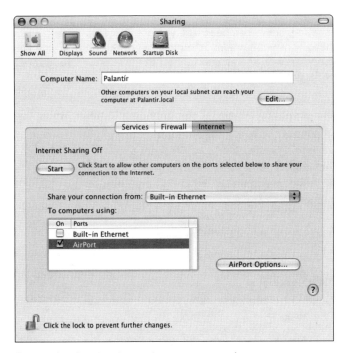

Figure 29-31: Sharing an Internet connection.

---

note When your Mac shares an Internet connection, the ISP sees only your Mac and its TCP/IP address. Your Mac, however, sees the local TCP/IP addresses of the computers on your local network that are sharing the connection. When another computer on your network sends a packet, the packet goes through your Mac, which stores tracking information about the packet before sending it off to the ISP. Incoming packets are received by your Mac and routed by it back to the final recipient on your network. This is all done through the magic of Network Address Translation (NAT).

Panther makes Internet sharing easy to set up. Just follow these steps:

1. Click the Share your connection from: pop-up menu and choose a network port on your Mac that connects to the Internet; for example, the Ethernet port on your Mac that connects to your ISP-supplied DSL modem.

2. Click check boxes in the To computers using list to select other active network ports on your Mac. The ports you select should be different from the port you selected in Step 1. Choosing the same port can create network problems for your ISP's other customers, and will possibly get your ISP so cheesed off that it will cancel your Internet account.

3. Click the Start button.

After Internet sharing is on, all the computers on your local network can use the Internet, courtesy of your Mac.

---

note   This might go without saying, but remember that if you put your Mac to sleep or turn it off, computers on the local network will lose their Internet connections. Also, if your firewall is on, other computers won't be able to connect to the Internet through yours (see Firewall and other Security Secrets, below).

Here are just some of the possible ways a Mac can provide Internet sharing:

◆ From an AirPort connection to an Ethernet port

◆ From a built-in modem connection to an Ethernet port

◆ From an Ethernet connection to an AirPort port

◆ From a Bluetooth modem connection to an Ethernet port

◆ From a Bluetooth modem connection to an AirPort port

◆ From an Ethernet connection to a FireWire port

◆ From an AirPort connection to a FireWire port

Secret

AirPort Options

When one of the checked network ports in the To computers using list is an AirPort port (say "AirPort port" three times — it's fun), it means that you have asked your Mac to become an AirPort base station and to create a local network that other AirPort-equipped Macs can join in order to use your Internet connection.

To help configure your Mac as a base station, the Sharing pane's AirPort Options button becomes enabled. Clicking it produces the dialog sheet (shown in Figure 29-32). From that sheet you can give your ad-hoc network a name, choose to enable encryption (don't think of it as a choice, though — just do it), create a network password, and choose a WEP key length.

A word about this last option. WEP (Wired Equivalent Privacy) is a protocol used at the bottom two layers of the OSI model to encrypt wireless transmissions. The longer the key, the harder the encryption is to crack. However, WEP on its own is not really a super-ultra-secure protocol even with a long key. It's more like the lock on your front door: it will keep out the casual intruder, but not someone armed with a crowbar and determination to get in. A newer protocol, WPA (Wi-Fi Protected Access) is available with the newest AirPort Extreme cards and base stations, and it provides much stronger security but it's still not totally secure. On the other hand, what is?

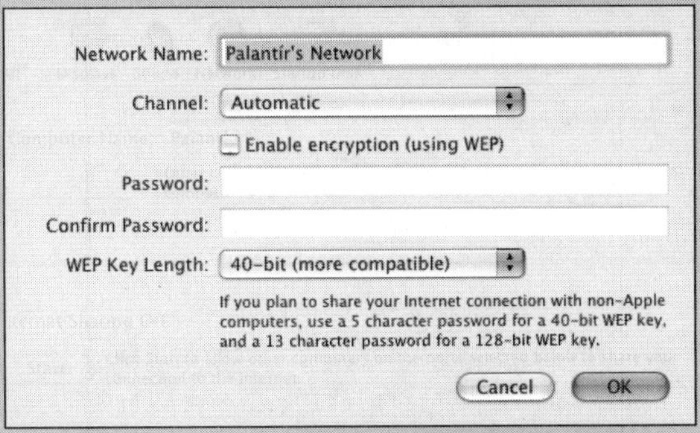

Figure 29-32: AirPort options for Internet sharing.

AirPort Base Station

If you have a portable Mac and just a few hundred bucks to spare, you would do well to consider getting an AirPort card and an AirPort base station. Even if you have a recent model desktop Mac, you might want to consider it. An AirPort base station makes creating a flexible, fully functional local area network a breeze and can significantly reduce the number of Ethernet cables snaking along your baseboards.

Connect the base station to the Internet (it can talk to cable modems, DSL modems, and regular old phone modems as well as Ethernet connections) and any Mac with an AirPort card can share its connection. With the more recent versions of the AirPort base station even non-AirPort-equipped Macs can share a connection if you connect the base station to the local Ethernet network that hosts those Macs — the newer models have two Ethernet ports, allowing the base station to bridge two different wired networks.

on the web Apple provides a useful manual on how to set up various network configurations using an AirPort. This manual, *Designing AirPort Extreme Networks,* is essential reading if you plan to create an AirPort network. It can be found online in Preview-friendly PDF format at www.apple.com/airport/pdf/DesigningAirPortNets-022-1036.pdf.

AirPort Basics

The key to managing an AirPort network is the AirPort Admin Utility (shown in Figure 29-33) located in the Applications⇨Utilities folder (of course).

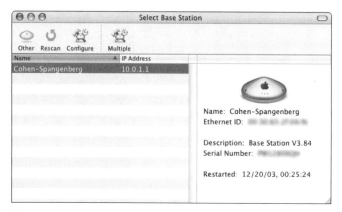

Figure 29-33: The AirPort Admin Utility.

Secret

Multiple Base Station Networks

The Multiple icon in the AirPort Admin Utility's main window, visible in Figure 29-33, lets you create a network that has more than one base station. You can use this to create what is called a *Wireless Distribution System* (WDS) that can cover areas larger than the signal of a solitary base station can cover. This can be useful for schools, small businesses, and large homes.

A WDS has one base station, called the *main* base station, that connects to the Internet. Other base stations share the main station's Internet connection. A base station that simply shares the main station's connection is called a *remote* base station; a base station that both shares the connection and that can transfer the connection to other base stations is called a *relay* base station. See the section, "The WDS Tab," ilater in this chapter.

To set up a base station, select it in the AirPort Admin Utility's window and click the Configure icon. AirPort Admin Utility displays a configuration window for the selected base station (shown in Figure 29-34).

The configuration window provides a summary of base station settings and buttons that let you quickly set or change basic configuration settings:

♦ **Name and Password:** This button provides a pane that lets you name the network that the base station creates, allows you to set a password for the network, and specify what kind of encryption the network uses.

♦ **Internet Connection:** This button shows a pane that lets you choose a connection method for Internet access. (Figure 29-35 shows some of the possibilities offered in the pane's Connect via: menu.) For each method, you fill in necessary information (e.g., account name, password) in the provided fields to establish the connection.

Figure 29-34: An AirPort Admin Utility configuration window.

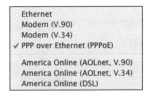

Figure 29-35: Some AirPort Internet connection possibilities.

◆ **Show All Settings:** This button gives you access to the full range of AirPort configuration settings, and that range is extensive. The result of pressing this magic button is described in the next section, "AirPort Advanced."

Oh, Gee — AirPort Extreme

Apple's original AirPort cards and base stations use a wireless technology standard known as IEEE 802.11b. (IEEE is the Institute of Electrical and Electronics Engineers and it is responsible for maintaining all sorts of computing and electrical engineering standards.) 802.11b uses the 2.4-GHz frequency band and can achieve speeds of up to 11Mbps, but will fall back to 5.5, 2, or even 1Mbps when there's interference.

Apple's new AirPort cards, base stations, and Macs use the newer IEEE 802.11g standard, which Apple has dubbed AirPort Extreme. 802.11g networks can achieve speeds of up to 54Mbps. Apple chose this standard over the competing 802.11a standard (which can achieve comparable speeds) because it is compatible with older 802.11b devices. Of course, 802.11g can only achieve its highest speeds on a good day, with a fair wind, no interference, and, most importantly, no 802.11b devices on the network; a mixed network of 802.11b and 802.11g devices won't achieve 802.11g's theoretical maximum speed but the 802.11g devices on the network will still transmit and receive information faster than their 802.11b counterparts.

AirPort Advanced

For special configuration needs or just more fine-grained access to a base station's settings, click the AirPort Admin Utility's Show All Settings button. The utility presents a tabbed interface (shown in Figure 29-36); the number of tabs differs depending on the model base station being administered. You can make a number of changes to the various panes under the tabs before you click the Update button, which applies the new settings and restarts the base station.

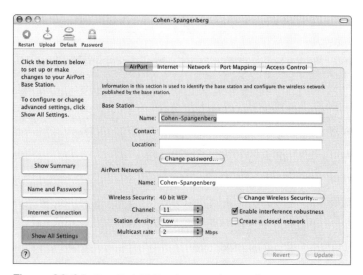

Figure 29-36: Detailed AirPort base station settings.

> **on the web** I said this previously, but it bears repeating: get Apple's manual, *Designing AirPort Extreme Networks*, especially if you go poking around the advanced settings that the AirPort Admin Utility makes available. The current version as of this writing is available at www.apple.com/airport/pdf/DesigningAirPortNets-022-1036.pdf. If that address changes, try going to Apple's AirPort page (www.apple.com/airport/); you should find a link to the latest version.

The AirPort Tab

The leftmost tab shows a pane that contains settings for the base station itself and for the network it creates. You can give the base station a name (the name you'll see when you browse for base stations in the AirPort Admin Utility's first window) and a password (which you need to enter in order to change the base station's settings). You can also provide contact and location information. (Corporate network administrators like this, because it lets them quickly find out where a base station is and who is running it . . . if the information is correct, of course.)

The pane's bottom half lets you set up the AirPort network itself. Here are some of the options. (Different options may appear depending on the model of the base station being set up.)

◆ **The Name field** is where you give a name to the network that the base station creates — this can be different from the base station's name; it is what users will see when they look for a wireless network with Internet Connect or the AirPort menu in the menu bar.

◆ **The Channel pop-up menu** is where you can choose a channel over which the base station broadcasts from. (You have eleven channels from which to choose.) If there are other base stations nearby, choose a different channel from theirs to reduce interference.

◆ **The Station Density pop-up menu** lets you choose Low, Medium, or High — the higher the setting, the more quickly the base station drops your signal in favor of another, closer station. (On the other hand, the higher settings make the AirPort ignore more interference than the lower settings.)

◆ **The Multicast pop-up menu** lets you choose a multicast rate. (Multicast is used for some streaming media.) The higher numbers limit the range of the network for such broadcasts.

◆ **The Change Wireless Security button** is where you can set the network's password as well as choose the security method and the encryption key length. Older AirPorts use WEP security only, but AirPort Extreme base stations can use the newer, more secure WPA protocol; however, older Macs with the 802.11b AirPort cards cannot join a WPA network. (See the secret, "AirPort Options," earlier in this chapter, for more on WEP and WPA.)

◆ **The Enable interference robustness check box** makes the AirPort network less susceptible to interference from other devices (like microwave ovens) at the expense of somewhat lower transmission speeds.

◆ **The Create a closed network check box** provides another measure of security. This hides the network's name: Users won't see it in Internet Connect's Network menu or on the menu bar's AirPort menu. To join the network, users must choose Other from one of those menus and then type the network's name into a dialog box. This is called "security through obscurity," which is far from a foolproof tactic, but it is still probably good enough to keep that creepy guy in the apartment next door from leeching off of your Internet connection.

The Internet Tab

You set up the method by which the AirPort base station establishes an Internet connection with the pane shown under the Internet tab. This pane features a Connect using pop-up menu that is remarkably similar to the Connect via pop-up menu (refer to Figure 29-35) that AirPort Admin Utility displays when you click the Internet Connection button. The contents of the rest of the Internet pane change depending on the connection method you choose, but you should be able to figure out the various options if you've read the preceding portions of this chapter. You'll see options for TCP/IP, modem, and so on that are similar to those shown in the Network preferences panes and in the Internet Connect application.

The Network Tab

The pane under the Network tab lets you control how the base station shares its Internet connection with devices on the AirPort network.

Figure 29-37 shows the pane that appears for a first generation AirPort base station; later models have some minor differences and enhancements. For example, the newest models have a built-in feature to enable remote users to dial in via modem to the AirPort base station, a feature to enable America Online parental controls, and some additional DHCP options.

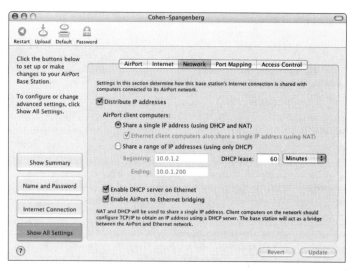

Figure 29-37: AirPort base station is a DHCP server.

The important thing to note is that the base station is both a DHCP server and a router: that is, it can assign IP addresses to devices on the network for a limited time (which you can specify) and it can connect two different networks together, passing data packets between them and making sure the packets get to the right local IP addresses using a technique called NAT (*Network Address Translation*).

Of course, you don't have to use the base station as a DHCP server — if you uncheck the Distribute IP addresses box, the base station will still act as a bridge between two networks, passing packets back and forth, but it won't perform any additional routing and it won't allow client devices to share an Internet connection.

> **tip**
>
> For most home and small business use, the default settings in the Network pane that enable DHCP and NAT are all you need; Apple's done a lot of hard work here to make sure that AirPort is as close to plug-and-play as anything as complicated as network administration can be. For more complex network situations, you should either work with your network administrator (if you have one) or consult Apple's manual, *Designing AirPort Extreme Networks*. (This is the third time I've made this plug, so there's no excuse for complaining that nobody told you. . . .)

The Port Mapping Tab

When a base station provides DHCP and NAT to allow devices on the network to share an Internet connection, it keeps track of the IP addresses it has assigned and it builds a list of the port numbers at each of those addresses that have sent information requests out onto the Internet (such as requests for Web pages over port 80). When the requested information comes back, the base station uses the list it built to route the information to the correct port number at the correct address.

This technique won't work, though, if one of the devices on the AirPort network needs to act as a publicly accessible Web or file server. In such cases, you need to give the device a manual IP address (rather than letting it request an address via DHCP). After you've done that, you can use the Port Mapping pane (shown in Figure 29-38) to assign the appropriate port numbers (such as port 80 for HTTP requests) to the IP address you've given the device that is performing server functions.

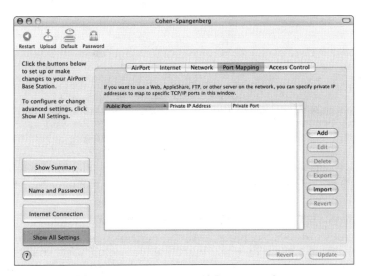

Figure 29-38: Port mapping on an AirPort network.

The Access Tab

The Access (or Access Control) pane lets you seal off your AirPort network's Internet sharing ability from any users except those privileged few that you specifically allow. The pane provides a list that you can fill with the AirPort ID numbers (also known as the MAC ID; see "The AirPort Tab," section earlier in this chapter) of just those devices that you want to allow on your AirPort network. This is more secure than a closed network, but it means that you have to visit the AirPort Admin Utility, and restart the network, every time you want to add a new user.

> **note** The absence of a wireless user's MAC ID from the Access Control pane's list of MAC IDs won't stop that user from joining your AirPort network; it simply will not allow the user to access a wired network connected to your base station (such as the Internet connection from your cable modem).

The Authentication Tab

This tab, which is available for later model AirPort base stations, provides settings to enable a base station to communicate with a RADIUS server (Remote Authentication Dial-In User Service). RADIUS servers are often used on corporate networks to provide network access security and accounting. If you don't have a RADIUS server, you'll never use this tab; if you do, you should work with that server's administrator (or consult the server's documentation).

> **note**   The Authentication settings and the Access Control settings work together. When a device requests to join the AirPort network, the base station first checks for the MAC ID in the Access Control list and then, if it isn't found, the RADIUS server's list. The device can only join the network if it is found on one of those lists.

The WDS Tab

If you have more than one late model AirPort base station, you can use this tab to set up a Wireless Distribution System. The pane under the WDS tab lets you specify whether the base station is a remote, a relay, or a main base station (see "Multiple Base Stations," earlier in this chapter). The settings options for a main base station include a list (by MAC ID) of each of the remote and relay base stations that comprise the WDS. The settings for a remote base station let you specify (by MAC ID) the main base station with which it communicates; a relay station's settings include a list of all of the remote base stations whose communications it is relaying.

If you need to set up a WDS, you really should consult Apple's *Designing AirPort Extreme Networks* manual. (Okay, this is absolutely the last time I'm going to mention it, I promise.)

Computer-to-Computer AirPort Networks

Two Macs with AirPort cards can establish an AirPort network even in the absence of an AirPort base station. Such ad hoc networks can be quite useful: You can use them to exchange files with colleagues at a business meeting, you can use them to play network games, you can use them to pass instant message notes via iChat in a boring class. (Notice that I said you *can* — I didn't say you *should*.)

Creating a computer-to-computer network is quite simple. Simply choose Create Network from the AirPort status menu in the menu bar (shown in Figure 29-39) or from the Network: pop-up menu in Internet Connect's AirPort pane.

Figure 29-39: Create Network command on the AirPort status menu.

You must enable the Allow this computer to create networks check box under the Network Preferences' AirPort settings tab to allow the Create Network command to appear on either of these menus.

Figure 29-40 shows the dialog box that appears when you choose the Create Network command. In the simplest case, you simply give your network a name and choose a channel. If you feel the need for a bit more security, you can click the Show Options button, which lets you specify a password for the network and choose the level of encryption it will use. Click OK and any other AirPort-enabled Macs in the immediate vicinity can see and join your network. And that's all there is to it. (I said it was quite simple.)

Figure 29-40: Creating a computer-to-computer network.

caution When you create a computer-to-computer network, you will lose your connection to any AirPort network you have previously joined. If the AirPort network was providing you with Internet access, you will lose that access until you leave the computer-to-computer network and rejoin your original AirPort network.

Panther's Firewall and Other Security Provisions

Get a Mac. Install Panther on it. Connect it to the Internet. Feel secure.

In fact, that's almost true. With three decades of field-testing, the Unix underpinnings of Panther make it a hard target for casual script kiddies to hack. But that's not to say that it's invulnerable; and when Panther has an Internet connection — remember, Panther *wants* to have one and will work hard to create one — your Mac becomes a target, whether defensively hardened or not.

The Internet is the medium by which most hacking occurs these days. That means that TCP/IP is the networking method involved in most attacks, which suggests that the way most attacks enter a target computer is through one of its IP ports (which, of course, you shouldn't confuse with your network ports, which you shouldn't confuse with your Mac's hardware ports; see "Ports, Real and Imaginary," earlier in this chapter).

Basically, when a network service (for example, a Web server, a file server, a media server) is running, it pays attention to information coming in on specific IP ports (see "Ports of Call," earlier in this chapter). Internet attacks come in the same way: through an IP port. Close a port (that is, don't allow any programs or processes to receive information from that port) and an attack can't get in on that port. Nor can valid service requests, of course; if no ports are open to incoming traffic, no Internet services on your Mac can respond to service requests.

The trick, then, to managing Internet security on your Mac, is to manage which ports will receive information and which services can access those ports. And that's what the Sharing preference pane in System Preferences is for.

The Sharing Services Tab

The Sharing preferences' Services tab shown in Figure 29-41 lists the built-in and pre-configured services in Panther you can share and offers a simple interface for enabling and disabling them: click a check box. Or click a service and then click the Start (or Stop) button. Your choice.

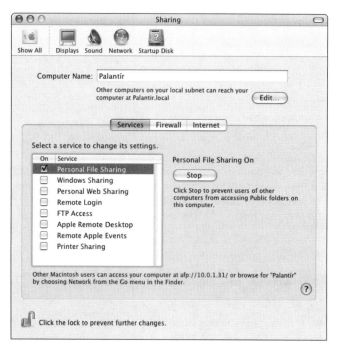

Figure 29-41: Preconfigured services you can share.

The Services tab provides most of the control you need for managing both Internet services and the IP ports that they use. When you enable a service in the list, Panther automatically opens the necessary ports that the service requires and routes traffic coming in to those ports to that service:

◆ **Personal File Sharing** lets you share files with other Macs on the network. Depending on how your Internet access is provided, Internet users from anywhere in the world can share your files; file sharing is described in more detail in "Sharing Files and Other Data," later in this chapter.

◆ **Windows Sharing** lets you share files with computers running Windows, using Windows file-sharing protocols. Note that Macs running Panther can also share files with you, because Panther understands Windows file-sharing protocols; Windows sharing is described in more detail in the next chapter.

◆ **Personal Web Sharing** turns your Mac into a standard Internet Web server, using the industry-standard Web server software, Apache. Web sharing is described in more detail in "Sharing Files and Other Data."

◆ **Remote Login** lets anyone running a Unix terminal application login to a command-line session on your Mac (if they have an account and a password). This service uses the SSH (Secure Shell) protocol, which is, as the name suggests, pretty secure. (Although an authorized user with command line access should never be considered innocuous.) Unix folk switching to the Mac really like this feature. Long-time Mac users will probably never use it.

◆ **FTP Access** lets anyone using an FTP program to post and retrieve files from your Mac using the venerable File Transfer Protocol that is almost as old as the Internet itself. FTP access is described in more detail in the next chapter.

◆ **Apple Remote Desktop** service lets your Mac be completely taken over by another Mac running the Apple Remote Desktop administration software. This program is very powerful, and is frequently used to manage classroom computers, business computers, and to provide help services. Leave this off unless you are in an environment where a network administrator requires it to be on. Note that even if you have this service on, you must be running the Apple Remote Desktop client on your Mac in order for someone to use the administration software to take over your machine.

◆ **Remote Apple Events** allows AppleScript events to be sent to applications running on your Mac from another machine on the network (and that includes the Internet); this can be useful in certain workgroup environments. The Remote Apple Events service requires an initial login and password, so it's not as though any script kiddie out there with AppleScript skills can take over your Mac — but AppleScript is powerful, and even an authorized user can cause havoc with a poorly written script. Leave this off unless you really need it, and turn it off when you're not using it.

◆ **Printer Sharing** allows other Macs to use a USB or other single-user printer connected to your Mac. This only works over a local network (in particular, only over your local *subnet*, which is usually the part of the network you can access without going through a router).

note   When you have Printer Sharing turned on, Panther also lets other users on your network send faxes through your Mac if you have set up faxing. Also, documents sent through your Mac to be printed will have their data stored temporarily on your Mac's hard disk, which can cause problems if disk space on your Mac is tight.

The Panther Firewall

There may be certain applications that need to respond to traffic over specific IP ports but are not listed in Panther's set of services; some such applications include iChat AV (for access via Rendezvous) and iTunes (for music sharing). For this reason, Panther gives you a Firewall tab in the Sharing preferences (see Figure 29-42). With it, you can block access to all IP ports except those that you specify, and you can label the sets of ports that go with each service.

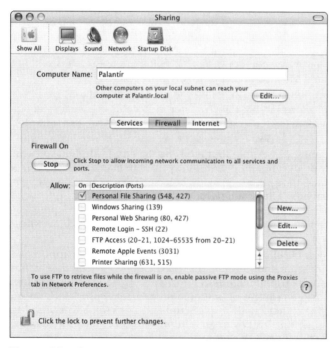

Figure 29-42: Ready, aim, firewall.

To turn on the Panther firewall, click the Start button. That's it; once on, no traffic will be allowed to establish a connection on any but the ports listed for each of the checked items in the Firewall pane's list.

Behind the Scenes — IPFW

Secret

Although the Firewall tab in the Sharing preferences has been present in Mac OS X since only Jaguar (10.2), Mac OS X has had a firewall from the start. Built into the Unix soul of Mac OS X is ipfw, a Unix command-line program: the "IP firewall and traffic shaper control program" according to its Unix man page. But IPFW is not a firewall either; it merely lets you create the rules that a lower level process, ipfirewall, running deep in Mac OS X follows when handling IP network traffic.

When you change the Firewall pane's settings, you are, in fact, actually creating sets of rules that IP firewall will follow as it monitors network traffic. The Firewall tab, however, only creates very simple sets of rules: IPFW allows you to exert much finer control over network traffic . . . if you are a hardy Unix command-line demi-god. If you are not so sanguine about braving the command line, but still would like to control the firewall with more precision than the Firewall pane allows, check out Brickhouse, a free program that provides a graphical front-end to IPFW (http://personalpages. tds.net/~brian_hill/brickhouse.html).

The Standard Ports

You might think that you can just click the check boxes in the Firewall pane to turn ports on and off for things like file sharing, FTP, and so on. After all, that's what check boxes do, right?

Not so fast. If you look closely, you'll notice that most of the items in the Firewall tab's list of port sets are actually disabled. Point your mouse at one of these faux check boxes and Panther will tell you what's going on (shown in Figure 29-43).

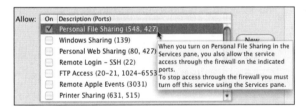

Figure 29-43: Panther handles the firewall settings for some services automagically.

In fact, the check boxes in the Firewall pane are disabled for each service listed in the Sharing preferences' Services tab. Panther handles those services' firewall needs when you use the Services tab to turn them on or off. But you can look at the list of services in the Firewall tab and find out which ports each service uses, and that's got to be worth something, right?

Creating, Editing, and Deleting Firewall Items

But, as noted, some applications not listed on the Services tab might have firewall needs, and, for those applications, you can create port lists that will be monitored for traffic (shown in Figure 29-44). And after you create them, you will be able to turn each of those sets of ports on and off in the Firewall list.

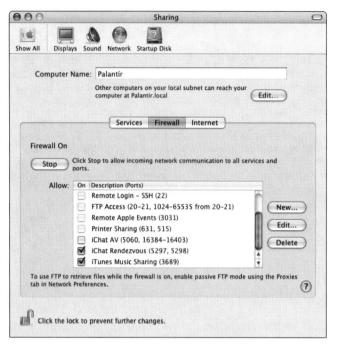

Figure 29-44: Port sets added to the Firewall list.

To create a new set of IP ports to add to the Firewall pane's list, click the New button. A dialog box appears (shown in Figure 29-45) that asks you for the ports you want to add.

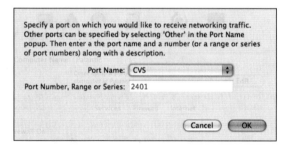

Figure 29-45: Creating a set of known ports . . . note the typo in the instructions.

The Port Name: pop-up menu (shown in Figure 29-46) contains Panther's predefined IP port sets for some common Internet services. Select an item and click OK to add its ports to the Firewall list.

> **note**
> As you add items from the menu, they appear in the Firewall list as you'd expect — but they vanish from the menu so you can't add them twice. Also as you'd expect, if you delete them from the Firewall list (using the pane's Delete button), they appear on the menu the next time you look.

Figure 29-46: Common port users.

To create a set of IP ports not on the menu, select the Other item from the menu. The Port Number, Range, or Series field becomes active, allowing you to enter the port numbers you want to monitor. Also, a Description field appears, into which you should enter a descriptive label so you'll know in the many happy days to come just why you created the port set in the first place.

The pane's Edit button produces the same dialog box (see Figure 29-45) as the New button, allowing you to modify the selected set of IP ports in the Firewall pane's list. (And, no, you can't edit the disabled standard items, just in case you were wondering.)

Sharing Files and Other Data

Before his spelling checker caught the error, John Donne wrote, "No Mac is an island." He knew what he was talking about, even if his spelling checker didn't. Put two or more Macs on the same network, and they can share files with each other, no floppy disks (remember those?), Zip disks, CDs, DVDs, USB memory devices, or portable FireWire hard drives required. Macs have been able to do this for the better part of two decades, and now Panther extends the Mac's inborn file-sharing abilities — sometimes for the better, and sometimes for the . . . well, not worse, but, perhaps, for the more confusing.

Sharing Your Files with Other Mac Users

You've already seen how you can share your Mac's files: click Personal File Sharing in the Services tab of Sharing preferences (see "The Sharing Services Tab," earlier in this chapter). There is no step three.

> **note**
> Personal File Sharing is the latest implementation of AFP (the Apple Filing Protocol), which lives between the presentation and application layers of the OSI model. AFP was once tied to the AppleTalk protocol, but, even before Mac OS X came on the scene, it was made compatible with TCP/IP. Note that AFP is an Apple file-sharing technology; while it is possible that other platforms may implement the ability to use it, in practice it will only be Macs on a network that will see the Personal File Sharing files provided courtesy of AFP.

But what does Personal File Sharing buy you? Back in the long, long ago (pre–OS X), when you enabled file sharing you could share any and all of the folders and files on your

Mac that you decided to make shareable. But Mac OS X, even in its third major version, has no obvious, simple method (such as the sharing controls available in the pre–Mac OS X system's Get Info window) that normal folk can use to make specific folders and files shareable or not.

> **note** Current file-sharing limitations are true of the Mac OS X most users are likely to have. However, Mac OS X Server is another matter. It has all the controls you would ever want for managing file sharing on a folder-by-folder, file-by-file basis. It also costs several times what the nonserver version of Mac OS X costs.

What Personal File Sharing on Mac OS X *does* do is share all the files contained in exactly *one* folder in each user account's home directory: the home directory's Public folder (shown in Figure 29-47). The Public folder is shared as *read-only* — this means that any Mac user, anywhere on the network, can copy the files you place in your Public folder, but that user can't change them on your Mac. Also, by default, Mac OS X creates one folder inside of the Public folder that is writeable but not readable (that is, *write-only*): the Drop Box folder. Other Mac users on the network can drop files *onto* the Drop Box folder, thus copying them to your Mac, but they can't open the Drop Box folder to see what is inside.

Figure 29-47: A typical Public folder.

Users and Groups in Mac OS X

Secret

Mac OS X, unlike Mac OS 9 and earlier, does not offer you an easy way to create file-sharing users and groups. Of course, you *can* create user accounts with Panther's Accounts preference pane, but these accounts are user accounts for use on the Mac itself: Each user account comes with a home directory, login privileges, and so on. Creating a user account just for file-sharing purposes is serious overkill. Similarly, users can be combined into groups using the powerful (and, hence, dangerous) NetInfo utility, but it ain't all that easy . . . and besides, these groups are Unix-style groupings of user accounts and are used for many other purposes than mere file-sharing. Again, serious overkill, and, unless you know what you are doing in NetInfo, you can quite easily make a blunder that will render your system inoperable.

There are several reasons for Mac OS X's Personal File Sharing limitations:

♦ **The Security Reason:** File sharing is a risky business in a world where hackers (the bad kind) abound, and each avenue into your machine's file system is a potential point of attack. Reducing the number of open directories and accessible files to a few well-known locations reduces the risk.

♦ **The Politeness Reason:** Mac OS X, unlike previous Mac systems, is assumed to be a multiuser system, which requires that the data owned by each user be protected from the accidental or deliberate depredations of other users — both on the same Mac as well as elsewhere on the network. When you turn Personal Sharing on in the Sharing Preferences you turn it on for *every* user account on that Mac, making the shared files of *all* user accounts on that Mac available, willy-nilly, to other users on the network; limiting share access thus decreases each user's risk from the mistakes or malice of other users.

♦ **The Cynic's Reason:** Apple can't very well charge more for Mac OS X Server if the regular version of Mac OS X provides the same features.

♦ **The Simplicity Reason:** For most people, having a single place to put the files they want to share, and a single place to pick up files that other people have given them, is much easier to understand and use than the file sharing capabilities in the pre–OS X environment.

Secret

SharePoints Brings Back the Good Old Days

Just because Apple hasn't provided the means for you to create file-sharing user and group accounts in Mac OS X doesn't mean that it isn't possible. Michael Horn has created an application to fill the gap that Apple has torn in the fabric of Mac OS X: SharePoints.

SharePoints lets you create user accounts that don't show up in your Login window and that don't have separate home directories: which is exactly what you want for file-sharing-only users. SharePoints also lets you create user groups, doing all the down-and-dirty work that you would otherwise have to do yourself with NetInfo. And, finally, SharePoints lets you set *any* folder to be shared that you like. Just about all the personal file-sharing functionality that Apple abandoned on the road to Mac OS X can be found in SharePoints . . . and maybe a bit more, too.

You can download SharePoints from http://hornware.com/sharepoints/. And it won't cost you more than you can afford, either: Michael Horn simply requests a donation if you like the product (you decide how much).

Web Sharing

When Mac OS X was built atop the core of a standard Unix distribution, one of the pretty little things that came wrapped in that core was the standard, open-source, Apache Web Server. Apple took advantage of Apache to create Personal Web Sharing, which, like Personal File Sharing, is turned on and off in the Sharing preference pane's Services tab (shown in Figure 29-48).

Unlike Personal File Sharing, which makes your files and folders available right in the Finder, Personal Web Sharing makes files available to other users on your network via a Web browser. You might want to use Web Sharing to make information (as opposed to files) available to others in a platform-independent manner. Heck, even a digital cell-phone can display Web pages these days.

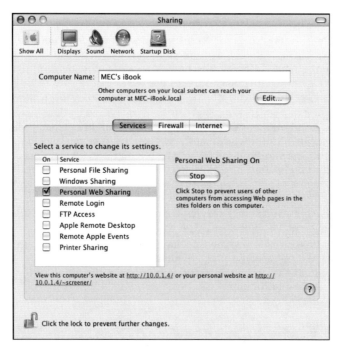

Figure 29-48: Web Sharing enabled in Sharing preferences.

Each user's home directory on your Mac has a Sites folder (shown in Figure 29-49), which gets published when you turn on Personal Web Sharing. For Web users, the address of these sites is of the form `http://<IP ADDRESS>/~<short user name>/` (for example, `http://10.0.1.4/~michael/`). In addition, a general Web folder is also published; it is located in Library⇨WebServer⇨Documents.

Figure 29-49: A user's personal Sites folder.

Web Addresses and Rendezvous

If you have a static IP address and an Internet connection, files that you share with Personal Web Sharing are available to the world; all any Internet user needs to access your shared files is your IP address and a Web browser. If you have a dynamic IP address (a more common situation for home users), your address can change every time you reboot or reconnect to the network. This makes your files less easily accessible to Internet users, because you'll have to have some way to inform them each time your IP address changes.

For users on your local network, especially those who employ browsers that can handle Rendezvous/ZeroConf protocols (Safari is such a browser), you can use your Mac's Rendezvous name (e.g., My-Computer.local), which the Sharing Preferences panel helpfully provides (visible near the top of Figure 29-48). Figure 29-50 shows a Rendezvous-style address being used in Safari's Address bar.

You don't have to be a Web master to take advantage of Personal Web Sharing. Most word processors can export Web pages, so you don't need to know a lick of HTML to make a publishable Web page. Also, most modern browsers can display things like PDF files, JPEG pictures, and QuickTime movies, too. Just drop copies of your files into your Web directory and you've published them (see Figure 29-50).

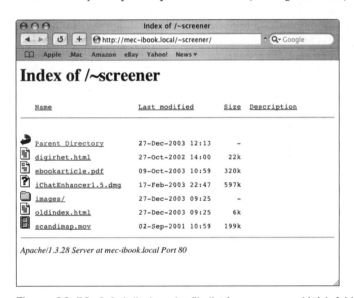

Figure 29-50: Safari displays the file list from a personal Web folder.

insider insight Apache, the Web server built into Mac OS X, gets its name not from the native American tribes of the southwest United States. Rather, this descendant of **the public domain HTTP daemon** that **Rob McCool** originally developed **at the National Center for Supercomputing Applications,** is called Apache because McCool's work was extended by other developers who added *patches* to it . . . it is literally *a patchy server.* It is also the most commonly used Web server on the Internet today.

Accessing Other Mac Users' Files

Panther changes how you connect to other Macs (or, indeed, servers in general) on your network. In its third generation, it seems that Mac OS X slowly wants to wean the Mac community from the old-style, server-volume-on-the-desktop model and move it toward a more Windows-like network-browser model.

What am I talking about? Here's what. Once upon a time, when Macs were truly a world unto themselves, file-sharing Macs on a network would appear listed in a program called the Chooser: Click a listed Mac, optionally provide a username and password, choose one of the *volumes* it was sharing (a volume being a shared folder or disk), and the volume would appear on your desktop like any other hard disk. In Mac OS X up until Panther, the Macs on the network would appear in the Network folder on your Mac, but after you opened one, it appeared on your desktop, too. Now, though, things have changed a bit.

The Network Browser Method

Figures 29-51 and 29-52 show, respectively, how a server appears in your Network Browser both before and after it is mounted (to see the Network Browser, click that lovely globe-like thing in your sidebar or use the Finder's Go⇔Network command).

Figure 29-51: The Network Browser before connecting to a server.

Cosmetic issues aside, this method of mounting servers should be very familiar to Windows users switching to the Mac: a quite similar process is used on Windows to connect to servers. What is new, for the Mac user, is that the mounted server does *not* appear on the desktop as it did in days of old. What once were called *volumes* are now called *sharepoints*, and you can access them *only* in the Network Browser — if that's from where you mounted them. (See the next section, "The Connect to Server Method," for another way to mount servers.)

Figure 29-52: A connected server's sharepoints in the Network Browser.

The Network Browser's connecting method is also slightly different. When you attempt to mount a server by double-clicking it or by clicking the Connect button, you still need to login (see Figure 29-53). But you no longer need to choose which volume to mount once you do: All the sharepoints to which you have access are available when you connect.

Figure 29-53: Connecting to a server hasn't changed much.

Disconnecting from a server mounted in the Network Browser is also, perforce, different: you can't drag the server to the Trash from the desktop, obviously, because it's not *on* the desktop. Instead, you select it in the Network Browser and choose Eject from the Action menu (shown in Figure 29-54) or select File⇨Eject from the Finder. Or you can drag the server's icon from the Network Browser to the Trash. (The Trash icon in the Dock changes to a Disconnect icon as you drag.)

note   **You can't eject sharepoints, only the server itself. It's all or nothing when you mount a server in the Network Browser.**

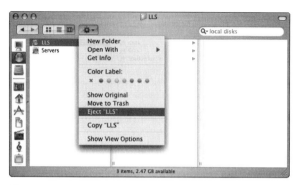

Figure 29-54: Ejecting a server with the Action menu.

The Connect to Server Method

Long-time Mac users may find the new Network Browser paradigm confusing. They would be right, too. Luckily, you can still have server volumes mount on your desktop if that's what you prefer.

The key is in the Finder's Go menu: the Connect to Server command. Using this command presents the Connect to Server window (shown in Figure 29-55).

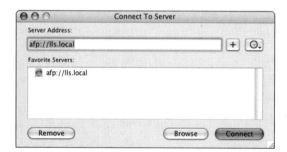

Figure 29-55: Connecting to a server, old school . . . sort of.

Type the server address in the Server Address field, click Connect, and your Mac attempts to contact the server. If successful, you get a chance to login, after which you get a choice of volumes to mount (shown in Figure 29-56). Choose a volume. (You can choose more than one if you like — Shift-click and ⌘-click both work.) It mounts on your desktop. Just like the old days.

> **note**
>
> The form of the server address you type can be an IP address or a Rendezvous-style name, prefaced with `afp://` (which stands for Apple File Protocol) if it is an AFP server (which is what your Mac uses for Personal File Sharing, and what Mac OS X Server uses for its AppleShare services). If you omit the protocol, the Connect to Network command assumes that you want an AFP server. For some other server protocols, see the next chapter.

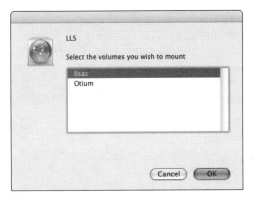

Figure 29-56: You can pick the volumes when you use the Connect to Server command.

If you think that typing server names into a dialog box is not very user-friendly, you are certainly not alone. However, you only have to do it once. You can use the Add to Favorites button (it looks like a plus sign) in the Connect to Server window to add that address to your list of favorite servers. After that, just double-click the server in the list of favorites to mount it.

> **tip** What's that? You forgot to add the server to your list of favorites? Not to worry: Click the Recent Servers button (it looks like a clock set to 5:15) to choose a server you've recently accessed from a pop-up menu. Panther remembers.

What's Missing with Shared Volumes

Secret

Veteran Mac users are used to some amenities with desktop-mounted servers that Panther's brave new world of networking doesn't seem to provide. Or does it?

- **Aliases**: In the past, you could make an alias to a mounted volume and, after you disconnected from the server, double-clicking the alias would cause the Mac to attempt to mount the server again. But, with Panther, an alias to a server volume (or to a sharepoint in the Network Browser, for that matter), doesn't work that way. All you'll get is an error message from the Finder if you attempt to double-click an alias of an unmounted volume or sharepoint.

- **Connect at Startup**: The old pre–OS X Mac system gave you the option of specifying which servers would automatically be mounted at startup. Mac OS X does not provide a similar facility.

Workarounds to both of these deficiencies are available courtesy of the AFP Internet location file type. You can make one of these files with a text editor, like TextEdit. Simply type a network location URL (for example, `afp://server.local/volume/`) as you would in the Connect to Server window, select the text, and drag it from the text editor to the Desktop. The Finder converts the dragged text to a Internet location file (shown in Figure 29-57). Double-click the file to have your Mac attempt to connect to the server.

continues

continued

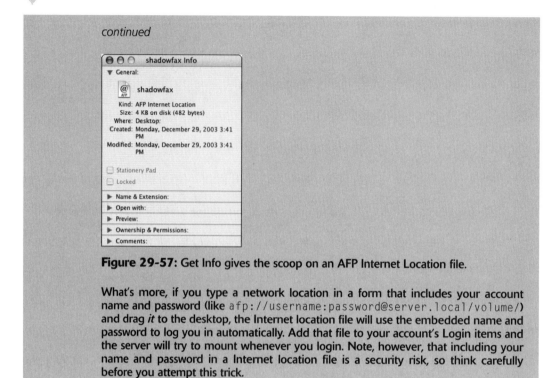

Figure 29-57: Get Info gives the scoop on an AFP Internet Location file.

What's more, if you type a network location in a form that includes your account name and password (like `afp://username:password@server.local/volume/`) and drag *it* to the desktop, the Internet location file will use the embedded name and password to log you in automatically. Add that file to your account's Login items and the server will try to mount whenever you login. Note, however, that including your name and password in a Internet location file is a security risk, so think carefully before you attempt this trick.

Summary

In this chapter, I talked about the protocols you may have heard of and probably some you haven't. After that, we looked at the networking preferences in depth so you could see how those protocols were set to be used.

We also took a good long look at AirPort and AirPort base station settings and options as a prelude to sharing files between Macs. Sharing files is a big deal, so I hope you read it all and what I had to say helped.

Hopefully along the way, I made it clearer how to connect your Mac to . . . whatever. If I didn't quite cover it in this chapter, my guess is that you need some more information about connecting a Mac to a PC. If that's the case, then you will find more information on that subject in the next chapter.

Mac/Windows Cross-Platform Networking

Chapter

30

♦ ♦

Secrets in This Chapter

♦ ♦

" Y ou can't get theah from heah . . ." — Punch line to an old Maine joke

Mac users set adrift on a Windows network have usually felt as lost as the beleaguered tourist in the old joke, even (or sometimes, especially) after asking for support from the Windows network management staff. Panther's cross-platform network-savvy features have changed all that. Not completely of course: Windows networks can be amazingly complicated, and even Windows users may find themselves stranded on a dead-end path in the backwoods when attempting to connect to one of the more arcane configurations that characterize Windows networks. However, Panther does give you a fighting chance to work and play nicely with your Windows-using brethren, and that's all that any Mac user can reasonably ask.

Secrets of Windows Network Jargon

The Mac culture has generated its share of jargon over the past twenty years. (I like to call such words "terms of art.") So, it should come as no surprise to find that the Windows culture has done the same . . . and it has, with bells on. Don't forget that the Windows/DOS culture grew out of the IBM culture, which is famous for having generated reams of some of the most obscure and forgettable jargon in human history. (These are the folk gave us terms like EBCDIC and ABEND.) When Mac users want to network with their Windows compadres, therefore, it's inevitable they're going to run into language difficulties. Below are some of the terms you're apt to encounter.

Active Directory

Active Directory is a Windows network's *directory service,* the set of tools, protocols, and data that a network needs in order to keep track of its users and resources. Active Directory lets network administrators monitor and manage things like user accounts, access privileges, passwords, home directories, e-mail addresses, workgroups, and so on.

Secret

Open Directory Is Your Network Compatibility Key

Apple does not pretend that just one directory service, or even two or three, are sufficient for a Mac living in today's inter-networked cross-platform environment. That's why they've developed *Open Directory,* an open-source component of Darwin (the underlying Unix core of Mac OS X).

Open Directory is not a directory service; rather, it is a framework for handling multiple directory services. It does this in two ways: by abstracting the features that various directory services offer (such as authentication, discovery of resources — like printers and file servers — and file sharing), and by providing a plug-in architecture for handling transactions with different directory services, such as Active Directory and Novell's eDirectory.

Built in to Open Directory are components that handle Microsoft's Active Directory, LDAP, NetInfo (which is what earlier versions of Mac OS X, and, before it, NextStep used), and more — Open Directory in Panther Server can even act as a Windows NT network's primary domain controller. (Yes, you can now run a Windows network on an Apple Xserve that's sitting on a rack in the back room — the world is changing, indeed.) As Mac OS X evolves, and Apple revises and tunes its directory service plug-ins, Open Directory will doubtless become even more cross-platform savvy than it already is.

Common Internet File System (CIFS)

The *Common Internet File System* (CIFS), introduced by Microsoft in 1996, is a protocol that is an essential part of Windows file sharing. CIFS lives in the presentation layer of the OSI model (discussed in Chapter 29). The protocol is a reworking and expansion of Microsoft's original *server message block* (SMB) protocol (see "SMB and Samba" later in this chapter). Some people mistakenly think that CIFS is simply another name for SMB; in fact, SMB is a part (albeit a core part) of CIFS.

Domain Controller

A server that maintains information about network resources for a specific part of a network and that provides access control is the domain controller. In older Windows networks, you may find a number of *primary domain controllers* (PDCs) and *backup domain controllers* (BDCs), and you need to log in to the one that maintains your account in order to use the network; on modern Windows networks using Active Directory, domain controllers share their information and users no longer need to access a specific domain controller to be allowed to use the network.

Lightweight Directory Access Protocol (LDAP)

The *Lightweight Directory Access Protocol* (LDAP) is a standard protocol. Published by the Internet Engineering Task Force (IETF), it lets programs acquire information from different directory services, as long as the directory service is designed to make its information available in LDAP format. Active Directory is such a directory service.

NetBIOS and NetBEUI

These are, and are not, the same thing, depending on the context, the time of day, the phase of the moon, and to whom you are talking. As is often the case when discussing Microsoft products, one name can often refer to more than one thing (e.g., Outlook) and several different names can often refer to the same product. So it is with these two.

> **note** NetBIOS and NetBEUI are not Microsoft inventions, by the way; they originated with IBM, back when IBM and Microsoft were the best of buddies.

NetBIOS, from one point of view, is an enhanced application programming interface (API) for the PC's basic input/output system (BIOS) that allows programs to access network information in much the same way that they can access local data. From another point of view, it is the collection of protocols that allow this access.

NetBEUI is the *NetBIOS Extended User Interface*, which has nothing to do with user interfaces that you or I might use; rather, it extends NetBIOS's capabilities and fills in some of the unspecified parts of the NetBIOS specification. (The *user* in this context is the computer, not the person sitting in front of it.)

In the early days, NetBIOS/NetBEUI were in some ways similar to AppleTalk (see Chapter 29), in that they were proprietary protocols for moving information on a LAN (Local Area Network). Again, like AppleTalk, individual machines had NetBIOS names to identify them on the network. Microsoft eventually put together a NetBEUI over TCP/IP implementation, much like Apple did with AppleTalk. In Windows XP, NetBEUI has withered away to a more-or-less unsupported protocol, but it is still around on many, many networks.

SMB and Samba

SMB is the Microsoft *server message block* protocol that underlies the file-sharing abilities of Windows (and DOS before it). SMB is a core part of Microsoft's CIFS (see earlier in this chapter).

Samba is both a Brazilian dance and an open source implementation of SMB. The SMB implementation was originally developed in Australia, not Brazil, in 1991 by Andrew Tridgell, a computer science doctoral student at the Australian National University, Canberra, who was frustrated by the inability of his Unix and Microsoft DOS-based computers to share files over a network. Being an old-fashioned hacker (that is, the good kind of hacker who only takes systems apart in order to improve them), he cobbled together a solution to his dilemma in just a few short weeks. From that humble beginning, Samba has become an almost essential package for Linux and Unix-based systems (like Panther) that require file-sharing capabilities with Windows systems.

Windows Internet Naming Service (WINS)

The *Windows Internet Naming Service* (WINS) provides a way for a Windows network to associate names with addresses, similar to how the Internet's *domain name system* (DNS) works. When you put your Mac on a Windows network, you often have to specify a WINS server to provide name resolution.

Workgroup

A *workgroup* is a name assigned to a group of related resources (user machines, shared printers, servers) on a Windows network; it's kind of like an AppleTalk zone name if you squint at it a bit. On a *peer-to-peer* Windows network (that is, one that doesn't rely upon a central server, directory services, name servers, and so on), you often see the name WORKGROUP used as the workgroup name. (This is a Windows default that Panther also uses, in its attempt to work and play well with Windows.) The servers, printers, and other resources to which you have access when you connect to a Windows network may change depending upon the workgroup name you use when connecting.

Secret

Panther Server Serves Up Windows File-Sharing Protocols

You don't need a copy of Windows Server and you don't even need an Intel-processor-based machine if you want to set up a Windows network. Apple's Panther Server can do all the basic Windows networking stuff you need: it knows Active Directory as well as AppleShare, and it can act as a Windows primary domain controller, provide native Windows authentication, use WINS for name resolution, and assign WINS and NetBIOS DHCP information to Windows clients. Oh, yes, it can also handle e-mail and file-sharing services for all your network clients, Mac, Unix, Linux, or Windows.

Apple's Xserve computers come with an unlimited client version of Panther server, so if you stick a rack-mounted Xserve in your server room, you can probably save a good chunk of folding green, and your Windows-using colleagues will be none the wiser.

Sharing Your Mac Network with Windows Users

On a small network, such as one that you might find in a home or a small business office, you probably won't find a network administrator or directory servers or all the other hoopla and folderol that you'll find in corporate computing environments, but you may still need to exchange information and resources with the occasional non-Mac user. Panther's built-in Windows compatibility features are intended to help you do just that.

Sharing Files with Windows Users

Seemingly, there's no trick to making your Mac's files available to Windows users on a local area network if that's all you need to do. Simply open System Preferences, click on the icon for Sharing, and turn on Windows Sharing (shown in Figure 30-1).

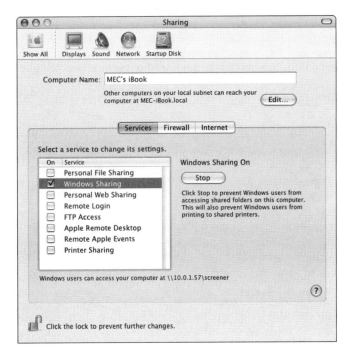

Figure 30-1: Windows Sharing enabled.

> **tip**
>
> When you turn Windows Sharing on, Panther also makes any shared printers connected to your Mac available to Windows users.

Not very hard, is it? Of course, there are a few hidden gotchas. First, Windows File Sharing will work for Windows users only if those users have account names and passwords on your Mac that they can use: Panther's Window Sharing does not allow for guest access. That means that you either have to

◆ **Give the Windows users your own account name and password** (which is a security hole the size of the galactic core)

◆ **Create a user account on your Mac that you will use for Windows file sharing only** and give the Windows users that account name and password (which is also a security hole, but a much smaller and more manageable one).

Neither of these two choices is very satisfactory. The first one opens your home directory to the Windows user, and when your home directory is open to a Windows system, it is vulnerable to any destructive *malware* (like a virus or a Trojan horse) that might have infected that Windows system. Let's face it: Your Windows-using chums may be trustworthy, but can you trust their OS?

The second choice means that you'll have to put all the files you want to share into the directory of the user account you created for your Windows users, which usually means that you'll have to drag the files you want to share into that account's Drop Box folder, then log in to that account and move them to where you want them to be finally located. Even with Fast User Switching, this process can be a tedious way to waste your time.

In short, if you need to share files directly from your Mac with a Windows user, the ability is there in Panther—half-baked, but there.

Secret

Better-Baked File Sharing with Some Third-Party Help

The insufficiencies, quirks, and resulting frustrations that Panther provides when you try to share your files with Windows users can largely be ameliorated by two products, one free and one not.

The free SharePoints software from http://hornware.com/sharepoints/ allows you to create "homeless" user accounts for file-sharing purposes. You can use this to make accounts for your Windows-using friends just like you can for your Mac friends. SharePoints also gives you some extra control over Panther's Samba server. SharePoints is further described in Chapter 29.

Even SharePoints can't fix some of the quirks in Panther's Samba server, though: all it does is provide a front end to manipulate various Panther configuration files. If your need to work with Windows users goes beyond Panther's built-in Windows compatibility features, Thursby's DAVE might be just the thing (www.thursby.com/dave/).

DAVE provides numerous features to make your cross-platform networking adventures much less adventurous. It understands several different types of security, provides compatibility with older and newer Windows networks, allows Mac users to share individual folders with Windows folk, supports Windows shortcuts (.LNK files), and more. It works with some of Panther's built-in capabilities and supersedes others to provide almost complete compatibility with various kinds of Windows networks.

caution

When you turn off Windows Sharing in the Sharing preferences, it doesn't always immediately turn itself off, no matter what the preference pane says. The SMB server on your Mac may stay on until you close System Preferences and maybe even longer if there are open connections to your Mac. (At least, that's what *I've* seen happen in Mac OS X 10.3.2, though, as always, your mileage may vary.)

To be sure that your Mac is no longer doing Windows Sharing behind your back, you can sleep and wake your Mac . . . that will usually break any open connections. When all else fails, shutting down completely (including powering off) and then restarting should do the trick.

Sharing an AirPort Base Station with Windows Users

One of the benefits of Apple's push to adopt industry standards over the last few years is that it has allowed Apple to pioneer new technologies that other non-Apple users will (eventually) use. AirPort is one of those technologies: Apple didn't invent it; the company took the 802.11b standard and packaged it so that it would work extremely well with Apple computers but wouldn't lock out others. Airport Extreme supports 802.11g and 802.11b cards in Macs or Windows based PCs.

A Windows computer with a wireless adapter that supports 802.11b can join any AirPort network. No special configuration needs to be used. All the Windows user has to do is enter the network password . . . oh, wait, um, maybe it's not all *that* simple.

When you set up an AirPort Base Station, you usually (and you really should) enable security by creating a network password in order to lock out unauthorized intruders and to protect your data. (Chapter 29 covers this in more detail.) However, the network password that you enter on your Mac when you want to join the network won't work for Windows users. That's because Apple's AirPort software converts the password you give it into a *WEP key*, a binary key for encrypting and decrypting the data that travels between your Mac and the base station. WEP keys are usually long strings of hexadecimal numbers, which are a pain to type and a pain to remember, but the AirPort software protects you from most of that pain.

Windows users have no such pain relief: to join an AirPort network, they will have to enter the actual WEP key itself. But how do you find it out? That's what the friendly little Password icon on the AirPort Admin Utility's toolbar is for. (Take a look at Figure 29-34, back in Chapter 29, to see it for yourself.) Click this icon and a sheet comes down that gives you the WEP key that Windows users will need to enter to join the network (shown in Figure 30-2). And it is *that* simple.

To connect to the AirPort network created by this base station from a computer not using AirPort software, you should use the following:

Hex equivalent password (WEP key): FBD0E1D438

OK

Figure 30-2: A hex key for Windows.

> **note** When joining an AirPort network, Windows users should also make sure that their *authentication method* (one of the options that the Windows wireless software provides) is set to *Shared;* if it is set to *Open,* the Windows computer may have trouble communicating with the AirPort network.

Networking in a Windows World

Yes, you and I know that the Mac — especially a Mac running Panther — provides a superior computing environment to the one offered by the machines and operating system that make up that *other* platform. And you know the platform I mean: the one that owns so much of the personal computer market that it has officially been deemed a monopoly. So, when it comes to putting your Mac on a network at school or work, the odds are good that it's a Windows network of some flavor to which you are connecting your Mac.

Connect to a Windows Server

You can connect to a Windows server using the Finder's Go➪Connect to Server menu item almost exactly as you would do to mount an Apple server (see Chapter 29). And, as with Apple servers, this technique mounts the server on the desktop (that is, if you have chosen to show mounted volumes on the desktop in your Finder preferences).

Windows servers use the SMB protocol, so the addresses you enter into the Connect to Server dialog box usually take the form `smb://<server address>`, where `<server address>` can be a URL, like `billsdisk.example.com`, the machine's NetBIOS name on the Windows local area network (see "Secrets of Windows Network Jargon," earlier in this chapter), or an IP address, as in Figure 30-3.

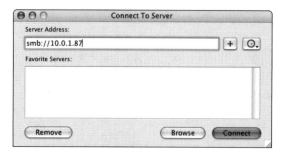

Figure 30-3: Connecting to a Windows server is done through the Connect to Server dialog box.

Secret

Getting Back to the Jaguar Connect Dialog Box

Some users may find the Panther version of the Connect To Server dialog box less friendly than the version in Jaguar. If you are one of those folk, AppleScript is your friend. Open the Script Editor, then type and run the following script to see the old-style (c. 2002) Connect To Server dialog box from Jaguar:

```
tell application "Finder"
    open location (choose URL showing File servers ù
    with editable URL)
end tell
```

You can find out more about AppleScript in Chapter 11.

When you click Connect in the Connect To Server dialog box, Panther presents its version of the Windows network Authentication dialog box (shown in Figure 30-4). Here's where you enter your keys to the Windows kingdom: your user account name, your password, and your Windows network workgroup.

SMB/CIFS Filesystem Authentication

Enter username and password for BALLMER:

Workgroup/Domain
WORKGROUP

Username
BILLG

Password
•••••••

☐ Add to Keychain

(Cancel) (OK)

Figure 30-4: Authentication, the Windows way.

After you've authenticated, you're almost done: You simply need to pick a *share* to mount on your desktop (shown in Figure 30-5), a *share* being Windows jargon for a directory on the server that is shared. (See? Windows isn't *always* complicated.) The share you choose appears on your desktop and in the Finder windows' sidebars, just like a shared Mac disk.

Figure 30-5: Pick a share to mount via SMB.

note When you click Connect in the Connect To Server dialog box, Panther may present the SMB Mount dialog box (shown in Figure 30-5) *before* it asks you to authenticate if the server offers more than one publicly accessible share. Click the Authenticate button in the dialog box to get to the Authentication dialog box shown earlier in Figure 30-4, or click Connect to mount a public share.

The SMB Address, Expanded Edition

In the Connect To Server dialog box shown earlier in Figure 30-3, you can, in fact, specify an address that includes your Windows workgroup, user account name, password, and the share that you want to mount all in one go, and completely bypass the subsequent dialog boxes. The expanded form of the SMB address looks like this:

```
smb://workgroup ;username:password@<server name or address>/share
```

It should be noted that while "workgroup" is the default name, not all workgroups are named "workgroup."

Note, though, that entering the share's address this way will transmit both your name and your password to the server *unencrypted*, and that is not something you necessarily want to do.

However, if you use the address format below, which omits the password, you will still see the authentication dialog box, but you won't have to choose a share in a separate dialog box, and the other portions of the authentication dialog box will be filled in for you.

```
smb://workgroup;username@<server name or address>/share
```

Remember, too, that you can use the Connect To Server dialog box's Add button (plus sign) to add such admittedly long and complicated addresses to the list of server addresses that the dialog box remembers, saving you some work the next time you need to connect to a server.

Browse to a Windows Server

To make Windows switchers feel right at home, all Apple has to add to the Network icon in the Panther Finder's sidebar is one word, *Neighborhood* — Panther's Network browser functions very much like the Network Neighborhood feature in Windows. You can click the Network icon, or choose Go⇨Network, or click Browse in the Connect To Server dialog box (refer to Figure 30-3) to see the Network browser (shown in Figure 30-6).

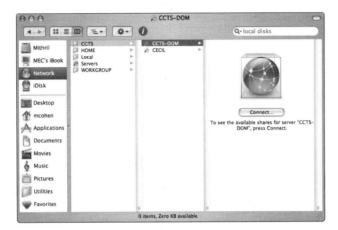

Figure 30-6: The Network browser sees servers and shares.

The Network Browser Changes to the Network browser

Secret

It's called the *Network browser*, not the *Network Browser*. Apple seems strangely insistent on this point. Starting in Mac OS 8.5, the Mac had a *Network Browser* application, but the name fell into disfavor in Mac OS X. (There's a Help document still in Panther, "Where is the Network Browser?" that's been around since Mac OS X 10.1.) Yet the Connect To Server dialog box in Panther has a Browse button that brings up the window in Figure 30-6, and Apple's Help documents refer to this window as the "Network browser," so the name seems to be the same—there's just been a change in typography.

The Network browser shows you the servers that you can browse on your network. You may also see folders in the browser, within which you will find servers. (Folders usually contain the servers for a particular workgroup.) Whether you can see a server in the Network browser depends on several things, some of which are in your control and some of which are not:

♦ **The server must be on the network to which you are connected.** Yes, this seems obvious, but sometimes machines are down or disconnected, and sometimes you may not be connected to the network to which you think you are connected. You can check your Network settings in System Preferences to find out which network ports are active and connected to which networks (see Chapter 29).

♦ **The server must be discoverable.** That is, it either must advertise itself as being available in some way, or some other computer on the network (such as a Windows domain controller) must advertise it.

♦ **Your Mac must be capable of receiving the server's advertisement.** For example, if you don't have Active Directory enabled in Panther's Directory Access utility (see later in this chapter), your Mac won't hear anything about servers being advertised by the Active Directory service and you won't be able to browse them.

So why browse instead of mounting a server on your desktop with the Connect To Server dialog box? You want to browse when

- ◆ **You're on a local network with a lot of different servers** and you frequently use a variety of them.
- ◆ **You're a Windows refugee** and you like the comfort of something that feels like your Network Neighborhood.

You want to use the Connect To Server method when

- ◆ **A server is not on your local network.**
- ◆ **You want it on your desktop.**

Secret

Getting the Most from the Directory Access Application

Panther uses two general methods to acquire information within a network environment: it listens for service advertisements using various protocols (such as AppleTalk, Rendezvous, and SMB), and it consults with various directory services on the network (such as Active Directory and NetInfo). Directory Access is the program (tucked safely into your Utility folder where Panther keeps the sharp tools) that lets you enable, disable, and configure Panther's various information-acquiring methods (shown in Figure 30-7).

In most cases, you will use Directory Access merely to turn things on and off. For example, if you don't have any AppleTalk devices on your network, your Mac doesn't need to spend time listening for AppleTalk packets, so you can turn that function off. Similarly, if you can't see any Windows servers on your network, and you *know* they're out there, you should check Directory Access to see if Active Directory and SMB are enabled.

You can configure a number of network services with Directory Access by clicking the Configure button, but, in most cases, you won't touch it before consulting with a friendly neighborhood network administrator — or even an unfriendly one. Playing around with service configurations without knowing what you are doing is a very easy way to hopelessly confuse your Mac.

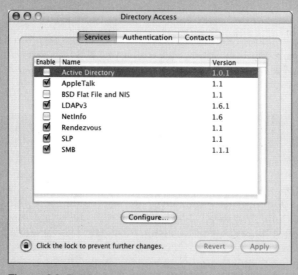

Figure 30-7: Directory Access helps you find your way.

note Servers or folders may not show up immediately in the Network browser when you first open it. Panther has to wait until a server advertises its availability or until a directory service returns information about the currently available workgroups, which can take a few seconds.

Click on a server in the Network browser, and, if you are using column view, you are offered a friendly Connect button; click it (or double-click the server if you are in list or icon view), and you are asked to authenticate (shown in Figure 30-8). After you authenticate, you are given access to any shares on the server to which you are entitled (shown in Figure 30-9). These shares appear *only* in Panther's Network browser; unlike shares mounted with the Connect To Server dialog box, they don't appear as volumes on your desktop.

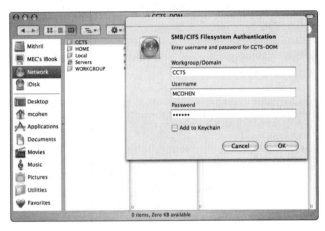

Figure 30-8: Halt and be recognized.

note Shares to which you do not have access and servers to which you have not connected have subtly different appearances in the Network browser than accessible shares or connected servers: they look slightly lighter than their counterparts, but not so light as to look disabled. Unfortunately, this subtle difference in appearance is easy to miss.

caution Rendezvous uses the suffix *.local* for servers on a local network. Network administrators setting up small networks using Active Directory often use the same name. (Word has it that some instructional examples for Active Directory setup use this, and network administrators may simply have copied the example.) This can create a conflict, making Windows servers in the *local* domain invisible. You can't resolve this conflict; your Windows network administrator has to do that.

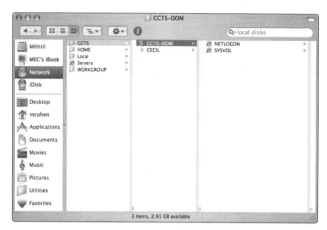

Figure 30-9: Windows shares in Panther's Network browser.

That's it: After you've mounted a Windows share, you can drag files and folders to it just like any other folder on your Mac.

Secret

Two Unfortunate Things About Browsing Windows Servers

The Network browsing abilities of Panther can make working in a Windows world more convenient, but the Panther's browser is not yet completely tame:

1 When you authenticate to a network share, it seems that all logged-in users on your Mac can see those shares in the Network browser. However, those users likely won't have permission to use those shares, and they won't be able to reauthenticate. This makes Fast User Switching less useful when you're working on a Windows network.

2 Panther offers you a Disconnect option both in the server's contextual menu and in its Action menu, but the menu item doesn't seem to work: After you're connected to a Windows server, you seem to stay connected until you completely disconnect from the network, at which point you'll see the dialog box in Figure 30-10 for each and every server you have mounted. If you often move your Mac laptop between locations and networks, this dialog box can get old real fast.

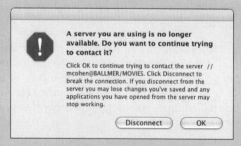

Figure 30-10: This is the warning you get when Windows servers go away.

Other Secrets of Cross-Platform Interoperability

Working in a cross-platform environment means more than just being able to shoot files across the network between two different platforms. You also have to be able to do something with the files once they've been exchanged.

Microsoft's Offices

Microsoft's monopoly extends beyond the Windows operating system (or systems — there are a number of various Windows versions out there):Tthe not-so-gentle-giant that lives at One Microsoft Way in Redmond, Washington, has a pretty strong lock on business productivity software as well. Yes, I'm talking about the ubiquitous, multifarious, Microsoft Office.

The current version of Office for Windows, Office 2003, comes in a variety of flavors, with a version for students and teachers, one for small businesses, one for professionals (such as information technology professionals and developers), and a "standard" version for just plain folk. None of these are completely compatible with each other (let alone the Mac); and when you consider that some Windows folk are running Office 2003 (of some form), some are running Office XP, some are running Office 2000, and some are running Office 97, you can begin to appreciate why compatibility is something of an ideal rather than a fact.

---

note The forthcoming-as-I-write Office 2004 for Macintosh has a Compatibility Reports feature that supposedly lets you know when you are using a feature that is incompatible with other versions of Office. This won't help you, of course, if folk using other versions of Office send you files that are incompatible with *your* version. C'est la vie.

Still, there's a good deal of compatibility between most of the versions of Office for Windows out there, and between them and the versions of Office that Microsoft makes available for the Mac OS X.

---

insider insight It should be common knowledge, but many people still don't realize that one of the core programs in the Office was ported from the Mac. Excel on the Mac came out in 1985, the year after the Mac was introduced, but it didn't appear in Windows until 1987. And although Word for DOS predated the Mac (it came out in 1983), the first version of it to support a graphical user interface was the Mac version, introduced in 1984 on the same day the Mac first appeared. Word didn't show up in Windows until 1989.

Office on Windows and Office on the Mac have these programs in common:

- ◆ **Word**
- ◆ **Excel**
- ◆ **PowerPoint**

Office on Windows also includes these programs, which do not appear in the Mac version:

✦ **Access** (database)
✦ **Publisher** (page layout)
✦ **InfoPath** (forms creation)
✦ **Outlook** (e-mail and scheduling).

Finally, Office on the Mac features Entourage, a Mac-only e-mail and scheduling program. Entourage also handles newsgroups.

Generally, the programs that the Mac and Windows versions of Office have in common are reasonably compatible, but you may run into some minor inconsistencies. If the following issues don't affect you, though, you can work in a Windows world and still let your Mac flag fly:

✦ **Word in Office X does not handle non-European characters very well;** though the underlying Word software on both platforms uses Unicode (the standard for multilingual character encoding), Word on the Mac does not display any characters that aren't in the Western European character set. (You'll see underscores only where, say, your Cyrillic text should appear.) The next version of Office for Panther, due by mid-2004, may fix this problem.

> **note**
>
> Panther's version of TextEdit is quite capable of opening and saving Word documents directly. Although it doesn't support anything like the full range of Word's features, for most standard business documents (such as memos, letters, or white papers), TextEdit does a rather credible job of filling in for Word. What's more, it will even display the Unicode characters in a Windows Word document that the Mac version of Word can't.

✦ **You can't embed fonts in the Mac version of Word (as you can with the creation of a PDF).**
✦ **Pictures inserted into Word and Excel documents on the Mac will sometimes appear as big red X's when moved to Windows, and vice versa.**
✦ **PowerPoint slides inserted into Excel documents on the Mac may look rough and distorted when viewed in Windows.**
✦ **PowerPoint on the Mac works well with embedded QuickTime media, but PowerPoint on Windows doesn't handle embedded QuickTime media.**
✦ **Programs written in Visual Basic for Applications (VBA) may not work;** the Mac version of Office uses version 5, while Office on Windows is more than a version ahead.
✦ **Forget about Office documents that use embedded ActiveX controls;** you won't find them on the Mac.

Secret

Entourage Can Now Be Used with Exchange Server

Outlook for Exchange, the Microsoft mailing and scheduling program built in to Office on Windows, is one of the thorns in the side of Mac users who wish to work with their Windows compatriots. Sure, we Mac users have Entourage, the mail counterpart in the Mac Office suite, and some of us find it just delightful to use as an e-mail client, but it just doesn't work as well with the Microsoft Exchange servers that handle e-mail and scheduling in many corporate settings. That is not to say that things haven't gotten better recently . . . they have. Somewhat.

The latest version of Entourage can now communicate directly with an Exchange server, just like Outlook can. "Hooray!" one might be tempted to cheer. Don't give in to that temptation, though: Entourage can only communicate with an Exchange server that has enabled *Internet Message Access Protocol* (IMAP), an Internet standard for handling remote mailboxes on a mail server. Recent versions of the Exchange server software *are* fully capable of supporting IMAP, but many mail server administrators are set in their ways and still use Microsoft's proprietary *Messaging Application Programming Interface* (MAPI) for mailbox access, which Entourage can't use.

Outlook for Exchange also has many powerful scheduling and collaboration features, only a rather small set of which is compatible with Entourage. With Entourage, you can see other Exchange users' calendars to help you schedule meetings, and you can synchronize your Entourage calendar with the Exchange server so you can work offline. But you can't schedule resources, you can't synchronize tasks, and you can't access public folders.

So, if you want to use your Mac in a corporate setting, Entourage may be able to help you fit in. Then again, it may not.

The Emulators

If you can't beat 'em, be 'em: that's the point behind emulators. But, where once was a thriving market in such items, the PC emulator market now pretty much boils down to just one application . . . and that application was recently acquired by Microsoft.

Virtual PC

Virtual PC, formerly produced by Connectix and now a *jen-you-wine* Microsoft product, creates a software version of an Intel-based microcomputer, complete with Windows software, right inside your Mac. And it works, too, surprisingly well: Even the bugs to which Windows is heir, as well as the virus vulnerabilities to which it is also heir, are present and accounted for.

insider insight

If you are a Linux junkie, and don't want to kill the Panther in your Mac for a PowerPC Linux replacement, you can run a version of Linux designed for Intel processors in the Virtual PC environment. Microsoft, doesn't officially support such behavior, of course (would you expect them to?) but it does work.

Requiring at least a 500MHz G3 Mac with 256MB of RAM and a couple of gigabytes of free hard disk space, Virtual PC lets you run almost any program that runs on Windows. However, there are many programs you absolutely won't want to run, because Virtual PC is slow, so slow that multimedia applications, games, and other applications that require a peppy processor behind them for a satisfactory experience most likely will frustrate you beyond endurance.

On the other hand, many things do work just fine in the Virtual PC emulator, and that makes this package almost essential for any Lone Mac Outpost on the Windows frontier:

◆ **Office 2003** on Virtual PC lets you avoid compatibility issues with your Windows coworkers, because it is the same Office that they use, and operates with only a hint of sluggishness in the emulated environment.

◆ **Windows networking works exactly like it does on Windows.** (You can even communicate over the network from the Virtual PC on your Mac with the Mac that's hosting it as though it were a different computer.)

◆ **You can copy and paste between Mac programs and Windows programs.**

◆ **Folders and removable media can be shared between your Mac and the PC inside it.**

Microsoft has pledged continued support and development of Virtual PC; in fact, it is included in Office X for the Mac Professional Edition and is slated to be part of the next Mac Office as well. Is Microsoft being sneaky here, trying to lure the Mac faithful to abandon their platform of choice? No, not really: they just want to sell as many copies of Windows as they can, and Virtual PC provides them with another opportunity to do just that.

Secret

The Sex Lives of PC Emulators

Virtual PC 6.1, the current version as I write, is incompatible with the new Power Mac G5s. The problem, though, is not the result of a dark Microsoft conspiracy to sabotage Apple's latest desktop powerhouse — Microsoft would be happier if there *were* no problem in the first place. No, the problem arises from sexual incompatibility: Intel processors implement *little-endian* byte sex. (that is, when numbers take up several bytes of storage, the bytes containing the least significant parts of the number are given the lowest memory addresses) while PowerPC processors implement *big-endian* byte sex (the most significant bytes have the lowest addresses).

G4 and earlier PowerPCs have a feature that can quickly reverse a number's byte sex, but the G5 does not. Virtual PC relies on that missing sex change operator, and can't operate without it. Microsoft promises that Virtual PC 7 will work around the byte-sex problem, and will be available by mid-2004.

PC-MacLAN

Sometimes a Windows machine may need to talk to Macs using Apple protocols, such as AppleTalk — think of a mixed network, with some older Macs, older Windows machines, and legacy printers and servers of various makes and configurations. PC MacLan, from Miramar (www.miramar.com) is made for such a case. It doesn't emulate a computer, like Virtual PC; instead, it more or less emulates an Apple network on a Windows PC. It does much more, too.

Sure, Panther (and, even more, Panther Server) can handle a lot of Windows networking chores, but not every Mac runs (or even *can* run) Panther. With PC MacLAN installed on the PCs, however, Windows users running various versions of Windows, and Mac users running various versions of the Mac OS (Classic and X) can exchange files and share printers almost transparently.

The package also includes DataViz's Conversions Plus package that lets PC users convert Mac files to file formats that they can use; PC Migrator, a PC program which lets Mac users copy whole disk volumes to Windows disks, automatically adding appropriate file extensions as it goes; and A.K.A., which provides the same file-extension voodoo as PC Migrator, but runs on the Mac.

You may never need the features that PC MacLAN provides, but it sure can come in handy when you do.

The Remote Controllers

If you can't beat 'em, and you can't be 'em, control 'em: that's the idea behind remote control software. For example, if you have, say, a Windows machine at your office, but you have a Mac at home, you can run programs on your remote-control-enabled office machine, move files on it, read mail on it, connect to servers from it — in short, do anything you could do while sitting in front of it — all from your Mac at home.

Remote Desktop Connection

A number of versions of Windows include either a feature called Terminal Services or one called Remote Desktop Services. If one of these services is running on a Windows machine, you can use Microsoft's Remote Desktop Connection (RDC) on your computer to display a desktop from the Windows machine and control it with your mouse and keyboard. Windows network administrators, for example, use Microsoft's RDC client to control the various servers under their jurisdiction remotely; similarly, help desk personnel often use RDC to help solve user support problems remotely. Now Mac users can join the party.

Microsoft has made a version of the RDC client available for Mac OS X, and they seem to be serious about continuing to do so, because they have updated it for Panther. You can grab a free copy from their Mactopia download site (www.microsoft.com/mac/downloads.aspx). It's not something you'll need unless you have a Windows computer you need to control, and it doesn't go in the other direction (not surprising because the Mac doesn't run Microsoft's Remote Desktop Services unless you're running Virtual PC). But, for what it does, it does it well and with little fuss.

---

note   Consumer versions of Windows do not run Remote Desktop Services. Only Professional or Server versions of Windows do that; for example, Windows XP Professional, Windows Server 2003, Windows 2000 Server, or the Terminal Services Edition of Windows NT Server 4.0.

Timbuktu

A full-featured, Mac-friendly remote control program, Timbuktu has been letting Macs control other Macs as well as PCs for years. Available from Netopia (www.netopia.com), the program does just about everything that Remote Desktop Connection can do, and a whole lot more.

With Timbuktu, you can observe another machine, control it, transfer files to and from it, and exchange text messages with the person sitting in front of it. The program can work over the Internet (shown in Figure 30-11) as well as local area networks, and even via modem. Of course, there is one catch: You have to install a copy of Timbuktu on both machines, and it isn't free; a cross-platform "twin pack" costs a couple hundred dollars.

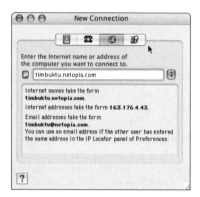

Figure 30-11: Timbuktu lets you control another machine almost anywhere on the Internet.

VNC

Midway between Netopia's Timbuktu and Microsoft's RDC in terms of features is Virtual Network Computer (VNC), an open source remote control package available from SourceForge (http://sourceforge.net or from http://www.realvnc.com). Originally developed by Olivetti, taken over by AT&T, and eventually released to the open source community, VNC works on a variety of platforms, including Mac OS X.

You need a VNC server running on the machine you wish to control, and a VNC client (such as Chicken of the VNC, shown in Figure 30-12) running on your Mac. Both servers and clients are free. You can't copy files with it, nor can you text message, but the price is right and, because the source code is freely available, you theoretically can add any of those features if they're important to you (assuming, of course, that you can read and write Objective C or C++).

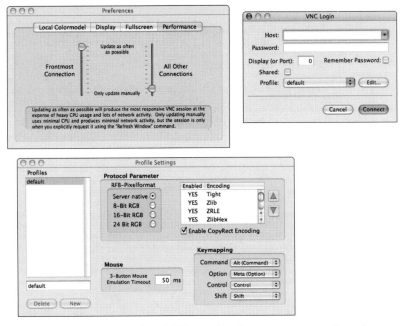

Figure 30-12: Chicken of the VNC provides free remote control goodness.

Summary

Living on a Mac in a Windows-dominated world is not the bleak struggle that it was a few years back. Panther's ability to connect to Windows networks of various stripes and flavors is unparalleled in Mac history. In fact, it can sometimes be easier to connect to a Windows network from a Mac than it is from a PC running Windows. Apple's ongoing commitment to open standards and interoperability suggests that things will only get better in this regard as time goes on.

Similarly, Microsoft's commitment to its Macintosh Business Unit (MBU), which develops such programs as Word, Excel, Entourage, Remote Desktop Connection, and, now, Virtual PC, shows no sign of going away. The MBU is a clear money-maker for Microsoft, and Microsoft has a decided preference for making money. Also third-party developers continue to find a profitable niche making products that bridge the gap between Macs and Windows PCs.

Macs may never dominate the computing world, but they no longer constitute an isolated island far from the shipping lanes. And who knows . . . island kingdoms have been known to conquer the world before.

Under the Hood: The World of Unix

♦ ◆ ♦ ◆ ♦ ◆ ♦ ◆ ♦ ◆ ♦ ◆ ♦ ◆ ♦ ◆ ♦ ◆ ♦ ◆ ♦ ◆

Secrets in This Chapter

◆ ♦

S o there it is, the command line, staring back at you with a cold, faceless expression, full of text, black on white, waiting for you to say something to it. The only thing it says to you is:

```
Last login: Fri Oct 31 09:28:52 on consle
Welcome to Darwin!
[Darknet:~] darkside%
```

"Welcome to Darwin!" It says. What?! Darwin? I thought I was using Mac OS X when I started up this computer, what is Darwin? Without a doubt, from the beginner Mac user to the extreme power user, anyone taking their first step into the Unix world will feel a little lost. Although you have the ability to talk to your computer in ways that you couldn't through the GUI, now you don't know what to say or how to say it. Learning where the underpinnings of OS X came from will give you a better understanding of how OS X works. And a little knowledge of basic BSD commands will get you using the Unix environment.

Before we go to what we have today, let's look at where we've been.

History

Mac OS X owes a lot of its existence not only to BSD but also to NeXTStep.

BSD Unix, short for Berkeley Software Distribution Unix, got its start at the University of California at Berkeley. Unix itself had been invented in 1969. It didn't attract a lot of commercial interest, however, until engineers from Berkeley added code to the kernel (or the core of the operating system)that allowed it to communicate on the Internet.

Secret

A Little More In-Depth History of Unix

BSD (Unix) can be traced to a project with Bill Joy in the summer of 1976. UNIX was critical to the development of computer science in the US and the world well before the addition of the TCP stack.

Today, Unix is still evolving. An army of open-source developers are constantly adding and/or modifying the Unix code to fit in the ever-changing world of technology. Over thirty years old, Unix is one of the most stable operating systems.

Apple co-founder Steve Jobs quit Apple to co-found NeXT Computer, which focused on offering the ultimate computer for the higher educational market, but which ended up with a computer that was way too expensive for the majority of potential buyers. The first NeXT computer was a monochrome computer with no floppy drive that cost $7,000. After a year of dismal sales of its NeXT computers, the company started to focus on developing software, and changed its name from NeXT Computer to NeXT Software. In 1996, Apple Computer bought NeXT Software and asked Steve Jobs to return to Apple as CEO and chairman. Steve agreed but only on an interim basis under the title of iCEO. A few years later, he dropped the interim status and became CEO once again.

NeXT computers shipped with its own operating system called NeXTStep, which ran on the Mach kernel with a BSD interface. Offering an advanced graphical user interface (GUI), it was truly ahead of its time. Today, much of the now abandoned NeXTStep (later named OpenStep after they stopped making hardware) lives on in Mac OS X. From the similar underpinnings to the similar look and feel, Mac OS X is almost a living reincarnation of the NeXTStep OS.

Figure 31-1 presents a simplified diagram of the OS X technologies. It's easiest to compare the underlying technologies of OS X to a pie or a cake, or maybe a pie-cake. The lowest level is like the crust, not very appetizing but important nonetheless. The stuff in the middle is like the cake itself. It's more tasty than the crust (which holds it all together), And then there is the frosting, the Aqua GUI which is the really tasty part. It's what everyone sees all the time and loves.

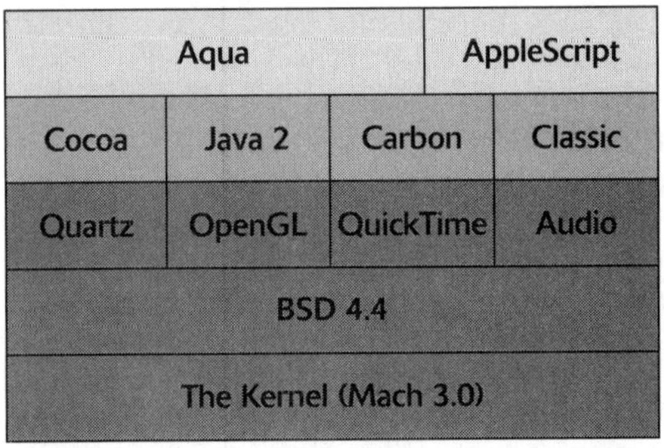

Aqua			AppleScript
Cocoa	Java 2	Carbon	Classic
Quartz	OpenGL	QuickTime	Audio
BSD 4.4			
The Kernel (Mach 3.0)			

Figure 31-1: The Mac OS X platform is made up of these different technologies.

Like NeXTStep, Mac OS X runs on the Mach 3.0 kernel, which interacts with common BSD commands. All commands interact with the kernel to some degree and through the kernel those commands interact with the hardware abstraction layer. The kernel is the core of the OS.

When Apple developed the underbelly of OS X, they modeled their BSD structure after FreeBSD, a common alternative OS. But unlike FreeBSD, Apple chose to keep the Mach 3.0 kernel, whereas FreeBSD has its own kernel.

OS X is truly a harmonious blend of technologies. It started with NeXTStep and is now the most popular version of Unix.

---

insider insight
The chief architect of FreeBSD is now a lead architect at Apple. Panther "synced" the code bases with the latest version of FreeBSD as much as possible.

But enough about history, let's dive right into the world of Unix and shine a light on this mysterious yet interesting topic.

How Not to Fear the Command Line

It seems hard to believe that using the command line could be any fun much less productive when you come from the pampered world of a graphical user interface (more commonly called a GUI, pronounced "goo-y" — say it with me, GOOO-Y). In the Unix world, your use of beautiful icons is stripped away, leaving you to depend on file suffixes. Click and dragging is no more, now you have to execute a command just to move, rename, or copy a file. Have no fear, understanding the command line is as easy as knowing that whatever you do on it, you can do also on the GUI, and vice versa. Just think of this as another way to talk to your Mac.

Understand that when you open a folder in the GUI you are executing a command. The command is saying, "I would like to move inside of this folder and see what is in it." Likewise, when you drag something from the desktop to another folder inside your home directory, you are executing another command, only this one says, "Move this file that is on the desktop and place it in that file in my home directory." This is what it is like in the command line. Instead of using your mouse, you have to rely on commands. But it is just as easy to learn a few letters that represent a command as it is to learn how to use a mouse.

A typical command structure is illustrated in Figure 31-2. The only part that is necessary is the command itself. The option, operator, and arguments are all optional. Let me explain what the command in the example does and it might make more sense. The command grep searches a given input. In Figure 31-2, the input is just the current directory. In other words, it will look at all the file and folder names and see if any of them have the word secrets and end with .txt. Those are two of the three arguments in the command structure. The last argument has to do with the operator. What the operator does is take whatever grep found and put it into a file called newfile. If newfile doesn't exist, it will make a new file and call it newfile. A *flag* or *option* will modify what a command does. Just about every command has flags. To see what they are and what they do, refer to the man pages (man grep). From this example, we can get a glimpse at the power of using the command line verses the GUI. Instead of manually looking through the, perhaps, thousands of files in a folder to find the name of a few you wanted, then create a text file and type the names of the matched files. But with Unix you did it all in a few seconds with one command.

Figure 31-2: The basic structure of a Unix command has the command itself and, optionally, an option, arguments, and operators.

The Unix file structure is a little more familiar and easier to understand. Because OS X is a true multiuser operating system, there is usually more than one user account on the computer. (Even if there is just one user that uses the computer, you should always have a second user account for troubleshooting purposes.) Think of the file structure as a large tree. The tree's trunk is the beginning, which in Unix is represented with the /. This is called the *root directory*. Everything is branched out from the root directory. For example, you're home directory is represented like this:

```
/Users/[Username]
```

The [Username] would be your name. As you can see, the *path* to your home directory started from the root directory (/). So we could say that your home directory (or home folder) is in the folder called Users that is in the root directory.

Another important feature of a multiuser operating system is permissions. Permissions allow your folders to be on the same computer as another person's folders without having to worry about the other person looking at your stuff. But user permissions on a Unix system do more than prevent unwanted people from looking at your files; they can also prevent other users from running certain programs or modifying your text files.

Permissions are set up in a way that gives users read, write, and execute permissions on every file and directory on the system. That's right. From the text file you have been working on to the picture you just imported to the application you just installed, they all have permissions. Permissions are given to three different groups of people; the owners, groups, and everyone else (also called Other by the OS X GUI). The owner is, of course, you, so you can set your own permissions. This is often handy if you don't want to edit a file, just set the permissions for that file to Read-only. In Unix, everyone is in a group. This is handy if you are working on a project with a group of friends and would like only that group of friends to be able to edit or see or just execute a file but not let anyone else be able to. The last group is for everyone. This would include anyone that logs into your computer as a guest.

Sometimes it's easiest to think of permissions of a file laid out in a chart. Figure 31-3 shows such a chart. On one side would be the modes of permissions (Read, Write, Execute) and on the other side would be who the permissions are for (User, Group, Other).

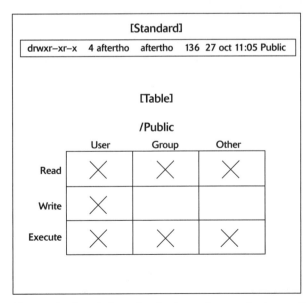

Figure 31-3: This line of code shows the standard way of showing permissions of a file (top) and the same permissions in a table for that same line of code (bottom).

The permissions given to a file (or directory) specify what you can do with it:

◆ **Read:** When a file is given this permission, the user is allowed to view the file. When Read is given to a directory, the user is allowed to view the content of the directory (but not go in it!).

◆ **Write:** Given the Write permission, a file is available to be edited, and a directory is allowed to have stuff put in it or be renamed.

◆ **Execute:** Execute permissions are given to files, but they usually only affect scripts or programs. If you give a text file Execute permission and you try to execute it, you will get an error. For a directory with Execute permission, you are allowed to go into that directory. This is different than having Read-only permission, which will allow you only to view the contents. You can also execute text files, if you make them executable , script files are text files. In Unix, all files have the potential to be executable, whether or not they contain executable commands is another matter.

Permissions shouldn't be something to worry about when you are new to Unix. But for now, be aware that everything has permissions, and that if you get a permissions error when you try to open a file, then you know that there must be something wrong with what permissions you have on that file (or in the case of an application, any associated files).

All this stuff about Unix can be a bit daunting. And, in fact, after reading this section about Unix, you will only understand a fraction of all there is to know. However, the point of this chapter isn't to teach you all there is to know about Unix, but rather to teach you how to teach yourself about Unix.

A good way to ease into using the command line is to give yourself permission to use the GUI whenever you don't feel comfortable with the command line. In fact, you are only handicapping yourself if you use just the command line or just the GUI.

Here's an example. Suppose you want to search through a folder of pictures, and that all of the filenames start with picture_ and end with .jpg and are numbered from 1 to 200. We only want a certain few of the pictures to be moved to a different folder.

In Unix we couldn't execute a command like

```
'mv picture_*.jpg /NewFolder'
```

This command would move *all* the pictures to the new folder. We want a selected few only, so we are forced to type every picture by name. Ugh! That would take too much time!

In the GUI, you could use your mouse and Shift-click on the pictures you want, then drag them over to the new folder. *Much* simpler!

You can see that in this case the command line isn't the right tool for the job. But there are times where the command line is the right tool for the job.

Most of the time, there is a way to do the same things in both the command line and the GUI. A good example is changing permissions. It is possible to change the permissions of a file in both the command line and GUI. Which is better? That's up to you. A person who knows Unix permissions well could finish ahead of a person using the GUI, yet a person who was proficient at the GUI could probably beat the Unix person. A true power user uses both.

Be Careful of Logging In as the Root User

On your road to exploring Unix, a very important hint that I would highly recommend is to *never become the root user if you don't need to be*. Hold on, I think this is so important, I'm going to say it again, *never become the root user if you don't need to be*. The root user, like the root directory is the top user. An analogy for the root user is like being the god of the computer. When you are root, you can do anything, permissions don't apply to you, you have the ultimate power to create, change, and destroy anything. Just as easy as I can make a typo, so too, could that typo easily cause major problems. So save yourself the trouble and *never become the root user if you don't need to be*.

Using the sudo Command to Avoid Logging In as the Root User

Another way of getting Root access without logging in as the Root user is to use the sudo command. Sudo allows a permitted user to act as the Root. Once a user has been authenticated, a timestamp is created and the user may then use sudo without a password for a default period of 5 minutes.

As with any new activity, practice makes perfect. A helpful tip is to keep the Terminal app in your Dock so you can open it once in a while to play around with. Jobs you know how to do well at the command line could save you time. Open it in your spare time to poke around, try new utilities, or, if you are bored enough, read the manual pages about new commands you don't yet know about. (See the next section on how to access the man pages.) Learn it at your own pace and before you know it, Unix will be just another everyday experience on your Macintosh.

Controlling Your Mac via Unix

Everyone should know how to be able to move around comfortably in any operating system, so we'll talk about how to do things in Unix that you already do everyday in the GUI. By the end of this section, you should be able to move around, make new folders and rename them, know how to delete files and folders, and finally know how to open and close an application. All this, without touching the mouse. . . .

> **tip** Just about every Unix command can be looked up to see what it does and how it should be used. You can find this information in what's commonly called the *man pages*. man is a command. It stands for manual and is used just like any other command. Just type **man**, then the *argument,* which, in this case, is the command name that you want to learn about, and press Enter. This can be used to look up any command mentioned in the book. Heck, even the man command has a man page (shown in Figure 31-4). A word of caution: the man pages are most often written by the programmers themselves and are often very dry to read. Still, they are helpful when you are stuck with an unfamiliar command.

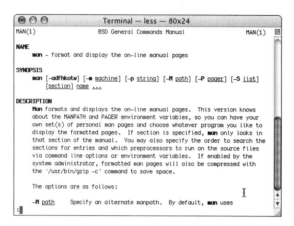

Figure 31-4: Terminal application showing a man page for the man command.

Listing the Contents of a Folder

The ls command *lists* what is inside of a directory. A cool feature of the ls command is that you don't even need to be inside of a folder to see what is in it (as shown in Figure 31-5 and in Figure 31-6).

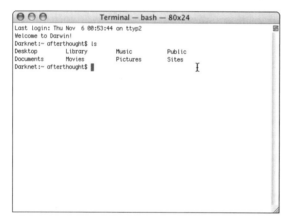

Figure 31-5: A screen shot of the ls command in action. When used in this example, it shows what is inside the current directory, which happens to be a home directory.

The ls command has many options that can be appended onto it. To see them all, refer to the man pages.

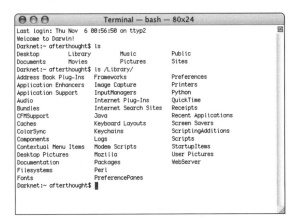

Figure 31-6: Using the ls command, you can list what is inside of a directory that you are not currently in. Even though I'm still in my home directory, I can list what is in the Library folder.

Changing Directories

The cd command is what you use to change directories. A directory is another name for folder. When you change directories, you can choose to type out the full path or the relative path. The full path would be the path where the directory is located starting with the root (/) directory. The relative path is like a shortcut. If you are already in your home directory and you would like to cd to your Pictures folder you would only have to type cd /Pictures, however typing cd /Users/[Username]/Pictures would work, too when [username] is your username (shown in Figure 31-7).

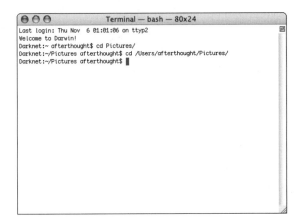

Figure 31-7: The cd command in action. Shown here is an example of using cd with the full path and relative path.

cd doesn't have a man page because it doesn't have any special options that go with it.

Creating a New Folder

Suppose you want to make a new folder. To do that you would use the mkdir command. This stands for *make directory*. To use this command you simply type mkdir, then the name you would like for the folder.

Unix is Case Sensitive

Names in Unix are case sensitive and don't use spaces like you normally do in the GUI. The names Pictures, pictures, and PictureS would represent three different folders. Also, if you have a folder called My Documents you would need to type it as My\ Documents. The backward slash is what's called an escape character. If this wasn't used, Unix would think you were trying to say something else to it after you named your folder My (shown in Figure 31-8).

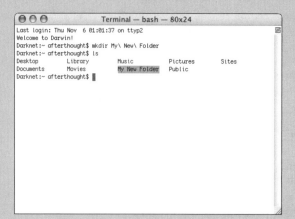

Figure 31-8: To make a new folder, use the mkdir command. Here mkdir is being used to create a new folder called My New Folder. Notice the use of the escape character that allows the use of a space in the naming of a new folder.

The mkdir command has a few different options but nothing that is of dire importance. Still, it's good to read what options you do have.

Renaming or Moving a Folder or File

Now that you have new folder called My New Folder, suppose you want to rename it something else, like My Old Folder. To do this, simply use the mv command. Now wait a minute, what does mv stand for? It actually stands for *move*. The mv command is actually two commands in one, which makes a lot of sense when you think about it. By *moving* a file into the *same* directory you are already in, you have the opportunity to call it something else in the process! Simply type mv, then the name of the file you want to rename, then the new name separated by a space! It's that easy(shown in Figure 31-9).

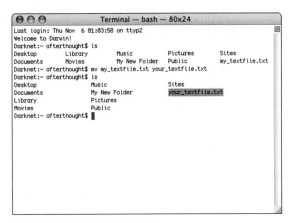

Figure 31-9: Renaming a file with mkdir; in this case my_textfile.txt is renamed your_textfile.txt.

To actually move a file is just as easy—this time you move it to a *different* directory. Type mv, then the name of the file (assuming you are in the same directory the file is already in), and then the path to where you want it moved. Again, the path can be relative or the full path(shown in Figure 31-10).

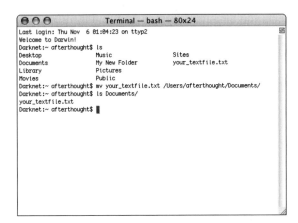

Figure 31-10: The mv command used to move the file your_textfile.txt to the Documents folder using the full path.

The man pages have a few extra options that could be used, but they are not used very often.

Secret

Using the Interactive Option to Avoid Mistakes

Always remember that whatever you delete in Unix is gone for good. This includes overwriting a file or folder. Unix can be fun, but you have to play by its rules. That's why when you are moving a file or folder you might want to use the -i (which stand for interactive) option. This will make Terminal display a message asking if you would like to overwrite the file or directory. Either check before you move anything or get into the habit of using -i with the mv command because Unix is never forgiving when it comes to deleting files.

Removing Directories or Files

Back to the folder you created with the mkdir command. To get rid of it, use the rm command. This of course stands for *remove* and can be used to remove files or directories. Rmdir is a variant of this command that allows you to delete directories just like rm –dr does.

The rm command is used much in the same way as all our other commands. To remove a file you would type rm, then the name of the file or directory. However, if it is a directory, you will want to use the -d option to indicate that it's a directory. But it won't delete a folder that is full, so you will want to use the -r option to delete anything inside the folder. See Figure 31-11.

tip When using more than one option, you can often combine the two options after one hyphen, like rm -dr [filenamefile].

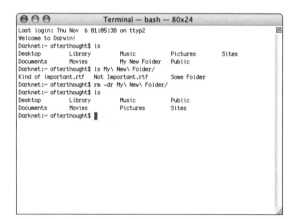

Figure 31-11: The figure shows the rm command and the -dr options hard at work.

The rm command has many important options in the man page. One such example is the use of -i, which displays a message before it deletes something, much the way the GUI does when emptying the Trash. Without it, the rm command would silently delete everything you asked it to.

Copying Files

The cp command takes care of your copying needs. If you hadn't guessed already cp is short for *copy* and is, again, used much the same way as mv or rm. Type cp, then the name of the file you want to copy, press space, then the name you want to call this copy. Like the mv command, you can also copy the file to a different folder in the same step. This is illustrated in Figure 31-12.

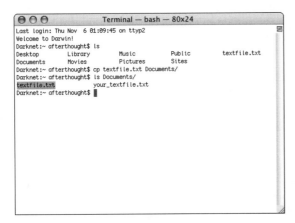

Figure 31-12: Copying files is pretty easy; the only hard part is to know where you want to copy them to!

Again, note that the cp command has many options that you can explore in the man pages. Probably the option you'll want to use the most is the -i option. This will make the Terminal display a message if it's going to overwrite a file if you name the new one the same as a file that already exists.

Opening an Application

Besides handling files and folders, you can start up applications from the Terminal instead of double-clicking on them in the GUI. You accomplish this with the open command. (Wow . . . you thought it was going to be another abbreviation, didn't you?) To do this, type open, then the application or the path to the application. For example, type open /Applications/iTunes.app and viola! iTunes opens in the GUI (shown in Figure 31-13).

open also opens any documents with their default application. For example, opening a Word file (with the .doc suffix) will start Microsoft Word if it's installed.

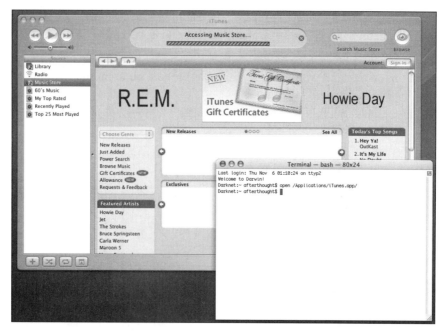

Figure 31-13: Our freshly opened iTunes application and the Terminal window showing the evidence of being the one that opened it.

Seeing What Applications Are Running

Now that you have an application running, you can look at how much RAM it is using and what percentage of the processor it is taking up. To do this, run a program in Terminal called top. Type `top`, then press Enter (as shown in Figure 31-14).

```
●○○            Terminal — top — 80x24
Processes: 67 total, 2 running, 65 sleeping... 172 threads        01:13:20
Load Avg: 0.57, 0.71, 0.74    CPU usage: 24.8% user, 26.4% sys, 48.8% idle
SharedLibs: num = 116, resident = 30.8M code, 3.03M data, 6.66M LinkEdit
MemRegions: num = 9573, resident = 217M + 20.3M private,  151M shared
PhysMem: 76.0M wired,  360M active,  189M inactive,  625M used, 14.4M free
VM: 5.63G + 82.9M   54002(0) pageins, 19090(0) pageouts

  PID COMMAND      %CPU   TIME   #TH #PRTS #MREGS  RPRVT  RSHRD  RSIZE  VSIZE
 1015 top         16.8%  0:02.00   1    16     26   336K   384K  1.79M  27.1M
 1014 bash         0.0%  0:00.02   1    12     15   132K   832K   752K  18.2M
 1013 login        0.0%  0:00.03   1    13     37   144K   376K   504K  26.9M
 1011 fix_prebin   0.0%  0:00.08   1    27     30   356K   656K  1.18M  27.4M
 1010 iTunes       0.7%  0:10.74   5   310    222  9.81M 17.0M+ 31.0M-  170M
  990 AppleSpell   0.0%  0:00.06   1    24     31   452K  1.15M  3.94M  35.8M
  941 Preview      0.0%  0:04.46   1    59    127  1.46M 12.1M+ 20.0M   144M
  915 Terminal     2.2%  0:13.02   4    88    160  2.17M+ 9.01M+17.7M-  143M
  914 SystemUISe   0.0%  0:02.30   1   270    226  1.57M  8.76M+ 6.28M+  142M
  911 Snapz Pro    0.0%  0:28.05   5   226    177  19.3M  19.7M  34.1M   186M
  908 Finder       2.2%  0:14.36   2   105    239  7.82M  20.9M  35.1M   187M
  906 Dock         0.0%  0:02.54   2    84    115   632K 12.7M+ 7.66M-  134M
  902 pbs          0.0%  0:00.43   2    32     41   604K  1.51M  4.84M  44.3M
  897 ATSServer    0.0%  0:01.33   2    51    129  1.17M  6.07M  4.09M  54.1M
  896 loginwindo   0.0%  0:01.75   4   241    154  1.77M  5.61M  5.84M   126M
  890 Preview      0.0%  0:01.45   1    64    165  3.33M  11.3M  8.01M   157M
```

Figure 31-14: Shown here is top running in Terminal; the application iTunes is open.

But what is all that stuff shown? Most of it will not be important to the new Unix user. However, a few things will be important to you. For example, top reveals the PID (Process ID) number of the applications that are open. Every open application receives a number that identifies it. There is a lot to learn about the top application that won't probably ever concern you, much of it having to do with nit-picky system performance; but top can be helpful if a program is misbehaving or being a processor hog. A good source for more information is, of course, the man pages.

Closing an Application

To close a running application, use the kill command. But there's a twist: you can't just type `kill iTunes.app` like you did to open it. This is where knowing the PID (Process ID) number comes in handy, because typing `kill`, then the PID number will shut down the application quicker than you can say, "I should save this. . . ."

Be advised that killing applications that are needed by the system in top could damage the system. The rule of thumb is, don't kill what you didn't start.

Secret

Using the Terminal to "Kill" an Application or Process

Let's say that an application is being really pesky and will not quit. For whatever the reason, it's the only application that you get the colorful spinning ball. You try killing the application with the kill command but it is still not quitting. Try kill –9 PID number. This will tell the application to immediately drop what it's doing and shut down. This isn't the best way to shut down an application but it can be used as a last resort.

Consult the man pages for a full list of everything you can do with the kill command. You wouldn't believe the many ways of killing an application!

Unix Secrets for the Rest of Us

If you want to use Unix and the Terminal application but don't want to be a Unix guru, you'll want to read the next section. Here we're going to go through some of the rules and processes that will get you going right away.

Enable the Root User

The root user is the most powerful user on the system. Root has the power to create, modify, or destroy anything. It's no wonder that Apple, by default, disables the root account. Typing su (which stands for *su*per user) and a password won't work. Instead, you have to enable a root user in the NetInfo Manager application, which is located in the Utilities folder.

In the NetInfo Manager application (after you enable root user) under the Security menu, pull down to Authenticate. After you supply an administrator username and password, you can go to Enable Root User, also on the Security menu (See Figure 31-15).

The OS asks you for a new password for the root account if this is your first time enabling root. After that, you're set! Now make sure you understand the dangers of being root (see the Secret earlier in this chapter about using the sudo option), and consider this your first, second, and final warning. Go back to Terminal and type in su , press Enter, and then supply the password you chose for the root account. Congratulations! You are now the root user. To exit from the root user just type exit and you are back to your old self again.

Figure 31-15: Here is where you enable the root user account.

Thinking Ahead and Using the Developer Tools

The Developer Tools, if installed, will solve a lot of problems as you journey forward in the Unix world. But Apple didn't preinstall the Developer Tools because the average user isn't going to be programming their own programs.

What problems you might ask? In the world of Unix, applications aren't installed with the ease of an installer. Usually, they come off the Internet as source code, or the raw files that contain the actual code that was written by the programming. Such code needs to be compiled before you are able to run it. The developer tools install the necessary compilers needed to compile most of the Unix programs you will install.

Cron Stands for Chronological

Most users don't know it but when they go to bed at night and leave their computer on, the computer is hard at work cleaning itself up. The scripts are scheduled by the cron daemon. A daemon is a program that runs in the background usually doing nothing until it is needed. Web server software like Apache is one example of this kind of program.

There are three cron scripts that OS X runs. On is run daily at 3:15 AM, another is run weekly at 4:30 AM on Saturdays, and the last is run once a month at 5:30 AM on the first day of the month. They do things like empty different cache files and correct any permissions problems. However, your computer must be *on* and not asleep to have these cron scripts run.

Secret

Using Third-Party Utilities to Run Cron Scripts

One great shareware utility to manually run the cron scripts is called Cocktail. Cocktail (available at http://www.macosxcocktail.com/) by Kristofer Szymanski. This handy utility can be used for those people who shut their computers down at night, and therefore don't give their computers the opportunity to run the Cron scripts.

This gem of a program will do everything from choosing a different start-up language to deleting files that you just can't get rid of. Lucky you, it's even a GUI application!

Retrieving a Lost Password

Get ready because we are reaching deep down into the depths of our knowledge of Unix and pulling out the big guns. This section will show you how to retrieve an encrypted OS X password, yes, even the root password.

What this will require is a fairly intermediate knowledge of Unix and a program called John the Ripper.

This could be used for invading the privacy of others. Passwords are there for a reason. We are providing this information for your own use on your own computer(s) in case you need to retrieve your own lost password.

We do not advocate or intend for this material to be used for anything illegal or unethical. In other words, *do not* mess around with this on someone else's computer just because you now know how. (Don't make me come over to your house!)

Let me lay out the story. You followed my tip above and enabled the root user account and gave it a password that you would never forget, only a week later you forget the password. Sure, you could start up off of the boot CD and reset the password, but it's bugging you to high heavens that you can't remember the password you said you wouldn't forget. Not willing to admit defeat, you roll up your sleeves and get ready to hack . . . yourself.

First, you need to have John the Ripper installed. When you get that installed, you need to get the encrypted password file off the system. All the user accounts and passwords are in the NetInfo Manager.

You want NetInfo Manager to give you all the user accounts and passwords that are on the system and put them into a file. To do this, execute the following command in the Terminal application:

```
nidump passwd . > ~/Desktop/passwordfile.txt
```

nidump is a command that spits out something from the NetInfo database. In this case, you told it to give us the password files, and the period means all of them. You also told it to pass whatever is spit out into a new file called passwordfile.txt placed on your desktop (see Figure 31-16).

Figure 31-16: You can see the encrypted password of the root account highlighted here.

Now move the password file into the John the Ripper directory. After that's done, switch back to the Terminal application and type `./john incremental:all passwordfile.txt`. The `./` tells the program to run. `incremental:all` is an option in John the Ripper that directs it to try its best to crack the password, and `passwordfile.txt` is the password file you got from nidump. Now the hardest part of all. You wait. You wait until it pops up with the user name and password of anything it was able to crack.

Understand that if you have a complicated password that involves number and letters and symbols it could take forever to crack, so be patient.

Introduction to X11

In the world of Unix, there are programs that have windows and buttons and menus. But to display all that, you need a *window manager* to interpret the code so that you are able to use your mouse to click and drag on things. Enter X11. Apple's X11 is the answer to the final piece of the Unix puzzle. With this, you can run true Unix applications on your Mac along side your native Cocoa applications. We'll look at how you can easily download and install these free Unix applications and identify which ones are worth looking at!

Getting Started

Leave it to Apple to decide that the average user won't want to run Unix applications. Well you aren't an average user anymore. You demand free applications and the ability to run them! Good! But first, you'll need to install X11 because, while Apple provides it, they don't install it for you. No bother, it should be on the third install disk of Mac OS X 10.3 Panther or on your system restore disk if your computer happens to be new enough. If none of these apply to you, you can always download it from the Apple site (`http://www.apple.com/macosx/features/x11/download/`). When it's installed, start it up! Don't be surprised if you seem a little disappointed. It looks a lot like the Terminal at first (see Figure 31-17), and that's because it is.

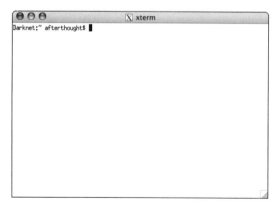

Figure 31-17: A view of X11 after you start it up. Nothing impressive — yet.

Fink to the Rescue!

So, now that you have your new X11 Window Manager, you can play with some free Unix applications! Here is a tip that will save you time and literally put thousands of applications at your fingertips: install Fink. Fink is a *package manager* utility, a program that assists you in downloading other programs that have been ported over to the Darwin (OS X) system. Currently Fink is at version 0.6.2. Download and install Fink by the instructions on Apple's Web site.

The most current version of Fink can be downloaded from that Apple Web site at
`http://www.apple.com/downloads/macosx/unix_open_source/fink.html`,
where you can also see some additional information about the application itself.

After you have done that, you simply type `fink list` in Terminal and hundreds of applications will stream across your Terminal window (see Figure 31-18). If you find one you want just type `fink install [app name]` where `[app name]` is the name of the application you would like to install. It's that easy. When it's finished close your Terminal window, open a new one, and type the name of the application you just installed!

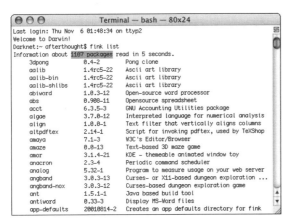

Figure 31-18: Fink gives you the opportunity to install hundreds of free applications.

Secret

The Etymology of Fink

The names of Unix programs can be odd, but usually have some sort of explanation behind them to justify their eccentricities. You'd think a program named Fink would be a marketer's nightmare, but the program that brings open-source Unix programs to the Mac OS is actually named from the German word for "finch," which is the kind of bird Charles Darwin studied on the Galapagos Islands and used to assert his theory of evolution. And as many of you know already, Darwin is the name of the kernel on which OS X is based. So, in a roundabout way, it makes sense, right?

A Few Recommendations . . .

The vastness of Fink can be a bit overwhelming, but here are a few recommendations of applications to use:

◆ **XMMS:** This is a great mp3 and audio player that is highly *skinable* (meaning you can make it look different). It's much like Window's own WinAmp.

◆ **KDE/Gnome:** Two of the best desktop environments in the Unix world. These two offer beautiful interfaces second only to OS X's own Aqua interface.

◆ **OpenOffice.org:** The king of all open source apps, this is your answer to a free version of Microsoft Office (see Figure 31-19). While not as chock-full of features, it will open and write Word documents. It also has programs much like PowerPoint and Excel. This is worth checking out.

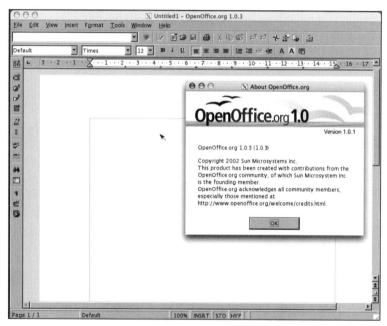

Figure 31-19: OpenOffice.org running on OS X. OpenOffice is a free alternative to Microsoft Office.

With the dream-team combination of X11 and Fink you have opened up a whole new arena of opportunity for your computer pleasure.

Summary

With luck, you aren't afraid of Terminal anymore and you are on the path to becoming a true Unix geek. (Just kidding.)

We've gone through some of the more simple commands via Terminal as well as a sophisticated series of commands to retrieve a lost password.

And I hope I've encouraged you to try X11 and Fink.

If nothing else, you get the idea that Terminal is another way (sometimes better and sometime worse) to talk to your Mac.

Troubleshooting

◆ ◆

Secrets in This Chapter

◆ ◆

Writing about troubleshooting your Mac always seems to feel like a compromise. We strut and tout the stability and the ease of use of our superior platform to our PC friends. We use phrases like "it just works" and "true plug-and-play" in earnest.

How many times have you been sitting with friends and have heard the latest office horror stories about the new runaway virus or blue screen of death? How many times have you sat smugly in a corner and, when asked about your own terrible technology trials, smiled and said simply . . . "I'm on a Mac!" (And if you haven't done this, you're missing out on one of the best reason's to own a Mac.)

The argument can be made that compared to the world of the PC; we are a lot more secure and stable. And so maybe we have the right to strut (a little) for our choice in this superior platform. But just between us — in the pages of this book, where no PC people will over hear us — we should talk about what to do when our stable, true plug-and-play computer *just doesn't work!*

Understanding the Problem

The Mac has changed a lot in the past couple of years. OS X (in any form) has presented new levels of stability and new challenges when that stability isn't working well.

Sometimes you don't know what the problem is. You just know that your computer isn't working well. And when that's the case, you either have to fix it yourself or find someone to pay to fix it. And so, the *real* first problem you have it to determine if you can handle fixing this on your own.

Before you get into the nuts and bolts of troubleshooting your OS, you need to look at this problem. If the difficulty is a software issue, then properly outfitted with the right software, hardware, and knowledge, you can probably take care of your own problems. If the difficulty is a hardware issue, you may be better off taking your sick Mac to certified technician and saving yourself the heartache.

Since about 80 percent of things that go wrong with a computer tend to be software related, most of this chapter covers strategies for these problems. But it's also worth covering the quickest ways to first determine if what you are dealing with is a hardware issue first.

Hardware Problem Test

Hardware problems can be anything from a kernel panic, a frozen start-up screen, a blinking folder with a question mark, or just a blank screen.

Some hardware problems are "easy." Your computer won't start up or you hear a nasty grinding sound. When these kinds of things happen, you know that it's time to take your computer into your service provider and check your backups.

But there are also less apparent kinds of hardware problems These kinds of hardware problems can drive you crazy. especially if they are intermittent or not consistent. Some of these kinds of hardware problems can act just like some software problems.

These are the kinds of problems that we need to look at. We need to determine if the problem you're dealing with is something that you can fix or not. This section will give you some simple things that you can try to determine if you are having a hardware problem.

Try the following steps in the order listed:

1. Make sure your computer and/or monitor are plugged into a good power source. I know this sounds like a silly thing to check, but it happens to the best of us.

2. Unplug all of your peripheral devices (printers, external drives, etc.) and restart your computer. If that fixed it, plug in one at a time until you determine which is the offending device. If you have older external ADB, Serial, and/or SCSI devices you will want to shut the computer and the device down between plugging those devices in and out of the computer to avoid damage to your computer.

3. If you are on a PowerBook or a tower, and your screen is completely blank, you should try a different monitor. It could be that your computer is working just fine. In the case of the PowerBook, if you find that an external monitor fixes the problem, then you will have to get your PowerBook into a certified repair shop to fix or replace the screen. In the case of the tower, you may need a new display.

4. Restart you Mac while holding down the Option key. This will bring your Mac up into the Boot screen. On this screen, you will see bootable volumes. If you see your HD on this screen, click on it and then click on the arrow on the right of the screen. If you have more than one bootable volume, try them all. If you don't see your HD on this screen, that doesn't mean that you've lost all of your data (yet). It just means that the computer doesn't recognize a valid system folder or that the drive is bootable.

5. The next step is to try to boot your computer from another source. Find the first (if there are more than one) installation CD or DVD that came with your computer, a new copy of a third-party disk repair utility on CD, or your new copy of Panther. To boot from a CD, place the CD in the computer and then restart holding the C key down. If this doesn't work, then try restarting your computer and holding the Option key down. If nothing has worked thus far, you're now starting to run out of possibilities.

6. If you use a third-party disk repair program on CD, *don't immediately run the program as soon as you have your computer up.* Running a disk recovery program can have some negative repercussions that I describe later. If you can see your HD and all of your data while your computer is booted from the CD, then you probably do not have a hardware problem. Skip ahead to the next section.

Secret

Why You Don't Need to Install Some Disk Utilities

Copies of third-party disk utilities like Norton Utilities, TechTool, Disk Warrior, and so on allow for the installation of the program on your computer. But you don't need to install them on your computer to get real value out of them. From my own experience, I always encourage my customer to save their hard-drive space and not install them.

These kinds of programs have real value because you can run them from a bootable CD. If you can't boot your current computer (holding down the C key) from your copy of one of these programs, then go get a new updated version of the CD today! And keep it close to your computer in case something terrible happens.

Do not download the update from the Web and then update your installed version of the program. That won't help you a whole lot if your updated disk repair program is on the volume (hard drive) that you need to recover with it.

If your disk repair CD comes with an antivirus program, that's okay to install and keep updated from the manufacturer's Web site.

7. If you can boot from a system install CD, then launch the Disk Utility from under the File menu. Don't format, erase, or partition anything. Just use the utility to see if the boot hard drive present. If there is, then you probably have a software problem. If there isn't, then you probably have a hardware problem.

8. The last thing that you can do, without cracking the case of your computer, is to see if you can see your computer's HD from another computer. To do this your computer must have a native FireWire (400 or 800) port. Hook your computer to another computer (with a native FireWire 400 port) and restart your computer while holding down the T key. If the screen is working at all and your HD is working, then you will have a blue screen show up with bouncing FireWire logo (as shown in Figure 32-1). Your Mac should come up as a mounted FireWire volume on the other Mac. You can restart the other Mac to make sure that it mounts. *If it does mount, you should take the opportunity to copy all of the data off before you do anything else.*

Figure 32-1: The blue screen and bouncing FireWire logo indicate that the computer has been started up in FireWire Target Disk Mode.

Secret

Duplicating the User with Target Disk Mode to Access User Files

If you find that you can see your computer mounted on the desktop of the new computer, but can't determine if there is anything in your user folder because it's locked (shown in Figure 32-2) you can get by that problem by fooling the other computer that you are the main user on your computer.

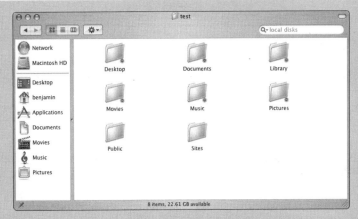

Figure 32-2: You might find the folders in the user folder locked with the permissions of the computer that is accessing the original computer in Target Disk Mode.

Create a new user on the other computer using your name, short username, and password (shown in Figure 32-3). Make sure you give administrative privileges to this user (as shown in Figure 32-4). Log out of the current user and log back in as your username.

Figure 32-3: Create a user that matches the user on the Target Disk computer.

continues

continued

Figure 32-4: You also need to let this duplicated user on the other computer have Administrative privileges.

You will probably find that you have complete access to all of your user folder directories.

If you have encrypted the files or have used FileVault in Panther, then this will not work well for you at all unless you have the encrypted files passwords and/or the Master Passwords for both users are set the same.

In addition to following the listed guidelines, it's also important to use your head. If you have just purchased new RAM or a new peripheral for your Mac and now your Mac isn't working well, you should start with what has changed recently. In the case of bad RAM or new cards (for example, PCI, PCI-X, AGP, PCMCIA, etc. . . .), you will have to open up your Mac and take them out. My suggestion is that if you didn't install those components in your Mac yourself, that you get the person who did to take them out.

If any of these procedures lead you to believe that your problem is software related rather than hardware related, move on to the next section of this chapter.

If none of these procedures yield any positive results for you, then you may be in over your head. Logic boards go out and hard drives die. It's a sad, cold reality of technology. You should never think in terms of "if my hard drive dies," but rather "when my hard drive dies."

When something like that happens, there are people out there that can help. That's what Macintosh certified technicians are for. If you don't have a relationship with one, then start one today!

Getting Your Computer to Boot Up

You've determined that the problems you are having are related to software and not hardware. You've eliminated peripherals and you're ready to start troubleshooting your problems. Right?

Wrong! First things first . . . have you gotten yourself to the point where you can make a back up of your data? If you are fortunate enough to be able to see your HD (in any form) and the data is all still there, then you have been given a small reprieve by the techno spirits. Don't waste it.

Now is the time to make sure you have a copy of everything before you start messing around with your OS. If you haven't got a backup system in place, then skip ahead to the last few sections of this chapter and read up on how to make a backup of your data. Then back up your HD! Now! Please do not proceed with any further troubleshooting your OS without this backup!

I'll wait while you do that. (Time passes. . . .)

Welcome back. Now that you've made yourself a good (as good at you could) backup of all of your data, you're ready to start working on fixing your software problems.

Assume that you can't boot up your system even in Safe mode (holding the Shift key down on startup), that you have a complete backup, and that you have verified that your data is still there. (You could also assume that you don't have access to any of these things and have no other options and nothing to lose, but that's a little negative to start out a troubleshooting session.)

> **note**
>
> Safe mode (sometimes calle Safe Boot) might be something that you haven't heard of before. In Safe Mode, only required items in the **Startup Items** and **Extensions** folders are loaded. This is very much like booting with "Extension Off" in Classic.
>
> And just like in the Classic version of this feature, some OS features or applications may not work in Safe Mode. Startup may also take longer than usual.
>
> This is not a regular working mode for your computer. You usually only use Safe Mode if you need to troubleshoot a problem and you can't start your computer up in any other way.

Situation

The hard drive will not come up. There is either a kernel panic on the screen, the screen is lit with nothing on it, the large Apple is on the screen and the round disk has been spinning for an hour, or there is a folder with a question mark on it.

Solution 1

Restore from a backup of the entire HD made just minutes before you had a system problem. (Just kidding.)

Since Solution 1 is not likely, proceed to Solution 2.

Solution 2

Put your utility CD/DVD (not an restore or installation CD/DVD) in the computer and boot (hold down the C key on restart) from a current copy of a disk repair utility like Norton Utilities. Then run the utility. If errors were found, then correct them if possible and restart. If you are unsure about how to restart on the appropriate startup volume, then hold down the Option key on the restart and select the correct volume on the Open Firmware screen.

Solution 3

If Solution 2 did not fix your problem, you need to move to this step. You'll need to reinstall the OS over the old one. To do this, find your most recent OS CDs. If you are reading this, it should be your Panther CDs or your computer's installation CD/DVD — whichever has the higher version of the OS on it. Proceed to Solution 3.

Put yourDisk 1 (of Panther) or your Restore CD/DVD in the computer and boot (hold down the C key on restart) from that CD/DVD. Then follow these steps:

1. When the installation window comes up, click on the Continue button (and agree to the licensing agreement) until you come to the Select a Destination screen.
2. Click on the volume where you want to reinstall the OS on top of the corrupt OS on your HD.
3. Then, before you click on the Continue button, click on the Options button.
4. This brings up a window with three choices. Choose the second one, Archive and Install. Also, make sure that you select Preserve Users and Network Settings with the appropriate check box (see Figure 32-5).

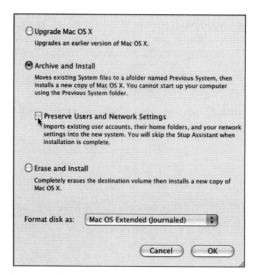

Figure 32-5: Choosing the Archive and Install option and then checking the Preserve Users and Network Settings option (as opposed to not choosing to preserve Users and Network Settings) will help make the software restoration less abrupt or invasive from the user standpoint.

5. Click OK.
6. Click the Continue button one more time and then the Install button to start the process.
7. When the installation is complete, restart your computer to see if you have retained your documents and settings.

When this is done, you may find that you will have to reenter some serial numbers and/or reinstall some applications. You may also need to use the software update to get your OS back up to the most recent version.

You also may find that now that you have a good working OS that you can move your home folder from your backup back into the Users folder — if you are missing a great deal of documents or settings from your restored home Users folder.

If you've gone through to Solution 3 and this didn't work — in other words you computer will not take an installation of the OS again, then you need to seek out professional help from someone like an Apple certified technician.

Troubleshooting Application Problems

In the days before OS X, you often had to combat extension and control-panel conflicts. Turning extensions on and off in the Extension Manager or starting up with extensions off. Now issues are frequently centered on permissions, preference corruption, and application-enhancer incompatibilities.

Situation

Every time you launch a certain application, it just quits. This kind of problem can extend to printers failing or applications quitting when documents are printed, as well as problems sharing or moving files.

Solution 1

Shut down your computer and restart it again. If you have an application problem that has happened just once, then you should see if it goes away or is corrected by a shutdown and restart.

Secret

Shutting Down Your Computer Every so Often Is a Good Idea

Shutting down your computer and then restarting it, as opposed to just restarting the computer, allows the Mac OS to perform additional hardware checks that it would not otherwise get from a restart.

If you don't usually shut your computer down, it's a good idea to do so every so often.

Solution 2

Check your crash log. This can give you valuable information about what the cause of the problem may be. The quickest way that I have found to look at a crash log is to open the Console program in the Utilities folder (located in the Startup Volume/Applications/Utilities directory) and select crash log from under the CrashReporter submenu under the /Library/Logs submenu under the Open Quickly submenu under the File menu (shown in Figure 32-6).

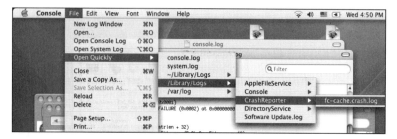

Figure 32-6: Choosing the crash log (for the application that just crashed) will allow you to see what has happened — and possibly why.

You can more easily navigate through all the logs by clicking on the Logs icon on the tool-bar of the Console Log (shown in Figure 32-7). This will show a hierarchical list of all of the logs.

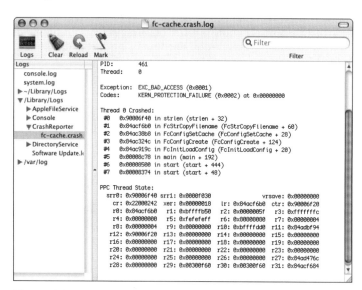

Figure 32-7: Clicking on the Logs icon allows easy access to all of the logs including the crash log.

Solution 3

Run Apple's Disk Utility (located in the Startup Volume/Applications/Utilities directory). By clicking on the startup volume, you can choose Verify Disk Permissions and Repair Disk Permissions (shown in Figure 32-8). Doing this every so often should be part of your maintenance regime.

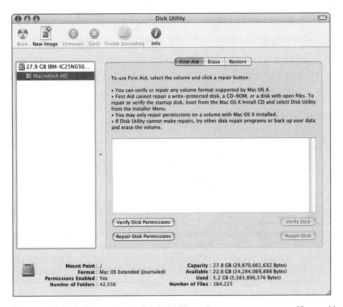

Figure 32-8: The Apple Disk Utility allows a user to verify and/or repair disk permissions on the startup volume.

Solution 4

Check your Activity Monitor (located in the Startup Volume/Applications/Utilities directory). This application (shown in Figure 32-9) allows you to see any processes or services that are running in the background that you may not want running. By double-clicking on the process, you can choose to sample (or take a more in-depth look at) or quit that process.

Some trial-and-error, good detective work, and this utility may help you figure out what the problem is.

> **caution** When "killing" processes, you must be careful. Killing the wrong process can leave your Mac in an unstable state. This kind of mistake is very common to people who aren't familiar with this Unix processes.

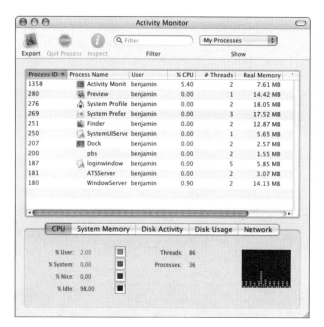

Figure 32-9: The Activity Monitor application shows you what is running that could be causing OS problems.

Solution 5

Find and remove the offending preference file. If you're running something like Suitcase, for instance and you find that it is quitting or not working well, you can easily find all of the preference files for Suitcase and delete them. This can lead to the loss of preference information and/or reinstallation of the program, so you should make sure you have a current backup of your user folder preferences and/or your system preferences before you start out on this route of troubleshooting.

As a rule, most user-specific preference preferences are kept in the Preferences folder in the Library folder, in the home folder.

Using Multiple Users to Find Problems

This is as good a place as any to give you my best secret for diagnosing your system.

One of the big problems for a Mac OS X user is determining where the problem is. There are four different places where fonts go. There are numerous Library folders and Preference folders. How are you supposed to know where the problem is?

The answer is the Test account.

Go into your System Preferences and add a new account called Test in the new Accounts panel (shown in Figure 32-10). Go to the Security tab and select Allow user to administer this computer (shown in Figure 32-11).

Figure 32-10: Create a test or control account by clicking on the Accounts icon in the System Preferences and then clicking on the Add button below the Login Options.

Figure 32-11: Make sure that you give the test or control account administrative privileges under the Security section of the Accounts preferences.

continues

continued

The next thing you need to do in this account is to log out of your current account and log into the Test account to make sure that you can.

After that, it's important that you do *nothing* to this account. Don't install new software. Don't set up new prefs. This is now your *control* on the experiment you call your computer.

If you find that something isn't working and you want to know if it's an overall system problem or a user-specific problem, log out of your account and into the Test account and try it. If the test account experiences the same problem, then the problem is system-wide. If the test account can do what your user account cannot, then go looking for the culprit within your home folder.

Solution 6

Check your application enhancers (third party "add-ins" or haxies you install into your OS) and background applications.

If you do determine that your problems are user-specific, make sure that you aren't running anything in the background that's old or conflicting with your version of the OS.

If you don't know and want to see if you are running anything that might be a problem, go back to the Activity Monitor (Startup Disk/Applications/Utilities). And look at the processes. A system free of background applications should look a lot like the one in Figure 32-9.

You should also check for application enhancers and haxies. These can usually be located on the bottom panel of the System Preferences window. Figure 32-12 shows the standard panels in System Preferences. The System Preferences window in Figure 32-13 shows that has a lot of things have been added that may or may not be causing problems. When diagnosing problems, these should be suspect.

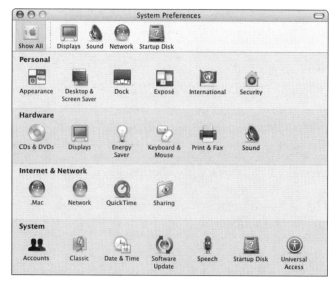

Figure 32-12: This is how your computer's panels in System Preferences look right after a clean installation.

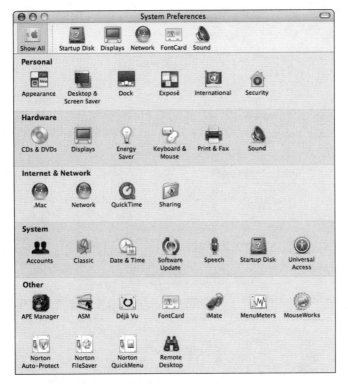

Figure 32-13: This is how the System Preferences window looks after application enhancers and haxies have been installed.

To remove some of these extra things, drag them out of the PreferencePanes folder (shown in Figure 32-14) in the Library folder in the Users folder (Home/Library/PreferencePanes).

Some of these may need to be uninstalled. Find the original installer and see if there is an Uninstall option when you launch the installer.

After you remove these, try restarting.

You should also check the other background applications that are running. Basically, any extra menu or application not provided by Apple should be suspect. To quickly test these, launch System Preferences and click on the Accounts icon. Click on the account you are in and then select the Startup Items button.

Here you will find a list of applications and extra (or background) services (shown in Figure 32-15) that the OS is launching for your account every time you start up. Try unchecking each one of them one at a time, logging out and logging back in to see if any of these are the culprit.

Figure 32-14: Some Application enhancers may reside in a folder in the user's Library called PreferencePanes.

Figure 32-15: The startup items for each account can be added or removed using the Add and Remove buttons below the listed items.

Secret

Take Some Screen Shots of Your Settings for Reference

As you change your settings, remove preference panels, and remove login items you may find it useful to keep track of what you've done so you can restore these items when you find the problem(s). A good method for doing that is to keep a log of your problems and to print out screen shots as you work on that log.

To make a screen shot of a specific window, type Command + Shift + 3. This will take a picture of your entire screen. To take a screen shot of a specific window, type Command + Shift + 4. This will turn your cursor into a crosshair. Click and drag it over the item(s) that you want to capture and then release.

The screen shots are saved to your desktop in PDF format. Make sure you open them up, crop what you don't need, and then print them out. Hard copy is necessary. Digital screen shots stored on your HD won't help you at all if your computer won't start up.

In Defense of Application Enhancers and Haxies

Application enhancers, haxies, and helper/background applications are not inherently bad. They are just not a part of the original OS. If you like and/or need one of these utilities in Panther that you liked so much in Jaguar, but it's causing system instability, then contact the software maker and find out if there is a Panther version available or coming out soon.

It's also not a bad idea to check online at places like Macfixit.com or Versiontracker.com to see if there are any reviews on your favorite haxie before loading it onto a new OS 10.3.

Solution 7

Check the permissions. You may find that your problems are limited to particular documents or a folder of documents. This can sometimes be caused by incorrect user permissions. To fix that, you need to highlight the document or folder and choose Get Info (⌘-I) from the File Menu (shown in Figure 32-16).

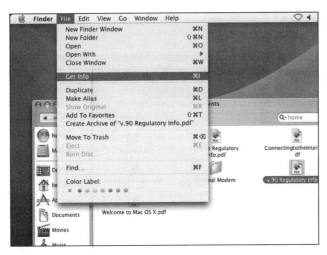

Figure 32-16: Highlight a file and select the Get Info (⌘-I) under the File menu in the Finder.

This opens an info box. Open the Ownership & Permissions section of the box by clicking on the triangle. Do the same on the Details triangle.

In order to change the permissions you will have to click on the small lock next to the Owner pull-down (shown in Figure 32-17). Then change the ownership of the document or folder to your username.

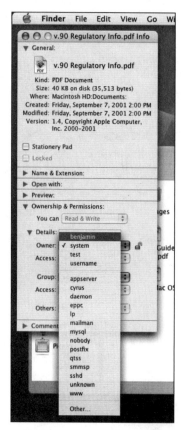

Figure 32-17: Changing the ownership of a file or folder of files in the Info dialog box may help to alleviate problems with those specific files.

When you are done, close the Info box. You are prompted to enter your password. Do so and try your document again. You may find that this has fixed your problem.

Solution 8

Try running a third-party disk utility like TechTool to diagnose and/or fix file, system, or volume structure problems.

Solution 9

Start from scratch. No one wants to hear this one, but sometimes that's the only option available. Systems can become so corrupt that your only recourse is to wipe the drive clean and install from scratch.

If you think you are at this point, you should consult a Macintosh technician to get confirmation first. It's a lot of work to reset all of your preferences and reinstall all of your applications.

Dealing with System Slowdowns

Between your computer not working at all and the desirable condition of your computer working perfectly, you will find a hazy region of computer (OS) behavior most generally characterized as "sluggish." We are, of course, talking about system slowdowns.

This section covers ways to get your system to respond as it did when you first installed the OS — or as close as you can get to it.

Why does your system slow down? That's a good question. There are a lot of reasons why it slows down, but usually it's because users have added things to the system.

Let's look at a few common areas that could be causing problems for you and what to do about them.

Your Services

Apple ships all of its computers and installs all of its OS's with the various services off. Services allow other computers to connect in some way with your computer. To look at those services, open System Preferences and click on the Sharing icon.

If you open the Sharing settings (shown in Figure 32-18) and find that all or most of the services are on, you might try turning a few off and seeing if that speeds you up a little.

---

tip There is a general misconception about file sharing and printer sharing. You do not need to have these on to access someone else's computer or a printer shared from another computer. Similarly, you do not need to have any of the rest of these services on to make contact with another computer that has these services on.

You only need to have these services on if another computer is trying to make contact (via one of these protocols) with your computer.

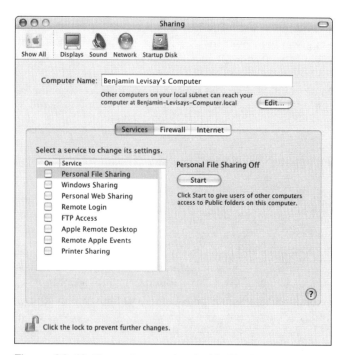

Figure 32-18: The various services inside Sharing in the System Preferences may cause the system to be slower. Turn off the services you don't need for faster system performance.

Classic Mode

One of the things that are possible in OS X is to launch OS 9.x in Classic mode. This is done either by launching a Classic application (which will also start Classic mode), by enabling Classic mode to start up every time the computer starts up, and/or by starting Classic from the Classic preference panel in the System Preferences.

Now, there are few applications left that don't have OS X–native versions. So, if you don't need Classic mode any more, you may want to make sure it's turned off.

To check the status of your Classic mode settings, open the System Preferences and click on the Classic icon (shown in Figure 32-19).

If Start Classic has been selected when you login, you might want to deselect it. If you launch an application that needs Classic mode, it will start it up for you. If you don't need it, it won't be running in the background slowing things down.

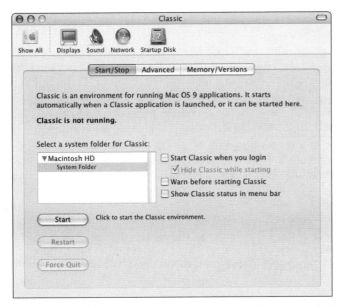

Figure 32-19: Turning off the automatic start of Classic mode, if you don't need Classic mode, is a great way to free up Ram and increase performance.

Fonts (Don't Get Me Started!)

A running gag around the office is about Benjamin the font fascist. And I admit it. I have strong opinions about fonts and font management. But under the same rationale that, "sometimes paranoid people do have people out to get them," I'd like you to humor me as we talk about the way you may have been messing up your system with your old fonts (Grin).

If you have been porting all of your *stuff* forward since OS 7.2 like I have, you have probably collected a font or two along the way. And if you're working in the design or print industry, you may have inadvertently collected a font or two from a customer file. (I say both of these things without being able to keep a straight face.)

And someone probably assured you that you could just move your fonts forward and everything would be okay — Right? *Wrong!!!*

Font management was desirable in pre–OS X computers, but I would say it's almost imperative in OS 10 and higher.

The first problem is that there are too many places to store fonts.

- There is a folder for fonts in the Library folder in each User folder.
- There is a folder for fonts in the Library folder in the System (OS X) folder.
- There is a folder for fonts in the Library folder at the top lever of the HD.
- There is a folder for fonts in the System Folder (OS 9).
- And there are numerous application-specific folders for fonts.

This begs the question, where should you put your old fonts? The answer to that depends on how many fonts you have.

If you are a home user and have a few fonts, you would put those fonts in the Font folder in the Library folder in your User folder. And then open Apple's Font Book (a new Panther feature) and turn off any that you don't like or want.

If, on the other hand, you are a graphic artist that was used to having 300 or more fonts in your old Fonts folder in the System Folder, *do not do this!* And if you have already done this, go to that folder and pull them all out!

Apple's new Font Book is a good beginning at an OS font management program, but it isn't robust or versatile enough to handle the font load of a graphic artist. For that you need something like Suitcase or Font Reserve (the latter now owned by Extensis, the maker of Suitcase). And if you were using a professional font management program, you wouldn't put them in your system or library folders. But I'm getting off topic.

To see if the fonts are slowing down your computer or maybe even upsetting your applications, pull the fonts out of the Fonts folder in the Library folder in your Users folder. If you've added fonts to one of the other places (that I mentioned in the bulleted points just listed), then you should try to sort through what you've added against what the system put in there.

> **tip**
>
> Don't add fonts to any directory except the Fonts folder within the User folder. That will allow you to use your Test account as a control for font-related issues.

I'll get off my soapbox now and move on. For more information on how to handle fonts, please see Chapter 23 in this book.

Clearing Your Caches

Cache information is typically stored as cache files. There are cache files for your entire system. There are cache files for your user settings. There are Internet caches that include favicons, history files, cookies, and download information. And there are virtual memory swap files.

> **note**
>
> A Favicon is a small image included on quite a few Web sites these days. This is the small custom icon that you see to the left of the URL in the address bar. Usually the Favicon represents the company's logo or Web site identity. Favicons also how up in BookMark lists. (See Chapter 18 for another look at Favicons.)

All of these things have their place. And some of these things contain user information that you will have to reset if you clear them. So, before you proceed any further in this section, it's important to stress the importance of a recent backup — a hard copy of your important settings, password information, and Internet settings. If you feel confident that you could reset your permissions for sharing, that you have your user folder backed up, and that your problem with slowdowns is dramatic enough that you are willing to try anything, then proceed.

There is a great little utility that I stumbled onto about a year ago that continues to be updated and that can help you with a myriad of system problems — including the clearing out of your caches. The name of the utility is Cocktail (current version 3.0.1 as I write this chapter). It was engineered and designed by Kristofer Szymanski and it can be found at www.macoscocktail.com. It's shareware and worth purchasing for $12. (Please be honest and support the makers of good utilities like this by paying for it.)

After you've purchased Cocktail, and downloaded and installed it, you will find it in your Applications folder. When you double-click it, it asks your password. After you enter your password, you find yourself at the main screen.

This utility does a lot of things, but here we're talking about clearing caches. To get to this section, click on the System icon on the toolbar of Cocktail and then click on the Cache tab (shown in Figure 32-20).

Here you will see seven choices for clearing your cache files. Keep in mind that clearing things like cookies may result in you having to sign in to all of your favorite sites from scratch. Similarly, the removal of other cache files could have repercussions to your user experience.

I have found that the following strategy works well for me:

1. Select one cache at a time and click the Clean button.
2. Log out and log back in as the main user (yourself).
3. Test the applications that seemed slow.
4. If the sluggish behavior still exists, then move to the next cache inside Cocktail.
5. Stop when you are satisfied with the results.

I usually leave my Cookies cache and my History cache until last because I have a great many sites that I log in tothat use Cookies.

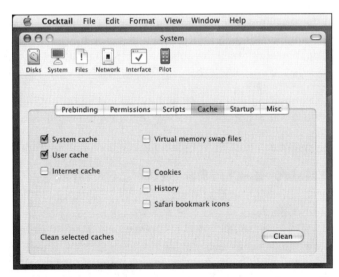

Figure 32-20: Cocktail will help you clean your caches out. Use this sparingly and only with a recent full backup to refer to.

caution You can also use Cocktail to (among other things) view logs, force empty the trash, fix permissions, and customize the interface.

It has a lot of power, which is why it makes you put in your password before it opens. It may also allow you to inadvertently damage your OS. Make certain you know what you're doing, have read the release notes, and have read the help files before you do something that you can't undo. If you don't know what an option is, don't use it.

And make sure you have a good backup. (Have I mentioned that before?)

There are other noteworthy utilities besides Cocktail. I cover a lot of them for you in the Appendix.

Running Third-Party Diagnostics and Optimizing Your HD

For years now, we've all been used to working with Tech Tool or Norton Utilities. Unless this is your first Mac, I'm sure you've run one of these at least once.

And as I said earlier in this chapter, you should have a current bootable copy of one of these. Which one you ask? I go back and forth on that. I have had times over the past few years when I've preferred one to the other. Now I keep a copy of everything on hand just in case. (And no, I'm *not* paranoid!)

Assuming you have one of these, it isn't a bad idea to run the disk utility and the optimizer every so often. I have customers that were told to run these once a week. My thought is that that's a little too much. I also have customers that were told to run these once a year. That's probably not enough.

My simple rule is to run these utilities when it seems like I need to run these utilities.

But before you run one of these, you should read the direction and disclaimers. They state quite clearly that the companies that make this software are not responsible for data loss as a result of running the software. That means if you run one of these utilities and something goes wrong, you could lose data.

Scared? Don't be. Just back your data up before you run one of these programs. If you think that's too simple and not practical, ask yourself this question: How much is your data worth?

A Few Words About Viruses and Security

Apple has received a lot of very positive press lately about how much better the Mac OS platform is than the Windows platform. And while Apple's security is good and the Mac OS is a more bulletproof OS, it is *not* impervious to viruses or worms or trojan horses.

One of the reasons that the Mac is not as targeted for viruses is that it accounts for a very small portion of computers used worldwide. Another reason is that Apple doesn't seem to offend people like Microsoft does. (This is just a harmless observation not a judgment.)

But is it possible for the Mac to get a virus? You bet it is! Just because it hasn't, doesn't mean it won't. And in the meantime, it can be an inconsiderate thing to inadvertently send PC viruses attached to Word documents to other people on PCs. Yes. That's right. Even though the Mac may not be affected, you can act as carriers for viruses already written.

One of these days, I'm sure that some enterprising young programmer with too much Jolt cola in his veins and too little regard for other people's property will engineer a monster Mac virus. And when that happens, the smug, overused phrase "Macs just don't get viruses" won't be much comfort.

So get yourself a virus protection program and keep the virus definitions updated. Most of the new virus protection programs have built-in virus updating support so that the applications can make contact with the servers and download new information about existing viruses.

If you choose not to scan everything that comes in, at least run your virus software on your computer overnight once a week or so to make sure you aren't carrying any PC viruses.

You should also pay attention to technology news. If you hear of a new virus, check to see if it will affect your OS. Chances are it won't but again, the day will come. . . .

Apple also releases security updates about once a month (or so) or whenever there is a security issue. It's a good idea to run the Software Update in System Preferences once a month (if you've set it to check manually like I have) to make sure you have the newest security update installed.

A little vigilance will ensure that you can continue to be smug around your PC friends for years to come.

Using the Terminal for Troubleshooting

It's important to remember that OS X is built on Unix. And because this is so, you have one more tool at your disposal to help in troubleshooting problems. There is a lot more information about Unix in the previous chapter if you are interested.

In this chapter, I'll show you a few ways to use the Terminal application that you may find helpful in troubleshooting your Mac.

If your computer will not boot properly, you can try booting into single-user mode (on startup hold down the Command and S keys) and running a utility called fsck.

◆ **note**

Single User Mode is something that is new to the world of the Mac since it evolved into a Unix environment. Single user mode occurs when you boot up a UNIX computer (OS 10.x is Unix) while holding down the "s" key (command -s on Mac OS X). This gives the user Root access to the computer where other commands can be use.

This is a fairly powerful thing to do. You should be careful that you understand what you're doing before you do something like this.

The man pages for fsck define it as a "file system consistency check and interactive repair" program. When you boot into single-user mode, you will see a screen that looks like this:

```
Singleuser boot - fsck not done
Root device is mounted read-only
If you want to make a modifications to files,
Run '/sbin/fsck -y' first and then '/sbin/mout -uw'
Localhost#
```

As it says, you will want to run the fsck program with the -y option. To do this, just type the following command line:

```
Localhost# /sbin/fsck -y
```

> **tip** It should be noted here that Unix is case sensitive. Text typed in the Terminal window that's "almost right" is wrong.

For those of you who are timid in Terminal, it's helpful to know that typing /sbin/fsck -y in Terminal does the exact same thing as clicking Repair Disk in the Disk Utility application. When it finishes, run it again until it reports that there are no more errors. When you are done, type reboot now and your computer should restart and boot without problems.

But let's say that the problem was something that happened out of the blue. Let's say you were trying to create some sort of startup script and something went wrong. Your computer won't boot all the way, so you can't get rid of the malfunctioning script. No fear. This can be fixed by using single-user mode also. After booting into single-user mode, you type:

```
Localhost# /sbin/mount -uw
```

What this does is change the start up disk permissions from Read-only to Read & Write. From here, you will be able to use the Unix commands to navigate and restore what your backup copy of the file. (You *did* make a back up copy, right?)

Finally, there is one other thing you could do with Terminal when access to your computer is not possible for some reason. This assumes, however, that you have turned on remote login in the Sharing tab of the System Preferences; an option that is *not* turned on by default, and that you have another computer that is running a version of OS X (or another Unix distribution). Normally when your computer appears frozen, it is still doing things in the background. Programs such as ssh or telnet are sometimes still operating just fine, yet your GUI seems to be stuck. Go to the other computer and type ssh *username@hostname* (this presumes ssh is installed and configured on the computer you are attempting to connect from).It should look something like the Figure 32-21.

From here you can either copy over any files you wish to have, and then make a backup copy (shown in Figure 32-22), kill the misbehaving application, or even reboot the computer.

Terminal — tcsh (ttyp1)
Last login: Mon Oct 27 18:39:07 on ttyp1
Welcome to Darwin!
tcsh: /sw/bin/init.csh: No such file or directory.
[Darknet:~] darkside% ssh other@the-Kat-box
other@the-kat-box's password:
Welcome to Darwin!
[the-Kat-box:~] other%

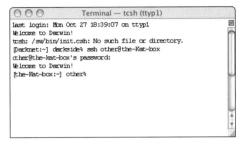

Figure 32-21: A Terminal login can help you determine if underlying processes are still working when the GUI is frozen.

Terminal — tcsh (ttyp1)
Last login: Mon Oct 27 19:12:18 on ttyp2
Welcome to Darwin!
tcsh: /sw/bin/init.csh: No such file or directory.
[Darknet:~] darkside% scp other@the-Kat-box:Documents/important.
txt ~/Desktop/
other@the-kat-box's password:
important.txt 100% 5 0.7K
B/s 00:00
[Darknet:~] darkside% ls Desktop/
important.txt
[Darknet:~] darkside%

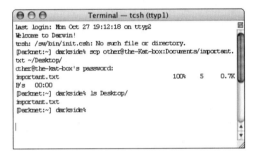

Figure 32-22: You can choose to make a secure backup copy from Terminal.

Figure 32-22 shows the use of the scp command (secure copy, like copying/sending data with ssh). It logs into the frozen computer and copies the important document, important.txt, over to the not-frozen computer. Then, in this example, that the file has been successfully copied over is verified.

Figure 32-23 shows top running on the remote computer. You can see that iTunes is running with a process ID number of 788. (Also note that the Finder is number 782.) If one of these applications is the suspected culprit to the nonresponsive computer, you need only kill it. To do this you would type `kill` then the PID (process ID) number (shown in Figure 32-34).

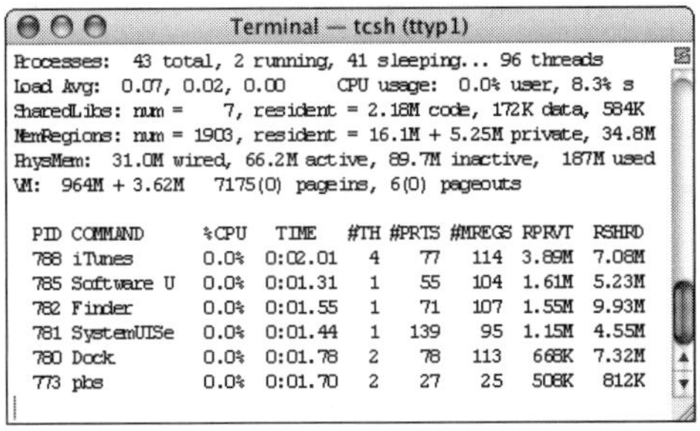

Terminal — tcsh (ttyp1)
Processes: 43 total, 2 running, 41 sleeping... 96 threads
Load Avg: 0.07, 0.02, 0.00 CPU usage: 0.0% user, 8.3% s
SharedLibs: num = 7, resident = 2.18M code, 172K data, 584K
MemRegions: num = 1903, resident = 16.1M + 5.25M private, 34.8M
PhysMem: 31.0M wired, 66.2M active, 89.7M inactive, 187M used
VM: 964M + 3.62M 7175(0) pageins, 6(0) pageouts
PID COMMAND %CPU TIME #TH #PRTS #MREGS RPRVT RSHRD
788 iTunes 0.0% 0:02.01 4 77 114 3.89M 7.08M
785 Software U 0.0% 0:01.31 1 55 104 1.61M 5.23M
782 Finder 0.0% 0:01.55 1 71 107 1.55M 9.93M
781 SystemUISe 0.0% 0:01.44 1 139 95 1.15M 4.55M
780 Dock 0.0% 0:01.78 2 78 113 668K 7.32M
773 pbs 0.0% 0:01.70 2 27 25 508K 812K

Figure 32-23: The Terminal can show you what applications are running with what Process ID number.

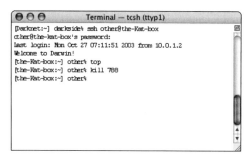

Figure 32-24: Knowing the process ID number allows you to choose which process to kill. Killing process ID number 788 in Terminal killed iTunes.

It should be noted here that kill does not always kill. The kill command sends a signal to the applicaiton. There are various levels of kill. kill-1 resets an application and kill-9 tells an aplication to die right now regardless of what it's doing or what process it's in.

You could have also killed PID 782 (the Finder). But be careful what you kill. The finder in this instance restarts when it's killed, but not all things do. You could end up making your problems worse.

And finally, you have the reboot option (shown in Figure 32-25). As you can see, even though the account other is an administrator account, you need to execute it as root, or with the sudo command (that we talked about earlier in this chapter).

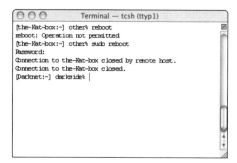

Figure 32-25: The Terminal will also allow us to reboot the computer.

Any additional information about the Unix tools you have just used can be referred to in the man pages (man is short for manual shown in Figure 32-26). Just type man [name of tool]:

```
Localhost# man scp
```

This will give you *all* the options that are available. However, man pages were, after all, written by technical writers for Unix users with some experience. Manual pages tend to be very dry and confusing, but they are worth looking at.

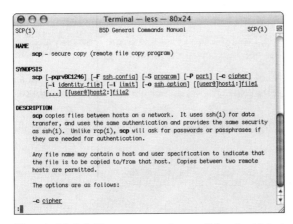

Figure 32-26: The user man (manual) for the Unix tools is available through Terminal for additional command-line information. This is an example of the man page for scp.

Planning Ahead

Hindsight is 20/20. We've all heard that before. It still irritates me every time I hear it because I always wonder if there was some way to get in front of the problem before it occurred. The only thing more irritating is *knowing for sure* you could have avoided the problem.

In this section, I show you that if you are properly outfitted that you can be prepared for the worst thing imaginable — data loss.

If you're a professional graphic artist and more than one day's worth of data loss is not acceptable, then you should really skip this section and consult a Macintosh service provider about some kind of automated AIT or DLT (tape-based) system on a nightly schedule. This section is meant more for the consumer or prosumer that doesn't have any kind of backup system or strategy at all.

> **note**
>
> My copy editor and my technical editor threw up "red flags" when the came across the work "prosumer." For a service provider who deals with the sale of computer equipment in the buisness market, this is a very commonly used term.
>
> Prosumer (pronounced proh.SOO.mur) is a consumer who is a novice or amature in computer user but who is knowledgeable (or needs) enough to require equipment that has some more robust or professional features ("professional" + "consumer"). In reality, this marks a separate level of marketing and purchasing power that falls somewhere between the comsumer and the corporate world. Many people who work at home on their computers (self-employed or other) can fall into the prosumer catagory.
>
> After doing a seach on the Internet, I found a cited example of the term on Word Spy (`http://www.wordspy.com/words/prosumer.asp`) from 2000.
>
> Example Citation: "In the parlance of the tech world, the new generation of digital film equipment is designed for the '**prosumer**,' the consumer who thinks of himself as a semi-professional."
>
> —Doug Bedell, "Digital video revolution," *The Dallas Morning News*, October 12, 2000

There are two parts to this. The first is equipment. The second is strategy. We'll start with the equipment, which includes hardware and some software.

Buying What You Need

This backup method assumes that you have a native FireWire port on your computer and that you are running a current version of the OS from an internal HD. If any of these suppositions are incorrect, you may have trouble getting this to work as it's laid out here.

You will need to purchase an external FireWire (400 or 800) hard drive that is more than twice as large as your internal HD. The ratio of internal hard drive storage space to external FireWire storage space should be 1 to 2or more.

You will also need a 6-pin to 6-pin FireWire cable, which usually ships with an external FireWire hard drive.

And you will need some kind of shareware or freeware clone utility. CopyCatX from SubRosaSoft (www.subrosasoft.com) and Carbon Copy Cloner from Bombich Software (www.bombich.com) are both great products that will work well for what you are about to do. Because of limited space in this book, I stick to Carbon Copy Cloner for the screen shot examples.

Preparing Your External Hard Drive

Plug your external HD into your computer via the FireWire cable and then launch the disk utility. Follow these steps:

1. Select the new external FireWire hard drive in left side of the Disk Utility window.
2. Click on the Partition button in the middle of the button row.

3. Under the Volume Scheme menu, select two partitions. Leave them at equal sizes. Each of these partitions should be slightly larger than your internal HD. If they aren't, then don't partition the drive.

4. Name each partition a variation of the name of your internal hard drive name. For instance if your internal HD is named Macintosh HD, then the top partition should be named something like Macintosh HD 1 and the bottom partition should be named something like Macintosh HD 2. This naming convention is to keep you from making a mistake in the future when you transfer data.

5. After you have named the partitions and named the external hard drive volumes, mark the names down in your computer log book or tape the names to the front of your external FireWire hard drive. (You'll thank me later when you don't have to think about it.)

If your internal hard drive is partitioned into more than one volume, then you will need to adjust your partitioning method in Step 2 and 3 to compensate. The end goal here is to have two empty partitions for each one of your internal volumes with the same storage space or better.

Using Carbon Copy Cloner

Now that you have your external FireWire hard drive prepared, you should see at least three volumes on your desktop. As I said before, if you have more than one volume, you're situation will be slightly different.

The next thing you need to do is to download a cloning program. We'll assume that you've downloaded a copy of Carbon Copy Cloner from bombich.com and have registered your copy of the great utility so that the author can afford to continue to update it for future versions of the OS. (It's the right thing to do.)

For this to run as smoothly as possible, I'd like to recommend that you turn off all other programs and services so that there is no chance of an error while your internal hard drive is cloned. I'm not suggesting that you boot into safe mode. That shouldn't be necessary, although it is an option if you have problems with this procedure. You should be okay if you just exit out of all other applications.

Next, you need to launch your copy by double-clicking on the double hard drive icon that is the application. Carbon Copy Cloner will launch and you will be given the opportunity to select the Source and Destination drives (shown in Figure 32-27).

For the Source Disk select your hard drive (that you want to copy from). When you select this, you will see all of the files and folders at the top level of the hard drive.

For the Target Disk select either of the numbered external FireWire partitions.

Next, click on the Preferences button. The preference dialog box appears (as shown in Figure 32-28). You can choose to allow Carbon Copy Cloner to repair the permissions before you clone your hard drive. I usually allow Disk Utility to do this prior to cloning. You can also choose to make the target disk bootable. This option should be selected so that you can boot your computer from the external partition.

The other preference settings have to do with synchronization; they are Disk Image options and ASR (Apple Software Restore) options. For the sake of this backup method, you can ignore these options and leave them at their default settings. The same is true of the Advanced settings. Just leave it alone until you have a reason to do otherwise.

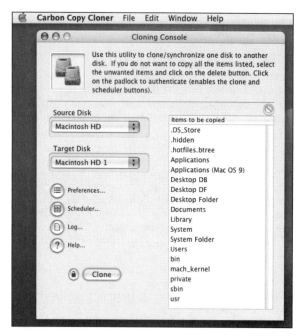

Figure 32-27: After you launch Carbon Copy Cloner, select the (startup) hard drive (that you want to copy from) as the Source Disk and the first external FireWire hard drive/partition as the Target Disk.

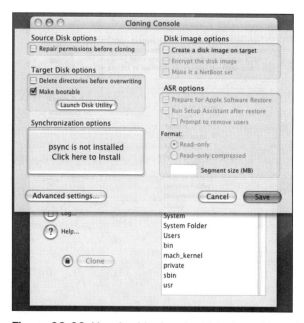

Figure 32-28: You should select the Make bootable option on in the Target Disk options. All of the other preferences can be left on their default settings.

Click Save to return to the main Cloning Consol. In order to start the cloning process, you need to click on the lock icon next to the grayed-out Clone button. This prompts you to enter your administrator password. Do so and click OK.

You're ready to clone your hard drive. Click on the Clone button and go do something else for a while.

When the cloning is done, it tells you that it is done.

Testing Your Cloned Hard Drive

Now that you've got a cloned hard drive, the best way to find out if it works is to start your computer up from that hard drive.

Open the System Preferences and select the Startup Disk icon. Select the volume named something like Macintosh HD 1 (the partition that was just the source for your clone) and set that to be your startup disk. Save that setting and restart your computer.

If you were successful, you will probably find that your desktop looks exactly like it did when you were starting up from your internal hard drive. You will be able to tell that you've started from your external partition by looking in the upper-right corner of the screen. Your startup volume should be at the top.

If your settings are such that you don't have your volumes mounted, then open a new Finder window. Hold down the Command key and click on the title at the top of the window. This will give you the path of the volume you have started up off of.

Another good way to check for the startup volume is to launch the Disk Utility application (located in the Utility folder in the Applications folder) and click on each partition in the First Aid panel. Only the permissions can be verified and repaired on the startup disk. All other volumes will allow you to verify or repair the entire disk.

When you are satisfied that your cloned volume is bootable and contains all your information, reopen the System Preferences and set your Startup Disk back to the internal hard drive. Then save your settings and restart your computer.

◆ tip

Because you are dealing with similarly named drives/partitions that contain almost identical duplicates of all of your files and directories, you shouldn't keep this external drive mounted on the desktop. You could make a mistake saving a file and mess everything up.

When you are done making a clone, dismount the external FireWire volumes by highlighting them and typing ⌘-E. Then disconnect the FireWire cable from the back of the computer and turn your external FireWire hard drive off.

You won't need it again until you're ready for another backup.

Congratulations. You just made a complete bootable backup of your hard drive. If your internal hard drive dies right now, you can have a service technician install a new hard drive and restore your computer to an absolute perfect clone of your computer prior to the drive's death.

If you have never done something like this before, you will probably find that you sleep better tonight than you have in a while.

But Why Are There Two Partitions?

The reason that there are two partitions is to give you options. Think of the first partition as a regular backup partition. If you decide to clone your hard drive once a day, once every two days, or even once a week, you are making a decision that you can live with one, two, or seven days worth of data loss (respectively).

The idea here is that every time you clone your internal hard drive, you will write over the first partition and replace those files with a fresh clone.

The process takes a while and so you may not want to do this every day. If you are extremely active with your computer, you may need to back up much more often than a casual user who can afford to lose a day or two's worth of e-mail.

But what happens if you deleted something last week that that you've already written over with a new clone? That's where the second partition comes in. Think of this partition as a vault partition. This is the partition that you select once a month (perhaps) or just before you do an extreme upgrade of your OS (say a Panther upgrade from Jaguar).

This will be left alone for a while. This partition will allow you to step backward for more than a day (since the day it was cloned) to recover data that you may have inadvertently deleted.

If nothing else, having two times the internal hard-drive storage space on an external hard drive can and will be useful. And if you're going to jump in and purchase an external FireWire hard drive, you might as well give yourself some options.

Surviving a Bad System Installation

Talking about "surviving a bad installation" is probably self-explanatory if you've adopted the backup strategy in the previous section. But just in case it isn't, let's go through it together.

Here are the steps:

1. You made a complete bootable backup of your hard drive using something like the equipment and software in the previous section.

2. You installed an upgrade of Panther over top of your Jaguar or OS 10.x.

3. You restarted and everything has gone to sour. Either your computer won't boot up or you find that your Panther is unusable for some reason.

4. So, you reconnect your external FireWire hard drive to your computer and turn it on.

5. If your computer locked or frozen, you'll have to hard start (if need be, by unplugging the power and plugging it back in and then hitting the on button) your computer.

6. As your computer starts up, hold down the Option key to enter the Boot screen.

7. Wait until you see the external bootable FireWire volume. Select that volume by clicking on it, and then click on the arrow button at the right of the screen. (Note: the clock may spin for a while during this step as the computer looks for bootable volumes.)

8. Let the computer boot from the volume on the external drive containing the most recent bootable backup of your hard drive (made just before your upgrade attempt).

9. Launch the Disk Utility and erase the internal hard drive (with the installed OS that just doesn't work).

10. Rename the internal hard drive the original name.

11. Launch Carbon Copy Cloner and set the Source Disk for the external volume that you booted from. Then set the Target Disk for the freshly erased and renamed internal hard drive.

12. Repeat the cloning process from the previous section, but in reverse (the external drive is the source and the internal drive is the target).

13. Launch System Preferences and click on the Startup Disk.

14. Select the freshly restored drive and then click on the Restart button to have your Mac reboot using the restored drive.

15. You should find that you are now booting from your internal hard drive running the system with all of the data and preferences you had just prior to your bad installation.

This doesn't tell you what went wrong or even how to fix it. What it does is to give you a choice to forgo the upgrade and return to a working OS so that you can get on with your work.

This will allow you time to research the problems and perhaps get some assistance.

It's good to have options.

Summary

Entire books have been written on troubleshooting system and application problems. The goal here was not to give you everything, but to give you some good basic strategies and techniques so that you can deal with disaster.

Here are the keys to dealing successfully with trouble:

♦ Have a backup plan.
♦ Have some bootable software utilities.
♦ Have an external storage solution.
♦ Find and develop a relationship with a certified Apple technician that knows more than you do.

If you follow these simple rules, you won't have to be a genius Mac OS troubleshooter. You can just be a smart Mac OS troubleshooter that sleeps well at night because your data has been backed up.

Third-Party Software and Web Resources

Appendix

This appendix is not just of list of shareware and other resources. Table A-1 lists all the third-party applications that I have discussed in the book. I also list here a few other products that I use and like but did not get a chance to write about in the book. Some of these are inexpensive shareware or donationware. Some are freeware. And some are full-blown commercial applications.

Table A-1: Third-Party Applications

Name	Web site address	Developer	Description	Chapter reference
ASM	www.vercruesse.de/software	Frank Vercruesse Products	Shareware customizable Finder Menu System Preference addition.	1 & 7
FruitMenu	www.unsanity.com/haxies/fruitmenu	Unsanity LLC	Shareware haxie to customize & enhance the Apple & contextual menus.	2
Classic Menu	www.sigsoftware.com/classicmenu	Sig Software	Shareware application that provides OS X with an Apple menu like Mac OS 9's.	2
Dock Detox	www.unsanity.com/haxies/dockdetox/	Unsanity LLC	Freeware haxie to remove notification icon bouncing in the Dock.	3
A-Dock X	http://jerome.foucher.free.fr/ADock.html	Jerome Foucher	Shareware side-dock with extra features.	3
Launcher	http://personalpages.tds.net/~brian_hill/launcher.html	Brian Hill	Shareware Cocoa adaptation of the Mac OS 7/8.x Launcher Control Panel.	3
Tinker Tool	www.bresink.de/osx/TinkerTool2.html	Marcel Bresink Software-Systeme	Freeware utility that allows you to access user settings that cannot be controlled by the System Preferences application.	3
Dockling	www.bkeeney.com/Utilities.html	Bkeeney Utilities	Shareware utility that helps you organize the Dock in an Apple menu-like structure.	3
Window-Shade X	www.unsanity.com/haxies/wsx/	Unsanity LLC	Shareware haxie that brings WindowShade functionality into Mac OS X.	3
Killdock	http://madej.ca/killdock/	Thomas Madej	Free application designed to enable or disable the Dock.	3
Dock Switcher	http://ilearnat.com/	iLearnAt.com	Shareware utility allows you to switch between multiple docks.	3

Name	Web site address	Developer	Description	Chapter reference
Déjà Vu	`http://propaganda prod.com`	Propaganda Productions	Shareware utility allows you to schedule unattended backups through a preference pane in your System Preferences.	4
More Internet	`www.monkeyfood.com/ software/more internet`	Diggory Laycock	Freeware app allows you to change all of your Internet protocols in one preference pane.	4
Share Points	`www.hornware.com/ sharepoints`	Michael Horn	Donationware application makes it easy to share any folder on your Mac.	4, 29, & 30
FontSight	`www.stone.com/ FontSight/`	Stone Design	Shareware program adds a visual font typeface menu to Cocoa applications.	7
FontCard	`www.unsanity.com/ haxies/fontcard/`	Unsanity LLC	Shareware haxie modifies the font menu in Carbon apps.	7
Photoshop CS	`www.adobe.com/ products/photoshop/ main.html`	Adobe, Inc.	Industry standard commercial graphics application is a powerful image and graphics editor.	7 & 9
ParaDocks	`www.pcv-soft.com`	PVC	Freeware application creates a hovering button bar of active applications.	7
PopApp	`www.people.cornell. edu/pages/pa44/ popapp.html`	Peter Ammon	Freeware utility creates a floating application circle about the cursor when a hot key is pressed.	7
Word Browser Plugin	`www.schubert-it. com/pluginword/`	Manfred Schubert	Freeware plug-in displays a text-only preview of Word documents in your Web browser.	8
Word X	`www.microsoft. com/mac/`	Microsoft Corp.	Commercial program is a powerful, industry-standard word processor.	8
Apple Works	`www.apple.com/ appleworks/`	Apple Computer, Inc.	Commercial software suite offers word processing, spreadsheet, and drawing capabilities.	8

(continued)

Table A-1 (continued)

Name	Web site address	Developer	Description	Chapter reference
Write	www.mariner software.com/	Mariner Software, Inc.	Word processing application features an easy-to-use interface.	8
Writer Express	www.nisus.com/ Express/	Nisus Software, Inc.	Easy-to-use word processor features a highly customizable interface.	8
ThinkFree Write	www.thinkfree.com/ products/pd_ write20.jsp	ThinkFree Corp.	Full-featured word processor is available as part of ThinkFree's Office suite.	8
Quark XPress	www.quark.com/ products/xpress/	Quark, Inc.	Quark's Flagship product is a full featured, robust layout program.	8
InDesign	www.adobe.com/ products/indesign/ main.html	Adobe, Inc.	Adobe's layout program provides tight integration with Adobe's other products and offers superb type controls.	8
Illustrator	www.adobe.com/ products/ illustrator/ main.html	Adobe, Inc.	Professional vector-editing program features powerful new 3D features and a bevy of creative drawing tools.	9
Freehand	www.macromedia. com/software/ freehand/?promoid= home_prod_fh_082403	Macromedia, Inc.	Commercial vector drawing program offers a full set of design tools and multipage document production.	9
GIMP (GNU Image Manipu- lation Program	www.MacGIMP.com	Archei, LLC	Commercial offering of the GNU image editing software can be used for image composition, image authoring or photo retouching.	9
Alien Skin Photoshop Plug-ins	www.alienskin.com/	Alien Skin Software, LLC	Commercial Photoshop filters provide a collection of versatile effects.	9
Auto FX Photoshop Filters	www.autofx.com/	Auto FX Software	Commercial image filters offer a wide range of photo enhancement solutions.	9
Via Voice	www.scansoft.com/ viavoice	Scansoft, Inc.	Commercial software adds enhanced voice-recognition capabilities to your Mac.	10

Name	Web site address	Developer	Description	Chapter reference
iListen	`www.macspeech.com`	MacSpeech, Inc.	Commercially available software offers dictation and voice command control for your Mac.	10
UI Element Inspector	`www.apple.com/ applescript/ uiscripting/02.html`	Apple Computer, Inc.	Free utility allows you easily determine the hierarchy of an object so you can translate it into AppleScript for control over the User Interface.	11
PreFab UI Browser	`www.prefab.com/ uibrowser/`	PreFab Software	Commercially available utility helps you control and monitor the user interface of most Mac programs.	11
QuicKeys	`www.cesoft.com/ products/qkx.html`	CE Software, Inc.	Commercially available software automates repetitive computer tasks with customized hot keys.	11
Acrobat Reader	`www.adobe.com/ products/acrobat/ readstep2.html`	Adobe, Inc.	Free application allows you to view and print PDF files.	12
MidiKeys	`www.manyetas.com/ creed/midikeys_ beta.html /`	Chris Reed	Free application turns your Mac keyboard into a MIDI keyboard.	13
Dent du MIDI	`http://homepage. mac.com/bery rinaldo/ddm/`	Bery Rinaldo	Freeware application takes standard midi files and generates separate files for each instrument.	13
Entourage	`www.microsoft.com/ mac/`	Microsoft Corp.	Commercially available e-mail program is part of Microsoft Office X.	18
Eudora	`www.eudora.com/`	Qualcomm Incorporated	Venerable commercial software is a powerful e-mail program.	18
Mailsmith	`www.barebones.com/ products/mailsmith/ index.shtml`	Bare Bones Software, Inc.	Commercial software is an e-mail client designed specifically for Mac users.	18
PowerMail	`www.ctmdev.com/`	CTM Development	Commercial software is a powerful, cross-platform e-mail client.	18

(continued)

Table A-1 (continued)

Name	Web site address	Developer	Description	Chapter reference
MSN for Mac OS X	www.msn.com	Microsoft Corp.	Free software (which works in tandem with a subscription service) offers e-mail and other Web-based services.	18
Mailblocks	www.mailblocks.com	Mailblocks, Inc.	Subscription based service helps you block unwanted e-mail.	18
Safari Enhancer	www.lordofthe cows.com/safari_ enhancer.php	Lord of the Cows.com	Donationware application enhances the functionality of Safari.	18
Spell Catcher X	www.rainmakerinc. com/products/ spellcatcherx/	Rainmaker Research, Inc.	Commercial software is a universal spell checker, thesaurus, and dictionary.	18
Gramma- rian Pro X	www.linguisoft.com	Linguisoft, Inc.	Commercial software is a universal interactive grammar and spell checker.	18
Excalibur	www.eg.bucknell. edu/~excalibr/	Rick Zaccone	Freeware program is a spell checker for your Mac.	18
Navigator	www.netscape.com	Netscape	Free program is a Web browser for your Mac.	18
Internet Explorer	www.microsoft. com/mac/	Microsoft Corp.	Free program is a Web browser for you Mac.	18
AOL Instant Messenger	www.aim.com	America Online	Free program is AOL's version of its instant messaging client.	19
Fire	www.epicware.com	Epicware, Inc.	Freeware program is an open source, multiplatform instant messenger client.	19
Proteus	www.indigofield. com/	Indigofield.com	Shareware program is an instant messaging application that works with most IM services.	19
iChat USBcam	www.ecamm.com/mac/ ichatusbcam/	Ecamm Network	Shareware program allows you use a USB Web cam with iChat AV.	19
iChat Streaming Icon	http://ichat. twosailors.com/	Twosailors Network	Shareware app changes your static buddy icon into an animation or a real video preview of yourself.	19

Name	Web site address	Developer	Description	Chapter reference
iBlog	www.lifli.com/	Lilifi software	Shareware application is a Web log authoring program that makes blogging a breeze.	21
Transmit	www.panic.com/ transmit/	Panic, Inc.	Shareware application is a powerful, flexible FTP client.	21
Photoshop Elements	www.adobe.com/ products/photo shopel/	Adobe, Inc.	Commercial program is Adobe's lite version of Photoshop.	21
Go Live	www.adobe.com/ products/golive/ main.html	Adobe, Inc.	Commercial program is Adobe's full featured WYSIWYG HTML editor.	21
Dream-weaver	www.macromedia. com/software/ dreamweaver/	Macromedia, Inc.	Commercial application is a powerful WYSIWYG HTML editor that offers tight integration with other Macromedia products.	21
Contribute	www.macromedia. com/software/ contribute/	Macromedia, Inc.	Commercial application allows non-technical users to update Web content.	21
Proof Master	www.proofmaster. net	Perfect Proof USA, Inc.	Commercially available software is a digital color proofing RIP for graphics arts professionals.	22
PDF U	www.ifthensoft.com/	If Then Software	Shareware utility that turns on hidden PDF services menu in 10.2.4 & higher.	22
Trans Type 2	www.fontlab.com/ html/transtype.html	FontLab	Commercial software offers quick conversion of fonts between Macintosh and Windows Formats.	23
Suitcase	www.extensis.com/ suitcase/	Extensis, Inc.	Suitcase is a commercially available font management software package.	23
Master Juggler	www.alsoft.com/ MasterJuggler/	Alsoft, Inc.	Commercially available software give you access to your font library and lets you store your fonts anywhere.	23

(continued)

Table A-1 (continued)

Name	Web site address	Developer	Description	Chapter reference
FontCard	www.unsanity.com/ haxies/fontcard	Unsanity LLC	Shareware haxie can be installed in the System Preferences that allows Carbon applications to sort fonts into families.	23
Silk	www.unsanity.com/ haxies/silk	Unsanity LLC	Silk is a shareware haxie that enables Quartz rendering in carbon apps that don't have Quartz support. It can also be used for font substitution.	23
Pop Char X	www.macility.com/ products/popcharx/	Ergonis Software	Commercial utility lets you easily view all the characters in whichever font you are currently using.	23
Font Reserve	www.extensis.com/ fontreserve/	Extensis, Inc.	Commercial font management software allows you to create a vault data base where all your fonts are stored.	23
Font Agent Pro	www.fontagent.com/	Insider Software, Inc.	Commercially available font tool helps you organize, manage, and repair fonts.	23
Sticky Brain	http://chronos. iserver.net/&/ products/index.html	Chronos	Shareware utility is a personal productivity application that helps organize all the miscellaneous information on your Mac.	23
Mactracker	www.mactracker.ca	Ian Page	Donationware utility gives you access to basic information about Apple products.	24
VueScan	www.hamrick.com/	Hamrick Software	VueScan is a commercial scanning program that works with most scanners.	25
OmniPage Pro	www.scansoft.com/ omnipage/mac/	Scansoft, Inc.	Commercial optical character recognition program allows you to scan pages and turn them into digital information you can edit.	25

Name	Web site address	Developer	Description	Chapter reference
Toast Titanium	`www.roxio.com/en/ products/toastwith jam/index.jhtml`	Roxio, Inc.	Commercial software helps you easily burn CDs and DVDs.	26
Brick House	`http://personal pages.tds.net/ ~brian_hill/ brickhouse.html`	Brian Hill	Shareware utility makes it easier to use the network firewall built in to OS X.	29
Virtual Network Computer	`http://source forge.net`	Open Source	Free software is an open source remote control package for your Mac.	30
Timbuktu	`www.netopia.com`	Netopia, Inc.	Commercial software allows you to operate distant computers as if you were sitting in front of them.	30
Remote Desktop Connection	`www.microsoft. com/mac/ downloads.aspx`	Microsoft	Free software allows you display a desktop from a windows machine and control it with your mouse and keyboard.	30
PC-Mac LAN	`www.miramar.com`	Miramar Systems, Inc.	Commercial application provides convenient networking between Macs and PCs, include pre-OS X Macs.	30
DAVE	`www.thursby. com/dave/`	Thursby Software systems, Inc.	Commercial software makes it easy to share files and printing across different platforms.	30
Cocktail	`www.macosx cocktail.com/`	Kristofer Szymanski	Shareware utility offers a set of maintenance tools and interface tweaks.	31, 32
Fink	`www.apple.com/ downloads/macosx/ unix_open_source/ fink.html`	SourceForge	Free package manager utility makes it easier to download UNIX programs that have been ported over to OS X.	31
X11	`www.apple.com/ macosx/features/ x11/download/`	Apple Computer, Inc.	Free utility offers the ability to run X Window System applications on your Mac.	31
Open Office	`www.openoffice. org/`	CollabNet, Inc.	Free software is a multi-platform office productivity suite that can run in the X11 environment	31

(continued)

Table A-1 *(continued)*

Name	*Web site address*	*Developer*	*Description*	*Chapter reference*
Copy CatX	www.subrosasoft. com	SubRosa Soft.com Ltd.	Fast and easy commercial utility for duplicating and OS X drive.	32
Carbon Copy Cloner	www.bombich.com	Mike Bombich	Shareware is a backup and cloning utility for Mac OS X.	32
Tinker Tool	www.bresink.de/ osx/TinkerTool.html	Marcel Bresink	Freeware application that gives you access to additional preference settings Apple has built into Mac OS X	Just a favorite of mine.
icns2 icon	www.icons.cx/	Icons CX	Freeware program that makes .icns files visible in the finder.	Super cool, a must have for those who make their own icons.
Snapper- head 4.6	www.bainsware.com/ snapperhead/	Bains Software	Donationware application that broadcasts a snapshot of your screen to those who enter your IP Address.	Just a favorite of mine.
CloakIt	www.citrussoft ware.com/cloakit. php	Citrus Software	Shareware application that makes it easy to create invisible folders on your Mac.	Just a favorite of mine
CronniX	www.koch-schmidt. de/cronnix/	Kock und Schmidt Systemtechnik GBR	Donationware Aqua front-end to the cron Unix tool that makes it easy to schedule execution of scripts.	Just a favorite of mine.
Graphic Converter	www.lemkesoft.de/ en/graphcon.htm	Lemke Software	Incredible shareware application that lets you view, edit, and convert most graphic files. Often called the "Rosetta Stone or Graphic File Formats."	An absolute must for graphics pros.
Lynx	www.apple.com/ downloads/macosx/ unix_open_source/ lynx.html	University of of Kansas	Free application is a text-only, super-fast, Web browser you run in the Terminal.	Will help establish geek cred.

Name	Web site address	Developer	Description	Chapter reference
iTerm	`http://iterm.sourceforge.net/`	Fabian and Ujwal S. Sathyam	Free application is a terminal emulation program that allows you to have tabbed terminal windows.	One-up the office alpha-geek with this one.
iCalViewer	`http://www.icalviewer.com/`	Karl Goiser	A Shareware desktop accessory and screen saver that you can use to show your iCal events moving in timeline.	My default Screensaver and a very useful desktop.

Other Online Resources

Although there are many online resources available, Table A-2 lists the ones that were used in this book or that I use on a regular basis.

Table A-2: Online Resources

Web site address	Developer	Description	Chapter reference
`www.apple.com/downloads/macosx`	Apple Computer, Inc.	Apple tracks and lists new OS X software.	2
`www.versiontracker.com`	TechTracker, Inc.	The most popular site to find, track, and get to Classic and OS X software.	2
`www.macupdate.com`	MacUpdate	Another site to find, track, and get Classic and OS X software.	Just a favorite of mine.
`www.macfixit.com`	TechTracker, Inc	Site that provides new and much more information about the Macintosh world.	32
`www.unicode.org/`	Unicode, Inc.	Site dedicated to the Unicode character encoding system.	Just a favorite of mine.
`www.lego.com`	The LEGO Group	Site dedicated to those fascinating building blocks you loved (and may still love) as a kid.	6

(continued)

Table A-2 *(continued)*

Web site address	Developer	Description	Chapter reference
www.apple.com/downloads/macosx/unix_open_source/	Apple Computer, Inc.	Site lists Unix and Open Source programs available for use on Mac OS X.	Just really cool, in a geeky way.
www.gimp.org	The GIMP Team	Site is where you track the development of the GIMP.	8
www.osxfaq.com/	OSXfaq	Site offers a Mac OS X and Mac OSX Unix tips of the day, plus the Inside Mac Internet radio show.	Just a favorite o' mine.
www.apple.com/store	Apple Computer, Inc.	Site is where you can find all your Apple products.	10
www.malcolmadams.com/itunes/scripts/scripts02.php.	Doug Adams	Find all kinds of AppleScripts to help enhance the performance of your Mac.	10
www.apple.com/applescript/apps/	Apple Computer, Inc.	Site is Apple's resource page for AppleScript.	11
www.apple.com/macosx/overview/	Apple Computer, Inc.	Site offers an overview of Panther and lists all the software that comes with the operating system.	Just a favorite of mine.
www.thegaragedoor.com	Victor Hookstra	Site offers a collection of tips and suggestions for getting the most out of GarageBand.	13
www.audio-units.com/	Florian Fink	Site offers many effects and instruments you can use with GarageBand.	13
http://developer.apple.com/sdk/#AppleLoops	Apple Computer, Inc.	Place to go for Apple's guidelines for creating audio loops for GarageBand and Soundtrack.	13
www.apple.com/iphoto/compatibility/camera.html	Apple Computer, Inc.	Apple's site for determining if you digital cameral is compatible with iPhoto.	14
www.apple.com/ilife/iphoto/hottips/	Apple Computer, Inc.	Check out this Web site for tips and hints on making the most of iPhoto.	14
www.ihffilm.com/ihf/videostandard.html	International Historic films, Inc.	Site features a list of countries and their video broadcast standards.	15

Web site address	Developer	Description	Chapter reference
www.apple.com/ ilife/imovie/ visual_effects.html	Apple Computer, Inc.	Apple lists an abundance of third-party plug-ins for iMovie on this site.	15
www.freeplaymusic. com	Freeplay Music, Corp.	Free background music for your iMovies.	15
www.icalworld.com/	iCal World	Publish your iCal calendar on the Web, with some added enhancements.	16
http://icalshare. com/	iCalShare	Huge directory of shared calendars, and a place to park you calendar as well.	16
www.apple.com/ ical/library/	Apple Computer, Inc.	Apple's iCal portal offers calendars to download that feature the holidays or even when your favorite sports team plays.	16
www.apple.com/ isync/	Apple Computer, Inc.	Home of Apple's iSync Web Page.	16
http://dns2go. deerfield.com	Deerfield.com	Make your Mac accessible anywhere by associating your current IP address with a domain name of your choice.	17
www.dyndns.org	Dynamic Network Services	Dynamic DNS services that direct a URL to your Mac even if you have a dynamic IP address.	17
www.no-ip.com	Vitalwerks Internet Solutions, LLC.	No-IP.com offers DNS services for Mac Users with dynamic IP Addresses.	17
www.tzo.com	Tzolkin Corporation	DNS service to those of us with dynamic IP Addresses.	17
http://hoohoo. ncsa.uiuc.edu/cgi/	NCSA HTTPd Development Teams	Introduction to the Common Gateway Interface, or cgi.	17
www.faqs.org/faqs/	FAQS.org	Archive of frequently asked questions about the Internet.	17
http://members. aol.com/voicepro/ custom.html	EVO, Inc.	Order a custom alert message from the voice behind AOL's famous, "You've got Mail" alert at this site.	17
http://homepage. mac.com/aamann	Andreas Amann	Freeware that enhances Mac OS X Mail and Eudora.	17

(continued)

Table A-2 *(continued)*

Web site address	Developer	Description	Chapter reference
www.clickfire.com/ viewpoints/articles/ favicons.php	Clickfire	Tutorial on how to make favicons, those nifty little pictures next to the URL in your browser.	Just a favorite...
www.mac.com/	Apple Computer, Inc.	Starting point to enter the world of .Mac, Apple's collection of online services.	20
http://davebarry. blogspot.com/	Dave Berry	Columnist Dave Barry's unofficial blog site.	21, and it cracks me up.
www.apple.com/ hotnews/	Apple Computer, Inc.	Get the latest Apple related news.	21
www.mac.com/1/ idiskutility_ download.html	Apple Computer, Inc.	Download the iDisk Utility. This is especially helpful if you have more than one iDisk.	21
www.apple.com/ macosx/features/ fontbook/	Apple Computer, Inc.	All the wonders of FontBook.	23
www.apple.com/ support/products/	Apple Computer, Inc.	Learn more about AppleCare.	24
http://wheretobuy. apple.com/locator/	Apple Computer, Inc.	Find an Apple products reseller.	24
www.apples pecialist.us/	Apple Specialist	Find the nearest Apple Specialist.	24
www.apple- history.com	Glen Sanford	Tons of information about Apple hardware through the years.	24
www.info.apple. com/support/ applespec.html	Apple Computer, Inc.	A quick look at Apple hardware.	24
www.megapixel.net	Megapixel.net	Great site to compare digital cameras.	25
www.apple.com/usb/	Apple Computer, Inc.	Apple's guide to the Universal Serial Bus.	27
www.mactech.com/ articles/mactech/ Vol.15/15.10/ WellConnectedMac/	Rich Morin and Doug McNutt	Article about the chaotic world of SCSI connections.	27
http://maccentral. macworld.com/ news/2003/10/30/ firewireissue/ index.php?redirect= 1081604203000	Jim Dalrymple	Article talks about the initial problems Panther had with certain FireWire devices.	27

Web site address	Developer	Description	Chapter reference
`www.oxsemi.com/ products/IEEE1394/ oxfw900.html`	Oxford Semiconductor	Information about the Oxford 900 FireWire Bridge chip.	27
`www.info.apple.com/`	Apple Computer, Inc.	Starting point for searching the Knowledge Base for instructions for installing hardware on your Mac.	28
`www.zeroconf.org/`	Stuart Cheshire	All the gory details on how Zeroconf, which Apple renamed Rendezvous, works.	29
`www.iana.org/ assignments/ port-numbers`	IANA	List of standard port numbers and their services.	29
`www.apple.com/ airport/pdf/ DesigningAirPort Nets-022-1036.pdf`	Apple Computer, Inc.	Download this PDF to get the manual on configuring an AirPort network configuration.	29
`www.apple.com/ airport/`	Apple Computer, Inc.	Apple's AirPort site.	29
`http://slacksite. com/other/ftp.html`	Jay Ribak	Information about PORT and PASV modes in FTP transactions.	29
`www.wordspy.com/`	Paul McFedries	Web site is devoted to *lexpionage*, the sleuthing of new words and phrases.	32

Index

continued

continued